THE KREMLIN LETTERS

THE
KREMLIN
LETTERS

**Stalin's Wartime Correspondence
with Churchill and Roosevelt**

edited by
DAVID REYNOLDS
and
VLADIMIR PECHATNOV

with the assistance of
ISKANDER MAGADEYEV and OLGA KUCHERENKO

YALE UNIVERSITY PRESS
NEW HAVEN AND LONDON

For information about this and other Yale University Press publications, please contact:
U.S. Office: sales.press@yale.edu   yalebooks.com
Europe Office: sales@yaleup.co.uk   yalebooks.co.uk

Set in Minion Pro by IDSUK (DataConnection) Ltd
Printed in Great Britain by Gomer Press Ltd, Llandysul, Ceredigion, Wales

Library of Congress Control Number: 2018948874

ISBN 978-0-300-22682-9

A catalogue record for this book is available from the British Library.

10 9 8 7 6 5 4 3 2 1

. . . I think I can personally handle Stalin better than either your Foreign Office or my State Department. Stalin hates the guts of all your top people. He thinks he likes me better, and I hope he will continue to do so.

Roosevelt to Churchill, 18 March 1942

If only Stalin and I could meet once a week, there would be no trouble at all. We get on like a house on fire.

Churchill, conversation with Colin Coote, 27 January 1944

In the history of diplomacy I know of no such close alliance of three great Powers as this, when allies had the opportunity of so frankly expressing their views.

Stalin, Yalta conference, 8 February 1945

Oleg Aleksandrovich Rzheshevsky
and
Warren F. Kimball,
who pioneered the way

CONTENTS

PLATES AND MAPS

Plates

Maps

ABBREVIATIONS

AAF	Army Air Forces (US)
AK	Home Army (Polish)
Alanbrooke	Field Marshal Lord Alanbrooke, *War Diaries, 1939–1945*, ed. Alex Danchev and Daniel Todman, London, 2001
ALSIB	Alaska–Siberia air bridge
AP RF	Archive of the President of the Russian Federation
APP	American Presidency Project: Speeches and Public Papers www.presidency.ucsb.edu
AVP RF	Foreign Policy Archive of the Russian Federation, Moscow
Barker	Elisabeth Barker, *Churchill and Eden at War*, London, 1978
Beaumont	Joan Beaumont, *Comrades in Arms: British aid to Russia, 1941–1945*, London, 1980
Butler	Susan Butler (ed.), *The Complete Correspondence of Franklin D. Roosevelt and Joseph V. Stalin*, New Haven, CT, 2006
CA	War Cabinet minutes, confidential annex (TNA)
CAB	Cabinet Office papers (TNA)
CAC	Churchill Archives Centre, Churchill College, Cambridge
Cadogan	David Dilks (ed.), *The Diaries of Sir Alexander Cadogan, OM, 1938–1945*, London, 1971
CCS	Combined Chiefs of Staff (US–UK)
CD	*The Churchill Documents*, ed. Martin Gilbert (vols 6–17) and Larry Arnn (vols 18–), Hillsdale, MI, 2008–

CHAR	Chartwell papers (CAC)
CHUR	Churchill papers (CAC)
Colville	John Colville, *The Fringes of Power: Downing Street diaries, 1939–1955*, London, 1985
Corr 1957	Ministry of Foreign Affairs of the USSR, *Correspondence between the Chairman of the Council of Ministers of the USSR and the Presidents of the USA and the Prime Ministers of Great Britain during the Great Patriotic War of 1941–1945*, 2 vols, Moscow, 1957
COS	Chiefs of Staff (UK)
DO	War Cabinet Defence Committee (Operations)
DVP	Foreign Ministry, Russian Federation, *Dokumenty vneshney politiki*, several volumes, Moscow, 1992–
EAM	National Liberation Front (Greece)
Eden	Anthony Eden, *The Eden Memoirs: The reckoning*, London, 1965
Eisenhower	Alfred D. Chandler, et al. (eds), *The Papers of Dwight D. Eisenhower: The war years*, 5 vols, Baltimore, MD, 1970
ELAS	Greek People's Liberation Army
FCNL	French Committee of National Liberation
FDRL	Franklin D. Roosevelt Library, Hyde Park, NY
FO	Foreign Office
Frieser	Karl-Heinz Frieser et al. (eds), *Germany and the Second World War*, Vol. 8: *The Eastern Front, 1943–1944*, Oxford, 2017
FRUS	US Department of State, *Foreign Relations of the United States*, several volumes, Washington, DC
FRUS Cairo and Tehran	*The Conferences at Cairo and Tehran* (1961)
FRUS Quebec	*The Conference at Quebec, 1944* (1972)
FRUS W and C	*The Conferences at Washington, 1941–1942, and Casablanca, 1943* (1968)
FRUS Yalta	*The Conferences at Malta and Yalta, 1945* (1955)
Gilbert 7	Martin Gilbert, *Winston S. Churchill*, Vol. 7: *1941–1945*, London, 1986
Gilbert 8	Martin Gilbert, *Winston S. Churchill*, Vol. 8: *1945–1965*, London, 1988
GKO	State Committee for Defence
Glantz/House	David M. Glantz and Jonathan House, *When Titans Clashed: How the Red Army stopped Hitler*, Lawrence, KS, 1995

Gorodetsky	Gabriel Gorodetsky (ed.), *The Maisky Diaries: Red ambassador to the Court of St James's, 1932–1943*, New Haven & London, 2015
Harriman	W. Averell Harriman and Elie Abel, *Special Envoy to Churchill and Stalin, 1941–1946*, New York, 1975
Harvey	John Harvey (ed.), *The War Diaries of Oliver Harvey, 1941–1945*, London, 1978
Herring	George C. Herring, Jr, *Aid to Russia, 1941–1946: Strategy, diplomacy, and the origins of the Cold War*, New York, 1973
Hinsley	F.H. Hinsley et al. (eds), *British Intelligence in the Second World War*, 4 vols, London, 1977–90
HSTL	Harry S. Truman Library, Independence, Missouri
IRC	International Red Cross
JACB	Papers of Sir Ian Jacob (CAC)
JCS	Joint Chiefs of Staff (USA)
JIC	Joint Intelligence Committee
JSSC	Joint Strategic Survey Committee
Kimball	Warren F. Kimball (ed.), *Churchill and Roosevelt: The complete correspondence*, 3 vols, Princeton, NJ, 1984
LC	Manuscript Division, Library of Congress, Washington, DC
Moran	C.M.W. Moran, *Churchill: Taken from the diaries of Lord Moran: The struggle for survival, 1940–1965*, London, 1968
MR	Map Room papers (FDRL)
NARA	National Archives and Records Administration, College Park, Maryland
NII	Scientific Research Institute (Russian)
NKVD	*Narodnyy Komissariat Vnutrennykh Del* – People's Commissariat for Internal Affairs
OGB	*Organy gosudarstvennoy bezopasnosti v Velikoy Otechestvennoy voyne*, 5 vols, Moscow, 2003
OSS	Office of Strategic Services (USA)
PCNL	Polish Committee of National Liberation
PM	Prime Minister
PPPR	Samuel I. Rosenman (ed.), *Public Papers of the Presidents: Franklin D. Roosevelt*, 13 vols, New York, 1938–50
PREM	Prime Minister's Correspondence (TNA)
PSF(D)	President's Secretary's File: Diplomatic (FDRL)
PSF(S)	President's Secretary's File: Safe (FDRL)
RDM	Russian Defence Ministry

Reynolds	David Reynolds, *In Command of History: Churchill fighting and writing the Second World War*, London, 2004
RG	Record Group
RGASPI	Russian State Archive of Social and Political History, Moscow
Ross	Graham Ross (ed.), *The Foreign Office and the Kremlin: British documents on Anglo-Soviet relations, 1941–45*, Cambridge, 1984
RSAFPD	Russian State Archive of Film and Photo Documents
Rzheshevsky	Oleg A. Rzheshevsky (ed.), *War and Diplomacy: The making of the Grand Alliance – Documents from Stalin's archive*, Amsterdam, 1996
SAMO	*Sovetsko-amerikanskiye othnosheniya vo vremya Velikoy Otechestvennoy voyny, 1941–1945*, 2 vols, Moscow, 1984
SANO	*Sovetsko-angliyskiye othnosheniya vo vremya Velikoy Otechestvennoy voyny, 1941–1945*, 2 vols, Moscow, 1983
Sherwood	Robert E. Sherwood, *Roosevelt and Hopkins: An intimate history*, New York, 1948
SOE	Special Operations Executive
Stavka	High Command (Soviet)
Stoler	Mark A. Stoler, *Allies and Adversaries: The Joint Chiefs of Staff, the Grand Alliance, and US strategy in World War II*, Chapel Hill, NC, 2000
SWW	Winston S. Churchill, *The Second World War*, 6 vols, London, 1948–54
Tamkin	Nicholas Tamkin, *Britain, Turkey and the Soviet Union, 1940–45: Strategy, diplomacy and intelligence in the Eastern Mediterranean*, London, 2009
TNA	The National Archives (UK), Kew, Surrey
UPP	Union of Polish Patriots
USAAF	United States Army Air Forces
WM	War Cabinet minutes (TNA)
WO	War Office papers (TNA)
Woodward	Sir Llewellyn Woodward, *British Foreign Policy in the Second World War*, 5 vols, London, 1970–76
WP	War Cabinet papers (TNA)

ACKNOWLEDGEMENTS

THIS BOOK IS THE result of lengthy research, conducted in a spirit of genuine international collaboration, as a carefully researched Russian text was revised and rewritten for an Anglophone audience. Along the way, we have accumulated numerous debts, which it is our pleasure to acknowledge here.

Financially, the work has been generously assisted by the Leverhulme Trust (Research Project Grant RPG–2015–156); the British Academy (Small Research Grant SG 100185) and the Russkiy Mir Foundation. Vladimir Pechatnov was also the grateful recipient of an Archives By-Fellowship at Churchill College, Cambridge and a research grant from The Roosevelt Institute, Hyde Park, New York.

We are also greatly indebted to the help of archivists at the following repositories: the Russian Federal Archive Agency (A.N. Artizov); the Russian State Archive of Social and Political History (O.V. Naumov, A.K. Sorokin, V.N. Shepelev); the Archive of the President of the Russian Federation, the Historical Documentary Department and the Foreign Policy Archive of the Russian Foreign Ministry (A.I. Kuznetsov, I.V. Fetisov, A.N. Zaleyeva); the Franklin D. Roosevelt Library, Hyde Park, New York (archivist Robert Clark); the Harry S. Truman Library, Independence, Missouri (archivist Rebecca Sowell); the Churchill Archives Centre, Cambridge University (director Allen Packwood). S.V. Kudryashov (German Historical Institute, Moscow) rendered great assistance in identifying and processing archival material. Moscow State Institute of International Relations (MGIMO), the Ministry of Foreign Affairs of Russia and the German Historical Institute, Moscow (N. Katzer) created favourable working conditions for the Russian research and provided organizational support. Vladimir Pechatnov is especially grateful to MGIMO President, Member of the Russian Academy of Sciences A.V. Torkunov, whose faith in and constant promotion of the project made its Russian version possible.

In Britain, David Reynolds acknowledges the assistance of Daniel Wunderlich and Edward Mayes in securing and administering the British funding, and the continued support of the Cambridge History Faculty and of Christ's College in his work.

The Foreign Policy Archive of the Russian Foreign Ministry, the Russian State Archive of Social and Political History, the Russian State Archive of Film and Photo Documents and the Russian Defence Ministry kindly allowed use of some material from their collections as illustrations. Other photo credits are indicated in the list of illustrations. Crown copyright documents composed by Winston Churchill and other members of the wartime British government are reproduced under the Open Government Licence, but are cited where possible from publicly available collections.

This publication greatly benefited from advice given by Member of the Russian Academy of Sciences, the late G.N. Sevostyanov, Honoured Scholars of the Russian Federation O.A. Rzheshevsky and V.L. Malkov. Two distinguished American historians of the Roosevelt era – Warren F. Kimball and David Woolner – made valuable critiques of the draft English text. Additional comment and advice were kindly provided by Kristina Spohr, Patrick Miles and Patrick Salmon of FCO Historians. We each owe a particular debt, as usual, to our long-suffering spouses: Margaret and Luba.

Our thanks to those at Yale University Press who have supported the project, particularly Robert Baldock, Rachael Lonsdale and Clarissa Sutherland, and to copy-editor Clive Liddiard. Yale's commitment to publishing this book, and also, later, an online edition of the whole correspondence, has been exemplary. Appreciation, too, for our agent Peter Robinson and assistant Matthew Marland at Rogers, Coleridge & White.

The book could not have been completed without the help of two immensely talented younger historians of the Second World War era whose linguistic, scholarly and compositional skills were invaluable. Iskander Magadeyev worked closely on the research and publication of the Russian edition; Olga Kucherenko, likewise, on translating the Russian material and in helping to prepare the English-language text. Both of them are acknowledged on the title page.

The Kremlin Letters is respectfully dedicated to two scholars – one Russian and the other American – who pioneered the way both in forging academic contacts across the Cold War divide and in setting an example for the editing of wartime documents. We are indebted to them as historians and as friends.

Finally, a word of mutual appreciation: this book shows that it is possible for two scholars from different, often frictional, political cultures to find common ground and complete a project that, we hope, will enhance historical research and also – in some small way – international understanding.

Cambridge and Moscow, May 2018

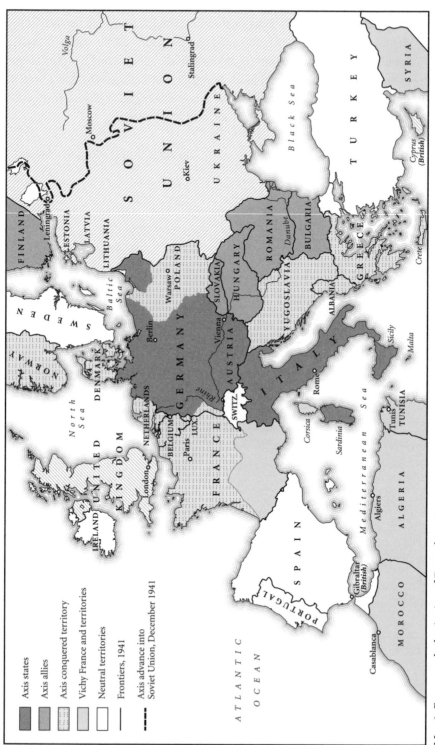

Map 1 Europe at the beginning of December 1941.

Legend:
- Axis states
- Axis allies
- Axis conquered territory
- Vichy France and territories
- Neutral territories
- Frontiers, 1941
- Axis advance into Soviet Union, December 1941

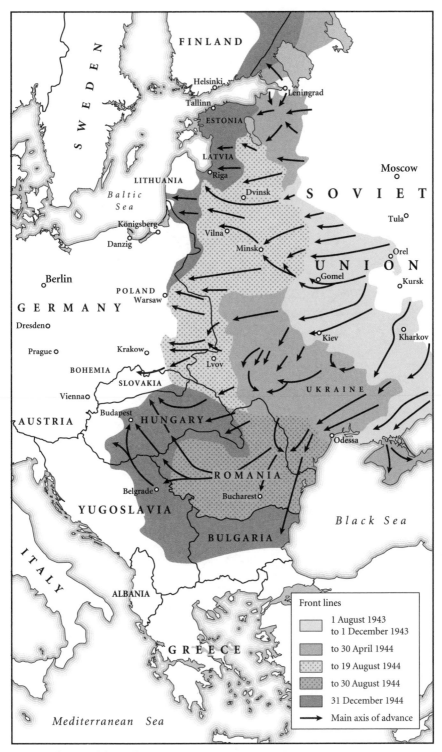

Map 2 Advance of the Red Army into Eastern Europe, 1943–44.

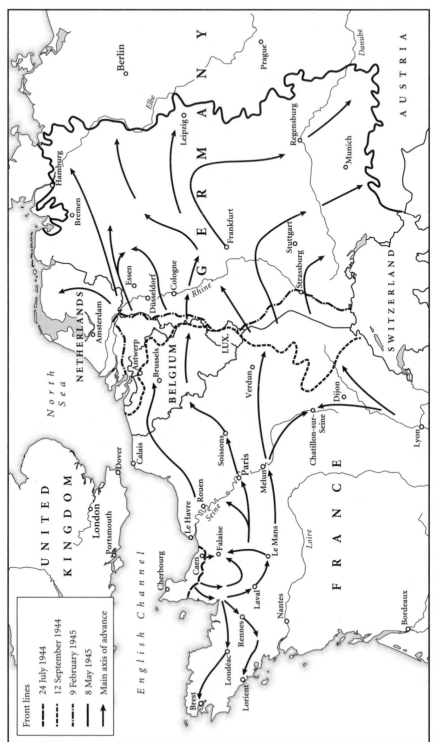

Map 3 Allied advance across Western Europe, 1944–45.

Front lines

	24 July 1944
	12 September 1944
	9 February 1945
	8 May 1945
	Main axis of advance

INTRODUCTION

THEY WERE THREE MOST unlikely musketeers. The offspring of an English lord and an American heiress, passionate in his defence of hierarchy and empire. A secretive 'squire' from the Hudson Valley, progressive in politics and obsessed with European imperialism. And a cold-blooded ex-terrorist, now determined to build up his power and that of his country in a hostile world. Yet for nearly four years, the 'Big Three' led one of the most effective alliances in history and, against the odds in the winter of 1941–42, achieved victory in 1945 over Hitler's genocidal regime and its allies in Rome and Tokyo. What is more, each member of this implausible trio became intrigued by the others and genuinely tried, in his distinctive way, to build personal relationships. As this book will demonstrate, their diplomatic triangle helped shape the outcome of the Second World War.

Winston Churchill, Franklin Roosevelt and Josef Stalin exchanged 682 messages between 22 June 1941, when Hitler invaded the Soviet Union (operation 'Barbarossa'), and Roosevelt's sudden death on 12 April 1945. Some are lengthy policy documents or chatty news bulletins about the battlefronts; others are brief acknowledgements or lists of supplies. *The Kremlin Letters* prints their most important exchanges in full – some 75 per cent of the total – especially those revealing the characters of the three men and their plans to meet, as well as exchanges on central issues such as the second front, the Arctic convoys and postwar spheres of influence. All the messages will appear later in an online edition.

The Big Three's correspondence was first published by the Soviet government in 1957, in Russian and in an English-language translation that was both comprehensive and accurate.[1] The work had been initiated by Stalin himself in 1950, as part of his campaign to rebut the Western 'Falsifiers of History'. But in late 1951, with publication imminent, the project was suddenly dropped and did not appear in print until the Khrushchev era, under the editorship of Foreign Minister Andrey Gromyko. Perhaps, it has been speculated, with a little polishing of the English text by two former Cambridge graduates then resident in Moscow: Guy Burgess and Donald Maclean. That the USSR was the first to publish the original documents, and so accurately, does not fit Western Cold War stereotypes about the secretive, manipulative Soviets, but Moscow was anxious to offset the selective use of Stalin's letters by Churchill and other Western war memoir-writers and their failure to acknowledge the huge Soviet role in defeating Hitler.[2]

Nevertheless, the documents were published 'raw', with very little background even from the Russian side. It is now possible to place the messages in their full international context, drawing on the archives of all three governments, especially recently opened Russian material from the Stalin archive and the files of the Foreign Ministry, and also private letters and diaries. The project database of some 5,000 documents includes the drafts of each message, records of discussions about them among advisers or in meetings such as those of the British Cabinet, and comments by the relevant ambassadors about how the messages were delivered and received by the three protagonists. In this way, the correspondence opens a multiplicity of windows into the diplomacy of the war. To reveal this, the volume therefore links the original messages in a connective editorial commentary to illuminate their full significance. The story unfolds in chronological chapters, each of which begins with a brief overview of the months in question. Messages and commentary together offer vivid insights into the diplomacy of what Churchill called the 'Grand Alliance' and Roosevelt the 'United Nations', and even more into the personalities of three remarkable, but very different, leaders whom the world crisis of 1940–41 had thrown together.

Churchill and Roosevelt were both quite open about their desire to build a personal relationship with the hitherto reclusive Soviet leader. Stalin also relished his new position at the top table of international politics, and was excited by the challenges of playing against (and with) his US and British interlocutors at a decisive juncture in history. Although some of the messages exchanged seem factual and formulaic, many were politically sensitive and highly personal. The various national archives reveal the care that all three leaders took over composition: mulling over what to say, when to say it, and in what tone – and then waiting anxiously for the response. That is why we also reproduce the more significant alterations that they made in successive drafts.

For the benefit of purists, it should be noted that there does not exist what could be called the 'definitive' text of a message. Not only were they translated from one language into another – Churchill once bemoaned to his Cabinet how 'the tone of the original was often lost in the process of translation'[3] – but most of them were also transmitted as secret telegrams, which meant enciphering and then deciphering the words. In the process, not only were synonyms substituted for the originals, but the word order was also routinely jumbled up to reduce the danger of ciphers being cracked by Axis decrypters. In a few cases, mistranslation caused misunderstanding and even offence – as when the English word 'diversion' in one of Churchill's letters in October 1943 was erroneously transliterated in the Kremlin as '*diversiya*' (Russian for 'subversion' or 'sabotage').[4] This volume therefore prints the versions of the messages that were sent or received in English by Churchill and Roosevelt, even though the translation from the Russian was often rough – especially in the case of the Soviet embassy in Washington in 1943–44, as Andrey Gromyko was finding his feet as the new ambassador. The point, however, is to see Stalin's letters in the form in which they were presented to the president and the prime minister.

To some readers, all this might seem an exercise in desiccated textual criticism. It is therefore worth spelling out what was at stake, especially for the benefit of those from the Facebook generation. In an era before mobile phones, emails, Skype and social media, and in a world where war had made international travel hazardous, telegrams were the prime means of communication. This was the only way that three unlikely allies could get the measure of each other. In fact, Roosevelt and Stalin did not meet in person until twenty-nine months after the onset of 'Barbarossa', at Tehran in November 1943; their second encounter, and the last, was at Yalta in February 1945. Even the peripatetic Churchill had just four sets of meetings with Stalin – the Tehran and Yalta summits, plus his solo visits to Moscow in August 1942 and October 1944. For most of the war, the Big Three did not do face-time.

Theirs, then, was largely an epistolary relationship, conducted through letters. History affords some celebrated examples of this form of personal interaction and self-revelation: one thinks of Cicero's letters to Atticus and other friends, or the erudite passion of Héloïse and Abelard, or Voltaire's correspondence with Catherine the Great and other luminaries of the Enlightenment. Indeed, during the eighteenth century the 'epistolary novel' became something of a cult genre, thanks to Samuel Richardson, Jean-Jacques Rousseau and Johann Wolfgang von Goethe – authors who unfolded their narratives through the letters of the main protagonists.[5] The correspondence that follows does not, of course, rank as a literary classic. Yet it deserves to be remembered because of the unique insights it offers into the personalities and minds of three of the most significant inter-national leaders of the twentieth century, and because their epistolary triangle formed a vital part of the strategic geometry of the Second World War.

The men and their ideas

Josef Stalin is the central figure in *The Kremlin Letters*, both because of the fresh insights from the new Russian material for Western readers and also because, most of the time, he was the one being courted by the other two. Small in stature – at five feet four inches (1.62 metres), he was probably an inch shorter than Churchill – and unprepossessing in appearance, with a blotchy face pockmarked from smallpox and a crooked left arm misshapen by a child-hood injury, Stalin was nevertheless the towering figure of modern Russian history, with whom his country is still struggling to come to terms. Earlier Cold War biographies portraying a dictator ruthlessly intent on power and fame, driven on by an abusive childhood in dirt-poor Georgia, have given way to more nuanced depictions. To quote biographer Stephen Kotkin,

> Stalin shatters any attempt to contain him within binaries. He was by inclin-ation a despot who, when he wanted to be, was utterly charming. He was an ideologue who was flexibly pragmatic. He fastened obsessively on slights yet he was a precocious geostrategic thinker – unique among Bolsheviks – who was, however, prone to egregious strategic blunders.[6]

These paradoxes are on full display in the messages that follow. But to understand what was said, we need to move beyond the realm of psychology to note two other features of Stalin, underlined by recent biographers. First, despite the cult of personality, his reliance on others – on his 'team' as Sheila Fitzpatrick has put it:

> Unchallenged top dog though he was, Stalin preferred – as his contemporaries Mussolini and Hitler did not – to operate with a group of powerful figures around him, loyal to him personally but operating as a team. These men were not competitors with him for leadership, but neither were they political non-entities or simply 'entourage', like his secretaries or secret policemen.[7]

Second, his skill in using words. Although Stalin was capable of mass murder to preserve his power and advance his goals, he recognized that the pen was often mightier than the sword. A poet in his Georgian youth, and well versed in the Russian language thanks to several years in an Orthodox seminary, Stalin acted throughout his political career as the 'editor-in-chief' of Soviet history. He was excellent on the small print – alert to grammar, punctuation and style – but, even more important, attentive to the big picture. Like Churchill, he had no doubt that if you left the 'verdict of history' to others, they would write *you* out of *their* story.

Teamwork and editorship were both essential in the composition of Stalin's telegrams, as is now clear from the material in the Stalin collection (*fond Stalina*) at the Russian State Archive of Social and Political History (RGASPI). The key team-player here was Vyacheslav Molotov, Stalin's deputy and the commissar for foreign affairs since 1939.[8] Reflecting on the wartime messages many years later, Molotov justly commented: 'Stalin and I drafted many of them together. Everything was done through me. It couldn't have been any other way.'[9] Molotov was himself an experienced wordsmith, having worked on the editorial staff of the party newspaper, *Pravda*, in its early years. In addition, as foreign minister from 1939, he was well versed in the intricacies of Soviet diplomacy: Stalin used him as a personal emissary to Churchill and Roosevelt in the summer of 1942. Molotov was notorious in the West for his workaholic temperament and dour rigidity, earning him nicknames such as 'Stone-Arse' and 'Mr Nyet'. Sometimes he used his own deputies, Andrey Vyshinskiy and Vladimir Dekanozov to prepare draft messages on minor issues. On more important matters, however, Molotov probably received verbal instructions from the 'Boss' himself, and then gave him a text. In any case, almost all drafts were presented to 'Comrade Stalin for approval' and then annotated by him with the words 'Agree' or 'Agree with amendments'. Often Stalin added whole paragraphs – using his blue, or sometimes red, pencil.

The twists and turns of Soviet diplomacy will be discussed more fully in subsequent chapters. But it is worth highlighting here a few key themes. In 1941 and 1942, Stalin's priority was to secure substantive Western aid. His precise agenda varied, but the two refrains were for a 'second front', ideally in northern France, and for a sustained supply line from Britain via the Arctic convoys to Arkhangelsk (Archangel) and Murmansk. Although the Soviet predicament eased during 1943, with the Red Army's victories at Stalingrad and Kursk, Stalin continued to treat the second front and the Arctic convoys as litmus tests of Western credibility as allies. When it became clear in June 1943 that there would be no landing in France that year, at the same time as Churchill suspended the Arctic convoys because of heavy losses, Stalin recalled his ambassadors from London and Washington – Ivan Maisky and Maksim Litvinov. Both were cosmopolitan intellectuals and accomplished linguists who had functioned in the past as adept double interpreters between Moscow and the West – sometimes even advising on the composition and presentation of the messages. But neither was a Kremlin insider, and both were now under suspicion in Moscow. Maisky and Litvinov were replaced by Fedor Gusev in London and Andrey Gromyko in Washington – more insular, often surly, protégés of Molotov – whose lack of diplomatic finesse and linguistic suppleness blunted Soviet diplomacy in the second half of the war.

Another vital concern in the Kremlin was the USSR's postwar borders. Stalin and Molotov raised this matter repeatedly in 1941–42, trying to extract from their new allies early and firm commitments. Faced, however, with a brick wall in London and especially in Washington, Stalin changed tack in May 1942, deciding to let the postwar borders be settled by the 'correlation of forces' as the war progressed – in other words, leaving the issue to the Red Army rather than the Foreign Ministry. Nevertheless, the question of frontiers came to the fore in the correspondence again in 1944–45 over the fate of the Balkans and especially Poland. By this time Stalin was in a strong military position, and he knew it; but he never entirely lost the fear that his allies might do a deal with Hitler behind his back. His unsatisfied curiosity about the flight to Britain in May 1941 of Deputy Führer Rudolf Hess is one example. Indeed, the fiercest exchanges in the whole correspondence occurred in March–April 1945, when Stalin accused his allies of trying to contrive a unilateral German surrender in the west via clandestine negotiations in Bern.

Even more than Josef Stalin, Winston Churchill was a man of words. Before the war, he had made his living by his pen, producing at various times pulp journalism, acute political commentary and substantial tomes of history, biography and memoir. He was also a political maverick, who changed parties twice during his career and was widely suspect in the 1930s as opportunist in tactics and erratic in judgement. Prime Minister Stanley Baldwin, who worked hard to keep Churchill out of office for much of the 1930s, joked that 'when Winston was born lots of fairies swooped down on his cradle' to smother him with gifts – 'imagination, eloquence, industry, ability' and so on, until another fairy, declaring that 'no one person has a right to so many gifts', denied him 'judgment and wisdom'.[10] But on a single overriding issue, the threat from Hitler, Churchill had proved more perceptive and outspoken than almost all his contemporaries. This sagacity ensured a return to office when war broke out in 1939, after a decade in the political 'wilderness', and then his appointment as prime minister in May 1940, just as the Nazi *Blitzkrieg* engulfed Western Europe. A soldier in his youth, Churchill was determined from the start of his premiership to take a firm grip on British strategy, and also to stamp his mark on foreign relations, especially with Britain's major allies. Convinced of his own persuasive powers and contemptuous of the Foreign Office, he relished personal diplomacy – what he would later call 'parleys at the summit' – first to woo Roosevelt and then to bond with Stalin. During the war, he travelled over 100,000 miles by air – usually in converted bombers that were unpressurized and badly heated, often skirting the edge of enemy airspace. When Churchill was visiting Moscow in October 1944, someone remarked that the Big Three were like the Holy Trinity. 'If that is so,' quipped Stalin, 'Churchill must be the Holy Ghost. He flies around so much.'[11]

For Churchill, therefore, the messages to his fellow leaders were a surrogate for conversation. Whereas Stalin, the editor, kept things short and sharp, Churchill tended to range expansively over policy and problems – drafting messages, as he liked to say, from mouth to hand. In other words, by dictation to secretaries, whose typescripts he would then edit – sometimes going through several versions. Some at least were written with an eye on posterity, because he was already planning the war memoirs that eventually appeared in six volumes from 1948 to 1954. For instance, after haggling with Stalin in January 1944 about whether or not Britain might have signed a compromise peace with Hitler in 1940, Churchill composed, but did not send, a message observing that 'we had better leave the past to history, but remember if I live long enough I may be one of the historians.'[12]

Not everything, however, was Churchill's own work. More routine messages were produced by the relevant departments, especially the Foreign Office but also the Chiefs of Staff Committee and his own private office. 'Looking at the messages and letters that go out under the P.M.'s signature,' his secretary and trusted adviser 'Jock' Colville opined in January 1945, 'I often think how difficult it will be for future historians to know what is "genuine Churchill" and what is "school of".'[13] Colville was, however, writing in the comfortable conviction that the records of the war would not be open to inquisitive scholars for many decades. In fact, most were made public in the 1970s. The prime minister's files at The National Archives (TNA) in Kew and supplementary documents in the Churchill Archives Centre (CAC) in Cambridge – many of them now online – help us pinpoint more precisely his authorial role in what he insisted on calling his 'Personal Correspondence' with Stalin and Roosevelt. An additional and distinctive feature of the British side of this epistolary triangle – as befits the more collegial system of Westminster and Whitehall – was the contribution of the Cabinet in approving and sometimes drafting key messages. On occasions, the minutes of Cabinet discussions shed additional light on the thinking behind the words.

Churchill's own foreign policy priorities were clear. Top of his list was the defeat of Hitler. As he said on the eve of 'Barbarossa', 'if Hitler invaded Hell, I would make at least a favourable reference to the Devil in the House of Commons'.[14] But his willingness to aid Stalin was always constrained by the limits of Britain's position, as a small island nation with extended global commitments amid a truly world war, and with an army that had to be virtually built up from scratch after Dunkirk. Haunted by the losses of the Somme and Passchendaele in the Great War, unnerved by the failure of the British troops for most of 1941–42 to win major victories, and fixated on the need to hold the Mediterranean as key to the British Empire's supply lines, Churchill wanted to concentrate on what he liked to call the 'soft underbelly' of the Axis – in other words North Africa and Italy – and in 1942–43 he was able to dictate strategy to Roosevelt because the bulk of America's newly raised combat troops were deployed in the Pacific. This focus on the Mediterranean lifeline to Britain's Asian empire also fitted with Churchill's adamant determination that, whatever the vicissitudes of war, 'I have not become the King's First Minister in order to preside over the liquidation of the British Empire'.[15]

In the first half of 1943, president and prime minister tried rather ineptly to deceive Stalin about when they would launch the second front, which prompted the Soviet leader to withdraw and then replace his ambassadors. By late 1943, Churchill's own priorities were shifting. A vehement anti-communist, he became more fearful as the tide turned against Germany that this would allow the Red Army to surge across Eastern Europe. Yet Churchill also hoped that good personal relations with Stalin might mitigate the consequences. For both leaders, Poland became the 'touchstone' of their relationship, particularly its postwar borders and its future government. Churchill's problem was that Stalin controlled much of the chess board by late 1944, thanks to the presence of the victorious Red Army in East and Southeast Europe. In any case, Churchill's forte was cards, not chess: he lacked Stalin's patience and guile during the endgame of the war. In fact, during 1945 the prime minister's conduct of relations became increasingly erratic, as he lurched from extravagant professions of faith in Stalin after Yalta in February 1945 to apocalyptic fears about the looming 'iron curtain', as victory dawned in the spring.

Of the three correspondents, Franklin D. Roosevelt was least involved in the nitty-gritty of composition. A significant number of 'his' messages emanated from the Pentagon because the US military were keen to use this top-level channel to go over the heads of the sticky Red Army bureaucracy. Even when the president initiated a message, he was usually content to take drafts from Harry Hopkins, the hard-driving former social worker from Iowa, who was his closest aide, Admiral William Leahy, officially 'chief of staff to the commander-in-chief' from July 1942, and later in the war Charles 'Chip' Bohlen, the State Department Russianist who interpreted for him at Tehran and Yalta. In his memoirs, Leahy recalled the president often saying, 'Bill, suppose you take a shot at this.' Leahy added: 'I always did, of course, and he always changed it.' The word 'always' is far too strong, but even when FDR did not alter a draft, he would generally read and approve it – even in his faltering final months, as Bohlen's memos from that time make clear.[16] The president's amendments often took the form of adding personal touches and encouraging noises to otherwise bureaucratic documents, because Roosevelt, like Churchill, had unbounded faith in the potency of his personal charm. A striking indication of this is his breezy observation in March 1942, quoted as an epigraph: without having ever met Stalin and after exchanging only a handful of messages, Roosevelt told Churchill that he could handle the Soviet leader better than anyone else, including the prime minister.

And yet FDR was also the 'Wheelchair President', struck down by polio before the age of forty and thereafter unable to walk unaided. Though still keen to travel, unlike Stalin (who was petrified of flying), but much less mobile than the globe-trotting Churchill, FDR had to rely on others to be his eyes and ears, especially Hopkins and also business tycoon W. Averell Harriman – both of whom served as crucial intermediaries with Churchill and Stalin.[17] But as the correspondence shows, the president was desperate for a personal meeting. In the spring of 1943, he even tried to set up one behind Churchill's back – leaving the PM mortified on discovering the deception. For FDR, more than Churchill, written communication was always intended to facilitate a real meeting of men and minds. There was something truly heartfelt about his opening greeting to Stalin at Tehran: 'I am glad to see you. I have tried for a long time to bring this about.'[18] It is, however, clear that Roosevelt's health never recovered from the gruelling trip to Tehran; the Yalta summit in the Crimea then finished him off. Roosevelt's courtship of Stalin proved in effect a death sentence. Whether the effort was worth the cost is one of the deeper questions that underlie this book.

Although far less of a details man than his two counterparts, FDR had a clear sense of where he was going in foreign policy. First, he believed that the Soviet Union, though 'run by a dictatorship as absolute as any other dictator-ship in the world',[19] was gradually emerging from its revolutionary phase into a more cooperative relationship with the outside world. He wanted to encourage that process; hence his decision in 1933 to open formal diplomatic relations, after successive Republican administrations had treated the USSR as a pariah state. In 1941, Roosevelt had no doubt that continued Soviet resistance was vital for Britain, as America's front line, and for the USA itself, and he extended Lend-Lease aid to the USSR despite fierce opposition from the political right, the Catholic Church and State Department hardliners. The hostility to the president's Soviet policy from most professional diplomats was a further reason why he used trusted intermediaries like Hopkins and Harriman to bypass the diplomatic establishment.

Secondly, Roosevelt believed that his people had to be pulled out of isolationism; even after Pearl Harbor, he feared the danger of its recrudescence once victory was won. The war therefore offered Americans what the State Department dubbed a 'Second Chance' to realize Woodrow Wilson's vision of an international organization, now in the form of the United Nations. To give the new UN real teeth, FDR believed it had to be built around the major powers – his 'four policemen': America, Russia, Britain and China. Without British and Soviet participation in particular, he was sure that the UN would be stillborn. His relationship with Churchill always mattered, but in the second half of the war he took it increasingly for granted. The crux for him in 1943–45 was to draw the USSR into what he called 'the family circle' of great powers.[20]

Creating a postwar United Nations organization on his terms became Roosevelt's prime objective, yet he never underestimated the difficulties. 'The tragedy of Wilson was always somewhere within the rim of his consciousness,' reflected speechwriter Robert Sherwood.[21] Wilson's frenzied campaign to mobilize the USA behind the League of Nations had precipitated the stroke in October 1919 that left him half-paralysed for the rest of his time in the White House. This double tragedy, political *and* personal, had particular poignancy for the Wheelchair President. Watching the movie *Wilson* in September 1944, Roosevelt was visibly shaken by the stroke scene. 'By God,' he muttered, 'that's not going to happen to me!' Less than seven months later, on 12 April 1945, FDR dropped dead from a massive cerebral haemorrhage.[22]

The triangle – and why it mattered

The relationship between the three leaders has been a subject of abiding interest for commentators and scholars.[23] Yet it has generally been studied without systematic research into their correspondence and the stories behind it. To take this dimension seriously throws additional light on the dynamic triangle formed by these larger-than-life personalities – a triangle that mattered for both the wartime and the postwar era. All three wielded enormous power not only over politics and foreign policy, but also over strategy and operations. Stalin and Roosevelt were, after all, commanders-in-chief, as well as heads of

government, while Churchill – though officially the 'king's first minister' – was
supreme commander in all but name. And each believed profoundly in his own
capacities as a manipulator of men. How they tried to handle each other and,
more broadly, how they played the game of triangular diplomacy are recurrent
features of their correspondence. Throughout 1941–45, none of them anticipated the Cold War, and they sought some kind of working relationship after
the defeat of Germany and Japan. But each tried to shape that relationship in
his own way, and it is here that we see some of the roots of the Cold War. This
is clear from *The Kremlin Letters*.

Although no ideological zealot, Stalin remained a Bolshevik in his basic
expectation of capitalist rivalry and encirclement. That said, the messages
confirm his greater respect for Roosevelt and his more difficult, often strained,
relationship with Churchill – a distinction conveyed by his remark to the
Yugoslav communist Milovan Djilas in June 1944: 'Churchill is the kind of man
who will pick your pocket of a kopeck if you don't watch him . . . Roosevelt is
not like that. He dips in his hand only for bigger coins.'[24] Although Molotov's
drafts did not usually differentiate when dealing with the two Western leaders,
Stalin often edited the texts to convey something of his respect for Roosevelt,
while toughening the wording to Churchill. His feelings about the president
reflected a complex interplay of considerations. Some were structural: the
superior military and economic power of the USA and also the relatively
detached geopolitical relationship with America, whereas the British Empire
was Russia's long-standing rival for power and position in Asia and the Near
East. Other considerations were more personal: Roosevelt's status as the initi-
ator of diplomatic relations with the USSR and the man who offered generous
wartime assistance in the form of Lend-Lease, in contrast to Churchill – notorious as a fierce anti-communist, who had championed Western intervention
against the Bolsheviks during the Russian Civil War. Harriman noted after
Tehran that Stalin 'spoke with the President as if with the most senior of all the
participants';[25] he was much more considerate of FDR than of Churchill, agreed
with him more often, and expressed his disagreement with greater restraint –
never indulging in the kind of jibes and needling with which he periodically
prodded the prime minister. The nicknames for the two leaders used in Soviet
intelligence reports – 'Captain' (*Kapitan*) for Roosevelt and 'Wild Boar' (*Kaban*)
for Churchill – was probably not accidental: Stalin's agents knew the outlook
and predilections of 'the Boss'.

Ideological differences aside, of course, Stalin never trusted anyone; and
thanks to extensive Soviet intelligence penetration of London and Washington,
he knew about Roosevelt's double plays, especially over the secret development

of the atomic bomb and the delays in opening a second front. Yet for Stalin, FDR was the most important means of implementing his grand strategy of defeating the common enemy and then securing the fruits of victory through an expanded Soviet sphere of influence in Europe and the Far East. On these territorial issues, Roosevelt was more accommodating than Churchill, largely due to the remoteness of the USA from Europe and a degree of distance between American and Soviet spheres of influence. The president, for instance, made no objection about transferring to the Soviet Union territories and rights in the Far East; on the British side, although Churchill was similarly accommodating at Yalta about former Japanese possessions, Foreign Secretary Anthony Eden did not feel it necessary to purchase Soviet entry into the Asian war. In Europe, FDR made it clear to Stalin at Tehran that the United States would not seriously impede the restoration of Soviet control over the Baltic states or dispute Soviet hegemony in Poland and Eastern Europe, so long as the USSR provided a veneer of democracy. Churchill, by contrast, was much more engaged – and often enraged – by these issues: Britain had officially gone to war for Poland in 1939, and entertained a particular interest in Greece and the Eastern Mediterranean. Although the State Department had a real hang-up about anything that smacked of 'spheres of influence' and Old World power politics, Roosevelt's determination not to get entrapped in European territorial squabbles and his repeated insistence that he could not keep US troops in Europe for more than a year or two reflected a worldview that suited Stalin. The president was interested in the grand architecture of global cooperation, not in the chessboard diplomacy of Europe's ever-shifting borders. In terms of both personality and policy, FDR was a known quantity and a manageable partner for Stalin; without him the future seemed much more uncertain.

For Roosevelt, in turn, Stalin's personality was crucial for achieving two essential foreign policy aims: maximizing the Soviet contribution to the struggle against the Axis and ensuring postwar cooperation, without which FDR believed there could be no lasting peace. This was why he was so keen to draw the USSR into the community of nations. His underlying assumption, shared with many Americans to the left of the political centre, was that they were witnessing a gradual convergence between the Soviet Union and the West. A quarter-century after the Bolsheviks seized power, the USSR under Stalin seemed to have developed into a country whose foreign policy was driven not by revolutionary expansion, but by national interest – in other words, a more 'normal' state, animated by *Realpolitik*. Related to this, Soviet society seemed in key areas to be in the process of gradual liberalization. Wartime signs included the abolition of Comintern – the revolutionary arm of Soviet foreign policy –

and the loosening of restraints on the Orthodox Church, both in 1943, together with the emphasis on historic Russian patriotism, rather than Marxist-Leninist ideology, as inspiration for the people's war effort. The president told Francis Spellman, the Catholic archbishop of New York, in September 1943 of his hope that in ten to twenty years 'European influences would bring the Russians to become less barbarian', and that 'out of forced friendship' with the USA and Britain might 'soon come a real and lasting friendship'.[26] FDR even admitted the possibility of mutual evolution – socialization of American capitalism and liberalization of Soviet socialism – capable in time of transcending the division of the world into two hostile systems. He was, after all, the 'New Deal' president, who in 1944 called for a 'Second Bill of Rights' to graft economic rights onto the political liberties enshrined in the US Constitution by the first Bill of Rights in 1791.[27]

All this reinforced his grand strategy of 'educating' the USSR through personal interaction with Stalin. The Soviet leader's evident power, his capacity to turn a great country one way or another, was here an apparent advantage. The man who could drive through the collectivization of agriculture and industrial mass production in barely a decade could, it seemed, also transform society and politics – if he was properly managed, which FDR saw as his own special task. In the president's opinion, the root issue was the Soviets' sense of insecurity and the consequent need to bring them in from the cold. Hence his efforts to avoid any impression of an Anglo-American bloc – especially before and during the Tehran conference, when he deflected Churchill's pleas for bilateral meetings – and his attempts in the last weeks of his life to restrain the prime minister from almost daily outbursts to Stalin because, as he said in a telegram on the day before he died, 'these problems, in one form or another, seem to arise every day and most of them straighten out'.[28]

Churchill's attitude to Stalin and the USSR was, in many ways, very different. Whereas FDR had an essentially optimistic vision of the future, the PM oscillated between hope and fear. In mid-January 1944, for instance, he wrote to Eden about 'the deep-seated changes which have taken place in the character of the Russian State' and 'the new confidence which has grown in our hearts towards Stalin'. Yet less than three months later, on 1 April, he told the Foreign Secretary: 'Although I have tried in every way to put myself in sympathy with these Communist leaders, I cannot feel the slightest confidence in them. Force and facts are their only realities.'[29] Nor did the PM espouse Roosevelt's leftist belief in convergence: Churchill's vehement opposition to socialism and communism had been the lodestar of his domestic and foreign policies ever since the 1920s. The prime minister also shared the 'orientalist' perceptions of

Russia that were widespread among the British establishment, speaking of their 'peasant' crudity and Asiatic 'barbarism', and likening them on occasions to 'baboons'. Even British diplomats who were leftist in inclination could not refrain from patronizing comments: 'It's too bad,' one wrote, 'that Stalin and Mol[otov] were not at Eton and Harrow, but what can we do about it?'[30] Nevertheless, Churchill did believe, especially after the Nazi-Soviet Pact, that he was dealing with a regime whose foreign policy was governed by considerations of *Realpolitik*, not ideology. As he declared in a radio address on 1 October 1939, 'I cannot forecast to you the action of Russia. It is a riddle wrapped in a mystery inside an enigma: but perhaps there is a key. That key is Russian national interest.'[31] And the key was held by Stalin.

On the importance of the Soviet leader and on the potential for communicating with him, Churchill and Roosevelt were therefore of one mind. Each in his different way believed it was possible to do business with the recluse of the Kremlin. This conviction was cemented by their brief but intense face-to-face meetings, when Stalin cut a very different figure from Hitler with his calculated rants, or Mussolini and his operatic bombast. The Soviet leader would sit quietly, often doodling, and then respond with remarks that were clear and pertinent – if often barbed. The cynical British diplomat Sir Alexander Cadogan summed up his performance at Yalta with unconcealed admiration, observing that while Roosevelt 'flapped around' and Churchill 'boomed', Stalin 'just sat taking it all in and being rather amused. When he did chip in, he never used a superfluous word, and spoke very much to the point. He's obviously got a very good sense of humour – and a rather quick temper.'[32] This was written in February 1945, after two major summits, but it should be noted that the amiable nickname 'Uncle Joe' had entered the private vocabulary of FDR and Churchill by August 1942, before either man had actually met Stalin. Indeed the belief that one could do business with the Soviet leader derived from the clarity and directness of the messages exchanged since June 1941. On paper, as well as in person, the dialogue was real – despite what was lost in translation.

Yet Stalin was not an easy man to measure. Averell Harriman, who talked with the Soviet leader dozens of times during the war, described him in 1975 as 'the most inscrutable and contradictory character I have known'. Stalin's frequent alternations between courtesy and brusqueness unsettled any feeling of a stable relationship. Churchill's explanation was that there were 'two forces to be reckoned with in Russia: (a) Stalin himself, personally cordial to me. (b) Stalin in council, a grim thing behind him, which we and he have both to reckon with.'[33] Roosevelt and Harriman also adopted this 'two Stalins' trope, attributing friction with Moscow to hardliners in the Politburo or to the failure of Molotov to pass on accurate information. Yet all this was wishful thinking. Even if Stalin was running a 'team', in Moscow itself no one had the slightest doubt who was 'Boss'.

Dealing with 'Uncle Joe', despite his apparent approachability, was therefore a delicate business. A further complication was that the Big Three relationship was not merely bilateral – Stalin and Churchill, Stalin and Roosevelt, Churchill and Roosevelt – but triangular and also volatile, which tended to leave one of the three feeling outnumbered or on the margins. Of course, the triangle was never equilateral, because Roosevelt and Churchill had a much closer relationship with each other than with Stalin. The volume of their bilateral correspondence was more than double their combined messages to the Soviet leader. They also met more often during the war years and spoke occasionally on the phone – drawing throughout on the benefits of a common language. At a deeper level, there existed a general British–American solidarity on most matters of Allied diplomacy, as well as an underlying consensus on political and social values – aside from colonies and trading blocs. The degree of awareness of the members of the Big Three about their partners' actions was also unequal: Roosevelt and Churchill constantly kept each other informed of their correspondence with Stalin, often coordinating their replies, whereas the latter could only guess (or infer from intelligence reports) what his two partners were saying to each other. This fundamental asymmetry always left him at a disadvantage against London and Washington.[34]

Yet the Churchill–Roosevelt relationship was never static. It was forged in 1940, when Churchill's determination to stay in the war after the fall of France ensured FDR's support for Britain as America's front line of defence; and it was strengthened in August 1941, with their first wartime meeting off Newfoundland, when they agreed the 'Atlantic Charter' of war aims and shared values. This would become a benchmark document for their relations with the USSR. After Pearl Harbor, with America now an ally, Roosevelt and Churchill met three times in little more than a year – twice in Washington and then in Casablanca – as they tried to formulate strategy for a global war in which they had to balance the containment of Japan in the Pacific with the prioritization of an early second front against Nazi Germany. On the latter, there was a fundamental divergence between the American desire for an early cross-Channel attack to relieve Russia and Churchill's more cautious peripheral strategy of 'closing the ring' on the Axis via North Africa and Italy.

In this period, Stalin was definitely in a weak position within the threesome. Allied aid to Russia, though significant, did not play a decisive role in turning the tide on Germany's Eastern Front. The victories at Stalingrad in January

1943 and Kursk the following July were won by the Red Army, and at huge cost. By the spring of 1943, the dynamics of the Big Three triangle were changing. Roosevelt never doubted the need for close cooperation with Britain – that remained axiomatic; but he now reached out more energetically to Stalin, seeing the Soviet leader as an ally both on wartime strategy (the invasion of France) and postwar diplomacy (for instance, European decolonization). His handling of the Tehran conference in November 1943 showed that on both the personal and the policy levels, he was aligning himself with Stalin. Churchill left Tehran very conscious that the two-plus-one dynamics of alliance politics had shifted against him. Sick and depressed, he sank into dire predictions of 'a more bloody war' that might 'wipe out civilization' and fumed that 'we've got to do something with these bloody Russians'.[35] This was one of Churchill's mood swings, and he soon shifted into a more positive mode; but his post-Tehran gloom showed an awareness that the power balance within the triangle was changing.

In the last year of the war, the interplay between the Big Three fluctuated even more. On strategy, Roosevelt was now the senior partner in the transatlantic alliance – pushing through the landings in Normandy and southern France against Churchill's continued forebodings, and also closing down the Mediterranean, where the British still dominated, as a major theatre of operations. All this accorded with Stalin's general preferences. On the other hand, the summer of 1944 saw the apogee of the Big Three's alliance, coordinating their operations on the continent of Europe as they converged on the Third Reich from east and west. On some matters of diplomacy that feature in the correspondence, Churchill and Roosevelt were at odds with Stalin, especially over the treatment of the Warsaw Uprising and the composition of a post-Nazi national government in Poland. Yet Roosevelt never let Poland get in the way of his broader vision of Soviet–American cooperation – concentrating on drawing the Soviets into the United Nations organization. In this phase, the dynamics were often two-plus-one, but the line-ups shifted from issue to issue. At Yalta, for instance, Stalin and Roosevelt were at odds over Poland, but both had little time for Churchill's wish to give France an occupation zone in Germany. Even so, the PM eventually got his way. As the end of the war drew near, the strains in the Alliance and the underlying suspicions became ever more apparent, but all three leaders still reposed considerable faith in their personal relationship. At Yalta, Stalin told Roosevelt and Churchill: 'While we are alive, there is nothing to fear. We will not allow dangerous disagreements.'[36]

Whether Roosevelt's death made a fundamental difference, or whether that 'what if' is just an illusion about great men and history, remains a matter of debate. Counterfactuals aside, however, this correspondence does make clear the central role of these three men in coordinating relations between their countries and thereby helping to determine the outcome of the war. Cooperation between such dissimilar political figures, from contrasting backgrounds and different political systems, was not guaranteed, and *The Kremlin Letters* is replete with friction and suspicion. But we should keep this in perspective. The Axis powers – Germany, Italy and Japan – had gained a remarkably strong geopolitical position by the spring of 1942 in Eurasia, North Africa and the Western Pacific. They were also much more alike as political regimes. Yet they never matched America, Britain and Russia in terms of military and diplomatic cooperation; Hitler patronized Mussolini and did not correspond with Tojo. The Big Three leaders, by contrast, were able to subordinate their contradictions to the main task of defeating a common foe.[37]

When Stalin extolled the unique frankness of their alliance – quoted as one of the epigraphs to this book – he was talking expansively during a well-lubricated Yalta dinner. But *in vino veritas*: theirs was indeed one of the closest working alliances in history. At a basic level, the Big Three's anti-Hitler coalition worked, whereas the Berlin–Rome–Tokyo Axis did not. This is also clear from *The Kremlin Letters*.

1

STRANGE ENCOUNTERS

(June to September 1941)

JUNE 1941 OPENED A totally new chapter in the Soviet Union's engagement with the United States and Great Britain. Yet relations never entirely escaped the shadow of the past, and we have to explore that history briefly in order to understand wartime tensions within the alliance triangle. The USA did not establish diplomatic relations with the USSR until 1933; Britain had done so in 1924 (though with a break in 1927–29). Stalin, mindful of Western intervention in the Russian Civil War, remained wary of a London–Berlin axis against Moscow: events such as Germany's admission to the League of Nations in 1926 and the Munich agreement of 1938 were seen in this light. For their part, British Conservatives feared a new Russo-German axis, as in the treaties of Brest-Litovsk (1918) and Rapallo (1922). Tentative attempts at collective security during the 1930s – promoted in Moscow by Foreign Minister Maksim Litvinov – were blighted by these historic suspicions, as well as by divergent security interests.

Neville Chamberlain's government was finally panicked out of appeasement in March 1939, when Hitler extinguished the independence of Czechoslovakia. In a belated attempt at deterrence, Britain offered Poland, clearly next on the Nazi hit-list, a guarantee of its independence. This commitment proved a hollow promise in 1939, because the British had neither the intention nor the capacity to send troops. Effective containment of Hitler would require the help of the Red Army, yet the chances of an accord with Moscow were prejudiced by the Polish guarantee, because of the USSR's rooted animosity to the Polish state and its desire to regain territory lost after the collapse of the tsarist empire and the war of 1920–21. Russo-Polish hostility would haunt relations between London and Moscow throughout the war. Once the flimsy nature of British diplomacy became clear to Stalin during the summer of 1939, he and Molotov – who had replaced Litvinov as foreign minister in May – were amenable to Hitler's overtures for an accord.

The consequent Nazi-Soviet Pact of August 1939 came as a bombshell in the West, cutting right across what had been the starkest ideological chasm of the 1930s. But in the short term it gave Stalin what he needed: assurance that a German invasion of Poland would not precipitate a war with Russia. Indeed the secret protocols of the pact facilitated a mutual partition of Poland in September 1939 and gave the USSR carte blanche to take over parts of Romania and the Baltic states of Estonia, Latvia and Lithuania, which had won their independence from Russia in bloody fighting after the Revolution. Germany was now expected to engage in a protracted war in the west with Britain and France, akin to 1914–18, that would exhaust all three powers and give the USSR precious years to complete its rearmament. The Nazi-Soviet Pact therefore looked like a brilliant act of diplomatic *Realpolitik* by Stalin – earning him *Time* magazine's ultimate accolade as 'Man of the Year' for 1939.

The following year, however, was undoubtedly Hitler's. In 1940, Britain and France were paid back with a vengeance for the errors of appeasement. The Nazi-Soviet Pact allowed Hitler to concentrate entirely on the Western Front. Aided by the good luck of his surprise thrust through the Ardennes, the Führer knocked France out of the war in four weeks – something that the Kaiser's best generals had failed to achieve in four years. Churchill, who took over as prime minister on 10 May, stilled Cabinet flutters about a possible compromise peace; but during the summer, Britain faced the threat of imminent invasion and then endured a grim winter of bombing by the Luftwaffe and the prospect of gradual strangulation of its supply lines by German U-boats. The Soviet situation was less precarious, but the pact of 1939 had backfired by allowing Hitler to gain dominance over continental Europe in 1940. Although Stalin moved preemptively into the Baltic states in June 1940, he now faced German power across new but unfortified borders in Eastern Europe. The Foreign Office hoped that this shared predicament might serve as the basis for closer Soviet–British relations, and in June 1940 it prepared a letter proposing discussions about how to 'resist German hegemony'. This was signed personally by Churchill as a way to ensure an audience with Stalin for the new British ambassador Sir Stafford Cripps.[1] But this overture had no effect and simply fed Stalin's suspicions that the British were trying to provoke him into war with Hitler, in order to relieve the pressure on them. Nor did it cut any ice in Moscow that Cripps was a leading pro-Russian member of the British left: what mattered for Stalin was pragmatism, not ideology. After a stiff three-hour meeting in the Kremlin on 1 July 1940, Cripps did not secure another audience with the Soviet leader until after 'Barbarossa', and Churchill received no reply to his message.

Whatever London might have hoped, Stalin was still trying to buy time by dealing with Hitler. In November, Molotov visited Berlin in search of a territorial deal over the Balkans, key to Russia's historic concerns about access to and from the Black Sea. His haggling over Bulgaria and Romania highlights another abiding theme of wartime diplomacy – spheres of influence in the Balkans – and foreshadowed the Churchill–Stalin 'percentages' deal of 1944. More immediately, the collapse of these Soviet–German talks triggered Hitler's Directive No. 21 of 18 December, ordering the Wehrmacht to prepare to 'crush Soviet Russia in a quick campaign, even before the conclusion of the war against England', so that Germany could gain complete control of continental Europe in 1941. 'After 1942,' he warned, 'the United States would be in a position to intervene.'[2]

The ensuing German build-up in Eastern Europe was tracked carefully in the Kremlin. From the autumn of 1940, the Soviet Interior Ministry (NKVD) provided a special operational file codenamed 'Venture' (*Zateya*), in which information on German intentions and dispositions was brought to Stalin's attention. But the Soviet leader, never fully trusting his own intelligence services, filtered this mass of data through his own assumptions, above all the twin beliefs that Hitler would not turn east until he had defeated Britain and that any invasion would follow a long war of nerves (as over Czechoslovakia in 1938 and Poland in 1939). Stalin was therefore determined to avoid anything that could be treated in Berlin as Soviet provocation. He viewed warnings of impending Nazi aggression sent by US Under-Secretary of State Sumner Welles on 1 March and Churchill himself on 3 April as deliberate attempts to push him into war with Germany. The prime minister's message proved particularly controversial. In his war memoirs, Churchill made a huge fuss about Cripps's failure to deliver the telegram until 19 April – and then only to Andrey Vyshinskiy, Molotov's deputy – even postulating that 'if I had had direct contact with Stalin I might perhaps have prevented him from having so much of his Air Force destroyed on the ground'.[3] This claim not only reveals Churchill's hubristic confidence in personal diplomacy, but also his utter failure to understand Stalin's almost paranoid mistrust of Britain. The stunning news that on 10 May Rudolf Hess, Hitler's deputy, had landed in Britain played into this worldview. Indeed, the Foreign Office ineptly encouraged Soviet agitation by a whispering campaign that the Hess mission (in all probability a maverick, solo act) reflected splits in the Nazi leadership and even presaged attempts to forge an alliance with Britain against Bolshevik Russia. Determined not to give Hitler any excuse to attack, Stalin avoided full mobilization right to the end. When Marshal Georgiy Zhukov, chief of the general staff, phoned him at 3.30 a.m. on 22 June to report German shelling and bombing all along the border and to request permission to retaliate, all that Zhukov could hear for several minutes was heavy breathing on the other end of the line.[4]

That morning, the Red Air Force lost 1,200 planes, an eighth of its total strength – mostly destroyed on the ground – and the Wehrmacht surged across the western USSR. A week later, finally coming to terms with the gravity of the crisis, Stalin muttered: 'Lenin founded our state, and we've fucked it up.' Whether he had a nervous collapse or was play-acting in order to sniff out possible opposition remains unclear. But he soon rallied, speaking to his people for the first time on 3 July and arrogating to himself the roles of commander-in-chief and defence minister, as well as party leader and head of government. Nevertheless, Hitler's 'surprise attack' – as it went down in Soviet official history – was a surprise largely of Stalin's own making, for which his people would pay a terrible price in the opening months of the war.[5]

In the West, too, the devastating opening of 'Barbarossa' would have lasting effects. It fed the widespread assumption in military circles that the Red Army – ravaged by Stalin's 1937 purge of the officer corps and then given a bloody nose by the Finns in the 'Winter War' of 1939–40 – was incapable of serious resistance. Most intelligence analysts in London and Washington reckoned that the Red Army would succumb within a month or two. On 4 July, Welles advised Laurence Steinhardt, the US ambassador to Russia, that it was believed that 'German troops would be able, if they desire so to do, to enter Moscow within a week', and advised him to start planning the evacuation of embassy staff to the east. In Britain, the prospect of a rapid Soviet collapse and consequent redeployment of the Wehrmacht to France revived fears for the security of Britain itself. British anti-invasion forces were ordered to be at peak readiness by 1 September.[6] Even though these alarmist predictions were soon revised, British and American military circles – many of them viscerally anti-communist – remained sceptical even into 1942 about the Soviet capacity for sustained resistance. This had a profound effect on their willingness to provide aid to Russia, given the huge deficiencies in their own rearmament.

At the top, however, Churchill and Roosevelt had to take the new relationship more seriously, if only to bolster Russian morale at a time when the Wehrmacht was sweeping all before it. The president was more forthcoming than the prime minister, but with his country officially neutral and public opinion still deeply sceptical about entering the war – especially in tandem with 'atheistic' Russia – he had to tread carefully. In the British case, relations quickly developed into a formal declaration of mutual help and no separate peace, which was signed on 12 July, but Churchill had no intention of allowing assistance for the Red Army to jeopardize Britain's own war effort, particularly in North Africa. This pitted him against Eden, his foreign secretary, and a few other politicians, especially Max Beaverbrook, the newspaper baron, who wanted to do much more for Russia and whose advocacy won widespread support in the country at large.

The debate about aid within London and Washington reflected an under-lying tactical difference – whether to adopt a quid pro quo approach that tied Western aid to Soviet cooperation on trade or intelligence, or else to operate in a generous, no-strings manner, on the assumption that the West needed to overcome rooted Bolshevik suspicions of the capitalists. In particular, this was Roosevelt's instinct, reinforced by the visit paid by his right-hand man, Harry Hopkins, to Moscow at the end of July. Indeed, it would guide his policy towards the USSR right through the war. Churchill's mood – in 1941 and later – was much more erratic, veering from cooperative noises to growling resentment in a way that infuriated advisers such as Eden. But his strategic preoccupation with the Mediterranean – leitmotif of his strategy in 1942–44 – was already clear by the autumn of 1941.

Once the agreement with Britain was signed, Stalin sent a succession of messages that made virtually no allusion to his previous pact with Hitler, but simply trumpeted the need for supplies from the West and also, in the British case, for troops either in the north or in the Caucasus. In these, he played on the value of Soviet resistance for the other two powers, and also on their presumed sense of guilt that the Russians were doing so much of the fighting. It is possible to read these messages simply as calculating diplomacy, written in a matter-of-fact manner with few salutations and little emotion. As such, they clearly struck home, eliciting florid and almost embarrassing tributes to Russian heroism from Churchill and Roosevelt. But some of Stalin's messages do have a raw quality, for instance his appeal on 3 September – hastily dictated to his secre-tary – for Churchill to 'open a second front this year somewhere in the Balkans or France' that would 'divert 30–40 German divisions from the Eastern Front'. This message and the surrounding telegrams to Ambassador Maisky in London convey something close to gut-churning panic. Here is another feature of this remarkable triangular correspondence: despite all the diplomatic frills and bureaucratic red tape, many of the messages are intensely human.

*****

Churchill's attempt to balance Britain's scarce resources with the need to keep open an eastern front was evident in his very first message to Stalin after the start of 'Barbarossa'. The prime minister declared Britain's support for the USSR over the BBC on the evening of 22 June, and was then urged to write in person to Stalin by Cripps – no longer *persona non grata* in Moscow, and also more bullish than most British observers about Soviet resistance. But Churchill resisted the ambassador's calls for immediate action. Avoiding any firm commitments, the PM saw the message largely as a way to break the ice. His final editing (in italics) played up hitherto modest British efforts and effusively praised Soviet resistance.[7]

Churchill to Stalin, sent 7 July 1941, received 8 July 1941[8]

We are all very glad here that the Russian armies are making such strong and spirited resistance to the utterly unprovoked and merciless invasion of the Nazis. *There is general admiration for the bravery and tenacity of the Soviet soldiers and people.* We shall do everything to help you that time, geography and our growing resources allow. The longer the war lasts the more help we can give. We are making very heavy attacks both by day and night with our Air Force upon all German-occupied territories and all Germany within our reach. About 400 aeroplanes made daylight sorties overseas yesterday. On Saturday night over 200 heavy bombers attacked German towns, some carrying three tons apiece, and last night nearly 250 heavy bombers were operating. *This will go on.* Thus we hope to force Hitler to bring back some of his air power to the West *and gradually take some of the strain off you.* Besides this the Admiralty have at my desire prepared a serious operation to come off in the near future in the Arctic, after which I hope that contact will be established between the British and Russian Navies. *Meanwhile by sweeping along the Norwegian coast we have intercepted various supply ships which were moving north against you.*

We welcome the arrival of the Russian Military Mission in order to concert future plans.

We have only got to go on fighting to beat the life out of the villains.

On 8 July, Cripps delivered the message in person to Stalin, who was clearly on edge but also conveyed a sense of confidence in ultimate victory. At this point, the Soviet leader seemed less interested in material aid than in political support. In keeping with his phobia about a Berlin–London axis, he pressed for a public and binding agreement between Britain and the USSR. The Hitler coalition, he said, 'should be opposed by a coalition': if the two countries were bound by a mutual assistance pact, 'then maybe there would be a prolonged and purposeful cooperation'. Stalin wanted this agreement to cover two main points: pledges of military aid and no separate peace.[9] Despite his bitter experience of the Nazi-Soviet Pact, Stalin apparently felt that the Western democracies would take contractual obligations more seriously than Hitler had done. A contract did not guarantee a commitment, but it strengthened cooperation and increased leverage.

Cripps recommended that London should seize the opportunity,[10] and Churchill immediately drafted a response to Stalin. His last paragraph antici-pated the interest of the United States – though still a neutral – in any postwar settlement. He told Eden that he wished to convene a meeting of the Cabinet to discuss the draft. Annoyed at the PM's intrusion onto his territory, Eden suggested that he handle the matter through Cripps and that, in general, the Churchill–Stalin channel should be used for issues of 'capital importance', because the prime minister should not 'become involved in the day to day details of diplomacy'.[11] Churchill, however, was not to be fobbed off, and the War Cabinet convened on the evening of 9 July to discuss this one item. Seeking a middle ground between an 'exchange of notes' (deemed too weak) and a formal treaty (too problematic and time consuming), the Cabinet couched the document as an 'Agreed Declaration', preferring that term to 'Agreement'. 'Rather afraid this is one of our famous half measures', noted Sir Alexander Cadogan, the permanent under-secretary at the Foreign Office (plate 23). The Cabinet decided to cut out the last part about postwar frontiers and American acquiescence (as shown below), because 'this might make difficulties for the Poles in their negotiations with the Russians'.[12]

The text was wired to Cripps early on 10 July – leaving Eden, according to Oliver Harvey, his private secretary, 'very fed up with the PM's monopolistic tendencies', reminiscent of the way Churchill had already taken over relations with Roosevelt. This was to be another recurrent pattern over the next four years.[13]

Churchill to Stalin, sent 9 July 1941, received 10 July 1941[14]

Ambassador Cripps having reported his talk with you and having stated the terms of a proposed Anglo-Russian agreed declaration under two heads, namely,

(1) Mutual help without any precision as to quantity or quality, and
(2) Neither country to conclude a separate peace,

I have immediately convened the War Cabinet, including Mr Fraser, Prime Minister of the Dominion of New Zealand, who is with us now. It will be necessary for us to consult with the Dominions of Canada, Australia, and South Africa, but in the meanwhile I should like to assure you that we are wholly in favour of the agreed declaration you propose. We think it should be signed as soon as we have heard from the Dominions, and published to the world immediately thereafter. ~~The details will fall naturally into their places in later discussion.~~

~~You will of course understand that at the victorious Peace Conference in which the United States will certainly be a leading party, our line would be that territorial frontiers will have to be settled in accordance with the wishes of the people who live there and on general ethnographic lines, and, secondly, that these units, when established, must be free to choose their own form of government and system of life, so long as they do not interfere with the similar rights of neighbouring peoples.~~

At 2 p.m. on 10 July, Cripps delivered this message to Stalin, together with a draft of the declaration sent by London. This would contain two provisions:

(1) The two Governments mutually undertake to render each other assistance of all kinds in the present war against Germany.
(2) They further undertake that during this war they will neither negotiate nor conclude an armistice or treaty of peace except by mutual agreement.

The Soviet leader's main request was that the document be called 'An Agreement for Joint Action', not merely a 'Declaration'. He also inquired about the intended period of the agreement. Cripps said that it would last for 'the duration of the war against Germany', which, as stated in draft article two, could only end when both their governments agreed to make peace. According to the Soviet record, Stalin jokingly asked: 'Is England afraid that the Russians will beat the Germans on their own and tell England that they don't want to deal with them?'[15] As a result of their discussion, a revised British draft was cabled to London and also to Washington. The Cabinet gave its consent, and Roosevelt his endorsement, once both had been assured that 'joint action' could not be construed in Russian as signifying a treaty of alliance. On 12 July, the agreement was signed in Moscow by Molotov and Cripps, together with a statement that it would take effect immediately. Thus Britain and the USSR segued cautiously into a new chapter in their relations – one that would have seemed inconceivable a month before.

The Soviet press enthusiastically presented the agreement as the creation of a 'real and powerful coalition of the great peoples of the Soviet Union and Great Britain'. The BBC Home Service interrupted its radio programmes to read out the full text of the agreement, while Churchill, speaking in the House of Commons on 15 July, proclaimed the agreement an 'Alliance' and called the Russian people 'our ally'.[16] But words were not matched by deeds. The British military – stretched by campaigns in Iraq, Crete, Egypt and Syria – remained doubtful of Soviet chances. General Noel Mason-MacFarlane, head of the British military mission in Moscow, was told bluntly by London that the Russians 'must save themselves, just as we have saved ourselves in the Battle of Britain and in the Atlantic'.[17] And the Soviet military mission to London received a distinctly cool welcome from David Margesson, the secretary of state for war. One of its members, Rear Admiral Nikolay Kharlamov, noted that 'Margesson did not shake our hands. Didn't offer us a seat … Listened … distractedly. And when he spoke, we realized that we were dealing with a staunch opponent of cooperation … He did not see any point at all in an Anglo-Soviet military alliance.'[18]

Meanwhile, the situation on the Soviet–German front continued to deteriorate. By 16 July, to Stalin's fury, the Wehrmacht had captured the city of Smolensk, on the main road to Moscow. That same day, his eldest son, Yakov Dzhugashvili, was taken prisoner. In this deepening crisis, Stalin decided to raise the stakes in what was his first message to Churchill. Alluding to the Soviet–British agreement and the PM's statement about the 'Alliance' between them, for the first time Stalin urged the opening of a new front against Hitler, although he did not yet use the adjective 'second'. He presented the idea of a cross-Channel landing in France, or else naval and air operations in northern Norway, as the logical next steps in their new relationship. And he sought to justify the USSR's westward expansion in 1939 under the Nazi-Soviet Pact as a life-saver in 1941, because it had given the Red Army more space within which to contain Hitler's 'sudden attack'.

Stalin to Churchill, sent 18 July 1941, received 19 July 1941[19]

Let me express my gratitude for the two personal messages you have addressed to me.

Your messages were the starting point of developments which subsequently resulted in agreement between our two Governments. Now, as you said with full justification, the Soviet Union and Great Britain have become fighting allies in the struggle against Hitlerite Germany. I have no doubt that, in spite of all the difficulties, our two States will be strong enough to crush our common enemy.

Perhaps it is not out of place to mention that the position of the Soviet forces at the front remains tense. The consequences of the unexpected breach of the

Non-Aggression Pact by Hitler, as well as of the sudden attack against the Soviet Union – both facts giving advantages to the German troops – still remain to be felt by the Soviet armies.

It is easy to imagine that the position of the German forces would have been many times more favourable had the Soviet troops had to face the attack of the German forces not in the regions of Kishinev, Lwow, Brest, Kaunas and Viborg, but in the region of Odessa, Kamenets Podolski, Minsk and the environs of Leningrad.

It seems to me, therefore, that the military situation of the Soviet Union, as well as of Great Britain, would be considerably improved if there could be established a front against Hitler in the west – northern France – and in the north – the Arctic.

A front in north France not only could divert Hitler's forces from the East, but at the same time would make it impossible for Hitler to invade Britain. The establishment of the front just mentioned would be popular with the British Army, as well as the whole population of Southern England.

I fully realise the difficulties involved in the establishment of such a front, I believe, however, that in spite of the difficulties it should be formed, not only in the interests of our common cause, but also in the interests of Great Britain herself. This is the most propitious moment for the opening of such a front, because now Hitler's forces are diverted to the east and he has not yet had a chance to consolidate the position occupied by him in the east.

It is still easier to open a front in the north. Here, on the part of Great Britain, would be necessary only naval and air operations, without the landing of troops or artillery. The Soviet military, naval and air forces would take part in such an operation. We would welcome it if Great Britain could transfer to this theatre of war something like one light division or more of the Norwegian volunteers, who could be used in north Norway to organise rebellion against the Germans.

The translation and typing of Stalin's message was done by Maisky himself, for reasons of secrecy, and he delivered the text personally to the prime minister's country residence, Chequers in Buckinghamshire, where Churchill was spending the weekend. After the PM had finished playing a board game with members of his family, the two of them went downstairs to a 'dreary drawing room' and sat on a sofa, while Churchill read the message carefully. 'He was evidently pleased – pleased at the very fact of having received a "personal message" – and did not try to conceal it,' Maisky noted in his diary. Churchill also expressed diplomatic approval of Stalin's defence of shifting Soviet borders west in 1939–40: 'Quite right! I've always understood and sought to justify the policy of "limited expansion" which Stalin has pursued in the last two years.'

But the prime minister was much more reserved about military operations, calling the idea of an invasion of France 'risky' and likely to 'end in disaster'. He showed interest only in possible operations in northern waters – phoning the Admiralty while Maisky was in the room to press the point. In order to sound more positive, Churchill pontificated about an air offensive, promising to 'bomb Germany mercilessly' and 'break the morale of the population' – something that would become a familiar refrain in 1941–43.[20]

The PM's reply to Stalin, sent via Cripps, reflected the line he had taken at Chequers – highlighting plans for naval operations off Finland and northern Norway. When Maisky saw a copy, he was not encouraged.[21] From Churchill's perspective, however, the message was a very full attempt to explain the geopolitical constraints on Britain: the strength of German defences in northern France, the difficulties of a Channel crossing, the campaigns in the Middle East and the Atlantic, and the constant need for air supremacy in order to mount any amphibious operations – as underlined by the abortive British landing at the Norwegian port of Namsos in April 1940 and the failure to hold Crete against German paratroopers in May 1941. Here, too, were lines of argument that would continue for the next two years.

Churchill to Stalin, sent 20 July 1941, received 21 July 1941[22]

I am very glad to get your message and to learn from many sources of the valiant fight and many vigorous counter-attacks with which the Russian armies are defending their native soil. I fully realise the military advantage you have gained by forcing the enemy to deploy and engage on forward Western fronts, thus exhausting some of the force of his initial effort.

Anything sensible and effective that we can do to help will be done. I beg you, however, to realise the limitations imposed upon us by our resources and geographical position. From the first day of the German attack upon Russia, we have examined the possibilities of attacking occupied France and the Low Countries. The Chiefs of Staff do not see any way of doing anything on a scale likely to be of the slightest use to you. The Germans have forty divisions in France alone, and the whole coast has been fortified with German diligence for more than a year and bristles with cannon, wire, pill-boxes and beach mines. The only part where we could have even temporary air superiority and air fighter protection is from Dunkirk to Boulogne. This is one mass of fortifications, with scores of heavy guns commanding the sea approaches, many of which can fire right across the Straits. There is less than five hours of darkness, and even then the whole area is illuminated by searchlights. To attempt a landing in force would be to encounter a bloody repulse, and petty raids would only lead to fiascos, doing far more harm than good to both of us. It would all be over without their having to move, or before they could move, a single unit from your fronts.

You must remember that we have been fighting all alone for more than a year, and that, although our resources are growing, and will grow fast from now on, we are at the utmost strain both at home and in the Middle East by land and air, and also that the battle of the Atlantic, on which our life depends, and the movements of all our convoys in the face of the U-boat and Focke-Wulf blockade, strain our naval forces, great though they be, to the utmost limit.

It is however to the North that we must look for any speedy help that we can give. The Naval Staff have been preparing for three weeks past an operation by sea-borne aircraft upon German shipping in Northern Norway and Finland, hoping thereby to destroy the enemy's power of transporting troops by sea to attack your Arctic flank. We have asked your Staff to keep a certain area clear of Russian vessels between July 28th and August 2nd, when we shall hope to strike. Secondly, we are sending forthwith some cruisers and destroyers to Spitzbergen, whence they will be able to raid enemy shipping in concert with your naval forces. Thirdly, we are sending submarines to intercept German traffic on the Arctic coast, although owing to perpetual daylight this service is particularly dangerous. Fourthly, we are sending a mine-layer with various supplies to Archangel. This is the most we can do at the moment. I wish it were more. Pray let the most extreme secrecy be kept until the moment when we tell you that publicity will not be harmful.

There is no Norwegian Light Division in existence and it would be impossible to land troops, either British or Russian, on German-occupied territory in perpetual daylight without having first obtained reasonable fighter air cover. We had bitter experiences at Namsos last year, and in Crete this year, of trying such enterprises.

We are also studying, as a further development, the basing of some British fighter air squadrons on Murmansk. This would require first of all a consignment of anti-aircraft guns, in addition to ground staff and equipment, then the arrival of the aircraft, some of which could be flown off carriers and others crated. When these were established our Spitzbergen squadron might possibly come to Murmansk. As soon as our naval forces are known to be in the North, we are under no delusion but that the Germans will immediately follow their invariable practice of opposing our forces with a strong force of dive-bombers, and it is therefore necessary to proceed step by step. All this, however, will take weeks.

Do not hesitate to suggest anything else that occurs to you, and we will also be searching earnestly for other ways of striking at the common foe.

Stalin took the message on the chin, evidently realizing – on advice from Maisky – that at this point it was impossible to change the prime minister's mind.[23] The debate about aid to Russia now shifted to military equipment. Responding to protests from Eden and others about the negativity of Churchill's message of 20 July, the Cabinet agreed to divert to Arkhangelsk 200 American Tomahawk (P-40C) fighter aircraft, sent under Lend-Lease and earmarked for the Middle East. Tomahawks were not used in Britain and, being American planes, it was assumed that the United States would take responsibility for spare parts and ground equipment. So this was the least costly concession that could be made.[24] Even so, Air Marshal Arthur 'Bomber' Harris, anxious to head off further diversions, told the Americans that Russian mechanics were 'blatantly incapable of efficient operation and maintenance of even familiar technology'. However, when the Americans carried out an assessment of the first shipment of Tomahawks, they reported with surprise that in just three and a half weeks, fifty Russian mechanics had assembled forty-seven aircraft, 'working in the pouring rain for fourteen hours a day without standard tools and technical manuals'. The Americans concluded that the Soviets were 'fully capable of effectively employing and repairing American aircraft equipment'.[25] In fact, Stalin had immediately sent the best aviation technicians to Arkhangelsk; they assembled the Tomahawks without any of the American help that Churchill's message clearly assumed would be necessary.

Churchill to Stalin, sent 25 July 1941, received 26 July 1941[26]

I am glad to inform you that the War Cabinet have decided, in spite of the fact that this will seriously deplete our fighter aircraft resources, to send to Russia as soon as possible 200 Tomahawk Fighter Aeroplanes. One hundred and forty of these will be sent from here to Archangel, and sixty from our supplies in the United States of America. Details as to spare parts and American personnel to erect the machines have still to be arranged with the American Government.

Up to two or three million pairs of ankle boots should shortly be available in this country for shipment. We are also arranging to provide during the present year large quantities of rubber, tin, wool and woollen cloth, jute, lead and shellac. All your other requirements from raw materials are receiving careful consideration. Where supplies are impossible or limited from here, we are discussing with the United States of America. Details will of course be communicated to the usual official channels.

We are watching with admiration and emotion Russia's magnificent fight, and all our information shows the heavy losses and concern of the enemy. Our air attack on Germany will continue with increasing strength.

This message from Churchill was delivered by Cripps next day, 26 July. According to the ambassador's report, Stalin expressed 'sincere gratitude' to the PM for the promised supplies, and then asked for urgent delivery of 10,000–12,000 tons of rubber.[27] On 28 July, Churchill sent an encouraging reply, wrapped as usual in what Eden called 'sentimental and florid' language that he and Foreign Office (FO) officials feared would 'have the worst effect on Stalin', who would consider 'guff' to be 'no substitute for guns'.[28] The main focus of Churchill's message was the impending visit to Moscow of the US president's right-hand man, Harry Hopkins. Although Churchill and Hopkins had first met only in January 1941, the PM quickly came to regard the indefatigable ex-social worker from Iowa with affection and respect, dubbing him 'Lord Root of the Matter' for his ability to get straight to the heart of any issue.

Churchill to Stalin, sent 28 July 1941, received 28 July 1941[29]

Rubber. We will deliver the goods from here or United States by the best and quickest route. Please say exactly what kind of rubber, and which way you wish it to come. Preliminary orders are already given.

Mr Harry Hopkins has been with me these days. Last week he asked the President to let him go to Moscow. I must tell you that there is a flame in this man for democracy and to beat Hitler. A little while ago when I asked him for a quarter of a million rifles, they came at once. He is the nearest personal representative of the President. The President has now sent him full instructions, and he leaves my house tonight to go to you. You will be advised of his arrival through the proper channels. You can trust him absolutely. He is your friend and our friend. He will help you to plan for the future victory and for the long-term supply of Russia. You could talk to him also freely about policy, strategy and Japan.

The grand resistance of the Russian armies in the defence of their soil unites us all. A terrible winter of bombing lies before Germany. No one has yet had what they are going to get. The naval operations mentioned in my last telegram to you are in progress. Thank you very much for your comprehension, in the midst of your great fight, of our difficulties in doing more. We will do our utmost.

Hopkins had been visiting London to concert plans for the first wartime meeting between Churchill and Roosevelt. American aid was now beginning to flow to Britain under the Lend-Lease Act passed in March 1941, but the extension of that programme to the USSR was problematic in Washington, because of ideological suspicion and doubts about Soviet resistance. Moreover, any orders that Moscow placed in America potentially conflicted with British needs – as in the case of the Tomahawk fighters. By late July, it was becoming clear that a coherent British–American policy towards Stalin depended on a much clearer appreciation of Russia's needs and its chances of survival. These imperatives lay behind Hopkins' sudden idea of paying a personal visit to Moscow, for which he sought the president's approval on 25 July. More generally, as he told Maisky, Hopkins wanted to 'bring Roosevelt and Stalin closer', because the Soviet leader was 'little more than a name' to FDR, who had no sense of Stalin as a human being. Hopkins saw himself as a vital intermediary between the Wheelchair President and the Kremlin enigma, trying to warm up their personal relations as he was already doing for FDR and Churchill. He described the latter role privately as being 'a catalytic agent between two prima donnas'.[30]

The Moscow visit came together very fast. Late on the evening of 27 July, John Gilbert 'Gil' Winant, the US ambassador in London, descended on the Russian embassy seeking visas for Hopkins and two aides, all of whom, he announced dramatically, were leaving for Russia in half an hour. It was after 11 p.m. and the consular office was locked up, so Maisky simply wrote his permission in each passport and affixed the embassy seal. Winant was then driven at speed to Euston Station, where Hopkins was about to leave for Scotland, from where he would commence a hazardous flight to Arkhangelsk and thence to Moscow. The US ambassador called in again on Maisky at midnight. 'I only just made it,' he exclaimed. 'The train was already moving.'[31]

Hopkins also carried with him a message from Roosevelt to Stalin, prepared with the help of Sumner Welles at the State Department. In this, his first communication to the Soviet leader, the president made clear that Hopkins was effectively his alter ego and, like Churchill, tried to bolster Soviet resistance with words, if not deeds.[32]

Roosevelt to Stalin, sent 26 July 1941, received 30 July 1941[33]

Mr. Hopkins is in Moscow at my request for discussions with you personally and with such other officials as you may designate on the vitally important question of how we can expeditiously and effectively make available the assistance which the United States can render to your country in its magnificent resistance to the treacherous aggression by Hitlerite Germany. I have already informed your Ambassador, Mr. Oumansky, that all possible aid will be given by the United States Government in obtaining munitions, armaments and other supplies needed to meet your most urgent requirements and which can be made available for actual use in the coming two months in your country. We shall promptly settle the details of these questions with the mission headed by General Golikov which is now in Washington. The visit now being made by Mr. Hopkins to Moscow will, I feel, be invaluable by clarifying for us here in the United States your most urgent requirements so that we can reach the most practicable decisions to simplify the mechanics of delivery and speed them up. We shall be able to complete during the next winter a great amount of matériel which your Government wishes to obtain in this country. I therefore think that the immediate concern of both governments should be to concentrate on the matériel which can reach Russia within the next three months.

I ask you to treat Mr. Hopkins with the identical confidence you would feel if you were talking directly to me. He will communicate directly to me the views that you express to him and will tell me what you consider are the most pressing individual problems on which we could be of aid.

May I express, in conclusion, the great admiration all of us in the United States feel for the superb bravery displayed by the Russian people in the defense of their liberty and in their fight for the independence of Russia. The success of your people and all other people in opposing Hitler's aggression and his plans for world conquest has been heartening to the American people.

By the time Hopkins arrived in Moscow, the Luftwaffe was mounting nightly air raids on the largely wooden city. Representatives of the British and US embassies and military missions were unable to travel freely, and they found it almost impossible to get clear information. Hopkins was no different: he never went near the front and left with little in the way of precise intelligence. But he had three conversations with Cripps (which helped him break out of the negativity of the US embassy) and six hours of talks at the Kremlin on 30 and 31 July (plate 5), which left him deeply impressed with the Soviet leader and his will to win. They discussed the need for a supply conference, to be held in Moscow, to harmonize Russian, American and British requirements. And, in an especially confidential conversation intended as a reply to FDR's message, Stalin impressed on Hopkins the importance of American entry into the war, adding that he would welcome US troops 'on any part of the Russian front under the complete command of the American Army'. According to Hopkins, he also 'repeatedly said that the President of the United States had more influence with the common people of the world today than any other force'. Hyperbole or not, this was language that Stalin would never have used to, or about, Churchill – an early sign of his differing estimation of his two allies.[34]

A few months later, in December 1941, Hopkins published an account of his mission to Moscow in the *American* magazine. Even allowing for the excesses of wartime propaganda and the worst American journalese, the piece conveyed Hopkins' genuine enthusiasm for Stalin.

> No man could forget the picture of the dictator of Russia as he stood watching me leave – an austere, rugged, determined figure in boots that shone like mirrors, stout baggy trousers, and snug-fitting blouse. He wore no ornament, military or civilian. He's built close to the ground, like a football coach's dream of a tackle. He's about five foot six, about a hundred and ninety pounds. His hands are huge, as hard as his mind. His voice is harsh but ever under control. What he says is all the accent and inflection his words need.[35]

Hopkins' positive report on Stalin strengthened the president's determination to extract more aid from the US military. Complaining about slow progress on 2 August, he noted: 'If I were a Russian I would feel that I had been given the run-around in the United States', and told his top administrator of aid to the USSR, 'please, with my full authority, use a heavy hand – and act as a burr under the saddle and get things moving'. FDR's priority was what could arrive during September because, he explained, 'after October 1st, we all doubt if there will be very active operations in view of rain, snow, frost, etc. and that if Germany can be held until then, Russia is safe until the Spring'. This proved, to put it mildly, a misplaced assumption.[36]

Meanwhile, on 31 July, Churchill followed up his message of the 28th with precise details of how Britain would supply 20,000 tons of rubber to the USSR. Coming as it did from Southeast Asia, this resource was easier to provide than shipments from Britain. Single-cargo vessels, loaded with rubber and sailing from Malaya to Vladivostok in August 1941, became one of the first tangible expressions of British aid to Russia.[37]

Despite Stalin's deft handling of Hopkins, the pressures on him were evident in the first written message he sent to Roosevelt on 4 August. Devoted entirely to Finland, this was drafted by Molotov and dispatched, without any changes, to Ambassador Umanskiy in Washington: 'You should immediately ask for an appointment with Roosevelt and inform him of the above', Umanskiy was instructed. 'Report on the results immediately.'[38] At the time, however, Roosevelt was already en route to his secret rendezvous with Churchill in Placentia Bay, off the coast of Newfoundland. So the ambassador translated the message and wrote a cover letter to the president, asking him to reply direct to Moscow.[39]

Without personal pleasantries, let alone words of appreciation about Hopkins, Stalin's letter bluntly urged the US government to apply pressure on Finland, which had now resumed its 1939–40 war with the USSR as a 'co-belligerent' of Nazi Germany. The strikes promised by Churchill against German bases in Finland and northern Norway had proved an expensive fiasco for the Fleet Air Arm, which lost fifteen planes on 30 July, and the raid on the port of Petsamo led the Finnish government to break off diplomatic relations with Britain. Stalin now asked Roosevelt to sever America's relations with Finland.

Stalin to Roosevelt, sent 4 August 1941, received 7 August 1941[40]

The Soviet Union holds that the question of restoring the neutrality of Finland and of detaching her from Germany is of utmost importance. The Soviet Government is in possession of most reliable information showing that the breaking off of relations between Great Britain and Finland and the blockade of Finland by Great Britain have not failed to produce desirable results and have caused conflicts within the governing circles of Finland. There are now voices audible in those circles in favor of neutrality and reconciliation with the Soviet Union.

Mr. Stalin is convinced that, should the Government of the United States consider it opportune to impress upon the Finnish Government the danger of a break in relations by the United States – the Finnish Government would be more resolute and acquire more courage in detaching itself from Nazi-Germany.

In this event the Soviet Government would be willing to make to Finland certain territorial concessions so as to facilitate her transition to a peaceful policy and the Soviet Government would be willing to conclude with Finland a new Peace Treaty.

This was not a particularly accomplished diplomatic debut. Stalin's clumsy appeal, bordering on a demand, must have raised eyebrows in the White House. Roosevelt made no direct answer, but Welles told Umanskiy two weeks later that, in response to Stalin's appeal, he had warned the Finnish envoy against continuing the war against the USSR, and mentioned that the USSR was willing to offer some territorial concessions to Finland. But, added Welles, acting in concert with the Foreign Office, this willingness should not be construed by the Finns as a sign of weakness, and he stressed Soviet determination and capacity to fight Germany to a finish.[41]

These overtures to Helsinki had no effect. By December, the British had slid into a state of war with Finland, but the USA maintained diplomatic relations with the Finns until the summer of 1944 – another example of divergence between London and Washington on the prickly question of how to handle relations with Russia's adversaries.

The first joint message from Roosevelt and Churchill to Stalin was composed on 14 August, at the end of their Newfoundland summit. Noting the complexities of what was already becoming a global struggle, they firmed up earlier discussions about a Soviet–American–British supply conference in Moscow with Averell Harriman leading the US team, and instructed their ambassadors there to hand Stalin the message on behalf of both countries.

The letter did not mention the so-called 'Atlantic Charter' drawn up hastily by British and American officials at Roosevelt's behest, setting out eight principles for 'a better future' on which the postwar world should be based. Churchill, who had hoped the meeting might presage an American declaration of war, had to accept merely a declaration of war aims, though he played up to his Cabinet the 'astonishing' association in this way of a neutral country with a belligerent power. But not everyone was impressed, with one minister damning the document's 'meaningless platitudes and dangerous ambiguities'. And in due course, the charter – especially article three on 'the right of all peoples to choose the form of government under which they live' – would cause significant diplomatic problems for both Churchill and Stalin, potentially challenging the position of the British Empire and Soviet territorial demands in Eastern Europe. Article four, about access on 'equal terms' to markets and raw materials, also reflected Roosevelt's desire to open up Britain's Imperial Preference trading arrangements. The charter was an early sign that the two leaders did not see eye to eye on empire.[42]

Roosevelt and Churchill to Stalin, sent 14 August 1941, received 15 August 1941[43]

We have taken the opportunity afforded by the consideration of the report of Mr Harry Hopkins on his return from Moscow to consult together as to how best our two countries can help your country in the splendid defence that you are putting up against the Nazi attack. We are at the moment cooperating to provide you with the very maximum of supplies that you most urgently need. Already many shiploads have left our shores and more will leave in the immediate future.

We must now turn our minds to the consideration of a more long-term policy, since there is still a long and hard path to be traversed before there can be won that complete victory without which our efforts and sacrifices would be wasted.

The war goes on upon many fronts and before it is over there may be yet further fighting fronts that will be developed. Our resources, though immense, are limited and it must become a question of where and when those resources can best be used to further to the greatest extent our common effort. This applies equally to manufactured war supplies and to raw materials.

The needs and demands of your and our armed services can only be determined in the light of the full knowledge of the many facts which must be taken into consideration in the decisions that we take. In order that all of us may be in a position to arrive at speedy decisions as to the apportionment of our joint resources, we suggest that we prepare a meeting which should be held at Moscow, to which we would send high representatives who could discuss these matters directly with you. If this conference appeals to you, we want you to know that pending the decisions of that conference we shall continue to send supplies and material as rapidly as possible.

We realise fully how vitally important to the defeat of Hitlerism is the brave and steadfast resistance of the Soviet Union, and we feel therefore that we must not in any circumstances fail to act quickly and immediately in this matter of planning the programme for the future allocation of our joint resources.

On 15 August, Steinhardt and Cripps delivered this message to Stalin, who expressed his thanks and said he would facilitate the supply conference in Moscow as soon as possible. Both the text of the letter and the reception of the ambassadors at the Kremlin were duly publicized by the Soviet government. Stalin himself seems to have been truly pleased by this high-profile signal of support from his Western allies.[44]

In his next letter, on 29 August,[45] Churchill reverted to the supply of materiel to Russia. The Tomahawks were on their way, and the PM was now expediting the provision of two squadrons of Hurricane fighters, with the promise of more if Stalin wanted. The planes and their crews arrived in the USSR on 7 September. Churchill also discussed Iran, where in 1939–40 Britain had vied for influence against Moscow and Berlin. Here, too, 'Barbarossa' transformed the situation: on 25 August, Soviet and British forces intervened to pre-empt a German coup. Not encountering any serious resistance, Soviet troops advanced into the northern provinces of Iran, while British troops and the Royal Navy occupied the southwest of the country and the ports of the Persian Gulf. Their forces jointly entered Tehran in mid-September, forcing the uncooperative Reza Shah to abdicate in favour of his son, and then gradually hammered out a treaty between the three governments that eliminated German influence, confirmed their respective spheres of influence in the north and south for the duration of the war, and granted the Allies unimpeded communications across the country. Between 1941 and 1945, 41 million tons of cargo were delivered via Iran – nearly a quarter of total Lend-Lease aid to Russia.[46]

Churchill's message also alluded to relations with Tokyo, where 'Barbarossa' had triggered intense debate about whether Japan should plunge the knife into Russia's back or take advantage of Russia and Britain's fight for life against Germany to win a sphere of influence in Southeast Asia. Tough words and action by Roosevelt and Churchill at the Atlantic conference were intended to act as a deterrent, but in fact they served to accelerate Japan's rush to war during the rest of 1941. Stalin, understandably, adhered to the neutrality pact he had signed in April with Tokyo.

On 26 August 1941, Maisky had an emotional conversation with Eden, in which – speaking, he said, personally – the ambassador expressed the 'growing dissatisfaction' in Moscow that Britain was offering 'very little' in the way of help. If Britain was not going to open a second front, it should be more liberal in providing military equipment. In response to Eden's explanations – British bombing of Germany, operations in Libya, Iran, etc. – Maisky declared: 'It's not enough to pinch the rabid beast's tail; it must be hit round the head with a club!'[47]

Maisky's report to Moscow on this interview elicited, most unusually, a personal telegram on 30 August from Stalin himself:

Your conversation with Eden regarding England's strategy fully reflects the mood of the Soviet people. I am glad that you have perceived the mood so well. Essentially Anglopra [the British government] assists the Hitlerites with its passive wait-and-see policy. The Hitlerites want to beat their opponents one by one – Russians today, English tomorrow. English passivity helps the Hitlerites. The fact that England applauds us and curses the Germans does not change anything. Do the English understand that? I think they do. So what do they want? I think, they want us to weaken. If this assumption is correct, we have to be careful with the English.

Stalin developed this theme by pointing to the recent redeployment of Germany's 'last thirty divisions from the West to our front' and the rapid deterioration of the Soviet position around Kiev and Leningrad. Clearly, he said, 'the Germans ignore the English threat in the West and consider it a bluff', and asked darkly 'why are the Germans so confident in the passivity of the English?' He warned Maisky that 'if the English do not open a second front in Europe in the next three to four weeks, we and our allies may lose. It is tragic, but it can become a fact.'[48]

Shaken by Stalin's message, Maisky responded the same day with a personal telegram. He urged a direct appeal from the Soviet leader to Churchill, which he would back up face to face, asking for a second front, or at least increased supplies. Maisky set out what he called the 'complicated knot of motives' – pulling in different directions – within which British policy was entangled, discouraging government circles (though not the public) from the idea of a second front:

1) Unshakeable belief in German invincibility on land.
2) A sense of complacency, since the Russians fight well, we need not hurry, we shall take our time and calmly implement our plans to prepare for a decisive offensive in 1942 or 1943.
3) A desire to weaken us – a tendency that is certainly evident in influential circles of the Conservative Party.
4) The English are ill-prepared for large-scale landing operations.
5) Fear of a new 'Dunkirk', which could undermine the position of the British government in the country and damage its reputation in America.

Despite London's mixture of complacency and fear, Maisky did not rule out a 'new push' for a second front: 'Churchill and others must understand at long last that if the USSR leaves the stage, the British Empire is finished.' He proposed either 'a personal message from Stalin to Churchill' or 'an extensive conversation between me and Churchill about the current situation'. He felt the former would be more effective.[49]

Stalin followed his ambassador's advice. His message to Churchill, dated 3 September, was dictated to Aleksandr Poskrebyshev, his dwarfish secretary, who wrote it down on small sheets of paper torn out of a pocket notepad (plate 3). Passing it on for encryption, Stalin added in blue pencil:

London, to Soviet Ambassador Maisky. I am sending you the text of my personal message to Churchil [sic]. Please translate and transmit to Churchil. I received your cipher and decided that I can use both of your recommended options – apply pressure by writing a personal letter and through you verbally.

The telegram developed the message he sent Maisky on 30 August, but now setting out the USSR's needs in dramatic terms: a landing in France or the Balkans that autumn sufficient to divert thirty or forty German divisions and guaranteed supplies of aluminium, planes and tanks to help replace the productive capacity lost in the German advance. Stalin also alluded to the epic evacuation programme of major factories, workers and families then under way, but noted that the relocated plants could not be up and running again in less than seven or eight months. The message ended with another handwritten post-script by Stalin to Maisky: 'Acknowledge receipt. Immediately report on the results of the discussion with Churchill.'[50] Judging by the marks on the document in Stalin's archive, the message was typed and encrypted in great haste, within ninety minutes, and dispatched at 10 p.m. on 3 September. 'My proposal has been accepted', Maisky noted with satisfaction in his diary. 'Firm, clear and ruthless words. No illusions, no sweeteners. The facts as they stand. The threats as they loom. A remarkable document.'[51]

Stalin to Churchill, sent 3 September 1941, received 4 September 1941[52]

Many thanks for your promise in addition to 200 fighters released by you formerly to sell to the Soviet Union another 200 fighters. I have no doubt that our pilots will be able to man them and to use them against the enemy.

I have to say however that these aircraft, which apparently could be put into action not immediately and not at one time, but in separate groups and at different moments, will not be in a position to bring about any substantial change at the Eastern front. They will not be in a position to bring about any substantial change not only because the war on such a tremendous scale requires a constant flow of a great number of airplanes. Still more important is the fact that for the last three weeks the position of the Soviet troops has deteriorated in such important regions as the Ukraine and Leningrad.

The relative stabilisation at the front, which was achieved some three weeks ago, was lately upset by the transfer to Eastern front of the 30–34 fresh German divisions and a tremendous number of tanks and aircraft. In addition the 20 Finnish and 26 Rumanian divisions have become more active. The Germans consider a danger in the West a bluff and do not hesitate freely to transfer all their forces from the West to the East. The Germans believe that they can beat all their enemies one by one; first the Russians and then the British.

As a result we have lost the greater part of the Ukraine and the enemy is now at the gates of Leningrad.

All these circumstances have brought some very unpleasant consequences. We have lost the iron ore of Krivoi Rog and a number of metallurgical works in the Ukraine. Further we have evacuated one aluminium works on the Dnieper and another from Tikhvin, one motor work and two aircraft factories in the Ukraine, two motor works and two aircraft factories from Leningrad – all of them could be put into operation again at their new places 7 or 8 months hence at the earliest.

This weakened our power of defence capacity and placed the Soviet Union in a position of mortal peril.

At this point, permissible to raise the question, where is the way out of this highly critical situation?

I believe there is only one possibility to remedy the position – it is to establish already this year a second front somewhere in the Balkans or France, which would be able to divert from the Eastern Front some 30 to 40 German divisions as well as to secure at the same time for the Soviet Union 30,000 tons of aluminium at the beginning of October and a minimum monthly delivery of some 400 aircraft and 500 tanks (small and medium size).

Without these two forms of help the Soviet Union may either be defeated or weakened to such an extent that for a long period it may not be in a position to help its Allies by active operations in the struggle against Hitlerism.

I am afraid that my message today will cause your Excellency the gravest concern. I cannot help it. Experience has taught me to face realities however unpleasant they may be and not to be frightened of [sic] to tell the truth however unwelcome it may be.

The Iranian affair in fact turned out not at all badly. The common operations of British and Soviet troops secured the issues in advance. So will it be always in the future wherever our forces act together. But Iran is only an episode. The outcome of the war will be decided of course not in Iran.

The Soviet Union as also Great Britain does not desire a war with Japan. The Soviet Union honours its treaty obligations, including its treaty of neutrality with Japan. If however Japan would break this treaty and attack the Soviet Union she will find a strong resistance on the part of Soviet forces.

In conclusion let me express my gratitude for your admiration for the deeds of the Soviet forces, which are waging a sanguinary war against the bandit hordes of Hitlerites for our common cause of liberty and freedom.

On 4 September, Vyshinskiy, the deputy foreign minister, delivered the message to Cripps, who forwarded it with an appeal that his government make 'a super-human effort' to offer the USSR 'very large and immediate help, otherwise it is doubtful if it is much good doing anything at all'.[53] In London, Maisky personally handed the roughly translated message to Churchill and Eden at 10 Downing Street at 10 p.m. on 4 September. The ambassador, according to Eden, 'emphasised with great earnestness the seriousness of the present situation' – potentially 'a turning point in history' – adding that 'if Soviet Russia were defeated, how could we hope to win the war?'[54] Churchill listened attentively, sucking on a cigar, but then recited his now familiar arguments that it was impossible to open a second front in Europe or to provide significant military supplies before the end of 1941. Alluding to Stalin's plea for 500 tanks a month, he said this was more than total current British production. He did not bother to add that he didn't have sufficient combat divisions in the whole of the British Army to engage thirty or forty German divisions. Churchill concluded: 'Only God, in whom you don't believe, can help you in the next 6–7 weeks' – saying this with what Maisky called 'half a smile'.[55]

Next day, the PM sought to instruct Cripps about British grand strategy. 'All our generals are convinced that a bloody repulse is all that would be sustained, or, if small lodgements were effected, that they would have to be withdrawn after several days.' Referring to the ambassador's plea for a 'super-human effort', he added sarcastically: 'you mean, I presume, an effort rising superior to space, time and geography. Unfortunately these attributes are denied us.' The PM also reiterated a point that was always in his mind about the consequences of the Molotov–Ribbentrop pact of August 1939: 'The situation in the West would be entirely different if the French front were in being, for then I have no doubt the invasion of Russia would have been impossible because of the enormous counter-attacks that could be immediately launched. No one wants to recrimi-nate,' he added archly, 'but it is not our fault that Hitler was enabled to destroy Poland before turning his forces against France, or to destroy France before turning them against Russia.'[56]

Churchill spent most of 5 September preparing his response to Stalin, cancelling his other engagements. In the morning, Eden convened a meeting of the chiefs of staff, to which Maisky and the head of the Soviet military mission in London were invited, so that they could hear for themselves Britain's stra-tegic rationale. The British military presented a raft of arguments against a diversionary landing in Europe, but this only served to confirm Maisky's previous assessment: 'One could sense that the chiefs of staff are simply hypno-tized by the might of the German war machine, and wholly deprived of initia-tive and boldness.'[57]

Meanwhile, Churchill showed a draft reply to the Cabinet for consideration. (This was an unusual occurrence – normally the PM jealously preserved his exchanges with Stalin and Roosevelt as 'personal correspondence' – and it shows that he recognized the gravity of the moment.) Stalin, he told his colleagues, 'was worthy of being told the truth and was capable of facing the facts of a situation', whereas Cripps ignored them in his emotional dispatches.[58] Following advice from the chiefs of staff, ministers discussed and ruled out diversionary operations in France or the Balkans, but the PM's draft reply, bypassing the question of supplies, was considered too negative in tone and content, especially by the Labour members.[59] Eden, Beaverbrook (the minister of supply) and the chiefs of staff suggested certain amendments, stressing sombrely:

> There are ominous signs that Russia is cracking. This is an historic telegram, possibly the most important which you have so far sent to the head of a Foreign State. Ministers and the Chiefs of Staff therefore feel that, at this critical stage in the war, the telegram should sound an encouraging note throughout, i.e. emphasis should be on the spirit of comradeship, willingness to share burdens and good cheer, and that as far as possible negative or discouraging information should be excluded.[60]

Churchill took account of these suggestions in the response he eventually sent to Stalin. Adopting Beaverbrook's suggestion, he committed Britain to providing half of Stalin's 'minimum' request – in other words, 200 planes and 250 tanks per month – expressing the hope that the other half would come from the United States. The PM was visibly pleased with the outcome of what amounted to a Russia Day for much of Whitehall. 'To celebrate this,' Eden noted in his diary, 'Winston insisted on a restaurant dinner and carried Max [Beaverbrook] and self off to [the] Ritz. Very good dinner, oysters, partridge, etc. and good talk. Winston at top of his form.'[61]

Churchill to Stalin, sent 5 September 1941, received 6 September 1941[62]

I reply at once in the spirit of your message. Although we should shrink from no exertion, there is, in fact, no possibility of any British action in the West, except Air action, which would draw the German forces from the East before the winter sets in. There is no chance whatever of a second front being formed in the Balkans without the help of Turkey. I will, if Your Excellency desires, give all the reasons which have led our Chiefs of Staff to these conclusions. They have already been discussed with your Ambassador in conference today with the Foreign Secretary and the Chiefs of Staff. Action, however well-meant, leading to only costly fiascos would be no help to anyone but Hitler.

The information at my disposal gives me the impression that the culminating violence of the German invasion is already over, and that winter will give your heroic armies a breathing space. This, however, is a personal opinion.

About supplies. We are well aware of the grievous losses which Russian industry has sustained, and every effort has been and will be made by us to help you. I am cabling President Roosevelt to expedite the arrival here in London of Mr. Harriman's Mission, and we shall try even before the Moscow Conference to tell you the numbers of aircraft and tanks we can jointly promise to send each month, together with supplies of rubber, aluminium, cloth, etc. For our part we are now prepared to send you, from British production, one-half of the monthly total for which you ask in aircraft and tanks. We hope the United States will supply the other half of your requirements. We shall use every endeavour to start the flow of equipment to you immediately.

We have given already the orders for supplying the Persian railway with rolling-stock to raise it from its present capacity of two trains a day each way up to its full capacity, namely, 12 trains a day each way. This should be reached by the spring of 1942, and meanwhile will be steadily improving. Locomotives and rolling-stock have to be sent round the Cape [of Good Hope] from this country after being converted to oil-burners, and the water supply along the railway has to be developed. The first 48 locomotives and 400 steel trucks are about to start.

We are ready to make joint plans with you now. Whether British armies will be strong enough to invade the mainland of Europe during 1942 must depend on unforeseeable events. It may be possible, however, to assist you in the extreme North when there is more darkness. We are hoping to raise our armies in the Middle East to a strength of three-quarters of a million before the end of the present year, and thereafter to a million by the summer of 1942. Once the German–Italian forces in Libya have been destroyed all these forces will be available to come into line on your southern flank, and it is hoped to encourage Turkey to maintain at least a faithful neutrality. Meanwhile we shall continue to batter Germany from the Air with increasing severity and to keep the seas open and ourselves alive.

In your first paragraph you used the word 'sell'. We had not viewed the matter in such terms and have never thought of payment. Any assistance we can give you would better be upon the same basis of comradeship as the American Lend-Lease Bill, of which no formal account is kept in money.

We are willing to put any pressure upon Finland in our power, including immediate notification that we will declare war upon them should they continue beyond the old frontiers. We are asking the United States to take all possible steps to influence Finland.

On 7 September, the day after receiving Churchill's response, the Soviet leader saw Cripps. 'I found Stalin very depressed and tired', the ambassador reported, with 'some return of the old attitude of suspicion and distrust'. (Stalin had evidently hoped to receive a more positive response from Churchill.) Cripps tried to find out what was behind the references to possible defeat in the Soviet leader's letter of 3 September. Perhaps a separate truce with the Germans? 'No,' said Stalin firmly. He explained that if they had to abandon the Donets Basin, with its coal mines and steelmaking, as well as Moscow and Leningrad – the centre for engineering industries – which he said was 'possible': they would have lost two-thirds of the production capacity for the front. As a result, the USSR would have to cease active hostilities and take up a defensive position, perhaps beyond the Volga.[63] Stalin's tone was confidential but blunt, perhaps hoping to shake up the British.

During the next week, the situation along the front continued to deteriorate. On 8 September, German and Finnish troops severed all land routes in and out of Leningrad, beginning a blockade that would not be fully lifted for almost 900 days, until January 1944. On the 13th, Stalin sent Zhukov to the city in an eleventh-hour bid to galvanize the city's hitherto inept defence effort. Meanwhile the German pincers closed around Kiev, and the city surrendered on 18 September, with the loss of more than half a million men killed or captured. The way was now open southward to Odessa and the Crimea. A week after Churchill's rejection of a second front, Stalin tried again – this time with a plea for direct military support on the Soviet–German front, either in the north or the south. A sign of his anxiety was the totally impossible figure of 25–30 divisions that he requested (a level of deployment greater than the whole British Army until the start of 1944).[64] In turn, Britain's offer of postwar financial compensation if the USSR felt it necessary to scuttle warships in Leningrad to stop them falling into German hands was hardly encouraging, and certainly not tactful.

Stalin to Churchill, sent 13 September 1941, received 15 September 1941[65]

In my last message I stated the viewpoint of the Soviet Government that the establishment of a second front is the most fundamental remedy for improvement of the situation with regard to our common cause. In reply to your message, in which you stress once more the impossibility of a second front at the present moment, I can only reiterate that the absence of second front simply favours the designs of our common enemy.

I have no doubt that the British Government desires to see the Soviet Union victorious and is looking for ways and means to attain this end. If, as they think, the establishment of a second front in the West is at present impossible – perhaps another method could be found to render the Soviet Union an active military help?

It seems to me that Great Britain could without any risk land in Archangel 25–30 divisions or transport them across Iran to the Southern regions of the U.S.S.R. In this way there could be established military collaboration between the Soviet and British troops on the territory of the U.S.S.R. A similar situation existed during the last war in France. The arrangement just mentioned would constitute a great help. It would be serious against the Hitler aggression.

I thank you very much for your promise to render us assistance by the monthly deliveries of aluminium, tanks and aircraft.

I can only welcome the intention of the British Government to render this assistance in aluminium, tanks and aircraft not on the usual commercial basis, but on the basis of comradeship and collaboration.

I hope the British Government will have ample opportunity of being convinced that the Soviet Government understands how to appreciate help from its Ally.

One remark in connection with the memorandum delivered on September 12th to Mr Molotov by the British Ambassador in Moscow Sir S. Cripps. In this memorandum it is said: 'If the Soviet Government would be compelled to destroy its naval vessels at Leningrad in order to prevent their falling into the enemy hands, His Majesty's Government would recognise after the war claims of the Soviet Government to a certain compensation from His Majesty's Government for the restoration of the vessels destroyed.'

The Soviet Government understands and appreciates the readiness of the British Government to make partial compensation for the damage sustained by the Soviet Union in case the Soviet vessels at Leningrad would actually be destroyed. There could be no doubt that such a course will be adopted should the necessity arise. However the responsibility for this damage would be not Britain's but Germany's. I think therefore that the damage after the war should be made good at the expense of Germany.

On 15 September, Maisky handed this message to Churchill, who tried to maintain his usual balancing act of reassurance without commitments. 'Thinking aloud', he said he was 'in principle' willing to send British troops to the USSR: indeed he 'would even consider it a matter of honour'. But he had to discuss the matter with his Cabinet and stressed the shortage of troops, given the commitment of 600,000 troops for the forthcoming offensive in Libya and the fact that there were fewer than a million trained and armed troops in Britain itself. The shortage of sea transport was also a problem. 'I don't want to mislead you,' Churchill told the ambassador. 'Even if the British Government decides to send an expeditionary force to you, it will not arrive before winter.' Anxious to accentuate the positives in the message, Churchill said how pleased he was that 'Mr Stalin has at last come to believe in our good intentions vis-à-vis the USSR'. Maisky sent an unvarnished account of the conversation to Moscow. 'From Churchill's musings today,' he concluded, 'it is clear to me that 25–30 divisions are out of the question. But it is important that the English actually begin such an operation, even with a small force at first. Then they would have to be drawn in deeper.'[66]

In volume three of his war memoirs, composed in 1950, Churchill observed that Stalin's request for 25–30 divisions was 'almost incredible' and that it 'seemed hopeless to argue with a man thinking in terms of such absurdities'.[67] Perhaps for that reason he evaded the question in his reply on 13 September, instead highlighting plans for the Moscow conference and for transport links across Iran. He spoke of examining possible 'military cooperation' on both north and south flanks, but without any specifics, and talked up the desirability of bringing the Turks into the war. Turkey would be another obsession of his wartime correspondence.

Churchill to Stalin, sent 18 September 1941, received 19 September 1941[68]

Many thanks for your message. The Harriman Mission has all arrived, and is working all day long with Beaverbrook and his colleagues. The object is to survey the whole field of resources, so as to be able to work out with you a definite programme of monthly deliveries by every available route and thus help to repair as far as possible the losses of your munition industries. President Roosevelt's idea is that this first plan should cover up till the end of June, but naturally we shall go on with you till victory. I hope that the Conference may open in Moscow on the 25th of this month, but no publicity should be given till all are safely gathered. Routes and methods of travel will be signalled later.

I attach great importance to the opening of the through route from the Persian Gulf to the Caspian, not only by railway, but by a great motor road in the making of which we hope to enlist American energies and organisation. Lord Beaverbrook will be able to explain the whole scheme of supply and transportation; he is on the closest terms of friendship with Mr Harriman.

All possible theatres in which we might effect military co-operation with you have been examined by the Staffs. The two flanks, North and South, certainly present the most favourable opportunities. If we could act successfully in Norway, the attitude of Sweden would be powerfully affected, but at the moment we have neither the forces nor the shipping available for this project. Again, in the South the great prize is Turkey; if Turkey can be gained, another powerful army will be available. Turkey would like to come in with us, but is afraid, not without reason. It may be that the promise of considerable British forces and supplies of technical material in which the Turks are deficient will exercise a decisive influence upon them. We will study with you any other form of useful aid, the sole object being to bring the maximum force against the common enemy.

I entirely agree that the first source from which the Russian Fleet should be replenished should be at the expense of Germany. Victory will certainly give us control of important German and Italian naval vessels, and in our view these would be most suitable for repairing losses to the Russian Fleet.

Reactions to this message fell into a now familiar pattern. Shown it by Eden on 18 September, Maisky complained about the absence of a clear answer to the request for a British expeditionary force, and warned of the unfavourable impact in Moscow. The foreign secretary wanted to do more for the Russians, and interceded with Churchill; but he was told firmly: 'All is governed by shipping. There is no objection to studying any plan but we must not encourage delusions that any large armies can be sent from Great Britain to fight in Russia.' The PM's eyes were firmly fixed on General Claude Auchinleck's impending offensive in Libya, from which he expected a decisive breakthrough in the Mediterranean.[69]

The supply discussions in London between Averell Harriman, Max Beaverbrook and their teams had been difficult, even acrimonious. The swashbuckling Canadian press baron tried to browbeat the Americans into ring-fencing existing US commitments to Britain before discussing aid to Russia. But Harriman was more than a match. His daughter noted that whereas Churchill was 'a gentleman', Beaverbrook was 'a ruffian' and 'luckily', she added, her father could 'talk both languages'. Beaverbrook had to tell the Cabinet's Defence Committee that the pledge of British and American help made by Churchill to Stalin on 5 September had 'proved in excess of U.S. intentions', because output estimates had now been cut back. He added: 'The promise of 400 aircraft and 500 tanks a month from October 1941 to June 1942, to which the United States of America and ourselves are committed, can be fulfilled by a sacrifice. That sacrifice will fall almost entirely on us.'[70] The chiefs of staff warned of the dire effects on British programmes and strategy, particularly the bombing offensive against Germany and the creation of new armoured divisions, while supporters of aid to Russia – especially Beaverbrook, Eden and Clement Attlee, leader of the Labour party – emphasized the need to avert a Russian collapse. Churchill tried to balance these competing pressures when framing the directive for Beaverbrook's mission to Moscow, instructing him to avoid providing hard statistics about production plans and not to promise much greater aid until mid-1942, when British–American production really got going – unless the United States did become a belligerent. The hollowness of British strategy at this stage in the war, before Pearl Harbor, is evident from this passage in Churchill's directive:

> The Russians will no doubt ask how you propose to win the war, to which our answer should be: 'By going on fighting till the Nazi system breaks up as the Kaiser's broke up last time.' For this purpose we shall fight the enemy wherever we can meet them on favourable terms. We shall undermine them by propaganda; depress them with the blockade; and, above all, bomb their homelands ceaselessly, ruthlessly, and with ever-increasing weight of bombs. We could not tell last time how and when we should win the war, but by not giving in and not wearying we came through all right.[71]

Or, as he liked to say in private, just KBO – keep buggering on.

2

'TWO RELATIVELY UNRELATED WARS'

(September to December 1941)

BEAVERBROOK, HARRIMAN AND THEIR teams arrived in Moscow on 28 September. Churchill and Roosevelt sent supportive messages, though the president's was embarrassingly revealed by German intelligence. The two emissaries had a friendly first meeting with Stalin, a difficult second session, and a more productive final meeting. This 'one-two-three' became a familiar pattern for Allied visitors to the Kremlin. Out of the week came a foundational agreement on American and British supplies to Russia, which they intended as some kind of surrogate for a second front. For all its deficiencies, the Moscow conference's decision in principle to share the resources of the three powers in the fight against a common enemy would eventually prove of great strategic importance, especially given the subsequent failure of Berlin and Tokyo to cooperate in any meaningful way.

The supply protocol cost the British dear – it was often implemented by diverting US supplies that would otherwise have gone to Britain – but in the first year they honoured it more fully than the Americans, still struggling to mobilize for global war. On the other hand, the USA was more generous about financial aid: FDR's messages of 30 October and 6 November offered the USSR a billion dollars of Lend-Lease aid, interest free (with repayment not beginning until five years after the war) and also $5 million of free medical supplies.[1] Stalin's appreciative message to FDR on 4 November, despite its somewhat stilted language, evinces a warmth of tone rarely found in telegrams to Churchill: another feature of the whole wartime correspondence. At this stage, however, the president – leading a country still deeply divided about getting into the war – was very much the third party in the triangle. Only six of the thirty-four messages that the three leaders exchanged up to Pearl Harbor emanated from the White House, and their impact was further diminished by delays in transmission (in one case five months) and by interception by German intelligence.

Throughout the autumn and winter of 1941, Stalin kept reminding London and Washington that the Russians were doing the bulk of the fighting. For how long, however, remained an open question in the West. On 15–16 October, with the Wehrmacht less than 100 miles from Moscow, panic spread through the capital and foreign embassies were hastily evacuated to Kuybyshev, some 500 miles to the east. Since Stalin and the Foreign Ministry eventually decided to stay in Moscow, this made communication among the Allies even more difficult.

The evacuation crisis, though not mentioned in the Big Three's messages, had an effect on relations. Churchill's attention was now focused on the impending 'Crusader' offensive against the Germans and Italians in North Africa which, with typical brio, he was talking up as a likely game-changer throughout the Mediterranean, perhaps drawing Turkey into the war on the Allied side. This was another of his cigar-smoke fantasies. To Roosevelt and Harriman, Churchill did not hold out much hope from the east, predicting that once Hitler had stabilized the Russian front deep in Russia's hinterland, he would turn back on Britain in 1942 and maybe against America in 1943. The PM's pessimism about the USSR was roundly attacked from Kuybyshev by Cripps, who warned on 30 October of the danger of conducting 'two relatively unrelated wars' without any real coop-eration. Stung by Cripps's barb that the British government was paying the USSR less high-level attention than it lavished on the ill-fated Greeks in the spring of 1941, Churchill agreed to send two senior generals to Moscow for ill-defined talks. This offer was conveyed to Stalin in a brusque message of 4 November, together with querulous expressions of doubt about the need for Britain to declare war on Finland, Hungary and Romania, whose troops were now fighting alongside the Wehrmacht in Russia. Stalin replied on 8 November, the day after his emotional review in a snowy Red Square of troops marching out to fight and die for Moscow. At the end of his tether, the Soviet leader did not mince words, calling British policy on the minor Axis states 'intolerable' and sarcastically saying that unless the British generals came with concrete plans for mutual mili-tary assistance and for shared war and peace aims, he saw no point in receiving them. Churchill was livid.

What is also evident, however, is that by the end of November 1941 the notoriously 'rough' Soviet leader was beginning to learn the language of diplo-macy. Alerted to Churchill's fury, he was persuaded to offer something close to an apology on 23 November and then, quite astonishingly, a week later to send a birthday greeting to Churchill himself. Stalin was not in the habit of wishing 'many happy returns' to a capitalist and imperialist, least of all one who had tried to strangle the Revolution in its cradle. Perhaps he was prompted to do so by Ambassador Maisky in London, whose role as double interpreter between the prickly pair is recurrent in the pages that follow (plate 6). That two-line message from Stalin on 30 November is one of the most striking documents in this chapter. Churchill replied with his own *billet-doux* – and relations were smoothed over for the moment. By this time, Cripps's cogent arguments and Stalin's anger had persuaded Churchill that he should treat the USSR as a serious ally and make a proper effort to concert their strategies and policies. At Cripps's suggestion, Eden was designated as the emissary. On 7 December, the foreign secretary set out on a special mission to Moscow – just as the war suddenly took a dramatic new turn.

*****

Churchill composed a letter to Stalin on 21 September for Beaverbrook to deliver in person. The PM combined his usual flowery rhetoric (plate 4) with information intended to show the limitations of Britain's position. Using material from the directive to the Beaverbrook mission, he emphasized that over the next nine months Allied aid to Russia would be mostly at Britain's expense. Churchill also underlined the smallness of his country's population compared with that of America or Russia, and the implications of this for the size of the British Army.

Beaverbrook handed over the letter during the mission's second meeting with Stalin on 29 September. The opening encounter the previous day had gone well, but now Stalin was angry and restless, pacing up and down, smoking continuously and impugning his allies' good faith. 'The paucity of your offers', he growled, 'clearly shows that you want to see the Soviet Union defeated.' The message from Churchill was treated in a similar way. Stalin ripped open the envelope, barely glanced at the contents and left the letter on the table, unread, for the rest of the meeting. Reminded of it at the end by Molotov, Stalin pushed it back into the envelope and handed everything to an aide. Harriman and Beaverbrook could not decide whether the whole meeting was a performance to unsettle them or reflected the intense strain upon Stalin. In the event, their third meeting proved calmer and more productive; in due course, they concluded that they had been victims of a standard Soviet diplomatic ploy. But Stalin's dismissive attitude to Churchill's letter may have reflected something else. The PM's instructions to Beaverbrook, on which the letter was based, had already been transmitted direct to the Kremlin by Soviet agents in London.[2]

Churchill to Stalin, sent 21 September 1941, received 29 September 1941[3]

The British and American Missions have now started, and this letter will be presented to you by Lord Beaverbrook. Lord Beaverbrook has the fullest confidence of the Cabinet, and is one of my oldest and most intimate friends. He has established the closest relations with Mr Harriman, who is a remarkable American, wholeheartedly devoted to the victory of the common cause. They will lay before you all that we have been able to arrange in much anxious consultation between Great Britain and the United States.

President Roosevelt has decided that our proposals shall, in the first instance, deal with the monthly quotas we shall send to you in the nine months period from October 1941 to June 1942 inclusive. You have the right to know exactly what we can deliver month by month in order that you may handle your reserves to the best advantage.

The American proposals have not yet gone beyond the end of June 1942, but I have no doubt that considerably larger quotas can be furnished by both countries thereafter, and you may be sure we shall do our utmost to repair as far as possible the grievous curtailments which your war industries have suffered through the Nazi invasion. I will not anticipate what Lord Beaverbrook will have to say upon this subject.

You will realise that the quotas up to the end of June 1942 are supplied almost entirely out of British production, or production which the United States would have given us under our own purchases or under the Lease and Lend Bill. The United States were resolved to give us virtually the whole of their exportable surplus, and it is not easy for them within that time to open out effectively new sources of supply. I am hopeful that a further great impulse will be given to the production of the United States, and that by 1943 the mighty industry of America will be in full war swing. For our part, we shall not only make substantially increased contributions from our own existing forecast production, but also try to obtain from our people an extra further effort to meet our common needs. You will understand, however, that our Army and its supply which has been planned is perhaps only one-fifth or one-sixth as large as that of yours or Germany's. Our first duty and need is to keep open the seas, and our second duty is to obtain decisive superiority in the air. These have the first claims upon the man-power of our 44,000,000 in the British Islands. We can never hope to have an Army or Army munitions industries comparable to those of the great Continental military Powers. None the less, we will do our utmost to aid you.

General Ismay, who is my personal representative on the Chiefs of the Staffs Committee, and is thoroughly acquainted with the whole field of our military policy, is authorised to study with your Commanders any plans for practical cooperation which may suggest themselves.

If we can clear our western flank in Libya of the enemy, we shall have considerable forces, both Air and Army, to cooperate upon the southern flank of the Russian front.

It seems to me that the most speedy and effective help would come if Turkey could be induced to resist a German demand for the passage of troops, or better still, if she would enter the war on our side. You will I am sure attach due weight to this.

I have always shared your sympathy for the Chinese people in their struggle to defend their native land against Japanese aggression. Naturally we do not want to add Japan to the side of our foes, but the attitude of the United States, resulting from my conference with President Roosevelt, has already enforced a far more sober view upon the Japanese Government. I made haste to declare on behalf of His Majesty's Government that should the United States be involved in war with Japan, Great Britain would immediately range herself on her side. I think that all our three countries should, so far as possible, continue to give aid to China, and that this may go to considerable lengths without provoking a Japanese declaration of war.

There is no doubt that a long period of struggle and suffering lies before our peoples, but I have great hopes that the United States will enter the war as a belligerent, and if so, I cannot doubt that we have but to endure to conquer.

I am hopeful that as the war continues, the great masses of the peoples of the British Empire, the Soviet Union, the United States and China, which alone comprise two-thirds of the entire human race, may be found marching together against their persecutors; and I am sure the road they travel will lead to victory.

With heartfelt wishes for the success of the Russian Armies, and of the ruin of the Nazi tyrants.

Roosevelt's message to Stalin, dated 17 September, was supposed to be transmitted in person by Harriman. It had the modest aim of making personal contact and offering words of encouragement, although FDR obliquely sought to remind the Soviet leader that his was not the only front in the war. The letter was, however, delayed by bad weather, and Harriman did not receive it before leaving London. Upon arrival in Moscow, he took the initiative himself to ask Roosevelt for 'a personal message' to the Soviet leader, stressing that Beaverbrook had delivered one from Churchill. A duplicate of the original message was then sent by telegram from Washington, and on 30 September Harriman handed it to Stalin. But the State Department had used a simple cipher which was cracked by the Germans, who trumpeted the message around the world as proof of Roosevelt's 'collusion' with the communists.[4]

This was not the last example of leakage of Big Three secret correspondence, with the Americans being particularly culpable in 1941–42. The president himself realized the unreliability of transmission through the State Department, telling Andrey Gromyko, the Soviet chargé d'affaires in Washington in April 1942, that the Soviet cipher system was 'more reliable'. FDR had already been informed by Churchill that the British had been able to crack American diplomatic ciphers.[5] Increasingly, the White House used the US Navy's more secure system to transmit the messages. Bypassing the State Department in this way also reflected FDR's general distaste for what he called the 'striped pants' set.

Roosevelt to Stalin, sent 17 and 29 September 1941, received 30 September 1941[6]

This note will be presented to you by my friend Averell Harriman, whom I have asked to be head of our delegation to Moscow.

Mr Harriman is well aware of the strategic importance of your front and will, I know, do everything that he can to bring the negotiations in Moscow to a successful conclusion.

Harry Hopkins has told me in great detail of his encouraging and satisfactory visits with you. I can't tell you how thrilled all of us are because of the gallant defense of the Soviet armies.

I am confident that ways will be found to provide the material and supplies necessary to fight Hitler on all fronts, including your own.

I want particularly to take this occasion to express my great confidence that your armies will ultimately prevail over Hitler and to assure you of our great determination to be of every possible material assistance.

Delivering this message, Harriman urged Stalin to establish direct contact with the president. 'Stalin said he was glad to hear this as he had previously felt he should not presume to address the President directly.'[7] His next letter, on 3 October, drafted by Molotov, did indeed address Roosevelt in person. The message was sent with Harriman; Stalin used Beaverbrook's presence in Moscow to send a parallel letter to Churchill.

Stalin to Roosevelt, sent 3 October 1941, received 16 October 1941[8]

Your letter has been presented to me by Mr Harriman. I avail myself of the opportunity to express to you the deep gratitude of the Soviet Government for having put at the head of the American delegation such an authority as Mr Harriman, whose participation in the proceedings of the Moscow Conference of the three powers has been so effective.

I have no doubt that you will do everything necessary to ensure the carrying out of the decisions of the Moscow Conference as speedily and completely as possible, particularly in view of the fact that the Hitlerites will certainly try to take advantage of prewinter months to exert every possible pressure on the front against the USSR.

Like you I have no doubt that final victory over Hitler will be won by those countries which are uniting now their efforts in order to speed up the annihilation of bloody Hitlerism – a task for the sake of which the Soviet Union now makes so great and heavy sacrifices.

In his memoirs, composed in the depths of the Cold War, Churchill wrote of the Moscow conference that the 'reception was bleak and the discussions not at all friendly', with little information or even hospitality. To capture the tone, he quoted an apocryphal story of an Intourist guide showing a Royal Marine officer around the city: 'This is the Eden Hotel, formerly Ribbentrop Hotel ... Here is Churchill Street, formerly Hitler Street ...' And so on, before the offer: 'Will you have a cigarette, comrade?' To which the marine replied: 'Thank you, comrade, formerly bastard.' In fact, the Moscow conference became a landmark in forging the coalition against Hitler. Despite Stalin's one-two-three ploy, the Western visitors felt themselves well treated, especially compared with the frigidity of previous diplomatic relations, and Stalin's banquet for his Western guests at the Kremlin was unprecedented. The conference resulted in the signing of the 'First Protocol' – a coordinated programme of British and American supplies to the USSR, running from 1 October 1941 to 1 July 1942. Beaverbrook told the British delegation firmly that they were 'not going to Moscow to bargain but to give'. This, he argued against the widely preferred quid pro quo approach, was 'the one way to break down the suspicious attitude' of Russia towards the West.[9]

During the Kremlin dinner, General Hastings 'Pug' Ismay, Churchill's military secretary, had a brief but instructive conversation with Stalin, which he reported to the Cabinet. The Soviet leader was insistent that 'tanks and aeroplanes decide war'. Ismay noted in his report that this was perhaps a recent discovery, and, if so, might explain why the Russians were mostly interested in Western tanks, anti-tank guns and anti-aircraft artillery (in which both the UK and the USA were themselves limited), rather than in field artillery and machine-guns, which the British were ready to offer in substantial amounts. Stalin also told Ismay that he fully understood why Britain could not open a western front at the moment, observing bluntly:

> The whole situation in Europe has changed. Never again can England rely on her Navy alone. She must have conscription and a large army in time of peace. There will always be 'Pétains' in France and therefore no reliance can be placed on the French army or people. Japan finds it possible to maintain a large army in addition to a large Navy. So why not England?

Ismay also lamented the lack of shared information: the Russian general staff told the British military mission 'precisely nothing'. This, he said, reflected the 'intense centralisation' in Russia and also 'the feeling of mutual distrust and dislike' that had prevailed between the two countries for over twenty years. As a result, Ismay believed that 'anything in the nature of joint planning' would 'in present circumstances be valueless'. But he expressed the hope that 'a new atmosphere' would be 'created by the punctual fulfilment of our promises of help'.[10]

In a letter of thanks for the Moscow conference, sent with Beaverbrook, Stalin did not miss the opportunity to remind the PM of the inadequacy of Allied aid so far.[11] Realizing the significance of the moment, Churchill called a meeting of the Defence Committee, at which specific arrangements were made for the first batch of deliveries that had been agreed in Moscow. The plan was approved in Cabinet on 6 October, together with the text of Churchill's telegram to Stalin announcing the start of deliveries. In what was for him the rare use of a foreign language, Churchill quoted the old Latin tag: 'He gives twofold who gives promptly.'[12]

Churchill to Stalin, sent 6 October 1941, received 7 October 1941[13]

I am glad to learn from Lord Beaverbrook of the success of the Tripartite Conference at Moscow. 'Bis dat qui cito dat.' We intend to run a continuous cycle of convoys leaving every ten days. The following are on the way and arrive at Archangel October 12th:

20 heavy tanks
193 fighters (pre-October quota).

Following will sail October 12th, arriving October 29th:

140 heavy tanks
100 Hurricanes
200 Bren carriers
200 anti-tank rifles and ammunition
50 2-pounder guns and ammunition.

Following will sail October 22nd:

200 fighters
120 heavy tanks.

Above shows that total of the October quota of aircraft and 280 tanks will arrive in Russia by November 6th. The October quota of Bren Carriers, anti-tank rifles and 2-pounder anti-tank guns will all arrive in October. 20 tanks have been shipped to go via Persia and 15 are about to be shipped from Canada via Vladivostok. The total tanks shipped will therefore be 315, which is 19 short of our full quota. This number will be made up in November. The above programme does not take into account supplies from the United States.

In arranging this regular cycle of convoys we are counting on Archangel to handle the main bulk of deliveries. I presume this part of the job in hand. Good wishes.

In his next letter to Stalin a few days later, Churchill again tried to substitute other kinds of aid for the sending of a British expeditionary force to the USSR, in this case offering to replace with British forces several Soviet divisions keeping order in Iran, so as to 'free' the latter to fight the Wehrmacht. Despite Churchill's solemn assurances that the British would not take advantage of the withdrawal of the Soviet troops from Iran, Stalin could not risk weakening his position in a country that boarded the USSR and that had been a source of historic rivalry between the two countries. Churchill's offer must have aroused suspicion, rather than encouraging confidence. The Soviet leader did not even reply.

Churchill to Stalin, sent 12 October 1941, received 13 October 1941[14]

I thank you for your letter of 3rd October. I have given incessant directions to accelerate the deliveries at Archangel, as reported to you in my telegram of the 6th October. Your request for 3,000 lorries will be met immediately from our Army stocks, but deliveries must not impede the flow of tanks and aircraft. We are asking Harriman to arrange a larger long-term programme from the United States.

About Persia. Our only interests there are: first, as a barrier against German penetration eastwards; and, secondly, as a through route for supplies to the Caspian Basin. If you wish to withdraw the five or six Russian divisions for use on the battle front, we will take over the whole responsibility for keeping order and maintaining and improving the supply route. I pledge the faith of Britain that we will not seek any advantage for ourselves at the expense of any rightful Russian interest during the War or at the end. In any case, the signing of the Tripartite Treaty is urgent to avoid internal disorders growing, with consequent danger of choking the supply route. General Wavell will be at Tiflis on the 18th October, and will discuss with your generals any questions which you may instruct them to settle with him.

Words are useless to express what we feel about your vast, heroic struggle. We hope presently to testify by action.

Stalin's failure to reply also reflected the dire military situation. Operation 'Typhoon', Hitler's new drive towards Moscow, broke through the so-called Mozhaisk Line – arching across the famous 1812 battlefield of Borodino. A final defence perimeter was hastily thrown together to protect the last sixty miles before the capital. As panic began to infect the city on 15 October, the British and US ambassadors were suddenly told at noon that they must evacuate their staff on a special train that evening. At the British embassy, across the Moscow river from the Kremlin, a bonfire was lit on the tennis court and vast piles of correspondence hastily burnt. Asked what should be done with the wireless, Cripps replied curtly: 'Smash it.' The Western diplomats took five days to travel to the city of Kuybyshev on the Volga, a rail journey of normally less than a day. For a few hours, a special train was ready to move Stalin east as well, until that plan was dropped. On 16 October, factories, shops and the Moscow Metro were closed. No buses or trams ran on the streets, and the sky was full of a sinister black 'snow' – ashes from thousands of offices burning their papers. Families fled with what possessions they could carry, while looters stripped abandoned shops and dwellings. One eyewitness likened Moscow to 'an ant heap', with little figures rushing in all directions. It was not until 20 October that the government got a grip on the crisis, placing the city under strict martial law.[15]

Meanwhile, Roosevelt had also been taking stock of the Moscow conference, including Stalin's message of 3 October that Harriman had brought back. 'What do you think – should I reply?' FDR asked Hopkins, 'especially given Stalin's apparent satisfaction, when Harriman told him that I would be happy to correspond with him directly?'[16] Hopkins urged the president to make a personal response: from his own meetings in Moscow 'it was clear that Stalin did not trust our Ambassador and other embassy staff' and probably 'would show a similar attitude towards the State Department, if prompted'.[17]

Roosevelt to Stalin, sent 13 October 1941[18]

We are shipping [in] October 94 light tanks and 72 medium 32-ton tanks with spare parts and ammunition. Most of these will leave the United States by October 15.

We are shipping 100 bombers and 100 of our newest fighter planes with spare parts and ammunition. These will be placed on ships during the next ten days.

We are shipping 5,500 trucks during October and large amounts of barbed wire. All other military supplies we promised for October are being swiftly assembled to be placed on ships.

Three ships left the United States yesterday for Russian ports. Every effort being made to rush other supplies.

In perhaps further evidence of the crisis atmosphere in Moscow, there is no trace of this message in the Russian archives.[19]

Nearly two weeks later, FDR told Stalin that the USSR had been brought within Lend-Lease. But ironically, in view of the president's desire to keep in personal touch, the message was sent via Tehran with the diplomatic mail and delayed. It did not reach the US embassy in Kuybyshev until 15 March 1942, and was finally delivered to the Kremlin next day – nearly five months after it had left the White House![20]

Roosevelt to Stalin, sent 25 October 1941, received 16 March 1942[21]

Mr Harriman has handed me your kind note dated October 3, 1941. I appreciate very much hearing from you.

A cable has already gone to you advising you that we can include the Soviet Union under our Lend-Lease arrangements.

I want to take this opportunity to assure you again that we are going to bend every possible effort to move these supplies to your battle lines.

The determination of your armies and people to defeat Hitlerism is an inspiration to the free people of all the world.

Roosevelt amplified the arrangements to be offered under Lend-Lease in a further message a few days later. This did arrive quickly, but in a bizarre form. It was transmitted by telegram to Steinhardt in Kuybyshev, but the ambassador decided that to relay it verbatim could compromise the US Navy code. (He assumed that the Soviets had already intercepted the message.) Eventually, after some delay, Steinhardt gave Vyshinskiy a memorandum paraphrasing the message, with the first person singular ponderously rendered into the third person, so that 'I have seen' became 'The President has seen'. As Steinhardt emphasized verbally, Roosevelt had approved all the decisions of the Moscow conference, and the USSR would also be allowed an interest-free loan of $1 billion to pay for Lend-Lease supplies. He added that 'from now on the Soviet government does not have to worry about the financial side of deliveries, in any case until the entire loan is spent'.[22] Until then, the Kremlin had been seeking funds to pay for supplies, having sent overseas ten tons of gold, the equivalent of $30 million, as a deposit for an American loan with which to pay for the materiel.[23]

Roosevelt to Stalin, sent 30 October 1941, received 2 November 1941[24]

I have seen the Protocol of the Conference held in Moscow and discussed the data contained therein with the members of our Mission.

I have approved all the items of military equipment and munitions and have directed that the utmost expedition be used to provide so far as possible the raw materials. I have ordered that the deliveries begin at once and be maintaining [sic] in the greatest possible volume.

In order to remove any financial obstacles I have also directed that arrangements be effected immediately whereby shipments up to the value of one billion dollars may be made under the Lend Lease act.

I propose, subject to the approval of the Government of the USSR, that no interest be charged on the indebtedness incurred as a result of these shipments and that the payments on such indebtedness by the Government of the USSR begin only five years after conclusion of the war and completed over a period of ten years thereafter.

I hope your Government can arrange to make special efforts to sell the United States such commodities and raw materials as may be available and of which the United States may be in urgent need. The proceeds of such sales to the Government of the United States to be credited to the account of the Soviet Government.

I want to take the opportunity to express the appreciation of this government for the expeditious way in which the supply conference in Moscow was handled by you and your associates and to assure you that the implications of that conference will be carried out to the limit.

I trust you will not hesitate to get in touch with me directly should the occasion require.

The following day, 31 October, Steinhardt handed Vyshinskiy a list of items to be delivered in addition to the supplies outlined in the First Protocol.[25] The ambassador asked for the list to be considered as a presidential message, 'for a telegram regarding this matter was received not from Hull, but from Roosevelt'.[26] FDR's open-handedness, at a time when Churchill seemed stingy and uncooperative, was appreciated in the Kremlin, and this is evident from Stalin's reply. Despite the stilted English of the State Department's translation, the tone was clearly very different from that of the messages which the Soviet leader was currently sending to 10 Downing Street.

Stalin to Roosevelt, sent 4 November, received 7 November 1941[27]

Although I have not yet received the text of your message, Mr Steinhardt, the Ambassador of the United States of America, on November 2, transmitted to me through Mr Vyshinsky an aide-mémoire setting forth the contents of your message to me.

In this connection permit me first of all to express complete agreement with your evaluation of the work of the conference of the three powers in Moscow, which is to be attributed in the greatest degree to the services of Mr Harriman and also Mr Beaverbrook who did everything possible for the successful conclusion of the work of the conference in the shortest time. The Soviet Government expresses its deepest gratitude for your statement that the decisions of the conference will be carried out to the maximum extent.

Mr President, the Soviet Government accepts with sincere gratitude your decision to grant the Soviet Union a non-interest bearing loan in the sum of one billion dollars to pay for supplies of armaments and raw materials for the Soviet Union, as exceptionally substantial assistance to the Soviet Union in its great and difficult struggle with our common enemy, bloody-thirsty Hitlerism. On behalf of the Government of the USSR, I express complete agreement with the conditions set forth by you concerning the granting of this loan to the Soviet Union, payments on which shall commence five years after the termination of the war and be made during the ten years after the expiration of this five year period.

The Government of the USSR is prepared to do everything possible in order to furnish the United States of America those goods and raw materials which are at its disposal and which the United States may need.

With respect to your proposal, Mr President, that personal direct contact should be immediately established between you and me, should circumstances require this, I share your desire with satisfaction and am prepared to do everything necessary to make this possible.

At 1 a.m. on 6 November, Vyshinskiy handed the letter and an English version to Steinhardt, adding that Stalin and Molotov wished to publish FDR's message in the Soviet press. The cautious ambassador questioned the political expediency of disclosing that a billion-dollar loan had been allocated bypassing Congress.[28] He added that Roosevelt had 'made similar decisions before with respect to England, and it was reported several months later, when American public opinion was conditioned for such measures'.[29] But the reaction in Washington to the Soviet request was much more positive. Hopkins told Gromyko that 'we couldn't have expected a better response from Moscow', and when the Soviet chargé met FDR the following day, he was clearly 'very satisfied' with Stalin's reply.[30] The president approved publication, but in a paraphrased form to prevent the Germans 'being able to decode our cyphers'. On 8 November, an account of Roosevelt's message and Stalin's response was published by the US State Department, and next day also in *Izvestiya*.[31]

After the flurry of messages in early October, Churchill did not write again to Stalin for three weeks. The almost marginal place of Russia in his strategic universe that autumn is best shown by a long and detailed letter that the PM sent to FDR on 20 October, marked 'For Yourself Only'. In it Churchill focused on Britain's oft-postponed, but now imminent, offensive in North Africa (operation 'Crusader'). The PM's underlying doubt about Soviet prospects, amid the panic in Moscow and evacuation of the government eastward, is evident from the following bleak scenario he offered the president:

> We must expect that as soon as Hitler stabilizes the Russian front, he will begin to gather perhaps fifty or sixty divisions in the west for the invasion of the British Isles ... One may well suppose his programme to be: 1939 – Poland; 1940 – France; 1941 – Russia; 1942 – England; 1943 –? At any rate, I feel we must be prepared to meet a supreme onslaught from March onwards.

Speaking to Harriman on 15 October, the PM had been less cryptic about 1943, observing 'maybe America'.[32]

We should, of course, remember that in the autumn of 1941 the United States was still neutral, and Churchill often exaggerated strategic dangers in the hope of pushing the president to ask a reluctant Congress to declare war. Even so, the message shows starkly his preoccupation with the Mediterranean and his scepticism about Russia.

Churchill's attitude did not go uncontested. Beaverbrook and Eden in Cabinet both urged some kind of troop commitment to aid the Soviets – if only to show signs of alliance solidarity. But the most cogent critique of Churchill's handling of Russia came from Cripps, who, as a fellow (yet rival) politician, argued back in a way that no professional ambassador would have dared to do. Faced with another message from the prime minister full of recriminations about the Molotov–Ribbentrop pact, mockery of the 'silly' idea of sending two or three divisions 'into the heart of Russia' to be 'cut to pieces as a symbolic sacrifice' and the 'madness' of upsetting plans for the North African offensive, Cripps responded by denouncing the apparent British preference for fighting its own separate war, 'to the great benefit of Hitler, instead of a single war upon the basis of a combined plan'. He noted that in the spring it had been 'thought worthwhile' to send both Eden, the foreign secretary, and Dill, the chief of the imperial general staff, to the Balkans in an ineffectual attempt to concert Greek resistance. 'And yet it could hardly be denied the Soviets are now more impor- tant to us as Allies than the Greeks ever were.' To Cripps, it seemed that 'we are treating the Soviet Government without trust and as inferiors rather than as trusted Allies. This attitude is similar to that which we have adopted ever since the Revolution and has been the cause of great resentment by the Soviets.' He referred specifically to 'the intervention by us on behalf of the White Russians' during the Civil War – a scarcely concealed dig at Churchill, who had been the government's most outspoken advocate of intervention. Each man, of course, had his own political and ideological agenda, but Cripps's essential point was valid: Churchill's government had treated the Russians quite differently from the Greeks and, indeed, the still-neutral Americans, with whom Britain had held extensive secret staff talks on strategy.[33]

Unyielding on even a token military commitment, Churchill felt obliged to be more forthcoming on strategic consultations. This was the crux of his next message to Stalin, sent on 4 November after discussion in Cabinet the previous day.[34] By offering to send to Moscow two senior British generals – Sir Archibald Wavell, commander-in-chief in India (who knew Russia and spoke the language), and Bernard Paget, commander-in-chief designate in the Far East – the PM hoped to kill two birds with one stone: to take account of the recom- mendations of Cripps and others about the need for real dialogue with the Kremlin, while also persuading Stalin of 'the limited possibilities of sending a British force to Russia' via either Murmansk or Persia.[35] In his message, Churchill also queried the persistent Soviet demand that Britain declare war on Germany's allies – Finland, Romania and Hungary – who were now at war with the USSR. Eden was sympathetic to Maisky's argument that this gesture would signal political cooperation at a time when military supplies were not forth- coming: '*Please* do it', the ambassador implored the foreign secretary on 21

October.[36] But Churchill, more concerned with American and Dominion opinion, procrastinated. Trying to sugar the pill, the PM reiterated in his message Britain's efforts to send supplies via the northern and southern routes, and also to put deterrent pressure on Japan.[37]

Churchill to Stalin, sent 4 November 1941, received 6 November 1941[38]

In order to clear things up and to plan for the future I am ready to send General Wavell, the Commander-in-Chief in India, Persia and Iraq, to meet you in Moscow, Kuibyshev, Tiflis or wherever you will be. Besides this, General Paget, our new Commander-in-Chief designate for the Far East, will come with General Wavell. General Paget has been in the centre of things here, and will have with him the latest and best opinions of our High Command. These two Officers will be able to tell you exactly how we stand, what is possible and what we think is wise. They can reach you in about a fortnight. Do you want them?

Do you yourself, Premier Stalin, think it good business that Great Britain should declare war on Finland, Hungary and Roumania at this moment? It is only a formality, because our extreme blockade is already in force against them. My judgement is against it because, firstly, Finland has many friends in the United States and it is more prudent to take account of this fact. Secondly, Roumania and Hungary: these countries are full of our friends: they have been overpowered by Hitler and used as a cat's-paw. But if fortune turns against that ruffian they might easily come back to our side. A British declaration of war would only freeze them all and make it look as if Hitler were the head of a grand European alliance solid against us. Do not, pray, suppose that it is any want of zeal or comradeship that makes us doubt the advantage of this step. Our Dominions, except Australia, are reluctant. Nevertheless if you think that it will be a real help to you and worth while I will put it to the Cabinet again.

I hope our supplies are being cleared from Archangel as fast as they come in. A trickle is now beginning through Persia. We shall pump both ways to our utmost. Please make sure that our technicians who are going with the tanks and aircraft have full opportunity to hand these weapons over to your men under the best conditions. At present our Mission at Kuibyshev is out of touch with all these affairs. They only want to help. These weapons are sent at our peril, and we are anxious that they shall have the best chance. An order from you seems necessary.

I cannot tell you about our immediate military plans any more than you can tell me about yours, but rest assured that we are not going to be idle.

With the object of keeping Japan quiet we are sending our latest battleship, the *Prince of Wales*, which can catch and kill any Japanese ship, into the Indian

Ocean, and are building up a powerful battle squadron there. I am urging President Roosevelt to increase his pressure on the Japanese and to keep them frightened, so that the Vladivostok route will not be blocked.

I will not waste words in compliments, because you know already from Lord Beaverbrook and Mr Harriman what we feel about your fight. Have confidence in our untiring support.

I should be glad to hear from you direct that you have received this telegram.

Roosevelt sent a message on 6 November, which enlarged on his previous generosity by pledging about $5 million from the American Red Cross (ARC) to cover roughly a third of the medical supplies promised by the USA and Britain as part of the protocol signed at the Moscow conference. Because the ARC was responsible to the US Congress (unlike its counterpart in Britain and many other countries), Roosevelt requested formal agreements between it and the Soviet Red Cross – a proposal to which Stalin readily agreed on 14 November.[39]

Meanwhile Stalin's relations with Churchill had reached a new low. The PM's message of 4 November had not gone down well in Moscow. Churchill's delay in declaring war on Germany's allies Finland, Hungary and Romania – which had been leaked in the British press – aroused serious doubts about the PM's sincerity. The proposed visit of the British generals with uncertain authority brought back memories of the fruitless military talks in August 1939 that had helped push the USSR into its pact with Nazi Germany: this idea was rejected by Stalin with unconcealed sarcasm. Here he was ignoring the advice of Maisky, who had proposed accepting the visit in order to sound out Britain's 'true intentions' and to pre-empt any claims from London that it had offered staff talks and Moscow had 'evaded them'.[40]

Stalin, however, was now moving to a different plane, seeking a formal Soviet–British alliance, including defined war aims. He had first raised the idea with Beaverbrook on 30 September, but the latter did not mention it to Churchill. Eden later told Maisky that London was ready to discuss such matters, but only in passing.[41] So Stalin decided to appeal to the prime minister direct, using as a peg Churchill's allusion on 4 November to the need to clarify Soviet–British relations. Bristling at the PM's insinuation that the Soviet authorities in Arkhangelsk were handling the aid inefficiently, he also accused the British of sending poorly packed cargo. His tone was terse and his ending abrupt. On a typed version of this document, Molotov wrote 'Comrade Stalin agrees',[42] which means that the draft was most likely prepared by Molotov on instructions from the Boss.

Stalin to Churchill, sent 8 November 1941,
received 11 November 1941[43]

Your message received on 7th November.

I fully agree with you that clarity should be established in the relations between the USSR and Great Britain. Such a clarity does not exist at present. The lack of clarity is the consequence of two circumstances

(a) There is no definite understanding between our two countries on war aims and on plans of the post war organisation of peace.

(b) There is no agreement between the USSR and Great Britain on mutual military assistance against Hitler in Europe.

As long as there is no accord on both these questions there can be no clarity in the Anglo-Soviet relations. More than that: to be quite frank, as long as the present situation exists, there will be difficult[y] to secure mutual confidence. Of course, the agreement on military supplies to the USSR has a great positive value but it does not settle, neither does it exhaust, the whole problem of relations between our two countries.

If the General Wavell and the General Paget, whom you mention in your message, will come to Moscow with a view to conclude agreement on two fundamental questions referred to above, I naturally shall be willing to meet them and to discuss with them these questions. If, however, the mission of the Generals is confined to the questions of information and to the consideration of secondary matters, it would not I think be worthwhile to intrude upon the Generals. In such a case it would also be very difficult for me to find the time for the conversations.

It seems to me an intolerable situation has been created in the questions of a British declaration of war on Finland, Hungary and Rumania. The Soviet Government raised this question with the British Government through the secret diplomatic channels. Quite unexpectedly for the USSR the whole problem – beginning with the request of the Soviet Government to the British Government and ending with the consideration of this question by the U.S.A. Government – received wide publicity. The whole problem is now being discussed at random in the press – friendly as well as enemy. And after all that the British Government informs us of its negative attitude to our proposal. Why is all this being done? To demonstrate the lack of unity between the USSR and Great Britain.

You can rest assured that we are taking all the necessary measures for speedy transportation to the right place of all the arms coming from Great Britain to Archangel. The same will be done with regard to the route through Iran. In this connection may I call your attention to the fact (although this is a minor matter) that tanks, planes [and] artillery are arriving inefficiently packed, that sometimes parts of the same vehicle are loaded in different ships, that planes, because of the imperfect packing, reach us broken.

On 11 November, Maisky gave this message to Churchill in his office in the Houses of Parliament. The PM read it and then jumped up from his chair, pacing the room. 'His face was as white as chalk and he was breathing heavily,' Maisky noted. 'He was obviously enraged.' The PM fumed about its tone and content, reminding Maisky that on 22 June he had immediately offered the USSR the hand of friendship, despite Stalin's previous accord with Hitler, and noting that Britain's war aims were encapsulated for the moment in the Atlantic Charter. Cooling down a bit, he declared, 'Right now I don't wish to respond to Stalin ... I might say a lot of undesirable things in the heat of the moment.' Instead he would take the matter to the Cabinet.[44]

'Later,' Eden recalled in his memoirs, 'we were to become only too familiar with the harsh tone of Marshal Stalin's messages to the Prime Minister, but the first example made a very disagreeable impression on the War Cabinet.'[45] Eden opined that behind the 'very suspicious' Soviet attitude was the fear that 'we and the United States would get together and leave them out of the settlement of matters at the Peace.' There was general agreement in Cabinet with the advice of Churchill and Eden to delay sending a formal reply, while making it clear via Cripps and Maisky that the government was 'pained and surprised at the tone and contents of the message'.[46]

From Kuybyshev, Cripps advised that Stalin's attitude would only be changed by a 'clear answer' on his two proposals – about an alliance agreement and the postwar settlement. He suggested that Eden should go to Moscow, together with the chiefs of staff. In further angry messages, the ambassador insisted that the policymakers in London had so far overlooked 'the fundamental importance of the issues which Stalin regards as touchstones of their sincerity in all-in-all collaboration' both during and after the war. Like Maisky, he urged London not to take too seriously Stalin's 'frank and blunt' mode of speaking, as a man who previously 'never had any real contact with Western ways and diplomatic usages'.[47] Cripps's argument made an impression on the leadership of the Foreign Office, where pressure was now mounting for a 'Volga Charter' – an Anglo-Soviet document on war aims – to complement the Atlantic Charter and 'make Stalin feel good'.[48] Churchill, however, categorically rejected any discussion of the postwar settlement. As a compromise, the Cabinet approved Eden's telegram to Cripps, expressing London's readiness for postwar cooperation but stressing that it was premature at this stage of the war to discuss the details.[49]

Meanwhile, on 12 November, Eden called in Maisky to express displeasure at the latest message and to seek explanation for its unusually harsh tone. Maisky argued that Stalin's requests were legitimate, but one should also 'make allowances' for the 'very great' strain of being supreme commander at such a desperate moment in Russian history. And he reminded Eden that Stalin, unlike the British, thought that the war was coming to a climax and 'would be over next year', which 'might account for the fact that he wished for early consultation about the post-war period'.[50] On the 14th, the foreign secretary advised the ambassador to organize a conciliatory signal from Molotov, which would allow Eden, as he put it, 'to build a bridge again'. Beaverbrook talked in similar vein. On 15 November, and again on the 19th, the ambassador cabled Moscow using these conversations to show the need for some kind of olive branch. Citing a 'fully reliable source' (actually Eden himself) he reported that the Cabinet was ready in principle to send three to four British divisions, which would 'pull others after them', and to begin negotiations on the issue of war aims and the postwar settlement, which Eden was authorized to do. Stalin underlined the words 'reliable source' and 'three to four British divisions'. Maisky said that the British government was 'waiting for some sort of a "conciliatory gesture" on our part, even my announcement on behalf of Comrade Stalin or Comrade Molotov that Churchill misunderstood or misinterpreted Comrade Stalin's message ... After such a "gesture" they would make an official démarche.'[51]

Eden had jumped at Cripps's idea of a Moscow visit, seeing it as a chance to strengthen his role in British–Soviet relations, which Churchill had monopolized since the start of 'Barbarossa'. The object of the visit, the foreign secretary told Cripps, 'would be to do all in my power to convince Stalin that our co-operation was loyal and whole-hearted now and would be so after the war'. But he also reminded the ambassador that Britain could not come up with a simple statement of war aims, because it was not yet clear 'what our conditions and problems will be, and we must not go ahead without America'.[52]

By now the Soviet leader had got the message. On the evening of 19 November, Maisky was sent something like the conciliatory cable for which he had been agitating. It is a remarkable document and deserves verbatim quotation:

My message to Churchill is exclusively of a business nature and does not impugn any members of the British government, especially Premier Churchill. I am too burdened with events at the front to pay even a minute's attention to personal affairs. It seems strange that the important issues concerning a military agreement and the postwar settlement, raised in my message, should be eschewed in favour of personal matters. If anyone is offended in this situation it is my homeland, since the question of Finland, raised by our government using a secret diplomatic procedure, was leaked to the press, which reported that England had rejected the Soviet proposal to declare war on Finland. Can it really be difficult to grasp that this has disappointed and humiliated my homeland? And yet, despite this, I have no complaints in that regard and wish to achieve only one thing – an agreement on mutual aid in Europe against Hitler and an agreement on the postwar settlement. That is my response to the wishes of Eden and Beaverbrook.[53]

A draft of this document has not been found in the Stalin archives, but it clearly reflects the Soviet leader's hand. Couched in a tone that combined wounded national pride with a statesmanlike readiness to forgive a justified grudge for the sake of the common cause, this was as near as the 'Man of Steel' would come to saying 'sorry'. Before delivery to the British, Maisky rephrased the text in third-person reported speech to avoid any impression of a direct apology, but the message was immediately welcomed by Eden and the FO as the 'olive branch' they had been seeking, and Churchill presented it in his memoirs as evidence that 'even Stalin seems to have felt that he had gone too far'.[54] The initial success of the long-awaited British 'Crusader' offensive in Libya, which opened on 18 November, had also softened the PM's own mood.

As Maisky had predicted, London's 'official démarche' was not long in coming. On 21 November, what was intended as a conciliatory telegram was in turn dispatched by Churchill. He prepared it in conjunction with Attlee, Beaverbrook and Eden. The FO would have preferred to handle the matter themselves, not least because Churchill – just like Stalin – did not 'do' apologies, so he still tried to fight his corner on Finland and on war aims, and took pains to warn the Kremlin that it would have to 'choose between troops and supplies'.[55] Yet the PM had delivered on Stalin's essentials: Britain's foreign secretary would come to Moscow accompanied by 'high military and other experts', with a remit to 'discuss every question relating to the war', including sending troops not only to the Caucasus, but right into the Red Army's front line on the southern front. It was also striking that Churchill – still notorious in Moscow as the most vehement counter-revolutionary – was now saying explicitly that ideological differences came second to shared geopolitical interests. The message was a clear move towards Stalin's proposals and towards the kind of alliance relationship that, as Churchill indicated in his opening paragraph, he had already cultivated with Roosevelt, even though America was still neutral.

Churchill to Stalin, sent 21 November 1941,
received 22 November 1941[56]

Many thanks for your message just received. At the very beginning of the war I began a personal correspondence with President Roosevelt which has led to a very solid understanding being established between us and has often helped in getting things done quickly. My only desire is to work on equal terms of comradeship and confidence with you.

About Finland. I was quite ready to advise the Cabinet to contemplate declaring war on Finland when I sent you my telegram of 5th September. Later information has made me think that it will be more helpful to Russia and the common cause if the Finns can be got to stop fighting, and stand still or go home, than if we put them in the dock with the guilty Axis Powers by a formal declaration of war and make them fight it out to the end. However, if they do not stop in the next fortnight and you still wish us to declare war on them we will certainly do so. I agree with you that it was very wrong that any publication should have been made. We certainly were not responsible.

Should our offensive in Libya result, as we hope, in the destruction of the German and Italian armies there, it will be possible to take a broad survey of the war as a whole with more freedom than has hitherto been open to His Majesty's Government.

For this purpose we shall be willing in the near future to send Foreign Secretary Eden, whom you know, via the Mediterranean to meet you at Moscow or elsewhere. He would be accompanied by high military and other experts, and will be able to discuss every question relating to the war, including the sending of troops not only into the Caucasus but into the fighting line of your armies in the South. Neither our shipping resources nor our communications will allow large numbers to be employed, and even so you will have to choose between troops and supplies across Persia.

I notice that you wish also to discuss the post-war organisation of peace. Our intention is to fight the war in alliance with you and in constant consultation with you to the utmost of our strength, and however long it lasts, and when the war is won, as I am sure it will be, we expect that Soviet Russia, Great Britain and the United States will meet at the Council table of victory, as the three principal partners and agencies by which Nazism will have been destroyed. Naturally the first object will be to prevent Germany, and particularly Prussia, from breaking out upon us for a third time. The fact that Russia is a Communist State and that Britain and the United States are not, and do not intend to be, is not any obstacle to our making a good plan for our mutual safety and rightful interests. The Foreign Secretary will be able to discuss the whole of this field with you.

It may well be that your defence of Moscow and Leningrad, as well as the splendid resistance to the invader along the whole Russian front, will inflict mortal injuries upon the internal structure of the Nazi regime. But we must not count upon such good fortune, but simply keep on striking at them to the utmost with might and main.

Stalin was clearly pleased with Churchill's message. It seemed to confirm the wisdom of his tactics, intended to shake up the British and get them to adopt his agenda. He even accepted Churchill's policy of giving the Finns a two-week ultimatum to stop fighting the USSR, rather than immediately declaring war. He particularly appreciated the PM's explicit acceptance of the Soviets as equal partners in the postwar settlement. The situation around Moscow had also improved somewhat, with the German offensive running out of steam – albeit within distant view of the Kremlin. Hence Stalin's quick and friendly reply.

Stalin to Churchill, sent 23 November 1941, delivered 25 November 1941[57]

Many thanks for your message. I sincerely welcome your wish as expressed in your message to collaborate with me by way of personal correspondence based on friendship and confidence. I hope this will contribute much to the success of our common cause.

On the question of Finland, the U.S.S.R. never proposed anything else – at least in the first instance – but the cessation of the military operations and the de facto exit of Finland from the war. If however Finland refuses to comply even with this in the course of the brief period you indicated, then I believe the declaration of war by Great Britain would be reasonable and necessary. Otherwise an impression would be created that there is no unity between us on the question of war against Hitler and his most ardent accomplices and that the accomplices of the Hitler aggression can do their base work with impunity. With regard to Hungary and Roumania we can perhaps wait a little while.

I support by all means your proposal of an early visit to the U.S.S.R. by the Foreign Secretary Mr Eden. I believe our joint consideration and acceptance of an agreement concerning our common military operations of the Soviet and British forces at our front as well as the speedy realisation of such an agreement would have a great positive value. It is right that consideration and adoption of a plan concerning the post-war organisation of peace should be founded on the general idea to prevent Germany and in the first place Prussia once more to violate peace and once more to plunge peoples into terrible carnage.

I also fully agree with you that the difference of the state organisation between the U.S.S.R. on the one hand and of Great Britain and the United States of America on the other should not and could not hinder us in achieving a successful solution of all the fundamental questions concerning our mutual security and our legitimate interests. If there are still some omissions and doubts on this score I hope they will be cleared away in the course of the negotiations with Mr Eden.

I beg you to accept my congratulations on the successful beginning of the British offensive in Libya.

The struggle of the Soviet armies against Hitler's troops remains to be tense. In spite however of all the difficulties the resistance of our forces grows and will grow. Our will to victory over the enemy is unbending.

Stalin's message was welcomed in Whitehall, but one point caused concern among the Cabinet and the military, namely his professed determination to reach an early agreement on the commitment of British troops to the Soviet–German front. Reminding the Defence Committee of their discussion about sending two British divisions and perhaps an Indian division to the Don, Churchill suggested that in view of the engagement of British forces in a major campaign in Libya and the recapture of Rostov-on-Don by the Red Army, the military situation had changed on both sides and planning should be revised. Indeed, added the prime minister, he always believed that sending British soldiers to Russia was 'like taking coals to Newcastle'. His preference was still 'giving the Russians as much equipment as possible'. The military supported him: Sir Alan Brooke (Dill's successor as chief of the imperial general staff) had no doubt that honouring the offer of troops 'would probably mean closing down the Libyan offensive'.[58] On 4 December, the War Cabinet, looking around for alternatives, agreed to scrape up some more supplies, while saying nothing to Stalin for the moment so as not to damage relations again.[59]

Striking evidence of the thaw was the greeting from Stalin for Churchill's birthday on 30 November. Most unusually for Soviet contacts with 'bourgeois' leaders, this gesture – probably prompted by Maisky – was intended to highlight the cordial nature of the new Allied relationship. Exchanging birthday greetings soon became a tradition in the Stalin–Churchill correspondence, but it is significant that the original initiative came from the Soviet leader.

Stalin to Churchill, sent 30 November 1941, received 30 November 1941[60]

Warmly congratulate you on your birthday. From the bottom of my heart wish you strength and health which are so necessary for the victory over the enemy of mankind – Hitlerism. Accept my best wishes.

On 3 December, Eden handed Maisky a greeting in response from Churchill, and asked the Soviet government for permission, which was given, to publish both messages in their two countries. This gesture was very likely the prime minister's idea.[61] In Moscow, the announcement for *Pravda* was carefully edited by Stalin himself.[62]

Churchill to Stalin, sent 3 December 1941, received 5 December 1941[63]

I thank you indeed for your most kind and friendly message on my birthday. Let me take this opportunity of telling you with what admiration the entire British people are watching the steadfast defence of Leningrad and Moscow by the brave Russian armies and how we all rejoice with you in the brilliant victory you have won at Rostov-on-Don.

Churchill still hoped to avoid going to war with Finland, but Eden rebelled. 'I do not see how my mission to Moscow would have any chance of success,' he told the PM, 'if I have to start with this question still unsettled.' He wanted to go to Moscow with what he called a 'full basket' – especially now Churchill and the military had reneged on the idea of sending troops. Eden was backed by the leaders of the British Dominions, who emphasized that any further delay would be 'regarded as weak' and 'would arouse suspicions in Russia'. The PM gave in with ill grace, blustering that the declaration of war on Finland would prove 'an historic mistake'.[64]

And so, on 6 December, Britain declared war on Finland, Romania and Hungary. The previous day the Red Army had launched its counteroffensive around Moscow, smashing into the exhausted Germans with fresh divisions from Siberia. And the nucleus of a British fleet was now in the South China Sea to deter Japan. In short, a favourable context had been created for Eden's Moscow visit, which promised to be a milestone in the development of the Soviet–British alliance. In the process, Stalin had started learning the arts of diplomacy and Churchill had been obliged to temper his rooted suspicion of Bolshevism.

Eden and his party – including Ambassador Maisky, by now a valued mutual interpreter between the two leaders – left Euston Station for the far north of Scotland at 1.15 p.m. on 7 December on a special sleeper train. But by the time they reached the naval base at Invergordon next morning to begin their voyage to Russia, not only Eden's visit but the whole war looked totally different.

3

'I CAN HANDLE STALIN'

(December 1941 to April 1942)

SOON AFTER EDEN'S TRAIN arrived at Invergordon on 8 December, he had to take an urgent phone call from Churchill. The prime minister was in a state of high excitement because of the news from Pearl Harbor. The Japanese attack on the United States, quickly followed by Hitler's declaration of war, transformed the international situation. Eden's visit to Moscow had been predicated on the fact that the British had only one major ally in the war and they desperately needed to improve relations with Stalin. Now suddenly a country with which Britain had already been entangled in a 'common-law alliance' had been catapulted into belligerency.[1] The United States was, moreover, a much more congenial partner than the Soviet Union for the half-American and passionately anti-communist Churchill.

It is fascinating to speculate about whether the PM would have authorized Eden's visit (or declared war on Finland) if the USA had entered the war a couple of weeks earlier. What one can say is that Pearl Harbor cut much of the ground from underneath Eden. This was apparent that very morning, when Churchill stated over the phone that he would immediately travel to Washington to concert policy with Roosevelt. Eden thought it madness for both prime minister and foreign secretary to be away from Britain at such a crucial moment, but his objections were brushed aside. On 12 December, five days after Eden, Churchill also set out from Euston on a special train for Scotland – in his case, bound for the Clyde and thence the Potomac. The symbolism was apt, and enduring: throughout the wartime Alliance, Churchill's first priority was always America, whereas Eden was more inclined to look east.

Pearl Harbor transformed relations with Russia in terms of strategy, as well as diplomacy. Japan's surprise strike on the US Pacific Fleet, in which more than 2,400 Americans died, was a national humiliation for the United States, generating a passionate desire to avenge this 'sneak attack'. It also exposed America's unreadiness for total war, and for several months Roosevelt was necessarily immersed in the multitudinous challenges of war mobilization. But it was also a precursor to a series of dramatic assaults on Western power across the Pacific and Southeast Asia. America quickly lost the Philippines, and Britain was stripped of Malaya and Singapore; the Japanese also overran all of French Indochina and the Dutch East Indies. By the spring, they were threatening India and Australia – vital sources of wealth and manpower for the British Empire. America and Britain were drawn into a major war of containment that distracted them from their preferred policy of 'Germany First'. Stalin, however, maintained the USSR's neutrality pact with Japan, deflecting pressure to join the Pacific War so that he could concentrate on the struggle for survival against Hitler. By the time the US Navy turned the tide by destroying much of the Japanese carrier fleet at the battle of Midway (4–7 June 1942), Japan had transformed the strategic geography of the Asia-Pacific theatre, enriching its empire with vast reserves of manpower and strategic raw materials, especially oil, tin and rubber. And although the Wehrmacht was held at the gates of Moscow in December 1941, Hitler opened a devastating new offensive in the spring, driving southeast towards the oilfields of the Caucasus via the strategic junction of Stalingrad. At the same time, the German–Italian armies in North Africa, led by Field Marshal Erwin Rommel, were closing in on Cairo.

By the summer of 1942, in fact, the Berlin–Rome–Tokyo Axis controlled over a third of the world's population and mineral resources.[2] Meanwhile, their foes in Moscow, London and Washington were in danger of spreading themselves too thinly over separate wars in Russia, North Africa and the Pacific. Ultimately, the Alliance worked and the Axis did not; but this outcome was by no means apparent in early 1942.

Churchill's visit to Washington was an important step in building a coalition. During the Arcadia conferences that he and Roosevelt held with their military advisers (22 December 1941 to 14 January 1942) they created the Combined Chiefs of Staff to oversee military policy, together with a network of 'combined boards' to harmonize the handling of munitions, shipping, supply and the like. The two allies also affirmed as top strategic priority the defeat of Germany, after which Italy and Japan would probably succumb; but this 'Germany First' strategy was not easy to follow in a situation of global war waged on many fronts with limited resources. An essential precondition of effective war management was the principle of 'unified command' in each theatre of operations, pushed through by General George C. Marshall, the US Army chief of staff. He had never forgotten his experiences in France as a young staff officer in the previous war, when the belated appointment in spring 1918 of General Ferdinand Foch as supreme Allied commander had been essential to curb the bickering between the British, French and Americans, in order to resist the new German onslaught and win the war. Marshall insisted that unified command meant 'one man in command of the whole theater – air, ground, and ships'. Mere 'cooperation' was not enough because of 'human frailties'. Those frailties were not only national, but also interservice: the US Navy's rivalry with the US Army, for instance, was as visceral as its suspicions of the Royal Navy. Marshall considered that securing approval of the principle of unified command at Arcadia was one of his major contributions to winning the war.[3] Behind the scenes, the British and Americans were also pooling their programmes to develop an atomic bomb and sharing signals intelligence gleaned from code-breaking through the British 'Ultra' project and the American 'Magic' intercepts. In all these ways, the alliance between Washington and London developed into perhaps the closest in the history of warfare. This anecdote told by Harry Hopkins may be apocryphal, but it was certainly apt. When in Washington, Churchill was given a room in the White House. On one occasion the president paid a visit, only to find his guest emerging wet, glowing and completely naked from the bath. Embarrassed, FDR started to withdraw, but Churchill beckoned him back: 'The Prime Minister of Great Britain,' he boomed, 'has nothing to conceal from the President of the United States.'[4]

Although overshadowed by Churchill in Washington, Eden's visit to Russia (15–22 December 1941) was a milestone in relations between London and Moscow – the first time a British foreign secretary had visited the USSR.[5] The main topic of discussion was the signing of a treaty of alliance between the two countries, but Stalin suddenly enlarged the agenda by demanding that the treaty include agreement on the USSR's postwar borders. This probably reflects his short-lived optimism after the Wehrmacht had been routed near Moscow, which the Soviet leader – erratic again in his geopolitical judgement – mistook for a sign of Hitler's imminent defeat. Hopeful of ending the war in 1942, he wanted to stake out the Soviet position for a future peace conference, so Molotov set up the Foreign Ministry's first commission on planning for the postwar settlement. Stalin's main territorial demand was the restoration and recognition of the USSR's borders before 22 June 1941 and the establishment of Soviet military bases in Romania in exchange for Moscow's recognition of British security interests in Western Europe. The June 1941 borders were, of course, those established under the Nazi-Soviet Pact of 1939 – giving the USSR control of eastern Poland, parts of Romania and the three Baltic states – and so Stalin's demand aroused intense debate with his two allies. In London, Eden was sympathetic and Churchill gradually came around during the early months of 1942; but Roosevelt and the State Department were strongly opposed to such a breach of the Atlantic Charter. The British felt caught between their two allies. 'Soviet policy is amoral,' Eden told the Cabinet. 'United States policy is exaggeratedly moral, at least where non-American interests are concerned.'[6] The issue rumbled on all through the spring.

Stalin's demands for more supplies and an early second front continued to occupy centre-stage in the Big Three's correspondence. After its abrupt entry into the war, the United States faced a full-scale crisis in the Pacific and a succession of devastating U-boat raids along its Atlantic seaboard. The consequent shortage of vessels to transport Lend-Lease cargo to the USSR led to the disruption of US deliveries under the First Protocol. And although the American military advocated an early frontal assault on 'Fortress Europe' as the best way to bring down the Third Reich, their slow rearmament and preoccupation with the Pacific left them in a weak position to challenge Churchill's 'peripheral strategy' of gradually closing the ring on Germany through operations in the Mediterranean backed by bombing, blockade and subversion. In March 1942, the US War Department's Operations Division under General Dwight D. Eisenhower developed outline plans for a full-scale invasion of northern France in the spring of 1943 (codenamed 'Roundup'). In case of imminent Soviet defeat or a 'sharp weakening' of Germany in the summer and autumn of 1942, a smaller landing was conceived, involving six to eight divisions (operation 'Sledgehammer'). These plans would form the subject of intense debate between London and Washington over the next year, with Moscow an interested but largely impotent bystander.

In early 1942, and indeed throughout that year, Churchill remained Stalin's main correspondent, seeing himself as broker of the West's relations with the Kremlin. FDR's messages were much more sporadic, often coming in short flurries with long gaps in between. Yet Roosevelt had a clear sense of where he wanted the Alliance to go. On 1–2 January, he and Churchill, together with the Soviet and Chinese ambassadors, followed by representatives of twenty-two other countries put their names to the 'Declaration of United Nations' about their 'common struggle against savage and brutal forces seeking to subjugate the world'. The term 'United Nations' was coined by Roosevelt and it was on his insistence that the declaration was explicitly based on the principles of the Atlantic Charter. And on 23 February, the president shared his globalist vision with the American people in one of his most successful radio 'fireside chats'. To an audience of 60 million (roughly 80 per cent of the potential adult audience), all primed to have maps open in front of them, he explained the geopolitical interrelationships of this 'new kind of war', which involved 'every continent, every island, every sea, every air lane in the world'. Urged afterwards by one friend to speak on the radio more often, he said he could not spare the time required. In any case, he added delicately, 'I think we must avoid too much personal leadership – my good friend Winston Churchill has suffered a little from this.'[7]

Within the president's global vision, Stalin bulked large. Roosevelt was beginning to tire of playing second fiddle to Churchill and sought ways to strengthen his own contact with the Kremlin. FDR entered the argument about Soviet borders, and then in April he suggested to Stalin for the first time that they meet *à deux*, keeping this proposal secret not only from Churchill, but also from the State Department. He did, however, convey to the PM the conviction that he could 'handle' Stalin better than the professional diplomats in Washington and London and, by implication, better than Churchill. Here was another sensitive topic for the future.

*****

Roosevelt's concern about the crisis in the Pacific was evident in his first exchanges with the Soviets after Pearl Harbor. On 8 December, clearly 'tired and preoccupied', he saw Stalin's new ambassador, Maksim Litvinov, and asked whether the USSR expected to be attacked by Japan. Litvinov 'expressed doubt that this was in Japan's interests'.[8] Three days later, when the ambassador confirmed that the USSR would not declare war at that time, the president asked the Foreign Ministry not to make this public, in order to tie down as many Japanese forces as possible, 'who would otherwise be free to act against England and America'.[9] On 14 December, Roosevelt summoned Litvinov again and handed him a letter for Stalin, urging the Soviets at least to join discussions in Moscow and in China to coordinate strategy. Stalin sent a polite but evasive reply.[10]

When Litvinov delivered this message on 19 December, the ambassador said that the president 'threw up his hands and began to repeat the vague and confusing explanations he had given me earlier'. Litvinov's appraisal was blunt:

> Things are not going well in the area of the Dutch East Indies and Singapore and all the Pacific positions may soon be lost. Roosevelt wants to create an appearance of enhanced diplomatic activity and all sorts of meetings, because the public demands allied actions and common plans.[11]

Moscow's wait-and-see tactics clearly seemed justified. When Roosevelt asked Litvinov about Soviet involvement in a proposed Pacific War Council, including representatives of the USA, Britain, the USSR and the Netherlands, the ambassador was instructed by Molotov on 24 December that 'we, unfortunately, cannot currently take part in this Council', being 'a power that is not a belligerent in the Far East'.[12] Litvinov's bleak prognosis of disaster for the Western Allies in Asia proved accurate and Stalin felt vindicated in his decision to maintain the neutrality pact with Japan at a time when London and Washington were at war against Tokyo. Nevertheless, the consequent asymmetry would be another source of imbalance and even tension among the Big Three.

Churchill was now en route to Washington, intent on preventing the Americans from focusing on Japan. While at sea, he sent Stalin a message promising to inform him 'fully' about the results of the conference. This was delivered in person by Eden on 16 December, who reported that Stalin was 'very happy with your message'.[13]

Churchill tried to warm up his relations with the Soviet leader with a reciprocal 'happy birthday' message on 21 December. Stalin politely responded, in turn congratulating the PM and the 'friendly' British Army on recent successes in Libya. Operation 'Crusader' (November–December 1941) was important both from a military point of view – it relieved the siege of the strategically important port of Tobruk – and psychologically as a morale-boosting victory over the German–Italian army. But losses were heavy and British forces were too depleted to reach their ultimate goals – the city of Tripoli and Libya's border with Tunisia.

Churchill to Stalin, sent 21 December 1941, received 21 December 1941[14]

I send you sincere good wishes for your birthday and hope that future anniversaries will enable you to bring to Russia victory, peace and safety after so much storm.

Stalin to Churchill, sent 27 December 1941, received 27 December 1941[15]

Thank you very much for your good courtesy on occasion of my birthday. I take this opportunity to express to you and the friends [sic] British Army my sincere congratulations in connection with your recent victories in Libya.

While in Washington, Churchill noted adverse reactions in the American media and in diplomatic dispatches to David Zaslavskiy's article in *Pravda* on

30 December, entitled 'Pétain methods in the Philippines'. With biting sarcasm, the author attacked the American surrender of the Philippines, comparing it to the behaviour of a 'ladybird', which 'flips over on its back, folds up its legs and surrenders to the mercy of its enemy'. The article contrasted these 'Pétain methods' with the heroic resistance of Leningrad and London against German air raids and, as the Foreign Office almost gloatingly commented, 'in fact accuses the Americans of cowardice'.[16] The article touched a sore spot, because Washington was painfully aware of the hasty evacuation of the Philippine capital Manila by General Douglas MacArthur, but his rear-guard action on the Bataan Peninsula was talked up by the American military and media for morale reasons. The pejorative assessment of MacArthur's actions in *Pravda* was sharply discordant with these sentiments, and Churchill decided to offer some 'friendly comment' about the dangers of such articles for Soviet–American relations. Stalin replied very diplomatically, denying official sanction of the article, while not condemning its sentiments.[17]

Churchill frequently congratulated Stalin on the Red Army's successes – with reason. The counter-offensive near Moscow, which started on 5 December 1941, when the temperature was fifteen degrees below zero and the snow a metre deep, brought one victory after another, as fresh Red Army troops, properly provisioned, pinched out the German bulge around Moscow. Hitler resisted calls for a general withdrawal, demanding that troops 'defend their positions fanatically'; he sacked several senior commanders and assumed direct command of the army.[18] But success then went to Stalin's head. At a Stavka (high command) meeting on 5 January, as Zhukov later recalled, the Boss unveiled his grand vision for future military actions: 'After their defeat near Moscow, the Germans are at a loss, they are poorly prepared for winter. Now is the perfect time to go to a general offensive.' The Red Army's task, he declared – pacing as usual around his office – was to 'drive them to the west without stopping, to force them to expend their reserves before spring'. Zhukov and others warned of insufficient resources for such a large-scale offensive on all fronts, but Stalin took no notice.[19] The gloom of the autumn had turned to hubris. And so, on 7 January, there commenced a general offensive by the Red Army along 800 kilometres of front, from the environs of Leningrad right down to Kharkov. It was tasked with ensuring the 'complete defeat of Hitlerite forces in 1942'.[20] Initial successes soon flagged, as troops moved beyond their tenuous supply lines and the Red Air Force gave up its permanent, heated airfields thereby having to make do, like the Luftwaffe, with frozen and inhospitable airstrips. 'By biting off more than his forces could chew, Stalin failed to eliminate the encircled German forces in front of Moscow and made only limited gains elsewhere.'[21]

Nothing of this backstory emerged in the Churchill–Stalin correspondence. The prime minister continued to send fulsome congratulations to the Red Army, and Stalin reciprocated with praise for British successes in North Africa.[22]

Although psychologically the relief of Tobruk was similar to the Moscow counter-offensive, the two operations were markedly different in scale. During operation 'Crusader', 237,000 soldiers were involved on both sides, with German and Italian losses (killed, wounded and missing) totalling 38,300, compared with 17,700 for the British,[23] whereas 7 million men were engaged in the Battle of Moscow, with the Germans losing 615,000 and the Soviets 958,000.[24]

Churchill to Stalin, sent 11 January 1942, received 15 January 1942[25]

I am very glad to receive your kind telegram, which reached me through M. Litvinov on 9th January. The papers here are filled with tributes to the Russian armies, and may I also express my admiration of the great victories which have rewarded the leadership and devotion of the Russian forces. I am emphasising in my talks here the extreme importance of making punctual deliveries to Russia of the promised quotas.

I send you every good wish for the New Year.

Stalin to Churchill, sent 16 January 1942, received 16 January 1942[26]

Received your message of 15th January. My sincere thanks for your good wishes for the New Year and in connection with the successes of the Red Army. My best greetings to you and to the British Army on their important successes in Northern Africa.

Roosevelt's next message to Stalin, on 9 February 1942, was purely informative. The president knew that promised supplies had not been delivered in full and on time because of the outbreak of war with Japan, the shortage of vessels and bureaucratic red tape in Washington. A US War Department report on supplies to the USSR for October–December 1941 stated that 298 of the promised 750 tanks had neither been delivered nor were in transit; for fighters and light bombers, the shortfall was much worse: respectively 780 of 900, and 747 of 828. Roosevelt ordered that the planned monthly targets should be adhered to from 1 January 1942, and that all the accumulated shortfall should be made up by 1 April.[27] Reporting on measures taken to remedy the situation, the president's message to Stalin was intended to mitigate this discontent.

Roosevelt to Stalin, sent 9 February 1942, received 11 February 1942[28]

Our shipments for January and February have included and will include 244 fighter planes, 24 B-25s, 233 A-20s, 408 medium tanks and 449 light tanks.

The reports here indicate that you are getting on well in pushing back the Nazis.

While we are having our immediate troubles in the Far East, I believe that we will have that area reinforced in the near future to such an extent that we can stop the Japs but we are prepared for some further setbacks.

I realize the importance of getting our supplies to you at the earliest possible date and every effort is being made to get shipments off.

Roosevelt had sent Stalin only a couple of messages in the two months since Pearl Harbor, both very businesslike, and he was by now keen to warm up the correspondence. Aware of this, Sumner Welles produced a draft message on 10 February, in case the president wanted to send something 'of a more personal nature'.[29] The draft dealt with two items of positive news – introducing the new US ambassador to the USSR, Admiral William H. Standley, and communicating the president's decision to provide a large new loan to pay for Lend-Lease goods. Back in September, Stalin had told Harriman and Beaverbrook sharply that Ambassador Steinhardt was a man who 'spread defeatist rumours', spoke 'disrespectfully' about the Russian government and 'did not believe in victory'. FDR got the message and cast around for a replacement. Harriman turned down the job, but recommended Standley, who had been a member of his mission to Moscow. Being a retired officer, used to obeying orders, and lacking any experience of the USSR, Standley probably commended himself to the president as a convenient but distinguished messenger boy.[30] When writing to Stalin, Roosevelt followed Welles' draft, except for deleting a final rather banal paragraph about problems with delivering Lend-Lease cargo.

Roosevelt to Stalin, sent 10 February 1942, received 14 February 1942[31]

I am much pleased that your Government has expressed its willingness to receive as the Ambassador of the United States my old and trusted friend, Admiral Standley. The Ambassador and I have been closely associated for many years. I have complete confidence in him and recommend him to you not only as a man of energy and integrity but also as one who is appreciative of and an admirer of the accomplishments of the Soviet Union, which, you will recall, he visited with Mr Harriman last year. Since his return from Moscow Admiral Standley has already done much to further understanding in the United States of the situation in the Soviet Union and with his rich background and his knowledge of the problems which are facing our respective countries I am sure that with your cooperation he will meet with success in his efforts to bring them still more closely together.

It has just been brought to my attention that the Soviet Government has placed with us requisitions for munitions and supplies of a value which will exceed the billion dollars which last autumn were placed at its disposal under the Lend-Lease Act following an exchange of letters between us. I propose, therefore, that under this same Act a second billion dollars be placed at the disposal of your Government upon the same conditions as those upon which the first billion were allocated. In case you have any counter suggestions to offer with regard to the terms under which the second billion dollars should be made available, you may be sure that they will be given careful and sympathetic consideration. In any event, it may prove mutually desirable later, in order to meet changing conditions, to review such financial arrangements as we may enter into now.

The problems connected with the effecting of the prompt delivery of the supplies already ordered by your Government have been, I know, the subject of a message from Mr. Harriman and I am confident that we shall achieve complete success in solving them.

Stalin sent his replies to Roosevelt almost simultaneously, and while his response to the letter of 9 February was rather dry, the second message was pointedly cordial, thanking the president for the new American loan and not quibbling about the details. It did, however, dangle hope that the charge might be written off at some later date because of the 'extremely strained' state of Soviet resources. Both documents were prepared by Molotov and approved without any changes by Stalin. Characteristically, he refrained from making direct criticism of the administration on the issue of supplies, despite having good reason to do so. In a memo to Stalin and Molotov, the foreign trade commissar, Anastas Mikoyan, stated that in the first three months of the First Protocol, 'Great Britain has been fulfilling its obligations more or less accurately, which cannot be said about deliveries from the United States.' Representatives of the US government, the memo concluded, 'give generous promises and then unceremoniously violate their obligations.'[32] Stalin's restraint probably stemmed not only from reluctance to offend FDR, but also from awareness that Roosevelt and Hopkins were doing everything in their power to improve the situation, while the US military and other bureaucratic agencies often sabotaged the president's instructions.[33]

Stalin to Roosevelt, sent 18 February 1942, received 19 February 1942[34]

I have received your message informing me of consignments of armaments from the United States for January and February.

I would like to emphasise the fact that at the present moment, when the peoples of the Soviet Union and their Army are exerting all their powers to thrust back, by their determined offensive, Hitler troops, the fulfillment of American deliveries, including tanks and aeroplanes, is of the utmost importance for our common cause, for our further success.

Stalin to Roosevelt, sent 18 February 1942, received 20 February 1942[35]

Acknowledging the receipt of your message of 13th February, I would like to say first that I share your confidence that the efforts of the newly-appointed Ambassador of the United States to the Union of Soviet Socialist Republics, Admiral Standley, of whom you speak so highly and in such warm terms, to bring our two countries still closer to one another, will be crowned with success.

Your decision, Mr President, to place at the disposal of the Soviet Government another billion dollars, in accordance with the law of the supply of armaments under the Lend-Lease Act, on the same conditions which applied to the first billion, is accepted by the Soviet Government with sincere gratitude. With regard to your inquiry I have to inform you that, at the present moment, in order not to delay matters, the Soviet Government is not raising the question of the modification of the conditions attaching to the granting by your Cabinet of the above-mentioned second billion dollars or of taking into consideration the extremely strained state of the resources of the USSR by the war against our common foe. At the same time I entirely agree with you and should like to express the hope that at a later date we shall be able jointly to fix a time when it will appear desirable to both of us to revise the financial agreements now concluded in order to pay special attention to the above-mentioned circumstances.

I should like to take this opportunity to draw your attention to the fact that the Soviet organizations when realizing the loan granted to the USSR are at present experiencing great difficulties with regard to the transport of armaments and materials purchased in the USA to USSR ports. We would consider the most suitable arrangements for the transports of armaments from America, in the circumstances, would be that which is successfully adopted for the transport of armaments from England to Archangel, but which heretofore has not been possible to apply to deliveries from the United States. According to this arrange-

ment, the British military authorities delivering armaments and materials designate the ships themselves, as well as organizing their loading in the port, and their
convoy to the port of destination. The Soviet Government would be extremely
grateful if the same arrangement for the delivery of armaments and the convoying
of ships to the USSR ports could be adopted by the United States Government
also.

The White House was responsive to Stalin's proposal to centralize American
supplies on the British model. 'I think this is important and that we should do
it,' the president wrote to Hopkins. 'Will you prepare reply for my signature?'[36]
The message, which also picked up Stalin's hint about payment for Lend-Lease,
was sent via Litvinov.

Roosevelt to Stalin, sent 23 February 1942, received 24 February 1942[37]

This will acknowledge your message of February 20.

I want you to know that at the appropriate time we shall be glad to re-consider
with you our agreement relative to the funds we are advancing under the Lend-
Lease Act. At the moment the all-important problem is to get the supplies to you.

I am having canvassed at once your suggestion relative to centralizing control
here of munitions being sent to Russia.

The further news of the successes of your Army heartens us very much.

I wish to send you my warm congratulations on the twenty-fourth anniversary
of the founding of the Red Army.

After this flurry of correspondence, there was another hiatus: Roosevelt and
Stalin did not correspond again for seven weeks, until mid-April.

On Eden's advice, Churchill also decided to congratulate Stalin on the anniversary of the Red Army, his bête noire when founded in 1918. The PM spent
time improving the FO draft and even attended a reception for Red Army Day
at the Soviet embassy.

Churchill to Stalin, sent 23 February 1942, received 24 February 1942[38]

The twenty-fourth anniversary of the foundation of the Red Army is being celebrated today after eight months of a campaign which has reflected the greatest
glory on its officers and men and which has enshrined its deeds in history for all
time.

On this proud occasion I convey to you, a the Chairman of the Defence
Committee of the Union of Soviet Socialist Republics, and to all members of the

Soviet forces, an expression of the admiration *and gratitude* with which the peoples of the British Empire have ~~learnt~~ *watched* their exploits and of our confidence in the ~~successful issue~~ *victorious end* of the struggle we are waging together against the common foe.

The Churchill–Stalin correspondence during February is less interesting for what was said than for what was not mentioned. Warm words from London about the Red Army and its triumphs masked growing awareness, derived from Bletchley Park's Enigma decrypts, that the Soviet counter-offensive was running out of steam. The Cabinet's Joint Intelligence Committee (JIC) was sure that the Germans would be in a position to mount a major new offensive once the weather improved in the spring, and that it would be directed southeast towards the oilfields of the Caucasus. This was also the view in Washington. The capacity of the Soviet Union to resist a second great onslaught was a matter of debate, even though doubts were not as deep as in the summer of 1941. This nagging uncertainty should be kept in mind when reading the Big Three messages that spring and when assessing the arguments between London and Washington about strategy and supplies for much of 1942.[39]

Nor was there reference in the correspondence to the February political crisis in Britain, as Churchill endured what his wife called 'the Valley of Humiliation', so different from the heady heights of 1940. Two dramatic events reverberated around the world and shook British confidence. On 13 February the German battlecruisers *Scharnhorst* and *Gneisenau* escaped from Brest, on the northwest coast of France, and raced up the Channel to safety in Wilhelmshaven. It seemed as if the Royal Navy and the RAF could not even police Britain's home waters. Two days later, on the 15th, Singapore fell to a smaller force of Japanese, and 80,000 soldiers of the British Empire surrendered – what Churchill later called 'the worst disaster and largest capitulation in British history'. The military conduct of the campaign had been a fiasco, but blame also attached to Churchill for his obstinate refusal to accept that what he liked to call the 'fortress' of Singapore was indefensible once the Japanese controlled the Malayan mainland. Britain's entire Asian empire seemed in jeopardy. On 19 February, Japanese planes bombed the city of Darwin, on the north coast of Australia, prompting the government in Canberra to recall for home defence three Australian divisions that had hitherto played a critical part in the campaign in North Africa. With India also threatened by possible invasion, panic spread through Madras and other coastal cities – highlighting the incompetence of the imperial authorities. The Indian Congress party girded itself for a major political challenge to British rule, while the nationalist leader

Subhas Chandra Bose called for armed struggle against the 'iniquitous' British regime and insisted that Germany, Italy and Japan were 'our natural friends and allies'.[40]

The abject surrender of Singapore was also a huge diplomatic embarrassment for the prime minister when dealing with his two main allies. Although the Americans had been kicked out of the Philippines, MacArthur managed to convert the rear-guard defence of the Bataan Peninsula into a propaganda triumph. And whatever the problems with Stalin's hubristic counter-offensive, the Russians were clearly taking on the bulk of the Wehrmacht. Oliver Harvey, Eden's private secretary, noted in his diary that Churchill was 'very grunty' about Russia. 'At the back of his mind and unconsciously, I believe, the P.M. is jealous of Stalin and the successes of his armies'.[41]

These setbacks brought to the boil protests about Churchill's war leadership. 'No man is indispensable', the *Daily Mail* warned darkly.[42] On 19 February, Churchill reshuffled his War Cabinet, getting rid of the divisive Beaverbrook, despite their old friendship, and including Stafford Cripps – now back from Russia and riding high in popular opinion as a champion of aid to Russia and of an early second front. Cripps, together with Eden, were now being talked of as possible replacements for Churchill. He 'is exhausted by his superhuman efforts', Harvey recorded in his diary on Friday, 27 February: 'We are all convinced that the PM cannot last much longer'. Churchill's daughter Mary noted that same day: 'Papa at very low ebb . . . He is saddened – appalled by events'.[43]

Churchill was then spending a long weekend at Ditchley Park, a country house in Oxfordshire, and the chance for reflection prompted him to dictate a long telegram to Stalin. He had already shared some of his woes with Roosevelt, receiving in return sympathetic messages and advice not to heed 'back-seat drivers'.[44] Less emotionally, but with a candour that was unusual in his dealings with the Kremlin, he now set out for Stalin the strategic effects of the Japanese tsunami. Faced with 'most serious difficulties' for the defence of Burma and India, he said he had been forced to redeploy the divisions that had been touted for the 'Levant-Caspian front' to support 'the left wing of the Russian Armies'. He also tried to explain the extended logistics of global war, with troopships for the Far East able to make at most three round trips a year. However, the PM did offer reassurance that Britain was adhering 'most strictly' to the protocol of monthly supplies agreed by Beaverbrook in October. Churchill passed the message to the FO for despatch to the Kremlin, but Cadogan considered it 'rather silly' – deploring its 'black' tone – and consulted Eden. After four days of haggling and re-drafting by Churchill and the FO, it was decided not to send the Soviet leader any overview of the war situation.[45]

On 9 March, however, Churchill did send Stalin a brief message. This included a telling reference to the long-running dispute with Moscow about recognizing the USSR's June 1941 borders, which shows just how far the February crisis had affected Churchill's mood. Stalin had raised the border issue during Eden's visit in December, as an integral part of the proposed treaty of alliance between the two countries. The British position, in conformity with the Atlantic Charter, was that no territorial issues could be agreed until the postwar peace conference. Stalin's insistence reflected his hopes that the Moscow counter-offensive might decide the war in 1942, and that the USSR needed to line up support now for its key demands. But Roosevelt and the State Department – mindful of the so-called 'secret treaties' between Britain, France and Russia in the First World War – were emphatic that the peacemakers after this war should start with a clean slate, and one on which the United States would be well placed to write as it wished. Back in Britain, Eden pressed the case for recognition, convinced that Stalin was 'a political descendant of Peter the Great rather than Lenin', for whom traditional Russian security concerns mattered more than the spread of communism. He told the Cabinet that Stalin considered the border issue 'the acid test of our sincerity' and strongly implied that it was more important to keep in with the Russians than with the Americans, if a choice became necessary. On 8 January, cabling from America, Churchill told Eden flatly that he was sticking to the Roosevelt line and fumed that the 1941 frontiers were 'acquired by acts of aggression in shameful collusion with Hitler'. His acid test, he told Eden sternly, was 'our sincerity to be involved in the maintenance of the principles of the Atlantic Charter, to which Stalin has subscribed. On this, also, we depend for our association with the United States.' Churchill hinted that he regarded this matter as a resignation issue.[46] Juggling its two great allies would always be a problem for Britain, but at this stage in the war Eden was always inclined to go further than Churchill in propitiating Russia. The PM's residual anti-Bolshevism played a part – Eden's politics were more left of centre – but the foreign secretary also shared the widespread assumption within the FO that the United States was again likely to turn its back on Europe after the war was over.

The War Cabinet debated the question on 6 February, with Beaverbrook and Eden strongly arguing the Soviet case, while the fiercely anti-communist Labour leader, Clement Attlee, denounced the idea as 'dangerous . . . wrong and inexpedient' – laying Britain open to 'pressure to make concessions right and left'. Churchill, now wavering, agreed that the issue should be put to Roosevelt, in what he called 'a balanced presentation' of the pros and cons.[47] But representations by the British ambassador in Washington, Lord Halifax, proved unavailing: Roosevelt, bolstered by Welles, stuck to their position and the president said that he would take up the matter personally with Litvinov. For Eden, FDR's objections and, worse, his interference in what was a Soviet–British issue were infuriating. Harried on the border issue by Maisky, he kept up the heat on Churchill all through February. Having blocked Churchill's 'bleak' draft of 27 February, on 6 March he urged the PM to write to FDR proposing strategic talks with the hard-pressed Stalin, without making an issue of the borders. Next day, a weary Churchill did what Eden asked, telling Roosevelt that the 'increasing gravity of the war has led me to feel that the principles of the Atlantic Charter ought not be construed so as to deny Russia the frontiers she occupied when Germany attacked her'.[48]

This was the message that Churchill mentioned in the first sentence of his telegram to Stalin two days later.

Churchill to Stalin, sent 9 March 1942, received 12 March 1942[49]

I have sent a message to President Roosevelt urging him to approve our signing the agreement with you about the frontiers of Russia at the end of the war.

I have given express directions that the supplies promised by us shall not in any way be interrupted or delayed.

Now that season is improving we are resuming heavy air offensive both by day and night upon Germany. We are continuing to study other measures for taking some of the weight off you.

The continued progress of the Russian armies and the known terrible losses of the enemy are naturally our sources of greatest encouragement in this trying period.

This was a message whose brevity belied its importance. The first sentence about borders signalled a new push by the Foreign Office to conclude the delayed treaty of alliance with Moscow. Churchill's second sentence, offering assurances about supplies, was also telling. This was another talismanic issue, especially in view of possible Soviet misreading of the resignation of Beaverbrook – hitherto the leading advocate of aid to Russia. There was also a pregnant reference to intensified air attacks on Germany. Air Marshal Arthur 'Bomber' Harris had been appointed head of RAF Bomber Command on 22 February, and he embarked on a relentless campaign of what was effectively area bombing of German industrial centres. This would become a key weapon in Churchill's limited strategic and diplomatic arsenal over the next year. And the cryptic references to studying 'other measures' for helping the Russians hinted at the debate about the second front that was hotting up that spring between London and Washington.

By the time Stalin replied to the prime minister, he had received a report from Litvinov about his meeting with Roosevelt on 12 March. The president had acted on his intention to engage in the Soviet–British negotiations: he told the ambassador that he accepted the validity of the Soviet demands about its western borders and did not foresee any differences of opinion on this matter after the war. However, FDR spoke against the conclusion of a secret agreement on this subject, citing the Atlantic Charter as well as the danger of negative domestic and international reaction. 'Roosevelt,' noted Litvinov, 'obviously hinted that the agreement should only be verbal, not formal.'[50] In Moscow, as in London, FDR's interference in Soviet–British negotiations aroused resentment. Molotov had already told Litvinov on 3 March: 'In this case we prefer to deal with one partner, namely the English.'[51] The Soviet response to Roosevelt, transmitted via Litvinov, merely acknowledged the president's suggestion and, in his reply to Churchill, Stalin made clear his wish to proceed bilaterally to a treaty that incorporated agreement on postwar borders. His mention in the message of 1942 as the turning-point year in the war indicated his continuing illusions about the Soviet offensive, but also served as a veiled reminder about the need for a second front.

Stalin to Churchill, sent 14 March 1942, received 16 March[52]

I am very grateful to you for your message handed in at Kuibyshev on March 12th.

I express to you the appreciation of the Soviet Government for your communication regarding measures you have taken to insure supplies to the Union of Soviet Socialist Republics and to intensify air attacks on Germany.

I express the firm conviction that the combined actions of our troops, in spite of incidental reverses, will in the end defeat the forces of our mutual enemy and that the year 1942 will be decisive in the turn of events at the battle front against Hitler.

As regards the first point of your letter dealing with frontiers of the Union of Soviet Socialist Republics, I think that it will still be necessary to exchange views regarding the text of a suitable agreement, in the event of its being accepted for the signature by both parties.

Maisky delivered this message on 16 March at the prime minister's country residence, Chequers, where he lunched with Churchill and Eden. With regard to the Soviet borders, the foreign secretary remarked that Roosevelt's intervention could complicate the signing of the Anglo-Soviet treaty. Churchill, alluding to the Atlantic Charter, admitted that 'I have, since the very beginning, been reluctant to recognize the 1941 borders, but, as Stalin was so insistent, I eventually agreed to do so', whereupon Maisky rather boldly advised them to 'consult' America but not seek its 'permission'. In general, he said, 'the British Government should appeal to its "American uncle" a little less often, and think a bit more about the independence of its policy'. Churchill and Eden listened, but did not comment. When Maisky asked what he thought of Stalin's assessment of 1942 as the decisive year of the war, 'Churchill's countenance darkened immediately' and he said with some irritation, 'I don't see how 1942 can become the decisive year.' Unlike 1941, he now faced three major enemies, not two, as well as a variety of new domestic and foreign problems. Maisky decided, as he put it, 'to take the bull by the horns', insisting that 'a crucial moment' in the war was approaching. If not stopped, Hitler's spring offensive would surge on beyond the Caucasus to Iran, Turkey, Egypt and India – linking up with Japan somewhere in the Indian Ocean and reaching out towards Africa. If Hitler succeeded, he would solve all his raw material problems, strip the USSR of vital territories and cause the 'collapse' of the British Empire. 'It's now or never' for the Allies, Maisky exclaimed, and Eden agreed. 'Perhaps you are right', Churchill muttered, but he was clearly in what Maisky termed a 'twilight mood'. The PM did, however, warm up when talking about British admiration for the Soviet war effort. 'Just imagine! My own wife is completely Sovietized … All she ever talks about is the Soviet Red Cross, the Soviet army.' He added with sly twinkle: 'Couldn't you elect her to one of your Soviets? She surely deserves it.' For Churchill, the second front had become, literally, a domestic issue.[53]

Correspondence between Churchill and Stalin was currently low-key. In a message of 20 March, the prime minister mentioned the visit by Beaverbrook to Washington without explaining its purpose. Beaverbrook told Maisky it was to intercede with Roosevelt about the Soviet borders.[54] Churchill also mentioned the possibility of the Germans using poison gas, thereby again seeking to show London's solidarity with the Soviet Union – albeit in carefully circumscribed ways. And he used the message to introduce his new ambassador to the USSR, Sir Archibald Clark Kerr – a career diplomat, unlike Cripps – who, in contrast to Steinhardt, was to play a prominent role in Soviet–British relations for the rest of the war (plate 23).

Churchill to Stalin, sent 20 March 1942, received 21 March 1942[55]

Many thanks for your reply of the 14th to my latest telegram. Beaverbrook is off to Washington where he will help smooth out the treaty question with the

President in accordance with the communications which have passed between us and between our Governments.

Ambassador Maisky lunched with me last week and mentioned some evidences that Germans may use gas upon you in their attempted spring offensive. After consulting my colleagues and the Chiefs of Staff, I wish to assure you that His Majesty's Government will treat any use of this weapon of poison gas against Russia exactly as if it was directed against ourselves. I have been building up an immense store of gas bombs for discharge from aircraft and we shall not hesitate to use these over all suitable objectives in Western Germany from the moment that your armies and people are assaulted in this way.

It is a question to be considered whether at the right time we should not give a public warning that such is our resolve, as the warning might deter the Germans from adding this new horror to the many they have loosed upon the world. Please let me know what you think about this and whether the evidence of preparations warrants the warning.

There is no immediate hurry, and before I take a step which may draw upon our citizens this new form of attack I must of course have ample time to bring all our anti-gas preparations to extreme readiness.

I trust you will give our new Ambassador an opportunity of presenting this message himself, and the advantage of personal discussion with you. He comes, as you know, almost direct from close personal contact with General Chiang Kai-shek, which he has maintained during the last four years. He enjoyed, I believe, the General's high regard and confidence. I hope and believe that he will equally gain yours. He is a personal friend of mine of many years standing.

Stalin received Clark Kerr on 29 March, spending two and a half hours with him in his Kremlin bomb shelter, sitting out yet another raid by the Luftwaffe. The ambassador – who had been granted special permission to make the twenty-hour journey from the boredom of Kuybyshev to present his credentials and deliver Churchill's letter – was a very different customer from the prudish Cripps. Having thought carefully about how to handle the interview, he gave the pipe-smoking Stalin some excellent English tobacco and they had a good man-to-man chat about pipes, sex and China, as well as discussing official matters such as the disposition of Wehrmacht divisions and the foreign policies of Sweden and Turkey. Stalin went out of his way to express thanks, and indeed surprise, that the British had fulfilled their supply commitments, comparing this favourably with the behaviour of the Americans. 'I had expected someone big and burly,' Clark Kerr wrote in a private letter to London. Instead he encountered 'a little, slim, bent grey man with a large head and immense white hands', who directed his gaze 'almost furtively, at my shoulder and not my face', always avoiding eye contact. Clark Kerr told Eden that they got on like 'two old rogues'. There is little doubt that Stalin found Clark Kerr agreeable company, and the ambassador was able to speak with increasing forthrightness to the Soviet leader. Whether that translated into real diplomatic benefits for Britain is, however, less clear.[56]

In his reply, Stalin readily endorsed Churchill's proposal on joint measures in the wake of any gas attack by Germany, and suggested similar action in respect of Finland. This did not elicit much sympathy from Churchill, but in a message of 9 April he did agree. Less grudgingly, he also assented to Stalin's proposal for direct contact between specialists in the USSR and Britain in the area of chemical defence, and offered supplies of mustard gas and of its antidote, bleaching powder, should the Soviets be in need.[57]

*****

Although Roosevelt did not correspond with Stalin between 23 February and 11 April, the president was now beginning to assert himself in foreign policy. Washington had recovered from the huge shock of Pearl Harbor – requiring the sudden conversion of the US armed forces and the American economy onto a war footing – and the president had taken in the full implications of the disasters that had befallen his British ally during February, especially Singapore. Both the power of Britain and the capacities of Churchill himself seemed to be waning: 1942 was clearly very different from 1940, and Roosevelt – though closely allied with Churchill – wanted to keep a certain distance. He told Henry Morgenthau, his treasury secretary and old friend, on 11 March:

> I do not want to be in the same position as the English. They promised the Russians two divisions. They failed. They promised them help in the Caucasus. They failed. Every promise the English have made to the Russians, they have fallen down on. The only reason we stand so well with the Russians is that up to date we have kept our promises.

Brushing aside the shortfalls on US supplies to Russia – noted to America's detriment by Stalin to Clark Kerr on 29 March – as simply the result of getting 'into the war ourselves', Roosevelt told Morgenthau: 'Nothing would be worse than to have the Russians collapse. I would rather lose New Zealand, Australia or anything else than have the Russians collapse.'[58]

The president made his thinking about Russia explicit in a chatty letter to Churchill on 18 March:

I know you will not mind my being brutally frank when I tell you that I think I can personally handle Stalin better than either your Foreign Office or my State Department. Stalin hates the guts of all your top people. He thinks he likes me better, and I hope he will continue to do so.

Considering that FDR had never met Stalin, and had exchanged little more than a dozen messages, this was pretty rich – but the breezy tone and lofty self-confidence were typical Roosevelt. The conviction that he could 'personally handle Stalin' became the lodestar of FDR's foreign policy until the day he died.[59]

Newly sceptical about the faltering British and determined to support Russia, the president took the initiative in the spring of 1942 in three areas of diplomacy. One was his intervention in the Soviet–British argument about borders. Another was his bold attempt to impose himself on Britain's imperial problems. On 10 March, with what he coyly described as 'much diffidence', he suggested to Churchill that it was time to concede self-government to India, offering as a model the Articles of Confederation under which the new United States had initially been governed after winning independence from Britain in 1783, before a new constitution was agreed. This, FDR argued, might galvanize Indian support for the war, as well as being 'in line with the world changes of the past half century and with the democratic processes of all who are fighting Nazism'. When the president reiterated his idea 'very frankly' a month later – warning of the reaction in America if self-government was not conceded and then India fell to the Japanese – Churchill was apoplectic. A complete diehard on India, he dictated a reply stating that he 'could not be responsible' for such a policy and predicting that 'Cabinet and Parliament would be strongly averse'. In the end he did not send the message, but conveyed its gist, including the threat of resignation, very bluntly to Harry Hopkins on 12 April, with what the latter described as a 'string of cuss words' that lasted 'for two hours in the middle of the night'.[60]

Roosevelt got the message and never mentioned India directly again. He did, however, press Churchill on what he considered the most important of his three initiatives: an early second front. Hopkins, together with Army Chief of Staff General George Marshall, had arrived in London on 8 April with detailed plans and a personal letter from the president. 'Your people and mine demand the establishment of a front to draw off pressure on the Russians,' FDR told Churchill, 'and these people are wise enough to see that the Russians are today killing more Germans and destroying more equipment than you and I put together.' The plan, he declared, 'has my heart and *mind* in it.' The American military, who had no doubt that the quickest way to defeat Germany was by re-establishing a western front in France, envisaged a massive landing of forty-eight Allied divisions on the Channel coast between Le Havre and Boulogne. Scheduled for 1 April 1943, this was codenamed 'Roundup'. Its essential prelude would be operation 'Bolero' – the build-up in the British Isles of the necessary forces and supplies to mount the invasion. At the same time, another operation, 'Sledgehammer', was outlined: in the event of a critical situation on the Soviet–German front, this aimed to land six to eight divisions in France in September 1942, in order to divert some of Hitler's forces from the east.[61]

Reinforcing his approach to Churchill, Roosevelt also sent a message to Stalin. This was drafted at the end of March, but then delayed until Hopkins had arrived in London. The president's deletions and additions (italicized) show how Roosevelt tried to make his proposal to meet Stalin *à deux* in Alaska or Siberia sound more concrete and attractive. He also cut out some of the background on America's strategic and logistic problems.[62] Since a personal meeting with Stalin was not possible in the immediate future, Roosevelt invited Molotov to Washington for discussions on the second front. He concealed this message not only from Churchill, but also from the State Department – personally handing it to Gromyko for transmission to the Kremlin, on the grounds that the Soviet embassy's encoding system was more secure.[63] The president did, however, inform Churchill on 1 April in a more general way that 'on word from you, when you have seen Harry and Marshall, I propose to ask Stalin to send two special representatives to see me at once'.[64]

Roosevelt to Stalin, sent 11 April 1942, received 12 April 1942[65]

It is unfortunate that geographical distance makes it practically impossible for you and me to meet at this time. Such a meeting of minds in personal conversation would be useful to the conduct of the war against Hitlerism. Perhaps if things go as well as we hope, you and I could spend a few *days* hours together next summer near our common border off Alaska. But, in the meantime, I regard it as of the utmost military importance that *we have the nearest possible approach to an exchange of views* I receive your advice and counsel at the earliest possible moment.

I have in mind a very important military proposal involving the utilization of our armed forces in a manner to relieve your critical Western Front. This objective carries great weight with me.

~~As you are aware, we have been conducting a delaying action in the Pacific, but it is my belief that matters in that ocean are now fairly well stabilized for the time being. Furthermore, our increasing production program has strengthened our weak spots and enabled me to turn my eyes toward consideration of diverting some German strength from the attack on your country on the Western Front.~~

~~One of the compelling reasons bearing on my proposal is that the shipping problem is our most difficult one. Therefore the voyage across the Atlantic for troops and munitions is much more militarily advantageous than the much longer voyage across the Pacific.~~

~~A number of alternatives in the European field must be considered.~~

Therefore, I wish you would consider sending Mr Molotov and a General upon whom you rely to Washington in the immediate future. Time is of the essence if we are to help in an important way. We will furnish them with a good transport plane so that they should be able to make the round trip in two weeks.

I do not want by such a trip to go over the head of my friend, Mr Litvinov, in any way, as he will understand, but we can gain time by the visit I propose.

I suggest this procedure not only because of the secrecy, which is so essential, but because I need your advice before we determine with finality the strategic course of our common military action.

I *have sent* ~~am sending~~ Hopkins to London relative to this proposal.

The American people are thrilled by the magnificent fighting of your armed forces and we want to help you in the destruction of Hitler's armies and material more than we are doing now.

I send you my sincere regards.

Stalin was very pleased with Roosevelt's message, especially the idea of an exchange of views on military and strategic issues with Molotov, which he saw as a sign that the Allies were finally ready for a serious discussion about opening a second front. Yet before making a final decision on Molotov's trip to Washington, Litvinov was instructed to find out from Roosevelt what questions he intended to discuss at the meeting. Reporting on his conversation with the president on 14 April, the ambassador confirmed that it was going to be about a landing in France – a point that Stalin picked up in his reply to Roosevelt.[66] It had already been decided in the Kremlin that Molotov would visit London to finalize negotiations on the Soviet–British treaty, so there was now an opportunity to kill two birds with one stone.

Stalin to Roosevelt, sent 20 April 1942, received 21 April 1942[67]

Let me thank you for the message which I received in Moscow the other day.

The Soviet Government agrees that it is necessary to arrange a meeting between V.M. Molotov and you for an exchange of opinions on the organization of a second front in Europe in the immediate future. Molotov can come to Washington with a competent military representative not later than May 10 to 15.

It goes without saying that Molotov will also stop in London for an exchange of opinions with the British Government.

I have no doubt that it will be possible to arrange a personal meeting between you and myself. I attach great importance to it, particularly in view of the important tasks facing our countries in connection with the organization of victory against Hitlerism.

Please accept my sincere regards and wishes of success in the fight against the enemies of the United States of America.

On 23 April, Admiral Standley was finally able to present to Stalin his credentials as the new US ambassador, twelve days after arriving in Russia. The meeting was rather different in tone from Clark Kerr's *entrée* a month before, because the admiral was formal in manner and lacked the Briton's rakish style. Transmitting the president's greetings and admiration for Russian fortitude, Standley said that he was instructed to bring up again the idea of a personal meeting. 'The President told me that he was sure that if the two of you could sit down and talk matters over, there would never be any lack of understanding between our two countries.' Stalin replied that he still had hopes that a meeting could be arranged. Standley also stated that Roosevelt regretted the delays in Lend-Lease deliveries, adding that it would be one of his main tasks to get these back on schedule, and he raised the question of improved air communications between the two countries, urging on Stalin the benefits of an Alaska–Siberia corridor. However, the Soviet leader firmly favoured Canada–Greenland–Iceland, not least because of the sensitivities of the other route for Soviet relations with Japan. As was his wont, Stalin went out of his way to needle his visitor and get a reaction, criticizing the American navy man for the US failure to develop convoys like the British and asking why they did not build cargo submarines. A stiff conversation – lacking Clark Kerr's rather daring human touches – it well encapsulated the limits of the Stalin–Standley relationship, which would become evident over the ensuing year.[68]

Meanwhile Hopkins and Marshall had returned from London. In his messages to Roosevelt about their talks, Churchill was at pains to praise the

American strategic plan as a 'masterly document', assuring him that the British 'wholeheartedly agree with your conception of concentration against the main enemy'. But the PM also mentioned 'one broad qualification', namely to do enough in the Pacific to 'prevent a junction of the Japanese and the Germans'.[69] And the detailed discussions exposed some of the weak spots in American strategy. Marshall was battling to prevent a drift of US resources to the Pacific. Seeking to preserve the more feasible 'Roundup' for 1943, he had to talk up the possibilities of 'Sledgehammer' in 1942 to head off the demands of MacArthur and the US Navy for an all-out campaign that year against Japan. Yet an 'emergency landing' in France by no more than eight divisions had little chance of success: privately, US planners said it 'should be considered a sacrifice for the common good'. And since they also knew they could not send any ground forces to Britain before 1 July, and only an estimated 66,000 by 1 October, the sacrifice would have to be made by British and Canadian troops.[70] The chiefs of staff in London were quite clear about this. 'The plans are fraught with the gravest dangers,' Brooke noted in his diary. He found Marshall 'very charming', but 'his strategical ability does not impress me at all!!' Focused on getting across the Channel, Marshall had apparently not considered what to do next: 'do we go east, south or west after landing? He had not begun to think about it!!' Brooke was determined not to jeopardize what he felt were much more viable operations in Southeast Asia and the Mediterranean. On the other hand, British leaders did not want to fuel Pacific-First pressure or seem backward in support for Russia, and so they kept many of their doubts to themselves. As 'Pug' Ismay, the PM's military secretary, later acknowledged, this dissimulation led to American feelings of 'broken faith' when British reservations became clear later in the summer.[71]

Nevertheless, Roosevelt had clearly grasped the situation by the time he met Litvinov on 21 April. The ambassador was delivering Stalin's message, but, to judge from the report he sent to Molotov, most of the conversation was about Britain – and it was very revealing. The president alluded to the visit by Hopkins and Marshall, 'intimating that their mission was unsuccessful'. He said that Churchill and the War Cabinet had 'called for a second front, but the general staff was against it, citing the overextended British position'. With the defence of Burma 'hopeless' and Ceylon 'most likely' to be abandoned as well, FDR stated that this would leave the Japanese in command of the Bay of Bengal and threatening lines of communication in the Arabian Sea. He 'spoke of continuous misfortunes of the English, and the recent loss of two cruisers and a battleship near Ceylon – what the English were calling a misfortune but he, Roosevelt, would characterize differently. He, obviously, wanted to say "bungling".' FDR's scarcely veiled contempt was all very different from the solicitous tone of his messages to Churchill. When Litvinov asked how these problems in the Far East related to the second front, for which, he argued, 'there were enough resources in the British Isles', the president

> agreed that there was no connection, saying that England was mouldering in inactivity [*ot bezdeystviya razlagayetsya*], while the Canadian units were eager to fight. Roosevelt then said with a laugh that the English were for a second front in principle. They wish to postpone until 1943, but the Americans insist on the creation of the second front straightaway.

Consequently, Litvinov told Molotov, 'Roosevelt thinks it advisable for you to make a stop-over in London on your way back, for you can then also speak on his behalf and put double pressure on the English.'[72]

The stage was therefore set for major trilateral discussions on two fundamental issues for the Alliance – the second front and postwar Soviet borders – with Britain diverging from its two partners on the former issue, and the United States at odds with the others on the second. Hitherto the key intermediaries between the Big Three leaders had been American or British – Hopkins, Harriman and Beaverbrook. In the spring of 1942, it was Russia's turn, as a most undiplomatic diplomat took to the air: Vyacheslav Molotov.

4

MOLOTOV THE GO-BETWEEN

(April to July 1942)

MARCH AND APRIL 1942 marked the 'quagmire season' (*rasputitsa*) when roads turned into mud during the spring thaw. The Wehrmacht and the Red Army regrouped for the summer campaign. Stalin's hubristic hopes, after turning the tide at Moscow in December, of ending the war in 1942 had clearly failed. And Hitler, though facing a huge manpower and equipment crisis that forced him to put the German economy on a 'total war' footing, remained in a very strong position, with the front stabilized from Leningrad to Taganrog and his troops still within 150 miles of Moscow. His plan for 1942 (operation 'Blue') envisaged a thrust southeast to secure the economic resources of the Volga basin and the Caucasus oilfields. As with 'Barbarossa' in 1941, the Nazi drive was aided by Stalin's misreading of German intentions: the Soviet leader had been deceived into believing that the main thrust would be directed against Moscow. His insistence on ill-prepared pre-emptive attacks further played into German hands: Timoshenko's counter-offensive at Kharkov on 12 May led within a week to a disastrous encirclement (17–22 May), reminiscent of the worst days of 1941. Once 'Blue' began in earnest on 28 June, the German advance southeast was swift and devastating. Having captured Rostov-on-Don on 23 July, a jubilant Hitler divided his forces in two for thrusts to the Caucasus and – fatefully – to Stalingrad.

For the USA, the main war was in the Pacific. During the spring, the Japanese continued their remorseless advance, conquering Burma and the Dutch East Indies in March. On 8 April, US forces surrendered on the Bataan Peninsula, and a month later the island fortress of Corregidor in Manila Bay fell, which meant that America had been driven out of the whole of the Philippines. Not until the naval battle of Midway on 4 June, when the Japanese lost four big aircraft carriers in an afternoon, did their progress slow. But they now controlled much of resource-rich Southeast Asia, as well as the Western Pacific. Not surprisingly, the Americans – public, politicians and strategists – were preoccupied with Asia, not Europe, in 1942. In Britain, by contrast, attention focused on North Africa, where the yo-yo war in the Egyptian desert had also reached a critical stage. The British surrender of Tobruk on 20 June to Rommel's inferior forces left the road to Cairo open. Adding insult to injury for Churchill, he received the news while conferring with Roosevelt in the White House. As he wrote in his memoirs, 'Defeat is one thing, disgrace is another.'[1]

The three Allies were therefore looking in different directions amid what was now, for America and Britain, a global war. Stalin, by contrast – fighting for his life in European Russia – maintained his neutrality pact with Japan. Yet the most striking difference between the three countries lies not in the extent of the conflict, but in its intensity. During the whole of the Second World War, only six Americans died from enemy action in the whole of the continental United States: a pastor's wife and five of her Sunday-school class who stumbled by chance on a Japanese balloon-bomb in a forest in Oregon on 5 May 1945.[2] For the British people, the worst of the Blitz had passed by 1942, though the so-called 'Baedeker Raids' in April–June on cultural targets such as Exeter, Norwich and Canterbury cost the lives of some 1,600 civilians. By contrast, for the second time in two years, the heartland of Russia was utterly ravaged by Hitler's 'war of extermination' (*Vernichtungskrieg*).

Roughly two-thirds of the Wehrmacht were deployed on the Eastern Front in 1942; during that year, the Red Army lost 2 million killed or missing.[3] Although the emergency evacuation eastward of some 1,500 big factories in 1941 helped salvage crucial productive capacity, the USSR's GDP in 1942 was less than 80 per cent of the 1941 figure. With defence industries accounting for over 60 per cent of GDP and the civilian economy stripped of manpower for the armed forces, food production plummeted and living standards collapsed. Most of the population had to survive on a grossly inadequate diet, in which ersatz bread predominated. During the depths of the grim siege of Leningrad, for instance, as one resident put it, 'we learned to make doughnuts out of mustard, soup out of yeast, hamburgers out of horseradish, and gelatin out of joiner's glue.' Such privation was the norm across the western Soviet Union in the first winter of Russia's war.[4]

This forms the military context for Big Three diplomacy during the spring and summer of 1942. A trio of issues continued to stand out: Allied supplies to

Russia, a British–Soviet treaty including acceptance of the USSR's 1941 borders, and – above all – the timing of a second front. Given the asymmetry between the Soviet war efforts and those of its two allies, trying to satisfy Stalin in these three areas became, for Churchill and Roosevelt, the essential litmus test of whether the Grand Alliance was working.

When the Moscow supply protocol was signed in October 1941, the war had been confined to Eurasia and North Africa. After Pearl Harbor, global war greatly complicated the logistical challenges, and the British chiefs of staff (COS) argued vehemently that they should no longer be held to the protocol. Worldwide war also stretched to the limits the Royal Navy and Britain's merchant fleet. In the first quarter of 1942, Britain lost twice the tonnage of shipping sunk in the last quarter of 1941. The 2,000-mile route of the Arctic convoys from Iceland to Arkhangelsk and Murmansk was particularly dangerous. So the COS urged Churchill to invoke the escape clause in the Moscow Protocol, which stated that 'in the event of the war situation changing and the burden of defence being transferred to other theatres of war, it will be necessary for the three countries concerned to consult together, and to decide what adjustment of the present arrangement is necessary'. Churchill, however, was adamant that Britain had to honour its supply commitments, because this was the only tangible support being provided to the beleaguered Russians at a time when British opinion was clamouring for a second front in France that he and the chiefs deemed suicidal. 'In this way alone,' he wrote in December 1941, 'shall we hold our influence over Stalin and be able to weave the mighty Russian effort into the general texture of the war.' Roosevelt took the same view, but the logistical chaos in Washington after Pearl Harbor had left Russian supplies at the mercy of US needs amid a medley of conflicting agencies, and so the United States was much further behind on the Moscow schedule of deliveries than Britain. Not until March did the White House begin to get a grip on the situation. 'The Russian protocol,' instructed Hopkins, 'must be completed in preference to any other phase of our war program.'[5]

Just at this time, the Germans strengthened their naval and air forces in northern Norway, spearheaded by the battleship *Tirpitz*, and the hours of darkness began to diminish to almost nothing. At the end of April, the British Cabinet decided to reduce the frequency and size of convoys, and this became a serious bone of contention between Churchill and Stalin in May. Their clash reached crisis point in mid-July, when the prime minister sent a long telegram regretfully announcing the postponement of convoys, after losing two-thirds of the ships in convoy PQ17. Stalin received this message just as his southern front was caving in, and he responded with imputations of bad faith and even cowardice. This seemed like a replay of their face-off in November 1941, but this time it would take more than an exchange of birthday greetings to resolve the row.

The dispute over the Anglo-Soviet treaty followed a different course. As his message to Stalin on 9 March showed, by the spring Churchill had come around on Eden's pressure that they should concede Soviet control of the Baltic states; but eastern Poland – the territory of a wartime ally – was a different matter. This deadlock eventually persuaded Stalin, on 22 April, to authorize Molotov to sort out the matter during his visit to Britain, which took place from 20 to 27 May. The Soviet leader agreed to this trip reluctantly and, throughout, kept his foreign minister on a tight rein, frequently demanding more information. In the end, the crisis was resolved when, against all expectations (not least Molotov's), Stalin accepted an alternative, more general treaty, pledging twenty years of friendship but without any references to territory. His U-turn occurred on 24 May, just when the disaster at Kharkov put paid to any lingering hopes of an early end to the war. After an unusually cordial exchange with Churchill about the treaty, Stalin focused his energies on trying to secure a second front in 1942.[6]

That issue had been downplayed during the winter, when prospects on the Eastern Front looked brighter; but it became urgent for Stalin in May, with the new German advance. Well aware of Churchill's resistance to a cross-Channel attack, Stalin concentrated here on Roosevelt, and a visit to the White House (29 May to 5 June) constituted the second leg of Molotov's extended foreign trip. The president did all he could to sound encouraging about the prospects for an early second front, infuriating General Marshall and the War Department. When Molotov visited London again en route home to Moscow (8–11 June), Churchill tried to damp down any hopes for 1942; but, as a counter-balance, he talked up Allied plans for 1943 in a way that created hostages to fortune and stored up more opportunities for Soviet resentment in the future. Still hopeful of action in 1942, Stalin acceded to FDR's request to reduce the shipping made available for supplies to the USSR on the grounds that this would free up tonnage for the second front. Perhaps for the same reason, in early July he acceded to a request that US bombers intended for Russia be diverted to Britain's battlefront in Egypt. But in the middle of the month, after the failure of a final effort by Marshall to persuade the British to mount a small-scale cross-Channel landing ('Sledgehammer') in 1942, Roosevelt overrode his JCS and backed Churchill's plan for an invasion of French Northwest Africa that autumn. When this became clear to Stalin, he told Churchill bluntly that the USSR could not accept the postponement of the second front until 1943 –

doing so in the same furious message to Churchill on 23 July that denounced his postponement of the Arctic convoys.

In addressing these three areas of controversy, Roosevelt did not live up to his airy assurance to Churchill in March that he could 'handle' Stalin. The bulk of the messages from April to July came from the prime minister, and most of those sent by FDR had been prepared by bureaucrats. The attempt by Roosevelt's close aide, Sumner Welles, to draft a more personal letter (20 July) was overtaken by events. The president was keen to set up an Alaska–Siberia air bridge to expedite the transfer of planes and to strengthen communications, and this issue accounts for a good deal of their correspondence in June and July; but the impetus and texts for these messages came from the US Army Air Force. Roosevelt's enthusiasm for the Russian alliance is most evident in his readiness, especially over supplies and the second front, to offer Stalin assurances (or at least rhetoric) that his advisers warned flew in the face of realities. The president did not seem to care: his main aim was to keep the Russians fighting through 1942.

It was therefore the surly Molotov who became, rather implausibly, the human go-between linking the Big Three leaders in the spring and early summer of 1942 (plates 7 and 8). His odyssey – physically gruelling, acutely dangerous and also highly stressful because of Stalin's micro-managing – was a trilateral version of his counterpart Eden's mission to Moscow in December 1941. The Eden visit had been a response to the epistolary flare-up between Churchill and Stalin in November 1941. But the second big clash between the two leaders, in July 1942, was resolved in a more dramatic way – and one that would move Big Three relations onto an entirely different plane.

*****

Stalin's main concern in his message to Churchill of 22 April was the draft Soviet–British political agreement – on which negotiations had progressed now that the Cabinet had decided to ignore American wishes and sign a treaty that accepted the USSR's June 1941 borders. Roosevelt and the State Department reluctantly acquiesced, and on 8 April the War Cabinet approved a new draft agreement, which was transmitted via Maisky to the Kremlin. This contained a provision, included to appease the Americans, that people in areas that the USSR would reoccupy had the right of emigration. But Eden was doubtful that Moscow would accept it, and that indeed proved the case.[7] In his 22 April telegram, Stalin said that Molotov would come to London to deal personally with the areas of disagreement – a proposal that Churchill readily accepted.

Stalin to Churchill, sent 22 April 1942, received 23 April 1942[8]

Recently the Soviet Government received from Mr Eden the drafts of two treaties between the USSR and Britain, which differed in some material respects from the texts of agreements which were under discussion while Mr Eden was in Moscow. In view of the fact that these drafts reveal fresh divergences which it would be difficult to resolve by correspondence the Soviet Government have decided, despite all the obstacles, to send Mr Molotov to London in order, by means of personal discussion, to dispose of all the matters which stand in the way of the signing of the agreements. This is all the more necessary because question of opening a second front in Europe (which was raised in the last message addressed to me by President of the United States, in which he invited Mr Molotov to go to Washington to discuss this matter) calls for a preliminary exchange of views between representatives of our two Governments.

Accept my greetings and my wishes for success in your fight against the enemies of Great Britain.

Churchill to Stalin, sent 24 April 1942, received 25 April 1942[9]

I am very grateful for your message of 23rd April, and we shall, of course, welcome M. Molotov, with whom I am confident we shall be able to do much useful work. I am very glad that you feel able to allow this visit, which I am sure will be most valuable.

In his message of 4 May, Roosevelt invited Molotov to fly to America on a US plane and stay in the White House. This was FDR's own idea, in an effort to show the importance he attached to the mission – and once more to signal his preference for personal relations with the Soviet leadership. He passed the message to Litvinov for transmission to Moscow[10] – another reflection of FDR's belief in the security of Soviet codes and his desire to keep the State Department at arm's length.

Roosevelt to Stalin, sent 4 May 1942, received 6 May 1942[11]

We are having grave difficulties with the northern convoy route and have informed Litvinov of the complications. You may be sure, however, that no effort will be omitted to get as many ships off as possible.

I have heard of Admiral Standley's cordial reception by you and wish to express my appreciation.

I am looking forward to seeing Molotov and the moment I hear of the route we shall make preparations to provide immediate transportation. I do hope Molotov can stay with me in the White House while he is in Washington but we can make a private home nearby available if that is desired.

In this message, Roosevelt also touched on an issue that was now becoming a major source of friction between the Allies – the Arctic convoys. On 24 April, the British Cabinet agreed to ease the pressure on the Royal Navy by reducing future Arctic convoys to three every two months, each of no more than twenty-five merchant ships, so as to ensure adequate escort protection.[12] This affected the Americans as much as it did the British, just when more US supplies and cargo vessels were at last becoming available. Roosevelt remonstrated with Churchill – warning that 'any word reaching Stalin at this time that our supplies were stopping for any reason would have a most unfortunate effect' – but the prime minister would only concede a possible increase of convoy size to thirty-five ships because the navy was 'absolutely extended'. FDR had to acquiesce, but, disingenuous as ever, he proposed on 1 May that, instead of sending a disheartening message to Stalin, the two of them should 'press the Russians to reduce requirements to absolute essentials', on the grounds that their preparations for the second front would 'require all possible munitions and shipping'.[13]

When the Cabinet made its decision on 24 April, it also urged that 'a request should be made, at a very high level, for increased Russian assistance in the defence of the convoys'.[14] But the Red Navy was the Soviet Cinderella service, deficient in ships and lacking clout to divert bombers and reconnaissance aircraft from the Red Army. The senior British naval officer in North Russia told London that the attitude in the Kremlin itself was effectively that 'these convoys are your only contribution. If you want them protected, send along the aircraft.' For Stalin, the issue was particularly urgent as he prepared for the inevitable German offensive in the spring. He wanted the maximum amount of Moscow Protocol supplies now, even if that meant relatively little later on. Yet the flow dropped dramatically during April, when only seven cargo vessels made it to North Russia, compared with twenty-nine in March – mostly because of heavy ice around Iceland. 'British and American fears of possible attacks by the Germans are exaggerated,' Molotov cabled Litvinov in exasperation on 25 April. He and Maisky were told to make strong representations in Washington and London.[15] Although convoy PQ15 reached Murmansk on 5 May with twenty-two of its original twenty-five ships intact, it could not fully make up the deficit. Hence, Stalin's urgent plea to Churchill on 6 May.

Stalin to Churchill, sent 6 May 1942, received 6 May 1942[16]

I have a request of you. Some 90 steamers loaded with various important war materials for the USSR are bottled up at present in Iceland or in the approaches from America to Iceland. I understand that there is a danger that the sailing of these ships may be delayed for a long time because of the difficulty to organise convoy escorted by the British Naval Forces.

I am fully aware of the difficulties involved and of the sacrifices made by Great Britain in this matter. I feel however incumbent upon me to approach you with the request to take all possible measures in order to ensure the arrival of all the above mentioned materials in the USSR in the course of May as this is extremely important for our front.

Accept my sincere greeting and best wishes for success.

In his reply, Churchill stressed the problems facing the Royal Navy (which lost two cruisers on the Arctic route in early May). Picking up on the Cabinet instruction of 24 April, he also emphasized the need for more naval and air assistance from the Soviet side. PQ15 had been assisted by the timely appearance of two Soviet destroyers, although the weather conditions were probably more decisive: thick fog kept the Luftwaffe on the ground.

Churchill to Stalin, sent 9 May 1942, received 11 May 1942[17]

I have received your telegram of May 6th and thank you for your message and greetings. We are resolved to fight our way through to you with the maximum amount of war materials. On account of the *Tirpitz* and other enemy surface ships at Trondheim the passage of every convoy has become a serious fleet operation. We shall continue to do our utmost.

No doubt your naval advisers have pointed out to you the dangers to which the convoys are subjected from attack by enemy surface forces, submarines and air from the various bases in enemy hands which flank the route of the convoy throughout its passage.

Owing to adverse weather conditions, the scale of attack which the Germans have so far developed is considerably less than we can reasonably expect in the future.

We are throwing all our available resources into the solution of this problem, having dangerously weakened our Atlantic convoy escorts for this purpose, and as you are no doubt aware have suffered severe naval casualties in the course of these operations.

I am sure that you will not mind my being quite frank and emphasising the need of increasing the assistance given by the U.S.S.R. Naval and Air Forces in helping to get these convoys through safely.

If you are to receive a fair proportion of the material which is loaded into ships in the United Kingdom and the United States, it is essential that the U.S.S.R. Naval and Air Forces should realise that they must be largely responsible for convoys, whether incoming or outgoing, when to the east of meridian longitude 28° east in waters which are out of sight of the Murmansk Coast.

The ways in which further assistance is required from the U.S.S.R. forces are as follows:

(a) Increased and more determined assistance from the U.S.S.R. surface forces;

(b) Provision of sufficient long-range bombers to enable the aerodromes used by the Germans to be heavily bombed during the passing of convoys in the North Cape areas;

(c) Provision of long-range fighters to cover convoys for that part of their voyage when they are approaching your coasts;

(d) Anti-submarine patrols both by aircraft and surface vessels.

When broadcasting tomorrow (Sunday) night I propose to make the declaration warning the Germans that if they begin gas warfare upon the Russian Armies we shall certainly retaliate at once upon Germany.

Rather than push the matter further, Stalin decided to send an emollient reply to Churchill and to use Roosevelt to put pressure on the British.

Stalin to Churchill, sent 12 May 1942, received 13 May 1942[18]

I have received your message of May 11 and thank you for the promise to arrange for maximum delivery of war materials to the U.S.S.R. We quite understand the difficulties which Great Britain is overcoming, and those heavy sea losses which you are suffering while accomplishing this big task.

As for your suggestion for the Air Force and Navy of the USSR to take more effective measures for protection of transports in the area mentioned by you, you may not doubt that on our part all possible measures will be taken immediately. It is necessary, however, to take into consideration that fact that our Naval Forces are very limited and that our Air Forces in their vast majority are engaged at the battlefront.

Please accept my best regards.

Stalin declined Roosevelt's offer to use an American plane to transport Molotov. Two state-of-the-art TB-7 bombers were prepared for the journey. Their trial run to Britain a few days earlier had gone well; on the way home, however, one of the aircraft was attacked and damaged both by a German plane and by Soviet fighters but made it back to Moscow.[19] Despite the apparent risk, the Kremlin decided to mount the mission without Allied escorts.

Stalin to Roosevelt, sent 15 May 1942, received 15 May 1942[20]

I thank you for the message conveyed through Ambassador Litvinov. I have already requested Prime Minister Churchill to contribute to the speediest overcoming of certain difficulties in connection with the transportation and convoying of ships to the U.S.S.R. Since the delivery of materials in May from the U.S.A. and England is of the utmost urgency, I make a similar request to you, Mr President.

The journey of Mr Molotov to the U.S.A. and England must be postponed for a few days owing to uncertain weather conditions. It appears that this journey can be made on a Soviet airplane both to England and to the U.S.A. I would at the same time add that the Soviet Government considers that Mr Molotov's journey should be accomplished without any publicity whatever till the return of Mr Molotov to Moscow, as was done when Mr Eden visited Moscow in December last.

In regard to the place of residence of Mr Molotov during his sojourn in Washington, Mr Molotov and I thank you for your kind suggestions.

The cryptic final sentence was clarified when Litvinov phoned Hopkins to say that Molotov accepted FDR's invitation to stay at the White House. In a rather amateur attempt to maintain confidentiality, Molotov was given the code name 'Mr Brown'.

It was, however, to Britain that Molotov would be coming first, where Churchill and his colleagues were keen to nail down the Soviet–British treaty without further meddling by the Americans. Just days before the foreign minister's arrival, the prime minister faced down a major protest from the chiefs of staff about continuing the Arctic convoys, which Admiral Pound privately described as 'a regular millstone round our necks' and 'a most un-sound operation with the dice loaded against us in every direction'. Churchill told the chiefs that both Stalin and Roosevelt would 'object very much to our desisting from running the convoys now', and argued that the operation would be justified if half the ships got through. 'The failure on our part to make the attempt would weaken our influence with both our major Allies. I share your misgivings but I feel it is a matter of duty.'[21] Informing Stalin of the despatch of PQ16 (actually delayed until 21 May), his message voiced his fears and gave a clear warning that future sailings were in the balance. This convoy consisted of thirty-five cargo ships, the maximum it was now felt could be safely escorted. The imminence of Molotov's visit doubtless strengthened the PM's doleful determination to put 'duty' before prudence.

Churchill to Stalin, sent 19 May 1942, received 20 May 1942[22]

A convoy of 35 ships sailed yesterday with orders to fight their way through to you. The Germans have about a hundred bombers in wait for these ships and escort. Our advisers think that, unless we are again favoured with weather which hampers the German air force, we must expect that a large proportion of the ships and the war materials contained in them will be lost.

As I mentioned in my telegram on the 9th May, much will depend on the extent to which your long-range bombers can bomb the enemy aerodromes, including that at Bardufoss, between the 22nd and 29th of this month. I know you will do your utmost.

If luck is not with us and the convoy suffers very heavy losses, the only course left to us may be to hold up the further convoys until we get more sea room when the ice recedes to the northward in July.

Molotov's plane landed at Dundee, on the east coast of Scotland, at 8 a.m. on 20 May, after a ten-hour flight from Moscow. He was then taken by train to London – meeting en route Ambassador Maisky (whom he cordially disliked) – and was accommodated in the prime minister's country residence at Chequers. This offered the anonymity and security the Soviets desired, while also signalling Molotov's special status as a VIP visitor. In his memoirs, Churchill referred to what he called 'the inveterate suspicion with which the Russians regarded foreigners', with anecdotes about Molotov's security men who demanded keys to all the rooms, and the women in black who guarded the rooms day and night, even when Molotov and his guards were at meetings in London. On the rare occasions when members of the Chequers staff were allowed to make up the beds, 'they were disturbed to find pistols under the pillows'. Churchill deleted from the proofs of his memoirs a story of how Grace Lamont, the curator at Chequers, went up to Molotov's room about 2 a.m. one night because a chink of light had been discerned through his curtains, in violation of the strict blackout. When she knocked on the door, it was unlocked and opened about a foot, whereupon Molotov confronted her with an automatic pistol. Being, as Churchill phrased it, 'a Scottish lady in her prime and of placid temperament', Miss Lamont was 'not at all taken aback'. She calmly explained the problem and Molotov immediately locked his door and attended to the curtain. The incident, said Churchill in this passage that he deleted in 1950, 'reveals one aspect of the gulf between the Soviet way of life and that of the Western powers'.[23]

The talks in London on 21–26 May (plate 9) focused on two key issues – the second front and the Anglo-Soviet treaty.[24] The opening days were intensely frustrating for Molotov. He cabled Stalin on 23 May to say that, despite showing 'particular personal attention' with meals together and a long late-night conversation at Chequers, Churchill 'is behaving with obvious lack of sympathy to me concerning the substance of the two main questions'. Probably, added Molotov, because he 'is waiting for new events on our front and is not in a hurry to agree with us at the moment'. On the question of a landing in France, the prime minister emphasized the lack of shipping and the need for air supremacy. On the draft treaty, although the British were now willing to concede postwar Russian annexation of the Baltic states, they wanted to include the right of emigration in the treaty, and they were also adamant that there could be no concessions on the border of Poland – whose independence had been guaranteed by Britain's treaty of alliance. Neither of these points was acceptable to the USSR. Molotov told Stalin grimly: 'I consider it pointless to return to Britain after my visit to the USA, because I see no prospects for improvement resulting from this. Most probably, the prospects for my trip to the USA are not favourable either, but the promise to go has to be kept.'[25]

Aware of Molotov's frustration, Churchill interceded with Stalin.

Churchill to Stalin, sent 23 May 1942, received 24 May 1942[26]

We have greatly enjoyed receiving M. Molotov in London and have had fruitful conversations with him on both military and political affairs. We have given him a full and true account of our plans and resources. As regards the Treaty, he will explain to you the difficulties, which are mainly that we cannot go back on our previous undertakings to Poland and have to take account of our own and American opinion.

I am sure that it would be of the greatest value to the common cause if M. Molotov could come back this way from America. We can then continue our discussions, which I hope will lead to the development of close military cooperation between our three countries. Moreover, I shall then be able to give him the latest development in our own military plans.

Finally, I hope that political discussions might also then be carried a stage further. For all these reasons I greatly hope you will agree that M. Molotov should pay us a further visit on his way home to you.

Stalin promised Churchill that Soviet air and naval forces would 'to their utmost' protect convoy PQ16. Twenty Ilyushin IL-4 bombers were relocated to the Arctic, and the Stavka ordered 'systematic strikes against enemy airfields in Bardufoss, Svartnesse, Tromsø, Hammerfest from 25 to 29 May'.[27]

Meanwhile, the Foreign Office tried to cut through the diplomatic deadlock by drawing up a completely new draft treaty. This avoided any territorial issues and simply committed the two countries to a wartime alliance and a twenty-year pact of mutual assistance. Its main point, Eden told the Cabinet, 'would be to offer the Russians, in place of the recognition of their frontier claims, a post-war alliance against German aggression until such time as a world-wide system for the maintenance of the peace has been evolved' – or in the event of such a system never coming into existence, for example 'because the United States declined to participate'.[28] This caveat reminds us of nagging British worries at this stage in the war that America might again revert to postwar isolationism – as after 1918.

On the morning of 24 May, Molotov forwarded the British text to Moscow with a brusque comment: 'We consider this treaty unacceptable, as it is an empty declaration which the USSR does not need.' Stalin's reply that evening was quite remarkable:

> We have received the draft treaty Eden handed to you. We do not consider it an empty declaration but regard it as an important document. It lacks the question of security of frontiers, but this is not bad perhaps, for it gives us a free hand. The question of frontiers, or to be more exact, of guarantees for the security of our frontiers at one or other section of our country, will be decided by force.

Stalin told Molotov to stop trying to amend the former treaties and adopt Eden's draft as the basis for an agreement, with two minor amendments. He instructed Molotov to 'sign the treaty as soon as possible and then fly to America'. Although the message addressed Molotov as usual in the familiar first-personal singular form, it was signed 'Instance' [*Instantsiya*] – a term signifying the Central Committee of the Communist Party of the Soviet Union that was used for particularly important cases. Molotov got the message – both literally and meta-phorically. That night he sent a reply that was almost grovelling: 'I shall act in accordance with the directive from the Instance and I believe that the new draft treaty can also have positive value. I failed to appreciate it at once.' Here is a particularly revealing insight into the relationship between Stalin and one of his closest associates. Widely regarded in the West as the tough guy, Molotov was ultimately Stalin's servant. And both men knew it.[29]

When FO officials drew up the draft treaty, they were not optimistic about the Soviet reaction. Eden hoped that Molotov would recognize the need not to return home empty-handed, given widespread expectations in both countries and internationally. Even if rejected by the Russians, he felt 'it would strengthen our position to have offered it'. Or *'faute de mieux'*, as his private secretary Oliver Harvey put it laconically. The sudden Soviet U-turn therefore came as a surprise. 'All very mysterious,' mused Harvey. On 25 May, the outstanding issues were dealt with 'most smoothly and rapidly' and the treaty was signed to considerable fanfare the following day. The new 'Twenty-Year Mutual Assistance Agreement' seemed to satisfy the government's dual desire to 'go as far as we can to dispel Russian suspicion of us without sacrificing our own principles'.[30] British policymakers were delighted. 'Our relations with the Soviet Union are now set on a completely different and much more satisfactory basis,' Eden told the Cabinet, to warm congratulations for his efforts. Churchill assured Roosevelt that the treaty was now 'entirely compatible with our Atlantic Charter', praising Molotov as 'a statesman' who had 'a freedom of action very different from what you and I saw with Litvinov'. Little did the PM realize who lay behind Molotov's sudden flexibility.[31]

The reasons for Stalin's volte-face remain opaque. Most likely, he saw the futility of further wrangling with his allies about recognition of the USSR's western borders. The US ambassador in London, John G. Winant, had made clear to Maisky and Molotov on several occasions that this would cause great offence in Washington. Winant also advised that it would be 'undesirable to complicate Roosevelt's position' in this way because, in his opinion, 'the second front was more important than the treaties'. Winant therefore served to bolster Molotov and Maisky in their conviction that FDR could put pressure on Churchill to override the opposition of the British chiefs of staff to a cross-Channel attack in 1942. Stalin also seems to have taken this view – mindful of new disasters on the front, where major operations had resumed after the spring thaw. The massive German pincer offensive around Kharkov wiped three rifle armies and a tank army off the Soviet order of battle by the time the encirclement was complete on 22 May. This followed closely on the heels of a similar disaster in the Crimea, where an inept campaign by Stalin's wilful crony Lev Mekhlis had led to the loss of three more armies. There was now a real danger that the entire southern flank of the Soviet front would collapse as the Wehrmacht ploughed on towards the Caucasus. And so Stalin focused on trying to secure an early second front and eschewed further diplomatic haggling – taking comfort, as he told Molotov, in the hope that he could gain more on the battlefield than at the negotiating table. However far-fetched that might have seemed in 1942, eventually he was proved right – though at enormous cost.[32]

Having received Churchill's message of 23 May, Stalin confirmed that Molotov would now stop over in London on his way home from Washington.

Stalin to Churchill, sent 24 May 1942, received 25 May 1942[33]

I received your last message on 24th of May. Viacheslav Molotov as well as I feel that it might be for him advisable on the return journey from the USA to stop in London to complete the negotiations with the representatives of the British Government on matters of interest to our two countries.

When they received the message on 25 May, 'Churchill and Eden were extremely happy and the premier immediately made it clear that he wanted very much to meet Comrade Stalin', recorded Maisky.

> Molotov supported the premier's intention and suggested that the meeting would undoubtedly be very useful and interesting, and that Comrade Stalin would be glad to see Churchill. Churchill brightened and said, 'As soon as we clear the north of Norway, we'll arrange our meeting in the conquered territories, and maybe even have the meeting of the three with the participation of President Roosevelt.'[34]

This was the first mention of a possible meeting between Churchill and Stalin: it would eventually take place in August.

After Molotov's return to Moscow, this next message from Churchill, along with Stalin's response (both very cordial in tone), was published in Soviet newspapers, with the exception of the paragraph concerning convoy PQ16.[35] With a friendship treaty scheduled to last until 1962, Soviet–British relations did indeed seem to be on a new footing.

Churchill to Stalin, sent 27 May 1942, received 28 May 1942[36]

We are most grateful to you for meeting our difficulties in the Treaty as you have done. I am sure the reward in the United States will be solid and that our three Great Powers will now be able to march together united through whatever has to come.

It has been a great pleasure to meet M. Molotov and we have done a great beating down of barriers between our two countries. I am very glad he is coming back this way for there will be more good work to be done.

So far all has been well with the convoy, but it is now at its most dangerous stage. Many thanks for the measures you are taking to help it in.

Now that we have bound ourselves to be Allies and friends for twenty years, I take the occasion to send you my sincere good wishes and to assure you of the confidence which I feel that victory will be ours.

Stalin to Churchill, sent 28 May 1942, received 28 May 1942[37]

I thank you very much for friendly feelings and good wishes expressed by you in connection with the signature of our new Treaty. I am sure this Treaty will be of the greatest importance for the future strengthening of friendly relations between the Soviet Union and Great Britain as well as between our countries and the United States and will secure the close collaboration of our countries after the victorious end of the war. I hope also that your meeting with Molotov on his way back from the United States will bring to an end that part of the work which was left uncompleted.

With regard to the measures concerning protection of convoys, you may be rest assured that in this respect everything possible on our side will be done now and in the future.

Please accept my most sincere good wishes as well as my fullest confidence in our complete joint victory.

Molotov reached the White House at 4 p.m. on 29 May, having been delayed a day and a half in Iceland because of bad weather. As soon as he arrived, 'somewhat unwashed and dishevelled', as he put it, the foreign minister plunged straight into discussions with Roosevelt – three on the first evening. Keen to build a special relationship with Stalin, the president unveiled his idea of an 'international police force' of the victor powers – America, Russia, Britain and China – to enforce the principles of the Atlantic Charter on Germany and Japan for a quarter of a century, until they had learned to curb their aggressive instinct. Churchill, he said, was resistant to the idea – talking vaguely about an updated League of Nations – but Roosevelt dismissed the League as 'inefficient' and believed that his power-based 'policemen' approach was the only answer. He told Molotov that 'Churchill would have to accept this proposal, if the USA and the USSR insisted on it'. Molotov's response was encouraging but non-committal, focusing instead on the issue of the second front. He insisted that if the Americans and British drew off forty German divisions to Western Europe, then Hitler's fate would be decided in 1942. Made aware by his military advisers of the lack of shipping to transport men and supplies across the Atlantic, Roosevelt offered Molotov only the possibility of operation 'Sledgehammer', using six to ten divisions. He told Molotov he wanted to 'take the risk', even if there was 'no guarantee of success'. According to the Soviet record, he added, 'It is necessary to make sacrifices to help the USSR in 1942. It is possible that we shall have to live through another Dunkirk and lose 100,000–120,000 men.'[38] What FDR did not make clear was that, because of the slowness of US mobilization and the commitments in the Pacific, the troops he was offering for sacrifice would mostly come from the British Commonwealth.

Molotov was not impressed with a possible landing on this scale. He admitted that the Red Army's southern flank was fragile and warned of a possible German breakthrough to the Baku oilfields, which would immensely strengthen Hitler and make the Red Army a much less formidable foe. If America postponed the second front until 1943, he stated bluntly, 'you will have eventually to bear the brunt of the war'. The president asked General Marshall if they could tell Stalin they were 'preparing a second front'. Marshall concurred, whereupon FDR – in a typically elastic rephrasing – 'authorized Mr Molotov to inform Mr Stalin that we expect the formation of a second front this year'. He also asked Molotov to reduce Soviet demands for supplies, in order to free up shipping for the 'Bolero' build-up of troops and supplies in Britain. Molotov was sceptical, fearing that there would be neither a second front nor sufficient supplies.[39]

The Soviet foreign minister had become increasingly frustrated. Having behaved with what the American record called 'unexpected frankness and amiability' – perhaps because 'the word had gone out from Mr Stalin to be somewhat more agreeable than is Mr Molotov's custom' – his demeanour on the final morning of talks, 1 June, was 'much more gruff and assertive', and there was real 'tension in the air'.[40] As in London, however, Molotov was then wrong-footed by 'the Boss' in a series of telegrams explicitly marked as coming from the 'Instance'. On 1 June, Stalin instructed him to tell FDR that the policeman idea was 'absolutely sound' and that it would be 'fully supported by the Soviet Government'. On 3 June, he complained that 'the Instance is dissatisfied with the terseness and reticence of your communications ... The Instance would like to know everything ...' Stalin added that the communiqué on the talks 'should mention, among other things, the subject of creating the second front in Europe and that full understanding has been reached in this matter'.

And in another 'Instance' telegram on 4 June, Stalin conceded Roosevelt's request to reduce shipping for Soviet supplies: 'In all probability this is needed by the USA and Britain to release tonnage for bringing troops to Western Europe in order to create the second front.' Acting on Stalin's instructions, Molotov made sure that the communiqué included this statement: 'In the course of the conversations, full understanding was reached with regard to the urgent task of creating a second front in Europe in 1942.'[41] This wording was, of course, ambiguous: it could signify that they agreed that the task of creating a second front was urgent, or that they actually agreed to mount a second front in 1942. Marshall had strenuously objected to including the date, but FDR was adamant. As he told Churchill, 'I am especially anxious that he carry back some real results of his Mission and that he will give a favorable account to Stalin. I am inclined to think that at present all the Russians are a bit down in the mouth ... we may be and probably are faced with real trouble on the Russian front and must make our plans to meet it.' The American diplomat Charles Bohlen later remarked rather archly that 'some people in the administration felt that encouragement, even when based on false premises, would stiffen the Soviet will.'[42]

At the time, Stalin seems to have been more optimistic than Molotov that his allies would indeed invade the continent of Europe in 1942, especially now that he had backed off on supplies in order to extract British agreement. He told Molotov on 7 June: 'You should press Churchill to organize the second front and start operations this year, taking into account that we are reducing our requests for supplies.'[43] But when Molotov began new talks in London on 9 June, he found Churchill more averse than ever to making any commitments about 1942. When Molotov mentioned FDR's comment about risking a 'second Dunkirk' and the possible sacrifice of 100,000 to 120,000 troops, the PM exploded angrily that 'we shall not win the war by doing such stupid things' and that he would rather resign than undertake an operation with no chance of success. Molotov replied defensively that he was only passing on Roosevelt's opinion, to which Churchill retorted 'I shall give him my opinion on this matter myself.' At the end of their meetings on 10 June, the PM gave Molotov an aide-mémoire, seeking to clarify FDR's vague but upbeat comments about 1942:

We are making preparations for a landing on the Continent in August or September 1942 ... It is impossible to say in advance whether the situation will be such as to make this operation feasible when the time comes. We can therefore give no promise in the matter, but, provided that it appears sound and sensible, we shall not hesitate to put our plans into effect.

Having carefully reserved the British position on 1942, Churchill was, however, far more expansive about the following year:

> Finally, and most important of all, we are concentrating our maximum effort on the organization and preparation of a large scale invasion of the Continent of Europe by British and American forces in 1943. We are setting no limit to the scope and objectives of this campaign, which will be carried out in the first instance by over a million men, British and American, with air forces of appropriate strength.[44]

Both Western leaders had therefore stuck out their necks about the second front – Roosevelt for 1942, Churchill for 1943. Their assertions did not persuade the Kremlin, but they did give it leverage that would be used in the months to come.

The Russians, British and Americans all felt able to take comfort from Molotov's shuttle diplomacy. But it had been a stressful few weeks. Stalin's dyspeptic telegrams to Molotov revealed his frustration at having to conduct diplomacy by proxy. Churchill's fury about a 'second Dunkirk' reflected not merely his sensitivity about Britain's military reverses, but also the difficulties of conducting relations with Russia in tandem with his increasingly assertive transatlantic ally. And Roosevelt – whose smooth tongue and confident manner were his most potent political weapons – was visibly uncomfortable and 'cramped', as Hopkins put it, by the ponderous nature of delayed dialogue through interpreters, especially when dealing with someone like Molotov, who lacked Litvinov's cosmopolitan manner.[45] In short, one senses that each of the Big Three was yearning to get up close and personal with his fellow leaders.

On 13 June, after Molotov's safe return to Moscow, the following exchange of messages was published in the Soviet press, in order to boost Russians and irritate the Axis.

Roosevelt to Stalin, sent 6 June 1942, received 8 June 1942[46]

I appreciate ever so much your sending Mr Molotov to see me. We had a very satisfactory visit and I shall await anxiously news of his safe arrival.

Stalin to Roosevelt, sent 12 June 1942, received 17 June 1942[47]

The Soviet Government shares your view, Mr President, as to the satisfactory results of Mr V.M. Molotov's visit to the United States.

I take this opportunity to thank you, Mr President, on behalf of the Soviet Government, for the cordial hospitality given to Mr Molotov and his staff during their sojourn in the United States.

Mr V.M. Molotov has safely returned to Moscow today.

After Molotov's shuttle diplomacy, both Churchill and Roosevelt tried to maintain the good mood by forwarding titbits of helpful intelligence. On 16 June, the prime minister alerted Stalin to possible threats to the northern convoy route, including even a possible attack on Murmansk. He talked vaguely about 'joint operations' and offered six RAF fighter squadrons in support – an offer that Stalin readily accepted.[48] On 17 June, a message from the president, prepared by the Army Air Forces (AAF), highlighted Japan's recent capture of two of the US Aleutian islands southwest of Alaska and the danger that air bases there could pose for both the American West Coast and the Soviet Far East. Anxious to develop an air supply route from Alaska to Siberia, Roosevelt urged Stalin to authorize secret staff conversations as soon as possible. The Soviet leader was anxious to avoid doing anything that might jeopardize the USSR's neutrality pact with Japan, especially in view of the grave situation on the Soviet–German front. But after the signing on 11 June of a Soviet–American mutual assistance agreement, the Kremlin agreed to establish the air route.[49]

Churchill's talk of operations in the Arctic reflected one of his recurrent obsessions: a landing in Norway. In a memo for the chiefs of staff on 1 June, he asserted that the limited German forces in northern Norway could easily be eliminated. Then,

> not only would the northern sea route to Russia be kept open, but we should have set up a second front on a small scale from which it would be most difficult to eject us. If the going was good, we could advance gradually southward, unrolling the Nazi map of Europe from the top.[50]

These breezy sentences exemplify that hubristic confidence in peripheral operations that infuriated Churchill's military advisers. At the Chiefs of Staff Committee on 8 June, it was noted that, as a 'second front', Norway was of limited value, because it had nothing of vital importance for Germany. Furthermore, the country's poor communications network would reduce the chances of a large-scale advance to the south. Enraged, Churchill told the military that they must concentrate on 'overcoming the many difficulties' rather than trying to judge 'whether the operation is desirable or not, which must be decided by higher authority'.[51] But the chiefs of staff stuck to their guns, informing the prime minister that 'we cannot at this stage offer a concrete plan'.[52]

The military and the Cabinet were, however, in agreement with Churchill on 11 June that 'we should not attempt any major landing on the Continent this year, unless we intended to stay there'. This stipulation was supposed to rule out suicide missions aimed at drawing off German troops and planes from the Eastern Front (though it did not prevent the disastrous 'hit-and-run' raid on Dieppe on 19 August). It was also agreed – building on the memo given to Molotov the previous day – that the 'Sledgehammer' landing in France in 1942 would only be launched 'in conditions which hold out a good prospect of success'. Churchill added that 'it seemed unlikely that these conditions would obtain'.[53] Armed with this consensus, Churchill flew to America on 17 June to meet Roosevelt for the first time since January. While there, he pressed for an Anglo-American invasion of French Northwest Africa (operation 'Gymnast'), so that the two allies 'would not stand idle in the Atlantic theatre' for the whole of the year.[54] The British exercised effectively a veto power on any cross-Channel attack in 1942: because of the slowness of American mobilization and the demands of the Pacific, most of the troops would be British and Canadian. FDR had always been interested in North Africa, and Churchill's case was strengthened by shocking news that the port of Tobruk and 33,000 troops had surrendered to Rommel's Afrika Korps. By the time Churchill left for home on 25 June, Roosevelt – despite continued opposition from General Marshall – was firmly inclined to 'Gymnast'.

For the moment, this was kept secret from Moscow. Indeed, it is striking that neither leader mentioned the Washington discussions in their next messages to the Kremlin – hardly likely to allay Stalin's ever-lurking suspicions. Churchill continued to jolly the Soviet leader along with friendly noises, including a fulsome message for the anniversary of Nazi Germany's attack on the USSR. Intended as a public relations gesture, the message was published in both the British and the Soviet press.[55]

For his part, Roosevelt did not send an anniversary message, perhaps preferring to avoid more empty rhetoric, but concentrated on trying to sort out the practicalities of the Alaska–Siberia air bridge. The AAF were keen to firm up arrangements in the next few weeks, before the ice set in, including a surreptitious American reconnaissance flight from the US base at Nome in Alaska to scout out the territory. Stalin was agreeable, but, in conversation with Ambassador Standley on 2 July, made clear his continued desire to keep everything low-key for fear of antagonizing Japan. Only Soviet pilots should do the flying, and the planning discussions should be held in Moscow, rather than in both capitals. After the meeting, Standley advised Washington that 'a large military mission will not be welcome at this moment.'[56] Accordingly, in another message composed by the AAF, Roosevelt informed Stalin on 6 July that General Follett Bradley would come to Moscow to handle the discussions for the Americans. Bradley remained until November 1942, while the details were worked out.[57]

On 4 July, Churchill asked Roosevelt to request Stalin to allow forty US Boston bombers – then at Basra, en route to the USSR – to be diverted to British troops in Egypt, facing an imminent German threat to Cairo. 'With Russia in the thick of the battle', the PM admitted to the president, 'this is a hard request and I shall quite understand if you do not feel able to do as I ask.'[58] FDR did pass on the British request, while framing it as a decision for Stalin to make in the light of the overall Allied war effort. Stalin promptly agreed, and Roosevelt sent a message of thanks – offering an additional 115 medium tanks as compensation. Churchill also expressed his gratitude for what was a striking Soviet gesture of Allied solidarity. Stalin expressed appreciation for the tanks but, characteristically, also took time out to tell the president that US tanks 'catch on fire very easily from the projectiles of anti-tank weapons striking the rear or sides', because they used high-grade and very vaporous gasoline. 'Our specialists', stated Stalin, 'consider that the diesel motor is most suitable for tanks.' FDR expressed his thanks and said that henceforth US tanks would use lower-octane fuel.[59]

Roosevelt to Stalin, sent 5 July 1942, received 6 July 1942[60]

The crisis in Egypt, with its threat to the supply route to Russia, has led Prime Minister Churchill to send me an urgent message asking whether forty A-20 bombers destined for Russia and now in Iraq can be transferred to the battle in Egypt. It is impossible for me to express a judgment of this matter because of limited information here. I am therefore asking you to make the decision in the interest of total war effort.

Stalin to Roosevelt, sent 7 July 1942[61]

In view of the situation in which the Allied forces find themselves in Egypt I have no objection to forty of the A-20 bombers now in Iraq en route to the U.S.S.R. being transferred to the Egyptian front.

Roosevelt to Stalin, sent 9 July 1942, received 10 July 1942[62]

I deeply appreciate your telegram authorizing transfer to Egypt of forty bombers. I am arranging to ship you at once one hundred and fifteen additional medium tanks with ammunition and spare parts. These tanks will be in addition to all tanks going forward as provided in July protocol.

Churchill to Stalin, sent 9 July 1942, received 11 July 1942[63]

I have just heard from President Roosevelt that you have consented to the transfer to our forces in Egypt of 40 Boston bombers which had reached Basra on their way to you. This was a hard request to make to you at this time, and I am deeply obliged to you for your prompt and generous response. They are going straight into the battle, where our aircraft have been taking heavy toll of the enemy.

*****

With relations already tense over the second front, July 1942 saw a major crisis over the Arctic convoys. Convoy PQ17 had sailed from Iceland for Arkhangelsk on 27 June. On the evening of 4 July, when it was in Arctic waters near Bear Island, Admiral Sir Dudley Pound, the first sea lord, ordered the convoy to scatter, fearful that the fabled German battleship *Tirpitz* had left its Norwegian port, against the advice of his intelligence staff. It was a fateful decision. Up to this point, the convoy had lost only three of the thirty-four merchant ships that had entered Arctic waters; but after the 'scatter' order, twenty-three were sunk by enemy aircraft or U-boats. Most historians have blamed Pound for his worst-case analysis about the *Tirpitz* and his tendency to micro-manage.[64]

At the time, however, this was covered up. Although the Cabinet's Defence Committee was adamant that there should be no interruption of the Arctic convoys 'when the great battle was raging on the Russian front',[65] the Royal Navy was under pressure to run equally hazardous convoys to Malta, a key stronghold in the battle for the Mediterranean. 'The fate of the island is at stake', Churchill told Pound: Britain must promise the besieged population that 'the Navy will never abandon Malta'.[66] On 13 July, the first sea lord told the Defence Committee bluntly that if the next Russian convoy sailed, he 'could not guarantee that a single ship would get through'. He added that all the chiefs of staff recommended suspension of these convoys for the moment. Faced with such categorical advice, the Defence Committee had little choice. Even Eden concurred, though very worried about the effect on the Russians at this time of three British 'negatives' in quick succession: on a second front in 1942, the diversion of the Boston bombers, and now on the convoys.[67]

On 14 July, Churchill sent Roosevelt the draft of a long message to Stalin about the PQ17 disaster and the decision to suspend Arctic convoys during the summer months of 'perpetual daylight'. FDR replied that he 'reluctantly' agreed with the decision and felt the message 'a good one'.[68] On the evening of the 14th, Ambassador Maisky was invited to dine with Churchill and Pound at Number 10. The PM's mood was grim. 'Three-quarters of the convoy perished – 400 tanks and 300 planes lie on the sea bed!' he exclaimed. 'My heart bleeds.' Having gone against naval advice in sending PQ17, Churchill told Maisky that after such losses the Cabinet had no choice but to suspend the convoys for the moment. Aghast, Maisky asked pointed questions about the 'scatter' order, and insisted that suspension of supplies would be catastrophic for the USSR, just when the German summer offensive had opened. Pound, to whom Maisky 'took the greatest exception', answered back strongly and was supported by Churchill, though 'without much enthusiasm', the ambassador felt.[69]

Churchill fretted and tinkered over his message to Stalin for several days.[70] But the nub of his case remained unchanged: namely, the dire warning at the end of paragraph two that if major battleships were lost, this could jeopardize control of the Atlantic and thus the chances of preparing for 'a really strong second front in 1943'. He tried to strike positive notes, talking about plans to drive the Germans out of northern Norway and to offer air support on Russia's 'southern flank', while admitting that nothing would be possible until the autumn, because of the need for darkness in the north and the imperative of beating Rommel in Egypt.

The PM also raised another sensitive question: the movement of three Polish divisions from the USSR to Palestine. These units had been formed in the summer of 1941, following the thaw in Soviet–Polish relations, mediated by Britain, after 'Barbarossa'. Stalin released Polish prisoners of war from Soviet camps and allowed them to form their own military units under the command of General Władysław Anders – himself fresh from the Lubyanka – and then in March 1942 agreed that Anders' army could gradually move to the Middle East. On 30 June, Molotov formally arranged with Clark Kerr the transfer of the three divisions to the British Army.[71] Although grateful for these reinforcements, Churchill was unhappy that they came with their family members – and he made both these points at the end of his long message to Stalin.

Churchill to Stalin, sent 17 July 1942, received 18 July 1942[72]

We began running small convoys to North Russia in August 1941 and, until December, the Germans did not take any steps to interfere with them. From February 1942 the size of the convoys was increased, and the Germans then moved a considerable force of U-boats and a large number of aircraft to Northern Norway and made determined attacks on the convoys. By giving the convoys the strongest possible escort of destroyers and anti-submarine craft, the convoys got through with varying but not prohibitive losses. It is evident that the Germans were dissatisfied with the results which were being achieved by means of aircraft and U-boats alone, because they began to use their surface forces against the convoys. Luckily for us, however, at the outset they made use of their heavy surface forces to the westward of Bear Island and their submarines to the eastward. The Home Fleet was thus in a position to prevent an attack by enemy surface forces. Before the May convoy was sent off, the Admiralty warned us that losses would be very severe if, as was expected, the Germans employed their surface forces to the eastward of Bear Island. We decided, however, to sail the convoy. An attack by surface ships did not materialise, and the convoy got through with a loss of one-sixth, chiefly from air attack. In the case of P.Q. 17, however, the Germans at last used their forces in the manner we had always feared. They concentrated their U-boats to the westward of Bear Island and reserved their surface forces for attack to the eastward of Bear Island. The final story of P.Q. 17 convoy is not yet clear. At the moment only four ships have arrived at Archangel, but six others are in Nova [sic] Zemlya harbours. The latter may, however, be attacked from the air at any time. At the best therefore only one-third will have survived.

I must explain the dangers and difficulties of these convoy operations when the enemy battle-squadron takes its station in the extreme North. We do not think it right to risk our Home Fleet eastward of Bear Island or where it can be brought under the attack of the powerful German shore-based aircraft. If one or two of our very few most powerful battleships were to be lost, or even seriously damaged, while the Tirpitz and her consorts, soon to be joined by the Scharnhorst, remained in action, the whole command of the Atlantic would be lost. Besides affecting the food supplies by which we live, our war effort would be crippled; and, above all, the great convoys of American troops across the ocean, rising presently to as many as 80,000 in a month would be prevented and the building up of a really strong second front in 1943 rendered impossible.

My naval advisers tell me that if they had the handling of the German surface, submarine and air forces in present circumstances, they would guarantee the complete destruction of any convoy to North Russia. They have not been able so far to hold out hopes that convoys attempting to make the passage in perpetual daylight would fare better than P.Q. 17. It is therefore with the greatest regret that we have reached the conclusion that to attempt to run the next convoy, P.Q. 18, would bring no benefit to you and would only involve dead loss to the common cause. At the same time, I give you my assurance that, if we can devise arrangements which give a reasonable chance of at least a fair proportion of the contents of the convoys reaching you, we will start them again at once. The crux of the problem is to make the Barents

Sea as dangerous for German warships as they make it for ourselves. This is what we should aim at doing with our joint resources. I should like to send a senior officer shortly to North Russia to confer with your officers and make a plan.

Meanwhile, we are prepared to despatch immediately to the Persian Gulf some of the ships which were to have sailed in P.Q. convoy. The selection of ships would be made in consultation with Soviet authorities in London, in order that priorities of cargo may be agreed. If fighter aircraft (Hurricanes and Aircobras [sic]) are selected, can you operate and maintain them on the Southern Front? We could undertake to assemble them at Basra. We hope to increase the through-clearance capacity of the Trans-Persian routes so as to reach 75,000 tons monthly by October, and are making efforts to obtain a further increase. We are asking the United States Government to help us by expediting the despatch of the rolling-stock and trucks. An increased volume of traffic would be handled at once if you would agree to American trucks for U.S.S.R., now being assembled in the Persian Gulf, being used as a shuttle service for transporting goods by road between the Gulf and the Caspian. In order to ensure the full use of capacity, we agree to raise the figure of loadings due to arrive in September to 95,000 tons and October to 100,000 tons, both exclusive of trucks and aircraft.

Your telegram to me on 20th June referred to combined operations in the North. The obstacles to sending further convoys at the present time equally prevent our sending land forces and air forces for operations in Northern Norway. But our officers should forthwith consider together what combined operations may be possible in or after October when there is a reasonable amount of darkness. It would be better if you could send your officers here, but if this is impossible ours will come to you.

In addition to a combined operation in the North, we are studying how to help on your southern flank. If we can beat back Rommel, we might be able to send powerful air forces in the autumn to operate on the left of your line. The difficulties of maintaining these forces over the Trans-Persian route without reducing your supplies will clearly be considerable, but I hope to put detailed proposals before you in the near future. We must first beat Rommel. The battle is now intense.

Let me once again express my thanks for the forty Bostons. The Germans are constantly sending more men and aircraft to Africa; but large reinforcements are approaching General Auchinleck and the impending arrival of strong British and American heavy bomber aircraft forces should give security to the Eastern Mediterranean as well as obstruct Rommel's supply ports of Tobruk and Benghazi.

I am sure it would be in our common interest, Premier Stalin, to have the three divisions of Poles you so kindly offered join their compatriots in Palestine, where we can arm them fully. These would play a most important part in the future fighting, as well as in keeping the Turks in good heart by a sense of growing numbers to the southward. I hope this project of yours, which we greatly value, will not fall to the ground on account of the Poles wanting to bring with the troops a considerable mass of their women and children, who are largely dependent on the rations of the Polish soldiers. The feeding of these dependants will be a considerable burden to us. We think it well worth while bearing that burden for the sake of forming this Polish army which will be used faithfully for our common advantage. We are very hard up for food ourselves in the Levant area, but there is enough in India if we can bring it there.

If we do not get the Poles we should have to fill their places by drawing on preparations now going forward on a vast scale for Anglo-American mass invasion of the Continent. These preparations have already led the Germans to withdraw two heavy bomber groups from South Russia to France. Believe me, there is nothing that is useful and sensible that we and the Americans will not do to help you in your grand struggle. The President and I are ceaselessly searching for means of overcoming the extraordinary difficulties which the geography, sea-water and the enemy's air power interposes. I have shown this telegram to the President.

Meanwhile in Washington, Sumner Welles, FDR's closest adviser in the State Department, seems to have become concerned at the bureaucratic nature of the correspondence between the White House and the Kremlin. FDR had not really followed up his assertion in March that 'I can handle Stalin'. On his own initiative, Welles drafted a letter for FDR to send to Stalin introducing General Bradley, hailing the new North Pacific air route, and representing the Bradley mission as a kind of surrogate for a personal meeting between the two of them. In the opening paragraph of the letter, which Roosevelt signed on 20 July, the president stated: 'It is still a matter of deep regret to me that thus far the pressure of events has rendered it impossible for us to meet and personally discuss various matters vitally affecting the common interests of the United States and the Soviet Union.'[73] There can be little doubt that these words, though prepared by Welles, came from FDR's heart. In the end, however, the president decided not to send the letter.

While the Roosevelt–Stalin correspondence remained little more than businesslike, Churchill's prolix attempts to justify British policy caught the Kremlin on the raw. After the Soviet disasters at Kharkov and in the Crimea in late May, on 28 June the Wehrmacht launched its summer offensive towards the Caucasus (operation 'Blue'). As in 1941, initial German success was compounded by Soviet intelligence failures. Stalin and the general staff were convinced that Hitler's main target would be Moscow, and they were slow to redeploy reserves to the south, even after capturing a full set of operational orders when a German plane crash-landed behind Soviet lines on 19 June. Stalin dismissed this as a 'plant' – part of German deception measures. He rejected one request for reinforcements with the scathing response, 'If they sold divisions in the market, I'd buy you five or six, but unfortunately they don't.'[74] As late as 5 July, the Stavka was convinced that the new offensive was just a feint before the main thrust against the Soviet capital. On the 7th, German forces reached the Don at Voronezh and then turned south down to Rostov at the mouth of the Don. After the city fell on 23 July, Hitler divided his forces, ordering Army Group A south to take the Caucasus oilfields, while Army Group B drove east to seize Stalingrad. In retrospect, German commanders identified the Führer's act of hubris as the beginning of the Stalingrad debacle; but at the time, it looked as if the Germans were carrying all before them. What military historians David Glantz and Jonathan House call 'the near-panic of this period' is illustrated by Stalin's order No. 227, *Ni Shagu Nazad!* ('Not One Step Back!') of 28 July. 'Panic-mongers and cowards must be destroyed on the spot. The retreat mentality must be decisively eliminated.' Anyone who surrendered was a 'traitor to the motherland' and must be summarily shot or transferred to a penal battalion. 'Blocking units' just behind the front line were to enforce the order, under instructions to shoot any soldier who wavered.[75]

It was amid this crisis that Churchill's wordy message of 17 July was received in the Kremlin, just before the fall of Rostov-on-Don. Stalin saw it as a double betrayal – the British were suspending Russia's Arctic supply line and refusing to mount a second front in 1942. Maisky, deeply disheartened, advised that when replying it was necessary to state 'that we were in fact being left to the mercy of fate by our Allies in the most critical moment for us'. He urged Stalin to take 'a hard stand' with Churchill, making it clear that 'if the second front is not opened in 1942, the war may be lost, or at the very least the USSR will be weakened to such an extent as to be unable to take an active part in the struggle'. Although Maisky found Stalin's eventual reply 'somewhat gentler' than he had expected, it was, in fact, another calculatedly undiplomatic message. Apart from putting his finger on the Admiralty's mishandling of PQ17, Stalin accused Britain of a lack both of 'goodwill' towards its ally and of readiness to fulfil its 'contracted obligations'. He came close to insinuations of cowardice. Nothing of the sort had been sent since November 1941.[76]

Although composed in the heat of the moment, Churchill's message and Stalin's rebuttal illustrated some fundamental differences in the two countries' approaches to the war. British wariness about the convoys and the second front reflected the concerns of an island nation, for which the sea lanes, and therefore the navy, were central to its security. For this, there was no parallel in the Russian experience – nor could there be for an essentially continental power. And Stalin's cold assertion that 'risk and losses' were the name of the game in warfare reflected not only a realistic approach to war, but also a cavalier attitude to human losses that could not be shared by a democratic leader, especially in Britain, which was still haunted by the ghosts of the Somme and Passchendaele.

Stalin to Churchill, sent 23 July 1942, received 23 July 1942[77]

I received your message of July 17. Two conclusions could be drawn from it. First, the British Government refuses to continue the sending of war materials to the Soviet Union via the Northern route. Secondly, in spite of the agreed communiqué concerning the urgent tasks of creating a Second Front in 1942, the British Government postpones this matter until 1943.

Our naval experts consider the reasons put forward to justify the cessation of convoys to the northern ports of the USSR wholly unconvincing. They are of the opinion that, with goodwill and readiness to fulfil the contracted obligations, these convoys could be regularly undertaken and heavy losses could be inflicted on the enemy. Our experts find it also difficult to understand and explain the order given by the Admiralty that the escorting vessels of the P.Q. 17 should return whereas the cargo boats should disperse and try to reach the Soviet ports one by one without any protection at all. Of course I do not think that regular convoys to the Soviet Northern ports could be effected without risk or losses. But in war no important undertaking could be effected without risk or losses. [You know, of course, that the Soviet Union is suffering far greater losses.[78]] In any case I never expected that the British will stop despatch of war materials to us just at the very moment when the Soviet Union, in view of the very serious situation on the Soviet–German front, requires these materials more than ever. It is obvious that the transport via Persian Gulf could in no way compensate for the cessation of convoys to the Northern ports.

With regard to the second question, i.e. the question of creating a second front in Europe, I am afraid it is not being treated with the seriousness it deserves. Taking fully into account the present position on the Soviet–German front, I must say in the most emphatic manner that the Soviet Government cannot acquiesce in the postponement of a second front in Europe until 1943.

I hope you will not feel offended that I expressed frankly and honestly my own opinion, as well as the opinion of my colleagues, on the points raised in your message.

Stalin's message was handed to Churchill by Maisky that evening at 10 Downing Street. The premier was in a bad mood, having received disheartening news from Egypt. After three weeks of bitter fighting, Rommel's advance had been halted at El Alamein, but despite vastly superior forces, the British Eighth Army had not been able to inflict a decisive defeat. 'In his distress,' Maisky noted,

> Churchill must have had a drop too much whisky. I could tell from his face, eyes and gestures. At times his head shook in a strange way, betraying the fact that in essence he is already an old man and that it won't be long before he starts sliding downhill fast. It is only a terrific exertion of will that Churchill remains fit for the fight.

After reading the message, the prime minister was both 'depressed and offended' – being particularly wounded by the charge of breaking obligations. He told the ambassador that he would not have accepted a message phrased in such terms, but for the stern fight of the Russians against Nazi Germany. The following evening, the War Cabinet echoed Churchill's indignation, but agreed with him that no reply should be sent, because 'a wrangle' would be 'of no advantage to either of us'. However, the perceived inaccuracies in Stalin's charges were carefully listed, and it was agreed that these should be conveyed orally to Maisky, together with a detailed briefing on the convoy problems.[79]

As with the similar clash in November 1941, it was Maisky and Eden – the diplomatic professionals – who moved things on. 'Two great men have clashed,' the foreign secretary remarked to the ambassador with a faint smile on 24 July. 'They've had a tiff ... You and I need to reconcile them ... Too bad they've never met face to face!' Maisky reflected in his diary: 'Churchill is hot-tempered, but he is easily appeased. After his initial emotional reaction, he begins to think and calculate like a statesman' and 'in the end he arrives at the necessary conclusions'. After the flare-up in late 1941, that process of reflection had led to Eden's visit to Moscow in December, Molotov's return visit to London and the signing of the Anglo-Soviet treaty. 'What will be the outcome of this?' Maisky pondered. 'We shall see.'[80]

Roosevelt was also prodding Churchill to think more capaciously, observing in a telegram on 29 July:

> We have got always to bear in mind the personality of our ally and the very difficult and dangerous situation that confronts him. No one can be expected to approach the war from a world point of view whose country has been invaded. I think we should try to put ourselves in his place. I think he

should be told, in the first place, quite specifically that we have determined on a course of action in 1942.[81]

Roosevelt was referring to the recent conclusion of the protracted 'essay contest' between London and Washington over operations in 1942. Over the previous two weeks, the British and American military had finally agreed to mount operation 'Torch', the new name for 'Gymnast', against French Northwest Africa that autumn. The US Army still favoured a limited cross-Channel attack in 1942: this would keep the focus on France for the major assault in 1942, and also aid the Russians. General Dwight Eisenhower, then head of War Department planning, believed that even if the odds of a successful landing were only one in two, and of maintaining a beachhead one in five, such risks would be justified by the 'prize' of keeping Russia in the war. This was an approach to losses closer to Stalin's view than to that of Churchill. The problem remained that most of the losses would not be American, so US planners were in a weak position in the transatlantic argument. After the American Joint Chiefs of Staff (JCS) returned empty-handed from another abortive visit to London in mid-July, they argued that the USA should now concentrate on the war against Japan. 'Just because the Americans can't have a massacre in France this year', Churchill sneered, 'they want to sulk and bathe in the Pacific.' Roosevelt, however, was determined that there must be action in Europe against Germany in 1942. In his most assertive act as commander-in-chief, FDR overruled the JCS and accepted Churchill's plans for Northwest Africa – confident, like the PM, that doing so would not prevent a full-scale invasion of France in 1943. By the end of July, therefore, they had something more concrete to tell Stalin.[82]

As Eden had hinted, there was also a strong feeling in the Foreign Office that Churchill should do the telling in person. Alarmed by the new coolness in relations, and fearful that Molotov had not relayed the British position accurately to Stalin, Ambassador Clark Kerr urged a face-to-face meeting between the leaders. If, he argued, no second front was projected for 1942, it would be necessary to explain the Anglo-American position in detail to Stalin and 'no one could do so more convincingly than the Prime Minister'. He also felt that a visit by one of Russia's Western allies might prove essential to shore up morale. 'If things continue to go badly and Russian morale crumbles, the visit may be the only hope to tip the scales.' Sir Alexander Cadogan, the permanent under-secretary at the Foreign Office, supported the idea of a prime ministerial visit. He was not sure how to play it, however, whether to 'lay our cards on the table for the Russians' or just try to 'calm' them. The former, he wrote, was very risky, but the latter, would 'doom the Prime Minister to an extremely unpleasant trip'. Cadogan did not believe the Russians would be content any longer with promises of 'jam tomorrow', adding 'I don't see how we are going to hold the next 3 months or so without exposing our hand a bit more to the Soviets.'[83]

Eden showed Clark Kerr's telegram to Churchill and supported the idea of a personal meeting with Stalin, especially since the trip could be combined with the visit to Egypt that the PM was already planning. Churchill, a believer in personal diplomacy who also loved exciting adventures, jumped at the idea, according to Eden. The foreign secretary told the War Cabinet that he thought a meeting with Stalin 'would be of the greatest value' and his colleagues agreed, though they were concerned about whether the PM's heart would stand the strain.[84]

At 12.30 a.m. on the night of 30–31 July, Maisky received a phone call asking him to come to 10 Downing Street immediately. Churchill was in what Maisky called 'one of those moods when his wit begins to sparkle with benevolent irony and when he becomes awfully charming'. With an impish smile, Churchill showed Maisky a piece of paper. 'Take a look. Is it any use?' The ambassador scanned it quickly. 'But of course! It's worth a great deal, a very great deal!' he responded. This was the text of the PM's message to Stalin, making encouraging noises about a resumption of the convoys in September and proposing a meeting between them to review the war together. As Churchill sat back sipping whisky and puffing contentedly on his 'irreplaceable' cigar, Maisky reflected that his earlier calculations had been 'fully vindicated': the PM had 'cooled down' and was now focused on meeting Stalin. The ambassador said he would cable the message to Moscow immediately.[85]

Churchill to Stalin, sent 31 July 1942, received 31 July 1942[86]

We are making preliminary arrangements (see my immediately following message) to make another effort to run a large convoy through to Archangel in the first week of September.

I am willing, if you invite me, to come myself to meet you in Astrakhan, the Caucasus, or similar convenient meeting-place. We could then survey the war together and take decisions hand-in-hand. I could then tell you plans we have made with President Roosevelt for offensive action in 1942. I would bring the Chief of the Imperial General Staff with me.

I am starting for Cairo forthwith. I have serious business there, as you may imagine. From there I will, if you desire it, fix a convenient date for our meeting, which might, so far as I am concerned, be between the 10th and 13th August, all being well.

The War Cabinet have endorsed my proposals.

Churchill's supplementary message made it clear that the hoped-for resumption of the Arctic convoys depended on the Soviets honouring their promises to provide air cover. The message can therefore be seen as a delicate riposte to Stalin's accusations about how the British had broken their obligations.

Churchill to Stalin, sent 31 July 1942, received 31 July 1942[87]

My immediately preceding message.

We are taking preliminary steps for sailing a convoy of 40 ships during the first week of September. I must make it clear, however, that there is little chance of even one-third of the ships getting through to you, as was the case in PQ17, unless the air threat to the German surface fleet in the Barents Sea is such as to deter the latter from operating against the convoy. As you are no doubt aware the situation has been discussed with Maisky and I understand the latter has communicated to you what we consider the minimum air cover to be indispensable.

Stalin replied to both Churchill's messages as soon as he received them. He seemed pleased with the premier's willingness to discuss the urgent questions in person, and asked Churchill to come to Moscow because he and his military staff could not leave the capital at such a critical moment. On the convoys, Stalin treated Churchill's message as a firm commitment to resume sailings in September, but promised to take 'all possible measures' to increase air cover.

Stalin to Churchill, sent 31 July 1942, received 31 July 1942[88]

On behalf of the Soviet Government I invite you to the USSR to meet the members of the Government. I should be very grateful if you could come to the USSR to consider jointly the urgent questions of war against Hitler, as the menace from these quarters to Great Britain, the United States, and the USSR has now reached a special degree of intensity.

I think the most suitable meeting-place would be Moscow, as neither I nor the members of the Government and the leading men of the General Staff could leave the capital at the moment of such an intense struggle against the Germans.

The presence of the Chief of the Imperial General Staff would be extremely desirable.

The date of the meeting please fix yourself in accordance with the time necessary for completion of your business in Cairo. You may be sure beforehand that any date will suit me.

Let me express my gratitude for your consent to send the next convoy with the war materials for the USSR at the beginning of September. In spite of the extreme difficulty of diverting aircraft from the battle-front, we will take all possible measures to increase the aerial protection of the convoy.

The message was cabled to Maisky on 31 July, for transmission to Eden, because Churchill had already left London for Cairo.[89] Privately, the foreign secretary expressed the hope that Maisky could join Churchill for his talks with Stalin:

> It would be so good if you could be their interpreter! One must be able to translate not only the words but the spirit of a conversation! You have the gift! The prime minister was telling me that when you interpreted during our talks with Molotov, he had the impression that the language barrier between him and Molotov had fallen, that it no longer existed.[90]

But Maisky's star was now waning in Moscow and he was not invited.

After more than a year of their wary alliance, during which Eden and Beaverbrook, Maisky and Molotov had acted in various ways as mutual interpreters, the 'two great men' (in Eden's sardonic phrase) were finally about to meet. It would prove a stormy and momentous encounter.

5

CHURCHILL'S 'LUMP OF ICE'

(August to October 1942)

DURING THE SUMMER AND autumn of 1942, relations between the Allies were largely determined by the situation at the fronts in this truly global war, and the mood fluctuated between periods of coldness and thaw. The main axis of communication was still between Stalin and Churchill, who continued to play the role of chief representative of the Western Allies but now in person, rather than on paper, with his trip to Moscow on 12–16 August 1942. What Churchill said in 1950 in his memoirs rings true: 'I pondered on my mission to this sullen, sinister Bolshevik State I had once tried so hard to strangle at its birth, and which, until Hitler appeared, I had regarded as the mortal foe of civilised freedom. What was it my duty to say to them?' The message he was bearing – 'No Second Front in 1942' – seemed like 'carrying a large lump of ice to the North Pole', yet the prime minister said he had felt sure it was his 'duty to tell them the facts personally and have it all out face to face with Stalin rather than trust to telegrams and intermediaries'.[1]

Duty or not, Churchill was right about the importance of meeting face to face. From now on, their correspondence would always be coloured by this personal contact. After a final boozy dinner in Stalin's apartment, Churchill left Moscow with a formidable hangover, but, more durably, an indelible impression of the dictator's strategic acumen and human magnetism. Charmed by the unexpectedly warm and personal hospitality on that last evening, after some bruising moments during the visit, he became convinced that he had finally met the 'real Stalin', and had 'looked into' his 'soul' or 'heart'. After that meeting, he told Ambassador Archibald Clark Kerr and his personal doctor

Lord Moran that Stalin was a 'great man' – 'I was taken into the family,' he exulted. 'We ended as friends.'[2] Even when the euphoria of that moment had evaporated, the prime minister was ready to explain Stalin's inflammatory statements against his allies as the effect of pressure from shadowy colleagues, such as the 'Council of Commissars.'[3] Within this 'two Stalins' perspective, he persuaded himself that Stalin, despite his tetchiness, was essentially a wise and moderate politician, but was periodically impeded by 'dark forces' within the Soviet leadership.

On the other side, so an unusually expansive Molotov told Clark Kerr a few days after the visit, 'Stalin was impressed by the Prime Minister's spirit and dynamic qualities.' Even certain 'rough places' in their talks were beneficial, 'because their roughness came from frankness and sincerity – two things that were essential as a foundation of understanding'. Hitherto, said the foreign minister, the two leaders 'had known each other only through the telegrams they had exchanged', but now that they had met and 'talked without reserve each one would be able to put a nice value on the messages of the other and to read them with completer understanding'.[4] That said, personal contact did not change Stalin's fundamental suspicion of Churchill – evident in his message to Maisky on 28 October, quoted near the end of this chapter.

The 'two Stalins' trope was also picked up at times by Averell Harriman, Roosevelt's special emissary, but it was keenly contested by the US ambassador in Moscow, Admiral Standley,[5] who was also at odds with the White House over what he called FDR's 'Santa Claus' attitude to Stalin – an open-handed approach to aid, within the limits of the resources available, rather than strictly quid pro quo. Standley was also aggrieved at being bypassed by another pair of presidential emissaries, Wendell Willkie and Patrick Hurley, who replicated Hopkins and Harriman a year before. This pattern reflected both Roosevelt's continued dislike for State Department channels and also the continuing failure of the Wheelchair President to forge a direct relationship with Stalin on paper or in person. Roosevelt had not been able to join Churchill in Moscow and lagged far behind the prime minister in the number and length of messages. There was, for instance, a long hiatus in communications from the White House between 22 August and 5 October – and neither of those messages were telegrams about policy, but rather letters of introduction, sent by hand. Moreover, in contrast with the Roosevelt– Standley impasse, the prime minister took advice from his ambassador in Moscow both verbally and in writing. On the other hand, Stalin's less frequent messages to Roosevelt again display flashes of warmth that are rarely found in his fuller and more businesslike correspondence with Churchill.

Despite the positive vibes after the August visit and Churchill's efforts to talk up how he had persuaded Stalin of the merits of 'Torch' in French Northwest Africa, the Kremlin continued to resent the failure to mount a second front in France in 1942. By October, relations had become extremely tense, because of another postponement of the Arctic convoys (this time on account of 'Torch') and the abrupt transfer by the British to the Americans of 150 Airacobra fighter planes which had been promised for the Stalingrad front. There were also new recriminations about Rudolf Hess, Hitler's deputy who had fled to Britain mysteriously on the eve of 'Barbarossa': these resurrected earlier suspicions about an Anglo-German conspiracy. The root problem in Big Three relations, as in the autumn of 1941, was the dire situation on the Soviet–German front, this time at Stalingrad, where the German Sixth Army was gradually occupying the city in a brutal siege. Stalin became almost totally immersed in the crisis, fretting about the lack of air cover and brooding over the planned counter-offensive scheduled for November.

In the totality of the war, the battle for Stalin's city was of a strategic magnitude and symbolic significance that eclipsed all else. But his two allies were also preoccupied with their own strategic crises, each of which were of real political moment. For Churchill it was the threat from the Afrika Korps in Egypt. 'Rommel, Rommel, Rommel, Rommel', he shouted on 8 August, marching around the embassy in Cairo. 'What else matters but beating him?' Throughout September and October, the PM chafed impatiently for the opening of a counter-offensive at Alamein.[6] And both he and Roosevelt, having debated for months the strategy and logistics for 'Torch', waited anxiously for the landings in Morocco and Algeria to take place. The president hoped (vainly) for a start date before the mid-term congressional elections on 3 November, to give his Democratic party a much-needed boost.

In these circumstances, it was hard for Churchill and Roosevelt to understand Stalin's preoccupations, or for the Soviet leader to get the measure of his allies. In early October FDR entertained fleeting fears that Stalin might seek a separate peace with Berlin; later in the month, Churchill and his Cabinet (in 'two Stalins' mode) speculated that the Red Army might now be playing a larger and more baleful role in Soviet foreign policy. The curtness of Stalin's messages (in reality a consequence of his focus on Stalingrad) occasioned particular debate in London – at an almost comical level in the case of the two-sentence telegram from the Kremlin on 13 October. For its part, Moscow exaggerated the mendacity of the British, suspecting them of deliberately seeking to undermine the Soviet Union. Those bleeding to death found it difficult to understand the reluctance of the Western Allies to spill some of their own blood against a common enemy at a critical point in the war. Even surrogate help could be misinterpreted. The offer to establish an Anglo-American air force in the Caucasus evoked memories in Moscow of the British occupation of Baku in 1918–19, during the Russian Civil War. American keenness for an Alaska–Siberia air bridge (ALSIB) to ferry aircraft expeditiously to the Russians aroused suspicions for a while that the USA was trying to entangle the USSR in its war with Japan.

Despite occasional wobbles, the Americans and British did not seriously doubt Russian chances of survival in 1942. There was concern in the late summer about the fragility of defences along the Caucasus, which might allow a German drive into Turkey and the Near East, but essentially both military commands believed that the USSR was likely to hold out and, even in the worst-case scenario, would draw off the main forces of the Wehrmacht.[7] Both leaders agreed. 'It looks as if Hitler's campaign against Russia will be a great disappointment to him,' Churchill remarked to Wavell on 7 October. 'I feel very sure the Russians are going to hold out this Winter,' Roosevelt told Churchill on 27 October, 'and that we should proceed vigorously with our plans both to supply them and to set up an air force to fight with them.'[8] Given such underlying confidence in Soviet survival, aid to Russia could never have the existential importance in London and Washington that Moscow demanded.

*****

When he received Stalin's invitation of 31 July to visit Moscow, Churchill was delighted, accepting with alacrity.

Churchill to Stalin, sent 1 August 1942, received 1 August 1942[9]

I will certainly come to Moscow to meet you, and will fix the date from Cairo.

Churchill had originally planned that his visit to Moscow would take place between 10 and 13 August, as mentioned in his message of 30 July. But he was forced to prolong his stay in Cairo because of the difficulties of finding a new commander for the embattled Eighth Army – a post that eventually went to Brooke's protégé, General Bernard Montgomery. He did not leave Cairo until 10 August, flying via Tehran, where liaison had to be arranged with Soviet air command for the journey to Moscow.

The prime minister did not want Britain to take all the blame for the absence of a second front in Europe in 1942. On 4 August, he told FDR: 'I should greatly like to have your aid and countenance in my talks with Joe. Would you be able to let Averell come with me? I feel that things would be easier if we all seemed to be together. I have a somewhat raw job.' The initiative here had come from Harriman, who felt strongly about the need to show British–American solidarity on the second front issue and, with Eden's support, tried the idea on Roosevelt. The president initially felt that it might create suspicion that Harriman was 'acting as an observer' – checking up on Churchill because of insufficient trust – but when the prime minister, primed by Eden, also made the request himself, FDR readily agreed and notified Stalin. Harriman caught up with the PM in Cairo on 8 August.[10]

Roosevelt to Stalin, sent 5 August 1942, received 6 August 1942[11]

I am asking Mr Harriman [to] proceed to Moscow to be at disposal of yourself and your visitor to help in any possible way.

Roosevelt often preceded the arrival of American representatives in the USSR with personal letters to Stalin in which he briefly described the purpose of the visit and the personality and political views of the visitor. Support from Wendell Willkie – the Republican candidate in the election of 1940 – was important for the president. Their foreign policy views coincided in many respects: they agreed that the United States could not revert to isolationism, and both were also keen critics of European colonialism. Roosevelt wanted Willkie to endorse his ideas about rapprochement between the USSR and the USA and to help, as titular head of the Republican party, in propagating them in America. The italicized words about Roosevelt's policy being one of 'real friendship with your government' were added by FDR to the typescript draft.[12]

Roosevelt to Stalin, sent 8 August 1942, received 9 August 1942[13]

I should like to have your frank opinion on the following plan which I think may be useful:

I am sending Mr Wendell Willkie to visit the Governments in Egypt, Saudi Arabia, Syria, Turkey, Iraq and Iran for the primary purpose of explaining to the Governments of these smaller countries the danger they run in a German victory and that their greatest hope for the future lies in the defeat of Nazi domination of the places of the Near East and the Middle East.

Mr Willkie much wants to visit the Soviet Union for a wholly different purpose. He wants to know about the wonderful progress made by the Russian people, in addition to seeing for himself the undying unity of thought in repelling the invader and the great sacrifices all of you are making.

He is, as you know, my recent opponent in the 1940 elections and is the head of the minority party today. He is greatly helping in war work and is heart and soul with my Administration in our foreign policy of opposition to Nazism *and real friendship with your government*. Personally I think that for the sake of the present and the future a visit by him to the Soviet Union would be a good thing. He would fly to the Soviet Union during the first half of September.

Please tell me confidentially and frankly if you would care to have him come for a very short visit.

Stalin reacted favourably – Willkie was known in Moscow as an active supporter of the president's foreign policy – and sent a brief reply promising that the American politician would be 'most cordially received'.[14]

Meanwhile Churchill was wending his circuitous way from Cairo via Tehran to Moscow in a converted Liberator bomber, without heating and with a mattress and some blankets on a shelf instead of a bed. The plane was not soundproof, and so it was virtually impossible to make oneself understood over the roar of the engines: he and Harriman passed notes to and fro. Above 12,000 feet, they had to suck on oxygen masks. Along the Mediterranean, across the Caspian and up the Volga, there was always a risk from stray German fighters. The US General Douglas MacArthur, no Anglophile, commented later that Churchill deserved a Victoria Cross, Britain's highest gallantry award, for the journey alone.[15] After a long day's flight from Tehran, guided by two Russian officers, the plane landed at Moscow's Central Airport about 5 p.m. on 12 August, to be welcomed by Molotov and other officials, diplomats and journalists. There was a guard of honour, and a band played the national anthems of the three Allies in turn. Brooke and his military staff, together with Sir Alexander Cadogan from the Foreign Office, did not arrive until a day later, because their Liberator had to return to Tehran due to a malfunction. They were eventually transported to Moscow in a more luxurious Soviet passenger plane (an American Douglas DC-3), equipped with armchairs, a gramophone and a Persian carpet on the floor.

Given his arrival late in the day after a taxing journey, the prime minister could easily have postponed seeing Stalin until next morning. But that was not Churchill's nature. Pumped up with excitement, he was driven to the Kremlin for his first encounter with the Soviet leader at 7 p.m. on 12 August. Harriman was also in attendance (plate 11).[16] The first two hours, during which Churchill explained in detail why there would be no cross-Channel attack in 1942, were, in his own words, 'bleak and sombre'.[17] Stalin insisted that one could not win a war without taking risks, nor really train troops without bloodying them in battle. Having got the bad news out of the way, the prime minister then explained operation 'Torch', even sketching a crocodile to depict his idea of attacking the 'soft belly' of the Axis in the Mediterranean, before striking at its 'hard snout' in France. Churchill felt that they parted after four hours in an atmosphere of goodwill. He returned to 'State Villa No. 7' (Stalin's dacha at Kuntsevo, which had been placed at his disposal during the visit) tired but elated.

At noon on 13 August, Churchill met Molotov to explain in more detail Britain's planned military operations, especially the convoy to relieve the siege of Malta and the RAF raids on Hitler's Europe. He also conveyed this to Stalin in a summary memo.[18] That evening, he went to the Kremlin at 11 p.m. for his second meeting. Stalin immediately handed him an aide-mémoire, which developed in a formal manner the criticisms he had made the previous evening, echoing in turn his letter of 23 July. The Soviet leader accused Churchill of breaking a promise made in June about opening a second front in 1942 and underlined the consequent damage to Russian morale and to the Red Army's operations. He even made the very serious charge that the Soviet high command had planned their military operations for the summer and autumn of 1942 on the expectation of a second front that year. Interestingly, this point was omitted, presumably in error, from the English translation of Stalin's aide-mémoire that Churchill sent to London and is shown below in square brackets. It clearly came up in the conversation, and the PM explicitly rebutted the idea in his written reply of 14 August.

Stalin to Churchill, sent 13 August 1942, received 13 August 1942[19]

As the result of an exchange of views in Moscow which took place on August 12th of this year, I ascertained that the Prime Minister of Great Britain, Mr Churchill, considered the organisation of a second front in Europe in 1942 to be impossible. As is well known the organisation of a Second Front in Europe in 1942 was pre-decided during the sojourn of Molotov in London, and it found expression in the agreed Anglo-Soviet Communiqué published on June 12th last. It is also known that the organisation of a Second Front in Europe has as its object the withdrawal of German forces from the Eastern Front to the West and the creation in the West of a serious base of resistance to the German-Fascist forces, and the affording of relief by this means to the situation of the Soviet forces on the Soviet–German front in 1942. [Needless to say, the Soviet High Command, in planning its summer and autumn operations, counted on a second front being opened in Europe in 1942.][20]

It is easy to grasp that the refusal of the British Government to open a second front in Europe in 1942 inflicts a moral blow to the whole of Soviet public opinion, which calculates on the creation of a Second Front, and that complicates the situation of the Red Army at the front and prejudices the plan of the Soviet Command. I am not referring to the fact that the difficulties arising for the Red Army as a result of the refusal to open a second front in 1942 will undoubtedly be detrimental to the military situation of England and the remaining Allies. It appears to me and my colleagues that the most favourable conditions exist in 1942 for the creation of the Second Front in Europe, inasmuch as seeing almost all the forces of the German army and the best forces to boot, have been withdrawn to the Eastern Front, leaving Europe an inconsiderable amount of forces, and these of inferior quality. It is unknown whether 1943 will offer conditions for opening a second front as favourable as 1942.

We are of the opinion therefore that it is particularly in 1942 that the creation of a Second Front in Europe is possible and should be effective. I was however unfortunately unsuccessful in convincing Mr Prime Minister of Great Britain thereof, while Mr Harriman, the representative of the President of the U.S.A, fully supported Mr Prime Minister in the negotiations held in Moscow.

After the document had been translated verbally and Churchill said he would respond in writing, Stalin launched into an extended critique of the British, indicting them of broken promises about supplies and the second front, and even implying that British soldiers were scared to fight. In the measured paraphrase of the British minutes, 'he felt that if the British Army had been fighting the Germans as much as the Russian Army, it would not be so frightened of them'. All this Stalin delivered, characteristically, in a low voice, rarely if ever looking his interlocutor in the eye. The bad effect was enhanced by poor translation: Major Charles Dunlop, the British interpreter, was translating Churchill into Russian, while Pavlov, his Russian counterpart, was rendering Stalin in English – both in violation of normal practice that an interpreter translates from a foreign language into his own. Churchill called Pavlov 'a very poor substitute for Maisky'. Bristling at Stalin's criticisms and frustrated by the halting translation, the PM eventually exploded into impassioned defence of his own sincerity, including a reminder that Britain had had to fight alone for a year in 1940–41. The tirade went on for about five minutes, during which neither interpreter had taken a note. Cadogan attempted a brief paraphrase, but Stalin, smiling, cut him off: 'I do not understand the words, but by God I like your spirit.' Somewhat stiffly, the conversation moved on to military matters and the meeting eventually ended about 12.45 a.m.

Churchill went to bed angry and confused about how to read Stalin's erratic moods.[21]

Next day, he sent the following analysis to the War Cabinet in London:

We asked ourselves what was the explanation of this performance and transformation from the good ground we had reached the night before. I think the most probable is that his Council of Commissars did not take the news I brought as well as he did. They perhaps have more power than we suppose and less knowledge. And that he was putting himself on the record for future purposes and for their benefit and also letting off steam for his own. Cadogan says a similar hardening up followed the opening of the Eden interview at Christmas, and Harriman says that this technique was also used at the beginning of the Beaverbrook mission.[22]

The idea of 'two Stalins' – friendly in person, but confrontational when pressed by his colleagues – dates from this time. British and American visitors also became used to the hot–cold technique of Soviet diplomacy. Looking back years later, Brooke offered another explanation. He surmised that 'Stalin insulted Winston with the purpose of finding out what his reactions would be, and of sizing up what kind of man he was' – and was then favourably 'impressed' by Churchill's outburst.[23] Whatever the explanation for Stalin's conduct at the second meeting – political, tactical or personal – at the time it left Churchill in a deeply aggrieved state.

What did the Soviet political and military leadership really think in the summer of 1942 about the possibility of an early second front? It is difficult to give a conclusive answer. On the one hand, Soviet diplomats and intelligence officers did not entertain high hopes. On 16 July, Maisky cabled from London: '1. In this year's campaign, we have to rely only on ourselves. 2. There will not be an effective second front in 1942 – except if Hitler collapses in the coming months and there is a scramble to get to Berlin, but it is too early to say.'[24] Litvinov wrote with similar pessimism on 30 July, after a meeting with Roosevelt: 'All this strengthens my conviction that the question of the second front cannot be budged.'[25] And on 31 July, a 'resident NKVD spy' sent the following information: 'The British Cabinet Defence Committee during its meeting on 25 July decided not to open a second front this year.'[26] Looking back in 1976, Molotov asserted bluntly that neither he nor Stalin believed in such a possibility, and said that they had pressured the Anglo-Americans on the matter only to gain moral advantage and obtain concessions on other issues.[27]

On the other hand, during Molotov's visit to Washington in May and June 1942, Stalin told him to accept Roosevelt's proposal to reduce US supplies to the USSR in order to prepare for the opening of a second front, although his foreign minister warned that this could lead to neither the second front nor deliveries.[28] It is unlikely that the supreme commander would have agreed to such a sacrifice at such a desperate moment if he had not believed FDR's assurances. Also relevant is Stalin's reaction to a report from Kirill Novikov, a counsellor at the Soviet embassy in London, who warned that Churchill was coming to Moscow to explain the Allies' refusal to open a second front in 1942. 'It can't be that the Allies refuse to open a second front this year,' Stalin commented.[29] It is possible that by putting the screws on Churchill in Moscow, the Soviet leader still hoped to force a change in his position, although he must have understood that it would take months to prepare such a large-scale operation. Whatever Stalin's thinking, though, he had nothing to lose by expressing his indignation. At the very least, it would shame Churchill and force him to defend and justify himself.

As promised, Churchill responded to the main points of Stalin's message in a memorandum on 14 August that built on what he had said at the Kremlin two days earlier. The mode of argument was characteristically Churchillian – casuistical, sometimes internally contradictory, but pugnacious. The prime minister sought to represent 'Torch' as a 'second front' against the Germans. This was strictly true, but he was using the term in a very different sense from Stalin, who only meant a large-scale assault on France. Churchill insisted that even the small 'Sledgehammer' lodgement operation on the Cherbourg Peninsula was likely to end in 'disaster' – meaning that this ruled it out because British opinion would not tolerate a 'futile' bloodbath. For Stalin, habituated to bloodbaths, such an argument was not decisive if the operation had a diversionary effect. In the second paragraph, Churchill argued that even a successful lodgement would 'not bring even a single division back from Russia'; two paragraphs later, he claimed that 'all the talk' about 'Sledgehammer' had misled Hitler and forced him to hold 'large air forces and considerable military forces on the French channel coast'. And responding to the charge of bad faith, he highlighted what he had said in his confidential aide-mémoire for Molotov on 10 June, namely that the British could give 'no promise' about 1942. Stalin, by contrast, placed his weight on the optimistic (if ambiguous) wording in both the American and British communiqués after Molotov's visits (4 June and 11 June) – noting that, unlike the aide-mémoire, those were public statements and therefore had an impact on morale.[30]

Churchill to Stalin, sent 14 August 1942, received 14 August 1942[31]

The best second front in 1942, and the only large-scale operation possible from the Atlantic, is 'Torch'. If this can be effected in October, it will give more aid to Russia than any other plan. It also prepares the way for 1943 and has the four advantages mentioned by Premier Stalin in the conversation of August 12th. The British and United States Governments have made up their minds about this and all preparations are proceeding with the utmost speed.

Compared with 'Torch', the attack with 6 or 8 Anglo-American Divisions on the Cherbourg Peninsula and the Channel Islands would be a hazardous and futile operation. The Germans have enough troops in the West to block us in this narrow peninsula with fortified lines, and would concentrate all their air forces in the West upon it. In the opinion of all the British Naval, Military and Air authorities the operation could only end in disaster. Even if the lodgment were made, it would not bring a single division back from Russia. It would also be far more a running sore for us than for the enemy, and would use up wastefully and wantonly the key men and the landing craft required for real action in 1943. This is our settled view. The CIGS [chief of the imperial general staff] will go into details with the Russian Commanders to any extent that may be desired.

No promise has been broken by Great Britain or the United States. I point to paragraph 5 of my Aide-Memoire given to Mr Molotov on the 10th June, 1942, which distinctly says: 'We can, therefore, give no promise.' This Aide-Memoire followed upon lengthy conversations, in which the very small chance of such a plan being adopted was made abundantly clear. Several of these conversations are on record.

However, all the talk about an Anglo-American invasion of France this year has misled the enemy, and has held large air forces and considerable military forces on the French Channel coast. It would be injurious to all common interests, especially Russian interests, if any public controversy arose in which it would be necessary for the British Government to unfold to the Nation the crushing arguments which they conceive themselves to possess against 'Sledgehammer'. Widespread discouragement would be caused to the Russian armies who have been buoyed up on this subject, and the enemy would be free to withdraw further forces from the West. The wisest course is to use 'Sledgehammer' as a blind for 'Torch', and proclaim 'Torch', when it begins, as the second front. This is what we ourselves mean to do.

We cannot admit that the conversations with Mr Molotov about the second front, safeguarded as they were by reservations both oral and written, formed any ground for altering the strategic plans of the Russian High Command.

We reaffirm our resolve to aid our Russian allies by every practicable means.

In addition to the aide-mémoire, Churchill sent another message to Stalin on 14 August, updating losses on the Malta convoy (operation 'Pedestal'). He was keen to show that the British were also shedding blood in the war. And given Malta's strategic importance for Britain amid the crisis in Egypt and planning for 'Torch', it was inevitable that he attached more importance to 'Pedestal' than to the Arctic convoys. 'Prolongation of life of Malta was worth the heavy cost,' Churchill cabled Pound on 15 August.[32] The day before, the Combined Chiefs of Staff in Washington gave the northern convoys the lowest priority in the allocation of merchant vessels and naval escorts.[33]

Sending Stalin his aide-mémoire about the second front had not proved cathartic for Churchill. Tired, frustrated, even petulant about what Stalin had said at their second meeting, he talked of going home straight away and sulked through most of a bibulous Kremlin banquet on the evening of the 14th. Apparently appreciating that he needed to make some amends, Stalin said at one point 'I am a rough man, not an experienced one like you', and asked that his 'roughness' not be misunderstood. The PM put on a pleasant face for some photographs taken with the Soviet leader, but then immersed himself in official papers, before suddenly saying 'Goodbye' and marching out, forcing Stalin almost to trot in order to keep up with him all the way to the waiting car. Back at the dacha, Churchill had a row with Cadogan about the proposed communiqué, told his doctor Lord Moran that he'd 'had enough' and 'ought not to have come', and announced he would not go near Stalin again. 'Goodbye' not 'Good night' was, he stated, quite deliberate.[34]

Next morning, both Moran and Cadogan urged Clark Kerr to intercede and ensure that Churchill met Stalin again before he left: reports of a rift among the Big Three would be disastrous for the Allied cause. The ambassador took his courage in both hands and enticed the grumpy Churchill outside for a walk – less confrontational than talking face to face, and also away from the Russian bugging devices. According to Clark Kerr's diary account, 'I talked, and he stomped in front of me among the fir trees. I addressed myself to a pink and swollen neck and a pair of hunched shoulders.' The ambassador said he had urged the PM to come to Moscow because he felt that 'immense good' would come from a personal meeting with Stalin. He told the neck that, having had 'great faith' in him, now he felt 'disappointed'. The shoulders turned round for a moment. Clark Kerr explained that at the first meeting Churchill had used his 'charm' to 'admirable effect', but then on day two had let Stalin get under his skin. You are 'an aristocrat and a man of the world', the ambassador told the PM, whereas the Russians were 'straight from the plough or the lathe ... rough and inexperienced'. Yet instead of loftily recognizing this, Churchill had taken offence. Another stop and stare. And this time a response: 'That man has insulted me. From now on he will have to fight his battles alone ... I represent a great country and I am not submissive by nature.' Clark Kerr pressed again. Had Churchill considered the consequences if Russia went down for want of Allied support? How many young British and American lives would have to be sacrificed to make this good? He must not 'leave Russia in the lurch', whatever Stalin had said to hurt his pride. Gradually Churchill mellowed. Seizing his chance, Clark Kerr asked him to tell Stalin he wanted another talk, just the two of them: given the Soviet leader's conciliatory mood the previous evening, such a meeting was likely to go well, especially if Churchill turned on the charm again. Suddenly the prime minister strode back to the dacha and summoned Cadogan to join them. Pointing at Clark Kerr, he declared: 'He says it's all my fault.' Then he chuckled. The black mood had clearly passed. Pavlov was summoned and within minutes a meeting was fixed up for 7 p.m. that evening at the Kremlin.[35]

The talk was businesslike, but after about ninety minutes Churchill got up to leave, explaining that his plane would take off at dawn next morning. Stalin then suggested they have a farewell drink or two. Churchill said he was 'in principle always in favour of such a policy', and so the two men adjourned to the Soviet leader's apartments on the other side of the Kremlin. In attendance was Churchill's new interpreter, Major Arthur Birse – son of a Scottish businessman and a Russian mother, born and raised in St Petersburg, who had fought for the Whites in the Civil War and now served with the British military mission in Moscow. Birse, though not a professional translator, was bilingual: as well as interpreting fluently, he also chatted easily with Molotov and even Stalin, despite his thick Georgian accent – which Birse likened to hearing 'a native of the remote Highlands of Scotland' speaking English. Churchill immediately warmed to Birse as 'a very good interpreter' and used him at all subsequent meetings with Stalin.[36]

In the private apartments, Churchill met the Soviet leader's daughter Svetlana – 'a handsome red-haired girl', as he described her – and then for the next few hours sampled a rolling banquet of 'choice dishes' and 'excellent wines', topped off about 1.30 a.m. by a 'suckling pig', into which Stalin hacked with gusto. Apart from a few gibes about the Royal Navy and the Arctic convoys, the Boss was in good humour – possibly heeding Maisky's advice that the key to getting on with Churchill was having 'a purely private chat on varied themes'. Topics of conversation included operations in Norway, the conference communiqué, Munich, Maisky ('he speaks too much', grunted Stalin), the liquidation of the kulak peasants in the 1930s, and a possible visit by Stalin to London

(Churchill promised 'a magnificent reception'). When the PM waxed eloquent about the military genius of his ancestor John Churchill, first duke of Marlborough and scourge of Louis XIV's armies, Stalin – with what Birse called 'a sly, mischievous look' – said he thought the duke of Wellington was 'a greater general' because he had defeated Napoleon, 'the greatest menace of all time'. Churchill also had a laugh at Roosevelt's expense, saying that when the president finally met Stalin, FDR 'would probably want him to do something about God!' Stalin, according to Birse, 'replied that he personally respected God and hoped that with God's help they would achieve victory'. (This exchange was omitted from the official British record.) The PM eventually escaped about 2.30 a.m., drove back to the dacha for a quick change, and got to the airport just in time to depart on schedule at 5.30. By then, to quote his memoirs, Churchill had 'a splitting headache, which for me was very unusual'. He was able to sleep off his hangover during the flight back to Tehran.[37]

Before flying on to Cairo, Churchill sent an appreciative message of thanks, which Clark Kerr delivered via Molotov.[38]

Churchill to Stalin, sent 16 August 1942, received 17 August 1942[39]

On arriving at Tehran after a swift and smooth flight I take occasion to thank you for your comradeship and hospitality. I am very glad I came to Moscow, firstly because it was my duty to tell the tale, and secondly because I feel sure our contacts will play a helpful part in furthering our cause. Give my regards to Molotov.

That final, late-night conversation with Stalin left a lasting impression on Churchill. 'I had a very good interpreter and was able to talk much more easily,' he cabled FDR and the Cabinet. 'The greatest good will prevailed and for the first time we got on to easy and friendly terms. I feel I have established a personal relationship which will be helpful.' Later, when back home, he was even franker to Maisky: 'All these formal meetings, minutes, experts and other things – all this is nonsense. It is important to know the soul of the person with whom you work. On that evening, or rather night, I saw Stalin's soul.'[40] Leaving aside the uncanny parallel with President George W. Bush's response when asked in 2001 about how he got on with Vladimir Putin,[41] there is no doubt that Churchill left Moscow convinced that he could work man-to-man with Stalin – as long as the dark political forces in the Kremlin allowed them to do so (the 'two Stalins' theory).

*****

Roosevelt regretted not being able to participate personally in the Moscow meeting. During the banquet on 14 August, Harriman reminded Stalin that the president was keen to meet him, and the Soviet leader replied that such a meeting was 'of great importance'. He expressed hope that it could take place during the winter, when he was 'not so preoccupied', perhaps in Iceland in December.[42]

Resuming their correspondence on 18 August, Roosevelt alluded to the recent US landings in the Solomon Islands, but stressed his conviction that Germany was 'our real enemy' and that Russia was 'bearing the brunt of the fighting and the losses'. His promise of one thousand tanks was welcomed in Moscow because of US tardiness compared with Britain in fulfilling its obligations hitherto. The italicized passages were inserted by FDR himself, in an effort to make the message seem more personal, even though most of the phrases must have sounded like empty rhetoric in Moscow.[43]

Roosevelt to Stalin, sent 18 August 1942, received 19 August 1942[44]

I am sorry that I could not have joined with you and the Prime Minister in the Moscow conferences. I am well aware of the urgent necessities of the military situation, particularly as it relates to the situation on the Russian front.

I believe that we have a toehold in the Southwest Pacific from which it will be very difficult for the Japanese to dislodge us. Our naval losses there were substantial but it was worth it to gain the advantage which we have. We are going to press them hard.

On the other hand, I know *very well* that our real enemy is Germany and that our force and power must be brought against Hitler at the earliest possible moment. You can be sure that this will be done *just as soon as it is humanly possible to put together the transportation.*

In the meantime, over 1,000 tanks will leave the United States in August for Russia, and other critical supplies, including airplanes, are going forward.

The United States understands that Russia is bearing the brunt of the fighting and the losses this year. We are filled with admiration of your magnificent resistance. Believe me when I tell you that we are coming as strongly and as quickly as we possibly can.

As usual, Stalin's response was brief and to the point. He highlighted the USSR's current need for trucks, on which the USA had fallen well behind the Moscow Protocol schedule, and also alluded deftly to the importance of more Arctic convoys.[45]

Stalin to Roosevelt, sent 22 August 1942, received 23 August 1942[46]

I have your message of August 18. I also regret you could not have participated in the conversations I recently had with Mr Churchill.

In connection with your remarks regarding shipment from United States during August of tanks and war materials, I would like to emphasize our special interest at present time in receiving from U.S. aircraft and types of armaments and also trucks, in greatest possible quantity. Furthermore, I hope all measures will be taken to guarantee most expeditious delivery of goods to Soviet Union especially by northern sea route.

Anxious to maintain some impression of personal contact, on the 22nd Roosevelt sent another chatty message, updating Stalin on plans for the visit by Wendell Willkie, discussed earlier in the month.[47]

On the night of 30 August, Rommel's forces launched an offensive south of El Alamein. For Germany, the battle of Alam Halfa was the last chance to rout the British Eighth Army before the arrival of Allied reinforcements. Churchill promptly notified Stalin, and sent an identical message to Roosevelt.[48]

The success in mid-August – albeit at heavy cost – of operation 'Pedestal' to relieve Malta allowed the redeployment of British naval forces to provide a powerful escort for the new convoy PQ18. Writing to Stalin on 6 September, Churchill emphasized the serious preparations for the convoy. To protect the forty merchant vessels, the British were deploying seventy-seven warships – an unprecedented number – including, for the first time, an escort carrier to provide direct air cover.[49] In his letter, Churchill also reported on the situation in Egypt, where Rommel's offensive had finally petered out. Contrary to Churchill's hopes in the message, the British counter-attack and operation 'Torch' had to be postponed for logistical reasons. The Eighth Army's new commander, General Bernard Montgomery, was determined to build up his forces and delayed his offensive against Rommel until 23 October; while 'Torch' did not commence until 8 November.

Casting around for other news to please Stalin, Churchill returned to the question of sending Anglo-American air forces to the southern flank of the Soviet–German front – which he and Harriman had raised when in Moscow.[50] Writing to Roosevelt on 30 August, he described the project as 'a long term policy in our cooperation with Russia and for the defence of the Persian oil fields'. But it is clear that Churchill's underlying concern was to protect the British Empire's strategic interests. In a note to the chiefs of staff on 23 July, he spoke of placing British forces on the Soviet–German front in order to 'defend the Caspian Sea and the Caucasus Mountains, and to encourage Turkey to preserve neutrality, and thus shield the whole Levant–Caspian sector'.[51] However, the idea of sending an Anglo-American air contingent to the region (codenamed 'Velvet') was not well received in Washington, because of commitments in North Africa and the Pacific. Thus, at the time Churchill wrote to Stalin on 6 September, the issue of deploying British and American squadrons to the Caucasus was still under discussion.

Churchill to Stalin, sent 6 September 1942, received 7 September 1942[52]

Convoy PQ18 with 40 ships has started. As we cannot send our heavy ships within range of enemy shore-based aircraft, we are providing a powerful destroyer striking force, which will be used against enemy's surface ships should they attack us east of Bear Island. We are also including in the convoy escort, to assist in protecting it against air attack, an auxiliary aircraft-carrier just completed. Further, we are placing a strong line of submarine patrols between the convoy and the German bases. The risk of an attack by German surface ships still, however, remains serious. This danger can only be effectively warded off by providing in the Barents Sea air striking forces of such strength that Germans will not risk their heavy ships any more than we will risk ours in that area. For reconnaissance, we are providing eight Catalina flying boats and three PRU [Photographic Reconnaissance Unit] Spitfires to operate from North Russia. To increase the scale of air attack, we have sent 32 torpedo-carrying aircraft which have suffered loss on the way, though we hope that at least 24 will be available for operation. These with 19 bombers, the 10 torpedo-carrying aircraft, 42 short-range and 43 long-range fighters which we understand you are providing, will almost certainly not be enough to act as a final deterrent. What is needed is more long-range bombers. We quite understand that the immense pressure put upon you on the main line of battle makes it difficult to supply any more Russian army long-range bombers. But we must stress great importance of this convoy in which we are using seventy-seven warships, requiring to take in 15,000 tons of fuel during the operation. If you can transfer more long-range bombers to the North temporarily, please do so. It is most needful for our common interests.

Rommel's attack in Egypt has been sharply rebuffed, and I have good hopes [we] may reach a favourable decision there during the present month.

The operation 'Torch,' though set back about three weeks beyond the earliest date I mentioned to you, is on full blast.

I am awaiting President's answer to definite proposals I have made him for bringing a British–American air contingent into action during winter on your southern flank. He agrees in principle and I am expecting to receive his plans in detail. I will then cable you again. Meanwhile I hope planning with regard to airfields and communications may proceed as was agreed, subject to your approval, by your officers while I was in Moscow. For this purpose we are anxious to send staff officers from Egypt to Moscow, in the first instance, as soon as you are ready for us to do so.

We are watching with lively admiration the continued magnificent resistance of Russian armies. The German losses are certainly heavy and winter is drawing nearer. I shall give, when I address the House of Commons on Tuesday, an account of my visit to Moscow, of which I retain the most pleasing memories, in what I hope you will regard as agreeable terms.

Please give my good wishes to Molotov and thank him for his congratulations on my safe return. May God prosper all our undertakings.

Stalin replied to Churchill next day. He was pleased that convoy PQ18 had sailed and appreciated the importance of its safe arrival in the Soviet Union. Despite the difficult situation on the Soviet–German front, he agreed to the deployment of Soviet long-range bombers to assist in protecting the convoy, as well as destroyers from his Northern Fleet. The safe arrival of most of PQ18 was therefore a notable example of Soviet–British cooperation.

Stalin to Churchill, sent 8 September 1942, received 9 September[53]

I received your message on September 7. I understand all-importance of safe arrival of convoy PQ18 in Soviet Union and necessity of taking measure[s] for its defence. Difficult as it is for us to transfer at the present moment an additional number of long-range bombers for this task, we have decided to do so. Today orders have been given to send additional long-range bombers for the purpose mentioned by you.

I wish you success in the outcome of operations against Rommel in Egypt, and also full success in Operation 'Torch'.

Replying to this on 12 September, Churchill thanked Stalin for allocating additional Soviet air units to protect convoy PQ18. He also detailed the latest tonnage of bombs dropped on Germany by the RAF, anxious to show that the British were striking at the heart of the Reich and knowing from their conversation in Moscow that Stalin was an enthusiast of bombing. Meeting Willkie on 23 September, the Soviet leader said that 'the bombing of Germany is very important, for it undermines the morale of the German population. The bombing undermines Hitler's authority and faith in him.'[54]

But the limited 'thaw' in Soviet–British relations that followed Churchill's visit to Moscow and the sailing of PQ18 was now coming to an end. On 15 September, Maisky received a telegram from Moscow stating that two days earlier the British War Office had notified the Soviet trade mission that it was removing 150 Airacobra P-39 fighters from PQ19 and replacing them with 280 trucks. 'And the British reported that allegedly the Soviet command agreed to this change.'[55] The ambassador was ordered to protest urgently to Eden, and to ensure that the fighters were reloaded on board. On 17 September, Eden told Maisky that the planes had been requested by Eisenhower for 'Torch' and that the transfer of 154 Airacobras, originally earmarked for the USSR from the British share of Lend-Lease, had been made with Churchill's approval. Maisky sought to ensure that 'compensation for the current loss is sent with the convoy no. 20' – lobbying Eden, Beaverbrook and Cripps.[56] The foreign secretary tried to 'mitigate the blows we are compelled to deal them' by offering the Russians additional Albemarles,[57] and also to explain the logistical challenges of the North African landings. 'They are so ignorant of naval matters,' Eden told Churchill, 'that I do not believe that they have hitherto ever understood that we could not, if we really tried, combine "Torch" with convoys and execute both at the same time.'[58] Or, as the prime minister put it pithily to the Commons on 8 September, the Russians were 'land animals', whereas the British were 'sea animals'.[59]

On 20 September, Stalin cabled Maisky:

> I consider English conduct on the question of Airacobras tremendously insolent. The English had no right to divert the cargo without our consent. The Englishmen's claim that the transfer occurred on the orders from the Americans is hypocritical. It is easy to see that the United States acted at the request of the English.'[60]

In fact, the British account was true, but Stalin's indignation is entirely understandable. The Russians had an acute need for fighters, especially on the Stalingrad front, where the Germans enjoyed marked air superiority. Moreover, in a similar situation in July, Stalin had given in to the Allies by transferring to them forty Bostons. He cabled Maisky in late October, 'I have little faith in operation "Torch". If, contrary to expectations, this operation succeeds, one can agree with the fact that the aircraft was taken from us for this operation.'[61]

The commander of the US Army Air Forces, General 'Hap' Arnold, received a mild warning from the management committee of the Soviet supply protocol, urging him to take account of 'the Russian temperament and the situation in which they are' and 'to limit the diversion of equipment intended for Russia as much as possible'.[62] But this was easier said than done, given the voracious demands of global war in the Mediterranean and the Pacific. At this point even Churchill began to get the message about logistics. On 21 September, he had a long briefing from Eisenhower when, apparently 'for the first time', Ike told Marshall confidentially, the PM became 'acutely conscious of the inescapable costs of TORCH' for other operations. Not only would it require cessation of the Arctic convoys for at least several months, it also called into question a second front in France in 1943. Although Marshall had made the latter point repeatedly, as did the Combined Chiefs of Staff in a definitive memo in June, Churchill 'expresses himself now as very much astonished to find out that TORCH practically eliminates any opportunity for a 1943 ROUNDUP'. For more than two hours Ike went over with the PM 'all the additional costs involved in the opening of a new theatre, in establishing a second line of communications, in building up new port and base facilities and in the longer turn-around for ships'.[63]

That night Churchill sent an anxious, rambling cable to Roosevelt. Although forty ships were already loaded for PQ19, it was now clear that the convoy could not be sent without delaying 'Torch' by three weeks. 'The time has therefore come to tell Stalin, first that there will be no PQ19 and secondly we cannot run any more PQ's till the end of the year, that is January. This is a formidable moment in Anglo-American-Soviet relations', he told the president. 'We are solemnly pledged to the supply of Russia and the most grave consequences might flow from failure to make good.' Churchill also alluded lightly to the implications for a second front in 1943. 'I gained the impression at the conference that ROUNDUP was not only delayed or impinged upon by TORCH but was to be regarded as definitely off for 1943. This will be another tremendous blow for Stalin.' Churchill therefore wanted to send a cable to the Kremlin coupling notification of an end to Arctic convoys until January with an offer to begin planning for a landing in Norway (operation 'Jupiter') – one of his obsessive hobby-horses that appalled both the British and the American military.[64]

Churchill's message arrived at the White House when Roosevelt was away on a two-week tour of the American heartland and West Coast (17 September to 1 October), officially to visit defence plants, but also to drum up votes for Democrats in the imminent mid-term congressional elections. Hopkins sent a rapid holding cable to 10 Downing Street: 'Urge very strongly that message to Stalin not be sent until you hear from President. Seems clear that what is said to Stalin now and what firm commitments we are prepared to make may be turning point in the war.'[65] Churchill therefore decided to delay his announcement about the suspension of convoys, and instead sent Stalin some intelligence titbits about monthly aircraft production in Germany and about possible German naval operations in the Caspian Sea.[66]

Stalin's reply on 3 October was like a cold shower, warning about the deteriorating situation at Stalingrad, where the German Sixth Army had opened a new offensive against the factory district in the north of the city, just a couple of miles from the Volga river. The Germans enjoyed significant superiority in most areas, with about 1,000 tanks to 700, and 10,000 guns and mortars against 7,000. Their air superiority, which Stalin estimated at two to one, was actually even greater – 1,000 aircraft against 389.[67] Because of this, in his letter Stalin emphasized the need for British and American fighters, even temporarily forgoing tanks and artillery; he personally inserted in the draft explicit mention of Spitfires and Airacobras.[68] There was an almost plaintive tone to some of the sentences: 'Even the bravest troops are helpless if they lack air protection.' The Soviet leader had told Willkie bluntly on 23 September that 'our recent failures in the south are explained by the lack of fighter air force, which is crucial.'[69]

Stalin also mentioned the safe arrival of convoy PQ18; most of the ships had reached Arkhangelsk on 21 September. Overall, the convoy lost thirteen merchant ships out of forty-four. Foreign Trade Commissar Anastas Mikoyan told Stalin caustically, '12 out of 13 ships were sunk in the area defended by the English.'[70] At the end of the message, Stalin expressed his opinion about the British intelligence on German combat aircraft production, estimating the figure at 2,500 not 1,300.[71]

Stalin to Churchill, sent 3 October 1942, received 3 October 1942[72]

I have to inform you that the situation in the Stalingrad area has deteriorated since the beginning of September. The Germans were able to concentrate in this area great reserves of aviation and in this way managed to secure superiority in the air of ratio 2:1. We had not enough fighters for the protection of our forces from the air. Even the bravest troops are helpless if they lack air protection. We more particularly require Spitfires and Aircobras [sic]. I told about all of that in great detail to Mr Wendell Willkie.

The ships with arms arrived at Archangel and are being unloaded. This is a great help. In view, however, of the shortage of tonnage we would be prepared temporary [sic] to forgo some forms of assistance and this way to reduce the amount of tonnage necessary if there could be secured the increased number of fighter aircraft. We would be prepared temporary to forgo our claims on tanks and artillery equipment if Great Britain and the USA could supply us with 800 fighters a month (approximately Great Britain 300 and the USA 500). Such a help would be more effective and would improve position at the front.

The information of your Intelligence to the effect that Germany manufactures not more than 1,300 combat machines a month is not confirmed by our sources. According to our information, the German aircraft works, together with the works in the occupied countries engaged in making of aircraft parts, are producing not less than 2,500 combat machines a month.

During the autumn, plans for the Alaska–Siberia air bridge – discussed by Roosevelt and Stalin in June and July – were gradually thrashed out. Although General Follett Bradley had flown from Washington to Moscow on 26 July, his negotiations did not proceed smoothly, and on several occasions came close to collapse.[73] The Soviets remained wary, as Molotov and Mikoyan noted to Litvinov, of the 'suspicious efforts of some Americans to inflate the significance of the route hoping to complicate our relationship with Japan'.[74] However, after Stalin met Bradley on 6 October, and representatives of the US War Department and the Soviet military mission in Washington discussed the matter on 8 October, the situation changed for the better, and at the end of October 1942 the route was inaugurated.[75] Although the ALSIB air bridge did not reach its target of 142 planes a month until April 1943, it would eventually play a major role in wartime aid. More than 8,000 US planes – over 50 per cent of the total provided to the USSR – arrived via this route (plate 10).[76]

Although Roosevelt was closely involved in Churchill's correspondence with Stalin over the PQ convoys, he did not communicate directly with the Kremlin for seven weeks after his message of 18 August. When he wrote again, on 5 October, it was to introduce yet another new personal emissary. Formerly secretary of war in the Hoover administration (1929–33), Patrick Hurley was a Republican from Oklahoma and a political ally of the president, who employed him as a personal envoy on a series of wartime missions until Hurley disgraced himself as a drunken buffoon while ambassador to China in 1944–45. To Stalin, Roosevelt used the pretext that Hurley was en route to the Antipodes and needed to convince the Australians and New Zealanders about the wisdom of the 'Germany First' strategy and the centrality of Russia's fight against Hitler, but the letter was mostly 'flannel'. (In fact, Hurley never actually reached New Zealand.) 'Hurley's task, like other envoys before him,' notes Warren Kimball, 'was to check Stalin's political pulse and to offer reassurances to the Soviet leader that the Americans would stay the course.'[77] The president also hoped that Hurley could glean first-hand information about the situation on the

Soviet–German front, about which the Soviets remained exceedingly cagey. The letter, drafted by Sumner Welles in his usual prolix style, was signed by Roosevelt on 5 October.[78] Hurley eventually handed it to Stalin during a long personal meeting on 14 November. He was then taken on a ten-day tour of the Stalingrad front, sending back a detailed report to FDR on 8 December.[79]

Roosevelt to Stalin, sent 5 October 1942, received 14 November 1942[80]

My dear Mr Stalin: I am giving this letter of presentation to you to General Patrick J. Hurley, former Secretary of War and at present United States Minister to New Zealand.

General Hurley is returning to his post in New Zealand and I have felt it to be of the highest importance that, prior to his return, he should be afforded the opportunity of visiting Moscow and of learning, so far as may be possible, through his own eyes the most significant aspects of our present world strategy. I wish him in this way, as a result of his personal experiences, to be able to assure the Government of New Zealand and likewise the Government of Australia that the most effective manner in which the United Nations can join in defeating Hitler is through the rendering of all possible assistance to the gallant Russian armies, who have so brilliantly withstood the attacks of Hitler's armies.

I have requested General Hurley likewise to visit Egypt, as well as Iran and Iraq, in order that he might thus personally familiarize himself with that portion of the Middle East and see for himself the campaign which is being carried on in that area.

As you know, the Governments of Australia and of New Zealand have been inclined to believe that it was imperative that an immediate and all-out attack should be made by the United Nations against Japan. What I wish General Hurley to be able to say to those two Governments after his visit to the Soviet Union is that the best strategy for the United Nations to pursue is for them first to join in making possible the defeat of Hitler and that this is the best and surest way of insuring the defeat of Japan.

I send you my heartiest congratulations on the magnificent achievements of the Soviet armies and my best wishes for your continued welfare.

Ambassador Standley was not in the loop about the Hurley visit. Earlier, he had been repeatedly snubbed by Willkie and not even informed about the content of the latter's conversation with Stalin.[81] Furious at being marginalized as a mere message-boy, and at odds with what he considered Roosevelt's policy of giving the USSR all it requested while asking virtually nothing in return, the ambassador decided to fly home and make his case in person. Meeting Standley on 6 October, Stalin asked him to take a message for the president, in which the Soviet leader developed ideas already mentioned to FDR on 22 August and Churchill on 3 October, as well as during his talk with Willkie on 23 September – highlighting the USSR's acute needs for fighters, trucks and aluminium, and employing similar figures.[82] A relatively new element, however, was the idea of letting the Soviet Union have US merchant ships to deliver goods via Vladivostok. The Americans could not deliver military cargo to Vladivostok, because they were at war with Japan.

The Kremlin did not, however, wait for Standley to deliver the message in person. On 8 October, Molotov sent it via the Soviet embassy in Washington: 'Since Standley will arrive in Washington probably not earlier than a week from now, you should go to Roosevelt and deliver the message from Comrade Stalin, explaining that you are doing so because of the urgency of the issues raised in the letter.'[83] On 11 October, the text was delivered to Hopkins in the White House.[84]

It is revealing of the jittery mood in Washington that news of Standley's trip alarmed FDR. He feared that the ambassador might be carrying a top-secret message from Stalin about a possible separate peace with Germany if the Allies did not increase their help to the USSR. Roosevelt shared his fears with Churchill in a cable on 5 October. The PM was sceptical, replying that he was puzzled as to what message Standley was bringing, but remarking 'I cannot believe it threatens a separate peace. So far the Russian campaign has been very adverse to Hitler, and though they [the Russians] are angry with us both they are by no means in despair.'[85]

Stalin to Roosevelt, sent 7 October 1942, received 11 October 1942[86]

Availing myself of the opportunity to send you a personal message afforded by Mr Standley proceeding to Washington, I would like to express a few considerations on the military supplies from the United States to the USSR.

It is reported that the difficulties with supplies are caused primarily by the shortage of shipping. In order to ease the shipping situation, the Soviet Government would agree to certain cuts in the American supplies of armaments to the Soviet Union. We should be prepared temporarily to have discontinued the supplies of tanks, guns, ammunition, revolvers and such like. At the same time, however, we are in extreme need of an increase in the supply of fighter planes of modern types (such as for instance Airacobras) and in getting under all circumstances certain kinds of other supplies. It should be borne in mind that Kittyhawk planes are not up to the mark in the fight against modern German fighter planes.

It would be good if the USA could in any case ensure our getting every month the following supplies:

500 fighters
8 to 10 thousand trucks
5,000 tons of aluminium
4 to 5 thousand tons of explosives.

In addition to this, it is important to get supply during 12 months of two million tons of grain (wheat), and also as much as possible of fats, food concentrates and canned meat. A considerable amount of these foodstuffs could be shipped via Vladivostok on Soviet ships, if the US consented to concede to the USSR at least 20 to 30 ships. I have already spoken to Mr Willkie about all this and am sure that he will communicate it to you.

As regards the situation at the front, you are of course aware that during the last few months the situation grew worse in the south, especially in the Stalingrad sector, due to the shortage of planes, particularly fighter planes. The Germans turned out to have a large reserve of planes. In the South the Germans have at least a double supremacy in the air, which prevents us from giving our troops cover. The practice of the war has shown that the most gallant troops are helpless if they are not shielded from the air.

After Stalin's downbeat 3 October message to Churchill, it was no longer possible to keep delaying news about the PQ convoys. Back from his inspection trip out west, and fearful that Standley might be bearing a message from Stalin about a separate peace, FDR urged Churchill 'most strongly' that they should not tell Stalin that PQ19 was being suspended. He asked the British to explore the idea of sending the convoy in small groups of two or three, with limited escort, in the hope of evading the Germans. 'I think it is better that we take this risk than endanger our whole relations with Russia at this time.' In London, however, the Admiralty made it clear that sending the convoy in small packages would use up as many escorts and that 'possibilities of evasion are slight'. The PM warned FDR that Maisky already knew the fate of PQ19, and told him that, although 'there has been advantage in the delay of a fortnight' in telling Stalin, 'which you proposed, I feel strongly that he should be told now'. On the evening of 7 October, following a discussion in the War Cabinet, he sent FDR a revised draft message to Stalin. After the president rewrote the third paragraph, about the Caucasus, the cable was duly sent by Churchill on the 8th and Roosevelt followed up later that day with another hortatory message of his own.[87]

Churchill to Stalin, sent 8 October 1942, received 9 October 1942[88]

We shall attack in Egypt towards the end of this month and 'Torch' will begin early in November. The effect of these operations must be either (a) to oblige the Germans to send air and land forces to counter our move, or (b) to compel them to accept new position created by our success, which would then create a diversion by threat of attack against Sicily and South of Europe.

Our attack in Egypt will be in good force. 'Torch' will be a heavy operation in which, in addition to United States Navy, 240 British warships and more than half a million men will be engaged. This is all rolling forward irrevocably.

The President and I are anxious to put an Anglo-American force on your southern flank and operate it under strategic control of Soviet High Command. This force would consist of following: British: 9 Fighter Squadrons, 5 Bomber Squadrons. United States: 1 Heavy Bombardment Group, 1 Transport Group. Orders have been issued by us to assemble this force and take their station so that they would be available for combat early in the New Year. Most of this force will come from Egypt as soon as they can be disengaged from the battle there, which we believe will be successful on our part.

In a letter, which M. Maisky delivered to me on the 5th October, you asked for a great increase in fighter aircraft supplies for Russia by this country and the United States. We will send you as soon as possible by the Persian Gulf route 150 Spitfires with equivalent of 50 more in the form of spares to be sent as they become available as a special reinforcement which we cannot repeat. This special reinforcement is over and above protocol supplies by the northern route so far as it can be used. President Roosevelt will cable separately about United States contribution.

I was greatly relieved that so large a proportion of the last convoy reached Archangel safely. This success was achieved only because no less than 77 warships were employed on the operation. Naval protection will be impossible until our impending operations are completed. As necessary escorts are withdrawn from 'Torch' they can again be made available in Northern waters.

Nevertheless, we intend in the meanwhile to do our best to send you supplies by the northern route by means of ships sailed independently instead of in escorted convoys. Arrangements have been made to sail ships from Iceland during the moonless period 28th October to 8th November. Ten of ours are preparing in addition to what Americans will do. The ships will sail singly at about 200-mile intervals, with occasional larger gaps, and rely on evasion and dispersion.

We hope to resume flow of supplies in strongly escorted convoys from January 1943.

It would, of course, greatly help both you and us if Germans could be denied the use of airfields in Northern Norway. If your Staffs could make a good plan, the President and I would at once examine possibility of cooperating up to the limit of our ability.

Roosevelt to Stalin, sent 8 October 1942, received 9 October 1942[89]

The Prime Minister has sent me copy of his message to you.

We are going to move as rapidly as possible to place an air force under your strategic command in the Caucasus. I am now trying to find additional planes for you immediately and will advise you soon.

I am also trying to arrange to have some of our merchant ships transferred to your flag to increase your flow of materials in the Pacific.

I have just ordered an automobile tire plant to be made available to you.

We are sending very substantial reinforcements to the Persian Gulf to increase the flow of supplies over that route and are confident that this can be done. We are sending a large number of engines and other equipment as well as personnel.

I am confident that our contemplated operation will be successful.

Everyone in America is thrilled by the gallant defense of Stalingrad and we are confident that it will succeed.

The Soviet ambassadors in London and Washington did not conceal their dissatisfaction with these messages. Maisky and his naval attaché Rear Admiral Kharlamov lobbied repeatedly for the British to send single ships, arguing that October in the Arctic was a period of darkness, when it was difficult to detect merchant ships from a plane, and the port of Arkhangelsk was still not iced up. Although the Soviet demand for more Spitfires was partially satisfied – halfway if only the planes are considered, or two-thirds if one includes the equivalent of '50 more in the form of spares' – Churchill described the transfer of the 150 fighter planes not as the beginning of a monthly supply, as Stalin had requested, but as one-off assistance. 'As you can see,' Maisky told Moscow, 'the British remain faithful to themselves: to make concessions "piecemeal". In particular, the story with Spitfires is similar to what happened with Hurricanes last year.'[90] In Washington, Litvinov used the references to 'Torch' to remind Roosevelt on 7 October of the Soviets' real goal of a second front. 'I asked,' the ambassador told Moscow,

whether the President believes that the landing was unfeasible. He replied that it would be possible when the enemy forces are weakened. I pointed out that if it gets quiet on the Eastern Front, Hitler will transfer his forces to the west and then the landing would be even less achievable. The President began to say unconvincingly that they are doing what is practically possible, and that Hitler would feel the planned blow on the flank.[91]

Roosevelt appreciated the need to give Stalin a clear answer about the assistance they would provide. Stalin did not need abstract promises; he wanted specific figures and a timetable of deliveries, especially for the all-essential fighters. The Americans were spurred by Churchill's letter of 8 October, which offered additional aircraft in excess of the Second Protocol. On 10 October, Hopkins wrote to Marshall that 'in view of the strategic situation, the President believes it desirable to give a positive answer to Stalin'. Although the 500 aircraft requested in Stalin's letter of 7 October were considered unrealistic, the delivery of 300 additional planes – 100 a month – was deemed feasible.[92]

Roosevelt to Stalin, sent 11 October 1942, received 12 October 1942[93]

Every possibility of increasing the number of fighter planes to be sent to Russia is being examined by me. The fact of the matter is that all Airacobra production is now going to fighting fronts immediately. While these urgent combat requirements make it impossible to increase the number of Airacobras for you at the moment, nevertheless I am hoping to increase our production of this type at the expense of other types in order to give you more planes. Also if our forthcoming operations which you know about turn out as successfully as they promise, we would then be in a position to release fighters.

Our heavy bombardment group has been ordered mobilized immediately for the purpose of operating on your southern flank. These planes and sufficient transports will go to the Caucasus at an early date. This movement will not be contingent on any other operation or commitment. Twenty merchant ships for use in the Pacific are also being made available to you.

In October we will ship to you 276 combat planes and everything possible is being done to expedite these deliveries. I shall telegraph you in a day or so in reference to explosives, aluminum and trucks.

Stalin's cryptic message to Churchill on 13 October produced confusion in Whitehall.

Stalin to Churchill, sent 13 October 1942, received 13 October[94]

I received your message of 9th October. Thank you.

Assuming that this referred to the PM's cable sent on 8 October, London struggled to understand why the Soviet leader had made no comment on Churchill's
concrete offers of an Anglo-American air force on his southern flank, of additional fighters and piecemeal merchantmen on the northern route. Sir Orme
Sargent, deputy under-secretary at the Foreign Office, thought 'Stalin's present
ill-temper and bad manners' were related to grievances about the second front
and perhaps old Bolshevik memories of Allied intervention in the Russian
Civil War stirred up by the offer of planes in the Caucasus.[95] Churchill, however,
thought he detected something more sinister. On 24 October, mulling over the
whole issue in a message to Roosevelt, he confessed himself 'frankly perplexed'
at the 'cryptic thank you' and the 'baffling' silence about his detailed proposals.
'I wonder,' the PM mused, 'whether anything has occurred inside the Soviet
Animal to make it impossible for Stalin to give an effective reply. It may be that
the Russian army has acquired a new footing in the Soviet machine.' Here
was another echo of the 'two Stalins' idea. Roosevelt, however, did not share
Churchill's anxieties. 'I am not unduly disturbed about our respective responses
or lack of responses from Moscow,' he replied on the 27th. 'I have decided that
they do not use speech for the same purposes that we do.'[96] And so, whereas it
had been the prime minister early in October who brushed away the president's frisson of anxiety about a possible Soviet compromise peace, it was FDR
three weeks later who calmed Churchill's momentary panic about some kind of
Kremlin power struggle. Both leaders were living on their nerves in that month
before 'Torch' and Alamein.

So what was behind Stalin's delphic response of 13 October? Documents
from his archive reveal that the Soviet leader carefully read Churchill's long
letter dated 8 October, underlining its most important parts, as well as what
was actually a translation error by Pavlov – who hastily transliterated the word
'diversion' in paragraph one as 'subversion' (*diversiya* in Russian).[97] Thus, he
knew its contents but chose not to answer himself, entrusting the matter to
Molotov, who eventually abandoned a draft complaining about reduced air
deliveries and simply sent the brief two-sentence acknowledgement.[98]

All this reveals not some deep political reason, which the British tried so
hard to discern, but the fact that Stalin and Molotov were intensely busy with
other more urgent matters. Stalin's main concern was to obtain the quickest
and most substantial help in the fight against Germany. By 13 October, he was
denied both a second front in Europe in 1942 and full convoys. He may not
have been against other forms of assistance, such as an Anglo-American air
force in the Caucasus or the operation in northern Norway. However, these
required coordination, negotiation and, most importantly, time to prepare and

execute, and were therefore immaterial at the moment. So Stalin and Molotov probably felt that a brief acknowledgement was preferable to yet more enervating exchanges with the prime minister.

On 14 October, Roosevelt followed up his message of the 11th with details about the delivery of trucks, explosives, wheat and other supplies.[99] The response was a terse acknowledgement by Molotov, similar to the one he had sent to Churchill. The point, once again, was clear: words were now irrelevant. Both literally and figuratively, it was time for the Allies to deliver.

Stalin to Roosevelt, sent 15 October 1942, received 16 October 1942[100]

I am in receipt of your message of 12 October and thank you for your communication.

Stalin to Roosevelt, sent 19 October 1942, received 21 October 1942[101]

I have received your message of October 16. My answer has been delayed because matters connected with the front have diverted my attention. The whole business now [is] entirely a matter of your cargoes reaching the Soviet Union within the time stated.

Stalin's October 1942 messages are among the most laconic in his correspondence with Churchill and Roosevelt. The situation around Stalingrad was now critical. Although Marshal Zhukov was preparing his grand pincers operation to encircle the besieging German Sixth Army (operation 'Uranus'), this was not scheduled until early November. On 15 October, a regiment of the 14th Panzer Division reached the bank of the Volga river. This cut off Red Army units to the north and threatened to roll south along the river bank to encircle other units of the embattled Soviet 62nd Army. The shortage of air support, which Stalin had repeatedly lamented to Churchill and Roosevelt, was painfully evident. The 8th Air Army was down to fewer than 200 planes of all types, of which only two dozen were fighters. From 19 October, Soviet diversionary operations were launched north and south of the city, which allowed shattered units to be pulled back across the Volga for rapid regrouping and reinforcement. But these assaults lasted only a few days. It remained an open question whether Stalingrad could hold out until Zhukov was ready to counter-attack.[102] In such circumstances, Stalin and Molotov were not bothered about their pen-pals in London and Washington.

Silence would have been the wisest policy on the Western side, but Churchill and Roosevelt could not restrain themselves. The prime minister contrived a postscript to his message of 8 October, while the president used Admiral Standley's arrival in Washington as his pretext.

Churchill to Stalin, sent 18 October 1942, received 19 October 1942[103]

I should have added that the 150 Spitfires are all armed with 2 cannons and 4 machine-guns.

Roosevelt to Stalin, sent 24 October 1942, received 26 October 1942[104]

Admiral Standley has handed me your personal note, copy of which you had previously sent me. Our ambassador has also given me a very full report of the situation in Russia as he sees it. He confirms reports we have already had of the strength and fighting qualities of your army and the urgent need of the supplies indicated by you. I fully recognize these needs.

To Roosevelt, Molotov sent another terse acknowledgement.[105] Churchill received nothing at all, and he did not write to Stalin again for another month. Under the surface, there was real irritation and suspicion. On 19 October, Stalin cabled Maisky: 'We in Moscow have an impression that Churchill is set on Soviet defeat in order then to connive with Hitler's or Brüning's Germany at the expense of our country.'[106] Maisky dared to disagree with his leader. 'The defeat of the Soviet Union would inevitably mean the end of the British Empire', and so, he said, any deal with Hitler or with Brüning, former chancellor of the Weimar Republic, would be unacceptable to British public opinion and especially Churchill, with his 'rabid anti-German feelings'.[107] On the 28th, Stalin elaborated on his fears:

> I still think that being a supporter of an easy war, Churchill is easily influenced by those who are set on the Soviet defeat, for our country's defeat and a compromise with Germany at the expense of the Soviet Union is the easiest form of war between Britain and Germany.
>
> Of course, the British will then realize that without the Russian front on the European continent, with France out of the game they, meaning the English, are doomed. But when will they realize this?
>
> We shall see.
>
> I doubt the English will support the northern operation. They just talk about it to keep up appearances.
>
> Churchill told us in Moscow that by early spring '43 one million Anglo-American forces would open a second front in Europe. But Churchill

evidently belongs to those statesmen who give a promise easily only to forget about it just as quickly or insolently break it.

He also vowed to bomb Berlin intensively throughout September and October. However, he has not fulfilled his promise and did not even bother to inform Moscow of the reasons for non-compliance.

Well, we shall remember what kind of allies we are dealing with.[108]

The tension in Soviet–British relations revived Stalin's old fears about Britain's collusion with Germany behind the back of the USSR. The prime symbol was Rudolf Hess, who had landed in Britain in May 1941. Soviet intelligence in Germany and Britain carefully monitored developments around Hess's mission; they emphasized his closeness and loyalty to Hitler, they

'The Matter of the Second Front'. On 6 October 1942, *Pravda* also got at the British by publishing veteran cartoonist Boris Yefimov's waspish caricature of a 'Conference of Military Experts'. The blimpish old generals, with names such as 'What-if-they-lick-us?', 'What's-the-hurry?' and 'Why-take-the-risks?', are being lectured by the dashing young 'General Guts' and 'General Decision', who may be intended to look like Americans. The clock is now well past the eleventh hour.

believed his mission had not been a sudden impulse, but a planned and coord-inated act.[109] According to the NKVD's London station, 'as the war progresses, Hess may become the centre of intrigue in favour of a compromise peace, and will be useful for the peace party in England and for Hitler.'[110] It was Hess's potential utility that apparently most troubled the Kremlin: why else would the British continue to offer him safe haven? Churchill most likely 'keeps him in reserve', as Stalin put it to Maisky on 19 October.[111] That day, *Pravda* published an article entitled 'Bring the criminal Hitlerite clique to justice', which asserted that

> the well-known criminal Hess had but to put on the uniform of a Hitlerite pilot and fly to England, and it seems he can now count on being able to hide from the international tribunal and avoid being held responsible for his countless crimes, thus turning England into a refuge for gangsters.[112]

The impetus for this article in *Pravda* was an official declaration made by Molotov on 14 October, in response to a British statement a week earlier regarding the punishment of war criminals. This had been issued after consul-tations with the USA and other Western allies, but not with Moscow. Such peremptory conduct was jarring to the Kremlin leadership. Their declaration stated that

> the Soviet Government considers it necessary to bring to justice without delay in the special international tribunal and to apply the full weight of the criminal law to all the leaders of Nazi Germany, who have already been caught over the course of the war by the authorities of the states, fighting against Nazi Germany.[113]

Among these leaders was Hess. The Soviets demanded his immediate trial.

The *Pravda* article caused indignation in Whitehall, which was at a loss as to why the Kremlin should undertake such an offensive and public démarche, rather than express its concerns privately. Clark Kerr was instructed to protest personally to Stalin. 'Anglo-Soviet relations almost as bad as they can be', noted Harvey in his diary on 26 October. He found the Hess furore deeply implau-sible. 'Do the Russians seriously think we are keeping him for some anti-Soviet move? Hess is quite mad and useless for any purpose.'[114] Eden and Maisky had a frank conversation on the matter. The ambassador reported that the foreign secretary 'was seriously agitated, anxious; he flushed, went pale, and raised his voice to a high pitch on several occasions'. According to Eden's account, he told

Maisky of his 'astonishment and keen displeasure' about the article: such language about Britain was 'intolerable between Allies'. Maisky eventually admitted that the *Pravda* article about Hess was a way of venting Moscow's 'grave disappointment' about Churchill's failing to live up to his 'promises' about the second front and the bombing of Berlin.[115]

On 26 October, the War Cabinet discussed the 'unfriendly attitude' that the Russians were adopting. Apart from the second front issue, various other explanations were adduced, including the idea that 'the Army was taking a larger part in the internal position of the country', a possible attempt to divert domestic criticism of military losses and even Russian fears that they 'would not be given their proper place at the Peace Conference'.[116]

Next day, Churchill advised Eden to 'treat the Russians coolly, not getting excited about the lies they tell, but going steadily on with our task. You should remember that the Bolsheviks have undermined so many powerful governments by lying, machine-made propaganda, and they probably think they make some impression on us by these methods.' Insisting it would be 'a great mistake to run after the Russians in their present mood', the PM assured the foreign secretary: 'the only thing that will do any good is fighting hard and winning victories ... Should success crown our efforts, you will find that we shall be in a very different position.'[117]

By the end of October 1942, the Big Three's correspondence was in a state of suspended animation. Each leader had to wait on events. The oft-delayed British offensive at Alamein had opened on 23 October, but the outcome was still in the balance. 'Torch' was scheduled for 8 November, and Zhukov's 'Uranus' for the following day. For each of the Big Three, deeds now mattered more than words.

6

CASABLANCA
A TABLE JUST FOR TWO

(November 1942 to January 1943)

IN THE END, NOVEMBER 1942 proved a month to savour for all the Big Three – a taste at last of real military triumphs.

On 4 November, after eleven days of bitter fighting, the German–Italian army started its long retreat from Alamein. The carnage in North Africa hardly compared with the Eastern Front – roughly 5,000 dead on both sides – but the political and morale value was immense. Montgomery had defeated Rommel; the British Army had finally beaten the Germans (even if a significant part of Rommel's infantry was Italian, while the Empire and Commonwealth contributed a goodly part of Monty's troops). Then, on 8 November, over 100,000 British and American troops, most of them without combat experience, landed in French North Africa (under Vichy government rule) at Casablanca, Oran and Algiers. The numbers involved were double those deployed in the notorious landings at Gallipolli in 1915; what is more, two of the Allied task forces had travelled 2,800 miles from Britain, and the third had sailed 4,500 miles across the Atlantic from the USA. Given the scale and hazards of the operation, it therefore came as a huge relief to both Churchill and Roosevelt when French resistance ceased within a couple of days. Both leaders had been acutely conscious of the risks they were running by forcing this operation on their generals. 'If Torch fails,' the prime minister told Eden, 'then I'm done for and must go.' Roosevelt was almost as worried. When the call about the landings came through, his hand was shaking as he took the phone. 'Thank God,' he exclaimed, 'thank God', on learning that the GIs were ashore with fewer casualties than expected.[1]

Eclipsing both Alamein and 'Torch' was 'Uranus'. At 07.20 on 19 November, a cascade of 'Katyusha' rockets heralded the opening of this massive counter-offensive to encircle the Axis armies besieging Stalingrad. After a massive two-month build-up, Soviet strength in the whole Stalingrad sector amounted to 1.1 million men, 900 tanks, 13,500 artillery pieces and 1,110 aircraft.[2] The Red Army targeted weak Romanian divisions protecting the flank of the German Sixth Army. Underestimating Russian capabilities, crippled by lack of fuel and paralysed by Hitler's usual 'stand fast' order, the army commander General Friedrich Paulus failed to react quickly enough, and within five days the Soviet pincers had closed around him and 330,000 troops. It would be another two months before Paulus and his army finally surrendered, with more than 90,000 troops marching off to Soviet POW camps, but the start of 'Uranus' marked the turning point on the Eastern Front.

Little wonder that Churchill entitled the 1942–43 volume of his war memoirs *The Hinge of Fate*. For each of the triumvirate, the 'hinge' turned in November 1942.

One can sense this in their correspondence. The tone becomes much warmer, with Churchill, for instance, writing to Stalin on 24 November about their 'trustful personal relations'. The two of them exchanged birthday greetings in November and December, repeating the pattern set in 1941. Yet their writing styles remained highly distinctive. Stalin consistently understated the scale of his operations and his great victory, whereas Churchill tended to talk up relatively small operations and unwisely anticipate future prospects.

Roosevelt was less prone to Churchillian verbiage. He and Stalin did not exchange birthday greetings and FDR remained a less frequent correspondent than the prime minister. As before, the Wheelchair President placed much faith in special envoys to act as his eyes, ears and mouth. Even though this practice may have irritated Stalin, it paid dividends in the case of General Patrick Hurley, who not only had an extended meeting with the Soviet leader, but was also given unique access to the Stalingrad front. FDR even considered sending General George Marshall, the US Army chief of staff, to convey the results of the Casablanca conference.

This summit in North Africa (12–24 January 1943) was necessitated by the slow progress of the Allies after the 'Torch' landings. Hopes had initially been high of reaching Tunis before Christmas, but the caution of the Allied advance and Hitler's rapid reinforcement of Tunisia made a quick victory impossible before the winter rains turned the desert sand and dirt roads into mud. This setback vindicated Marshall's earlier warnings that 'Torch' would divert and distract from a cross-Channel attack – as Churchill had belatedly appreciated.

So the Allies needed to discuss what they would do in 1943. Roosevelt suggested a conference of senior staffs, but Churchill favoured a top-level meeting of the three leaders; this was duly proposed to Stalin on 2–3 December. Stalin, however, declined the invitation, citing the pressures of military operations. This was perhaps his main reason, but, as Churchill surmised, the Soviet leader probably realized he could do little to force the second front on his allies at this stage and was wiser to save his presence for a later time, when he would enjoy greater bargaining power. Roosevelt, however, was unwilling to take 'no' for an answer; he urged Stalin to reconsider, and even offered to delay the meeting into March. The Soviet leader stuck to his guns, but Roosevelt would continue to press for a face-to-face meeting.

During December 1942, the correspondence again turned tetchy. Stalin had resumed his needling about a second front (or at least unequivocal statements of Allied plans), but Churchill remained evasive. He and Roosevelt were facing up to the gravity of the Allies' shipping crisis – especially shortages of assault craft that were essential to mount amphibious landings, and of escort vessels to protect the merchant ships carrying essential supplies across the Atlantic and Pacific, as well as into Arctic waters. In December, Stalin abruptly went into reverse on the idea of sending an Anglo-American air force to the Caucasus, ostensibly because the fighting was now shifting north, but probably also because the Kremlin, mindful of Allied military intervention during the Russian Civil War, did not want their personnel on Soviet soil. And when Roosevelt, pressed by the Pentagon, kept banging on insensitively about sending US squadrons to the Soviet Far East, just in case Japan declared war, Stalin got very peeved. Understandably, he saw this as an American effort to drag the USSR into the Pacific war at a time when his country was fighting for its life against Hitler. The result was the first unpleasant message from Stalin to Roosevelt, which infuriated FDR, though he decided not to reply.

The atmosphere was therefore tense by the time Churchill, Roosevelt and their staffs convened at Casablanca (12–24 January 1943). Theirs was a table just for two (plate 12), yet they knew Stalin was waiting impatiently for juicy morsels from the feast. But the outcome was largely a victory for the British Mediterranean strategy, with the next target Sicily, while maintaining troops in Britain in case of a sudden German collapse. It was already widely assumed in London and Washington that the real second front would be postponed until 1944. Rather than despatch Marshall as personal emissary, as FDR casually suggested at one point, they decided to send a carefully worded joint message summing up the conference in a general way – presumably realizing that sending a messenger would only invite cross-examination about the unpalatable message. Stalin's reply was studiously polite, but it put Churchill and Roosevelt on the spot by requesting details and timings for the 'concrete operations' they now planned in order to defeat Germany in 1943. This would become his refrain over the next few months.

*****

Churchill's pride and excitement almost jumps off the page in his message of 5 November to Stalin, announcing the defeat of Rommel's army at Alamein and the imminent opening of 'Torch'. (He followed up on the 7th, with other breathless messages updating German losses and warning of a German air raid on Baku.[3]) The phrase 'political difficulties about which you expressed concern' refers to Stalin's comments in the Kremlin on 12 August that the operation was 'not sufficiently thought-through politically' and that 'it would be more beneficial to have de Gaulle or any other French general participate in this operation'.[4] Despite Churchill's complacent assurance that these issues had been 'satisfactorily solved', the anger of General Charles de Gaulle – the Free French leader – at his exclusion from 'Torch' would prove a major headache for Britain and America in the weeks ahead.

The turn of the tide in Egypt allowed Churchill to push ahead with the idea of a British–American air force in the Caucasus. But the most striking symbol of warmer relations with Moscow was Churchill's cryptic final sentence of congratulations on the upcoming anniversary of the October Revolution – words that this inveterate enemy of Bolshevism surely never imagined he would ever utter.

Churchill to Stalin, sent 5 November 1942, received 5 November 1942[5]

I promised to tell you when our army in Egypt had gained a decisive victory over Rommel. General Alexander now reports that enemy's front is broken and that he is retreating westwards in considerable disorder. Apart from the troops in the main battle, there are six Italian and two German divisions in the desert to the south of our advance along the coast. These have very little mechanical transport or supplies, and it is possible that a very heavy toll will be taken in the next few days. Besides this, Rommel's only line of retreat is along the coastal road which is now crammed with troops and transport and under continuous attack of our greatly superior Air Force.

Most Secret – for yourself alone. 'Torch' is imminent on a very great scale. I believe the political difficulties about which you expressed concern have been satisfactorily solved. The military movement is proceeding with precision.

I am most anxious to proceed with the placing of 20 British and American squadrons on your southern flank as early as possible. President Roosevelt is in full accord and there is no danger now of a disaster in Egypt. Before anything can be done, however, it is necessary that detailed arrangements should be made about landing grounds, etc., between your Officers and ourselves.

Kindly let me know as soon as possible how you would like this consultation to be arranged. The squadrons it is proposed to send were stated in my telegram of October 8th (Foreign Office No. 268), in accordance with which we have been making such preparations as were possible pending arrangements with you.

Let me further express to you, Premier Stalin, and to M. Molotov, our congratulations on the ever-glorious defence of Stalingrad and on the decisive defeat of Hitler's second campaign against Russia. I should be glad to know from you how you stand in the Caucasus.

All good wishes for your anniversary.

Despite the fears of some in Moscow about possible Western ambitions in the Caucasus, Stalin initially accepted Churchill's offer of twenty British and American squadrons, and on 8 November proposed discussions on the detailed arrangements. In keeping with the warmer tone of relations, he congratulated the prime minister on victory at Alamein and sent best wishes for the success of 'Torch'. Responding to the PM's request for an update on the Caucasus, he again underlined the shortage of air power.[6]

Stalin to Churchill, sent 8 November 1942, received 9 November[7]

Your message received on the 5th November.

My congratulations on the successful development of the military operations in Egypt. Let me express my confidence that now you will be able to completely annihilate the Rommel's gang and his Italian allies.

We all here hope for the success of the 'Torch'.

Many thanks for your communication that you and President Roosevelt have decided in the near future to send to our Southern front the 20 British and American squadrons. A speedy arrival of these 20 squadrons would be a very valuable help. The necessary consultation between the British, American and Soviet representatives on the preliminary arrangements could be best organised first in Moscow and later in case of need directly in the Caucasus. I am already informed that the USA will send for this purpose the General E.E. Adler. I will wait for your communication on who will be appointed to represent Great Britain.

The situation on our Caucasian front deteriorated somewhat as compared with October. The Germans succeeded in capturing the town Nalchik. They are

approaching Vladikavkas where severe fighting is going on at present. Our difficulty here is our weakness in the fighter aircraft.

Let me express my gratitude for your congratulations in connection with the
anniversary of the USSR.

When Maisky delivered this brief but cordial message to Churchill on
9 November, he found the PM in what he called 'a state of excitement because
of successes in Africa'. Having looked at the envelope in some trepidation,
Churchill was pleased with what he read. 'That's better,' he declared. 'I want
to work with Stalin as a friend.' But, he asked, just what had been going on?
'No responses to my letters for a long time and then I get a "thank you" and
haven't the slightest idea how to interpret it.' Still tanked up, the PM went on to
outline his scenario for the future actions of Anglo-American forces after
'Torch' – the capture of Sicily and Sardinia, the conclusion of war with Italy,
bringing Turkey into the Alliance and mounting operations in the Balkans. He
called all this a 'second front in 1943'. The ambassador immediately poured
cold water on what Churchill said, asking about the promised invasion of the
north of France and stressing that 'the Italian-Balkan plans go round and round
the problem' of how to defeat Hitler. The PM backed off, telling the ambassador
'don't tell Stalin anything just yet. This is just an initial sketch. I'll write to him,
so he may know my thoughts from me.' Maisky, however, did relay Churchill's
words to Moscow – adding 'do not give me away, lest Churchill is less talkative
next time'.[8]

Following up on what he had said to Maisky, on 13 November Churchill
sent a detailed letter to Stalin, copying it to Roosevelt for information.[9] He
filled out plans for the deployment of air squadrons to the Caucasus, explaining
that Air Marshal Peter Drummond, an Australian who was deputy commander-
in-chief of the RAF in the Middle East, would lead the British team in the planning – together with the American General Elmer Adler (mentioned in Stalin's
message of 8 November). The two officers and their staffs arrived in Moscow
on 21 November, but their negotiations soon ran into what proved an insuperable obstacle: the Soviets wanted the planes, but not British and American
pilots.[10]

Churchill spent most of the message expatiating on Allied successes in
North Africa and speculating about future prospects – indulging his love of
broad-brush scenarios, in contrast to the terse, matter-of-fact manner of the
Soviet leader. In particular, he mentioned the deal concluded by the US high
command in Algiers with Admiral François Darlan, commander-in-chief of
the Vichy French armed forces, who ordered a ceasefire and stopped further

resistance to the Allied troops. On 13 November, Eisenhower appointed Darlan high commissioner in French North Africa. The 'dirty deal' with Darlan sparked huge controversy in Britain and America, and became a feature of subsequent Big Three correspondence until the admiral's assassination on Christmas Eve.

Amid all this detail, Churchill made no mention of a key Soviet concern – resumption of the Arctic convoys. Maisky had asked about this when he met the PM on 8 November. Churchill 'agreed to reconsider the issue', Maisky told Stalin, 'but with such a look that did not induce much optimism'.[11]

Churchill to Stalin, sent 13 November 1942, received 14 November 1942[12]

Many thanks for your messages of the 8th and 10th November, which have both reached me.

I have appointed Air-Marshal Drummond to represent Great Britain in the Staff discussions between the Soviet, American and British representatives on the preliminary arrangements for the employment of the twenty British and American squadrons on your Southern Front. Air-Marshal Drummond has been ordered to leave Cairo for Moscow with a small party of Staff Officers forthwith.

Important success has rewarded our operations both in Egypt and in French North Africa. We have already penetrated deeply into Cyrenaica. Tobruk has just been recaptured. The so-called Panzer Army is now reduced to a very small, hard-pressed band with hardly a score of tanks and we are in hot pursuit. It seems to me almost certain that Benghazi will soon be recovered and that the enemy will try to escape into Tripolitania, holding a line at Agheila. He is already evacuating stores from Benghazi and is endeavouring to open new improvised and restricted bases in the Gulf of Sirte.

The 'Torch' is flaming well, and General Eisenhower and our own Commanders have every hope of obtaining complete control of French North Africa and building up a superior air power at the tip of Tunisia. This is all in the intention of further aggressive operations. All the great troop convoys have moved, or are moving so far, safely across the Ocean and from Great Britain. We hope to create a strong anti-German French army in North Africa under General Giraud.

The political reactions in Spain and Portugal have been most satisfactory and the danger of Gibraltar harbour and airfield being rendered unusable has ceased for the present to be a grave anxiety. The German invasion of Vichy France which was foreseen by us and also by you in our conversations is all to the good. The poisonous and paralysing influence of Vichy on the French nation will decline, and the whole people will soon learn to hate the Germans as much as they are hated in the occupied zone. The future of the Toulon fleet is obscure. The Germans have not felt themselves strong enough to demand its surrender, and are reported to intend to respect Toulon. Admiral Darlan, who is in our power, has asked the fleet to sail for West African ports. Whether this order will be obeyed is still doubtful.

A great reversal of the situation along the whole African shore has taken place and may be counted on. If we can open a passage for military traffic through the Mediterranean our shipping problem will be greatly eased and we shall come into far closer contact with Turkey than has hitherto been possible. I am in communication with President Roosevelt who is delighted at the success of the American enterprise. The whole position must be reviewed in a few days, with the intention of further vehement action. I will let you know as soon as possible what our ideas for the future are. You know, I am sure, how anxious we are to take off you some of the undue weight which you have steadfastly borne in these last hard months. Meanwhile I am proceeding on the assumption that you are still confident that the Caucasus range will not be penetrated in the winter months.

On 14 November, Stalin wrote to both Churchill and Roosevelt.[13] Most of the text was similar – containing advance intimation of the Stalingrad counter-offensive and good wishes for the success of 'Torch' – but the letter to FDR included an allusion to Stalin's meeting that day with General Patrick Hurley, bearer of Roosevelt's letter of 5 October. At the height of the Stalingrad crisis, the Boss had no time for protocol visits. 'I do not want to receive General Hurley. I'm at the front, busy', he told Molotov peevishly after an initial request from the US embassy.[14] The president's frequent use of special envoys seems to have grated on Stalin. In February 1943, he told Clark Kerr, according to the Soviet minutes, 'Roosevelt calls everyone whom he sends to the USSR his special representatives. In Comrade Stalin's view, this is wrong ... Churchill is more serious about it.'[15] Perhaps this was intended to flatter the British, but Stalin had put his finger on a difference of approach between the two Western leaders: Churchill tried to engage Stalin through his own (prolix) words, as on 8 November; whereas the Wheelchair President relied more on VIP proxies to get through to the Soviet leader.

In the end, however, Stalin agreed to FDR's request to see Hurley, and the meeting paid off, just as the president hoped.[16] The general was allowed to make a ten-day visit to the battle zone: he visited the Southwestern Front – a key part of the Stalingrad encirclement operation, where he conferred with its commander, General Nikolay Vatutin – and he also toured the southern flank in the Caucasus. Hurley's upbeat report became for Roosevelt the first direct evidence of what was going on at Stalingrad and on the Eastern Front in general during this critical phase of the war. Upon his emissary's return, the president sent Molotov the following extract from his letter to Hurley: 'Your excellent report, coupled with everything that you say about the magnificent operations and excellent morale of the Russian armies, gave me greatest pleasure.'[17]

Stalin to Roosevelt, sent 14 November 1942, received 14 November 1942[18]

I am very grateful to you for your letter, which General Hurley has handed in today. General Hurley and I have had a long talk on strategy. It seems to me that he has understood me and is satisfied that the strategy that is now being followed by the Allies is correct. He asked to be allowed to see one of our fronts and, in particular, to go to the Caucasus. He will be afforded an opportunity to do so.

There were no major changes on the Soviet–German front during the last week. We expect to begin our winter campaign in the nearest future. Preparations for it are now going on. I shall keep you informed as to the progress of this campaign.

We here are all highly gratified by the brilliant successes of American and British armed forces in North Africa. Allow me to congratulate you upon this victory. With all my heart I wish you further successes.

In his reply, Roosevelt alluded appreciatively to Stalin's meeting with Hurley, and mentioned recent American naval successes in repulsing Japanese forces attempting to recapture the island of Guadalcanal, a thousand miles northeast of Australia. But FDR also emphasized to Stalin that he and Churchill were in 'complete agreement' about the Germany First strategy, despite countervailing pressures from Australia and New Zealand. The president again alluded to the value of face-to-face meetings – 'with you and your staff'.

Roosevelt to Stalin, sent 19 November 1942, received 21 November 1942[19]

I am glad you have been so kind to General Hurley.

As you can well recognize, I have had a problem in persuading the people of Australia and New Zealand that the menace of Japan can be most effectively met by destroying the Nazis first. General Hurley will be able to tell them at firsthand how you and Churchill and I are in complete agreement on this.

Our recent battles in the South-west Pacific make the position there more secure, even though we have not yet eliminated attempts by the Japanese to extend their southward drive.

The American and British staffs are now studying further moves in the event that we secure the whole south shore of the Mediterranean from Gibraltar to Syria. Before any further step is taken, both Churchill and I want to consult with you and your staff, because whatever we do next in the Mediterranean will have a definite bearing on your magnificent campaign and your proposed moves this coming Winter.

I do not have to tell you to keep up the good work. You are doing that, and I honestly feel that things everywhere look brighter.

Operation 'Uranus' opened on 19 November, and within five days the Red Army's pincers had closed around the rear of the German Sixth Army: the besiegers became the besieged. Stalin decided to inform his allies promptly, sending identical messages to Churchill and Roosevelt on 20 November. His final sentence about Soviet operations developing 'not badly' shows Stalin's customary wariness about blowing his trumpet too early – being innately cautious, even superstitious about such things.[20]

Stalin to Churchill, sent 20 November 1942, received 20 November 1942[21]

We began offensive operations in the Stalingrad area – in the North Western and in the Southern sectors of the front. The first stage of these offensive operations has as its main task to capture the railway line Stalingrad–Lihaya and to dislocate communications of the Stalingrad group of the German forces. In the North Western sector the German front is broken on the stretch of 22 kilometres and in the southern sector on the stretch of 12 kilometres. The operations are developing not badly.

Against the backdrop of military success for both their countries, the Stalin–Churchill correspondence loosened up. On 24 November, Churchill sent one of his longer messages to Stalin, couched in a particularly expansive tone. The opening paragraph, about their 'trustful personal relations' and their 'duties to the great masses', sounded almost as if he and Stalin were both democratic statesmen. The PM went on to confirm that the next Arctic convoy would sail just before Christmas. But the psychology behind the rest of his message is not easy to fathom. Churchill went into considerable detail about his plans for Turkey, Syria and even Italy. Although he ended with a few lines about building up strong British and US forces in southern England, this was in order to keep the Germans pinned down in the Pas de Calais and to be 'ready to take advantage of any favourable opportunity' in France – hardly the ringing affirmation of the second front that Stalin wanted to hear. Churchill, of course, had already been indiscreet about British priorities when talking to Maisky on 9 November, but it is surprising that he now sent a carefully composed message that could only have confirmed Stalin's worst suspicions about Allied strategy.

Churchill also alluded in passing to the mounting storm in Britain and America about Eisenhower's deal with Darlan; the word 'rogue' was the PM's own addition. He insinuated, as Roosevelt had said publicly on 17 November, that the arrangements made were only temporary until their armies had gained a firm grip on French North Africa. Molotov also seemed worried. After a conversation with him, Clark Kerr warned Eden of the danger that Darlan might grow into 'a second Hess' in the Soviet mindset.[22]

Churchill to Stalin, sent 24 November 1942, received 25 November 1942[23]

It gave me the very greatest pleasure to receive your warm and heartfelt congratulations. I regard our trustful personal relations as most important to the discharge of our duties to the great masses whose lives are at stake.

Although the President is unable with great regret to lend me twelve American destroyers for which I asked, I have now succeeded in making arrangements to sail a convoy of over thirty ships from Iceland on December 22. The Admiralty will concert the operation with your officers as before. The Germans have moved the bulk of their aircraft from the north of Norway to the south of Europe as a result of 'Torch'. On the other hand, the German surface forces in Norway are still on guard. The Admiralty are pleased so far with the progress of the Q.P. convoy, which has been helped by bad weather and is now under the protection of our cruisers which have been sent out to meet it.

I have communicated to President Roosevelt some preliminary ideas about Turkey and have found that he independently had formed very similar views. It seems to me that we ought all of us to make a new intense effort to make Turkey enter the war on our side in the Spring. For this purpose I should like the United States to join in an Anglo-Soviet guarantee of the territorial integrity and status of Turkey.[24] This would bring our three countries into line, and the Americans count for a lot with the Turks. Secondly, we are already sending Turkey a considerable consignment of munitions, including 200 tanks from the Middle East. During the winter by land route, or coasting up the Levant, I shall keep on sending supplies of munitions to Turkey together, if permitted, with experts in plain clothes for training and maintenance purposes. Thirdly, I hope by early spring to assemble a considerable army in Syria drawn from our Eighth, Ninth and Tenth Armies, so as to go to help Turkey if either she were threatened or were willing to join us. It is evident that your operations in the Caucasus or north of it may also exercise a great influence. If we could get Turkey into the war we could not only proceed with operations designed to open the shipping route to your left flank on the Black Sea but we could also bomb heavily from Turkish bases the Roumanian oilfields which are of such vital importance to the Axis in view of your successful defence of main oil supplies in the Caucasus. The advantage of a move into Turkey is that it proceeds mainly by land and can be additional to offensive action in the Central Mediterranean, which will absorb our sea power and much of our Air power.

I have agreed to President Roosevelt's suggestion that we each send in the near future, if agreeable to you, two high British officers and two Americans to Moscow to plan this part of the war in 1943. Pray let me know if you agree.

I hope you realise, Premier Stalin, that shipping is our limiting factor. In order to do 'Torch' we have had to cut our Trans-Atlantic escorts so fine that the first half of November has been our worst month so far. We and the Americans have budgeted to lose at the rate of 700,000 tons a month and still improve our margin. Over the year the average loss has not been quite so bad as that, but this first fortnight in November is worse. You who have so much land may find it hard to realise that we can only live and fight in proportion to our sea communications.

Do not be disturbed about the rogue Darlan. We have thrown a large Anglo-American army into French North Africa and are getting a very firm grip. Owing to the non-resistance of the French Army and now to its increasing support, we are perhaps fifteen days ahead of schedule. It is of the utmost consequence to get the Tunisian tip and the naval base of Bizerta at the earliest moment. The leading elements of our First Army will probably begin their attack immediately. Once established there with over-powering Air, we can bring the war home to Mussolini and his Fascist gang with an intensity not yet possible.

At the same time, by building up a strong Anglo-American army and Air Force in Great Britain and making continuous preparations along our south-eastern and southern coasts, we keep the Germans pinned in the Pas de Calais, etc., and are ready to take advantage of any favourable opportunity. And all the time our bombers will be blasting Germany with ever-increasing violence. Thus the halter will tighten upon the guilty doomed.

The glorious news of your offensive is streaming in. We are watching it with breathless attention. Every good wish.

On 25 November, the president sent a particularly chatty message to Stalin, striking a bullish note about recent successes at Guadalcanal and about his hopes that heavy bombing would soon undermine Italian morale and force the country out of the war – a frequent theme of his conversations with Soviet representatives in Washington.[25]

Replying to Churchill's message of 24 November, Stalin thanked him for preparing a new Arctic convoy and also expressed 'full agreement' with the idea of getting Turkey into the war and holding staff talks among representatives of the Big Three. Of particular interest is his reaction to Churchill's comment about the 'rogue' Darlan. In a draft of the message for Stalin's approval, Molotov had denounced the deal in no uncertain terms:

> As for Darlan, the suspicions about him seem quite legitimate to me. In any case, serious decisions regarding North African affairs should be based not on Darlan and people like him but those who can be an honest ally in the relentless struggle against Hitler's tyranny, with which I am sure you would agree.

But Stalin clearly considered such moralizing to be prissy and indeed missing the essential point: namely that the 'dirty deal' had actually helped ensure the success of the Allied landings.[26] So he replaced Molotov's angry sentences with his own very expressive phrase about the necessity in wartime to use 'even the devil and his grandma' (plate 13). Here is another reminder that, although Stalin's diplomacy relied heavily on Molotov, ultimately the Boss wrote the script. Stalin made some other amendments to the text. He added a pointed question to the paragraph about the troop build-up in England, reminding Churchill of his 'promise' to open a second front in 1943. And he replaced Molotov's last paragraph, which expressed thanks for Churchill's congratulations about the Stalingrad success, with more specific information about the counter-attack and about operation 'Mars', being mounted west of Moscow to deter the Germans from sending reinforcements to Paulus's Sixth Army.[27]

Stalin to Churchill, sent 27 November 1942, received 28 November 1942[28]

Thank you for your message, which I received on the 25th November. I fully share your view on the importance of developing our personal relations.

I am grateful to you for the measures you are taking to send a big new convoy to Archangel. I realise that in view of the considerable operations in the Mediterranean Sea this constitutes great difficulty for you.

I am in full agreement with you and President Roosevelt on the question of Turkey. It would be desirable to do everything possible to have Turkey enter the war on our side in the spring. That would be of great importance in order to accelerate the defeat of Hitler and his accomplices.

It seems to me that the Americans used Darlan not badly in order to facilitate the occupation of Northern and Western Africa. The military diplomacy must be able to use for military purposes not only Darlans but 'even the devil himself and his grandma'.[29]

I paid close attention to your communication that you and the Americans do not relax preparations along your southeastern and southern coasts in order to keep the Germans pinned in the Pas de Calais, etc. and that you are ready to take advantage of any favourable opportunity. I hope this does not mean that you change your mind with regard to your promise given in Moscow to open a second front in Western Europe in the spring of 1943.

I am in full agreement with President Roosevelt's suggestion and your wish to arrange in Moscow conversations of the representatives of the three General Staffs to prepare the respective military plans for 1943. We are ready to meet the British and American representatives whenever you wish.

In the Stalingrad operations we were so far successful partly because of snowfall and fog which hindered the activities of the German aviation.

We have the intention to start in the next few days active operations on the central front in order to pin here the enemy forces and to prevent the transfer of any portion of them to the south.

The Soviet leader's line about 'the devil and his grandma' made an impression on Eden. 'Yours is such an expressive language,' he told Maisky. Yet, the ambassador noted, Eden was 'in a state of great anxiety about the story with Darlan, disquiet which largely derives from the fear that the Americans might be playing an independent game that does not correspond fully to England's interests'.[30] Stalin was not alone in comparing Darlan to the devil. Quoting a 'Balkan' proverb, Roosevelt told a press conference: 'My children, you are permitted in time of great danger to walk with the Devil until you have crossed the bridge.'[31] In Moscow, British diplomats noted that Molotov was soon repeating Stalin's phrase about Darlan with some relish. Junior Soviet officials, like Maisky and Molotov initially, had been very dubious about using Darlan – all of which strongly suggests that the decision to endorse US policy had been taken by Stalin himself.[32] But Clark Kerr warned that the Darlan deal constituted a dangerous precedent for the Americans organizing governments in the liberated territories without any consultations with Moscow. 'The Russians claim that the problems of political administration which will arise in each country over time are as much theirs as they are ours and the Americans'. North Africa is the first and it will set a precedent.' He added, 'The Russians are not in the mood to be excluded from anything.'[33]

Churchill read out Stalin's telegram to the Cabinet on 30 November. He noted its 'very cordial' tone, but also its reference to the PM's 'promise' in August. According to the Cabinet minutes, Churchill said that the changing military situation 'made it all the more incumbent upon us to start a Second Front in Europe in 1943. Our present activities in the Mediterranean, important though they were, could only be regarded as an inadequate contribution compared with the efforts which Russia was making.'[34] The previous day, also alluding to Stalin's message, he had told the chiefs of staff bluntly:

I certainly think that we should make all plans to attack the French coast, either in the area of the Channel or in the Bay of Biscay, and that July 1943 should be fixed as the target date. Judging from the conditions on the Russian front, it does not look as if Hitler will be able to bring back any large force from the east to the west. He now has to watch the southern coast of France as well. The battles on the Russian front have already greatly modified and may fundamentally change the overall situation.

These comments about crossing the Channel in July 1943 are a reminder that, despite Churchill's recurrent obsession with the Mediterranean, his strategic thinking was more volatile than the 'bulldog' image suggests.[35]

On 27 November, with 'Uranus' going well, Stalin caught up on his correspondence and replied warmly to FDR's messages of the 19th. Picking up on the current mood of confidence in London and Washington that they would control all of North Africa by Christmas, he expressed his hope that the campaign 'may influence the whole military situation in Europe' and allow the Allies to develop 'offensive operations' on the continent. To this end, he agreed that Big Three staff talks were desirable.

Stalin to Roosevelt, sent 27 November 1942, received 27 November 1942[36]

I thank you for your message, received by me on November 21. I fully understand your desire to make the present military situation clear to the people of Australia and New Zealand, and the need for your attention to operations in the south-west Pacific.

As regards operations in the Mediterranean, which are developing so favorably, and may influence the whole military situation in Europe, I share your view that appropriate consultations between the Staffs of America, Great Britain and the U.S.S.R. have become desirable.

Greetings and my best wishes for new successes in further offensives.

The end of November 1942 constituted one of the warmest moments in Soviet–British relations during the war. London had decided to resume the Arctic convoys; and the Allies had at last tasted success on their respective battlefields. British diplomats were pleased at the improvement in relations with Moscow. They placed considerable weight on a speech by Stalin on 6 November to mark the twenty-fifth anniversary of the Bolshevik Revolution in which he referred to 'the steadily growing friendship among the members of the Anglo-Soviet-American coalition' and 'their amalgamation into a united fighting alliance'. A memo by the FO's Northern Department, endorsed by Cadogan, stated: 'Stalin's speech of November 6th last may safely be taken as announcing to the Soviet Union the decision of the Soviet Government to give the policy of collaboration with this country and the United States a trial.'[37]

In the same vein, Stalin stressed the personal nature of his correspondence with Churchill – as in 1941 extending to the prime minister best wishes for his birthday on 30 November, to which the PM sent an appreciative reply (plate 14). A further round of messages followed for Stalin's birthday in December.[38]

*****

With plans for 1943 now pressing on the minds of all the Big Three, the need for coordination seemed acute. Although on 27 November, Stalin had agreed with Roosevelt about a tripartite meeting of their military staffs, Churchill took a different view, arguing that the issues needed to be thrashed out in a Big Three meeting. 'What about proposing it for January?' he asked the president, noting that 'Stalin talked to me in Moscow in the sense of being willing to come to meet you and me somewhere this winter, and he mentioned Iceland.'[39] Urged on by Harry Hopkins, Roosevelt took up the idea of a summit. For months, he had wanted to meet Stalin in person and he was rather jealous that the more mobile Churchill had stolen a march on him. He proposed to the PM that all three should meet in North Africa around 15 January 1943, working on the (erroneous) assumption that 'Tunis and Bizerte should have been cleared up and Rommel's army liquidated before the conference.' However, before sending this message to Churchill, FDR removed Harry Hopkins' draft sentences about it being 'essential that you and I have a thorough understanding before the conference takes place', adding instead, 'I think that you and I understand each other so well that prior conferences between us are unnecessary.'[40] This would become a familiar pattern for the rest of the war: the president wanted to engage with Stalin on his own, rather than giving the impression that the Soviet leader was facing a firm Anglo-American front – which was Churchill's consistent line.

Both leaders sent Stalin the proposal for a North African meeting on 2–3 December, with the initiative for the idea ascribed to Roosevelt.

Roosevelt to Stalin, sent 2 December 1942, received 5 December 1942[41]

The more I consider our mutual military situation and the necessity for reaching early strategic decisions, the more persuaded I am that you, Churchill and I should have an early meeting.

It seems to me that a conference of our military leaders alone will not be sufficient, first, because they could come to no ultimate decisions without our approval and, secondly, because I think we should come to some tentative understanding about the procedures which should be adopted in event of a German collapse.

My most compelling reason is that I am very anxious to have a talk with you. My suggestion would be that we meet secretly in some secure place in Africa that is convenient to all three of us. The time, about January 15th to 20th.

We would each of us bring a very small staff of our top army, air and naval commanders.

I do hope that you will consider this proposal favorably because I can see no other way of reaching the vital strategic decisions which should be made soon by all of us together. If the right decision is reached, we may, and I believe will, knock Germany out of the war much sooner than we anticipated.

I can readily fly, but I consider Iceland or Alaska out of the question at this time of the year. Some place can, I think, be found in Southern Algeria or at, or near, Khartoum where all visitors and press can be kept out. As a mere suggestion as to date would you think of sometime around January 15?

Churchill to Stalin, sent 3 December 1942, received 4 December 1942[42]

The President tells me that he has proposed a meeting for us three in January somewhere in North Africa.

This is far better than the Iceland project we talked over in Moscow. You could get to any point desired in three days, I in two, and the President in about the same time as you. I earnestly hope you will agree. We must decide at the earliest moment the best way of attacking Germany in Europe with all possible force in 1943. This can only be settled between the heads of the Governments and States with their high expert authorities at their side. It is only by such a meeting that the full burden of the war can be shared according to capacity and opportunity.

But Stalin declined the invitation to meet his two allies, sending almost identical replies (once differences of translation are set aside), apart from prodding Churchill again about the second front.[43] 'Stalin's absence was his own choice – and his mistake,' observes historian Warren Kimball. 'He missed a chance to shape the very strategies he criticized.'[44] The Soviet leader's excuse – intense pressure of affairs of the front – was quite convincing, but probably not the only reason. Fear of air travel, reluctance to venture outside the NKVD security net, a desire to strengthen his military-strategic position before entering into decisive discussions of grand strategy – these also probably played a part. During the Casablanca conference, when Roosevelt was pondering Stalin's motives for absence, Churchill told him (according to the account he gave Maisky):

> Stalin is a realist. You can't catch him with words. Had Stalin come to Casablanca, the first thing he would have asked you and me would have been: 'How many Germans did you kill in 1942? And how many do you intend to kill in 1943?' And what would the two of us have been able to say? We ourselves are not sure what we are going to do in 1943. This was clear to Stalin from the very beginning. So what would have been the point of him coming to the conference?[45]

Stalin to Churchill, sent 6 December 1942, received 6 December 1942[46]

Your message of December 4 received.

I welcome the idea of a meeting of the three heads of the Governments being arranged in order to fix a common line of military strategy.

To my great regret, however, I will not be in a position to leave the Soviet Union. Time presses us and it would be impossible for me to be absent even for a day as it is just now that important military operations of our winter campaign are developing. These operations will not be relaxed in January, probably to the contrary.

I am waiting your reply to the paragraph of my preceding letter dealing with the establishment of the second front in Western Europe in the spring of 1943.

The operations in the Stalingrad area as well as on the central front are developing. In the Stalingrad area we are keeping a large group of the German troops surrounded and hope to annihilate them completely.

Having received Stalin's response, Churchill told Maisky that he understood the 'seriousness' of Stalin's concerns, but regretted that the meeting would not take place, because he had planned to urge an early opening of a second front in 1943, despite American resistance. As Maisky told Moscow:

I have the impression that the Americans and the English use a second front in Western Europe as a ball: when Roosevelt insisted on the second front in 1942, Churchill objected, and now when Churchill is in favour of the second front in 1943, Roosevelt opposes it. Essentially both cherish the same idea – the idea of an 'easy war' for themselves.[47]

Roosevelt was put out, even irritated, by Stalin's refusal to come to Casablanca and tried again, dangling as bait 'matters of vital importance' that could only be discussed in person, and even proposing to reschedule the meeting for March.[48] In his reply, Churchill evaded a direct answer to Stalin's question about the second front, citing the need for a joint decision with Roosevelt.

Roosevelt to Stalin, sent 8 December 1942, received 10 December 1942[49]

I am deeply disappointed that you feel you cannot get away for a conference with me in January. There are many matters of vital importance to be discussed between us. These relate not only to vital strategic decisions but also to things we should talk over in a tentative way in regard to emergency policies which we should be ready with, if and when conditions in Germany permit.

These would also include other matters relating to future policies about North Africa and the Far East which cannot be discussed by our military people alone.

I fully realize your strenuous situation now and in the immediate future and the necessity of your presence close to the fighting front.

Therefore, I want to suggest that we set a tentative date for meeting in North Africa about March first.

Churchill to Stalin, sent 12 December 1942, received 13 December 1942[50]

In your message to me of November 27 in the last sentence of paragraph 5 and also in your message of December 6, you ask specifically about a second front in 1943. I am not able to reply to this question except jointly with the President of the United States. It was for this reason that I so earnestly desired a meeting between the three of us. We both understand the paramount military reasons which prevent you from leaving Russia while conducting your great operations. I am in constant communication with the President in order to see what can be done.

In a carefully balanced letter, Stalin politely turned down FDR's offer to meet in March 1943, not January, suggesting that they discuss whatever urgent problems the president had in mind through correspondence. He did not miss the opportunity to remind Roosevelt of the 'promises' made to open a second front at the latest by the spring of 1943, offsetting this unpleasant reminder with a compliment about the Americans' skilful use of Darlan. Although the translation was very literal in places – 'waterway' signifies that Darlan had been brought into the tidal flow of the Allies – the tone captured something of the Russian original: patiently polite, but somewhat patronizing, as if dealing with an errant child.

Stalin to Roosevelt, sent 14 December 1942, received 14 December 1942[51]

I, too, must express my deep regret that it is impossible for me to leave the Soviet Union either in the immediate future or even at the beginning of March. Front business absolutely prevents it, demanding my constant presence near our troops.

So far I do not know what exactly are the problems which you, Mr President, and Mr Churchill intended to discuss at our joint conference. I wonder whether it would not be possible to discuss these problems by way of correspondence between us, as long as there is no chance of arranging our meeting? I admit that there will be no disagreement between us.

Allow me also to express my confidence that the time is not being lost and that the promises about the opening of a second front in Europe given by you, Mr President, and by Mr Churchill in regard of 1942 and in any case in regard of the spring of 1943, will be fulfilled and that a second front in Europe will be actually opened by the joint forces of Great Britain and the United States in the spring of the next year.

In view of all sorts of rumors about the attitude of the Union of Soviet Socialist Republics toward the use made of Darlan and of other men like him, it may not be unnecessary for me to tell you that, in my opinion, as well as that of my colleagues, Eisenhower's policy with regard to Darlan, Boisson, Giraud and others is perfectly correct. I think it is a great achievement that you have succeeded in bringing Darlan and others into the waterway of the Allies fighting Hitler. Some time ago I made this known also to Mr Churchill.

Annoyed by Stalin's obduracy and his needling, Roosevelt did not reply to this message. Instead, he responded with a reminder of his own: about the deployment of the Anglo-American air force units in the Caucasus (operation 'Velvet'), which had been hanging fire since mid-November. By now it had become apparent to the Soviets that 'Velvet' would require a transfer to the Caucasus of 22,000 personnel, and delivery of up to 30,000 tons of cargo via the Persian Corridor – equal to its monthly capacity – at the expense of supplies to the Soviet Union. The Soviet counter-proposal – to send just the aircraft, without crews and maintenance personnel – was rejected by the Allied representatives, and this brought negotiations to a standstill.[52] Replying to Roosevelt, Stalin said that there was no longer any need to send squadrons to the Caucasus, since the worst fighting was taking place elsewhere – reminding Roosevelt again that the Soviets needed planes, not pilots. The president responded briefly on 21 December, promising to expedite aircraft deliveries.[53]

On 29 December, Churchill came clean to Stalin about the delay in mopping up North Africa. Contrary to earlier hopes of reaching Tunis by Christmas, he now had to confess that tough German resistance had slowed progress – though, characteristically, he put the best possible gloss on the situation. The PM was able to give more positive news about continuing the Arctic convoys. He and Roosevelt had now agreed that, despite Stalin's non-attendance, they would meet *à deux* near Casablanca.[54] Relaying this last piece of information cryptically to the Soviet leader, Churchill used language that could not have boosted the Kremlin's confidence – avoiding the magic words 'second front' and again stressing the tightness of shipping. In his brief acknowledgement of 5 January, Stalin kept up the pressure, telling Churchill, 'I will be very grateful for information on the results of these conversations.'[55]

Churchill to Stalin, sent 29 December 1942, received 30 December 1942[56]

We are deeply encouraged by the growing magnitude of your victories in the south. They bear out all that you told me at Moscow. The results may be very far-reaching indeed.

The Axis are making good their bridgehead on the Tunis tip, which we nearly managed to seize at the first rush. It now looks as if fighting there will continue through January and February. I hope General Alexander's Army will be masters of Tripoli early in February. Rommel will very likely withdraw towards the Tunis tip with his forces, which amount to about 70,000 German troops and as many Italians, two-thirds of all of them administrative. The warfare on the African coast is very costly to the enemy on account of heavy losses in transit and at the ports. We shall do our utmost to finish it as quickly as possible.

The December PQ convoy has prospered so far beyond all expectation. I have now arranged to send a full convoy of thirty or more ships through in January, though whether they will go in one portion or in two is not yet settled by the Admiralty.

For yourself alone, I am going to visit President Roosevelt soon in order to settle our plans for 1943. My supreme object is for the British and Americans to engage the enemy with the largest numbers in the shortest time. The shipping stringency is most severe. I will inform you what passes.

A day later, Stalin received another message from Roosevelt. After Moscow had refused operation 'Velvet' in the Caucasus, the president again raised the issue of sending an American air force to the USSR, this time Siberia. He was under pressure from the US military to establish air bases in the Far East for their own war with Japan. The final version of the telegram was prepared by Admiral Leahy, on behalf of the Joint Chiefs, who were trying to use the high-level channel to go over the top of the stolid Soviet military bureaucracy. It was nodded through by FDR just before the New Year without any changes.[57] The result was a heavy-handed message, setting out in great detail (right down to naming specific Soviet officers) what the Americans wanted in a theatre that was peripheral to Stalin's strategic concerns, but where he was acutely sensitive about US efforts to embroil him in an undesired war.

Roosevelt to Stalin, sent 31 December 1942, received 1 January 1943[58]

In the event that Japan should attack Russia in the Far East, I am prepared to assist you in that theater with an American air force of approximately 100 four-engined bombardment airplanes as early as practicable, provided that certain items of supply and equipment are furnished by Soviet authorities and that suitable operation facilities are prepared in advance. Supply of our units must be entirely by air transport, hence it will be necessary for Soviet Government to furnish such items as bombs, fuel, lubricants, transportation, shelter, heat and other minor items to be determined.

Although we have no positive information that Japan will attack Russia, it does appear to be an eventual probability. Therefore, in order that we may be prepared for this contingency, I propose that the survey of air force facilities in the Far East, authorized by you to General Bradley on October 6 be made now, and that the discussions initiated on November 11 on your authority between General Bradley and General Korolenko be continued.

It is my intention to appoint General Bradley, who has my full confidence, to continue these discussions for the United States if you so agree. He will be empowered to explore for the United States every phase of combined Russo-American operations in the Far East theater and based upon his survey to recommend the composition and strength of our air forces which will be allocated to assist you should the necessity arise. He will also determine the extent of advance preparations practicable and necessary to insure effective participation of our units promptly on initiation of hostilities. His party will not exceed twenty persons to fly into Russia in two American Douglas DC-3 type airplanes.

If this meets with your approval, I would suggest that they proceed from Alaska along the ferry route into Siberia, thence under Russian direction to the headquarters of the Soviet armies in the Far East, and thence to such other places in Russia as may be necessary to make the required survey and discuss operating plans.

It would be very helpful if an English-speaking Russian officer such as Captain Vladimir Ovnovin, now in Washington, or Captain Smolyarov in Moscow, is detailed to accompany General Bradley as adjutant and liaison officer.

I seize this opportunity of expressing my admiration for the courage, stamina and military prowess of your great Russian armies as reported to me by General Bradley and as reflected in your great victories of the past month.

The president's message of 31 December must have revived Stalin's long-standing concerns that the Americans wanted to draw the Soviet Union into a premature war with Japan. The placement of the US air force in the Far East would be a flagrant violation of the Soviet–Japanese neutrality pact, while the proposed survey of Soviet military facilities in the Far East also smacked of espionage by the Americans. An inaccuracy in Pavlov's translation did not help:

the relatively neutral term 'survey' (*osmotr*) was turned into the seemingly intrusive 'inspection' (*inspektsiya*).[59] Nevertheless, in his reply Stalin simply reiterated what he had said about the Caucasus, namely that America should send the bombers, without their pilots, to the Soviet–German front.[60]

Despite Stalin's clear statement, Roosevelt persisted. Belatedly aware that his failure to think carefully about the Pentagon draft he okayed on 30 December had caused problems, he took time to edit their material on this occasion – adding, among other changes, the passages about General Marshall italicized in the text. But in fact, the president only dug himself in deeper by still pushing for General Bradley to be allowed to conduct a preliminary survey of Siberia.

FDR's offer to send Marshall to Moscow to discuss the whole strategic situation fits with the president's habit of sending VIP visitors to get the measure of Stalin – a particular concern since the Soviet leader was not coming to Casablanca. Nevertheless, this latest piece of Roosevelt improvisation came out of the blue at a meeting of the JCS on 7 January. After some discussion about plans for Casablanca, according to the official minutes:

> The President then asked General Marshall if he thought that he, General Marshall, should go to Moscow.
> General Marshall said, 'What would I be expected to accomplish there?'
> The President replied that the visit would be particularly for the purpose of giving impetus to the Russian morale. He said that Mr. Stalin had been invited to confer with the President and Mr. Churchill on two occasions but had been unable to do so. He said that he thought that Mr. Stalin probably felt out of the picture as far as Great Britain and the United States were concerned and also that he has a feeling of loneliness.

FDR mentioned some topics that he intended to discuss with Churchill at Casablanca – including the doctrine of 'unconditional surrender', the postwar disarmament of the Axis, and plans for a Big Three meeting in the summer – and suggested that Marshall 'could be the emissary to inform Mr. Stalin of these results'. The army chief of staff, probably taking a very deep breath, indicated that he would prepare to visit Moscow.[61]

Roosevelt to Stalin, sent 8 January 1943, received 10 January 1943[62]

After reading your reply to my radio[gram] concerning the Far East, I am afraid I did not make myself clear.

As I previously explained reference South Caucasus, it is not practicable to send heavy bombers to Russia at this time other than in existing organized units.

Our proposal regarding the 100 planes referred to a situation which would occur if hostilities were actually to break out between Japan and Russia. Under such conditions, we calculated that by regrouping our air units in the Pacific Theater, 100 planes in organized units could be concentrated in Eastern Siberia because their action as well as your battle there would enable us to reduce our air strength elsewhere in the Pacific Theater.

My radio [message] was intended to be in the nature of anticipatory protective planning against a possibility only. The immediate action recommended was in reference to the survey and discussions by General Bradley with Soviet officials. Only by such preliminary survey and advance planning will it be possible to render reasonably prompt assistance in the event of an outbreak of hostilities in Siberia.

I should like to send General Marshall to Moscow for a visit in the very near future and, if this can be arranged, I hope that you will be able to discuss this matter with him at that time.

He will be able to tell you about the current situation in Africa and also about planned operations for balance of this year in all war theaters. I think this will be very helpful and he will have the latest news. Meanwhile I would appreciate an early reply to my proposal of December 30 that General Bradley and his party proceed without delay to the Far East for survey and staff discussions.

My deep appreciation for the continuing advances of your armies. The principle of attrition of the enemy forces on all fronts is beginning to work.

Still optimistic about the prospects in North Africa, Churchill had told the chiefs of staff on 29 December to examine 'whether combined and concurrent operations can be organised from the West and South' in 1943 against Hitler's Europe – in other words, landings in France and in Sicily or Sardinia. On 5 January, the COS brought him back to reality: the available assault ships and landing craft would be 'insufficient to mount more than one large-scale amphibious operation at a time'. And even this would be on a dangerously limited scale, even in August 1943 – with the capacity to land no more than four divisions in France, or three divisions in Italy, during the crucial first forty-eight hours of the operation, when troops were struggling to establish a beachhead.[63]

The dire shortages of landing and assault vessels were facets of a larger shipping crisis. In October 1942, Churchill sent Roosevelt a long letter about 'some of the major points governing our joint action in the war', stating bluntly: 'First of all, I put the U-boat menace. This, I am sure, is our worst danger', with the

prospect of '700,000 tons a month loss'. Not only did this 'cripple our war energies and threaten our life' in Britain because of the country's reliance on
imports, but 'it arbitrarily limits the might of the United States coming into the
struggle. The Oceans, which were your shields, threaten to become your cage.'
On 30 November, Roosevelt replied that he wanted 'to give you the assurance
that from our expanding fleet you may depend on the tonnage necessary to
meet your import program'. He also said that the US Navy Department would
confer with British naval staff in Washington about the distribution of the 336
escort vessels that the USA expected to produce in 1943. This letter was,
however, never shared with the JCS and, in any case, 'Torch', the Pacific theatre
and the U-boats all took their toll of shipping – which proved the Achilles' heel
of the British–American war effort in 1943.[64]

The shipping crisis also figured in a message Churchill sent to Stalin on 10
January 1943, informing him about another hiatus in proposed Arctic convoys,
caused by a shortage of escorts, at a time when the Battle of the Atlantic was at
its height. The January sailing to Russia was therefore reduced from thirty
merchant vessels to nineteen, but Churchill said they would send full convoys
in February and in March. Before the PM wrote to Stalin, Maisky had already
got wind of the news. Referring to Churchill's 'promise' to Stalin in his letter of
29 December, the ambassador asked Eden and the Admiralty to fulfil this obligation.[65] Churchill exploded with rage:

> Monsieur Maisky is not telling the truth when he says I promised convoys
> of 30 ships in January and February. Maisky should be told that I am getting
> to the end of my tether with these repeated Russian naggings and that it is
> not the slightest use trying to knock me about any more. Our escorts all
> over the world are so attenuated that losses out of all proportion are falling
> upon the British Mercantile Marine.[66]

But the diplomatic Eden did not reprimand Maisky when they met on
11 January; the ambassador told Moscow that Eden said Churchill had 'made a
mistake by giving such a definite promise'.[67] Stalin reacted calmly to this
message in a brief reply on 16 January.[68]

Churchill to Stalin, sent 10 January 1943, received 12 January 1943[69]

The December convoy has now been fought through successfully and you will
have received details of the fine engagement fought by our light forces against
heavy odds.

The Admiralty had intended to run the January convoy in two parts of fifteen ships each, the first part sailing on about 17th January, and the second part later in the month. Since it is clear from the experience of the last convoy that the enemy means to dispute the passage of further convoys by surface forces, it will be necessary immediately to increase our escorts beyond the scale originally contemplated for January. A still further increase will be necessary for later convoys owing to the increased hours of daylight.

We have therefore had to revise our arrangements. Instead of running the January convoy in two parts we will sail 19 ships (including two oilers) instead of the 15 originally contemplated on 17th January. This will be followed on about the 11th February by a full convoy of 28 to 30 ships. Thereafter we will do our utmost to sail a convoy of thirty ships on about 10th March, but this is dependent on the Americans assisting us with escort vessels. If they cannot provide this assistance this convoy could not sail until 19th March at the earliest.

Roosevelt's letter of 8 January about the Far East was apparently the final straw for Stalin. The president's reiteration of his proposal to send air units to the Far East, despite Stalin's categorical statement on 5 January that they only wanted planes for the Soviet–German front, led the suspicious Soviet leader to the conclusion that the Americans sought to involve the USSR in 'their war', while keeping clear of Russia's struggle. Stalin also took umbrage over the proposed visit by Marshall. On another occasion, Stalin might have received the US Army chief of staff, but in current circumstances he deemed such a visit undesirable and brusquely asked what the point was. Also irritating was Roosevelt's obsession with General Bradley's proposed 'survey' of potential air bases in Siberia. In Pavlov's translation, the unfortunate word 'inspection' crept in again, and Stalin heavily underlined it.[70] Given all these irritations, the Soviet leader departed from his usual polite tone with Roosevelt and sent what was really his first sharp message to the president, tinged with irony. His reply made extensive use of the term 'inspection', and not only firmly declined all the president's proposals but also stepped on a sore spot by alluding to the Allies' slow progress in North Africa. Although the handwritten draft came from Molotov, the latter must surely have acted on instructions from Stalin.

After seeing the correspondence, Maisky predicted that Roosevelt would 'probably take offence' at Stalin's reply, but felt 'it can't be helped! The Americans need to be taught a lesson. They really do fancy themselves to be the salt of the earth and the mentors of the world.'[71]

Stalin to Roosevelt, sent 13 January 1943, received 13 January 1943[72]

I wish to express my gratitude for your decision to send 200 transport planes to the Soviet Union.

As regards sending bombing avio-units to the Far East, I made clear in my previous messages that what we want is not avio-units, but airplanes without fliers, as we have more than enough fliers of our own. This is in the first place.

In the second place, we want your aid in airplanes not in the Far East, where the USSR is not in a state of war, but at the Soviet–German front, where the need for aviation aid is particularly acute.

I do not understand your suggestion that General Bradley should inspect Russian military objectives in the Far East and in other parts of the USSR. It would seem obvious that Russian military objects can be inspected only by Russian inspectors, just as American military objects can be inspected only by American inspectors. In this respect there must be no misunderstanding.

As regards General Marshall's journey to the U.S.S.R., I must say that his mission is not quite clear to me. I would ask for elucidation as to the purpose and aims of the journey, so that I could consider this question in full consciousness of what it entails, before giving an answer.

My colleagues are concerned over the slowing down of operations in North Africa and, moreover, as it is said, not for a short time, but for a long period. May I have some information from you on this point?

Roosevelt did not reply to Stalin's icy message, resisting the temptation to respond in the same vein; but he vented his feelings while at Casablanca – as Churchill told Maisky and Eden later. The British clearly shared Stalin's reaction to the president's ham-fisted démarche about the Soviet Far East: Churchill laughingly called it 'a remarkable message', while, according to Maisky's diary, 'Eden's face was a picture of horror when he heard of the proposal to send 100 bombers' to Siberia. 'Well,' said Churchill, 'Roosevelt was, frankly speaking, enraged by Stalin's message and wanted to send an abusive reply. But I managed to talk him out of it. I told him: listen, who is really fighting today? Stalin alone! And look how he's fighting! We must make allowance. The president eventually agreed and thought better of starting a row with Stalin.'[73]

*****

Churchill and Roosevelt descended on Casablanca in high spirits – almost like schoolboys who had skipped class. FDR suggested that he and Hopkins adopt the aliases Don Quixote and Sancho Panza. 'However did you think of such an impenetrable disguise?' Churchill asked with heavy irony. He suggested 'Admiral Q' and 'Mr P', adding 'NB We must mind our P's and Q's.'[74] The conference venue was the plush Hotel Anfa, in the suburbs of Casablanca, where the two leaders and the Combined Chiefs of Staff (CCS) held a gruelling series of meetings from 12 to 24 January. On the main strategic issue, the second front, their options were severely limited. As Marshall had consistently warned, the logistical implications of 'Torch' had already made a full-scale invasion of France ('Roundup') unlikely in 1943; by the New Year, a combination of slow progress in North Africa, the shipping crisis and the shortage of landing craft ruled out anything but a smaller 'lodgement' on the continent ('Sledgehammer'). Even this was predicated on the assumption that 'the German strength in France decreases, either through withdrawal of her troops or because of an internal collapse'. It would not be the operation Stalin wanted – a full-frontal assault on Hitler's 'Fortress Europe', risking substantial losses in order to draw the Wehrmacht back from the Eastern Front.[75]

In their final report, dated 24 January, the CCS distinguished three types of amphibious operation from the UK. Since these decisions would cast a long shadow over Big Three relations, they should be quoted precisely:

(1) Raids with the primary object of provoking air battles and causing enemy losses.
(2) Operations with the object of seizing and holding a bridgehead and, if the state of German morale and resources permit, of vigorously exploiting success.
(3) A return to the Continent to take advantage of German disintegration.

Under (2), the CCS identified an operation against the Cotentin Peninsula (south from the port of Cherbourg), with a target date of 1 August 1943. They also agreed to set up a US–UK planning staff, whose directive would include 'provision for a return to the Continent under (3) above with the forces which will be available for the purpose in the United Kingdom month by month'. A draft of this passage had contained an additional sentence: 'The directive will also make provision for the planning of an invasion of the Continent in 1944.' But this sentence was deleted from the final version, even though it reflected the clear sense of the CCS – namely that, to quote the head of the US Army Air Force, General 'Hap' Arnold, 'it looked very much as if no continental operations on any scale were in prospect before the spring of 1944'. Brooke agreed, but added that 'we should definitely count on re-entering the Continent in 1944 on a large scale'.[76]

Given the need to do something once North Africa was liberated, the conference agreed to prepare an invasion of Sicily (operation 'Husky') in July, with Eisenhower as supreme Allied commander. Nothing was said about what would happen after that. Early in the conference, Brooke explicitly ruled out 'any further operations in Italy from Sicily in 1943, unless Italy collapsed completely', but he saw the island as a convenient base from which to intensify Allied bombing 'to put Italy out of the war'. Marshall was not happy about the strategic drift. The US Army chief of staff remained focused on invading France as the key to Germany's defeat, and warned that 'every diversion or side issue from the main plot acts as a "suction pump"'.[77] He clearly feared that 'Husky' could have that effect in 1943, just like 'Torch' in 1942; but as the conference developed, he and his American colleagues were not able to resist concerted British pressure. This was partly on account of deep and unresolved differences between the US Army and the US Navy about the priority given to France over the Pacific; but it was also due to the fact that the British arrived with a large and informed planning staff, backed by a floating war room of maps, charts and statistics on the headquarters ship HMS *Bulolo*. As US Army planner General Albert Wedemeyer ruefully put it (adapting Julius Caesar): 'We came, we listened, and we were conquered'.[78]

All this meant that the Allies, to use Maisky's metaphor, would continue to pinch the 'tail' of the Nazi beast, rather than hit it 'round the head with a club'.[79] Although Roosevelt and Churchill had kept open the possibility of some kind of cross-Channel invasion in 1943, they knew that the results of Casablanca were not likely to please Stalin. So they decided to report to him in a special joint letter, which was drafted by the CCS on 21–22 January, reworked by Hopkins and Harriman, and discussed by the two leaders on the nights of 23 and 24 January. 'Our idea,' Churchill told the War Cabinet, 'is that this statement should set out combined intentions but should contain no promises.' The joint letter superseded FDR's earlier, vague idea of sending Marshall as another special envoy – probably because of Stalin's cool reception of that idea, but also because Roosevelt and Churchill wanted to minimize discussion with the Kremlin.[80]

It was important not only to inform the Kremlin, but also to proclaim to the world the unity of the anti-Hitler coalition. The summit communiqué, also carefully drafted, stated:

Premier Stalin was cordially invited to meet the President and Prime Minister, in which case the meeting would have been held very much farther to the east. He was unable to leave Russia at this time on account of the great offensive which he himself, as Commander-in-Chief, is directing.

The President and Prime Minister realized up to the full the enormous weight of the war which Russia is successfully bearing along her whole land front, and their prime object has been to draw as much weight as possible off the Russian armies by engaging the enemy as heavily as possible at the best selected points.

Premier Stalin has been fully informed of the military proposals.[81]

The statement about Stalin being 'fully informed' was an exaggeration, because the joint message to him had been deliberately vague. Nevertheless, the Western leaders did not deceive themselves about the Kremlin's reaction. 'Nothing in the world would be acceptable to Stalin as an alternative to our placing 50 or 60 divisions in France by the spring of this year,' Churchill told the Cabinet. 'I think he will be disappointed and furious with the joint message. Therefore I thought it wise that the President and I should both stand together. After all our backs are broad.'[82]

Churchill and Roosevelt to Stalin, sent 26 January 1943, received 27 January 1943[83]

We have been in conference with our military advisers and have decided on the operations which are to be undertaken by the American and British forces in the first nine months of 1943. We wish to inform you of our intentions at once. We believe that these operations, together with your powerful offensive, may well bring Germany to her knees in 1943. Every effort must be made to accomplish this purpose.

We are in no doubt that our correct strategy is to concentrate on the defeat of Germany, with a view to achieving an early and decisive victory in the European theatre. At the same time, we must maintain sufficient pressure on Japan to retain the initiative in the Pacific and the Far East and sustain China and prevent the Japanese from extending their aggression to other theatres such as your Maritime provinces.

Our main desire has been to divert strong German land and air forces from the Russian front and to send Russia the maximum flow of supplies. We shall spare no exertion to send you material assistance by every available route.

Our immediate intention is to clear the Axis out of North Africa and set up naval and air installations to open:

(i)   an effective passage through the Mediterranean for military traffic, and

(ii) an intensive bombardment of important Axis targets in Southern Europe.

We have made the decision to launch large-scale amphibious operations in the Mediterranean at the earliest possible moment. Preparation for these operations is now under way and will involve a considerable concentration of forces, including landing craft and shipping in Egyptian and North African ports. In addition, we shall concentrate in the United Kingdom a strong American land and air force. These, combined with the British forces in the United Kingdom, will prepare themselves to re-enter the continent of Europe as soon as practicable. These concentrations will certainly be known to our enemies, but they will not know where or when or on what scale we propose striking. They will, therefore, be compelled to divert both land and air forces to all the shores of France, the Low Countries, Corsica, Sardinia, Sicily and the Levant, and Italy, Yugoslavia, Greece, Crete and the Dodecanese.

In Europe we shall increase the Allied bomber offensive from the United Kingdom against Germany at a rapid rate and by midsummer it should be double its present strength. Our experiences to date have shown that day bombing attacks result in the destruction and damage to large numbers of German fighter aircraft. We believe an increased tempo and weight of daylight and night attacks will lead to greatly increased material and morale damage in Germany and rapidly deplete German fighter strength. As you are aware, we are already containing more than half [the] German Air Force in Western Europe and the Mediterranean. We have no doubt that our intensified and diversified bombing offensive, together with the other operations which we are undertaking will compel further withdrawals of German air and other forces from the Russian front.

In the Pacific it is our intention to eject the Japanese from Rabaul within the next few months and thereafter to exploit the success in the general direction of Japan. We also intend to increase the scale of our operations in Burma in order to reopen our channel of supply to China. We intend to increase our air force in China at once. We shall not, however, allow our offensives against Japan to jeopardise our capacity to take advantage of every opportunity that may present itself for the decisive defeat of Germany in 1943.

Our ruling purpose is to bring to bear upon Germany and Italy the maximum forces by land, sea and air which can be physically applied.

Ambassador Standley and Lacy Baggallay, the British chargé, were instructed to deliver personally to Stalin the message from Roosevelt and Churchill about Casablanca, which they did together on the night of 26–27 January.[84] The Kremlin gave the text very serious attention. Probably on Stalin's instructions, Molotov even ordered that Pavlov's translation should be checked against the rendition into Russian by the British embassy. 'Semantic differences are not found,' Foreign Ministry staff reported. 'The only difference between the two translations is that Pavlov's translation reads better in Russian (editing, style).'[85]

Baggallay reported to London that Stalin's reaction to the message was restrained. Having read the text, he stated tersely that he had 'no questions'. Stalin 'had a good poker face', Standley noted; he looked at Molotov and handed him the message without comment. Privately, however, the two Allied diplomats noted the message's 'incompleteness' and 'vagueness' about upcoming operations. Standley suggested that this was deliberate, admonishing Stalin for not going to Casablanca. Be that as it may, concluded Baggallay in his report, 'Stalin is apparently expecting something more specific.'[86]

Two short messages from Churchill to Stalin, dated 27 and 29 January, concerned the PM's forthcoming visit to Turkey. This had aroused a good deal of debate within the Cabinet. Eden and Attlee tried to dissuade Churchill from going, believing there was no compelling reason for Turkey to change its policy of neutrality and that the time was therefore not ripe for such a visit. Churchill, however, seizing on information from the British ambassador in Ankara, believed that he could accelerate Turkey's entry into the war by playing up Soviet victories on the Eastern Front and Allied successes in the Mediterranean. He also exploited US agreement at the conference that Britain should 'play the hand' in Turkey, just as America was taking the lead with China. Churchill duly informed Stalin of this meeting, while putting out a cover story that he was actually going to Moscow.[87]

Although the USSR had a special interest in access through the Straits to the Black Sea, Churchill's unconcealed passion for the Eastern Mediterranean was unlikely to reduce Stalin's doubts about his commitment to the second front. These were evident in his response to Churchill and Roosevelt's joint message about Casablanca. In his reply, unchanged from Molotov's draft, the Soviet leader asked explicitly to be informed about 'the concrete operations planned' and 'their timing'. For the moment, he refrained from further comment, hoping (or pretending to hope) that the Allies would hold to their commitment to open a second front in 1943. But he could easily see that his allies were hedging their bets – insinuating a readiness to invade France, while focusing their attention and resources on the Mediterranean. Over the next few months, the failure of Churchill and Roosevelt to come clean with Stalin would create a major rift in the Alliance.[88]

Stalin to Roosevelt and Churchill, sent 30 January 1943, received 30 January 1943[89]

I received your friendly joint message on the 27th January. I thank you for the information on the decisions taken in Casablanca regarding operations to be carried out by American and British armed forces in the course of the first nine months of 1943. As I understand that by the decisions taken regarding Germany you yourselves set the task of crushing it by opening a second front in Europe in 1943, I should be very obliged to you for information on the concrete operations planned in this respect and on the scheduled times of their realization.

As regards the Soviet Union, I can assure you that the armed forces of the USSR will do everything in their power to continue the offensive against Germany and her allies on the Soviet–German front. Circumstances permitting, we expect to finish our winter campaign in the first half of February of this year. Our troops are tired, they need rest and will hardly be able to continue the offensive beyond that time.

*****

By dawn on 31 January 1943, Red Army troops had cleared virtually all of central Stalingrad, working from cellar to cellar with grenades and flame-throwers. 'Russians at the entrance,' Paulus's headquarters staff signalled at 07.35. 'We are preparing to surrender.' Russian emissaries descended into the stinking basement, and a couple of hours later the German commander came up into daylight – his gaunt, stubbled face captured in dozens of photos.[90]

On 3 February, German radio finally admitted that the battle was over, but assured listeners that generals, officers and men had 'fought shoulder to shoulder to the last bullet'. During three days of official mourning, with solemn music and masses for the dead, Göring and Goebbels tried to elevate the 'heroes' of Stalingrad to the level of the Spartans who sacrificed themselves at Thermopylae against the 'Asiatic' hordes. But Stalingrad could not be mytholo-gized. A few days later, rumours began circulating about mass surrenders from Paulus downward. Most Germans realized that their country had suffered a major defeat, that talk of conquering Russia was now pie in the sky, and that they now had to face an apparently endless war of attrition. One black joke told of Wehrmacht soldiers on the Eastern Front who had read a strange word – 'Peace'. No one knew what it meant. After the query went all the way up to battalion HQ, the commander found the answer in a recently published dictionary: 'Peace, way of life unfit for human beings, abolished in 1939.'[91]

Stalingrad was *the* turning point in Hitler's war. And it made the Soviets think. One catches this in Maisky's diary. After savouring the capture of Paulus, two dozen generals and some 90,000 men, he mused: 'If in spite of all our efforts a second front were not to be opened, would this really be an unalloyed misfortune? I doubt it.' Of course, he admitted, no second front would mean higher Russian losses. 'But what about the long run? Here the balance might be different.' First, 'all the glory for defeating Germany would be ours', boosting the prestige of the USSR and of communism. Second, if Britain and America stayed on the sidelines, they 'would emerge from the war with weak and inexperienced armed forces, while the Red Army would become the most powerful army in the world'. This would 'tip the international balance of power in our favour'. And third, 'the Red Army would stand a good chance of entering Berlin first and thereby having a decisive influence on the terms of peace and on the situation in the post-war period'. Maisky summed up:

So which course of events would be more advantageous for us in the final analysis?

Hard to say. At first glance, a second front would seem preferable. But is that really the case?

Time will tell.[92]

7

SECOND FRONT WHEN?

(February to April 1943)

FEBRUARY 1943 BEGAN WITH news of the German surrender at Stalingrad. The twenty-fifth anniversary of the Red Army, later that month, became the focus of celebrations in both Allied countries, and Roosevelt and Churchill each went out of his way to praise Stalin's military genius. Now that the Red Army was winning, the Soviet leader had moved from wearing traditional Bolshevik party attire (the 'peasant' clothing noted rather derisorily by the British when Churchill visited Moscow in August 1942) to full-dress military uniforms. In his Kremlin office, pictures of Engels, Marx, Lenin and other communist ideologues were replaced by heroic generals from the Russian past, especially the wars against Napoleonic France, such as Alexander Suvorov and Mikhail Kutuzov.

During February, Stalin gradually extracted from his allies fuller details of what had been agreed at Casablanca. Roosevelt still tried to be vague, but Churchill was more candid, speaking with considerable frankness to Maisky (probably when in his cups) late on 8 February. Stalin indicted both his allies for their slowness in clearing the Axis out of Tunisia – April was now the predicted date, not February – and for their intention to invade France in August or September, urging that this should be done in spring or early summer to help the Red Army. But this letter of 16 February was couched more in sorrow than in anger – unlike some of his messages in 1941 and 1942 – pointing out the 'undesirability' of such a delay for 'our common interests'. To appreciate his tone, it is worth noting that there were considerable hopes in Moscow after Stalingrad of a rapid German collapse in 1943. These evaporated in late March, after Field Marshal Erich von Manstein's counter-offensive in the Ukraine (known in Germany as the Donets Campaign and to the Russians, more precisely, as the Donbas and Kharkov operations), which drove the Red Army back more than a hundred kilometres before the spring thaw put an end to serious campaigning until the summer.

With the war quietening down for the moment on the Eastern Front, Churchill shifted gears in his correspondence – acutely conscious, as he put it on several occasions to British and US policymakers, that they were holding down perhaps a dozen German divisions, compared with the 185 facing Stalin.[1] Not only did he play up every phase of the campaign in Tunisia, even though this served to show just how slowly the British and US armies were advancing, but he also sent upbeat reports on virtually every bombing raid on Germany mounted as part of the strategic bombing offensive agreed at Casablanca. His clear intention was to show that this was a surrogate second front. The prime minister also sent a remarkably full and candid account of British global dispositions and shipping constraints on 11 March, seeking to explain why a cross-Channel attack was so problematic. In this he laid bare information that Roosevelt had been at pains to conceal about how few US divisions would be available in Britain by August, because of the campaigns in North Africa and the Pacific. This elicited another message of complaint from Stalin to both his allies on 15 March about the continued slippage in North Africa and the centrality of a second front, not successes in the Mediterranean, for Allied victory. Yet, once more, he pulled his punches – talking about the 'grave danger' of further delays in invading France and the 'apprehension' he felt at the 'vagueness' of their statements – without going ballistic.

Stalin was also surprisingly muted when told by Churchill at the end of March about another suspension in the Arctic convoys – this time until at least late summer, because of German naval deployments and then the priority of the planned invasion of Sicily. Possibly this reflects the Soviet leader's growing subtlety, guided by Maisky, in dealing with Churchill – playing on his sense of noblesse oblige and his feelings of guilt at the weight of the war falling on Soviet shoulders. The PM's almost boyish delight on 31 March at Stalin's dismissal as 'scoundrels' of those claiming that Britain was just watching the war was fully reported by Maisky to the Kremlin. Both Stalin and Churchill were clearly developing an 'epistolary' relationship in the early spring of 1943, based on an attempt to understand the other's psychology. Churchill was particularly explicit about this, explaining the perplexing alternation of warm and hard messages from the Kremlin through what was now, since the Moscow visit in August 1942, his idée fixe about 'two Stalins' – which postulated a Soviet leader who liked Churchill personally, but who often had to take account of his hardline colleagues. This remarkable misapprehension of the power dynamics in Moscow would continue to shape the PM's perceptions of the USSR in 1943, and indeed for the rest of the war.

The absent partner in all this was Roosevelt. The few messages he sent to Stalin during these months were mostly formulaic – praise for Red Army victories – and usually composed by others, with very little presidential amendment. And he sent no messages at all between 23 February and 26 April. Although that period included a two-week tour of military bases in April,[2] the president was generally content for the PM to take responsibility for the difficult messages on strategy and the convoys. But he did put down a marker of sorts in a message about the second front on 22 February, which was only forwarded to the PM ten days later. In his turn, Churchill was at pains to conceal from FDR the information on US dispositions that he had sent to Stalin on 11 March. In short, there were now signs that the two leaders were trying to deal with Stalin in their own ways. For Roosevelt, the fascinations of cultivating a pen-pal were distinctly limited. What he wanted was a face-to-face relationship.

The president was also firming up his vision of the postwar world, as Eden discovered when he paid a lengthy visit to Washington in late March 1943. FDR made clear that the 'real decisions' would be taken by America, Britain, the USSR and China – insisting that the Chinese should be one of the 'policemen', despite Eden's scepticism. He was also emphatic about Germany's 'total surrender' and the need for an orderly but rapid process of European decolonization – suggesting that Britain give Hong Kong back to China as a 'good will' gesture.[3]

On 30 March, at the end of Eden's visit, the president told a press conference that they had spent some time discussing the postwar peace, and then added 'I hope and expect that we will be continuing discussions along these lines with the Russian Government in the very near future.' A reporter jumped in:

'Is there anything more specific we can have on this? This summer, do you plan ...'

'No, not today,' the president shot back, amid laughter.

'Is hope still "springing eternal" about Mr Stalin?'

'Yes.'

'Do you expect a surprise visit?'

'What?'

'Do you expect to be surprised by somebody arriving?'
'You can never tell.'

The delphic president, as always, was playing his own game.[4]

*****

Churchill's talks with Turkish leaders on 30–31 January in Adana did not produce any significant reorientation of Turkey's policy towards the Allies. However, Churchill did not abandon his cherished idea of drawing Turkey into a war against the Axis. Reporting to Stalin on the talks, Churchill was deliberately upbeat – expressing the opinion that Turkey would enter the war 'before the year is out'. He also urged the Soviet leader to allay historic Turkish fears of Russia and said that he had told them that 'the safest place for Turkey was to have a seat with the victors, as a belligerent, at the peace table'. Stalin sent a polite reply, clearly indicating his expectation that the Turks would continue to sit on the fence.[5]

In his letter, Churchill also addressed Stalin's concern about the slowing down of the Allied offensive in North Africa – blaming bad weather, overstretched lines of communication and the enemy's strong defensive positions. Despite the fact that Montgomery's Eighth Army took Tripoli earlier than expected, on 23 January, its port had been destroyed by the Germans and took time to repair.[6] Although Churchill's explanations of slow progress were valid, they cannot have impressed Stalin. To a leader directing millions of men in costly but spectacularly successful operations across the vast expanse of the wintry Eastern Front, Churchill's problems across a few hundred square miles of muddy desert would not have seemed unsurmountable.

The Soviet victory at Stalingrad was front-page news all over the world. In public tributes, Churchill and Roosevelt each went out of his way to highlight Stalin's personal role as military supremo. At a press conference on 1 February, Churchill praised 'the tremendous feat of arms performed by our Russian Ally under the general command and direction of Premier Stalin, a great warrior, and a name which will rank with those most honoured and most lasting in the history of the Russian people'.[7] Roosevelt's congratulatory message, transmitted in an uncyphered telegram to Stalin, was couched explicitly as coming from one commander-in-chief to another. On White House orders, the message was passed to the US press and published on 5 February. Next day, Roosevelt's greetings and a polite response from Stalin were printed in the Soviet press.[8]

Roosevelt to Stalin, sent 4 February 1943, received 5 February 1943[9]

As Commander-in-Chief of the Armed Forces of the United States of America I congratulate you on the brilliant victory at Stalingrad of the armies under your Supreme Command. The 162 days of epic battle for the city which has for ever honored your name and the decisive result which all Americans are celebrating today will remain one of the proudest chapters in this war of the peoples united against Nazism and its emulators.

The commanders and fighters of your armies at the front and the men and women, who have supported them, in factory and field, have combined not only to cover with glory their country's arms, but to inspire by their example fresh determination among all the United Nations to bend every energy to bring about the final defeat and unconditional surrender of the common enemy.

Stalin's main concern was the paucity of information about what Churchill and Roosevelt had decided at Casablanca. After receiving their broad-brush summary of discussions, Stalin had asked pointedly on 30 January for details of 'the concrete operations planned' and of their timing. The response was prepared with great care in London, and Churchill's draft message was then coordinated with Roosevelt. The president was initially happy to nod it through ('I wholly approve') in a brief, chatty message to the PM that he probably dictated himself. But when this was shown to the Joint Chiefs, they were far from pleased and requested amendments to two key paragraphs (see 9 February, below): about Italy (b) and the cross-Channel assault (d). On the first, Churchill's draft had stated that in July or earlier, they intended to 'attack Italy across the Central Mediterranean with the object of promoting an Italian collapse, and establishing contact with Yugoslavia'. Alert for signs of Churchillian mission creep, the Joint Chiefs replaced 'attack Italy' with 'seize Sicily' (as agreed at Casablanca) and turned the reference to Yugoslavia hinting at a possible Balkan campaign into the vaguer phrase 'with the consequent effect on Greece and Yugoslavia'. As to France, they objected to Churchill's sentence giving a detailed enumeration of the forces likely to be used: 'We are aiming at August for a heavy operation across the Channel, for which between seventeen and twenty British and US divisions will be available, of which four to seven will be US divisions, with a gross strength of fifty thousand each.' Admiral Ernest King, chief of naval operations, warned FDR that the paragraph 'promises <u>much more</u> than can be done, even though the word used is "aiming"'. This paragraph was replaced with a more general statement about 'pushing preparations to the limit of our resources for a cross-channel opera-tion in August' or else September, and the rider that timing must depend on 'the condition of German defensive possibilities' at that moment. FDR nodded through those changes equally insouciantly, adding only a request: 'Please inform Stalin that I approve of this message.' Churchill accepted the American revisions and resisted the efforts of Brooke and his own military to remove the August–September date for the possible invasion of France, to avoid Britain being tied down.[10]

This transatlantic exchange was important. Whereas Churchill tried to address Stalin's desire for concreteness with almost reckless precision, the JCS – militarily prudent, but taking risks diplomatically – had emasculated his message. The president did not seem to care either way. Yet this telegram would set the tone of relations with Stalin for 1943 because, even after being moder-ated by the Americans, it could be construed as almost a promise – especially bearing in mind the near commitment about 1943 made in Churchill's memo to Molotov of 10 June 1942. Making matters worse for the British was the PM's loose tongue on the evening of 8 February, just before the revised message was sent to Stalin. The PM had returned only the day before after his two-week odyssey around the Mediterranean. When Maisky arrived punctually for his 10.30 p.m. meeting to deliver Stalin's telegram on Turkey, Churchill was nowhere to be seen. He eventually appeared in his siren suit, bleary-eyed with tousled hair, having only just got up from a post-prandial nap. Soon, however, he became extremely loquacious – perhaps lubricated by the 'bottle of whisky' that Maisky studiously noted at the start of the long account of the evening that he wrote in his diary and sent to the Politburo.

The ambassador quickly moved the PM off Turkey and onto the plans concocted at Casablanca. Churchill showed him the draft Stalin message he had sent to Roosevelt and the president's reply, which contained, as Maisky inaccurately put it, 'some (insignificant) amendments to Churchill's proposals'. The ambassador's account not only provided a full summary of each paragraph of the PM's draft, but also added extra detail from Churchill himself. Especially striking was what the PM was reported as saying about the potential scope of the Italian operation: 'If the Italians' resistance proves weak or a pro-Allied coup happens in Italy by that time, the British and Americans will make for the north of the Apennine Peninsula, and from there head west to southern France and east to the Balkans.' None of this had been agreed at Casablanca. Even more imprudent was what Churchill let slip about capabilities for a cross-Channel assault, claiming that the British would be able to assign twelve to fifteen divisions.

'But the Americans?' Maisky asked.

Churchill stopped and shrugged. 'Right now the Americans have only one division here!'[11]

Maisky was astonished.

'The Americans have sent nothing since November,' Churchill explained.

'How many American divisions do you expect by August?'

'I wish I knew,' replied Churchill with what Maisky called 'comical despair'. When talking to Stalin in August, he said, he had been working on the assumption that the Americans would have sent twenty-seven divisions to Britain by 1943 – 'just as they had promised'. (This was, of course, before 'Torch' intervened.)

'Now the Americans promise to send only 4–5 divisions by August!' he exclaimed. 'If they keep their word, then the cross-Channel operation will be carried out with 17–20 divisions.'

'What if the Americans deceive you once again?'

Churchill thought for a moment. 'I'll carry out this operation whatever happens.'[12]

This was a remarkable conversation. Of course, Maisky enjoyed colouring his accounts of meetings with Churchill, but whether or not the PM used the exact words ascribed to him, the ambassador had captured the essence of the PM's original draft message to Stalin – which the Americans had tried to conceal. As with most of Maisky's important cables, copies of his report – sent on the morning of 9 February[13] – were distributed to all Politburo members. After reading it, the Soviet leadership would have had little confidence in the 'information' on Allied strategy for 1943 that Churchill provided later that day in the sanitized telegram.

Nor would the Kremlin have been impressed on the 14th by some Churchillian hyperbole about how the liberation of Rostov-on-Don left him 'without power to express' Britain's 'admiration and gratitude'.[14]

Churchill to Stalin, sent 9 February 1943, received 12 February 1943[15]

Your message of 30th January. I have now consulted the President and the matter has been referred to the Staffs on both sides of the Ocean. I am authorised to reply for us both as follows:

(a) There are a quarter of a million Germans and Italians in Eastern Tunisia. We hope to destroy or expel these during April, if not earlier.

(b) When this is accomplished, we intend in July, or earlier if possible, to seize Sicily with the object of clearing the Mediterranean, promoting an Italian collapse with the consequent effect on Greece and Yugoslavia and wearing down of the German Air Force; this is to be closely followed by an operation in the Eastern Mediterranean, probably against the Dodecanese.

(c) This operation will involve all the shipping and landing craft we can get together in the Mediterranean and all the troops we can have trained in assault-landing in time, and will be of the order of three or four hundred thousand men. We shall press any advantage to the utmost once ports of entry and landing bases have been established.

(d) We are also pushing preparations to the limit of our resources for a cross-Channel operation in August, in which both British and US units would participate. Here again, shipping and assault-landing craft will be limiting factors. If the operation is delayed by the weather or other reasons, it will be prepared with stronger forces for September. The timing of this attack must, of course, be dependent upon the condition of German defensive possibilities across the Channel at that time.

(e) Both the operations will be supported by very large United States and British air forces, and that across the Channel by the whole Metropolitan Air Force of Great Britain. Together, these operations will strain to the very utmost the shipping resources of Great Britain and the United States.

(f) The President and I have enjoined upon our Combined Chiefs of Staff the need for the utmost speed and for reinforcing the attacks to the extreme limit that is humanly and physically possible.

Stalin replied to his two partners separately, though the text was essentially the same.[16] He expressed dismay about the slowness in cleaning up Tunisia, and urged them to invade France in the spring, rather than delay until August–September. He also asserted that Hitler had transferred twenty-seven divisions (an exaggeration) to the Eastern Front because of the slackening of operations in Tunisia 'for some reasons'. Despite what could have been taken here as an insinuation of Allied treachery, Stalin's general tone was exhortatory rather than inquisitorial – urging his allies to get a move on and cross the Channel because 'simultaneous pressure on Hitler' on two fronts 'could achieve great results'.

It is worth noting that, like early 1942 after the counter-attack before Moscow, victory at Stalingrad had somewhat gone to the head of the Boss and the Stavka high command. They were further emboldened by recapturing the Ukrainian city of Kharkov on 16 February. Amid this heady atmosphere, Soviet strategic aims had expanded far beyond the simple defeat of German forces in southern Russia; the Stavka sought to collapse enemy defences along virtually the entire Eastern Front.[17] If, as seems to be the case, at this point the Soviet leadership sniffed the chance of victory in 1943, that helps to explain the disappointed rather than angry tone of Stalin's message.

Stalin to Churchill, sent 16 February 1943, received 16 February 1943[18]

I received your message concerning the contemplated Anglo-American military operations on the 12th February. Many thanks for your additional information on the Casablanca decisions. I cannot refrain, however, from making certain observations on your message, which as you state represents the viewpoint of the President.

It is evident from your message that, contrary to your previous calculations, the end of operations in Tunis is expected in April instead of February. I hardly need to tell you how disappointing is such a delay. Strong activity of the Anglo-American troops in North Africa is more than ever necessary at this moment when the Soviet armies are still in a position to maintain their powerful general offensive. With simultaneous pressure on Hitler from our front and from your side we could achieve great results. Such a situation would create serious difficulties for Hitler and Mussolini. In this way the intended operations in Sicily and the Eastern Mediterranean could be expedited.

It is evident from your message also that the establishment of the second front, in particular in France, is envisaged only in August–September. It seems to me the present situation demands the greatest possible speeding up of the action contemplated, i.e. of the opening of the Second Front in the west at a considerably earlier date than indicated. In order not to give the enemy any respite, it is extremely important to deliver the blow from the West in the Spring or early Summer and not to postpone it until the second half of the year.

We have reliable information to the effect that since the end of December, when the Anglo-American operations in Tunis for some reasons was slowed down, the Germans transferred 27 divisions, including 5 Panzer divisions, from France, Belgium, Holland and Germany itself to the Soviet–German front. Thus, instead of helping the Soviet Union by diversion of the German forces from the Soviet–German front, the position of Hitler was alleviated. It is just because the military operations in Tunis slackened, Hitler was able to throw in some additional troops against the Russians.

All this brings to the conclusion that the sooner we will jointly take advantage of Hitler's difficulties at the front, the more reasons we will have to expect his early defeat. Unless we will take all this into consideration, unless we will use the present moment to our common interest, it may well be that the Germans, after having a respite which will enable them to remuster their forces, may once more recover their strength. It is clear to everyone of us how undesirable it would be to allow this to occur.

I deemed it necessary to send this reply also to Mr Roosevelt.

Many thanks for your very warm congratulations on the liberation of Rostov. Our troops today captured Kharkov.

Maisky was unable to deliver Stalin's message in person to Churchill, because the PM, worn down by his travels around the Mediterranean, had been taken ill with pneumonia, so Maisky saw Eden instead. The foreign secretary showed the paper to the bed-ridden PM, who said that 'every observation' in it was 'fair and just' and that he would respond as soon as possible.[19] Maisky pressed Eden to reconsider what had been agreed at Casablanca in the light of the current military situation, arguing that the war might end in 1943 if the Soviet offensive were bolstered by a 'sufficiently strong blow from the west' in the form of an invasion of France. 'Sicily, Italy, and so on can be delayed because, if the second front lives up to expectations,' he said, 'the question of the Mediterranean will be solved by itself.' According to Eden's account of the meeting, Maisky stated firmly that, after the capture of Kharkov and Rostov, 'the Soviet Government believed that there was a much greater chance of finishing the war this year than had seemed possible even a month ago.'[20]

Churchill's promised reply was delayed by his pneumonia: between 19 and 25 February, he did not dictate any minutes, and whiled away the time in bed by reading a novel – an unnatural activity that shows just how ill he was. The trip to Casablanca had also undermined Roosevelt's health: he succumbed to influenza in late February and found it hard to shake off. But he needed to respond to Stalin's 16 February rebukes about Allied strategy. A first draft on 18 February from his chief of staff, Admiral Leahy, was followed next day by a longer text prepared by General Marshall and Field Marshal Sir John Dill, head of the British Staff Mission in Washington. This went into more explanatory detail about the weather conditions in Tunisia ('reported to be the rainiest winter in that area for many years') and blamed the delay in mounting the second front 'solely' on the shortage of shipping – stating that 'we are using a considerable portion of our shipping and escort vessels, both British and American, to send supplies to you'. The draft also contained a long paragraph about the combined air offensive, as a result of which 'a considerable portion of the German air force is now maintained in Western Europe against Anglo-American operations'.[21] Roosevelt did not use the text from Marshall and Dill, and sent only an abbreviated version of Leahy's draft, whose clotted phrases and clichéd praise cannot have impressed Stalin. Perhaps because of his illness, the president did not consult Churchill before sending off the message on 22 February. This was to cause some problems in March.

Roosevelt to Stalin, sent 22 February 1943, received 23 February 1943[22]

I have received your message of February 16th in which you present certain considerations that you had communicated to Mr Churchill in reply to his message to you of February 12th.

I regret equally with you that the Allied effort in North Africa did not proceed in accordance with the schedule, which was interrupted by unexpected heavy rains that made the roads extremely difficult for both supplies and troops en route from our landing ports to the front lines and made the fields and mountains impassable.

I realize fully the adverse effect of this delay on the common allied effort and I am taking every possible step to begin at the earliest possible moment successful aggressive action against the Axis forces in Africa with the purpose of accomplishing their destruction.

You are fully informed in regard to the wide dispersion of America's transportation facilities at the present time and I can assure you that we are making a maximum effort to increase the output of ships to improve our transportation.

I understand the importance of a military effort on the Continent of Europe at the earliest practicable date in order to reduce Axis resistance to your heroic army, and you may be sure that the American war effort will be projected on to the Continent of Europe at as early a date subsequent to success in North Africa as transportation facilities can be provided by our maximum effort.

We wish that the success of your heroic army, which is an inspiration to all of us, will continue.

On the same day, perhaps to offset this message, Roosevelt also sent Stalin formal congratulations on the twenty-fifth anniversary of the Red Army. The day was widely celebrated in Britain as well, where the government had sidestepped the twenty-fifth anniversary of the Bolshevik Revolution in November 1942, but was now under intense public pressure to applaud the Soviet forces. The climax was a huge pageant in the Royal Albert Hall, addressed by Eden, with special music and readings and a giant hammer-and-sickle flag in the background. 'How times change!' mused Maisky in his diary, recalling the Civil War less than a quarter-century before, when it was Churchill 'who led the crusade against the Bolsheviks'.[23]

On 25 February, Churchill apologized for his slow response to Stalin's message of 16 February about the second front, promising 'more information' in 'a few days'. In fact, he did not reply for another two weeks, filling in with a sequence of brief but enthusiastic news updates on 2, 4 and 6 March about how many tons of bombs the RAF had dropped on Berlin, Hamburg and then Essen. To these Stalin replied with polite appreciation.[24]

It was not until 11 March that Churchill finally sent his response to Stalin's message of 16 February. He had actually dictated the main points straight away on the 18th and gave them to Eden and Ismay, who suggested amendments. Because of Churchill's illness, work on the text lapsed until 3 March, when the chiefs of staff produced an updated draft prepared on his directions. This was then shared with Roosevelt on 4 March as a proposed joint message, only to elicit a copy of the rather general answer that FDR had sent Stalin off his own bat on 22 February, with an apology for not sending it to Churchill earlier. 'In view of my reply to Mr. Stalin,' the president added, 'it does not seem advisable that your message should be considered a joint message from both of us.'[25] This news caused understandable irritation in London, which Eden did not conceal from Maisky on 9 March,[26] but it did allow Churchill to send a reply that was better tailored to British concerns.

Churchill's draft had always included a long explanation of the problems faced in Tunisia – such as weather, lines of communication and German reinforcements – because he wanted Stalin to grasp the peculiar difficulties of the campaign. Increasingly aware since Stalingrad of the magnitude of the Soviet war effort, he also wished to explain the very different challenges facing Britain. Freed now from the obligation to concoct a joint reply, he added a remarkably detailed description of British deployments around the world and of the global supply lines on which his island nation depended.

These new paragraphs constitute Churchill's fullest and most intelligent attempt to get across to Stalin the problems Britain faced in mounting a second front. He also provided data about the US troop presence in Britain, explaining that it had fallen far short of the twenty-seven divisions anticipated in mid-1942, because of the demands of 'Torch' and the shipping crisis. This was the kind of information that Roosevelt had struck out from the joint message to Stalin on 26 January, after Casablanca; nor was it in the vague Roosevelt–Leahy telegram of 22 February. For the first time, therefore, Churchill had come clean in a formal message about British and American capabilities for a 1943 second front – though he had, of course, already blabbed much of this in his late-night chat with Maisky on 8 February, which the ambassador had passed on to Moscow.

Two other points about the message are significant. First, it attempted to rebut Stalin's argument on 16 February that Hitler was exploiting the Allies' passivity in Tunisia to redeploy fresh troops to the Soviet front. The chiefs of staff suggested to Churchill, based on intelligence data at the time, that much of this movement was due to simple rotation of German troops between Western and Eastern Europe, in order to relieve and replace battle-weary units.[27] And in the final paragraph, Churchill made clear again that the British and Americans would only cross the Channel when Hitler's power was on the wane, because a 'premature' attack would 'lead to a bloody repulse'. For the British, this had always been the limiting condition governing a cross-Channel attack – stated emphatically by Churchill when in Moscow on 14 August 1942 – that it should be the *coup de grâce* rather than *guerre à outrance*. That was never an argument that found much favour with a ruthless warlord who had been waging total war for nearly two years.

Churchill to Stalin, sent 11 March 1943, received 12 March 1943[28]

Mr Roosevelt has sent me a copy of his reply to your full message of February 16. I am well enough to reply myself.

Our first task is to clear the Axis out of North Africa by an operation the code name of which is in my immediately following [message]. We hope that this will be accomplished towards the end of April, by which time about a quarter of a million Axis troops will be engaged by us.

Meanwhile all preparations are being pressed forward to carry out Operation 'Husky', which is the new code word (see my immediately following telegram), in June, a month earlier than we had planned at Casablanca.

Plans are also being investigated for operations in the Eastern Mediterranean such as:

(a) Capture of Crete and/or Dodecanese, and
(b) A landing in Greece.

The timing of these operations is largely governed by the result of 'Husky' and the availability of the necessary assemblage of shipping and landing craft. The assistance of Turkey and the use of Turkish air fields would, of course, be of immense value. At the right time I shall make a request of them.

The Anglo-American attempt to get Tunis and Bizerta at the run was abandoned in December because of the strength of the enemy, the impending rainy season, the already sodden character of the ground and the fact that communications stretched 500 miles from Algiers and 160 from Bone through bad roads and a week of travelling over single-track French railways. It was only possible to get supplies up to the Army by sea on a small scale owing to the strength of the enemy air and submarine attack. Thus it was not possible to accumulate petrol or other supplies in the forward areas. Indeed, it was only just possible to nourish the troops already there. The same was true of the air, and improvised air fields became quagmires. When we stopped attacking there were about 40,000 Germans in Tunisia apart from Italians and from Rommel who was still in Tripoli. The German force in North Tunisia is now more than double that figure, and they are rushing over every man they can in transport aircraft and destroyers. Some sharp local reverses were suffered towards the end of last month, but the position has now been restored. We hope that the delays caused by this setback will be repaired by the earlier advance of Montgomery's army which should have six divisions (say 200,000 men) operating from Tripoli with sufficient supplies against the Mareth position before the end of March. Already on March 6 Montgomery's army repulsed Rommel's forestalling attack with heavy losses. The British and American armies in the northern sector of Tunisia will act in combination with Montgomery's battle.

I thought that you would like to know these details of the story, although it is on a small scale compared with the tremendous operations over which you are presiding.

The British Staffs estimate that about half the number of the divisions which were sent to the Soviet–German front from France and the Low Countries since last November have already been replaced mainly by divisions from Russia and Germany, and partly by new divisions formed in France. They estimate that at the present time there are 30 German divisions in France and the Low Countries.

I am anxious that you should know for your own most secret information, exactly what our military resources are for an attack upon Europe across the Mediterranean or the Channel. By far the larger part of the British Army is in North Africa in the Middle East and in India and there is no physical possibility of moving it by sea back to the British Isles. By the end of April we shall have five British divisions, or about 200,000 men, in Northern Tunisia in addition to General Montgomery's army of some six divisions and we are bringing two specially trained British divisions from Iran, sending one from this country to reinforce them for 'Husky' a total of fourteen. We have four mobile British divisions, the two Polish divisions, one Free French division and one Greek division in the Middle East. There is the equivalent of four static divisions in Gibraltar, Malta and Cyprus. Apart from the garrisons and frontier troops, there are ten or twelve divisions formed and forming in India for reconquering Burma after the monsoon and reopening contact with China (see my immediately following message for the code-word of this operation). Thus we have under British command, spread over a distance of some 6,300 miles from Gibraltar to Calcutta, thirty-eight divisions including strong armoured and powerful proportionate Air forces. For all these forces active and definite tasks are assigned for 1943.

The gross strength of a British division, including Corps, Army, and Line of Communication troops, may be estimated at about 40,000 men. There remain in the United Kingdom about 19 formed divisions, 4 Home Defence divisions and 4 Drafting divisions, of which 16 are being prepared for a cross-Channel operation in August. You must remember that our total population is 46 millions and that the first charge upon it is the Royal Navy and Mercantile Marine, without which we could not live. Thereafter comes our very large Air Force, about 12 hundred thousand strong, and the needs of munitions, agriculture and air raid defence. Thus the entire manhood and womanhood of the country is, and has been, for some time fully absorbed.

The United States had the idea in July last to send 27 divisions, of a gross strength each of between 40 and 50 thousand men, to the United Kingdom for the invasion of France. Since then they have sent seven divisions to the Operation 'Torch' and three more are to go. In this country there is now only one American division and no more are expected for two months at least. They hope to have four divisions available by August in addition to a strong air force. This is no disparagement of the American effort. The reason why these performances have fallen so far short of the expectations of last year is not that the troops do not exist, but that the shipping at our disposal and the means of escorting it do not exist. There is in fact no prospect whatever of bringing anything more than I have mentioned into the United Kingdom in the period concerned.

The bomber offensive from the United Kingdom has been going steadily forward. During February over 10,000 tons of bombs were dropped on Germany and on German-occupied territory, and 4,000 tons have fallen on Germany since the beginning of March. Our Staffs estimate that out of a German first-line strength of 4,500 combat aircraft, 1,780 are now on the Russian front, the remainder being held opposite us in Germany and on the Western and Mediterranean fronts. Besides this, there is the Italian Air Force with a first-line strength of 1,385 aircraft, the great bulk of which is opposed to us.

With regard to the attack across the Channel, it is the earnest wish of the President and myself that our troops should be in the general battle in Europe which you are fighting with such astounding prowess. But in order to sustain the operations in North Africa, the Pacific, and India, and to carry supplies to Russia the import programme into the United Kingdom has been cut to the bone and we have eaten, and are eating, into reserves. However, in case the enemy should weaken sufficiently we are preparing to strike earlier than August, and plans are kept alive from week to week. If he does not weaken, a premature attack with inferior and insufficient forces would merely lead to a bloody repulse, Nazi vengeance on the local population if they rose, and a great triumph for the enemy. The Channel situation can only be judged nearer the time, and in making this declaration of our intentions there for your own personal information, I must not be understood to limit our freedom of decision.

Churchill sent two other telegrams on 11 March – one of which applauded the recent Soviet film about Stalingrad and promised to reciprocate with a new British documentary about Alamein. These two films were shown publicly in the UK and USA under the titles *Heroic Stalingrad* and *Desert Victory*.[29]

On 13 March, the prime minister sent another bombing update. But this was an excuse to ask Stalin to keep 'between you and me' paragraphs eight to ten of his long message of 11 March – in other words, the paragraphs beginning 'I am anxious ...', 'The gross strength ...' and 'The United States...' This ploy was a rarity in the Big Three correspondence: the PM using Stalin to conceal something from the president. He had already told the FO that he did not plan to share the message with the Americans and that, if this proved necessary, those paragraphs should be omitted – noting that the Americans 'might be vexed by the disclosure of their actual military dispositions'. This strengthens the impression that Churchill was trying to shift some of the blame for delays and uncertainties over the second front from London to Washington. On the 15th, Stalin duly promised to keep those paragraphs confidential.[30]

By this time, serious problems had arisen on the Soviet front. Kharkov, captured by the Red Army on 16 February, was retaken by the SS Panzer Corps on 14 March. This reverse was but one facet of the successful German counter-offensive masterminded by Manstein. Once again, hubris in Moscow played a part: 'Stalin and his subordinates continued to believe that they were on the verge of a great victory.' They wanted to build on their successes at Stalingrad and in the south by mounting a broad advance further north to destroy Hitler's Army Group Centre in the Ukraine and thrust across the Donets basin to the Dnieper River. This placed huge strains on an exhausted Red Army. Surprisingly high German morale and strong support from the Luftwaffe allowed Manstein to turn the tide from early March, driving the Soviet troops back beyond Kharkov to Belgorod and the Donets River, helped by the arrival of the spring thaw, which prevented any immediate Soviet fightback. The result was a large Soviet bulge around the city of Kursk – which would become the focus for both sides in the summer of 1943.[31]

It was against this background that Churchill's long telegram of 11 March was received in the Kremlin. Stalin read the message very carefully – pencil in hand, as was his wont – underlining the most disturbing parts.[32] As with his message of 16 February, Stalin wrote individually on 15 March to Churchill and Roosevelt, but in almost identical terms.[33] The draft came from Molotov, but the Boss added greater precision and fuller argument. He zeroed in on their vagueness about dates and their slow advance in Tunisia – repeating his accusations about the consequent redeployment of Wehrmacht divisions to the Soviet front, and thereby dismissing Churchill's claim about troop rotation. He reminded both partners of what they had said in the past – that the second front would happen 'no later than' the spring or early summer of 1943. But he pulled his punches at the end, simply warning 'how dangerous' further delay would be 'from the viewpoint of our common cause'. What 'dangerous' meant was left, for the moment, unspecified.

Stalin to Churchill, sent 15 March 1943, received 15 March 1943[34]

I received your reply to my message of the 16th of February.

It is evident from this reply that the Anglo-American operations in North Africa have not only not been expedited, but on the contrary they are being postponed till the end of April. Even this date is not quite definite. Thus, at the height of our fighting against the Hitler troops, i.e. in February–March, the weight of the Anglo-American offensive in North Africa has not only not been increased but there has been no development of the offensive at all, and the time limit for the operations set by yourself was extended. Meanwhile Germany has succeeded in transferring 36 divisions (including 6 armoured divisions) from the West against the Soviet troops. It is easy to see what difficulties this created for the Soviet armies and how the position of the Germans on the Soviet–German front was alleviated.

Fully realising the importance of 'Husky', I must however point out that it cannot replace the second front in France. Still, I welcome by all means the contemplated acceleration of this operation.

Now, as before, I see the main task in hastening of the second front in France. As you remember, you admitted the possibility of such a front already in 1942 and in any case not later than the spring of 1943. There were serious reasons for such an admission. Naturally enough I underlined in my previous message the necessity of the blow from the West not later than in the spring or early summer of this year.

The Soviet troops spent the whole winter in tense fighting, which continues even now. Hitler is carrying out important measures with a view to replenish and increase his army for the spring and summer operations against the USSR. In these circumstances, it is for us extremely important that the blow from the West should not be put off, that it should be struck in the spring or in the early summer.

I studied your observations, contained in the paragraphs 8, 9 and 10, on the difficulties of the Anglo-American operations in Europe. I recognise these difficulties. Notwithstanding all that, I deem it my duty to warn you in the strongest possible manner how dangerous would be, from the viewpoint of our common cause, further delay in the opening of the second front in France. This is the reason why the uncertainty of your statements concerning the contemplated Anglo-American offensive across the Channel arouses grave anxiety in me, about which I feel I cannot be silent.

On 15 March, Stalin sent two other telegrams to Churchill. One of them informed the PM about an American proposal to exploit the formation of a new government in Helsinki by offering US mediation in the Soviet–Finnish war. By formally notifying Churchill as well, Stalin wanted to signal that he was punctilious about obligations to his allies – in this case with reference to the Soviet–British treaty of 1942, which ruled out separate negotiations with Germany and her allies. In reply, Churchill kept his distance – suggesting that US feelers 'might not be altogether premature', while indicating that 'you will be the best judge of the right tactics'.[35]

Stalin's other message on 15 March was a response to the PM's telegrams of the 11th and 13th. Stalin's amendments (insertions italicized, deletions in strikethrough) added emotion ('with all my heart') and candour (about the loss of Kharkov). The Soviet leader also inserted the line about sending Churchill a copy of the documentary film *Stalingrad.*

Stalin to Churchill, sent 15 March 1943, received 15 March 1943[36]

I received your message of the 6th and 13th March, on the successful bombing of Essen, Stuttgart, Munich and Nuremberg. *From the bottom of my heart* I welcome the British aviation striking hard against the German industrial centres.

Your wish that paragraphs 8, 9 and 10 of your message of the 11th of March should be considered as a special military communication will be respected.

Many thanks for your congratulations on the capture of Viazma. *Unfortunately we had to evacuate Kharkov today* one cannot be sure of our success near Kharkov.

As soon as we will receive your film on the 8th Army, which is mentioned in your special message of the 11th of March, I will see it myself and take care that

it should be shown widely to our army and population. I fully realise how important it will be for the cause of our fighting friendship. *Let me send you personally
our Soviet film 'Stalingrad'.*

Churchill forwarded Stalin's telegram of 15 March to Eden, then on his visit to
Washington, attaching his own message of 11 March for delivery to Roosevelt,
but without the sensitive paragraphs 8–10. He also transmitted Stalin's 15
March cable about the RAF bombing and the war films, calling it 'a friendly
personal telegram which Stalin sent evidently to take the edge off the official
one'.[37] Churchill struggled to understand the contrast between these two
messages. Being an emotionally affective person, easily swayed by the mood of
the moment, he found it hard to imagine the psychological complexity of Stalin
– cold-blooded, yet a consummate actor – who could put on a variety of guises
in quick succession, from frosty harshness to chatty warmth. So he again
resorted to his 'two Stalins' concept, cabling Eden that the pair of telegrams
dated 15 March

> emphasize the feeling that has been growing in my mind that there are two
> forces to be reckoned with in Russia:
> (a) Stalin himself, personally cordial to me,
> (b) Stalin in council, a grim thing behind him, which we and he have to
>   reckon with.[38]

That evening, the PM also drew the attention of the Cabinet to the 'different
tone' of these two messages. According to the minutes: 'The first might well
have been sent by Premier Stalin after consultation with some official body',
whereas the second Churchill 'took to be a personal message from Premier
Stalin, who was anxious to preserve good relations with him'.[39] While Churchill
might have been right about Stalin's intentions, he did not seem to suspect that
the only 'official body' with which Stalin consulted in drafting this message was
his foreign minister. In the end, both the PM and the president chose not to
respond directly to Stalin's message, probably because nothing they could say
would mollify him.

    Churchill and Stalin continued to exchange friendly messages about the
British war news and about the films of their recent victories. On 28 March, the
PM reported on the latest raid on Berlin and the Eighth Army's 'left hook'
around the Mareth Line in southern Tunisia. His enthusiasm for the *Stalingrad*
film was widely shared in Britain: when the film was shown in cinemas, it
helped raise thousands of pounds for the Hero City. Stalin's praise for *Desert*

Victory is particularly interesting: the vivid word 'scoundrels' (*podletsy*) was his own insertion in Molotov's draft.[40]

Churchill to Stalin, sent 28 March 1943, received 29 March 1943[41]

Last night 395 heavy bombers flung 1,050 tons on Berlin in 50 minutes. The sky was clear over the target and the raid was highly successful. This is the best Berlin has yet got. Our loss was 9 only.

After a check the battle in Tunis has again taken a favourable turn, and I have just received news that our armoured troops of the enveloping movement are within 2 miles of El Hamma.

I saw the Stalingrad film last night. It is absolutely grand and will have a most moving effect on our people.

Stalin to Churchill, sent 29 March 1943, received 29 March 1943[42]

I received your message of the 28th March.

I congratulate the British Air Force on the new big and successful bombing of Berlin.

I hope the British armoured units will be able to use to the full advantage the improvement in the Tunis situation and will not give any respite to the enemy.

Yesterday, together with my colleagues, I have seen the film 'Desert Victory', which you have sent me. It makes a very strong impression. The film depicts magnificently how Britain is fighting and stigmatises those scoundrels (there are such people also in our country) who are asserting that Britain is not fighting but is merely an onlooker. Impatiently I will wait a similar film on your victory in Tunis.

The film 'Desert Victory' will be widely shown in all our armies at the front and among the widest masses of our population.

It seems that Stalin's praise was genuine. Asked by Clark Kerr on 12 April about the improvement of Britain's image in the USSR, he replied, according to the Soviet record:

'Desert Victory' does a great deal in this regard, and we plan to disseminate it widely among the public and in the Red Army. He, Comrade Stalin, must say that both in the army and on the home front there are people who having little understanding of the war, think that one can quickly and easily open a second front. There are people who think that England is not fighting but watching from the sidelines. But this is not the opinion of the government and the high command of the Red Army. There are no people in the government who would think this way. In our country there are also hidden enemies of our alliance with Britain and our country, who say that England is not fighting. But these people are few and we punish them. At one time we arrested these people and the English chided us for this, but now it is clear that it had to be done.

On hearing this astonishing outburst – equating critics of the alliance with Britain with 'enemies of the people' (*vragi naroda*), a notorious Soviet anathema – Clark Kerr replied that Stalin's statement would be 'received in London with great satisfaction'.[43]

That word 'satisfaction' did not even begin to capture the response when Maisky handed Stalin's message to Churchill on 31 March. According to the ambassador's diary, when Churchill got to the phrase about 'scoundrels', his face was 'convulsed by a spasm, he shut his eyes for a moment, and when he opened them I could see tears'. Churchill was so excited that he jumped up from his chair. 'The deepest thanks to Stalin!' he exclaimed. 'You have never brought me such a wonderful message before.' Maisky decided this reaction was both 'genuine' and also something of 'an act' – reflecting what he called the PM's 'emotional-artistic temperament': at times 'Churchill, like a good actor, gives vent to his emotional temperament and does not prevent genuine tears from watering his eyes.' Theatrics aside, Maisky believed the word 'scoundrels' had deeply touched the prime minister. 'He must have perceived in it longed-for recognition of his war effort of these past three years. And from whose lips? . . . From Stalin's! This could and must have moved Churchill deeply and brought tears to his eyes.'[44]

Yet, how sincere was the praise that Churchill took at face value? We shall never know, but it is worth noting the conjecture of Christopher Warner, head of the FO's Northern Department, who detected in Stalin's compliment hidden sarcasm. 'Do you take Joe's reference to there even being some in Russia who thought we were not pulling our weight, as a leg pull?' he asked Clark Kerr in a private letter. 'I confess that I am inclined to do so.'[45] After all, hadn't many of Stalin's messages in 1941–42 insinuated that the British were not fighters but spectators? Whatever the Soviet leader's intentions, he was fully informed by Maisky about Churchill's effusive reaction – and doubtless bore it in mind for future correspondence.[46]

Churchill's emotions were particularly on edge when Maisky visited him on 31 March, because he was actually expecting Stalin's response to a message the PM had sent on 29 March stating that the Western Allies had decided to suspend yet again the Arctic convoys. This decision had been brewing for some time, due to the shortage of merchant ships and escorts. As in 1942, the convoys became a victim of the 'soft underbelly' strategy, this time with the Sicily landings ('Husky') taking the place of 'Torch'. The chiefs of staff had pressed the case for suspension at the beginning of March, and Churchill at first tried to resist. 'This is a most grave matter,' he told them.[47] However, military advice prevailed, and on 18 March the Cabinet approved cessation of the convoys until August. After a few days of procrastination, Churchill decided he must break the bad news to Stalin, telling Eden on the 25th: 'A frank and immediate declaration of our inability will come as shock to him, but successive evasions and postponements will inspire him with suspicions of our intentions and our honesty.' Quoting the old proverb, Churchill concluded philosophically: 'I think we might just as well be hung for a sheep as a lamb.'[48]

Conscious that Maisky's staff paid close attention to the loading and movement of ships, Churchill pressed Roosevelt to agree that he should now write to Stalin. The PM's draft of his proposed message made much of the part that the 'menacing' presence at Narvik of a powerful German battle-fleet played in preventing the March and May convoys and buried the need for escorts to 'support our offensive operations in the Mediterranean' in the body of the message. The president agreed that Stalin had to be informed, but made two amendments to the draft. He deleted a sentence of Churchill's about still hoping to send one more convoy before May, if the disposition of German surface raiders left 'a reasonable chance of getting through', and, as partial compensation, added that the USA would 'materially increase shipments via Vladivostok'. After despatching the telegram to Stalin, Churchill asked Roosevelt to send a 'supporting message', which he felt sure would be 'most helpful'. The president, however, having suggested his tweaks to the PM's cable, was then happy to let him take the flak.[49]

Churchill's one-sentence message, sent the same day, about the latest raid on Berlin was intended to ameliorate somewhat the bad news about convoys.[50]

Churchill to Stalin, sent 30 March 1943, received 30 March 1943[51]

The Germans have concentrated at Narvik a powerful battle fleet consisting of *Tirpitz, Scharnhorst, Lutzow,* one 6-inch cruiser and 8 destroyers. Thus the danger to the Russian convoys which I described in my message to you of July 17 last year has been revived in even more menacing form. I told you then that we did not think it right to risk our Home fleet in Barents Sea, where it could be brought under the attack of German shore-based aircraft and U-boats without adequate protection against either, and I explained that if one or two of our most modern battleships were to be lost or even seriously damaged while *Tirpitz* and other large units of the German Battle Fleet remained in action, the whole command of the Atlantic would be jeopardised with dire consequences to our common cause.

President Roosevelt and I have therefore decided with the greatest reluctance that it is impossible to provide adequate protection for the next Russian convoy and that without such protection there is not the slightest chance of any of the ships reaching you in the face of the known German preparations for their destruction. Orders have therefore been issued that the sailing of March convoy is to be postponed.

It is a great disappointment to President Roosevelt and myself that it should be necessary to postpone March convoy. Had it not been for the German concentration, it had been our firm intention to send you a convoy of 30 ships each in March and again in early May. At the same time we feel it only right to let you know at once that it will not be possible to continue convoys by the Northern Route after early May, since from that time onwards every single escort vessel will be required to support our offensive operations in the Mediterranean, leaving only a minimum to safeguard our lifeline in the Atlantic. In the latter we have had grievous and almost unprecedented losses during the last three weeks. Assuming 'Husky' goes well we should hope to resume convoys in early September, provided that the disposition of German main units permits and that the situation in the North Atlantic is such as to enable us to provide the necessary escorts and covering force.

We are doing our utmost to increase the flow of supplies by Southern Route. The monthly figure has been more than doubled in the last 6 months. We have reason to hope that the increase will be progressive and that figures for August will reach 240,000 tons. If this is achieved, the monthly delivery will have increased eightfold in twelve months. Furthermore, the United States will materially increase shipments via Vladivostok. This will in some way offset both your disappointment and ours at the interruption to Northern convoys.

On 31 March Maisky told the PM that the news about the convoys left him 'simply astounded'. What effect, he asked, would it have on the mood of the Red Army and the people? 'This is the third summer that they are waiting for a second front from their Western Allies.' And now, Russia was being asked to accept that convoys would probably be suspended until darkness set in – in November or December.

Churchill became emotional. 'It seems strange,' he declared, 'but our entire naval supremacy is based on the availability of a handful of first-class combat units. Your people may not understand this, but your Government must!'

He paced around, then added: 'I considered it my duty to tell Stalin the whole truth. You mustn't deceive an ally.' Suddenly he came up very close, looked straight into the ambassador's eyes and asked, 'Will it mean a rupture with Stalin or won't it?'

Maisky said that the Soviet leader would speak for himself, but did warn that Churchill's decision would arouse 'very strong feelings' in Stalin. 'I don't want a break up. I don't!' the PM exclaimed. 'We, the three great powers should be together. This is the foundation of everything.'[52]

Maisky's vivid report of their conversation reached Moscow while Stalin was mulling over his reply to Churchill's convoy telegram. How far this influenced him is impossible to say. But it could well be that he realized the decision was irrevocable, so there was no point in contesting it and getting into an argument. Given Churchill's evident embarrassment, it may have seemed more productive to play on his feelings of guilt to gain moral advantage that could be exploited on other issues. At any rate, Stalin touched the PM to the quick with his stoic and restrained response to news that he called 'catastrophic'.

Stalin to Churchill, sent 2 April 1943, received 2 April 1943[53]

I have received your message of the 30th March conveying to me that the necessity compels you and Mr Roosevelt to stop convoys to the USSR till September.

I understand this unexpected action as a catastrophic diminution of supplies of arms and military raw materials to the USSR on the part of Great Britain and the United States of America, as transport via Pacific is limited by the tonnage and not reliable, and the southern route has a small transit capacity. In view of this, both just mentioned routes cannot compensate for the discontinuation of transport via the northern route. You realise of course that the circumstance cannot fail to affect the position of the Soviet troops.

Whatever the motivation for Stalin's asymmetric response, its impact was immense. Maisky himself was surprised at the tone: 'far milder than I had expected', he wrote in his diary. According to the ambassador, on 2 April Churchill was 'staggered by this. He had been very gloomy and tense when I arrived. I could feel that he was expecting a sharp, abusive response. He put on his glasses and slowly, reluctantly unfolded the message, as if trying to postpone the moment when he would have to swallow the bitter pill. And then this!'[54]

After pacing around the Cabinet table, Maisky reported to Moscow, Churchill unburdened his emotions:

Tell Stalin that his response is a magnanimous and courageous reply. That's how I perceive it. Such a reply makes me feel doubly obliged to do absolutely all that is humanly possible to compensate the USSR for the suspension of the northern convoys. And I am working like an ox to do so.

After a couple more turns around the Cabinet room, Churchill added: 'With this response Stalin has shown once again how great and wise a man he is. I want to work with him without fail. I will work with him. When the war ends I'll spare no effort to help restore Russia.' Then, a moment later – according to Maisky's message to Moscow, Churchill suddenly said, 'We are moving towards a new era – it will be the "Russian century".' Here was a striking twist on Henry Luce's proclamation in 1941 of the dawning 'American Century'. The remark, Maisky observed, 'was, of course, calculated', but he was struck that Churchill 'found it necessary to make it: so far, in the eight years that I have known him, he had never once expressed himself in this way'. The phrase 'Russian century' did, however, echo – consciously or not – a point that Maisky himself had asserted to Eden on 10 March.[55]

Making due allowance for Maisky's capacity for hyperbole and also some degree of calculation on Churchill's part, the latter's positive reaction to Stalin's message was genuine. 'P.M. delighted with it. He may be right,' noted the ever-cautious Cadogan. Forwarding the text to Roosevelt on 2 April, Churchill dubbed it 'a very natural and stout-hearted response', which 'makes me the more determined to back this man with every conceivable means'. As on 30 March, he urged the president to send a supporting message of his own – 'it could only do good' – but again FDR ducked out.[56]

Churchill also corresponded with Clark Kerr in Moscow: 'Let me know what you think of Joe's reply about the convoy business. My own feeling is that they took it like men.' The ambassador said he, too, 'had been prepared for a very tart reply' and was 'surprised by Joe's moderation'. Clark Kerr, like Stalin, understood Churchill's sense of *noblesse oblige* – which he himself had played upon during the turbulent Moscow visit of August 1942. He told the PM that Stalin 'believes in your good faith and will, I think, take from you more than from anyone else', but urged that 'a blow taken in good part calls for a word of praise'.[57]

The PM accepted his ambassador's advice. On 6 April, he sent Stalin a message whose opening paragraph struck the note of appreciation and solidarity that Clark Kerr had recommended:

I acknowledge the force of all you say in your telegram about the convoys. I assure you that I shall do my utmost to make any improvement which is possible. I am deeply conscious of the giant burden borne by the Russian Armies and their unequalled contribution to the common cause.

Churchill went on to give considerable detail about the latest raids on Essen, Kiel and Paris, and about the renewed campaign in Tunisia – about which he added further updates.[58]

Stalin replied on the 7th in a warm message of congratulations about the raids and Tunisia – though with perhaps a hint of sarcasm in the word 'finally'.

Stalin to Churchill, sent 7 April 1943, received 7 April 1943[59]

I have received your two messages of the 6th April, as well as your message of today concerning an important advance of your troops in Tunisia.

I congratulate you on this serious success. I hope that this time the Anglo-American troops will finally defeat and destroy Rommel and other Hitler gangs in Tunisia. It will be of the greatest importance for our common cause.

I welcome the bombing of Essen, Berlin, Kiel and other industrial centres of Germany. Every blow delivered by your Air Force to the vital German centres evokes a most lively echo in the hearts of many millions throughout the width and breadth of our country.

Churchill's next message, on 10 April, explained what the British government was doing to try to compensate for the shortfall of aircraft deliveries to the USSR via the Arctic route. The PM showed remarkable determination in seeking to mitigate the effects of the cancellation of the convoys. On Tuesday, 6 April, he had sent an 'Action This Day' minute to key ministers, telling them that 'every effort' must be made to ferry the planes to southern Russia via the RAF base at Takoradi in West Africa. 'The whole matter must be regarded as of the highest importance and urgency, as I want to telegraph Stalin tomorrow if possible, Thursday at the latest.'[60] After rapid study and consultation, the ministers offered the PM the options that he then outlined in his letter to Stalin, including the offer of an additional sixty Hurricane IIDs – specially equipped for tank-busting – which had been used to great effect in North Africa. The Air Ministry warned that because of the shortage of shipping and spare parts, the planes could not be put into operation before September or October; it recommended that the PM mention the time factor to avoid future disappointment. But Churchill did not want to spoil the impression of British generosity by any such qualifications. Amendments (italicized in the text) were made by the PM to a draft of 9 April.[61]

Churchill to Stalin, sent 10 April 1943, received 11 April 1943[62]

In the two *cancelled* convoys JW 54 and JW 55, there were 375 of your Hurricanes and 285 of your Airocobras and Kittyhawks. The latter were part of the American quota. We are working day and night to make a plan for sending you all these aircraft as rapidly as possible by other routes.

The Airocobras and Kittyhawks might go via Gibraltar and North Africa to Abadan. The Hurricanes have not sufficient range to manage the flight to Gibraltar, so they have to go by sea to Takoradi or Casablanca, be assembled there, *be tropicalised* and fly on to Tehran *where we can de-tropicalise them*. Alternatively, *if Tunis is conquered soon we may be able to pass* a number of Hurricanes by sea through the Mediterranean and erect them in Egypt or Basra. Each of these alternatives presents its difficulties. There is also a big problem in transporting the large number of spares which accompany the aircraft. Nevertheless, we shall overcome these difficulties.

It has also occurred to me that you might like to have some of our 40-mm cannon fighter Hurricanes for your operations against German armour on the Russian front. During the recent fighting in Tunisia these have met with success against Rommel's tanks. One squadron of 16 aircraft destroyed 19 tanks in four days. The aircraft is known as Hurricane II D and carries two 40-mm cannon with 16 rounds of ammunition per gun and two .303-inch machineguns with 330 rounds per gun. In other respects it is similar to Hurricane II C, except that it is 430 lbs heavier and approximately 20 mph slower. I could send you a maximum of 60 of this type of aircraft. *Let me know whether you would like them*. They would probably have to go via Takoradi and could be worked into the plan which is being made for the Hurricanes, Airocobras and Kittyhawks from the convoys.

With the President's approval, Mr Harriman is collaborating with us in making the plan. I hope to telegraph to you *next week* giving you our concrete proposals. I am determined that you shall have the aircraft as soon as it is humanly possible to get them to you.

On 11 April, Churchill sent the latest news about Tunisia and the bombing of Germany. As with several of these bulletins about air raids, his optimism the morning after was not vindicated by subsequent reports. Although Churchill said that the RAF had hit Duisburg and Frankfurt 'hard', it did not do so accurately because of the fog he mentioned. The PM also referred to the contribution of the Aid to Russia Fund, established in October 1941 under the auspices of the British Red Cross and headed by his wife, Clementine. The £3 million already raised by what was generally known as 'Mrs Churchill's Fund' provided tangible evidence of public sympathy in Britain for the Russian people, but, as the PM and his wife were well aware, it was also diplomatically useful given the limits of British military aid.[63]

As Stalin noted in his reply on 12 April, the Red Air Force was now in a position to mount its own attacks on East Prussia, targeting cities such as Königsberg, Danzig and Tilsit. He also mentioned receiving General Giffard Martel, the new head of the British military mission. Unlike most senior British officers in Moscow, Martel was not an ingrained anti-Bolshevik. He had shown an interest in Soviet tank doctrine before the war, and witnessed Red Army manoeuvres in 1936. In a meeting attended by Molotov and Clark Kerr that was reported in the Soviet press,[64] the general had an animated conversation with Stalin about military matters. He said that the British Army had 'learned to beat the Germans in the desert, but only the Russians know how Germans fight in the European theatre of war' – adding that the British had 'a lot to learn from the Russians'. Stalin replied graciously, 'We will learn from one another.'[65]

Churchill to Stalin, sent 11 April 1943, received 12 April 1943[66]

All Nazi-Fascist forces are falling back to the line Enfidaville of which I told you. Our armour has broken through from the west towards Kairouan. The Eighth Army has been pushing northwards and we are preparing to deliver a weighty punch by the First Army. Great pains are being taken for a heavy toll of an escape by sea. I hope to have good news for you soon from Africa. There are still over 200,000 of the enemy in the net, including wounded, and we have 25,000 prisoners so far apart from killed, which last may be put from 5,000 to 10,000.

Air. We sent 378 aircraft to Duisburg and repeated with about 100 the next night. Last night 502 went to Frankfurt. We hit both of these places hard but were hampered by heavy cloud. I hope you got the short film of the devastations and also the photographs. I am having these sent regularly to you as they might please your soldiers who have seen so many Russian towns in ruins.

I am trying to arrange to push some fast ships through the Mediterranean as soon as it is open to carry your priority cargoes to the Persian Gulf. These cargoes will include some of the specially selected drugs and medical appliances purchased by my wife's Fund which will shortly reach three million pounds and has been raised by voluntary gifts from both poor and rich. This Fund is a proof of the warm regard of the British people for the Russian people.

Stalin to Churchill, sent 12 April 1943, received 12 April 1943[67]

I received your messages of the 10th and 11th April.

The speedy development of the Anglo-American advance in Tunis constitutes an important success in the war against Hitler and Mussolini. I wish you to kill the enemy and capture as many prisoners and trophies as possible.

We are delighted that you are not giving respite to Hitler. To your strong and successful bombings of the big German cities we add now our air raids on the German industrial centres of East Prussia. Many thanks for the film depicting the results of the bombing of Essen. This film as well as the other films which you promise to send us will be widely shown to our army and population.

The contemplated deliveries of fighters from the cancelled convoys are of great value to us. I am also grateful for your offer to send us 60 Hurricanes II D armed with 40 mm cannon. Such planes are very needed, especially against heavy tanks. I hope that your and Mr Harriman's efforts to secure the despatch of 'planes to the USSR will be crowned with a speedy success.

Our people highly appreciate the warm feelings and sympathy of the British people which have found expression in the creation of the Aid to Russia Fund mentioned by you. Please convey to your wife who is at the head of the fund my thanks for her untiring activities in this sphere.

I received today the Lieutenant-General Martel who delivered to me your letter. Of course General Martel will be given every assistance in his study of the Red Army and its fighting experience.

When Churchill read the message on 14 April, he was 'pleased, even heartened', Maisky told Moscow. 'The paragraph devoted to Mrs Churchill made a particularly strong impression on him. I should explain that Mrs Churchill has a strong influence on her husband. He shares with her all the news and asks her advice on all matters. This I have noticed more than once in the pre-war years, and it is still so.'[68] Here was another example of the useful intelligence that the veteran ambassador (in post since 1932) could provide – his own wife worked closely with Clementine on the Aid to Russia Fund – and Stalin probably kept the point in mind. When Mrs Churchill visited Moscow in the spring of 1945, at a nadir in relations between the two governments, she was accorded the warmest possible welcome by Stalin and Molotov.

'I continue to have very agreeable correspondence with Joe,' Churchill told Roosevelt on 15 April.[69] So he kept playing the same tunes, on bombing and Tunisia. He also repeated his offer made in March 1942 of issuing a warning to Hitler that any use of poison gas by the Wehrmacht on the Eastern Front would be followed by British retaliation on Germany itself. Although the chiefs of staff judged that the chances of the Germans starting chemical warfare, 'though less remote than hitherto', were 'still small', Churchill's offer was another gesture of alliance solidarity. Stalin supported Churchill's proposal, and on 20 April a statement was duly issued, confirming Britain's readiness to retaliate in kind if the Germans used gas against the USSR. To drive home the point, it also stressed that British gas resources had 'greatly increased since last year'.[70]

*****

In the early months of 1943, therefore, relations between the Big Three seemed surprisingly pleasant. Faced with unpleasant news about further delays over the second front and another suspension of the convoys, Stalin had pulled his punches – pointing out the impact on the USSR but avoiding recriminations. For his part, Churchill worked hard to cultivate Stalin, feeding him juicy titbits of news about the battle for Tunisia and the bombing of Germany. After the 12 April meeting at the Kremlin, Clark Kerr wrote home to the FO, 'I've never seen Stalin in sunnier temper. Indeed, for the moment the Kremlin seems full of sunlight.'[71] And when Churchill met Maisky at lunchtime on the 21st, he made the telling observation: 'Now we are much closer to one another than a year ago.'[72]

A few hours later, Stalin sent a message to both his allies that transformed the mood completely.

8

POLES APART

(April to July 1943)

GERMAN REVELATIONS IN MID-APRIL about the Katyn graves sparked a new crisis in Big Three relations – one that threatened the unity of the Alliance and raised deeper questions about the morality of international relations. In 1943 there was already strong circumstantial evidence that the Poles exhumed near Smolensk had been executed by the Soviets, and Stalin's direct responsibility was confirmed in the 1990s after the demise of the USSR. Yet from the moment the graves were discovered, the Soviet leader went onto the attack, accusing the Nazis of the crime, implicating the Polish government-in-exile in London in a German cover-up and using that as a pretext to break off diplomatic relations with the London Poles. This left him free in due course to promote an alternative Polish government in Moscow – which became a major issue in 1944–45.

It was a brilliant but utterly cynical display of propagandistic diplomacy by Stalin, which managed to put Churchill and Roosevelt, rather than him, on the defensive. Both his allies regarded relations with the Poles as secondary to the Big Three Alliance. Even though the Foreign Office had little doubt about who was to blame for Katyn, the prime minister became increasingly impatient with the most outspoken anti-Soviet elements of the London Poles, whom their premier, General Władysław Sikorski, seemed unable to control. Stalin was Churchill's priority. On 2 May, the PM resumed his regular updates about the bombing of German cities and Allied progress in North Africa, making much of the final victory in Tunisia on 13 May, which at last gave the Western Allies something tangible to set against Stalingrad. He was particularly pleased by the warm appreciation of the British and American contributions to the war in Stalin's May Day message to the Soviet people and the world.

Roosevelt also played up the North African campaign, but as usual, he did not devote a Churchillian degree of energy and detail to the correspondence itself. The president's preferred strategy remained to send VIP personal emissaries to build mutual trust, gain intelligence about the Kremlin recluse and, above all, prepare the way for a personal meeting, and this reached its apogee in May, with the Davies mission to Moscow. Joseph E. Davies was an old crony of FDR, who had served as US ambassador to Russia in 1936–38. He arrived in the Soviet capital on 19 May, telling all and sundry that he was bearing a secret letter from the president, the contents of which he could reveal only to Stalin himself. This snub was the last straw for the long-suffering Ambassador Standley – at a time when Churchill was using his British counterpart, Clark Kerr, as a regular and trusted source of advice. Roosevelt's initiative also entailed deliberate deception of the prime minister. True to his thinking since March 1942, FDR proposed to Stalin that they hold an informal, small-scale meeting *à deux*, excluding Churchill, and he kept 10 Downing Street in the dark about all this for a month and a half. When the PM finally discovered what was going on, FDR flatly lied that it was Stalin who wanted the one-on-one meeting. Roosevelt's proposal and his duplicity were both signs of the changing balance within the Big Three relationship at this mid-point in the war.

The idea of a Roosevelt–Stalin meeting came to nothing, mainly because of the freeze in Moscow's relations with the West after Stalin was told formally on 2 June that no second front in France would be mounted until the spring of 1944. Churchill, Roosevelt and their staffs had met in Washington from 12 to 25 May, seeking to hammer out their operational plans for 1943. This was hard enough to do just between the British and Americans, and a Soviet presence would have complicated the detailed discussions about global priorities and logistics; but the failure to send even a pro forma invitation to Stalin allowed the Soviet leader to complain of non-consultation when he received the unpalatable news. Making matters worse, this news was conveyed to him in a 'joint message' from the two leaders that in fact came largely from General Marshall and took the form of an unvarnished digest of operational decisions. Replying in two forensic messages, Stalin quoted back at his partners their past predictions and promises about a second front since the summer of 1942. Although he omitted some of their qualifying sentences about weather, enemy strength, etc. that had been included as wiggle-room, the account was essentially accurate and the effect devastating – Churchill and Roosevelt had been giving the Russians the runaround on strategy for two years. Reactions to his messages in

Washington and London were true to form: FDR avoided getting into a long argument, whereas Churchill's innate desire to explain, extenuate and defend himself verbosely against accusations of bad faith only added fuel to the flames. Unlike Stalin, Churchill did not understand the power of silence.

*****

Stalin's telegram about the discovery of the Katyn graves is one of the most vituperative messages he sent to his two Western allies. Its tone was even more striking because of the warmth of recent exchanges with Churchill. As a piece of statecraft, the text is also remarkable because it was a tissue of lies, based on the precept that the best form of defence is attack. Churchill and Roosevelt had frequently been either economical or elastic with the truth when corresponding with Stalin, but neither of them had engaged in systematic and knowing misrepresentation on this scale. What's more, they were both pretty sure that he was lying. Yet the exigencies of the Alliance required them to bite their tongues. For the Big Three, April 1943 was one of their 'unfinest hours'.

Between 1988 and 1992, Mikhail Gorbachev and especially Boris Yeltsin finally opened up the relevant documentation, which was then published by a joint Polish–Russian commission of archivists and historians. This confirmed that the shooting of these Polish officers, soldiers and intellectuals had been formally approved on 5 March 1940 by Stalin, Molotov and an inner circle of the Politburo, on the recommendation of NKVD chief Lavrentiy Beria. The Poles had been captured by the Red Army in September 1939, when Poland was overrun, and were regarded in the Kremlin as the hostile core of any revived Polish state. The executions, perhaps 22,000 in all, took place during April and May 1940 at various locations in Belorussia and the Ukraine. Hitherto, Stalin's usual policy for dealing with 'enemies of the people' had been mass deportation to remote regions where the victims would simply be worked to death. But the Soviet penal system had been overwhelmed by some 250,000 Polish POWs taken in 1939. Stalin had a visceral hatred of the Poles and saw eastern Poland as a rightful part of the Russian Empire, while most of the prisoners were vehement anti-Soviets, whom the NKVD categorized as 'counter-revolutionaries'. All these factors help to explain the mass killing of 1940, which Stalin probably assumed would never be uncovered.[1]

But three years later, on 13 April 1943, Berlin announced the discovery of over 4,400 graves in Katyn Forest, near Smolensk, attributing the shootings to the USSR in 1940. Moscow quickly retaliated by blaming it on the Germans during the invasion of 1941. Then on 16 April, the Polish government-in-exile in London issued a statement saying that, when they began to form an army in

Russia in 1941 from released POWs, it became clear that some 15,000 officers and men could not be accounted for. It asked that Berlin's claims be investigated by the International Red Cross (IRC), even though any such investigation would have to be arranged with the Wehrmacht, which controlled the area around Smolensk. The Germans seized their chance to support the request for an IRC investigation, which the Soviet media then denounced as evidence of collusion between the Polish and German governments.

Stalin took the same line with Churchill and Roosevelt. The Kremlin was already at odds with the London Poles, headed by General Sikorski, over the treatment of former Polish POWs and deportees in the USSR, and also over the claim to the USSR's 1941 borders, so the Soviet leader may well have been looking for an opportunity to break off diplomatic relations. At any event, on 22 April, Molotov instructed Aleksandr Bogomolov, ambassador to the exiled Allied governments in London, to terminate immediately relations with the Sikorski government, though 'without discontinuing formal relations with the Poles'.[2] This would leave him in a position to identify, or even create, a group of Polish politicians with whom he could work – such as communist exiles in Moscow. Stalin wished to give his allies some prior notification of his action, sending almost identical messages.[3] To put them on the defensive, he blasted the Poles for 'collusion' in a German 'campaign of calumny' against the USSR. This collusion, he claimed, was tantamount to their making a *de facto* break in relations, and so he was simply reciprocating. It was a breathtaking display of diplomatic chutzpah.

Stalin to Churchill, sent 21 April 1943, received 21 April 1943

The Soviet Government considers that the attitude taken of late by the Polish Government vis-a-vis the Union of Soviet Socialist Republics is completely abnormal and contradicts all the rules and usages of relations between the two Allied States.

The slanderous campaign hostile to the Soviet Union started by the German fascists in connexion with the murder of the Polish officers near Smolensk perpetrated by themselves on the territory occupied by the German troops was immediately seized by the Government of General Sikorski and is being avidly fanned by the Polish Governmental press. The Government of General Sikorski has not only not treated the vile fascist calumny against the Union of Soviet Socialist Republics with the contempt it deserves but it did not find it necessary even to put any question in this connexion to the Soviet Government or ask for any explanation.

The Hitlerite authorities, after perpetrating a monstrous crime against the Polish officers, are staging now a comedy of 'investigation' in which they use some of the

Polish pro-fascist elements carefully selected by the Germans. In the occupied Poland, where everything is under Hitler's heel, no honest Pole can open his mouth.

The International Red Cross is called for the purpose of this 'investigation' by both the Hitler Government and the Polish Government. In the atmosphere of terror with its gallows and mass extermination of peaceful population, the International Red Cross is forced to take part in the comedy of 'investigation' of which the producer is Hitler. It is obvious that such 'investigation' – conducted in addition behind the back of the Soviet Government – cannot be trusted by any honest man.

The fact that the campaign hostile to the Union of Soviet Socialist Republics broke out simultaneously in the German and Polish press, and is being conducted in the same direction, cannot leave any doubt that between the enemy of the Allies – Hitler – and the Government of General Sikorski there exist contact and understanding with regard to this hostile campaign.

At a time when the peoples of the Soviet Union are sheding [sic] their blood in the most difficult struggle against Hitler Germany [sic] and making the greatest possible efforts to defeat the common foe of all the freedom-loving democratic countries, the Government of General Sikorski delivers a treacherous blow to the Soviet Union to serve the cause of Hitler's tyranny.

All these circumstances compel the Soviet Government to state that the present Polish Government, which descended so low as to come to an understanding with Hitler Government [sic], put de facto end to the Allied relations with the Union of Soviet Socialist Republics and took up a position of hostility to the Soviet Union.

In view of the foregoing the Soviet Government came to the conclusion that it is necessary to interrupt relations with this Government.

I think it incumbent upon me to inform you on the above and I hope that the British Government will understand the necessity of this step which has been forced on the Soviet Government.

Given the importance of Stalin's letter, Maisky decided to deliver it to Churchill in person on Good Friday, 23 April, even though the latter was paying a rare wartime visit to Chartwell, his country house in Kent. As usual, the ambassador's diary account and his report to Moscow present him as being in full command of the conversation; but Churchill's memoir portrays Maisky arriving in a state of 'unusual perturbation' and conducting himself with a mixture of 'appeal alternating with bluster'. The ambassador surely knew that the Soviet government was following a high-risk strategy and that the British in particular – with treaty commitments to the Poles – might react badly to his démarche. In fact, however, Churchill was philosophical. His line to Maisky, as to Sikorski, about the officers was 'if they are dead, they could not be resurrected'.[4] Maisky records him saying 'Even if the German statements were to prove true, my attitude to you would not change. You are a brave people. Stalin is a great warrior, and at the moment I approach everything primarily as a soldier who is interested in defeating the common enemy as quickly as possible.'[5]

This was also the view of the Cabinet. On 19 April, they agreed with Churchill and Eden that the Poles should maintain diplomatic relations with Moscow and concentrate on practical issues, such as the return of Poles remaining in the USSR.[6] Neither Clark Kerr nor the FO believed the Soviet account, but all agreed to turn a blind eye in the interests of Allied unity. Only Sir Owen O'Malley, British ambassador to the Polish government-in-exile, dug more deeply into the limited evidence, concluding grimly: 'We have in fact perforce used the good name of England like the murderers used the little conifers to cover up a massacre.' But reluctantly, O'Malley saw no alternative at present, in view of the 'immense importance of an appearance of Allied unity' and 'the heroic resistance of Russia'. He could only suggest lamely that 'the voice of our political conscience' should be 'kept up to concert pitch', thereby 'predisposing ourselves' to speak the truth at a more propitious time after the war. In fact, successive British governments decided, on FO advice, to stick to this 'not proven' silence throughout the Cold War, until being embarrassingly wrong-footed in 1988 by the 'New Thinking' in Moscow.[7]

In what Harvey called a 'soothing reply', the PM tried to restrain Stalin from an irrevocable break with the London Poles. It was based on an FO draft on 20 April, which Churchill then edited, as he put it, to be 'more consistent with my style of conversation' with Stalin.[8]

Churchill to Stalin, sent 24 April 1943, received 25 April 1943[9]

Ambassador Maisky delivered your message to me last night. We shall certainly oppose vigorously any 'investigation' by the International Red Cross or any other body in any territory under German authority. Such investigation would be a fraud, and its conclusions reached by terrorism. Mr Eden is seeing Sikorski today and will press him as strongly as possible to withdraw all countenance from any investigation under Nazi auspices. Also we should never approve of any parley with the Germans or contact with them of any kind whatever and we shall press this point upon our Polish Allies.

I shall telegraph to you later how Sikorski reacts to the above points. His position is one of great difficulty. Far from being pro-Germen or in league with them, he is in danger of being overthrown by the Poles who consider that he has not stood up sufficiently for his people against the Soviets. If he should go, we should only get somebody worse. I hope therefore that your decision to 'interrupt' relations is to be read in the sense of a final warning rather than of a break and that it will not be made public at any rate until every other plan has been tried. The public announcement of a break would do the greatest possible harm in the United States, where the Poles are numerous and influential.

I had drafted a telegram to you yesterday asking you to consider allowing more Poles and Polish dependants to go into Iran. This would allay the rising discontent of the Polish army formed there and would enable me to influence the Polish Government to act in conformity with our common interests and against the common foe. I have deferred sending this telegram in consequence of yours to me in hopes that the situation may clear.

Churchill and Eden applied considerable pressure to the London Poles, who, on 30 April, withdrew their request to the International Red Cross, citing the difficulties of organizing such an investigation. But this was too late. Already on 25 April, Molotov had summoned the Polish ambassador, Tadeusz Romer, at midnight and handed him a note on the severance of relations.[10] The Kremlin was clearly in a hurry: Stalin sent Churchill a formal statement of the break late on 25 May, even before Molotov met Romer, and the Soviet note was published next day in *Evening Moscow*, not in the national newspapers as was customary. Developing his line that the Soviet Union was the injured party, Stalin explained his haste by reference to pressure from 'my colleagues' and from 'indignant' public opinion. His message crossed, and rendered irrelevant, a message from Churchill, trying to maintain Soviet–Polish relations: this insisted that Sikorski had simply made a 'mistake' in appealing to the Red Cross rather than being guilty of 'collusion' with the Germans and promised to restrain the Polish press from 'polemics'.[11]

Stalin to Churchill, sent 25 April 1943, received 25 April 1943[12]

I received your message concerning the Polish affairs. Many thanks for your interest in the matter. I would like, however, to point out that the interruption of relations with the Polish Government is already decided and today V.M. Molotov delivered a Note to this effect. Such action was demanded by my colleagues as the Polish official press is ceaselessly pursuing and even daily expanding its campaign hostile to the USSR. I was obliged also to take into account the public opinion of the Soviet Union, which is deeply indignant at the ingratitude and treachery of the Polish Government.

With regard to the publication of the Soviet document concerning the interruption of relations with the Polish Government, I am sorry to say that such a publication cannot be avoided.

Churchill consulted with Roosevelt about Katyn and shared his messages. The president did not receive Stalin's telegram of 21 April until the 24th, being on a trip to Mexico. Aided by Admiral Leahy, FDR prepared a draft reply and asked Hull for comments, as became his practice with correspondence on the Polish question. The secretary of state deleted just a single word, though an important one: 'stupid' before 'mistake' in the second paragraph.[13] The president's letter largely repeated the PM's arguments, with an additional reference to the potential role of Churchill as an intermediary.

Stalin's reply to Roosevelt was more detailed than his message to the prime minister. He adopted a tone of pained reasonableness about Sikorski, expressing a willingness to think the best of his motives, but accusing him of letting himself be used as a 'tool' in Hitler's 'anti-Soviet campaign'. The Soviet leader also turned his partners' rhetoric about preserving the unity of the Alliance against them, arguing that they had a duty to prevent one ally from acting 'inimically' against another, in ways that benefited the enemy. Yet there was also suppleness behind Stalin's apparent rigidity: the verb *preryvat'*, translated into English in the first sentence as 'severance' of relations, can also mean 'interrupt'.[14]

Roosevelt to Stalin, sent 26 April 1943, received 27 April 1943[15]

Your telegram was received by me while on my inspection trip out West. Your problem is well understood by me but I do hope that in this present situation you can find means to label your action as a suspension of conversations with the Polish Government-in-exile rather than a complete severance of diplomatic relations.

In my opinion Sikorski has in no way acted with the Hitler gang but instead he has made a mistake in taking up this particular matter with the International Red Cross. Also Churchill will find ways and means, I am inclined to think, of getting the Polish Government in London to act in the future with more common sense.

If I can help in any way, please let me know, particularly with reference to looking after any Poles which you may desire to send out of the Soviet Union.

In the United States, incidentally, I have several million Poles, a great many of them being in the Navy and Army. All of them are bitter against the Nazis, and the situation would not be helped by the knowledge of a complete diplomatic break between yourself and Sikorski.

Stalin to Roosevelt, sent 29 April 1943, received 29 April 1943[16]

I received your answer, unfortunately, only on April 27, whereas the Soviet Government was obliged to take a decision for the severance of relations with the Polish Government on April 25.

Since the Polish Government, throughout nearly two weeks, not only did not continue, but also intensified in its press and radio, a campaign which was hostile to the Soviet Union and advantageous only to Hitler, public opinion in the U.S.S.R. grew extremely indignant over this conduct, and postponement of the decision of the Soviet Government became impossible.

It is conceivable that Mr Sikorski himself has no intention of cooperating with Hitler's gangsters. I should be only too glad if this supposition turned out to be correct. I do, however, consider that Mr Sikorski allowed himself to be led by certain pro-Hitler elements, either within the Polish Government or in its entourage, and as a result the Polish Government, very possibly involuntarily, became a tool in Hitler's hands in the anti-Soviet campaign of which you are aware.

I, too, believe that Premier Churchill will find a way to bring the Polish Government to reason and to help it proceed in future to act according to the dictates of common sense. I may be wrong, but I believe that one of our duties, as allies, consists in preventing any one ally from acting inimically, to the comfort and gratification of the common foe, against any other ally.

As regards Polish subjects in the Soviet Union and their further destinies, I can assure you that the Soviet authorities have always treated them as friends and comrades, and will continue to do so in the future. It is therefore clear that there is not, nor can be, any question of their being deported from the Soviet Union. Should they themselves wish to leave the U.S.S.R., the Soviet authorities, which have never put obstacles in the way of this, do not intend to do so in future, and will render them all possible assistance.

Stalin's statements that the break had already taken place dismayed London and Washington. The British were particularly annoyed, having made considerable efforts to resolve the confrontation with the Poles. 'In recent weeks everything had been going so well,' lamented Eden during a meeting with Maisky on 29 April. 'Our relations with you were getting better, I would even say better than ever before, and all of a sudden such a blow.' According to Harvey, the foreign secretary was frankly 'at a loss to see what Stalin is up to', but he discerned troubling echoes of the Czech crisis of September 1938: 'It is too like Hitler and Benes to be pleasant.'[17]

In any case, the fact that Stalin did not even wait for an answer from his allies before breaking with the London Poles showed that he was not consulting, but merely informing. 'The stubbornness which they have shown in handling the question,' cabled Clark Kerr from Moscow, 'suggests that what they have done is only part of a preconceived plan.' He felt it would be 'wise not to exclude the possibility that the next step may be the setting up of a Polish government in this country with which they would establish diplomatic relations'.[18] This danger was discussed in Cabinet on the evening of 27 April, together with the need to restrain both the Polish press in London and Maisky's weekly *Soviet War News*, which damned the Poles with choice phrases, such as 'accomplices of the cannibal Hitler'.[19] The Ministry of Information duly leaned on the Poles, while Churchill and Cadogan ticked off the Soviet ambassador. 'We kicked Maisky all around the room, and it went very well,' Cadogan recorded with satisfaction, though one would not know this from Maisky's own diary and his report to Moscow which, as usual, represented the British as eating out of his hand.[20]

Churchill had fired off a message to Stalin, but Clark Kerr took the most unusual step of delaying delivery because of his concern about its content and tone. Eden and Cadogan then persuaded the PM to rebalance the text, which, according to Cadogan, had been 'a little hard on the Poles and a little soft on the Russians'. In particular, they added the new opening paragraph expressing Churchill's 'disappointment' that Stalin had acted unilaterally – thereby playing the Allied unity card back against the Soviet leader.[21] The fourth paragraph was a warning shot about trying to form a Moscow-based Polish government – an idea that, in his reply to Churchill, Stalin rejected as an invention of Goebbels' propaganda.[22]

Churchill to Stalin, sent 28 April 1943, received 30 April 1943[23]

I cannot refrain from expressing my disappointment that you should have felt it necessary to take action in breaking off relations with the Poles without giving me time to inform you of the results of my approach to General Sikorski, about which I had telegraphed to you on April 24. I had hoped that, in the spirit of our Treaty of last year, we should always consult each other about such important matters, more especially as they affect the combined strength of the United Nations.

Eden and I have pointed out to the Polish Government that no resumption of friendly or working relations with Soviet Russia is possible while they make charges of an insulting character against the Soviet Government and thus seem to countenance the atrocious Nazi propaganda. Still more would it be impossible for any of us to tolerate inquiries by the International Red Cross held under Nazi auspices and dominated by Nazi terrorism. I am glad to tell you that they have accepted our view and that they want to work loyally with you. Their request now is to have dependants of the Polish army in Persia and the fighting Poles in the Soviet Union sent to join the Polish forces you have already allowed to go to Iran. This is surely a matter which admits of patient discussion. We think the request is reasonable if made in the right way and at the right time and I am pretty sure that the President thinks so too. We hope earnestly that, remembering the difficulties in which we have all been plunged by the brutal Nazi aggression, you will consider this matter in a spirit of collaboration.

The Cabinet here is determined to have proper discipline in the Polish press in Great Britain. Even miserable rags attacking Sikorski can say things which German broadcast repeats open-mouthed to the world to our joint detriment. This must be stopped and it will be stopped.

So far this business has been Goebbels' triumph. He is now busy suggesting that the USSR will set up a Polish Government on Russian soil and deal only with them. We should not, of course, be able to recognise such a Government and should continue our relations with Sikorski who is far the most helpful man you or we are likely to find for the purposes of the common cause. I expect this will also be the American view.

My own feeling is that they have had a shock and that after whatever interval is thought convenient the relationship established on July 30, 1941, should be restored. No one will hate this more than Hitler and what he hates most is wise for us to do.

We owe it to our Armies now engaged, and presently to be more heavily engaged, to maintain good conditions behind the fronts. I and my colleagues look steadily to the ever closer cooperation and understanding of the USSR, the United States and the British Commonwealth and Empire, not only in the deepening war struggle but after the war. What other hope can there be than this for the tortured world?

Despite the hints of criticism in Churchill's text, it must have been clear to Stalin that he had ridden out the storm. In fact, within a couple of weeks of the German revelations, it can be justly said that 'the Soviet leadership had managed to produce a position of strength from a potential position of great weakness'.[24] He had adroitly severed relations with the London Poles, freeing him at some later point to create a puppet Polish government in Moscow, while appearing as a generous ally by representing himself as willing to help the Polish army and its dependants leave the USSR.[25] It was a virtuoso piece of Machiavellian diplomacy.

As was now the norm, Roosevelt let Churchill do the heavy lifting in correspondence with the Kremlin. In fact, he did not write again to Stalin about Katyn. But the president approved of Churchill's stance, as is evident from a long message to the PM which was not eventually sent. In this draft, FDR said he agreed that Sikorski was the 'most helpful' Polish leader available from the perspective of the common cause, that the creation by Moscow of a 'rival Polish

Government' must be 'avoided at all costs', and that they should all keep off the 'underlying territorial dispute' between Poles and Russians. 'The winning of the war is the paramount objective for all of us,' FDR insisted. 'For this unity is essential.'[26]

Churchill continued to treat Katyn as an unfortunate irritant in what had seemed an improving relationship. 'I think it would be a pity,' Churchill cabled Clark Kerr on 2 May, attaching his next message to the Kremlin, 'that our Polish discussions with Stalin should interrupt the more or less weekly flow of friendly messages I have been sending him about operations. I am sure these give him pleasure and maintain our indispensable contact.' Trying to get relations on to a matey footing, he told the ambassador that, when giving Stalin the message, 'if you like, and if the going is good, say I should like him to give me a fighting Pole for every German I take in Tunisia from now on, and a Polish dependant, woman or child, for every Italian'. Jokes like that, he admitted, were 'in questionable taste, but there are moments and situations when they have their uses'.[27]

'I warmly agree that flow of messages should not be interrupted,' Clark Kerr cabled. 'I like your joke and shall enjoy putting it to him, for I think he will like it too.'[28] The ambassador had his chance a few days later. Getting the message across did not prove straightforward, but once Stalin got the point, Clark Kerr reported that 'it gave him a good laugh'. The Soviet leader then quipped that Churchill 'would catch many more Germans than he had fighting Poles' and that no Italian was 'worth a Polish woman' – so the deal would not be fair on either of them. In any case, he added, Churchill would need all his Italians to build roads, because 'that was all the Italians could do'. Pavlov's version of the talk was less colourful, but he did record another one-liner from Stalin, warning Churchill not to miscalculate: 'Sometimes a woman is better than an Italian.' Whatever the exact nature of this conversation – probably somewhere in between the ambassador's embellishments and the Soviet interpreter's dryness – it is clear that Stalin and Clark Kerr enjoyed exchanging a bit of racist, sexist banter to jolly along Anglo-Soviet relations.[29]

And so, on 2 May, Churchill sent another of those detailed reports on the bombing of Germany and the endgame in Tunisia by which he hoped to engage Stalin's interest as a fellow supreme commander, and also show that the Western Allies were now striking hard at the enemy. The cable began with an appreciation for Stalin's May Day speech, which suggested that Churchill's message was finally getting through. In it, Stalin had linked hard-won Soviet successes on the Eastern Front with those of the Western Allies, whose troops had 'routed the Italo-German troops' in North Africa, while their airmen struck 'shattering blows at the military and industrial centres of Germany and Italy, foreshadowing the formation of the second front in Europe'. Thus, Stalin declared, 'for the first time since the beginning of the war, the blow at the enemy from the East, dealt by the Red Army, merged with a blow from the West, dealt by the troops of our Allies, into one joint blow'. It was a deft tribute which, Churchill told Stalin, he had read 'with the utmost satisfaction and admiration'.[30]

Conscious of having retrieved the situation over Katyn, Stalin did not let Churchill's letter sent on 28 April stand as the last word. On 4 May, he batted back the PM's comments about Allied unity, reiterating his claims that the British should have restrained the Poles. And his fierce rebuttal of Hitlerite 'rumours' about the creation of a new Polish puppet government in Moscow was, for the first time, tied to the idea that the Big Three should take it upon themselves to 'improve the composition of the present Polish government' in London, in order to 'strengthen the united front of the Allies against Hitler'. The Kremlin's tactic of blasting the London Poles as fascist collaborators, combined with Churchill and Roosevelt's reluctance to challenge the Soviet version of Katyn, was now giving Stalin an opportunity to question the Polish government-in-exile's right to speak for Poland. He would later exploit this opportunity to the full.[31]

Stalin to Churchill, sent 4 May 1943, received 6 May 1943[32]

In sending to you my message of the 21st of April on the interruption of relations with the Polish Government, I was guided by the following considerations: the Poles started a notorious anti-Soviet press campaign on the 15th April; this campaign was aggravated first by the statement of the Polish Defence Ministry and then by the statement of the Polish Government of the 17th April. Nobody in London opposed the campaign and nobody warned the Soviet Government about its coming although it is very difficult to think that the British Government had no inkling of the contemplated campaign. It seems to me that taking account of the spirit of our Treaty it would have been natural to prevent one ally from delivering a blow against another, more particularly so when such blow renders a direct help to our common enemy. In any case, this is my understanding of the Allied obligations. However, I deemed it my duty to convey to you the viewpoint of the Soviet Government on the questions of Soviet–Polish relations. As the Poles continued to kindle their scandalous anti-Soviet campaign, it could not be expected that the patience of the Soviet Government had no limit.

You write that you will discipline the Polish press. Many thanks for that. I doubt however that it would be easy to bring to reason the present Polish Government, its entourage of pro-Hitler bawlers and its unrestrained press. In spite of your statement that the Polish Government is prepared to collaborate loyally with the Soviet Government, I have little faith in its ability to keep its word. There are so many pro-Hitler elements in the entourage of the Polish Government and Sikorski is so helpless and so terrorized by these elements! Even assuming that Sikorski would like to be really loyal, it is hardly conceivable that he would be in a position to do so.

With regard to the rumours spread by the Hitlerites concerning the formation of a new Polish Government in the USSR, all these canards must be refuted. Our Ambassador has already told you about that. This however does not exclude the possibility for Great Britain, the USSR and the USA to take measures in order to improve the composition of the present Polish Government. Such action would be desirable with a view to strengthen the united front of the Allies against Hitler. The sooner this would be done, the better.

Mr Eden, after return from the USA, intimated to Mr Maisky that among the supporters of President Roosevelt there are people who consider the prospects of the present Polish Government uncertain. They do not know whether it will be able to return to Poland and assume power, although they would like to retain the services of Sikorski personally in a leading position. It seems to me that, in the estimate of the present Polish Government's prospects, the Americans are very near to the mark.

On the question of the Polish subjects in the USSR, whose number is not very large, as well as on the question of the families of the Polish soldiers evacuated to Iran, it should be stated that the Soviet Government never put obstacles in the way of their exit from the USSR.

I received your message on the recent events in Tunis. Many thanks for your communication. I am delighted at the successes of the Anglo-American troops and I wish them still more success.

*****

On 29 April, Churchill proposed to Roosevelt that he come to Washington to decide future strategy in the wake of victory in Tunisia. He was particularly keen to confirm arrangements for 'Husky' – the invasion of Sicily. The president agreed on 2 May and, as host of the meeting (codenamed 'Trident'), he notified Stalin. Since the Soviets were not invited, Roosevelt promised to keep the head of the Soviet Purchasing Commission in the USA, General Aleksandr Belyayev, informed about the discussions.[33]

Roosevelt to Stalin, sent 5 May 1943, received 7 May 1943[34]

I want you to know that Mr Churchill is coming to Washington next week to discuss our immediate next steps. We will of course keep General Belyaev currently informed.

Meeting *à deux* made sense in military terms, because the British and Americans would be discussing difficult issues of Mediterranean strategy; but Roosevelt was sensitive to the diplomatic implications of not inviting Stalin. On the same day, he composed another letter to the Soviet leader, pressing again the proposal he had periodically floated for an informal personal meeting between the two of them. Although FDR presented the idea as contingency planning for a sudden German collapse, postwar issues were clearly also on his mind, because he explicitly ruled out the inclusion of Churchill. This reflected the president's conviction that he and Stalin did not carry the same 'imperialist' baggage as the prime minister when thinking about the future. The proposed meeting place – the shores of the Bering Straits – would be as far from Britain as possible.

FDR's overture required considerable delicacy, so he again resorted to a trusted personal emissary – this time Joseph E. Davies, the US ambassador to Moscow in 1936–38, who had been given the job in return for his wife's lavish contributions to FDR's campaign.[35] The president personally informed Litvinov on 5 May about the idea of a personal meeting 'without Churchill'.[36] As Litvinov remarked soon afterwards in a note on US policy, Roosevelt 'believed that with regard to certain postwar issues it would be easier for him to come to an agreement with us rather than with Great Britain, and I am inclined to think that this explained his persistent proposals to meet Comrade Stalin'.[37] Churchill also knew about Davies' mission, even before Roosevelt's message of 5 May, because the garrulous emissary had already spilled the beans to a member of the British embassy in Washington. Davies told David Bowes-Lyon, the queen's brother, on 24 April, that he would be going in May to Moscow as a special envoy 'with the full authority of the President' and 'would be in a position to make agreements with the Soviet Government should it be possible to do so'. This news – conveyed by Davies 'in the strictest confidence' – was immediately relayed to Eden and Churchill in London. The British did not know the contents of Roosevelt's letter, but they were well aware that something big was afoot.[38]

Roosevelt to Stalin, sent 5 May 1943, received 20 May 1943[39]

I am sending this personal note to you by the hands of my old friend, Joseph E. Davies. It relates solely to one subject which I think it is easier for us to talk over through a mutual friend. Mr Litvinov is the only other person with whom I have talked about it.

I want to get away from the difficulties of large Staff conferences or the red tape of diplomatic conversations. Therefore, the simplest and most practical method that I can think of would be an informal and completely simple visit for a few days between you and me.

I fully appreciate the desirability for you to stay in daily touch with your military operations; I also find it inadvisable to be away from Washington more than a short time. There are two sides to the problem. The first relates to timing. There is always the possibility that the historic Russian defense, followed by taking the offensive, may cause a crack-up in Germany next winter. In such a case we must be prepared for the many next steps. We are none of us prepared today. Therefore, it is my belief that you and I ought to meet this summer.

The second problem is where to meet. Africa is almost out of the question in summer and Khartoum is British territory. Iceland I do not like because for both you and me it involves rather difficult flights and, in addition, would make it, quite frankly, difficult not to invite Prime Minister Churchill at the same time.

Therefore, I suggest that we could meet either on your side or my side of Bering Straits. Such a point would be about three days from Washington and I think about two days from Moscow if the weather is good. That means that you could always get back to Moscow in two days in an emergency.

It is my thought that neither of us would want to bring any Staff. I would be accompanied by Harry Hopkins, an interpreter and a stenographer – and that you and I would talk very informally and get what we call 'a meeting of the minds'. I do not believe that any official agreements or declarations are in the least bit necessary.

You and I would, of course, talk over the military and naval situation, but I think we can both do that without Staffs being present.

Mr Davies has no knowledge of our military affairs nor of the post-war plans of this Government, and I am sending him to you for the sole purpose of talking over our meeting.

I greatly hope that our forces will be in complete control of Tunisia by the end of May, and Churchill and I next week will be working on the second phase of the offensive.

Our estimates of the situation are that Germany will deliver an all-out attack on you this summer, and my Staff people think it will be directed against the middle of your line.

You are doing a grand job. Good luck!

Stalin sent identical greetings to Churchill and Roosevelt on the Allies' long-awaited victory in Tunisia, and these two documents were published in the Soviet press. On 10 May, church bells once again rang across Britain in celebration – echoing the jubilation after Alamein and 'Torch'. The last remnants of the German–Italian forces surrendered on 12–13 May; the Allies netted about a quarter of a million prisoners.[40]

Stalin to Roosevelt, sent 8 May 1943, received 7 May 1943[41]

I congratulate you and the gallant American and British forces on the brilliant victory which has led to the liberation of Bizerte and Tunis from Hitlerite tyranny. I wish you continued success.

Conscious of Stalin's rooted suspicions about Allied military plans, Churchill decided to placate him with some encouraging hints about the purpose of 'Trident' being to 'settle further exploitation in Europe after "Husky" and also to discourage undue bias towards the Pacific'.[42] The PM also responded positively to Stalin's message of 4 May about Poland – unlike Eden, who had a stiff meeting with Maisky about it. The Soviet ambassador, Eden told Clark Kerr, showed 'little willingness to accept that there might be a Polish point of view', and at one point criticized the British government for being 'too tolerant' of Polish feelings. 'I had to remind him', declared Eden, 'that we went to war because of Poland.'[43] Churchill, however, was much more upbeat – cabling Eden when en route to America: 'Further reflection increases my feeling that Polish government made almost foolish and improper blunder and that it is necessary for the future of Poland that there should be substantial reconstruction. I am glad you are already beginning to speak in this sense to Sikorski.'[44]

The PM prepared a draft reply to Stalin that laid most of the blame on the London Poles and their Russophobe hangers-on. He invited Eden to 'check and amend in any way you think fit', whereupon the foreign secretary revised the message to take a firmer line with Moscow and sought support from the War Cabinet. His colleagues agreed that Churchill's draft, in Eden's words, 'virtually committed us to bring about changes in the Polish Government' as almost the precondition for any renewal of Soviet–Polish relations. Eden's revision cut this out, and instead warned Stalin that Sikorski could hardly be expected to reconstruct his government 'under foreign pressure'. His colleagues suggested various other amendments to the fulsome tone of Churchill message.[45] Cadogan – almost as cynical about British politicians as he was about most foreigners – noted later in his diary: 'It amuses me to see how, in his absence, *every* member of the Cabinet makes, simultaneously, sweeping suggestions.' If the PM were present, he noted, 'every rabbit would crouch dumb'. Although Churchill, by then in Washington, had asked to 'see the final result before you send it', this seems not to have been done.[46]

Churchill to Stalin, sent 12 May 1943, received 13 May 1943[47]

I am much obliged to you for your message about the Polish affair.

The Poles did not tell us what they were going to do and so we could not warn them against the peril of the course which they proposed to take.

The Polish press will be disciplined in future, and all other foreign language publications.

I agree that Polish Government is susceptible of improvement, though there would be a great difficulty in finding better substitutes. I think, like you, that Sikorski and some others should in any event be retained. But you will, I hope, agree that it is hardly possible for a Prime Minister to reconstruct his Government under foreign pressure. If Sikorski did so, he would probably have to go, and we should not get anyone as good in his place. Therefore he probably cannot make changes at once, but I will take every opportunity to urge him to this direction as soon as may be. I will discuss this with President Roosevelt.

I note your intimation that it is not policy of the Soviet Government to put obstacles in the way of the exit of Polish subjects in USSR or of families of Polish soldiers, and will communicate with you further on this subject through the Ambassador.

Many thanks for your message about the occupation of Tunis and Bizerta. The question is now how many do we catch.

Seeking to move on from Katyn and compensate for the cancellation of the Arctic convoys, Churchill sent Stalin a sweetener about a new shipment of Hurricane fighters via the southern route through Basra.[48] Although the PM, as usual, was making as much as he could of British aid to Russia, the weight of contribution between the two Western allies was now shifting markedly. In 1941–42, Britain had fulfilled its pledges under the First Supply Protocol far more effectively than the USA, but by the time the Third Protocol was under discussion in June 1943, the balance was the other way around. America was promising far more and would deliver even more than it had promised – including military hardware that enhanced the Red Army's mobility as it took the offensive, such as jeeps, trucks and railroad flat cars. Britain, facing growing manpower shortages and now fighting in earnest in the Mediterranean, was struggling to provide for its own expanding army and air force. The Air Ministry, for instance, was reluctant to release modern Spitfire fighters and Mosquito fighter-bombers, and instead kept providing reconditioned Hurricanes (known in Russia as 'flying coffins') – a practice that was greatly resented in Moscow.[49]

But the Americans were gilding the lily in their own way. On 18 May, Roosevelt sent Stalin a crisp US estimate of 'Axis losses in North Africa from December 8, 1940, to May 12, 1943' – 625,000 personnel; 'not less than 2,100 tanks; 2.2 million tons of merchant shipping', and so on. He did not point out that over those two and a half years the British and their allies had done virtually all the fighting until the final six months. After some thought, Molotov's office 'decided not to reply'.[50]

Joseph Davies breezed into the Soviet capital on 19 May carrying the president's secret message and a copy of the self-promotional movie about his ambassadorship, *Mission to Moscow*. The following evening, Standley accompanied him to the Kremlin. 'Our President,' the ambassador announced stiffly, 'has intimated that he does not want me to be present when his letter is delivered. With your permission, Mr Stalin, I will withdraw.' Once this had happened, Davies read out the letter, while Pavlov translated. Stalin doodled throughout, but then asked why Churchill was to be excluded from the proposed meeting. Davies said that the prime minister would be kept informed, but he had different ideas about colonialism and imperialism. If Stalin and Roosevelt were to meet, Davies opined, they would certainly come to an understanding.

'I am not sure,' Stalin replied.

'Well, from what I know of what you both have done, I am sure.'

'But understanding is not enough,' Stalin observed sternly. 'There must be reciprocity and respect.'

The Soviet leader launched into a *tour d'horizon* of postwar issues, spiced with barbs aimed at the London Poles, doodling all the while. But then he looked up abruptly and told Davies: 'I think your President is right. I think he represents America, as I understand it. He is a great man. I believe in him. You may tell your President I agree with him and it is necessary that we meet, as he suggests.' After studying a map, Stalin suggested somewhere in Alaska – Nome or Fairbanks – as an appropriate mid-point (plate 15).[51]

While awaiting a formal letter in reply, Davies busied himself in Moscow by promoting himself and his film, to the private amusement of the Russians and the British embassy. He continued to keep Standley at arm's length, stating that he did not know what was in Roosevelt's letter because it was written in Russian, and claiming that, although he and Stalin had talked for two and a half hours, they did not discuss its contents. The Soviet leader finally produced a response, which suggested that he and Roosevelt defer the meeting until July or August because of the impending German offensive around Kursk – about which Moscow already had accurate intelligence. In a typical dig, he also cited uncertainties about the second front as another imponderable.[52] Davies took the letter back with him to Washington – bypassing Standley again. The existence of what the FO called 'the famous secret letter' had become common gossip in Anglo-American circles in Moscow – US correspondents concluded that the president was trying to set up a Big Three meeting – but exactly what Roosevelt had proposed and how Stalin had responded remained for the moment unknown.[53] The Davies visit was also a very public humiliation for Admiral Standley. 'Our embassy is just across the street from the Kremlin,' wrote Moscow correspondent Quentin Reynolds, 'and Ambassador Standley is never too busy to walk over to the Kremlin with a letter.'[54]

Stalin to Roosevelt, sent 26 May 1943, received 3 June 1943[55]

Mr Davies has handed me your message.

I agree with you that this summer, possibly as early as June, the beginning of a new large-scale offensive of Hitlerites is to be expected on the Soviet–German front. Hitler has already concentrated against us about 200 German divisions and as many as 30 divisions of his allies. We are preparing to meet the new German offensive and to launch counter-attacks but we experience a shortage of airplanes and aircraft fuel. Now it is of course impossible to forsee all the military and other steps that we shall have to take. This will depend upon the developments at our front. Much will depend also on how speedy and active will be the Anglo-American military operations in Europe.

I have mentioned these important circumstances to explain why my present answer to your proposal cannot be quite definite now.

I agree with you that such a meeting is necessary and that it should not be postponed. But I ask you to appreciate duly the importance of the circumstances set forth just because the summer months will be extremely serious for our Soviet armies. As I do not know how the events will develop on the Soviet–German front in June, I shall not be able to leave Moscow during that month. Therefore I would suggest that our meeting should be arranged in July or August. In case you could upon receipt of my communication agree to the time of our meeting suggested by me, I would arrive in the place of our meeting at the fixed time.

As to the place of the meeting, this will be communicated to you by Mr Davies personally.

I agree with you as to the limitation of the number of your and my advisers.

I thank you for sending Mr Davies to Moscow, who has a knowledge of the
Soviet Union and can unbiasedly judge of things.

Davies' mission coincided with Stalin's decision to dissolve the Comintern, the
Communist International, whose task had been to direct the operations of
communist organizations around the world. This was publicized on 22 May.
Although diplomats in London and Washington did not anticipate the cessation of Moscow's support for foreign communist parties – rightly so, because
the functions of Comintern were simply absorbed by the International
Department of the Central Committee – the decision was perceived in Allied
capitals as a Soviet retreat from the public goal of world revolution, and therefore a move that would strengthen the anti-Hitler coalition. Churchill's initial
reaction was that the news of Comintern's dissolution was 'very fine and full of
hope for the future'; he even thought of sending Stalin a message to this effect,
but never did, perhaps seeing snags or probably being too busy in Washington
with Roosevelt.[56] At a Politburo meeting on 21 May, Stalin explained the
Comintern's dissolution as a pragmatic response to changing international
circumstances. Some communist parties were seeking to overthrow their
governments (for example, in Germany and Italy), whereas those in Britain, the
USA and other Allied countries 'had the task of supporting their governments
to the fullest for the immediate destruction of the enemy'.[57]

The 26 May marked the first anniversary of the Soviet–British treaty of alliance. London and Moscow exchanged warm greetings, and Molotov gave a
formal breakfast to celebrate the occasion. It seemed that Allied relations were
once again picking up. 'I think we can congratulate ourselves (and thank you),'
Warner wrote to Clark Kerr, 'that the Polish imbroglio seems to have been kept
in an entirely separate compartment from general Anglo-Soviet relations and
seems to have had no ill-effect upon them.'[58]

However, a new storm was about to break following the 'Trident' meetings
in Washington on 12–25 May. And this storm could not be easily contained; in
fact, it precipitated the worst crisis to date in relations among the Big Three.

*****

'Trident' proved a particularly fraught Anglo-American conference. The underlying source of friction on strategy remained the same: the US desire for an
early cross-Channel attack on Hitler's Europe, against the British preference to
gradually force a German collapse by first gaining control of the Mediterranean
and then knocking Italy out of the war. The debate was further complicated by
conflicting service interests: the US Navy still fixated on the Pacific, while both

air forces gave pride of place to the strategic bombing of Germany. The struggle was more intense than Casablanca because the US Joint Chiefs – smarting at their humiliation there – had greatly improved their staff structure and conference support, especially on home soil, so that they could fight their corner as tenaciously as the British. So heated were the arguments that on several occasions the Combined Chiefs of Staff sent virtually all their aides out of the room, so that they could let off steam at each other in closed session and then hammer out compromises without losing face.[59]

The delayed victory in North Africa and the continued insecurity of the Atlantic had by now ruled out a cross-Channel attack in the campaigning season of 1943, at least on the Anglo-American definition of acceptable risk – a definition that Stalin had never accepted. At 'Trident', the two sides eventually settled on 1 May 1944 for the invasion of France, but Churchill and Brooke hoped to extract a firm commitment to follow up the capture of Sicily ('Husky') with the invasion of Italy. Marshall, however, feared that this would repeat the 'vacuum' effect of the North African landings the previous year, which had 'sucked in more and more troops', and preclude a sufficient troop build-up in Britain to mount the cross-Channel attack on schedule. He warned strongly against 'a prolongation of the war in Europe, and thus a delay in the ultimate defeat of Japan, which the people of the U.S. would not tolerate'. Brooke, by contrast, argued that an invasion of Italy could precipitate the collapse of Mussolini's regime and force Hitler to divert divisions from the Eastern Front to shore up his southern flank. He suggested that ceasing operations in the Mediterranean after capturing Sicily, in order to cross the Channel, would actually 'lengthen the war'. Brooke's underlying assumptions about France were as pessimistic as those he entertained about Italy were optimistic: that, at best, the Allies could only land sufficient troops and equipment to hang onto a beachhead in 1944 (for example the Brest Peninsula), and that no major breakout operations 'would be possible until 1945 or 1946'. He cited the experience of 1914–18, when there had been 'some 80 French divisions available on our side' for major assaults on the Western Front, and it still took four years to break the Germans.[60]

The 'strategy' of both sides was therefore dependent on a good many speculative assumptions. No simple resolution of the arguments was possible, and all the CCS could do was try to paper over the cracks. By 20 May, they had agreed on a compromise form of words: after Sicily, the Allied commander-in-chief in the Mediterranean should mount such operations as were 'best calculated to eliminate Italy from the war and to contain the maximum number of German forces'. This formulation left open whether to invade Italy (the British ambition) or simply to capture Sardinia – the more modest and self-contained US alternative, in order to utilize otherwise idle troops in 1943. An additional proviso, that 'each specific operation' would have to be approved by the CCS, was intended by the Americans to prevent yet more mission creep. Brooke was content with these compromises, aware of how close they had all come to spilling blood. He was therefore incensed when Churchill tried to overturn the tenuous accord during a meeting at the White House on 24 May, by pressing for an explicit commitment to invade Italy. 'As a result he created situation of suspicion in the American Chiefs that we had been behind their backs, and has made matters far more difficult for us in the future!!' Brooke exploded in his diary. 'There are times when he drives me to desperation!'[61]

Churchill lost that skirmish – the CCS's Italian compromise became enshrined in the conference conclusions – but he went on to win the struggle. After Washington, he returned home via Algiers and Tunis, determined to press Eisenhower into firm and urgent plans for post-'Husky' operations. Coyly he suggested to the president that, to avoid any impression of 'undue influence' by the British, he would like to take Marshall with him, and Roosevelt agreed. But without the president and his own staff in support, Marshall was less able to hold the line against the prime minister's authority, rhetoric and cunning. By the end of their meetings with Eisenhower on 3 June, Churchill had ensured that the minutes included enough uncontested statements about the value of the 'capture of Rome' to set down a firm marker for further action if Sicily fell quickly. No wonder the PM wrote in his memoirs, 'I have no more pleasant memories of the war than the eight days in Algiers and Tunis'![62]

Before Churchill left Washington, he and the president had spent a good deal of their final evening together trying (and failing) to finalize a message for Stalin, summarizing the 'Trident' conclusions. So, on the plane to Algiers, the PM gave that task to the long-suffering Marshall, who managed within two hours to produce a typed fair copy, with which Churchill was delighted. He wrote later, 'I was immensely impressed with the document, which exactly expressed what the President and I wanted, and did so with clarity and compre-hension not only of the military but of the political issues involved.'[63]

Reading the message today, it is hard to understand the PM's enthusiasm. George Marshall was no wordsmith: he had simply pulled together passages from the conference conclusions in language that was often ponderously bureaucratic and made little attempt to present the unpalatable conclusions from a perspective that seemed sympathetic to the Soviets. This was not Marshall's fault, and nor was diplomacy his métier. What is astonishing is the way this all-important message was nodded through by the two political leaders. Perhaps Roosevelt was exhausted and Churchill consumed by his trip to Algiers. Whatever the reason, the PM and Brooke approved Marshall's text on the plane without any change. The president's only amendment was to incorporate support for Russia into the Allies' 'first priority' – rather than placing it 'next in priority' (as in Marshall's draft), or fourth out of five (as in the conference conclusions).[64]

This token upgrade of Russia at the start was belied by the detail later in the document. There was no attempt to apologize for delays in delivering on past 'promises', or to offer the kind of explanatory detail about the global and logistical constraints that Churchill had developed so skilfully in his message of 11 March. For reasons that are not clear, the two leaders did not even bother to include a conciliatory preamble from their earlier draft, framed with due politeness to Stalin and including the phrase 'Nearly all the decisions enumerated below were made only after they had been measured against the yardstick of their aid to your country's war effort.' The Soviet leader would probably have regarded such a preamble as fluff, but without any effort at sugar-coating, Marshall's bald statement of the conference conclusions was almost gratuitously offensive in tone, as well as content.[65]

Roosevelt to Stalin, sent 2 June 1943, received 4 June 1943[66]

I am sending you through Ambassador Standley the recently approved decisions of our Combined Chiefs of Staff. These decisions have the joint approval of both Mr Churchill and myself. In view of their extremely secret nature I am asking Ambassador Standley to deliver them to you personally.

Roosevelt to Stalin, sent 2 June 1943, received 4 June 1943[67]

In general, the overall strategy agreed upon is based upon the following decisions:

a) To give first priority to the submarine menace, the security of our overseas lines of communication, and to employ every practicable means to support Russia.

b) To prepare the ground for the active or passive participation of Turkey in the war on the side of the Allies.

c) To maintain an unremitting pressure against Japan for the purposes of continually reducing her Military power.

d) To undertake such measures as may be practicable to maintain China as an effective Ally and as a base for operations against Japan.

e) To prepare the French forces in Africa for active participation in the assaults on Axis Europe.

With reference to (a) above regarding submarines, the immediate results of the recent deployment of long-range aircraft with new equipment and special attack groups of naval vessels give great encouragement, better than one enemy submarine a day having been destroyed since May 1. If such a rate of destruction can be maintained it will greatly conserve, therefore increase, available shipping and will exert a powerful influence on the morale of the German submarine armada.

With reference to the support of Russia, agreement was reached as follows:

a) To intensify the present air offensive against the Axis Powers in Europe. This for the purpose of smashing German industry, destroying German fighter aircraft and breaking the morale of the German people. The rapid development of this air offensive is indicated by the events of the past three weeks in France, Germany and Italy, Sicily and Sardinia, and by the growth of the United States heavy bomber force in England from some 350 planes in March to approximately 700 today with a schedule calling for 900 June 30, 1,150 September 30, and 2,500 April 1. The British bomber force will be constantly increasing.

b) In the Mediterranean the decision was taken to eliminate Italy from the war as quickly as possible. General Eisenhower has been directed to prepare to launch offensive immediately following successful completion of HUSKY, (viz the assault on Sicily,) for the purpose of precipitating the collapse of Italy and thus facilitating our air offensive against Eastern and Southern Germany as well as continuing the attrition of German fighter aircraft and developing a heavy threat against German control in the Balkans. General Eisenhower may use for the Mediterranean operations all those forces now available in that area except for three British and four American divisions which are to participate in the concentration in England, next to be referred to.

c) It was decided that the resumption of the concentration of ground forces could now be undertaken with Africa securely in our hands and that, while plans are being continuously kept up to date by a joint U.S.–British Staff in England to take instant advantage of a sudden weakness in France or Norway, the concentration of forces and landing equipment in the British Isles should proceed at a rate to permit a full-scale invasion of the Continent to be launched at the peak of the great air offensive in the Spring of 1944. Incidentally, the unavoidable absorption of large landing-craft in the Mediterranean, the South-West Pacific and the Aleutian Islands has been our most serious limiting factor regarding operations out of England.

We have found that undertakings listed utilize our full resources. We believe that these operations will heavily engage the enemy in the air and will force a dispersion of his troops on the ground to meet both actual attacks and heavy threats of attack which can readily be converted into successful operations whenever signs of Axis weakness become apparent.

Standley presented this message to Stalin and Molotov at 11 p.m. on 4 June in an air-raid shelter some eighty feet under the Kremlin (because of a Luftwaffe raid). While Pavlov translated, Stalin 'listened attentively to the message, showing no evidence of surprise. He exhibited no reactions other than stating that he understood the general purport of the message and after careful study for two or three days would make a reply.'[68]

After Davies returned from Moscow, he reported to Roosevelt on his meeting with Stalin and delivered the Soviet leader's reply to FDR's secret letter. The president was pleased that his initiative had been well received and clearly now assumed that their meeting would take place later in the summer. He sent a cordial reply, including greetings to Molotov ('Mr Brown') (plate 16). The sensitivity with which this message was composed stands in striking contrast to the heavy-handedness of the Marshall message about strategy that the president had approved virtually unchanged.

Roosevelt to Stalin, sent 4 June 1943, received 5 June 1943[69]

I am very grateful to you for your courtesy extended to my government and me in your cordial reception of Ambassador Davies. He has returned safely, bearing your letter. I am happy that you and I are in complete agreement in principle on all the matters contained in your letter and I will await your further communication in accordance with your letter and your understanding with Mr Davies.

My warm personal regards, with my kind remembrances also to Mr Brown.

Stalin carefully studied his partners' message of 2 June, underlining key points. He did not try to challenge the Allied plans. His reply – sent to Roosevelt and copied to Churchill – simply accused them of flagrantly violating previous commitments and warned darkly that their decisions would have serious consequences for his country.[70] After his editing, Molotov's muscular text became more precise and succinct. The Soviet leader referred particularly to the joint letter of 26 January, after Casablanca, and to the PM's detailed follow-up on 9 February. In both cases, Stalin – like his partners – was playing with words. In the first message, Churchill and Roosevelt had said that the operations they planned, 'together with your powerful offensive, may well bring

Germany to her knees in 1943': the phrase 'may well' was a familiar Churchillism that talked up future prospects while avoiding firm pledges. In Stalin's message, this passage was rendered as a 'decision' to 'force Germany on her knees in 1943'. And when summarizing the message of 9 February (which had given the intended dates for a cross-Channel attack as either August or September 1943), Stalin omitted the next sentence, which Churchill clearly intended as the limiting condition in both cases ('The timing of this attack must, of course, be dependent upon the condition of German defensive possibilities across the Channel at that time').

But these Kremlin word games did not affect the larger point. Stalin had reason to complain that his allies had led him along with hints and provisos, nudges and winks, fine words and crossed fingers. He went right back to Molotov's shuttle diplomacy in 1942, especially Churchill's aide-mémoire of 10 June and the Soviet–American communiqué issued two days later. It was difficult to dispute his striking sentence about the Red Army 'fighting for two years ... not only for its own country but also for its Allies ... almost in single combat'.

Stalin to Roosevelt, sent 11 June 1943, received 11 June 1943[71]

Your message in which you inform me about certain decisions on the questions of strategy made by you and Mr Churchill I received on June 4. I thank you for the message.

As is apparent from your message, these decisions are in contradiction with those made by you and Mr Churchill at the beginning of this year, regarding the terms of the opening of the second front in Western Europe.

You of course remember that in the joint message of January 26 of this year you and Mr Churchill informed me about the decisions made at that time to divert considerable German land and air forces from the Russian front and to force Germany on her knees in 1943.

Later Mr Churchill on his behalf informed me on February 12 about the more precise terms of the British–American operation in Tunisia and in Mediterranean, as well as on the Western coast of Europe. It was said in this message that preparations for the operation of forcing the Channel in August 1943 were energetically being carried out by Great Britain and the United States, and should weather or other reasons have prevented it, then this operation would be prepared for September 1943 with the participation of larger forces in it.

Now, in May 1943, you and Mr Churchill made the decision postponing the British–American invasion of Western Europe until the spring of 1944. That is the opening of the second front in Western Europe, which was postponed already from 1942 to 1943, is being postponed again, this time until the spring of 1944.

This decision creates exceptional difficulties for the Soviet Union, which has already been fighting for two years, with utmost strain of its strength, against the main forces of Germany and her satellites, and leaves the Soviet Army, fighting not only for its own country but also for the Allies, to its own strength, almost in single combat with yet very strong and dangerous enemy.

Is it necessary to say what painful and negative impressions will be made in the Soviet Union, upon its people and its Army, by the new postponement of the second front and by leaving our Army, which has made so many sacrifices, without expected serious support from the British–American armies?

As to the Soviet Government, it does not find it possible to agree with this decision, made, besides, without its participation and without attempt to discuss jointly this most important question, and which decision may result in grave consequences for the future progress of the war.

Stalin's blunt response hardly came as a surprise. 'The main trouble,' Warner told Clark Kerr, was that in 'our wholesale appeasement period we made rash prom-ises to the Russians, which we cannot fulfil. It may have been worth it, but I much doubt it.' Warner could only hope that the 'bombshell' (as he called it) of 'Trident' would be defused in the same way as Katyn, 'without a lengthy and serious dislocation of general Anglo-Russian relations'.[72] Commenting himself on Stalin's message, Clark Kerr advised London that it was 'becoming more and more urgently necessary to arrange a full dress meeting' of the three leaders:

Nothing short of this seems likely to avert the consequences of this new postponement which cannot but confirm Stalin and his people in their deep-seated belief from which they were just beginning to emerge, that we and the Americans are not really playing fair but are deliberately allowing the Russians to bleed themselves to death.[73]

In Washington, as partial compensation for 'Trident', the president wanted to send additional supplies to the USSR. Hopkins managed to squeeze addi-tional aluminium from the War Production Board and extra planes from the Army Air Forces. FDR was particularly keen on the latter, instructing the AAF that 'from the point of view of carrying out our strategic concept of the war we should do everything possible to strengthen Russia this summer' and that planes were 'the quickest and best way'.[74]

Whereas Roosevelt sought to sweeten the pill of 'Trident' with gifts, Churchill tried to do so with words. On 12–13 June, he prepared what he called an 'entirely good-tempered' reply and sent it to the president for his opinion. In the draft, following Clark Kerr's advice, he pressed the importance of a Big Three meeting and again urged the merits of the British naval base at Scapa Flow in the Orkney Islands as a venue. 'All this,' the PM told the president coyly, 'makes me anxious to know anything you care to tell me about your letter sent to him by Mr Davis [sic] and the answer which has been received from him.' Like the US press corps in Moscow, Churchill seems to have assumed that FDR had proposed a tripartite meeting, which of course was not the case. For his part, FDR decided not to send Stalin a brief and rather anodyne message that had been drafted on 14 June for his signature, which included the remark that a meeting of the three of them that summer 'would be very helpful' – apparently because he was still hoping to hold the meeting *à deux*, as proposed via Davies. Eventually Roosevelt sent a message to London on 18 June saying 'I heartily approve of your reply' and promising that Harriman would arrive in London within a few days with news 'about the letter Joe Davies brought from Moscow for me'.[75]

Churchill's letter to Stalin exhibited some similarities with his message of 9 February after Casablanca, trying to offer reasons or rationalizations for the decisions made at 'Trident' and so crudely transmitted to Moscow on 2 June. The PM made valid points about the contribution that the Mediterranean front was now beginning to make to the total Allied war effort, and pressed for a Big Three meeting in a tone that showed he was still not aware of FDR's Davies démarche. His message was replete with the usual slippery 'Churchillisms', as in the statement that the strategic bombing offensive 'may well have a decisive effect' and 'should have produced a massive return' by the autumn. More seriously, the PM dented his credibility by suggesting that the absence so far of any German summer offensive might indicate that 'the unexpectedly rapid defeat of the Axis forces in North Africa has dislocated German strategy'. This just two weeks before operation 'Citadel' was unleashed around Kursk! And his breezy prediction that once Italy had been forced out of the war, the Germans would 'make a new front either on the Alps or the Po' was an early hint of a fatal misconception underlying his Italian strategy, namely that Hitler would surrender most of the country and not fight for Rome.

Churchill was now very fed up with the Soviets. He told Clark Kerr on 19 June that, although choosing to send Stalin 'a soft answer', he believed that 'no apology is called for from us' and told the ambassador to

> adopt a robust attitude to any further complaints. They themselves destroyed a second front in 1939 and 1940 and stood by watching with complete indifference what looked like our total obliteration as a nation. We have made no

reproaches, and we did our best to help them when they were in turn attacked. Nothing will induce me in any circumstances to allow what at this stage I am advised and convinced would be a useless massacre of British troops on the Channel reaches [*sic* – see note] in order to remove Soviet suspicions. I am getting rather tired of these repeated scoldings, considering that they have never been actuated by anything but cold-blooded self-interest and total disdain of our lives and fortunes. At the proper time you might give him a friendly hint of the danger of offending the two Western powers whose war-making strength is growing with every month that passes and who may play a helpful part in the Russian future. Even my own long-suffering patience is not inexhaustible.[76]

This was probably the hard message Churchill would have liked to send Stalin, except for the exigencies of Allied diplomacy. Having thereby vented his indignation and indulged his taste for bombast, the prime minister duly despatched his 'soft answer' to the Kremlin, with Roosevelt now chiming in briefly and somewhat disingenuously in support.

Roosevelt to Stalin, sent 18 June 1943, received 20 June 1943[77]

As I was away when your message came, I am a few days late in answering it. I am in full accord with what the Prime Minister telegraphed you. I assure you that we are really doing everything that is possible at this time.

I trust you will appreciate that our shipping situation is still tight, though we are cheered by the progress of our campaign against the submarines for the past two months, giving us a net gain in shipping available.

Churchill to Stalin, sent 20 June 1943, received 20 June 1943[78]

I have received a copy of your telegram of about [*sic*] the 11 June to the President. I quite understand your disappointment but I am sure we are doing not only the right thing but the only thing that is physically possible in the circumstances. It would be no help to Russia if we threw away a hundred thousand men in a disastrous cross-Channel attack such as would, in my opinion, certainly occur if we tried under present conditions and with forces too weak to exploit any success that might be gained at very heavy cost. In my view and that of all my expert military advisers we should, even if we got ashore, be driven off as the Germans have forces already in France superior to any we could put there this year, and can reinforce far more quickly across the main lateral railways of Europe than we could do over the beaches or through any of the destroyed Channel ports we might seize. I cannot see how a great British defeat and slaughter would aid the Soviet armies. It might, however, cause the utmost ill-feeling here if it were thought it had been incurred against the advice of our military experts and under pressure from you. You will remember that I have always made it clear in my telegrams sent to you that I would never authorise any cross-Channel attack which I believed would lead to only useless massacre.

The best way for us to help you is by winning battles and not by losing them. This we have done in Tunisia, where the long arm of British and United States sea power has reached across the Atlantic and ten thousand miles around the Cape and helped us to annihilate great Axis land and air forces. The threat immediately resulting to the whole Axis defensive system in the Mediterranean has already forced the Germans to reinforce Italy, the Mediterranean islands, the Balkans and Southern France with land and air forces. It is my earnest and sober hope that we can knock Italy out of the war this year, and by doing so we shall draw far more Germans off your front than by any other means open. The great attack that is now not far off will absorb the capacities of every port under our control in the Mediterranean from Gibraltar to Port Said inclusive. After Italy has been forced out of the war, the Germans will have to occupy the Riviera, make a new front either on the Alps or the Po and above all provide for the replacement of the thirty-two Italian divisions now in the Balkans. The moment for inviting Turkish participation in the war, active or passive, will then arrive. The bombing of the Roumanian oilfields can be carried through on a decisive scale. Already we are holding in the West and South of Europe the larger part of the German Air Forces and our superiority will increase continually. Out of a first-line operational strength of between 4,800 and 4,900 aircraft Germany, according to our information, has today on the Russian front some 2,000 compared with 2,500 this time last year. We are also ruining a large part of the cities and munition centres of Germany, which may well have a decisive effect by sapping German resistance on all fronts. By this coming autumn this great air offensive should have produced a massive return. If the favourable trend of anti-U-boat warfare of the last few months continues, it will quicken and increase the movement of the United States forces to Europe, which is being pressed to the full limit of available shipping. No one has paid more tribute than I have to the immense contribution of the Soviet Government to the common victory and I thank you also for the recognition which you have lately given to the exertions of your two Western Allies. It is my firm belief that we shall present you before the end of the year with results which will give you substantial relief and satisfaction.

I have never asked you for detailed information about the strength and dispositions of the Russian armies because you have been, and are still, bearing the brunt on land. I should, however, be glad to have your appreciation of the situation and immediate prospects on the Russian front and whether you think a German attack is imminent. We are already again in the middle of June and no attack has been launched. We have some reason to believe that the unexpectedly rapid defeat of the Axis forces in North Africa has dislocated German strategy and that the consequent threat to Southern Europe has been an important factor in causing Hitler to hesitate and to delay his plans for a large-scale offensive against Russia this summer. It is no doubt too soon to pronounce decidedly on all this, but we should be very pleased to hear what you think about it.

At the end of your message you complain that Russia has not been consulted in our recent decisions. I fully understand the reasons which prevented you from meeting the President and me at Khartoum, whither we would have gone in January, and I am sure you were right not to relinquish even for a week the direction of your immense and victorious campaign. Nevertheless the need and advantage of a meeting are very great. I can only say I will go at any risk to any place that you and the President may agree upon. I and my advisers believe Scapa Flow, our main naval harbour in the north of Scotland, would be most convenient, the safest and, if secrecy be desired, probably the most secret. I have again suggested this to the President. If you could come there by air at any time in the summer you may be sure that every arrangement would be made to suit your wishes and you would have a most hearty welcome from your British and American comrades.

In another attempt to offset the negative effects of 'Trident', Roosevelt took advantage of the second anniversary of 'Barbarossa' to pay tribute to the Soviet people and their supreme commander for heroic resistance to the Nazi invasion. The message, drafted by the State Department, was sent in an open telegram published in the American and Soviet media. Stalin sent his thanks – but with a sting in the tail: 'I am convinced that the sooner we deliver our joint united blows from the west and east against the enemy, the sooner victory will come.'[79]

A few days later, Churchill sent another message to Stalin concerning Soviet recognition of the Free French leader Charles de Gaulle as the future ruler of France. Never easy, Roosevelt and Churchill's relationship with the Gallic general had by then become really strained. FDR's animosity towards him was almost poisonous, but both leaders considered de Gaulle to be a loose cannon, an ambitious careerist who lacked strong support in France, and someone viciously hostile towards *les Anglo-Saxons*. They preferred the more moderate and tractable figure General Henri Giraud, commander-in-chief of the French forces in North Africa, and indeed much of their time at the Casablanca conference in January had been taken up with trying to create a shotgun marriage between de Gaulle and Giraud. In late May, infected by the Gallophobic atmosphere of the White House, Churchill asked the Cabinet to 'consider urgently whether we should eliminate de Gaulle as a political force and face Parliament and France on the issues'. The Cabinet, however, refused to support the PM. Eden noted drily in his diary: 'Everyone against and very brave about it in his absence.'[80]

At the beginning of June, the French Committee of National Liberation (FCNL) was created in Algiers, under Giraud and de Gaulle; but the latter intended to supplant his rival and then use the committee as the embryo for a postwar French government. On 17 June, Roosevelt renewed his pressure on Churchill by sending one of his most vituperative telegrams to the PM about the urgent need to 'divorce ourselves from De Gaulle' because he had 'proven to be unreliable, uncooperative, and disloyal to both our Governments' and also 'interested far more in political machinations' than in 'the prosecution of the war'.[81]

To make matters worse for Churchill, the Kremlin took a far more positive view of de Gaulle than did the White House – because of the support he enjoyed in France, his evident antipathy to Vichy and, not least, his independence from American control. On 19 June, Molotov informed Clark Kerr that the USSR was prepared to recognize the FCNL.[82] This prompted Churchill's anxious missive to Stalin, warning darkly that de Gaulle might endanger the security of the Sicily invasion and arguing that, if the Soviet Union unilaterally extended recognition, this could force him and Roosevelt to reveal publicly their dissent and thereby weaken Allied unity. In his reply, Stalin made clear that he dissented completely from Churchill's position on de Gaulle and recognition, but agreed to back off, provided his allies would do nothing further without consulting Moscow. Molotov surmised to Maisky that Britain and America were seeking 'a complete subordination of de Gaulle to Giraud' or even 'de Gaulle's elimination'.[83]

Churchill to Stalin, sent 23 June 1943, received 23 June 1943[84]

I am concerned to hear through Monsieur Molotov that you are thinking of recognising the French National Committee of Liberation recently set up at Algiers. It is unlikely that the British, and still more that the United States Government, will recognise this Committee for some time and then only after they have had reasonable proof that its character and action will be satisfactory to the interests of the Allied cause.

Since he arrived at Algiers, General de Gaulle has been struggling to obtain effective control of the French Army. Headquarters cannot be sure of what he will do or of his friendly feelings towards us if he obtained mastery. President Roosevelt and I are in entire agreement in feeling that de Gaulle might endanger the base and communications of the armies about to operate in 'Husky'. We cannot run any risk of this, as it would affect the lives of our soldiers and hamper the prosecution of the war.

Originally there were 7 members of the Committee but the number has now been expanded to 14, and we cannot be sure of its action. General Eisenhower has therefore, in the name of both United States and the British Governments, notified the Committee that General Giraud must remain the Commander-in-Chief of the French Army and have effective power over its character and organisation. Undoubtedly this will cause discussion in the House of Commons as well as in the United States, and the President and I will have to give reasons, of which there are plenty, for the course we have taken. If the Soviet Government had already recognised the Committee, the mere giving of these reasons and the explanations would reveal a difference of view between the Soviet Government and the Western Allies, which would be most regrettable.

We are very anxious to find a French authority to which all Frenchmen will rally, and we still hope that one may emerge from the discussions now proceeding at Algiers. It seems to us far too soon to decide upon this at present.

Churchill's 'soft answer' on the second front elicited a very hard response from the Kremlin, which was copied to Roosevelt.[85] With forensic intensity, Stalin once more dissected the statements made by Churchill over the previous two years, again somewhat selectively, as in the omission from the 9 February 1943 extract of Churchill's limiting condition about the state of German defences. Stalin also seems to have misconstrued, deliberately or not, Churchill's reference in the opening of his 20 June message to throwing away 100,000 men as the total force he was planning to commit to the cross-Channel attack, rather than as an intolerable level of casualties. But the main thrust of Stalin's indictment was again difficult to deflect, namely that Churchill had always been at pains to set out the difficulties of invading France, so the commitments he did make about 1943 must surely have been given after taking full account of those constraints. Stalin packed his most powerful punch into the peroration: the second front was now an issue of 'confidence' between the Allies, given the 'modest' Anglo-American losses and the 'colossal sacrifices' of the Soviet armies.

Stalin to Churchill, sent 24 June 1943, received 24 June 1943[86]

I received your message of 19th [sic] June.

I fully realise all the complexities involved in the organisation of the Anglo-American invasion of Western Europe, particularly in bringing of troops across the Channel. These complexities were obvious from your messages.

Indeed in reading your messages received by me in the course of 1942 and 1943 I was sure that you and President had the full understanding of the difficulties involved in such operation. I was also sure that you and President in making preparations for invasion were taking into account all these difficulties and all the efforts necessary for overcoming the difficulties. Last year you informed me that the landings of the Anglo-American troops in Europe on a grand scale will take place in 1943. In your memorandum delivered to V.M. Molotov on the 10th June 1942 you stated: 'Finally, and most important of all, we are concentrating on the organisation and preparation of a large scale invasion of the Continent of Europe by British and American forces in 1943. We are setting no limit to the scope and objectives of this campaign, which will be carried out in the first instance by over a million men, British and American, with air forces of appropriate strength.'

At the beginning of this year you told me twice – on behalf of yourself and President – of your decision concerning invasion of Europe by Anglo-American troops with a view 'to divert strong German land and air forces from the Russian front'. At the same time you had in mind 'to bring Germany to her knees in 1943' and fixed the moment of invasion as not later than September.

In your message of the 26th January you said:

'We have been in conference with our military advisers and have decided on the operations which are to be undertaken by the American and British forces in the first nine months of 1943. We wish to inform you of our intentions at once. We believe that these operations, together with your powerful offensive, may well bring Germany to her knees in 1943.'

In your next message received by me on the 12th February you fixed more exactly the time of invasion and in this connection stated:

'We are also pushing preparations to the limit of our resources for a cross-Channel operation in August, in which both British and US units would participate. Here again, shipping and assault-landing craft will be limiting factors. If the operation is delayed by the weather or other reasons, it will be prepared with stronger forces for September.'

In February when you were writing about the plans and time table of invasion of Europe, the difficulties of the operation in question were more considerable than at present. Since that time the Germans suffered a number of defeats: they were pushed back and had heavy losses on our front in the South; they were beaten and ejected from North Africa as a result of the Anglo-American action; in the U-boat war they experience far greater difficulties than ever before while the Anglo-American preponderance has considerably increased. It is well known also that the Anglo-American aviation dominates now the sky of Europe and that the navies and mercantile marine of Great Britain and the United States are at present stronger than hitherto.

Thus all the conditions necessary for the opening of the second front in Western Europe in the course of 1943 not only not deteriorated but on the contrary considerably improved.

Under such circumstances the Soviet Government could not think that the British and American Governments will change the decision on the invasion of Europe in 1943 taken at the beginning of this year. On the contrary the Soviet Government had every reason to expect that the Anglo-American decision will materialise, that the necessary preparations were being carried out and that the second front in Western Europe at last will be opened in 1943.

Therefore when you are writing now that 'it would be no help to Russia if we threw away hundred thousand men in a disastrous cross-channel attack', I have only to remind you of the following:

First, on your memorandum of June 1942 in which you talked of the preparation of invasion involving not hundred thousand but one million men in the first instance.

Second, on your February message in which you mentioned the great preparatory measures for invasion of Western Europe in August–September of this year. It seemed obvious that this operation had to be carried out not with hundred thousand men, but with an adequate number of troops.

When you now say 'I cannot see how a great British defeat and slaughter would aid the Soviet armies' – is it not clear that such a statement is groundless as far as the Soviet Union is concerned? Is it not clear also that it is in contradiction to the above mentioned responsible decisions concerning the energetic preparations for the Anglo-American invasion in 1943 on which the success of the whole operation should solely depend.

I do not desire to dwell on the fact that your last responsible decision on the cancellation of your former decisions concerning invasion of Western Europe was taken by you and President without participation of the Soviet Government and without any attempt to invite its representatives for talks in Washington although you could not be unaware of the fact that the role which the Soviet Union is playing in the war against Germany and its interest in the question of the second front are not inconsiderable.

It goes without saying that the Soviet Government cannot put up with such disregard of the most vital Soviet interests in the war against the common enemy.

You are writing that you fully understand my disappointment. I must say that: here is not simply the question of disappointment on the part of the Soviet Government, here is the question of its confidence in the Allies which is severely tried by the above happenings. One should not forget that on all this depends the possibility to save millions of lives in the occupied regions of Western Europe and Russia and reduce the colossal sacrifices of the Soviet armies with which the losses of the Anglo-American troops could be considered as modest.

Churchill did not take that lying down. 'I was sorely tempted to send no answer,' he wrote to Clark Kerr, 'but I consider that I must be on record as immediately repulsing the insulting charges of breach of faith which he makes.' As soon as he received Stalin's angry letter, the PM started composing an indignant reply. The draft was coordinated with the chiefs of staff, who made only small clarifications, but recommended a cooling-off period before sending the message, as on a previous occasion when dealing with a 'carping telegram' from the Kremlin. But Churchill would brook no delay.[87] The arguments in his letter were familiar. Britain had stood alone in 1940–41. It had then aided the USSR 'to the best of our limited means'. What Stalin called 'promises' were 'views' that had been 'continually modified by events'. And, once more, the Churchillian over-egging of the pudding, in this case hypothesizing that, because of his own 'Mediterranean strategy', Hitler's summer campaign in 1943 might prove a pale reflection of 1941 and 1942. By now the Kremlin knew that Germany's Kursk offensive would begin any day.

Churchill to Stalin, sent 26 June 1943, received 27 June 1943[88]

I am sorry to receive your message of the 24th. At every stage the information I have given you as to our future intentions has been based upon the recorded advice of the British and American Staffs, and I have at all times been sincere in my relations with you. Although until 22nd June 1941 we British were left alone to face the worst that Nazi Germany could do to us, I instantly began to aid Soviet Russia to the best of our limited means from the moment that she was herself attacked by Hitler. I am satisfied that I have done everything in human power to help you. Therefore the reproaches which you now cast upon your Western Allies leave me unmoved. Nor, apart from the damage to our military interests, should I have any difficulty in presenting my case to the British Parliament and the nation.

The views of our Staffs, which I have shared at every stage, have been continually modified by the course of events. In the first place, although all shipping has been fully occupied, it has not been possible to transport the American Army to

Britain according to the programme proposed in June 1942. Whereas it was then hoped that twenty-seven American divisions would be in Great Britain by April 1943, in fact there is now, in June 1943, only one, and there will be by August only 5. This is due to the demands of the war against Japan, the shipping shortage, and above all the expansion of the campaign in North Africa, into which powerful Nazi forces were drawn. Moreover, the landing craft which in January of this year we proposed to make available for a cross-Channel enterprise, have either not fully materialised up to date or have all been drawn into the great operation now impending in the Mediterranean. The enemy's uncertainty as to where the blow will fall and what its weight will be has already, in the opinion of my expert advisers, led to the delaying of Hitler's third attack upon Russia, for which it seemed great preparations were in existence six weeks ago. It may even prove that you will not be heavily attacked this summer. If that were so, it would vindicate decisively what you once called the 'military correctness' of our Mediterranean strategy. However, in these matters we must await the unfolding of events.

Thus not only on the one hand have the difficulties of a cross-Channel attack continually seemed greater to us and the resources have not been forthcoming; but a more hopeful and fruitful strategic policy has been opened to us in another theatre, and we have the right and duty to act in accordance with our convictions, informing you at every stage of the changes in our views imposed by the vast movement of the war.

The PM keenly awaited an answer from Moscow, not least because the altercation with Stalin came at an unusually sensitive moment in his relations with Roosevelt. On 24 June, Harriman had finally told him of FDR's proposal for a one-on-one meeting with Stalin. The PM immediately sent an indignant telegram to the White House, warning in his most grandiloquent style of the 'gravity of the issue' and the 'use that enemy propaganda would make' of a meeting from which the British Commonwealth and Empire were excluded: 'many would be bewildered and alarmed thereby'. Churchill's pain was not salved by FDR's casuistic answer that he simply wanted to explore Uncle Joe's postwar thinking, rather 'as did Eden for you a year ago'. The president included a bare-faced lie: 'I did not suggest to UJ that we meet alone but he told Davies that he assumed (a) that we would meet alone and (b) that he agreed that we should not bring staffs to what would be a preliminary meeting' before a Big Three summit. This blatant act of deception by FDR was not forgotten by Churchill, being both a personal affront and also an intimation of the growing power of the Big Two as against Britain.[89]

But, after reflection, Churchill detached his hurt feelings from the state of Big Three relations at this delicate moment, sharing his concerns with the president in a message on 28 June. First, he mentioned Stalin's 'very unpleasant reply' about the second front, which he forwarded to the president together with his own reply. Second, Stalin had suddenly summoned home Litvinov from Washington and Maisky and Bogomolov from London for what were cryptically termed 'consultations'. Third, Churchill – like Roosevelt – was puzzled at the absence of a German summer offensive, into which he now read more than simply the effects of Allied success in the Mediterranean. Putting all three issues together, he was clearly beginning to wonder if Stalin was considering a negotiated peace with Hitler. Seeds of anxiety had sprouted, even though the PM tried to stamp on them firmly in his message:

> Anthony and his Foreign Office are definitely of opinion that no decisive Volte-face is impending in Russia. Myself, I do not see how they could do it having regard to the deeds done between the German and Russian masses and to what would appear to be the Russian interest in the future world.

All that said, as Churchill's recent allusions made clear, he had not forgotten that Stalin had been Hitler's friend in 1939–41. Under these circumstances, Churchill told the president on 29 June that he would 'no longer deprecate' a Roosevelt–Stalin meeting, and indeed considered this 'important' if it could be arranged.[90]

That same day, increasingly anxious about the mood in Moscow, he cabled Clark Kerr: 'I shall be most interested to know what you can gather of the reaction to my patient response to Stalin's offensive message.' Churchill asked how he should read expressions such as 'the Soviet government will not put up with such treatment' which, he said, raised 'various questions in experienced minds' – in other words, about a break in diplomatic relations. 'Personally,' he added portentously, 'I feel that this is probably the end of the Churchill–Stalin correspondence from which I fondly hoped some kind of personal contact might be created between our countries. There is certainly no use in making it a vehicle of recriminations.' The PM told the ambassador, 'As you were the first to suggest my visit to Moscow, I should be most glad to hear what you think.'[91]

Put on the spot, Clark Kerr offered a revealing interpretation of what bugged the Russians and how to deal with this. He adopted the same tone as the previous summer, when trying to prevent Churchill from flouncing out of Moscow after his difficult second meeting with Stalin – combining frank advice to the PM with snooty badinage about the 'rough' Russians. In his reply now, he went back before the 'Trident' letter to the joint message after

Casablanca, emphasizing that 'as seen from Moscow there is a weakness in our case ... Our weakness lies not in our inability to open this second front but in our having let him believe we were going to do so.' This was indeed fair comment. Clark Kerr said that Stalin had 'picked up upon this weakness and has expressed himself in very forthright terms', but then added 'I do not think he meant to be offensive.' The ambassador likened Stalin's recent messages to the 'straight talking' that the two leaders did in Moscow, and told Churchill 'it would be a mistake to take amiss such stuff as this when it comes from a man as rough and green and bad-mannered as Stalin.' Clark Kerr admitted 'it is melancholy to reflect that we must willy-nilly co-operate with this man not only in the beating of Hitler but in the years that will follow, and that upon this co-operation depends millions of lives and to a large extent the future of the world.' But this was the situation facing Britain. 'I can therefore only urge you to expend your much tried patience with the old bear and to deal with him as with the bear he is. Honey and bites of meat and the stick when he deserves it.' After this jokey condescension, Clark Kerr finished by pooh-poohing the PM's darker thoughts. 'I by no means share your view that this need be the end of the Churchill–Stalin correspondence', though he suggested 'letting matters simmer' for a bit, rather than firing off another missive. As for a separate peace: 'I do not think there is much chance of his running out of the war and probably early success of Husky and what is to follow will go a long way towards getting him in tune again.'[92]

On 2 July, Churchill went over with Maisky, who was about to return to Moscow, what he had also aired with Clark Kerr. The PM said he was 'getting rather tired of being scolded and did not see much use in keeping up a personal correspondence if it only became a vehicle for recrimination'. Like Clark Kerr, Maisky deprecated any such rupture, saying that Stalin was 'harsh in his manner' and opined that when the correspondence 'contained agreeable, smooth things, it did good', but 'perhaps even more good when blunt things could be said on either side without any harm'. He kept urging Churchill 'not to attach importance to the tone of the messages'. When the PM alluded to that nagging phrase 'The Soviet Government cannot put up with ...' and asked whether it had 'any sinister inference or was merely scolding', Maisky said it was the latter. Churchill reiterated his desire to work with Stalin and said that Eden was willing to go to Russia for talks if Stalin thought this desirable. That, of course, had been the way that the two leaders moved on from their confrontation in November 1941, which led to the foreign secretary's visit the following month. Summarizing Churchill's record of the conversation for Clark Kerr, Eden discreetly omitted the PM's sly parting dig at Maisky:

Before he left, I mentioned, as if discontentedly, that Sir Archibald Clark Kerr always took the Russian view in everything ... and that I supposed it was inevitable that ambassadors should largely take the point of view of the countries to which they were accredited. Indeed, within limits, it was perhaps desirable that they should do so. I was sure that he (M. Maisky) had always made the best case for the English to Russia, as well as for Russia to England, and that was why his mission to England had been so memorable. On this, he took his leave very cordially.[93]

In Maisky's account of the meeting sent to Moscow, he omitted any reference to their discussion of the correspondence, and instead gave a colourful rendition of Churchill's reaction to Stalin's letter. Churchill, said the ambassador, insisted that when he gave Stalin his promises, he 'sincerely believed in the possibility of their fulfilment. There was no conscious deception.' But, the PM continued, 'we are not gods, we make mistakes. War is full of all sorts of surprises ... We have to change plans on the go.' During the conversation, the ambassador added, Churchill returned on several occasions to Stalin's words at the end of the message about 'confidence' in the Allies. This phrase, said Maisky, 'clearly haunted Churchill and caused him great embarrassment'.[94]

The PM never received an answer to his message of 26 June. Instead, Stalin let his allies brood on the implications of the withdrawal of ambassadors. Maisky had received Molotov's call to return to Moscow on the 25th,[95] in other words on the day after Stalin's angry retort to Churchill's letter of 20 June, which had apparently been the last straw for the Soviet leader. Officially, Maisky and Litvinov were summoned home for consultations, but as veteran diplomats, they understood that they were unlikely to return to their posts. The announcement, Maisky cabled Moscow on 29 June, made an impression on Eden 'similar to an exploding bomb'. From his words 'one could gather that he associated my summons to Moscow with Comrade Stalin's message of 24 June, and perceived it all as a clear sign of the deterioration of relations between the USSR and Great Britain'. A month later, the foreign secretary was still trying to read the tea leaves when he discussed Maisky's recall with the Soviet chargé d'affaires Arkadiy Sobolev.[96]

Typical of the way in which Churchill downplayed the Polish issue, no mention was made in the correspondence of the momentous news on 5 July of the death of General Sikorski. The Polish leader had been killed late the previous evening, when the plane in which he was travelling crashed into the sea immediately after take-off from Gibraltar. A British court of inquiry two days later blamed the jamming of the elevator controls, but could not explain how this had happened; at the same time it ruled out sabotage and asserted that the crash was an accident. Given the contradictions in this official account, the mysterious death of the charismatic Polish leader has proved fertile terrain for conspiracy theorists, with the Germans and the Soviets fingered most frequently; but there remains no clear evidence that the crash was other than an accident. Whatever the explanation, the demise of Sikorski removed the one figure among the London Poles who was able to maintain some kind of hold over his fractious followers and also a pragmatic sense of balance in relations with the USSR.

As for the freeze in correspondence with the Kremlin, Churchill was the first to thaw. He resumed contact on 8 and 10 July, by announcing the start of operation 'Husky' in Sicily. Kursk had finally opened on 5 July, as he admitted rather convolutedly in his final paragraph on the 8th.

Churchill to Stalin, sent 8 July 1943, received 9 July 1943[97]

Operation 'Husky' is now imminent. It comprises the oversea movement of half a million men in which 1600 large ships and 1200 special landing vessels are employed. The enemy have 300,000 men in 'Huskyland'. Much depends on the first impact. I will let you know how the battle goes as soon as I can see clearly.

Meanwhile we have sunk 50 U-boats for certain in 70 days.

I hope all is going well on your battlefront. The German accounts seem confused and embarrassed.

Churchill to Stalin, sent 10 July 1943, received 10 July 1943[98]

Both British and United States Armies seem to be getting ashore all right. The weather is improving.

There was no reply. Given the edginess in London about what was going on in the Kremlin, the absence of any message from Stalin all through July was deeply disconcerting. Eden raised this with Sobolev, who made inquiries and reported on 29 July that he had been told by Moscow that Stalin was away at the front and would not return until 8 August, but would then 'certainly send a reply' to the PM. 'Good,' Churchill noted, adding drily: 'I shall await the happy day.'[99]

On 12 July, Secretary of State Cordell Hull told Andrey Gromyko, the Soviet chargé d'affaires in Washington now that Litvinov had left, that a US submarine had accidentally sunk a Soviet trawler in the region of the Aleutian

Islands and that two Soviet sailors had died. Hull expressed his government's deep regret. This incident gave Roosevelt a pretext for another message to Stalin. The meat of this came in the cryptic last paragraph, with another nudge about a Roosevelt–Stalin meeting. (The president inserted the words 'still' and 'to you and me'.) FDR also mentioned the idea to Lord Halifax, the British ambassador in Washington, on 7 July. Halifax told Churchill that FDR said 'he was not unhopeful of UJ agreeing to meet him', but this would depend on how Stalin 'judged his own military situation'. If the meeting did come off, 'he thought he might get something out of him on his real thought about one day joining in on Japan' – in other words entering the Pacific War.[100]

Roosevelt to Stalin, sent 15 July 1943, received 16 July 1943[101]

I am deeply sorry for unfortunate sinking of one of your ships in North Pacific and have directed every possible future precaution.

Although I have no detailed news, I think I can safely congratulate you on the splendid showing your armies are making against the German offensive at Kursk.

I hope to hear from you very soon about the other matter which I still feel to be of great importance to you and me.

Receiving no reply, Roosevelt discussed the silence with Davies, who composed a brief message of his own to Stalin on 22 July. Hopkins asked Gromyko to pass this on.[102] The chargé d'affaires did so on the same day in a despatch to Molotov: 'Roosevelt through Hopkins asked me to convey to Comrade Stalin the following appeal from Davies: "To Marshal Stalin. I am a little concerned that we haven't heard anything from you regarding my last conversation with you. Could you let us know in the near future?"'[103]

Stalin answered neither Roosevelt nor Davies. He perfectly understood Roosevelt's coded phrase, circling it twice in the translation,[104] but by that time any desire to meet the president had apparently evaporated after absorbing the 'Trident' decisions. Not only did it seem necessary to show the Allies his dissatisfaction, but the meeting itself had become meaningless because the main strategic decisions had been made without Soviet participation. Throughout July, Stalin left Roosevelt, like Churchill, to stew in the juice of his own anxieties.

9

FIGHTING BACK
UKRAINE AND ITALY

(August to September 1943)

THE SUMMER OF 1943 changed the face of the war in Europe. The two great arenas of battle were the Ukraine and Italy.

Hitler's third great summer offensive in the USSR, codenamed 'Citadel', opened on 5 July, with the intention of pinching out the Kursk salient by armoured attacks from north and south. But this time, unlike 1941 and 1942, the Soviet high command had properly anticipated the German thrust, concentrating troops and armour with a superiority of something like 2.5 to 1 in order to hold the Kursk bulge. Zhukov discouraged any attempt at a preemptive offensive, telling Stalin bluntly on 8 April, 'It would be better if we wear the enemy down along our defence line, destroy his tanks, and then by bringing in fresh reserves finally finish the main enemy forces in a general offensive'.[1] After two years of working with Stalin, Zhukov – like Brooke with Churchill – was anxious to temper his boss's itch for premature offensives. In massive armoured battles over a week in early July – at their peak involving 1,200 tanks on either side – the Red Army held the Wehrmacht and then moved onto the offensive – towards Orel north of the bulge and against Belgorod and Kharkov to the south.

Despite the Red Army's large-scale preparations, the Wehrmacht was taken by surprise when the Soviet onslaught opened on 12 July, and after two weeks of fierce fighting it was forced to retreat. Overcoming stiff resistance, Soviet troops liberated Orel and also Belgorod on 5 August. Not only was any further threat to Moscow eliminated, but the Red Army was also now driving into the Ukraine, recapturing Kharkov on 23 August and pushing close to Kiev during

September. But in the process heavy losses were incurred and, as usual, it was hard to supply and refit units that had moved far from their base areas, or to secure good intelligence. In a rare use of airborne troops, General Nikolay Vatutin tried to seize a bridgehead over the Dnieper River just south of Kiev on 24–25 September, but the operation was ineptly planned and executed: the paratroopers landed on top of a Panzer division and were cut to pieces.

Despite this late setback, the Red Army's summer victories were spectacular – a tribute not only to hugely superior numbers and near-indifference to casualty levels, but also to a revolution in Soviet conduct of warfare at all levels, from strategy and intelligence to tactics and all-arms cooperation. 'By mid-1943, Stalin had come to trust his commanders and staff officers as professional leaders, and they had justified this trust by learning the painful lessons of mechanized warfare.'[2] Even Churchill, whose war memoirs glossed over the Soviet story, stated that the 'three immense battles at Kursk, Orel and Kharkov, all within a space of two months, marked the ruin of the German army on the Eastern Front.'[3] Although German historians have warned against exaggerating the impact of Kursk – noting that the Wehrmacht lost only 252 tanks and 54,000 men, while the Red Army, even though in defensive positions, lost at least 177,000 men – they admit that, on a psychological level, the failure for the first time of a German summer offensive in the USSR 'had a symbolic impact that is hard to overestimate.'[4]

Meanwhile, on 10 July, while 'Citadel' hung in the balance, Allied forces invaded Sicily – led again by Eisenhower. Brushing aside feeble Italian resistance, they drove rapidly across the island. Hitler immediately called a halt to the 'Citadel' offensive and began to transfer some reserves from Germany to protect his southern flank. The 'two-front' war on the European continent that he had feared and Stalin had pressed for, was now becoming a reality.[5] In view of the brittleness of Italian morale and the current weak German presence, Ike told the CCS on 18 July that he and his commanders considered 'the mainland of Italy as the best area for exploitation with a view to achieving our object of forcing Italy out of the war and of containing the maximum German forces'. Delighted that his obsession about the 'soft underbelly' of the Axis seemed finally to be vindicated, Churchill talked of knocking out Italy in 1943 and maybe finishing the war in 1944 – heady hopes that Roosevelt and Eisenhower seemed to share, especially when Mussolini was overthrown and arrested on 25 July. In the Commons two days later, Churchill licked his lips at 'the downfall of one of the principal criminals of this desolating war' and indicated that Britain and America had no desire to 'break down the whole structure and expression of the Italian state', as long as the country's new rulers agreed to its unconditional surrender and were then ready to cooperate against 'our prime and capital foe', Nazi Germany. He and Roosevelt now prepared for an urgent meeting with the CCS in Quebec in mid-August, in order to plan future strategy and decide the fate of Italy.[6]

July 1943 was therefore a month of drama and exultation for all the Allies. 'A memorable moment', Brooke noted in his diary on learning of Mussolini's fall. Recalling Churchill's words after victory at Alamein in November 1942, he added: 'at last a change over from "the end of the beginning" to "the beginning of the end"!'[7] The Kremlin leadership also felt much more confident. In discussions with foreign diplomats, officials in the party's International Department began to speak of the imminent defeat of Germany; as did Solomon Lozovskiy, one of Molotov's deputy commissars for foreign affairs, when talking to the Chinese ambassador in Moscow on 10 August – the first time the latter had heard such talk directly from Soviet leaders. The following day, the whole diplomatic corps was brought back to Moscow from Kuybyshev in a convoy of trains.[8]

But as victory appeared on the horizon, so planning the peace became more urgent. London, Washington and Moscow could all see advantages in continued cooperation: that now seemed axiomatic. Yet cooperation did not preclude competition. All three Allied governments were now beginning to manoeuvre for postwar position. In particular, events in Italy obliged Stalin to enter Allied diplomacy in earnest, lest he be marginalized. Once the battle of Kursk was decided, he finally resumed communication with his two partners on 8–9 August. And then, during one of the most intense rounds of Big Three correspondence – climaxing in seventeen messages over less than two weeks (2–12 September) – Stalin seized the initiative again, as he had in April after the Katyn revelations. The Soviet leader politely resisted Roosevelt's continued nudges about an early meeting between the two of them, using, as always, the demands of 'the Front' as his excuse, while also renewing his proposal that, when they eventually did meet, Churchill should be included as well. To give himself time before that summit, and to force his allies to show their hands, Stalin also proposed a preliminary meeting of 'responsible representatives'. This idea quickly developed into the conference of foreign ministers, eventually held in Moscow in October. Although each leader tried to arrange both the conference and the summit in places that suited him, Stalin capitalized on the evident relief in London and Washington that he had broken his ominous six-week silence. As Churchill put it, the 'Great Bear' was again 'speaking, or at least growling'.[9] Exploiting their mood, the Soviet leader secured agreement that the foreign ministers would meet in Moscow in October, and the Big Three at the end of November in Tehran – the most desirable venue for him outside the USSR. Stalin had finally decided to embark on summit diplomacy in earnest, and would do so at a time and place of his own choosing. It is striking that Roosevelt never used his own disability as an argument in support of a more convenient location.

Stalin also tried to insert himself in the Italian imbroglio, conscious that if London and Washington were allowed to determine the fate of Hitler's main Axis partner, this would set significant precedents for the future. His allies, however, considered that they were doing all the fighting in Italy and also wanted to maximize Italian cooperation against Germany once the country had surrendered. London and Washington were certainly not of one mind about the future of Italy – the Americans had no time for Churchill's monarchist zeal to revive the royal house of Savoy – but they did agree that what Ike called 'military expediency' was the prime imperative, not diplomatic niceties. The Darlan deal in November 1942, despite the embarrassing publicity generated, was the precedent to be followed. On the other hand, they recognized that conceding some kind of Soviet involvement in arrangements for Italy would allow them to claim a similar role when the Red Army – now rapidly pushing west – entered the satellites and conquests of the Axis in Eastern Europe. They therefore accepted Stalin's proposal to create a three-power military–political commission for Italy which, he hoped, would also deal with future defectors from the Axis cause. But they had no intention of letting this get in the way of Eisenhower's military operations or allowing it to bolster the position of the communists in post-fascist Italy – as became evident during the autumn. The struggle over the commission would set a precedent for Poland in 1945.

August and September 1943 saw a temporary, but interesting, shift in the dynamics of the Big Three correspondence on the Western side. Churchill spent five weeks in North America, much of it in the company of Roosevelt. Allowing for sea voyages both ways, he was away from London for a month and a half – from 4 August to 19 September – his longest absence to date during the war and one that caused growing irritation in Westminster and Whitehall. Apart from his usual love of getting away, Churchill believed that, by staying on hand at such a crucial moment, he could significantly influence US policy, and also concert a common line with FDR towards Stalin. In London, however, his extended stay in America was not popular. 'While his influence on the President in military matters may be excellent,' noted Oliver Harvey in the FO, 'the President's influence on him in political matters is disastrous. The P.M.'s American half comes up more and more.'[10] Eden himself was also exasperated. 'I am most anxious for good relations with U.S.,' he wrote in his diary, 'but I don't like subservience to them.' He felt that Churchill, 'by prolonging his stay in Washington, strengthens that impression'.[11] Geoffrey Wilson, a leading Russophile in the FO, observed of the PM on 8 August: 'His statement the other day about consulting the Americans and informing the Russians was no slip of the tongue. It's his deliberate policy and it's going to land us in one hell of a mess.'[12]

At the Moscow end of the relationship, Stalin's growing effectiveness on the international stage was always constrained by his suspicious and autocratic nature. As he re-engaged with his allies after the summer freeze, he did so through new and very different emissaries in both London and Washington. Maisky and Litvinov, recalled at the end of June over the second front, were replaced respectively by Fedor Gusev and Andrey Gromyko (plates 17 and 18). Both were young career Soviet diplomats and Molotov protégés, born in the 1900s, and therefore totally unlike their predecessors – cosmopolitan socialists from an older generation (Litvinov was born in 1876, Maisky in 1884). The job of the new men, as Stalin and Molotov made clear to London, was to 'sign agreements' rather than engage in 'exchanges of views' – an admonition that the Foreign Office did not take sufficiently seriously.[13] Hopeful that the summer friction had been just a temporary blip in an improving relationship, they even lobbied for Maisky's return – a gambit that only served to reinforce Kremlin suspicions. Maisky was allowed back to London for just a few days at the end of August to wind up his affairs, cutting a mournful figure in conversations with Eden. By comparison, Gusev and Gromyko were at times almost messenger boys, with the British being particularly rude and contemptuous about the former. 'If Maisky is like a robin or a wren,' Clark Kerr told the FO, 'Gusev is like a sea-calf and apparently no more articulate.' After a dinner in Gusev's honour in October, Brooke wrote that 'Frogface' was 'certainly not as impressive as that ruffian Maisky was!'[14]

Distrustful as ever, Stalin and Molotov had deprived themselves of two experienced and perceptive observers in the key Allied capitals, men with the ability and independence to interpret Kremlin thinking to their hosts, and also to explain Western reactions to Moscow – ideal double interpreters, as Churchill had jokingly suggested to Maisky on 2 July. From now on, Stalin's messages and Western replies would be transmitted in a vacuum, as it were, just when effective communication between the Big Three mattered more than ever.

*****

Roosevelt sent congratulations about Orel,[15] but Churchill decided not to: he was still resentful of Stalin's lack of response to his message about the invasion of Sicily. 'Shouldn't the President have ended his greetings with: "Perhaps it hasn't escaped your attention that significant military operations have commenced in the Mediterranean, which have already led to the resignation of Mussolini?"' he told Harriman sarcastically.[16] According to Arkadiy Sobolev, the Soviet chargé in London, on 26 July Eden said that the PM was 'concerned' that he still had not received an answer to his last two letters to Stalin on 8 and 10 July, adding: 'I keep reassuring the prime minister, pointing out that Stalin was at the front during that time, and this may explain the delay. Nevertheless, I considered it my duty to inform you about this.'[17] It is unlikely that this was the reason for Stalin's silence: he went to the front only once during these weeks, and not for long. Naturally, he was preoccupied with July's decisive military operations, but probably he was trying to keep Roosevelt and Churchill in suspense and push them into further moves.

Washington and London's main concern was how to inform Stalin about the upcoming 'Quadrant' meeting of Roosevelt, Churchill and the CCS, scheduled for Quebec in mid-August. According to Oliver Harvey, Churchill hoped that he could 'persuade the Americans to agree to opening up our operations in Italy at the expense of future operations cross-Channel'. If, however, the Russians were present – Stalin, Molotov or even a Soviet general, 'who would support steadily American views' – then Churchill feared he 'might well be overwhelmed'. Yet it was deemed equally dangerous to keep Stalin in the dark and then present him with a fait accompli, especially given his outrage in June about the outcome of the 'Trident' meeting and then his unsettling silence throughout July. 'We are getting seriously worried about relations with Stalin,' Harvey noted at the end of the month.[18]

The issue was therefore delicate and British discussions about it shed interesting light on the place of the personal correspondence in Big Three relations. Clark Kerr felt strongly that Stalin was still smarting from his exclusion from 'Trident' and continued postponement of a second front. 'As time goes on,' the ambassador observed, 'I feel more and more that the only approach to these people is one of absolute frankness' – whatever the consequences. He therefore favoured inviting Stalin or Molotov to attend the meeting, accepting the possibility that they might bring military advisers. If the invitation were declined (which, he said, was 'not improbable'), then it would be appropriate for Eden to offer to visit Moscow and provide a briefing on what had been agreed. Cadogan agreed 'we *must*' invite Stalin, but Churchill was averse to even a symbolic gesture of this sort, telling Eden angrily on 1 August that there could be 'no question of inviting the Russians to this particular meeting', because it was simply a follow-up to earlier British–American discussions about the

Mediterranean theatre and would also deal with the war against Japan, in which the USSR was not a belligerent. Stalin could have 'no grievance' about being excluded, because over the summer he had declined repeated invitations to meet them. Rather than invite the Russians, Churchill continued petulantly, 'it would be better to call the meeting off altogether. I would far rather put up with Stalin's bad manners than be deprived of the means of carrying on this war effectively by consultation in regard to our own armies between Great Britain and the United States.'[19]

On the PM's instructions, the British therefore reverted to an earlier sugges-tion from Eden. They informed Stalin about the conference at the last minute, on 7 August, a day before 'Quadrant' became public knowledge. And they did so via a Foreign Office telegram to the Moscow embassy drafted by Cadogan and approved by Eden and Churchill – a low-key and impersonal mode of communication, presumably intended to avoid seeming to break the silence at the top, with the PM's views reported third-hand. In his memoirs, Eden said the message was 'sent as from the War Cabinet'.[20] Clark Kerr was instructed to deliver it 'to Stalin or Molotov'; he gave it to the latter on the 8th.

In it, the conference was presented as being about matters that concerned only Britain and America – plans for the Mediterranean and crossing the Channel, plus the war against Japan – but the reference to 'pressing forward our preparations for "Overlord"' was, to say the least, disingenuous, given Churchill's private intentions about Italy. To sweeten the pill, the last paragraph reiterated that 'the Prime Minister still hopes that a meeting between the three Heads of Government may be possible before long' – adding that Scapa Flow still seemed to him the best venue 'for all parties', but repeating 'his will-ingness to go to any rendezvous which is convenient for the Marshal and the President'.[21]

This carefully contrived (non-)message from Churchill prompted Stalin to break his long silence. On 8 August, he finally replied to Roosevelt, backing out of his earlier agreement via Davies to a summer meeting between the two of them. Stalin's aversion to air travel, his obsession with personal security and his sensitivity about the prestige of the USSR made him disinclined to meet Roosevelt and Churchill away from Soviet territory. And although the situation on the Soviet–German front had improved dramatically compared with 1942, the Soviet Union was still fighting on its own territory. Further victories would strengthen its diplomatic position, so Stalin was therefore in no hurry for a summit.

Molotov drafted the message, but the last four paragraphs were added by Stalin. It seems that the Soviet leader had decided to avoid reneging outright on a meeting *à deux* by proposing Churchill's possible participation as well. Yet he also spoke, rather vaguely, about a gathering of 'responsible representatives' as an alternative to a meeting of the three heads of government. The White House received this in the form of a rather clunky translation by the Soviet embassy.

Stalin to Roosevelt, sent 8 August 1943, received 8 August 1943[22]

Only now, having come back from the front, I can answer your message of July 16th. I have no doubt that you take into account our military position and will understand the delay of the answer.

Contrary to our expectations, the Germans launched their offensive not in June, but in July, and now the battles are in full swing. As it is known, the Soviet Armies repelled the July offensive, recaptured Orel and Belgorod, and now is putting the further pressure upon the enemy.

It is easy to understand that under the present acute situation at the Soviet–German front, a great strain and utmost vigilance against the enemy actions are required from the Command of Soviet troops. In connection with the above, I have at the present time to put aside other questions and my other duties, but [for] the primary duty – the direction of action at the front. I have frequently to go to the different parts of the front and to submit all the rest to the interests of the front.

I hope that under such circumstances you will fully understand that at the present time I cannot go on a long journey and shall not be able, unfortunately, during the summer and autumn to keep my promise given to you through Mr Davies.

I regret it very much but, as you know, circumstances are sometimes more powerful than people who are compelled to submit to them.

I consider that a meeting of the responsible representatives of the two countries would positively be expedient. Under the present military situation, it could be arranged either in Astrakhan or in Archangel. Should this proposal be inconvenient for you personally, in that case, you may send to one of the above-mentioned points your responsible and fully trusted person. If this proposal is accepted by you, then we shall have to determine a number of questions which are to be discussed at the conference and the drafts of proposals which are to be accepted at the meeting.

As I have already told Mr Davies, I do not have any objections to the presence of Mr Churchill at this meeting, in order that the meeting of the representatives of the two countries would become the meeting of the representatives of the three countries. I still follow this point of view on the condition that you will not have any objections to this.

I use this opportunity to congratulate you and the Anglo-American troops on the occasion of the outstanding success in Sicily which are resulted in the collapse of Mussolini and his gang.

Thank you for your congratulations sent to the Red Army and the Soviet people on the occasion of successes at Orel.

Next day, 9 August, having received the message about Quebec from the British government, Stalin and Molotov clarified their reference to a meeting of 'responsible representatives'. They decided firmly on holding such a gathering before any meeting of the Big Three and communicated the news to Churchill in a message handwritten by Molotov, adapting the cable to FDR, and then lightly edited by the Boss.[23] This decision allowed Stalin to postpone the summit, for which he was not yet ready, stressing again his obligations 'at the front', while laying the groundwork for the Big Three meeting at a lower, official level. Thus, the idea of a conference of foreign ministers – eventually realized in October – had been conceived.

Stalin to Churchill, sent 9 August 1943, received 9 August 1943[24]

I have just returned from the front and already had time to become familiar with the message of the British Government dated 7 August.

I agree that a meeting of the Heads of the three Governments is absolutely desirable. Such a meeting must be realized at the first opportunity, having arranged with the President the place and time of this meeting.

At the same time I ought to say that in the existing situation on the Soviet–German front I, to my regret, have no opportunity to absent myself and to leave the front even for one week. Although we have had several successes at the front lately, an extreme strain on the strength and exceptional watchfulness are required in regard to the new possible actions of the enemy from the Soviet troops and from the Soviet Command just now. In connection with this I have to visit the troops on that or other parts of our front more often than usual. In the circumstances at the present time I am not able to visit Scapa Flow or any other distant point for a meeting with you and the President.

Nevertheless, in order not to postpone an examination of the questions which interest our countries, it would be expedient to organize a meeting of the responsible representatives of our States, and we might come to an understanding in the near future concerning the place and time of meeting.

Moreover, it is necessary beforehand to agree on the scope of the questions to be discussed and the drafts of the proposals which have to be accepted. The meeting will hardly give any tangible result without that.

Taking this opportunity I congratulate the British Government and the Anglo-American troops on the occasion of their most successful operations in Sicily which have already caused the downfall of Mussolini and the break-up of his gang.

London and Washington were delighted by Stalin's message. 'This is much better than I had dared to hope for, and a great relief', Eden cabled Churchill in Quebec. 'Should we not now at once agree a meeting in principle, time, place, personnel and agenda to be decided later?' He ended with a sigh: 'Joe is unaccountable.'[25] At the War Cabinet on 11 August, 'general satisfaction was expressed with the tone and content' of the message. Keen to pre-empt likely negative publicity about the USSR's absence at Quebec, the Cabinet felt it 'necessary to accelerate preparations for the conference proposed by Premier Stalin'.[26]

It is hard to judge how far the Soviet leader's démarche was carefully calculated, but at any event his 'unaccountable' nature had again paid off. Given the mounting anxiety among the Allies caused by his prolonged silence, such an unexpected and constructive proposal, couched in friendly tones, was greatly appreciated. As urged by Eden and the Cabinet, Churchill sent a swift and enthusiastic reply. No longer grumpy, he congratulated Stalin on Orel and Belgorod and resumed the practice of spicing up his missives with highlights of Allied bombing of Germany – in this case the onslaught on Hamburg from 25 July to 3 August (operation 'Gomorrah') – promising to send photographic evidence of the devastation. 'This we know for certain,' he told Stalin, 'eighty per cent of the houses in Hamburg are down.' As for the naval war, the PM reported that in May, June and July the Allies had been destroying U-boats 'at the rate of almost one a day'. These months indeed marked decisive victory in the battle of the Atlantic, which finally enabled the Allies to move men and supplies in relative safety for operations in Europe. Yet Churchill's promise in the message to exploit success in Sicily 'to the full without prejudice to "Overlord"' was at odds with his private equivocations. The latest spasm of détente between the Allies did not signify full candour.[27]

Roosevelt and Churchill discussed their next joint letter to Stalin at Hyde Park, the president's country home on the Hudson River north of New York, where they spent a few days before the Quebec conference. They made what Churchill called a 'renewed final offer' to meet Stalin after their own conference, proposing Fairbanks, Alaska, as the venue. 'If he accepts it will be a great advantage,' the PM told Roosevelt; 'if not, we shall be on very strong ground.'[28] The Allies also informed Stalin of their rapid victory in Sicily, which ended with the capture of Messina on 17 August by General George Patton's Seventh US Army, whose troops had beaten Montgomery's British troops to the city by a couple of hours. In their letter, Roosevelt and Churchill also agreed to the idea of a meeting of foreign ministers, emphasizing that it must be purely 'exploratory', in order to retain the Big Three's ultimate authority. This was a point that worried the PM, who noted the 'dangers' that the meeting 'might only focus and define grave differences without having the power to smooth them by overall Agreement'.[29] It was for this reason, Hopkins told Eden, that the president had wanted to meet the Soviet leader alone, because he 'could say things to Stalin' that he 'would not allow others to say for him'. Both Hopkins and Eden could see the necessity of discussing sensitive issues such as the second front and the USSR's western borders at the level of heads of government, but despite such reservations, Stalin's idea of a lower-level ministerial meeting had already gained unstoppable momentum.[30]

Roosevelt and Churchill to Stalin, sent 18 August 1943, received 20 August 1943[31]

We have both arrived here with our staffs and will probably remain in conference for about ten days. We fully understand the strong reasons which lead you to remain on the battlefronts, where your presence has been so fruitful of victory. Nevertheless, we wish to emphasize once more the importance of a meeting between all three of us. We do not, repeat not, feel that either Astrakhan or Archangel are suitable but we are prepared ourselves, accompanied by suitable officers, to proceed to Fairbanks in order to survey the scene in common with you. The present seems to be unique opportunity for a rendezvous and also a crucial point in the war. We earnestly hope you will give this matter once more your consideration. Prime Minister will remain on this side of the Atlantic for as long as may be necessary.

Should it prove impossible to arrange the much needed meeting of the three heads of government, we agree with you that a meeting of the foreign office level should take place in the near future. The meeting would be exploratory in character as, of course, final decisions must be reserved to our respective Governments.

Generals Eisenhower and Alexander have now completed the conquest of Sicily in thirty-eight days. It was defended by 315,000 Italians and 90,000 Germans, total 405,000 soldiers. These were attacked with thirteen British and United States Divisions and with a loss to us of 18,000 killed and wounded. 23,000 German and 7,000 Italian dead and wounded were collected and 130,000 prisoners.

Apart from those Italians who have dispersed in the countryside in plain clothes, it can be assumed that all Italian forces in the island have been destroyed. Masses of guns and munitions are lying scattered about all over the island. Over 1,000 enemy aircraft have been taken on the airfields. We are, as you know, about soon to attack the Italian mainland in heavy strength.

Allied success in Sicily and Mussolini's fall raised the question of Italy's capitulation and subsequent treatment. Because the debate cast an enduring shadow over Big Three relations, some background is required.

Part of the problem was differences between London and Washington. The president wanted to stick 'as close as possible to unconditional surrender', whereas Churchill said he would 'deal with any Non Fascist Italian Government which can deliver the goods', meaning the maximum possible control of Italian territory and demobilization of the country's armed forces.[32] An ardent royalist, Churchill also hoped to restore the royal house of Savoy, whereas Roosevelt saw total surrender as the prelude to creating a more modern and democratic Italy. When Mussolini was suddenly overthrown, the two leaders had not yet worked out an agreed surrender document from which Eisenhower could deal with the new government of Marshal Pietro Badoglio. The FO had drawn up a detailed set of conditions, known as the 'Long Terms', but these were not acceptable to Washington because they did not amount to unconditional surrender. To cut through the impasse, Eisenhower – learning from his North African nightmare – drew up the so-called 'short terms' to deal with essential military matters and allow him to establish a 'Military Government' in Italy.

Given that Italy was Hitler's main European ally and the first major Axis state to withdraw from the war, this question was of cardinal importance for the Big Three as a whole. Although the country was firmly in the domain of the Anglo-American armies, Moscow was determined to participate not only on grounds of principle and equity, but also because a quarter of a million Italian troops had been engaged in the Stalingrad campaign. US and British diplomats understood the danger of brusquely excluding the USSR from Italian affairs and argued that Moscow should at least receive prompt updates on the Italian situation. Otherwise, warned Standley from Moscow, the Soviet leadership 'would have plausible ground for believing or affirming that a sufficiently cooperative attitude had not been shown' towards them.[33] Moreover, an exclusionary policy could seriously boomerang. After talking with Eden, Ambassador Winant wrote home to Washington, presciently: 'When the tide turns and the

Russian armies are able to advance we might well want to influence their terms of capitulation and occupancy in Allied and enemy territory.'[34] Eden promised Sobolev that before the surrender conditions were presented to the Italians, they would be 'communicated to the Soviet government and discussed with them in full accordance with the Anglo-Soviet treaty of alliance'.[35] Molotov underlined these lines in the chargé's dispatch. Sobolev, however, believed that these assurances were mere 'eyewash' and that there was a 'conspiracy' between the British and US governments. He suspected that when the surrender terms had been finalized and agreed, 'at the last minute they will be given to the Soviet government for consideration'.[36]

Sobolev's suspicions were exaggerated, but not unwarranted. On 30 July, the British government informed the USSR about the conditions of Italy's capitulation, to which Moscow stated it had no objections.[37] On 3 August, Clark Kerr handed Molotov the so-called 'short terms' of surrender concerning military matters. Consultations with Moscow ceased after this, but the events surrounding Italy's capitulation continued to move very fast. The story of Darlan in North Africa was repeated: amid the heat of battle, the British and Americans were inclined to deal with any figure of authority able to ensure not merely Italy's withdrawal from the war, but also some kind of 'co-belligerency' with the Allies. This became possible from 15 August, when emissaries of the Badoglio government met secretly with the British ambassador in Madrid. Writing on 18 August to the War Cabinet and FO, Churchill stated: 'The President and I are deeply impressed with the advantages of inducing Italy to change sides, which would save much time and blood in the struggle with the Germans.' If this were done rapidly, he said, it could prevent Hitler 'occupying Rome and setting up a Quisling administration' or 'the whole country sliding into hopeless anarchy'. The PM added coyly: 'There is no need to inform the Russians at this stage as the whole design will either come to nothing or be productive of important Military advantage.'[38]

The following day, however, the two leaders decided to bring Stalin into the loop, perhaps because the story was already leaking out. They informed him of Badoglio's offer of unconditional surrender in return for co-belligerency, but slid around their intended reaction – ostensibly dismissing any 'bargain' while noting the 'advantages' that 'might follow' from Italy changing sides, including perhaps helping to prevent the establishment of a German client government. The word 'bargain' had been carefully calculated: Churchill ruled out a direct quid pro quo, but suggested that, once Italy had surrendered, 'effective action' by the Italians to frustrate a German occupation 'would be regarded by the victorious Allies as a valuable service and would render further cooperation possible against the common foe'.[39] Roosevelt and Churchill also reported at length on negotiations with the Portuguese dictator António Salazar on the use of the Azorean islands for air and naval operations against German U-boats – codenamed 'Lifebelt'. This half of their message was as lengthy as the first, even though operations from the Azores were hardly as important as the future of Italy. The two leaders probably did not simply want to communicate an equivocal discussion of the Badoglio overtures, and so added some Churchillian-style titbits by way of padding. Indeed, it is likely that the cable was largely the PM's work. The instructions to Eisenhower about how to handle the emissaries from Badoglio, showing how the 'non-bargain' was envisaged, were sent to Stalin as a separate telegram.[40]

Even bearing in mind Kremlin irritation at Allied arbitrariness in Italy (for instance, use of the term 'United Nations' in the purely Anglo-American instructions given to Eisenhower), the Soviet reaction to this joint message seems surprisingly petulant. Perhaps this stemmed from Molotov, who wrote the letter without Stalin's discernible involvement – telling Clark Kerr, implausibly, that the Soviet leader was not in Moscow.[41] The foreign minister latched onto some unfortunate omissions in the cabled version of the letter – which Clark Kerr corrected on the 22nd, the day the Soviet response was dispatched – and used them to pose an accusation of unconscionable negligence that made a mockery of Allied assurances to keep Moscow 'fully informed' about Italy. Despite its almost insulting tone, the letter did contain an important proposal for the establishment of an Allied Commission in Italy, which must certainly have been agreed with Stalin.

For more than a week, Clark Kerr and the FO puzzled over why the Kremlin had worked itself up into such a state. Had they taken offence at the repeated use of 'we', failing to understand that this phrase referred to Churchill and Roosevelt, rather than the Big Three? Was the message another expression of resentment at the postponement of the second front or, perhaps, a 'twisted way' of conveying dislike at Soviet exclusion from Allied 'intimacies'? Depending on their general disposition towards Russia, British diplomats either gave Moscow the benefit of the doubt or read the message as confirming their worst suspicions. Christopher Warner, the hardline head of the FO's Northern Department, opined loftily, 'I am told that the Russians sometimes behave in this childishly crude way.'[42] On 31 August, Eden expressed 'bewilderment' at the message's 'sharply polemical tone', complaining to Maisky that Stalin seemed 'prepared to turn a purely technical mistake by a cryptographer into an unfriendly act of political significance'.[43]

Stalin to Roosevelt and Churchill, sent 22 August 1943, received 25 August 1943[44]

I have received your message on the subject of the negotiations with the Italians and the new armistice terms for Italy. I thank you for the information.

M. Sobolev was told by Mr Eden that Moscow was fully informed of the negotiations with Italy. I have to say however that the statement by Mr Eden does not correspond with reality as I have received your message, long passages of which are omitted and which has no concluding paragraphs. It is necessary in view of this to state that the Soviet Government is not informed about the British and American negotiations with the Italians. Assurance was given by Mr Kerr that within a short time he will receive the complete text of your message, although three days have passed and I have not yet been given the complete text of the message by Ambassador Kerr. I cannot understand how this delay could have occurred during the transmission of information on such important a matter.

I believe the time is ripe to organize the military-political commission of representatives of the three countries, Great Britain, the USSR, and the United States, with the purpose of considering the questions concerning the negotiations with the different Governments dissociating themselves from Germany. Until now the matter stood as follows: Great Britain and the United States made agreements but the Soviet Union, just as a passive third observer, received information about the results of the agreements between the two parties. I have to tell you that it is impossible any longer to tolerate such a situation. I propose to establish this commission and to assign Sicily at the beginning as its place of residence.

I am waiting for the complete text of your message on the negotiations with Italy.

Churchill and Roosevelt received this letter in Quebec on 24 August, and were taken aback by its unexpectedly sharp tone. 'We are both mad,' FDR declared at dinner. After looking at the cable, Harriman wondered why. 'As it was a bit garbled, and badly translated and paraphrased, I could not find that it was one about which to be irritated.' He also thought their attitude inconsistent when, a few weeks before, they had worried about the Russians 'playing a lone hand', observing, 'one can't be annoyed with Stalin for being aloof and then be dismayed with him when he rudely joins the party'. Ismay and Eden agreed with Harriman, but Churchill was not placated. His (somewhat disingenuous) attempt to keep the Soviet leader informed had prompted yet another reprimand, very sharply phrased. 'Stalin is an unnatural man,' Churchill declared sombrely. 'There will be grave troubles.' He even predicted 'bloody consequences' – using the words, Harriman noted, 'in the literal sense'. When Eden suggested things were not that bad, Churchill growled, 'There is no need for you to attempt to smooth it over in the Foreign Office manner'.[45]

Churchill may have been in a dark mood. His doctor told Eden that the PM appeared to be 'unduly depressed by troubles that are not immediate and to be unable to shake them off'.[46] In a cable to the War Cabinet on 25 August, Churchill griped at length about Stalin's message. Although very positive about the Quebec conference itself, he added: 'The black spot at the present time is the increasing bearishness of the Soviet Russia.' Stalin, he added, had 'absolutely no ground for complaint', because the Western Allies had kept him fully informed about the Italian terms, and he had 'studiously ignored our offer to make a further long and hazardous journey in order to bring about a tripartite meeting'. The PM stated that the president was also 'very much offended at the tone of this message'. Nevertheless, he continued, 'I do not think that these manifestations of ill temper and bad manners are preparations to a separate peace with Germany as the hatreds between the two races have now become a sanitary cordon in themselves.'[47]

While a weary Churchill – in need, as he himself admitted, of a few days' break – went out of his way to take offence at a botched telegram, Roosevelt, though initially cross about the Kremlin message, was more inclined to treat it all as a storm in a teacup and to pursue his larger agenda. Gromyko cabled Molotov:

> Today, 25 August, at 9.30 a.m. General Watson asked me to visit him at the White House. He said that he had received instructions from the President (who is still in Canada) asking me to report to Comrade Stalin that he, Roosevelt, and Churchill would very much like to receive in the coming days from Comrade Stalin an answer to their offer to hold a meeting in Fairbanks. Churchill remained here in the US to receive a response. Tomorrow he arrives at Roosevelt's estate near New York, 'Hyde Park'. Roosevelt will return from Canada at the beginning of next week, in any case not before Monday. Watson showed me the text of the aforementioned message from Roosevelt and Churchill dated 18 August, sent to Comrade Stalin.[48]

Next day, 26 August, another, more conciliatory missive from Stalin was received in Washington, responding to the 18 August joint message. Dated 24 August, it reiterated that Stalin could not attend a Big Three in Alaska because of the situation at the front – placing the onus, as he often did, on the opinion of 'my colleagues'. The message raised no objection to the instructions given to Eisenhower, but cited the lack of detailed information so far provided about Italy as further evidence of the need for the tripartite military–political commission he had proposed. Its work should not be merely 'exploratory', but pave the way for 'definite decisions' by their three governments. Again, the draft was handwritten by Molotov and showed no signs of editing by Stalin.

Stalin to Churchill and Roosevelt, sent 24 August 1943, received 26 August 1943[49]

I have received your joint message of August 19th.

I entirely share your opinion and that of Mr Roosevelt about the importance of a meeting between the three of us. In this connection I beg you most earnestly to understand my position at this moment, when our armies are carrying on the struggle against the main forces of Hitler with the utmost strain and when Hitler not only does not withdraw a single division from our front but on the contrary has already succeeded in transporting, and continues to transport, fresh divisions to the Soviet–German front. At such a moment, in the opinion of all my colleagues, I cannot without detriment to our military operations leave the front for so distant a point as Fairbanks although, if the situation on our front were different, Fairbanks undoubtedly would be very convenient as a place for our meeting, as I said before.

As regards a meeting between representatives of our states and in particular of representatives in charge of foreign affairs, I share your opinion about the expediency of such a meeting in the near future. This meeting, however, ought not to have a purely exploratory character but a practicable and preparatory character in order that after that meeting has taken place our Governments are able to take definite decisions and thus that delay in the taking of decisions on urgent questions can be avoided. Therefore I consider it indispensable to revert to my proposal that it is necessary in advance to define the scope of questions for discussion by representatives of the 3 Powers and to draft the proposals which ought to be discussed by them and presented to our Governments for final decision.

Yesterday I received from Mr Kerr additions and corrections to your and Mr Roosevelt's message, in which you informed me about the instructions sent to General Eisenhower in connexion with the conditions of surrender worked out for Italy in the negotiations with General Castellano. I and my colleagues think that the instructions given to General Eisenhower correspond entirely to the aim of the unconditional surrender of Italy and therefore cannot lead to any objections on our part.

But I think the information so far received is quite insufficient in order to be able to judge what measures are necessary on the part of the Allies during the negotiations with Italy. This circumstance confirms the necessity for the participation of a Soviet representative in taking decisions in the course of the negotiations. Therefore I think the time has fully come for the establishment of a military-political commission of representatives of the 3 countries which I mentioned to you in my message of August 22nd.

Even before this telegram arrived in London, the War Cabinet had advised Churchill to accept the Soviet proposal for a tripartite commission on Italy. Its deliberations on 25 August were guided by a telegram from Clark Kerr, who told Eden that, although 'the presence of a Soviet representative (suspicious and probably inarticulate until prompted by Moscow) will be a nuisance', the proposal should be accepted 'without demur' because 'immediate and full Soviet participation in our debates about Italy would go a long way not only to stilling grievances but, more important, towards laying the foundations of real cooperation in the settlement of Europe'. The ambassador also detected a longer-time advantage: 'The admission of the Soviet government to our present councils would open the door to ourselves and the Americans when the time came to provide for the future of Finland and Eastern Europe.'[50] By the time the War Cabinet's advice reached Churchill, refreshed after a few days' rest and fishing, he and Roosevelt had also seen the message from Stalin dated 24 August. Both welcomed its new tone. The president sent a brief message agreeing in principle to 'the meeting on the Foreign Office level' and to 'the Tripartite Commission', using unchanged a draft provided by the PM.[51]

In the meantime, the two leaders sent another joint message to Stalin, about the outcome of the 'Quadrant' conference. Prepared by Brooke and Leahy and unaltered by Roosevelt and Churchill, this brief review of British and US strategy skated over all the points that mattered to Moscow.[52] No indication of the date of the cross-Channel attack, or of its initial scale (in fact, at this stage intended as a puny three-division force). And no explanation of how forces would be apportioned between the Mediterranean campaign (to be 'pressed vigorously') and the build-up for France – the crucial issue of Anglo-American dispute, because the British wanted to keep their options open so as to exploit the flux of events in Italy. Characteristically, Churchill tried to do this head on at Quebec – by repeatedly arguing that there should be clear conditions for 'Overlord', such as the number of German divisions and the strength of the Luftwaffe in northern France. Brooke was more Machiavellian, seeking wiggle room in the small print of the documents, and his diary is peppered with anger not only about the obtuseness of the Americans (who seemed to see strategy as a set of rigid 'legal contracts'), but also about the 'prima donna' antics of his boss

– 'temperamental like a film star, and peevish like a spoilt child' – who could 'never see a whole strategical problem at once' and became obsessed with 'some isolated operation'. Brooke's habitual conviction that he alone knew what to do was accentuated by righteous indignation at being passed over for command of 'Overlord', because Churchill deemed it diplomatically necessary to give that plum job to an American.[53]

Given all the disagreements, it is perhaps not surprising that the cable to Stalin was couched so generally. But in terms of how it was likely to go down in Moscow, it was as ill-judged as the Marshall message in May after 'Trident'. On this occasion, however, Stalin did not bother to reply, perhaps because there was now no chance of a second front in 1943.

It is also noteworthy that Roosevelt and Churchill said nothing about their agreement in Quebec on 19 August concerning the joint effort to build an atomic bomb, the 'Manhattan' project, in which the USA was now very much the senior partner. Their memorandum on 'Tube Alloys' (codeword for the atomic bomb) addressed a number of issues, including postwar commercial use of atomic energy; but its most important diplomatic provisions were that Britain and America would not use the weapon on 'third parties' without 'each other's consent'. Nor would either 'communicate any information about Tube Alloys to third parties except by mutual consent'. In terms of overall foreign policy, Roosevelt still adhered to the 'four policemen' concept he had outlined to Molotov back in May 1942, namely a grand alliance of the UK, USA, USSR and China. Indeed, his diplomacy in 1943, especially the Davies mission and the quest to meet Stalin, underlined his concern with building that alliance. But his keenness to cooperate with the Soviets did not extend to nuclear issues. In the words of historian Martin Sherwin, 'there could still be four policemen, but only two of them would have the bomb'.[54]

Despite the secrecy of his Western allies, Stalin did get the message. A military intelligence report on the signing of the nuclear agreement arrived in Moscow Centre via GRU intelligence channels in early September.[55]

Roosevelt and Churchill to Stalin, sent 25 August 1943, received 26 August 1943[56]

In our conferences at Quebec, just concluded, we have arrived at the following decision as to military operations to be carried out during 1943 and 1944.

The bomber offensive against Germany will be continued on a rapidly increasing scale from bases in the United Kingdom and Italy. The objectives of this air attack will be to destroy the German air combat strength, to dislocate the

German military, industrial and economic system, and to prepare the way for a cross Channel invasion.

A large-scale building-up of American forces in the United Kingdom is now under way. It will provide an initial assault force of British and American divisions for cross Channel operations. A bridgehead in the Continent once secured will be reinforced steadily by additional American troops at the rate of from three to five divisions a month. This operation will be the primary British and American ground and air effort against the Axis.

The war in the Mediterranean is to be pressed vigorously. Our objectives in that area will be the elimination of Italy from the Axis alliance and the occupation of Italy, as well as Sardinia and Corsica, as bases for operations against Germany.

Our operations in the Balkans will be limited to the supply of Balkan guerrillas by air and sea transport, to minor raids by Commandos, and to the bombing of strategic objectives.

We shall accelerate our operations against Japan in the Pacific and in Southeast Asia. Our purposes are to exhaust Japanese air, naval and shipping resources, to cut Japanese communications and to secure bases from which to bomb Japan proper.

Having agreed with Stalin's idea of creating a commission on Italian affairs, his allies began to think through the practicalities. The question of including the French was particularly sensitive because of FDR's aversion to de Gaulle. Pressed repeatedly by Eden, Churchill had just concluded a long battle with the Americans about 'recognition' of the French Committee of National Liberation (FCNL), where de Gaulle was now largely in control. The president, in unusually casuistic mode, preferred the term 'acceptance', arguing that 'recognition' would be 'distorted to imply that we recognize the Committee as the government of France as soon as we land on French soil'. In the end, the British and US governments each endorsed the FCNL in its own preferred language and with qualifications, on 27 August. Stalin, who on 26 June had grudgingly deferred to Churchill's request for delay, now immediately declared unconditional Soviet recognition of the FCNL 'as the representative of state interests of the French Republic and the leader of all French patriots'.[57] The next question was whether to let the French have a seat on the commission for Italy. Churchill knew the Americans would not be keen, and Eden and Attlee feared that the Soviets might see French membership as a device to outvote the USSR. But bearing in mind the Kremlin's sympathies towards the FCNL, the PM sought Stalin's support first, in the hope that this would weigh with Roosevelt. He was jubilant when the Soviet leader promptly agreed.[58]

*****

A flurry of Big Three correspondence in the first two weeks of September was prompted by the fast-moving consequences of the invasion of Italy and intensified by Churchill and Roosevelt's fancy footwork between joint and individual messages to avoid seeming to gang up on Stalin.

On 3 September, British and Canadian troops of Montgomery's Eighth Army crossed the Strait of Messina and landed on the toe of Italy (operation 'Baytown'). That same day Badoglio's emissaries secretly signed the 'short terms', establishing a ceasefire between Italian and Allied forces. The armistice was kept secret for the moment, but when Badoglio tried to back-pedal – fearing insufficient Allied support against inevitable German retaliation – Eisenhower called his bluff by announcing Italy's surrender on 8 September. Next day, using the scarce landing craft hastily recycled from 'Baytown', the US Fifth Army under General Mark Clark, with British divisions in support, mounted operation 'Avalanche' – a landing at Salerno, up Italy's west coast, intended to take nearby Naples, which was logistically essential as a major port. This poorly planned and inadequately resourced operation was nearly thrown back into the sea: for more than a week it hung in the balance. Worse still for the Allies, as soon as the armistice was announced, German forces moved in, taking over all of unoccupied Italy within four days and brutally disarming the Italian troops. At least half a million became slaves in the German war economy.[59] The main plus for the Allies was the surrender of most of the Italian fleet.

On 2 September, Roosevelt and Churchill sent Stalin a preview of events in Italy, as usual mostly drafted by the PM.[60] Clark Kerr had already given Molotov the proposed 'long terms' of surrender which, five days later, the foreign minister authorized Eisenhower to sign on behalf of the USSR.[61] Given the fast-moving situation in Italy, the two Western leaders now told Stalin that they assumed he would approve the 'short terms' in the interests of maximizing Italian support against Hitler as soon as possible. But in a sentence added by Roosevelt, the message stated explicitly that 'we are of course anxious that the Italian unconditional surrender be to the Soviet Union as well as to Britain and the United States'.[62]

The message from Roosevelt to Stalin on 4 September dealt with the Italian commission and the proposed meeting of Big Three 'representatives'. It was actually prepared in close concert with Churchill, then staying in the White House, but the two leaders agreed to make what the PM called 'separate communications to the Russians, similar in principle but differing in expression', because 'we thought it a good thing that all our communications to them should not be identical'. Churchill sent his own message about the Italian commission the following day, taking pains to underline that it could not 'override' the authority of the three governments or 'interfere' in Eisenhower's conduct of military matters.[63]

Despite differences of emphasis between the two leaders, the device of separate messages was rather transparent, and Stalin doubtless saw through it. In case he did not, Churchill's speech at Harvard on 6 September made clear his devotion to the ideal of Anglo-American cooperation – rooted in 'ties of blood and history', of 'law, language, literature' and 'above all, the love of personal freedom'. The PM even singled out its embodiment in Eisenhower's HQ in Italy, where, he said, the two nations were 'completely intermingled'.[64]

With regard to what became the conference of foreign ministers, Roosevelt told Stalin he was anxious to send his confidant, Under-Secretary of State Sumner Welles, rather than the latter's superior, Cordell Hull. The president also said that Welles would be accompanied by Averell Harriman, another trusted adviser, who had visited Moscow in 1941 and 1942 and whom FDR was lining up to replace Ambassador Standley.

Roosevelt to Stalin, sent 4 September 1943, received 6 September 1943[65]

The Prime Minister and I are both happy at the idea of the political and military meeting on the State Department level.

I think it should be held as soon as possible. What would you think of a date about September twenty-fifth?

In regard to location, the Prime Minister has suggested London or somewhere in England, and I would be willing to have my representatives go to either of these if you also think it best. However, I am inclined to the thought of a more remote spot where also the membership of the meeting would be less surrounded by reporters. I would be inclined to Casablanca or Tunis. I do not object to Sicily, except that the communications from and to there are more difficult.

The political representatives would, of course, report to their respective Governments because I do not think we could give plenary powers to them. They could be advised on military developments by attaching one or two military advisers to them, though I do not want to have the meeting develop at this stage into a full-scale Combined Chiefs' conference.

If Mr Molotov comes and Mr Eden I would wish to send Mr Hull, but I do not believe the latter should make such a long journey and I would, therefore, send the Under Secretary of State, Mr Welles. Mr Harriman would go with Mr Welles because he has such a good knowledge of all shipping and commercial matters. For an American military adviser, I will try to send somebody from my Joint Staff who is in complete touch with the work of the Combined Staffs.

The tenacity and drive of your Armies is magnificent and I congratulate you again.

While this coming conference is a very good thing, I still hope that you and Mr Churchill and I can meet as soon as possible. I personally could arrange to meet in a place as far as North Africa between November fifteenth and December fifteenth. I know you will understand that I cannot be away from Washington for more than about twenty days because, under our constitution, no one can sign for me while I am away.

Turning now to a Commission to sit in Sicily in connection with carrying out of further settlements with Italy, why not send an officer to Eisenhower's headquarters where he would join the British and Americans who are now working on this very subject?

I have no objection to adding a French member to their meetings because we are now in the midst of equipping ten or eleven of their divisions in North Africa. However, I think it would be very unwise to let the French take part in discussions relating to the military occupation of Italy. If the Italians go through with the surrender terms already signed, I hope they will be able wholeheartedly to assist the occupation troops. On the whole, the Italians greatly dislike the French and if we bring the French into occupation discussions at this time the civil and military elements in Italy will greatly resent it.

We can discuss the problem of consulting the Greeks and Yugoslavs later on.

On 5 September, Churchill set out his own views on the conference of foreign ministers. Like the president, he wanted to minimize the discussion of military matters – offering a separate meeting of 'technical' specialists if Stalin wanted to get into the detailed reasons for delays in the second front. With regard to the conference venue, he advocated Britain – being, he said, 'the midway point' between Washington and Moscow – while Roosevelt, though not totally opposed, preferred somewhere in North Africa. Privately they did not rule out the Soviet capital, if Stalin insisted, but, as Eden observed to Churchill, 'it would be a mistake both psychologically and politically for the United States Government and we to show too much eagerness to go to Moscow'.[66]

Churchill to Stalin, sent 5 September 1943, received 6 September 1943[67]

The conference of Foreign Ministers.

I was glad to get your message of August 25th in which you agree to an early meeting of Soviet, United States and British representatives in charge of Foreign Affairs. If Monsieur Molotov comes we will send Mr Eden.

The conference even thus constituted could not, of course, supersede the authority of all Governments concerned. We are most anxious to know what your wishes are about the future and will tell you our views so far as they are formed. After that the Governments will have to decide and I hope we may be able to meet personally somewhere. I would if necessary go to Moscow.

The political representatives might require to be assisted by military advisers. I would provide a general officer, Sir Hastings Ismay, who is my personal representative on the Chiefs of Staff Committee and conducts the Secretariat of the Ministry of Defence. He could supply arguments and facts and figures on the military questions involved. I believe the United States would send an officer similarly qualified. This I think would be sufficient at this stage for the meeting of Foreign Ministers.

If, however, you wish to go in technical detail into the question why we have not yet invaded France across the Channel and why we cannot do it sooner or in greater strength than is now proposed, I should welcome a separate technical mission of your Generals and Admirals coming to London or Washington, or both, when the fullest possible exposition of our thought, resources and intentions could be laid before them and thrashed out. Indeed I should be very glad that you should have this explanation to which you have every right.

We are disposed to think that Britain being the midway point would be the most convenient place for the meeting, though it might be preferred to hold it outside London. I have made this proposal to the President but he has not given me a final decision upon it. If England were agreeable to you, I should be glad of your support in the proposal.

I hope we can aim at assembling the conference early in October.

On 7 and 8 September, Stalin responded to the flurry of messages from Roosevelt and Churchill. First, to both of them he confirmed that the USSR assented to Eisenhower signing the 'short terms' of Italy's surrender.[68] Then he answered separately their individual letters about the Italian commission, the foreign ministers' meeting and the Big Three summit, but using almost identical content and phrasing. Molotov seems to have prepared both drafts, and

1 & 2. **Prime time**
The Big Three at Tehran, with photographers, 29 November 1943.

3. **Stalin's** *cri de coeur*
3 September 1941. Stalin wanted a second front before the end of 1941, sufficient to divert from the east thirty or forty German divisions.

109

-5-

and suffering lies before our peoples, but I have great hopes that the United States will enter the war as a belligerent, and if so, I cannot doubt that we have but to endure to conquer.

I am hopeful that as the war continues, the great masses of the peoples of the British Empire, the Soviet Union, the United States and China, which alone comprise two-thirds of the entire human race, may be found marching together against their persecutors; and I am sure the road they travel will lead to victory.

His Excellency
Monsieur Joseph Stalin.

4. **Nice words from Churchill**
21 September 1941.

5. Special envoy
Harry Hopkins in Stalin's
Kremlin office, July 1941,
with Lenin at work in the
background.

6. Diplomatic interpreter
Ivan Maisky clinks glasses
with Churchill in the Winter
Garden of the Soviet embassy
in London, 29 August 1941.

7 & 8. **The go-between**
The intrepid Vyacheslav Molotov lands in Scotland, 20 May 1942, with the indefatigable interpreter Vladimir Pavlov at his side. Below, he is waved off from Washington on 4 June 1942 by Admiral Ernest J. King (left), Ambassador Litvinov, Secretary of State Cordell Hull and General George C. Marshall.

9. New friends
On the veranda at 10 Downing Street, Maisky and Molotov take a photo call with Churchill, May 1942. Clement Attlee, the Labour leader, is next to Molotov, and Foreign Secretary Anthony Eden stands to Churchill's left.

10. The Alaska–Siberia air bridge
Soviet and US airmen pose in front of a P-63 fighter delivered under Lend-Lease, Ladd Field, Alaska, 1943.

11. First meeting
Churchill and Stalin in the Kremlin, August 1942, with the US envoy Averell Harriman in the middle and Molotov on the right.

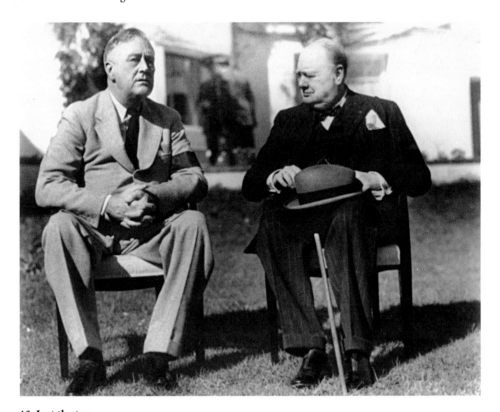

12. Just the two
Stalin was otherwise engaged when Roosevelt and Churchill conferred at Casablanca, January 1943. The battle of Stalingrad had reached its climax.

13. **Stalin the editor**
Molotov's draft to Churchill on 26 November 1942 damned the Allied pact with Vichy politico Admiral Darlan in Algiers. But the boss's blue pen altered the whole tone, commending the Darlan deal as a matter of necessity: in war, one must use 'even the devil and his grandma' for military purposes.

14. **'Most grateful'**
Churchill to Stalin, 1 December 1942.

THE WHITE HOUSE

WASHINGTON

[handwritten letter in Roosevelt's hand]

Roosevelt

15. **Behind Winston's back**
Joseph E. Davies with Stalin and Molotov in the Kremlin, May 1943, having delivered a letter from the president proposing a Roosevelt–Stalin meeting without Churchill.

16. **Mission accomplished**
FDR's thank-you on 4 June 1943 for Stalin's hospitality to Davies. 'Mr Brown' was the not-so-opaque codename used for Molotov during his 1942 visit to the USA.

17 & 18. **Molotov's new boys**
In the summer of 1943 Andrey Gromyko (left) was appointed ambassador in Washington and Fedor Gusev (right) took over in London.

19. **The other three**
Cordell Hull, Anthony Eden and Vyacheslav Molotov at the Moscow conference of foreign ministers, October 1943.

20. Waiting for Roosevelt
The new US secretary of state Edward Stettinius (left) and Molotov (front centre), along with
Gromyko (behind them) and Pavlov (right), watch the president's plane *The Sacred Cow* coming in
to land at Saki airfield for the Yalta conference, February 1945.

21. Two little giants
Stalin and Churchill in the Livadia Palace at Yalta, February 1945.

22. **The waning president**
Roosevelt enjoys a lighter
moment in the courtyard of the
Livadia Palace, February 1945.

23. **British diplomacy goes
to work**
Sir Archibald Clark Kerr,
Britain's ambassador to Moscow,
and Sir Alexander Cadogan,
permanent under-secretary at
the Foreign Office, pictured at
Potsdam, July 1945.

24. Ebb tide
Churchill hosts a dinner for Stalin and FDR's successor Harry S. Truman at Potsdam, 23 July 1945. Three days later he was no longer prime minister.

then edited the cable to Churchill in the light of Stalin's comments on the message to Roosevelt.[69] The Soviet leader reiterated the urgent need to create the military–political commission on Italian affairs, brushing aside the token invitation of a Soviet representative at Eisenhower's headquarters.[70] As for the foreign ministers, Stalin again underlined his wish for a thoroughly prepared agenda and, for the first time, proposed Moscow as the venue: this was inserted by Stalin himself in the draft message to Roosevelt. Finally, on the question of a summit of leaders, he justified its proposed location on grounds of the magnitude of the fighting on the Soviet–German front, where 'more than 500 divisions are engaged on both sides' – an unsubtle reminder to the Western Allies that his war was far bigger than theirs. As a seeming concession, however, Stalin offered to hold the summit outside the USSR, though near the Soviet border, in a country where all three had embassies – for example, he said, Iran. Thus the idea of Tehran emerged in the Big Three's correspondence. In the final line of congratulation about Allied successes in Italy, the adjective 'brilliant' was also added by Stalin.

Stalin to Roosevelt, sent 8 September 1943, received 9 September 1943[71]

Your message in which you touched upon several important questions I received on September 6th.

First. I still consider, as I did before, that the question of the creation of the Military-Political Commission of the representatives of the three countries with its residence at the beginning in Sicily or in Algiers is the most urgent one. Sending of a Soviet officer to the Staff of General Eisenhower can by no means substitute the Military-Political Commission, which is necessary for directing on the spot the negotiations with Italy (as well as with other countries dissociating themselves from Germany). Much time has passed, but nothing is done.

As to the participation of the French representative in this Commission, I have already expressed my opinion on this subject. However, if you have any doubt, in this case this question can be discussed after the Commission is created.

Second. I consider that the beginning of October, as the Prime Minister suggested, would be convenient time for the meeting of our three representatives and I propose as the place of the meeting – Moscow. By that time the three Governments could have reached an agreement regarding the questions which have to be discussed as well as the proposals on those questions, without which (agreement) the meeting will not give the necessary in which our Governments are interested.

Third. As to our personal meeting with participation of Mr Churchill, I am also interested to have it arranged as soon as possible. Your proposal regarding the time of the meeting seems to me acceptable. I consider that it would be expedient to choose as the place of the meeting the country where there are the representations of all three countries, for instance, Iran. However, I have to say that the exact date of the meeting has to be defined later taking into consideration the situation on the Soviet–German front where more than 500 divisions are engaged in the fighting in all, and where the control on the part of the High Command of the USSR is needed almost daily.

Fourth. I thank you for congratulations on the occasion of the successes of the Soviet Armies. I take this opportunity to congratulate you and Anglo-American troops on the occasion of the new brilliant successes in Italy.

On 9 September, the president held a brief meeting with Gromyko, who told Moscow that Roosevelt 'asked me to give him the English translation of Comrade Stalin's message of 8 September' because 'he does not want to send Comrade Stalin's messages to the State Department for translation for security reasons'. An English text was duly prepared at the Soviet embassy and delivered to the White House.[72] This practice would continue, with Gromyko himself usually acting as translator. Roosevelt was willing to accept occasional flaws in Soviet translation, rather than risk leaks of information through US diplomats, of whom he continued to have a low opinion.

Also on the 9th, Roosevelt and Churchill updated Stalin on the formal Italian surrender and on the 'Baytown' and 'Avalanche' operations.

Roosevelt and Churchill to Stalin, sent 9 September 1943, received 10 September 1943[73]

We are pleased to tell you that General Eisenhower has accepted the unconditional surrender of Italy, terms of which were approved by the United States, the Soviet Republics and the United Kingdom.

Allied troops have landed near Naples and are now in contact with German forces.

Allied troops are also making good progress in the Southern end of the Italian peninsula.

After digesting Stalin's messages to them on 8 September, Roosevelt and Churchill coordinated their thinking while sending separate replies, with the PM – as usual – inclined to spell things out in greater detail. For the Italian commission, Churchill appointed the Tory MP Harold Macmillan as his representative at Eisenhower's HQ. Roosevelt chose the US diplomat Robert Murphy, a veteran of the fraught negotiations with the French over 'Torch', who had worked closely with Macmillan over the Casablanca conference. Both leaders reiterated that the commission would not have executive powers.

On the conference of foreign ministers, they deferred to Stalin about holding the meeting in Moscow. But both leaders pushed back a bit on the location of the summit – Roosevelt said that Egypt would be more convenient for him than Tehran, while Churchill's own stated preferences were Cyprus or Khartoum, both in Britain's domain. Yet both messages also made clear their intense desire for a summit. Roosevelt ended his cable with 'I really feel that the three of us are making real headway', while Churchill reiterated his willingness to 'come anywhere, at any time, at any risk, for such a meeting' and averred portentously that on it 'may depend not only the best and shortest method of finishing the war, but also those good arrangements for the future of the world which will enable the British and the American and Russian nations to render a lasting service to humanity'.[74] Reading such sentiments, Stalin must surely have realized that he could stick to his guns – and he did.

The Salerno landing and the Italian surrender forced the Germans to transfer reserves to Italy. Sending brief congratulations on 10 September, Stalin said these developments would 'considerably facilitate the actions of the Soviet armies at the Soviet–German front' – a rare acknowledgement of direct Allied help to the Red Army.[75]

Soviet forces also enjoyed a major success of their own at the Black Sea city of Novorossiysk, one of the last Wehrmacht strongholds in the Caucasus, whose imminent capture was mentioned by Stalin. Although Russia's war is usually regarded in the West as an entirely land affair, the Novorossiysk operation also involved the Red Navy, with a naval bombardment and an amphibious landing across the bay to take the city and relieve the heroic Russian sailors who had denied the Germans full control of the port. The liberation of Novorossiysk obviously pleased Stalin. As recalled by the navy minister, Admiral Nikolay Kuznetsov, on 16 September he 'gleefully' listened to Yuriy Levitan – the familiar voice of Radio Moscow – reading out his own celebratory Order of the Day as supreme commander. 'Then we all watched fireworks. The Supreme was smiling. "Good job," he said, stroking his moustache.'[76]

Stalin received the diplomatic messages from Churchill and Roosevelt on the same day, 11 September. Since they covered the same ground, Stalin replied in a single letter. He took advantage of the Allies' agreement on the establishment of a commission in Italy, and hastened to declare in writing that this issue was now resolved. His choice of Andrey Vyshinskiy as the Soviet representative testified to the importance that Moscow attached to the commission, which, as his message also showed, he assumed and intended would handle not merely Italy, but also other Axis countries in due course. Stalin also continued to request urgently the texts of Anglo-American proposals for discussion at the Moscow conference, while ignoring Churchill's invitation to indicate the 'main points' that he had in mind. Moscow would be the first high-level tripartite meeting and also essential preparation for the first summit, so the ever-wary Stalin naturally wanted to ascertain his allies' intentions and plan the conference proceedings. On the Big Three meeting itself, Stalin held fast to Tehran – though deftly presenting this as assent to what Churchill had said.

Stalin to Churchill and Roosevelt, sent 12 September 1943, received 12 September 1943[77]

I have received your messages of September 10th.

The question of the creation of the Military-Political Commission we may consider in general to be solved. Vice-Chairman of the Council of People's Commissar for Foreign Affairs, Mr A.Y. Vyshinsky, whom you know well, was appointed by the Soviet Government as its plenipotentiary. Mr A.E. Bogomolov, Ambassador of the USSR to the Allied Governments in London, was appointed as Vice-Plenipotentiary. They will take with them the group of the responsible military and political experts and the small technical staff.

I think that the beginning of work of the Military-Political Commission can be set for September 25–30. I have no objections regarding Algiers as the place of work of the Commission at the beginning, having in view that the Commission itself will decide the question of expediency of its going to Sicily or to any other place in Italy.

I find that the consideration[s] of the Prime Minister regarding the functions of the commission are sound, but I consider that some time later we shall be able to determine more precisely the functions of the Commission regarding Italy as well as other countries, taking into consideration the first experience of the Commission's work.

As to the question of the meeting of our representatives, I propose to consider as agreed upon that Moscow be the place of the meeting, and October 4, as President suggested, be the date of it.

I still consider, as I did before and about what I had previously written to you, that in order to make this meeting successful, it is necessary to know in advance text of the proposals which British and the American Governments have and which are to be considered at the meeting of the three representatives. I, however, do not propose any limitation regarding the agenda.

As to the meeting of the heads of the three Governments, I do not have any objection regarding Tegeran [Tehran] as the place of the meeting, which (Tegeran) is more appropriate than Egypt where the Soviet Union does not have its representation.[78]

Churchill was very pleased with what he privately called Stalin's 'civil telegram'. But on 13 September, in his final talk with FDR at Hyde Park, they rejected as 'undesirable' the Soviet demand not only to furnish a full agenda for the foreign ministers' meeting but also to 'indicate beforehand our view on each point'. And they also still hoped to change Stalin's mind about the venue for the summit. 'If all else fails President will go to Teheran,' Churchill cabled Eden, 'but this is really hard measure and should be resisted so far as possible.'[79] Later that day, on the train to Halifax, Nova Scotia, for his voyage back across the Atlantic, the PM drafted a reply to the Soviet leader, expressing his general satisfaction but also re-opening Tehran. Underlining the president's 'real constitutional difficulty', he again suggested Egypt or perhaps Beirut. He even suggested a meeting at sea in 'one of the harbours of Egypt or the Levant or possibly Cyprus' and said the British 'could place a fine ship entirely at your disposal and you could send on ahead all your advance party, cypher staff, etc., so as to be completely independent of us, and at the same time in constant contact with your own war front'. Churchill sent the draft to Roosevelt for 'final approval', but the president did not reply until 4 October: 'I think your idea of enticing Uncle Joe to the Mediterranean with the offer of ship is excellent, but I am not sure whether or not I have told you this.' By then Churchill had sent a different message, on 25 September, telling FDR on 5 October: 'Not hearing from you, I did not persist in the ship enticing idea but I don't think it would have been accepted by Uncle Joe anyway.' The PM was surely right: Stalin would have rejected the offer of a British ship on grounds of status and also security – presuming that the vessel was bugged.[80]

*****

With Churchill on the high seas from 14 to 19 September, the tempo of Big Three correspondence eased. Meanwhile events in Italy continued to move fast. On 12 September, German paratroopers carried out a daring glider mission to rescue Mussolini from captivity in a mountain hotel and spirit him to safety. So, instead of being handed over to the Allies under the armistice terms, the former Duce was installed by Hitler at the head of a puppet regime in northern Italy, known as the Salò Republic.

Meanwhile Badoglio, though ineffectual, commanded considerable popular support and was increasingly working with the Allies. On 18 September, Eisenhower asked that, 'on the basis of military necessity', he should be allowed to treat the Badoglio government as a *de facto* co-belligerent and 'from time to time to lighten the provisions of the military armistice' in order to help the Italians wage war against the Germans. Roosevelt and Churchill agreed. The president also proposed, again on Ike's advice, that both the Allied military government in Italy and the functions earlier envisaged for the Armistice Control Commission would now be merged into an Allied Commission under Eisenhower as the Allied commander-in-chief. This would ensure that the USSR could not play a real part in the pacification and reshaping of Italy. Churchill agreed on 21 September, but he still wanted Badoglio to accept the long terms, so that the Allies would enjoy full freedom of manoeuvre. Four days later, FDR indicated his consent, so long as Badoglio stopped stalling and signed quickly.[81]

The next round of Churchill–Stalin messages was composed against this background. On 21 September, the PM proposed measures to boost support for the Badoglio government, using the Mussolini *coup de théâtre* and the German occupation of most of the peninsula to reinforce the case for his preferred policies in Italy.

Churchill to Stalin, sent 21 September 1943, received 21 September 1943[82]

Now that Mussolini has been set up by the Germans as head of a so-called Republican Fascist Government, it is essential to counter this movement by doing all we can to strengthen the authority of the King and Badoglio who signed the armistice with us and have since faithfully carried it out to the best of their ability, and surrendered the bulk of their fleet. Besides, for military reasons we must mobilise and concentrate all the forces in Italy which are anxious to fight or at least obstruct the Germans. These are already active.

I propose therefore to advise the King to appeal on the wireless to the Italian people to rally round the Badoglio Government and to announce his intention to build up a broad-based, anti-fascist coalition government, it being understood that nothing shall be done to prevent the Italian people from settling what form of democratic government they will have after the war.

It should also be said that useful service by the Italian Government's army and people against the enemy will be recognised in the adjustment and working of the armistice; but that while the Italian Government is free to declare war on Germany this will not make Italy an ally but only a co-belligerent.

I want at the same time to insist on the signing of the comprehensive armistice terms which are still outstanding, even though some of those terms cannot be enforced at the present time. Against this Badoglio would be told that the Allied Governments intend to hand over the historic mainland of Italy, Sicily and Sardinia to the administration of the Italian Government under the Allied Control Commission as it is freed from the enemy.

I am putting these proposals also to President Roosevelt and I hope I may count on your approval. As you will readily understand, the matter is vitally urgent for military reasons. For instance, the Italians have already driven the Germans out of Sardinia and there are many islands and key points which they still hold and which we may get.

On 22 September, Stalin responded positively to Churchill's proposal, but sought to pin him down on two points of importance to Moscow. First, Badoglio must make a public commitment to Italy's entry into the war against Germany as a co-belligerent with *all* the Big Three Allies. Second, Stalin wanted to be sure that when Churchill said that some of the armistice terms 'cannot be enforced at the present time' he was simply referring to German control of much of Italy, rather than (as was actually the case) expressing a desire to soften the terms of unconditional surrender.[83]

Stalin's vigilance about Italian affairs reflected awareness that a struggle for influence was now boiling up among the Big Three. On 22 September, the US chargé d'affaires in Moscow, Maxwell Hamilton, passed on Roosevelt's directive to Eisenhower, including the provision for him to head an Allied Commission in Italy, which would emasculate the tripartite military–political commission. Molotov's reply, not surprisingly, was negative: the USSR, though not opposed to Italy fighting alongside the three Allies against Germany, resisted any easing of the surrender terms, rejected the idea of the Allied Commission and insisted that the military–political commission should direct all the military, political and administrative issues for Italy, except for military operations themselves.[84] But this was a point on which London and Washington would not yield. As historian Warren Kimball has observed, they 'would have liked to avoid setting a precedent for exclusion that Stalin could use against them, but the dangers of letting the Russians into Italy seemed too great, particularly with the Italian Communists so strong'.[85] This struggle between the Allies about influence in Italy in 1943 paved the way for much more fraught arguments about Eastern Europe in 1945.

Stalin's files contain a particularly tantalizing document. This is a draft message to both his allies, dated 25 September, which proposed for discussion at the Moscow conference the conclusion of a military-political alliance of the Big Three. Modelled on the Soviet–British treaty of 1942, the agreement would ensure 'further strengthening of our military alliance in the fight against Hitler's Germany, as well as further development of our cooperation in the postwar period in the interest of peace and international security'. This, it was stressed, 'should not be a mere declaration, but should be the agreement which defines long-term political relations between our countries, both during the war and in the postwar period.'[86] Regardless of why Stalin shelved the draft, the fact that such an idea was entertained in the Kremlin underlines the Soviet desire in late 1943 to build a long-term relationship with America and Britain.

On 25 September came news of a major victory in the centre of the Red Army's long battlefront – the liberation of Smolensk. It is possible that Stalin's only trip to the front, in early August 1943, was directly linked to preparation for this operation, for which the Soviets had built up a crushing superiority. Victory was again won at massive cost – over 450,000 casualties, against 50,000 for the German Fourth Army[87] – but the triumph was hugely symbolic. In 1941, the fall of Smolensk had opened up the road to Moscow; in 1943, capture of the 'Smolensk gate' between the Dnieper and Western Dvina rivers would allow the Red Army to drive into the Baltics and Belorussia.[88] It was also hugely heartening for morale. Churchill sent 'personal congratulations' from himself and Eden, which Stalin duly acknowledged.[89]

With regard to the conference of foreign ministers, Roosevelt's original plan to send Welles to Moscow instead of Hull was thwarted by the veteran secretary of state himself. His long-running personal and political feud with the undersecretary of state had climaxed that summer. Sensitive as ever about his status, Hull declared that, wherever the conference might be held – 'anywhere between here and Chungking' – 'I would be there myself', even though he suffered from acute claustrophobia and had never before flown in an aeroplane.[90] The president particularly needed support for his internationalist foreign policy in the US Senate, where Hull, a former senator, enjoyed great prestige, so he felt obliged to consent. Welles' homosexual liaisons were being leaked to the press and, after a stubborn rear-guard action to protect his friend, Roosevelt announced Welles' resignation on 25 September. Equally embarrassing, having only two weeks before 'cheerfully' accepted Moscow as the venue for the foreign ministers' conference, that same day the president asked Stalin to move the meeting to London, so that the ailing Hull, now in his seventies, could attend more easily. FDR edited the draft substantially – a sign of the importance of the issue – personally composing the first and third paragraphs. He then pressed the embassy in Moscow to solicit a speedy Soviet response.[91]

Roosevelt to Stalin, sent 25 September 1943, received 28 September 1943[92]

I regret that I feel it necessary to reopen the question of the meeting of the Foreign Ministers, but on further consideration I am most anxious that Secretary Hull attend in person in the meeting with Mr Molotov and Mr Eden.

Mr Hull would find the long flight to Moscow extremely difficult for physical reasons. Would it be possible, therefore, for the conference to be held in England? It would, I believe, be a great advantage to all of us if Mr Hull could personally attend the conference.

I feel sure the British would be willing to make the change. Could the date be made October 15 for the opening session?

Churchill's message on 25 September 'pondering' security arrangements for Tehran reflects not only his restless mind and love of cloak-and-dagger activities, but also his growing (if erratic) efforts to make Stalin feel he was being treated properly as an equal. The last two sentences were probably intended as a compliment. Churchill's solicitude was evident in other messages at this time to British officials. For instance, when told that Stalin's stipulation (22 September) that Italy must declare it was now fighting on the side of all three Allies had arrived too late for inclusion in the king's surrender message, he issued a stern rebuke: 'This is a serious omission and may cause offence to Marshal Stalin. The support of the Russians for our policy is most valuable.'[93]

Churchill to Stalin, sent 25 September 1943, received 27 September 1943[94]

I have been pondering about our meeting of Heads of Governments at Teheran. Good arrangements must be made for security in this somewhat loosely-controlled area. Accordingly I suggest for your consideration that I make preparations at Cairo in regard to accommodation, security, etc., which are bound to be noticed in spite of all praise-worthy efforts to keep them secret. Then perhaps only two or three days before our meeting we should throw a British and a Russian brigade round a suitable area in Teheran, including the airfield, and keep an absolute cordon till we have finished our talks. We would not tell the Persian Government nor make any arrangements for our accommodation until this moment comes. We should of course have to control absolutely all outgoing messages. Thus we shall have an effective blind for the world press and also for any unpleasant people who might not be as fond of us as they ought.

I suggest also that in all future correspondence on this subject we use the expression 'Cairo Three' instead of Teheran which should be buried, and also that the code name for the Operation should be 'Eureka' which I believe is Ancient Greek. If you have other ideas let me know and we can then put them to the President. I have not said anything to him about this aspect yet.

Roosevelt's request to move the foreign ministers' conference to London was delivered to the Kremlin on 27 September. Stalin responded with a polite refusal.

Stalin to Roosevelt, sent 28 September 1943, received 28 September 1943[95]

Today I have received your message of September 27th.

I share your opinion regarding the desirability of the Secretary of State Mr Hull's presence at the forthcoming conference of the representatives of the three governments.

At the same time I have to inform you about great difficulties which could have appeared in case of change of the decision, previously agreed upon, regarding Moscow as the place of the forthcoming conference.

The fact is that in case the conference would not be held in Moscow but in Britain, as you propose, Mr V.M. Molotov could not have come to the conference at the appointed time, whose presence at the conference I consider to be necessary. Mr V.M. Molotov's departure from the USSR, at least in the near future, is absolutely impossible because, as you know, Mr A.Y. Vyshinsky, the Deputy Commissar for Foreign Affairs, will very soon go to Algiers.

Besides, as it is known, the press in the United States and Britain has already widely published the information that the forthcoming conference will take place not elsewhere but in Moscow and, therefore, the choice of a new place for the conference could cause undesirable perplexities.

I have no objections against October 15th as the date of the conference.

It is assumed that by that time the agenda of the three partite conference will be finally agreed upon among the three Governments.

Stalin's reasons were no more convincing that those behind Roosevelt's original request, but the choice of Moscow was of fundamental political importance to the Soviet leader. He was not going to budge.

10

FACE TO FACE
MOSCOW AND TEHRAN

(October to December 1943)

WITH THE WINTER DARKNESS approaching, the Soviets were anxious for their allies to resume the Arctic convoys, suspended in May because of the long summer days and the shipping demands of the Sicily and Italy campaigns. But Churchill's 1 October proposal for resumption – proffered as an act of generosity and hedged around with conditions, especially about the treatment of British seamen – provoked such a caustic reply from Stalin about Britain's 'obligations' that the PM was tempted to stop the convoys. The issue was eventually sorted out between the two foreign ministers, Eden and Molotov, and the convoys duly resumed – henceforth with fewer losses as the German naval presence in northern waters diminished, especially after the sinking of the battleship *Scharnhorst* on Boxing Day. But the brief row between the two leaders raised some revealing sidelights on their correspondence. Stalin, ever suspicious, liked to treat agreements as binding 'contracts'; Churchill – who could play the eel as well as the bulldog – was more inclined to view them as statements of intent.

The convoy row also exposed the problem of translation. In Washington, Andrey Gromyko – who formally presented his credentials as the new Soviet ambassador on 4 October – was now well established as translator of most of Stalin's messages, despite the many infelicities in his work, because of Roosevelt's ingrained suspicions of the State Department. In London, however, the approach was very different. Churchill had no time for Gusev – whom he did not receive again until 3 March 1944 – and blamed some of the set-to over convoys on 'very crude' renditions into English by the Soviet embassy and what was consequently 'lost in the process of translation'.[2] Yet there was also a shortage of competent Russianists available to the Foreign Office. So the translation gap remained a nagging anxiety in the Big Three's epistolary relationship.[3]

The situation in Italy remained in flux. At the beginning of October, Hitler shifted policy dramatically, deciding to hold Rome and conduct a defensive battle as far south as possible. Churchill's hopes of a quick and spectacular Italian triumph were dashed, and he became locked in a long and eventually futile argument with the Americans about continuing to 'nourish' the British-led campaign in Italy, rather than building up what would be American-dominated invasions of northern and southern France in 1944. On 13 October, the Badoglio government finally declared war on Nazi Germany: henceforth Italian units would fight with the British and US armies to liberate their country. Meanwhile Churchill and Roosevelt continued to emasculate the competence of the new Mediterranean Commission. Though the Soviets were unhappy, Stalin did not try to fight this. He now had more important issues on his mind than Italy: the upcoming conference of the foreign ministers in Moscow (19–30 October) and the first summit of the Big Three themselves at Tehran (28 November–1 December).

The Moscow conference (plate 19) proved surprisingly productive. Eden, Hull and Molotov agreed to set up a European Advisory Council of senior offi-cials, based in London, to start serious postwar planning. They also signed a declaration committing their countries to continue wartime cooperation beyond victory, by 'establishing at the earliest practicable date a general inter-national organization, based on the principle of the sovereign equality of all peace-loving States'. The Americans ensured that Nationalist China also signed what became the Four-Power Declaration, despite reservations from the USSR and Britain – neither of which shared Roosevelt's faith in war-ravaged China as the world's great power. And in private, Stalin assured Hull that the Soviet Union would enter the war against Japan once Germany had been defeated. In addition to these positive achievements, the atmosphere in Moscow was deeply encouraging for the British and US delegations. 'As far as I can judge the mood of these incalculable people,' Eden cabled Churchill, 'they are now in the current to move with us in all matters, provided that they can be made to feel that they are in all things our equals and that were are holding nothing back.' He added that he had not sufficiently appreciated 'how far these people have suffered from a feeling of exclusion which the extent and scope of their victories has only served to intensify'. From this perspective, the Big Three meeting was the natural next step.[4]

But where to hold that meeting entailed an extended diplomatic tug-of-war between the White House and the Kremlin, which absorbed much of their correspondence from mid-October. In September, Stalin had won the battle for Moscow as the venue for the foreign ministers, and he was eventually also successful in ensuring that the summit would take place in Tehran – the furthest he could go outside the USSR while remaining in secure communication with Moscow. The president tried all sorts of ploys to avoid travelling 6,000 miles to the Iranian capital – most of all touting the demands of the US constitution, which he chose to interpret very strictly, but also supposed pressure from his Cabinet. Stalin simply turned these arguments back on the president – we Russians also have a constitution, my colleagues are equally insistent – and also played his trump card: my war is bigger and more important than yours. FDR finally conceded on 8 November, announcing with a flourish that he had resolved his hitherto insuperable constitutional difficulties. Throughout their exchanges, it is striking that the Wheelchair President never mentioned his own infirmity.

In the course of this protracted argument, Stalin – as with Churchill over the convoys – intensified the pressure by not replying for a couple of weeks. And as in July, he and Molotov were quite ready to tell fibs about the supreme commander being unable to deal with messages because he was away at the front. Underlying the trial of strength over Tehran, like the convoys, was the determination of Stalin and Molotov that the Soviet Union should be treated as an equal by its two Western partners. In October and November 1943, they got their way. The British and Americans were coming to them.

Indeed, during the summit Roosevelt actually stayed in the Soviet embassy compound. Conventionally this has been interpreted as a concession on grounds of security in a city where Nazi death squads were rumoured to be on the loose. But evidence from the Soviet archives, deployed here for the first time, shows that Roosevelt himself angled secretly for this invitation, anxious to spend as much time as possible with the reclusive Soviet leader after eighteen months of trying to arrange a meeting. To this end, he not only kept Churchill at arm's length, but also sided with Stalin when the latter goaded the prime minister over dinner. The transcript of the Big Three meetings demonstrates Stalin's careful mastery of the issues and his superior skill as a diplomatist, regularly keeping his silence but then speaking out in a terse and timely manner at key moments. The Soviets had one overriding objective at both Moscow and Tehran, reflecting the dominant theme of Stalin's messages since 'Barbarossa', namely 'measures to shorten the war' and specifically the second front. In a decisive intervention on 29 November, he set down three essential aims for the conference: to confirm the strategic priority of France over Italy, to set a firm date for 'Overlord', and to appoint its supreme commander. All three aims were achieved during and just after the summit – to the satisfaction of both Stalin and Roosevelt.

Although Churchill may have come off worst in this triangular diplomacy, the mood during the summit and afterwards was remarkably harmonious. Roosevelt's cosying-up to Stalin was predicated on the assumption of a firm and enduring relationship with Churchill; the Soviet leader's baiting of the PM was balanced by moments of good humour and even warmth between the two of them. Both Roosevelt and Churchill had no doubt that the Big Three's talks were vital: 'on them depend the hopes of the future world', declared Roosevelt, while Churchill told Stalin at the end of the year: 'I only wish we could meet once a week.' Both of them felt that Tehran was a milestone in relations with the man they privately referred to as 'Uncle Joe' or 'UJ'. The year that the Russians would call *perelom* ('the turning point') ended with an impressive degree of good feeling among three leaders who had finally met in person. The question was whether that mood would be maintained on paper as the war neared its climax and the challenges of the peace could no longer be put on one side.

*****

Responding to the fast-changing Italian situation that autumn, the Western Allies continued to erode the terms of Italy's 'unconditional' surrender. Marshal Badoglio had reluctantly signed the 'long terms' on 29 September, but he implored Eisenhower to make some changes before publication, to prevent fascist propaganda about the 'dishonourable surrender' undermining the Italian army's loyalty to the new government. Arguing again on grounds of military expediency, Eisenhower strongly urged these points on the US and British governments. Specifically, he asked to change the title to 'armistice' not 'surrender', and to remove the first paragraph, which spoke of the 'unconditional surrender' of the Italian armed forces. As compensation, it would be stated that the terms had been accepted 'unconditionally' by the Badoglio government. Eisenhower said the Allies would lose nothing by agreeing to these 'modifications', because the short and long terms already signed 'give us full control and amount to complete capitulation by Italy'. Roosevelt put Eisenhower's request to Stalin on 1 October.[5]

Eisenhower also urged Roosevelt and Churchill to make a public statement explaining Italy's new status as a 'cobelligerent' with the Allies. The president agreed and General Marshall drafted a joint declaration, which was sent to Churchill. The PM, however, thought there would be 'a good chance of getting

UJ in too' and considered a few days' delay 'relatively unimportant compared with the value of getting Russian participation'. His redraft was accepted by Roosevelt and sent to Stalin on 1 October. It stated that the Allies accepted 'the active cooperation of the Italian nation and armed forces as a co-belligerent in the war against Germany', and also affirmed that after the war 'nothing can detract from the absolute and untrammelled right of the people of Italy by constitutional means to decide on the democratic form of government they will eventually have.[6] The Soviet leader agreed to the modification of the 'short terms' and to the joint declaration.[7]

By October, the Arctic convoys were again an issue of contention with Moscow. When Churchill announced their suspension in the spring, he added that 'assuming "Husky" goes well we should hope to resume convoys in early September'. As usual, Churchill added various conditions, such as German naval dispositions and the availability of British escorts; but, on 21 September, with no resumption in sight, Molotov handed Clark Kerr a memo stating that further postponement of convoys was 'quite unjustifiable', given the heavy burdens on the Soviet armies at the front and emphasizing the 'very great importance' that the USSR attached to this matter.[8] This brusque message caused a stir in London, and Churchill felt obliged to explain the situation to Stalin. The PM told the chiefs of staff, 'it is our duty if humanly possible to reopen these convoys'. When the military raised various possible problems, he told them 'naturally I am not going to make a solemn contract with Marshal Stalin, and we must safeguard ourselves against unforeseeable contingencies', but he did not agree with them that Britain's naval situation would be as 'strained' as in 1942–43.[9]

In his letter to Stalin of 1 October, the PM detailed Britain's worldwide naval commitments and presented his offer of four monthly convoys almost as a matter of goodwill, rather than a 'contract' or 'bargain'. Churchill then used this apparent act of benevolence to press for a quid pro quo in return: namely that Stalin permit an increase in the number of British service personnel in Arkhangelsk and Murmansk, and improve their working conditions – all of which had long been a bone of contention between the two governments. This row also reflected a clash of cultures, between Stalinist restriction and Western liberties: any British presence on Soviet soil would be viewed with suspicion in the Kremlin. Molotov's testy memo therefore offered a way out of the impasse. 'Now that the Russians have asked for a reopening of these convoys,' Churchill told his ministers on 25 September, 'we are entitled to make a very plain request to them for the better treatment of our personnel in North Russia.'[10] Eden's staff produced a laundry list of grievances, which formed the basis of the second half of the PM's message.

Churchill to Stalin, sent 1 October 1943, received 1 October 1943[11]

I have received your request for the reopening of convoys to North Russia. I and all my colleagues are most anxious to help you and the valiant armies you lead to the utmost of our ability. I do not therefore reply to the various controversial points made in Monsieur Molotov's communication. Since 22nd June, 1941, we have always done our best in spite of our own heavy burdens to help you defend your own country against the cruel invasion of the Hitlerite gang, and we have never ceased to acknowledge and proclaim the great advantages that have come to us from the splendid victories you have won and from the deadly blows you have dealt the German armies.

For the last four days I have been working with the Admiralty to make a plan for sending a new series of convoys to North Russia. This entails very great difficulties. First the battle of the Atlantic has begun again. U-boats have set about us with a new kind of acoustic torpedo, which has proved effective against escorting vessels when hunting U-boats. Secondly, we are at very full stretch in the Mediterranean, building up an army in Italy of about 600,000 men by the end of November and also trying to take full advantage of the Italian collapse in the Aegean Islands and Balkan Peninsula. Thirdly we have to provide our share of the war against Japan in which the United States are greatly interested and whose people would be offended if we were luke-warm.

Notwithstanding the above it is a very great pleasure to me to tell you that we are planning to sail a series of four convoys to North Russia in November, December, January and February each of which will consist of approximately 35 ships, British and American. Convoys may be sailed in two halves to meet operational requirements. The first convoy will leave the United Kingdom about 12th November, arriving North Russia ten days later, subsequent convoys at about 28-day intervals. We intend to withdraw as many as possible of the merchant vessels now in North Russia towards the end of October and the remainder with the returning convoy escorts.

However I must put it on record that this is no contract or bargain but rather a declaration of our solemn and earnest resolve. On this basis I have ordered the necessary measures to be taken for sending these four convoys of 35 ships.

The Foreign Office and Admiralty however request me to put before you for your personal attention, hoping indeed that your own eye may look at it, the following representations about the difficulties we have experienced in North Russia.

If we are to resume the convoys we shall have to reinforce our establishments in North Russia which have been reduced in numbers since last March. The present numbers of Naval personnel are below what is necessary for our present requirements, owing to men having to be sent home without relief. Your civil authorities have refused us all visas for men to go to North Russia even to relieve those who are seriously overdue for relief. M. Molotov has pressed His Majesty's Government to agree that the number of British Service personnel in North Russia should not exceed that of the Soviet Service personnel and Trade Delegation in this country. We have been unable to accept this proposal since their work is quite dissimilar and the number of men needed for war operations cannot be determined in such an unpractical way. Secondly, as we have already informed the Soviet Government, we must ask to be judges of the personnel required to carry out operations for which we are responsible. Mr Eden has already given his assurance that the greatest care will be taken to limit the numbers strictly to the minimum.

I must therefore ask you to agree to the immediate grant of visas for the additional personnel now required and for your assurance that you will not in future withhold visas when we find it necessary to ask for them in connection with the assistance that we are giving you in North Russia. I emphasise that of about 170 naval personnel at present in the North over 150 should have been relieved some months ago, but Soviet visas have been withheld. The state of health of these men who are unaccustomed to the climate and other conditions makes it very necessary to relieve them without further delay.

We should also wish to send a small medical unit for Archangel to which your authorities agreed but for which the necessary visas have not been granted. Please remember that we may have heavy casualties.

I must also ask your help in remedying the conditions under which our Service personnel and seamen at present find themselves in North Russia. These men are of course engaged in operations against the enemy in our joint interest and chiefly to bring Allied supplies to your country. They are, I am sure you will admit, in a wholly different position from ordinary individuals proceeding to Russian territory. Yet they are subjected by your authorities to the following restrictions which seem to me inappropriate for men sent by an ally to carry out operations of the greatest interest to the Soviet Union:

(a) No one may land from one of HM ships or from a British merchant ship except by a Soviet boat in the presence of a Soviet official and after examination of documents on each occasion.

(b) No one from a British warship is allowed to proceed alongside a British merchantman without the Soviet authorities being informed beforehand. This even applies to the British Admiral in charge.

(c) British officers and men are required to obtain special passes before they can go from ship to shore or between the two British shore stations. These passes are often much delayed with consequent dislocation of the work in hand.

(d) No stores, luggage or mail for this operational force may be landed except in the presence of a Soviet official and numerous formalities are required for the shipment of all stores and mail.

(e) Private service mail is subjected to censorship although for an operational force of this kind censorship should, in our view, be left in the hands of the British Service authorities.

The imposition of these restrictions makes an impression upon officers and men alike which is bad for Anglo-Soviet relations and would be deeply injurious if Parliament got to hear of it. The cumulative effect of these formalities has been most hampering to the efficient performance of the men's duties and, on more than one occasion, to urgent and important operations. No such restrictions are placed upon Soviet personnel here.

We have already proposed to Monsieur Molotov that as regards offences against Soviet law committed by personnel of the Services and of ships of convoys, they should be handed over to the British Service authorities to deal with. There have been a few such cases, no doubt partially at any rate due to the rigorous conditions of service in the North.

I trust indeed, Monsieur Stalin, that you will find it possible to have these difficulties smoothed out in a friendly spirit so that we may each help each other and the common cause, to the utmost of our strength.

Churchill was not alone in his concern about security should the Big Three meeting take place in Tehran. In August, a team of Soviet security experts had visited the Iranian capital to conduct a thorough reconnaissance. On 15 October, the 131st motorized infantry regiment of NKVD border guards arrived in Tehran. Its personnel began patrolling the streets, guarding the Soviet embassy, the shah's palace, the post office and other key installations, including, in due course, the buildings where the Tehran conference was eventually held. Estimates of the total Soviet security detail vary from 500 to 3,000 men.[12]

Not surprisingly, Stalin disliked Churchill's proposals on 25 September for British and Soviet troops to throw a cordon around Tehran, preferring a less conspicuous presence – and also one that the USSR controlled. He disingenuously suggested that 'a sufficient police guard' for each leader would provide adequate security.

Stalin to Churchill, sent 3 October 1943, received 3 October 1943[13]

I received your message of the 27th September concerning the forthcoming meeting of the three Heads of the Governments. I have no objection to the diverting preparations which you intend to carry out in Cairo. Regarding your proposal to throw British and Russian brigades round a suitable area in Cairo–3 several days in advance of our meeting in that city, I find this measure inexpedient as it would cause an unnecessary sensation and would decamouflage the preparations. I suggest that each of us should take with him a sufficient police guard. In my opinion this would be enough to secure our safety.

I have no objection to your other proposals relating to the forthcoming meeting, and I agree with those conventional denominations which you propose to use in the correspondence concerning this meeting.

Roosevelt and Churchill did not expect great results from the foreign ministers' conference in Moscow. Both of them were determined to reserve the serious business for their own summit. In his 4 October letter to Stalin, composed by Hopkins with a few presidential tweaks, FDR reiterated the purely 'preliminary' nature of the Moscow conference, but also gave Stalin a clear hint that he would welcome combined pressure on the British about the cross-Channel attack.

Roosevelt to Stalin, sent 4 October 1943, received 5 October 1943[14]

I have your wire and our delegation will be in Moscow on October fifteenth.

While I do not look upon this conference as one that will plan or recommend military strategy, I have no objection and, indeed, would welcome the fullest exchange on your proposal relative to an expedition directed against France.

General Deane is a member of our mission and will be fully informed of our plans and intentions.

I agree that this is a three-power conference and that the discussion on our proposal should be limited to the future intentions and plans of these powers exclusively.

This would, in no way, preclude a wider participation at a later date and under circumstances which would are mutually acceptable to our three governments.

I am sure that we are going to find a meeting of minds for the important decisions which must finally be made by us. This preliminary conference will explore the ground and if ~~points of difference~~ *difficulties* develop at the meeting of our foreign ministers, I would still have every confidence that they can be reconciled when ~~the three of us~~ *you and Churchill and I* meet.

It looks as if American and British armies ~~We~~ *should be in Rome in another few*
weeks.

The president's breezy last sentence about the Allied entry into Rome
proved totally mistaken. His prediction was, however, based on a range of
Enigma intercepts of German signals which led British and American
intelligence staff to believe that the Germans would not seriously contest
southern Italy, but would pull back northwards, maybe to a line from Pisa to
Rimini. But then Hitler – aware of the slow pace of the Allied advance and
reports that landing craft were being moved from the Mediterranean to Britain
– executed a dramatic U-turn, reminiscent of his decision to fight for Tunisia
in November 1942. Substantial reinforcements were sent to Field Marshal
Albert Kesselring's command in Italy, and new orders were issued that the
Germans must fight for Rome. And fight they did. The Allies did not enter the
Italian capital until 4 June 1944, just before D-Day. What to do about the Italian
quagmire would become a major bone of Anglo-American contention in
1943–44.[15]

*****

Stalin's letter of 6 October could only intensify Roosevelt's concerns about the
upcoming conference of foreign ministers. At Moscow, the Soviet leader clearly
wanted to start discussing the second front, whereas the president wished to
reserve grand strategy for the Big Three meeting. As for America's main agenda
item, an Allied declaration about peace, security and disarmament, the Kremlin
ruled out any participation by Nationalist China – which Roosevelt (unlike
both his partners) regarded as one of the essential 'four policemen' of the
postwar world. Stalin and Molotov were at their most casuistic here: since it
had already been agreed that the meeting would concern itself only with Big
Three matters, by definition that ruled out any declaration involving four
powers.

Stalin to Roosevelt, sent 6 October 1943, received 6 October 1943[16]

I received your message of October 4th.

As regards the military questions, i.e. British–American measures of short-
ening of the war, you already know the point of view of the Soviet Government
from my previous message. I hope, however, that in this respect a preliminary
meeting of the three will bring useful results, having prepared our future important decisions.

If I understood you correctly, at the Moscow conference will be discussed questions concerning only our three countries and, thus, it can be considered as agreed upon that the question of the declaration of four nations is not included in the agenda of the conference.

Our representatives have to do everything possible to prevent possible difficulties in their responsible work. It is understood that the decisions as such can be made only by our governments and I hope they will be made at my personal meeting with you and Mr Churchill.

Best wishes to the American and British Armies to fulfill successfully their mission and enter Rome, which will be a new blow inflicted on Mussolini and Hitler.

It took Stalin nearly two weeks to reply to Churchill's message of 1 October about the resumption of convoys and the status of British personnel in Russia's northern ports. When the answer arrived on 13 October, it was not at all to the PM's liking. Instead of expressing gratitude, Stalin insisted that the resumption of convoys was a matter of contractual obligation for the British, reminding him of the shortfall in deliveries under the Third Supply Protocol. He stated that Churchill's attempt to present resumption as a token of goodwill failed to appreciate that the deliveries had been factored into Soviet production plans, and claimed that Churchill's refusal to acknowledge his 'obligations' represented 'a kind of threat' to the USSR. Nor did the Soviet leader bend at all on the position of British military personnel in northern ports, reiterating the Foreign Ministry's argument that they should be treated on a principle of 'reciprocity and equality' with Soviet personnel in Britain.

Churchill's message 'seems to have caught Stalin in a rough mood', commented Clark Kerr, 'but I fancy that I see more of Molotov's hand than of his in the reply'. The prime minister – in line with his 'two Stalins' thesis – also wondered about authorship, telling Roosevelt

> I think or at least I hope this message came from the machine rather than from Stalin as it took 12 days to prepare. The Soviet machine is quite convinced it can get everything by bullying and I am sure it is of some importance to show that this is not necessarily the case.[17]

In this case, they were both mistaken: Stalin used a draft from Molotov as his base, but toughened it by replacing a tepid expression of appreciation for the resumption of convoys with the insulting lines about the PM proffering this as an act of goodwill and by accusing the British of trying to recruit Russians as spies. Later, during the Moscow conference, Stalin told Eden that the most upsetting part of Churchill's message had been the way he presented the resumption of convoys as a 'gift' to the USSR.[18]

Stalin to Churchill, sent 13 October 1943, received 13 October 1943[19]

I received your message of October 1st informing me of the intention to send four convoys to the Soviet Union by the northern route in November, December, January and February. However, this communication loses its value by your statement that this intention to send Northern convoys to the USSR is neither an obligation nor an agreement but only a statement which, as it may be understood, is one that the British side can at any moment renounce regardless of any influence it may have on the Soviet armies at the front. I must say I cannot agree with such posing of the question. Supplies from the British Government to the USSR, armaments and other military goods, cannot be considered otherwise than as an obligation, which by special agreement between our countries, the British Government undertook in respect of the USSR, which bears on its shoulders, already for the third year, the enormous burden of struggle with the common enemy of the Allies – Hitlerite Germany.

It is also impossible to disregard the fact that the Northern route is the shortest way which permits delivery of armaments supplied by the Allies within the shortest period to the Soviet–German front, and the realization of the plan of supplies to the USSR in appropriate volume is impossible without an adequate use of this way. As I already wrote you earlier, and as experience has shown, delivery of armaments and military supplies to the USSR through Persian ports cannot compensate in any way for those supplies which were not delivered owing to the absence of delivery of equipment and materials by the Northern route which, as it can be well understood, were taken into account when planning the supplies for Soviet armies. By the way, there was a very considerable decrease in the delivery of military goods sent by the Northern route this year in comparison with those received last year; and this makes it impossible to fulfil the established plan of military supplies and is in contradiction to the corresponding Anglo-Soviet Protocol for military supplies. Therefore, at the present time, when the forces of the Soviet Union are strained to the utmost to secure the needs of the front in the interests of success against the main forces of our common enemy, it would be inadmissible to have the supplies of the Soviet armies depend on the arbitrary judgment of the British side. It is impossible to consider this posing of the question other than a refusal of the British Government to fulfil the obligations it undertook, and as a kind of threat addressed to the USSR.

Concerning your mention of controversial points allegedly contained in the statement of Mr Molotov, I have to say that I do not find any foundation for such a remark. I consider the principle of reciprocity and equality proposed by the Soviet side for settlement of visa question in respect of personnel of the Military Missions to be a correct and indeed a just one. The reference to the difference in the functions of the British and Soviet Military Missions to exclude the usage of that principle, and that the numbers of the staff of the British Military Mission must be determined by the British Government only, I consider to be unconvincing. It has already been made clear in detail in the previous aide-memoires of the People's Commissariat for Foreign Affairs on this question.

I do not see the necessity for increasing the number of British servicemen in the north of the USSR since the great majority of British servicemen who are already there are not adequately employed, and for many months have been doomed to idleness, as has already been pointed out several times by the Soviet side. For example, it can be mentioned that owing to its non-necessity, the question of the liquidation of the 126th British port base in Archangel was put forward several times, and only now the British side have agreed to liquidate it. There are also regrettable facts of the inadmissible behaviour of individual British servicemen who attempted, in several cases, to recruit, by bribery, certain Soviet citizens for intelligence purposes. Such incidents, offensive to Soviet citizens, naturally gave rise to incidents which led to undesirable complications.

Concerning your mention of formalities and certain restrictions existing in Northern ports, it is necessary to have in view that such formalities and restrictions are unavoidable in zones near and at the front, if one does not forget the war situation which exists in the USSR. I may add that this applies equally to the British and other foreigners as well as to Soviet citizens. Nevertheless the Soviet authorities granted many privileges in this respect to the British servicemen and seamen, about which the British Embassy was informed as long ago as last March. Thus, your mention of many formalities and restrictions is based on inaccurate information.

Concerning the question of censorship and prosecution of British servicemen, I have no objection if the censorship of private mail for British personnel in Northern ports would be made by the British authorities themselves on condition of reciprocity, and also if cases of small violations committed by British servicemen which did not involve court procedure would be given to the consideration of the appropriate military authorities.

Churchill's first reaction to Stalin's message was 'I'll stop convoys'. He drafted a message for Eden to give Stalin, insisting that he could make no 'guarantee' about the convoys and stating that the British government would be 'very glad' to withdraw its personnel from North Russia once 'assured that it is not the desire of the Soviet Government to receive the Convoys under the modest and reasonable conditions which the British Government consider necessary'. But then on reflection, Churchill decided to make a three-pronged response, mixing conciliation, consultation and self-assertion. The first convoy was already being loaded, so he decided to let the convoys go ahead – 'in the interests of the war effort', he told the Cabinet. But he asked Eden, when in Moscow, to raise the servicemen issue with Stalin and also disabuse him of any idea that the 1 October message was intended as a 'threat'. Thirdly, the PM decided to take the most unusual step of formally refusing to accept Stalin's 'offensive' message. This he duly did when the new Soviet ambassador, Gusev, came to 10 Downing Street on 18 October for his first official visit.[20]

Churchill was so pleased with his démarche that he dictated a note of what happened, and later included it in his war memoirs. According to his account, after exchanging pleasantries with Gusev, the PM came to the point:

> I said very briefly that I did not think this message would help the situation, that it had caused me a good deal of pain, that I feared any reply which I could send would only make matters worse, that the Foreign Secretary was in Moscow and I had left it to him to settle the matter on the spot and that therefore I did not wish to receive the message, which I then handed back to him in an envelope.

When the ambassador remonstrated, saying he had been instructed to deliver the message, Churchill said, 'I am not prepared to receive it', and in a friendly but firm manner ushered the Soviet envoy to the door. So, the PM concluded, Stalin's message could now be treated as '*nul et non avenu*' – diplomatic language for 'null and void'.[21]

Gusev was in an invidious position: not only had his official debut been blighted, but he also faced a difficult job explaining things to the Boss. Nevertheless, the young ambassador kept his nerve. This is how he described the conversation in his dispatch to Moscow:

> Churchill received me in his office at Downing Street. At first glance, Churchill's watery eyes gave me an impression that he was drunk, and in the course of the conversation this was confirmed, for he reeked of wine. He really was drunk. At the meeting, after the customary greetings upon acquaintance, Churchill sat me down at the table and, smoking a cigar, said something along the following lines ...

Gusev then gave a rendition of the conversation that corroborates Churchill's, except for a more detailed description of his own resistance to the PM's attempts to hand him back the unfortunate envelope: 'In the doorway, Churchill shook my hand and literally shoved the packet in my hand, turned around and walked to the desk.' Under the circumstances, Gusev told Moscow, 'I decided it unnecessary to talk to Churchill again or return the packet to him through his Secretaries.' He added that there were no notes on the message, but the top right-hand corner of the first page had been cut off, perhaps because it had been annotated by Cadogan. With deft banality, Gusev concluded, 'I ask for your guidance.'[22]

Was the prime minister actually inebriated, or did the ambassador exaggerate for self-justification? Cadogan, a career diplomat with thirty-five years' experience, made no complaint about Churchill's actions, noting in his diary: 'It's a strong measure to return a communication, but this, after all, was not an official note – only an item in an exchange of personal messages, and was damned offensive.' Handing it back showed Stalin he could not 'wipe his boots on us.'[23]

When Eden took up the matter with Stalin and Molotov in the Kremlin on 21 October, the two-hour meeting began 'stickily' – according to his account. 'The Prime Minister is offended and will not accept my reply,' declared Stalin. 'I understand that Mr Churchill does not want to correspond further with me. Well, let it be so.' Eden denied that this was the case – Churchill had simply resented the apparent imputations of bad faith – and stated that the PM had instructed him to discuss the whole issue with the Soviet leader while in Moscow. This seemed to relax the tension and there ensued a businesslike discussion, during which Stalin made the telling remark that, as the foreign secretary put it, 'if our people would treat his people as equals we could have as much personnel as we liked'. Eden noted in his diary:

> Joe was friendly enough to me personally, even jovial. But he still has that disconcerting habit of not looking at one as he speaks or as he shakes hands. A meeting with him would be in all respects a creepy, even a sinister experience if it weren't for his readiness to laugh, when his whole face creases and his little eyes open. He looks more and more like bruin.[24]

In this easier atmosphere and amid the goodwill generated by the Moscow conference, Molotov agreed to be more cooperative about visas and hospital facilities, and allowed the British to increase the 383 British personnel in northern ports by 10 per cent without additional Soviet permission. Those who committed minor offences would henceforth be handed over to the British authorities, and two seamen imprisoned for drunkenly beating up an obstreperous Soviet functionary were released.[25]

Although the row had blown over, the exchanges had been revealing on both sides. Churchill's dramatic ploy of handing back Stalin's message clearly had an effect in Moscow, especially when coupled with Eden's conciliatory meeting and a readiness to resume the convoys. Here was British diplomacy that, for once, successfully combined the stick with the carrot. On the other side, Stalin's reference to treating the Russians as 'equals', like his insistence that the convoys were a commitment between allies, not an act of Churchillian *noblesse oblige*, underlined the ingrained status sensitivity that Clark Kerr had for months been trying to convey to London. Stalin's obduracy about convening the foreign ministers' conference in Moscow and the Big Three summit on ground of his own choosing in Tehran was part and parcel of that same attitude.

The two messages that had aroused so much ire also raised the larger issue of translation. As noted in the Cabinet minutes for 18 October, Churchill

> said that he thought it would be a great advantage if the Russians delivered their messages in Russian and let us arrange for their translation. He felt sure that the translations made were often very crude and that the tone of the original was often lost in the process of translation.

The following day, he told Eden that either the FO translated the messages into English or the Soviet embassy transmitted both its translation and the original Russian text.[26] On 22 October, Christopher Warner, head of the FO's Northern Department, which handled relations with the USSR, raised the matter with Gusev, suggesting that the Soviet embassy should seek advice from FO officials in complicated cases. The new ambassador was naturally aggrieved; when he asked for specific examples of distortion in the embassy's translations, Warner could not provide any. Reporting to Moscow, Gusev remarked caustically:

> Warner's talk about the accuracy of translation shows clearly that after Churchill's boorish antics with the return of the message from Comrade Stalin, they are trying to find justifications for such conduct and, by talking about stylistic nuances, somehow to smooth out and dispel the bad impression.[27]

Thus, the Soviet ambassador not only covered up for the embassy's work, but suggested that the British were trying to shift the blame onto the Russians.

Warner, too, was talking the talk: as he admitted to Eden, the Northern Department had not enough officials with a good knowledge of the Russian language, and they themselves often turned to Soviet embassy staff for clarifications.[28]

Churchill's next message was a proposal for a declaration by the three powers about Nazi atrocities in the occupied territories. The immediate impetus was the shooting in cold blood by the Germans of a hundred Italian officers on the island of Kos in the Dodecanese, which had disturbed the PM profoundly. Churchill suggested the idea to the War Cabinet on 8 October, in the hope of deterring further German 'frightfulness' by warning that perpetrators would be sent back to the countries in question 'for judgment'. The Cabinet agreed and the draft declaration was sent to Stalin and Roosevelt.[29]

The Soviets had been raising the issue of responsibility for the Nazi crimes for some time. Although Stalin did not respond directly to Churchill, on 25 October Vyshinskiy handed the Allied ambassadors an aide-memoire, which accepted the British draft and proposed minor amendments to highlight the 'heinous crimes' committed on Soviet territory. Instructed by Roosevelt, the State Department asked the US ambassador in Moscow to reach agreement with the Soviets on Churchill's draft, and to synchronize publication of the declaration with the end of the Moscow conference, in order to 'let the world know that the fate of these unfortunate peoples was not forgotten at the trilateral meeting'.[30] The text of the 'Moscow Declaration' was published on behalf of Roosevelt, Stalin and Churchill.[31]

A tug of war continued over where to hold the summit – about which, Roosevelt told Stalin on 14 October, he was 'much disturbed'.[32] In order to secure a location that he preferred, the president made as much as possible of his responsibilities under the US constitution (article 1, section 7) to return bills that had passed the Congress with his signature within ten days. His was a very rigid interpretation: the clause specified that the ten days began after the bill had been presented to him, and also that a bill automatically became law after that period had elapsed, even if the president had not signed. But constitutionality was not the fundamental issue. What mattered for Roosevelt, like Stalin, was comfort (given FDR's physical condition), as well as prestige: as with many summits throughout history, the length of the journey could be taken as an inverse measure of status. By going all the way to Tehran, Roosevelt would clearly be paying court to Stalin. The president suggested various alternative venues, while also stressing the importance he attached to the three leaders meeting in person.

Roosevelt to Stalin, sent 14 October 1943, received 15 October 1943[33]

The problem of my going to the place you suggested is becoming so acute that I feel that I should tell you frankly that, for constitutional reasons, I cannot take the risk. The Congress will be in session. New laws and resolutions must be acted on by me after their receipt and must be returned to the Congress physically before ten days have elapsed. None of this can be done by radio or cable. The place you mentioned is too far to be sure that the requirements are fulfilled. The possibility of delay in getting over the mountain – first east-bound and then west-bound – is insurmountable. We know from experience that planes in either direction are often held up for three or four days.

I do not think that any one of us will need Legation facilities as each of us can have adequate personal and technical staffs. I venture, therefore, to make some other suggestions and I hope you will consider them or suggest any other place where I can be assured of meeting my constitutional obligations.

In many ways Cairo is attractive, and I understand there is a hotel and some villas out near the pyramids which could be completely segregated.

Asmara, the former Italian capital of Eritrea, is said to have excellent buildings and a landing field – good at all times.

Then there is the possibility of meeting at some port in the Eastern Mediterranean, each one of us to have a ship. If this idea attracts you, we could easily place a fine ship entirely at your disposal for you and your party so that you would be completely independent and, at the same time, be in constant contact with your own war front.

Another suggestion is in the neighborhood of Bagdad where we could have three comfortable camps with adequate Russian, British and American guards. This last idea seems worth considering.

In any event I think the press should be entirely banished, and the whole place surrounded by a cordon so that we would not be disturbed in any way. What would you think of November twentieth or November twenty-fifth as the date of the meeting?

I am placing a very great importance on the personal and intimate conversations which you and Churchill and I will have, for on them depend the hopes of the future world.

Your continuous initiative along your whole front heartens all of us.

Stalin's position on the venue was, however, unyielding. 'The Soviet Government does not intend to swerve from the previously scheduled meeting point with Roosevelt,' Molotov informed Gromyko on 12 October. 'Cairo or some cruiser cannot be accepted for these purposes.'[34] The Soviet leader knew how long the president had been looking forward to this meeting, and also that, as Gromyko confirmed on 4 October, he was willing to accept Tehran as a last resort. So in this psychological game of 'chicken', Stalin enjoyed a massive tactical advantage. His editing of Molotov's draft (additions in italics) served to strengthen his most compelling argument, namely that he was acting as commander-in-chief on the most crucial front of the war. The underlined sentence was omitted by Gromyko from the English translation given to the White House, apparently by mistake: it does appear in the Russian text that he also submitted.

Stalin to Roosevelt, sent 19 October 1943, received 19 October 1943[35]

In regard to the place of the forthcoming meeting of the three heads of the three Governments, I want to tell you the following.

Unfortunately, not one of the places proposed by you for the meeting instead Tegeran is acceptable to me. It is not a matter of security, *for that does not worry me*.

In the course of the operations of the Soviet troops during the summer and fall of this year, it became evident that our troops can continue their offensive operations against the German Army, *and summer campaign may overgrow into winter one.*

All my colleagues consider that these operations demand daily guidance on the part of the Supreme Command, and my personal contact with the Command. In Tegeran conditions are better, since there are wire telegraph and telephone communications with Moscow, what cannot be said about the other places. That is why my colleagues insist on Tegeran as the place of meeting.

I agree that the representatives of press must not be present at the meeting. I also accept your proposal to set November 20th or 25th as possible date of the meeting.

Mr Hull has safely arrived in Moscow, and I hope his direct participation in the Moscow meeting of the three countries will do a great good.

But the president kept trying. He immediately dictated a response to his secretary, Grace Tully – a practice that was rare in his correspondence with Stalin – and then showed it to Hopkins, who, on top of various small textual changes (including the insertion of 'categorically' in paragraph five), suggested omitting one entire sentence (struck through). By doing that, he tacitly admitted that it was implausible to equate the constitutional duties of a head of state with the role of commander-in-chief on the cusp of an epic military victory. Rather desperately, the president cast around for alternative locations and additional arguments, further developing his deliberately selective interpretation of the US constitution. He also dramatized the consequences of not meeting. Once again, however, there was no *cri de coeur* about what was surely the most troubling issue: his own disability.

Roosevelt's message was cabled to Hull in Moscow. 'In reply to my several messages,' the president stated in his cover letter, 'the Marshal has shown no realization of my obligations.' He asked the secretary of state to deliver the message and 'explain to him orally the definite and clear reasons which are not actuated by personal desires but are fixed by our Constitution. This is not a question of theory; it is a question of fact.'[36] Given the importance of the message, the US embassy in Moscow made its own translation into Russian; both texts were handed by Hull to Stalin on 25 October.

Roosevelt to Stalin, sent 21 October 1943, received 25 October 1943[37]

I am deeply disappointed in your message received today in regard to our meeting.

Please accept my assurance that I fully appreciate and understand your reason for requiring daily guidance from the Supreme Command and your personal contact with the Command which is bringing such outstanding results. This is of high importance.

And I wish you would realize that there are other vital matters which, in this constitutional American Government, represent fixed obligations on my part which I cannot change. Our Constitution calls for action by the President on legislation within ten days of the passage of such legislation. That means that the President must receive and return to Congress, with his written approval or veto, physical documents in that period. I cannot act by cable or radio, as I have told you before.

The trouble with Teheran is the simple fact that the approaches to that city over the mountain often make flying impossible for several days at a time. This is a double risk; first, for the plane delivering documents from Washington and, second, for the plane returning these documents to the Congress. I regret to say that, as head of the nation, it is impossible for me to go to a place where I cannot fulfill my constitutional obligations. ~~These obligations are fully as important in the winning of the war by you and me as your obligations in the field.~~

I can assume the flying risks for documents up to and including the Low Country as far as the Persian Gulf, through a relay system of planes, but I cannot assume the delays attending flights in both directions into the saucer over the mountains in which Teheran lies. Therefore, with much regret I must tell you categorically that I cannot go to Teheran and in this my cabinet members and the Legislative Leaders are in complete agreement.

Therefore, I can make one last practical suggestion. That is that all three of us should go to Basra where we shall be perfectly protected in three camps, to be established and guarded by our respective national troops. As you know, you can easily have a special telephone, under your own control, laid from Basra to Teheran where you will reach your own line into Russia. Such a wire service should meet all your needs, and by plane you will only be a little further off from Russia than in Teheran itself.

I am not in any way considering the fact that from United States territory I would have to travel six thousand miles and you would only have to travel six hundred miles from Russian territory.

I would gladly go ten times the distance to meet you were it not for the fact that I must carry on a constitutional government more than one hundred and fifty years old.

You have a great obligation to your people to carry on the defeat of our common enemy, but I am begging you to remember that I also have a great obligation to the American Government and to maintain the full American war effort.

As I have said to you before, I regard the meeting of the three of us as of the greatest possible importance, not only to our peoples today, but also to our peoples in relation to a peaceful world for generations to come.

It would be regarded as a tragedy by future generations if you and I and Mr Churchill failed today because of a few hundred miles.

I repeat that I would gladly go to Teheran were I not prevented from doing so because of limitations over which I have no control.

I am suggesting Basra because of your communications problems.

If you do not like this, I deeply hope you will reconsider Bagdad or Asmara or even Ankara in Turkey. The latter place is neutral territory, but I think it is worth considering and that the Turks might welcome the idea of being hosts though, of course, I have not mentioned this to them or anybody else.

Please do not fail me in this crisis.

Roosevelt sent a copy of the message to Churchill, adding: 'I hope you can find some way of having Eden back this up.' Churchill said he would, but observed that Ankara did not seem feasible because of security and the problem of flying over the Taurus Mountains (which rise to 10,000 or 12,000 feet). In fact, the PM was less concerned about when and for how long they met Stalin than with trying to arrange another British–American meeting with the Combined Chiefs of Staff to review strategy in the light of the new situation opening up in the Mediterranean. This was a proposal that FDR was keen to resist, at least until after the Big Three summit, arguing that 'at the moment it seems to me that consideration of our relations with Russia is of paramount importance'.[38]

Further light on Stalin's obduracy about Tehran is shed by his conversation with Eden on 21 October. The Soviet leader explained that Tehran was the best place 'not on account of security but of communications'. Eden's account continued:

> The Marshal said he greatly regretted the inconvenience for the President and would have been only too glad to travel further, but the opportunities now existing in the war happened only once in half a century. He said this with every appearance of sincerity. I think that he genuinely wants the meeting, but I do not believe he is prepared to go to a place where he has not a Legation through which he can keep in hourly secret touch with Moscow. At one point he said that he would greatly regret it if the meeting had to be put off until the spring, but it might be better so. I said that I thought such a postponement would be an immense disappointment to the world. The Marshal did not dispute this.[39]

Playing the triangular game in his way, Stalin was now using Eden to send a signal to the PM, intimating that the summit could be seriously delayed if Roosevelt did not accept Tehran. On 25 October, he elaborated the point about secure communications to Hull, and Molotov did the same with Harriman, the new US ambassador, telling him that after years of Soviet occupation in northern Iran, the Russians 'had direct telegraph and telephone to Teheran under their complete control, policed by Soviet troops'.[40]

Stalin was in no hurry to answer Roosevelt, knowing that the clock was now ticking insistently in Washington because of the time it would take for a sea and air journey to anywhere in the Middle East. 'No word from U.J. yet,' moaned FDR to Churchill on 25 October.[41] Adding further pressure, Stalin told Eden and Hull that if the president and PM would not come to Tehran, he would send Molotov to meet them in Basra – a consolation prize that was hardly attractive. Judging it vital to exploit the new cooperative mood created by the Moscow conference, Eden urged Churchill to press Roosevelt to accept Tehran. Hull, for his part, told the president that Stalin was 'immovable' on the issue.[42]

Stalin sat on Roosevelt's message of 21 October for two weeks, finally replying on 5 November. Even Gromyko's plodding translation could not entirely conceal the playful sarcasm of Stalin's tone. Since the US president had cited the (fictitious) opposition of his Cabinet and congressional leaders to his going as far as Tehran, the Soviet leader invoked the (equally fictitious) resistance of his colleagues to their supreme commander venturing far outside the Soviet borders. At the end – proffered, tongue in cheek, as a bright idea and helpful suggestion – Stalin repeated his offer of sending Molotov to Basra. Since Roosevelt had made so much of the requirements of the US constitution, Stalin took pains to mention that the USSR also had a constitution which, he said, would allow Molotov to act with all the powers of the head of government. Stalin clearly took pleasure in calling his allies' bluff.

Stalin to Roosevelt, sent 5 November 1943, received 5 November 1943[43]

Mr Hull has transmitted on October 25 your latest message to me and I had a chance to talk with him regarding it. My reply has been delayed because I was sure that Mr Hull had transmitted to you the contents of the eventuated talk and my views regarding my meeting with you and Mr Churchill.

I cannot but give consideration to the arguments you gave regarding the circumstances hindering you from travelling to Teheran. Of course, the decision of w[h]ether you are able to travel to Teheran remains entirely with yourself.

On my part, I have to say that I do not see any other more suitable place for a meeting than the aforementioned city.

I have been charged with the duties of Supreme Commander of the Soviet troops and this obliges me to carry out daily direction of military operations at our front. This is especially important at the present time, when the uninterrupted four-month summer campaign is overgrowing into a winter campaign and the military operations are continuing to develop on nearly all the fronts, stretching along 2,600 kilometers.

Under such conditions for myself as Supreme Commander, the possibility of travelling farther than Teheran is excluded. My colleagues in the Government consider, in general, that my travelling beyond the U.S.S.R. at the present time is impossible due to the great complexity of the situation at the front.

That is why an idea occurred to me about which I already talked to Mr Hull. I could be successfully substituted at this meeting by Mr V.M. Molotov, my first deputy in the Government, who at negotiations will enjoy, according to our Constitution, all powers of the head of the Soviet Government. In this case the difficulties regarding the choice of the place of meeting would drop off. I hope that this suggestion could be acceptable to us at the present time.

Convinced at last of Stalin's intransigence, Roosevelt gave in. To save face, he claimed that he had suddenly found a way to solve his problem with Congress by flying, if necessary, to Tunisia and back in order to sign a bill. On Hopkins' advice, the president deleted from the draft any mention that he had invited the Chinese Nationalist leader Chiang Kai-shek to come to Cairo 'for a few days', perhaps not wanting to alarm Stalin too soon with this news. The letter also contained an invitation to the Soviets to participate in the pre-conference meeting in Cairo (codenamed 'Sextant') between the US and British military staffs. Initially FDR had considered this idea as a fallback if no summit with Stalin were possible. As he told Churchill on 26 October, the Moscow foreign ministers' conference appeared to mark 'a genuine beginning' of real collaboration between the three Allies, and he wanted to 'further stimulate this cooperation and particularly to increase the confidence of Stalin in the sincerity of our intentions'. He persisted in the idea even when Churchill vehemently objected to opening up the British–American discussions, advised by the US Joint Chiefs that it was vital to show the Soviets that 'they cannot doubt our good faith'.[44]

Eden supported the president: he believed that it was important to strengthen the new Soviet sense of equality with the Western Allies. But Churchill was playing his own deep game. The arguments he advanced against a Soviet presence in Cairo were a rag-bag of special pleading:

> I do not know of any really high officer of the Russian army who can speak English. Such a representative would have no authority or power to speak except as instructed. He would simply bay for an earlier second front and block all other discussions . . . it would probably mean that they would want to have observers at all future meetings and all discussions between us would be paralysed.

Underlying this rant was Churchill's bid in October and November to tilt the hard-won agreement on Allied strategy away from 'Overlord', because of what he called the 'gleaming opportunities' suddenly opening up in Italy and the Mediterranean. He candidly shared with Roosevelt his fears about a landing in Normandy, doubting not the ability of Allied troops to 'get ashore', but whether they could hold the beachhead against German counter-attacks. On three occasions between 17 and 27 October he told the president that he was more 'anxious' about 'Overlord' than any of the campaigns in 1941, 1942 or 1943 – indeed 'any other with which I have been involved'.[45] In Churchill's view, Cairo was his chance to bring the Americans to their senses about the 'prizes' to be grabbed in the Mediterranean. He did not want the Russians to get in his way. Or, as Oliver Harvey put it, the PM seemed to believe 'we are still fighting a different war from the Russians'.[46]

Roosevelt's decision to ignore Churchill's pleas to exclude the Soviets from Cairo was one sign of his growing independence in Big Three interactions – though his request in the message to Stalin to send a general who could speak English was perhaps intended as a sop to one of the prime minister's arguments.

Roosevelt to Stalin, sent 8 November 1943, received 9 November 1943[47]

Thank you for your message of November fifth which Mr Gromyko was good enough to deliver.

I hope to leave here in a few days and to arrive in Cairo by the twenty-second November.

You will be glad to know that I have worked out a method so that, if I get word that a bill requiring my veto has been passed by the Congress and forwarded to me, I will fly to Tunis to meet it and then return to the Conference.

Therefore, I have decided to go to Teheran and this makes me especially happy.

As I have told you, I regard it as of vital importance that you and Mr Churchill and I should meet. The psychology of the present excellent feeling really demands it even if our meeting last only two days. Therefore, it is my thought that the staffs begin their work in Cairo on November twenty-second, and I hope Mr Molotov and your military representative, who I hope can speak English, will come there at that time.

Then we can all go to Teheran on the twenty-sixth and meet with you there on the twenty-seventh, twenty-eighth, twenty-ninth or thirtieth, for as long as you feel you can be away. Then Churchill and I and the top Staff people can return to Cairo to complete the details.

The whole world is watching for this meeting of the three of us. And even if we make no announcements as vital as those announced at the recent highly successful meeting in Moscow, the fact that you and Churchill and I have got to know each other personally will have far-reaching effect on the good opinion within our three nations and will result in the further disturbance of Nazi morale.

I am looking forward with keen anticipation to a good talk with you.

Stalin sent Roosevelt a brief thank-you for agreeing to come to Tehran. He accepted the president's proposals for their meetings, and also the invitation for Molotov and a Soviet military representative to attend the Cairo conference.[48]

Roosevelt's deal with Stalin on two key issues – he would go to Tehran and the Soviets would participate in 'Sextant' – had been achieved through bypassing Churchill. Aware of the premier's refusal to invite the Soviets to Cairo, Roosevelt apparently decided to present him with a fait accompli. Nor did he send Churchill a copy of his 8 November U-turn on Tehran, allowing him to learn about it indirectly via Clark Kerr, who had been informed by Harriman.[49] Churchill was aggrieved about the lack of candour, which Roosevelt tried to justify on the grounds that he had only just heard that Stalin would definitely go to Tehran. As for Soviet participation in 'Sextant', FDR said 'it would be a terrible mistake if U.J. thought we had ganged up on him on military action'. Churchill, of course, conceived those Cairo meetings as a high-stakes bid to change America's strategy, which Roosevelt had every intention of resisting, and the Russian presence would be a convenient buttress to his position. President and premier were clearly at odds on policy, and Roosevelt's duplicitous treatment of Churchill – as over the Davies letter in May – showed again his shifting priorities within the Big Three relationship. The president ended his message, 'I am just off. Happy landing to us both.'[50] This was FDR at his most infuriating.

Hoping still to get something of what he wanted, the PM sent Stalin a telegram on 12 November indicating that he welcomed the Soviet presence at Cairo for military discussions, but trying to keep the Soviets away for the first few days – to permit the CCS talks about Europe that he so desired and also about the war against Japan. 'For the latter subject,' he said, 'it is hoped that Chiang Kai-shek himself and a Chinese military delegation may be present.' Churchill sent a draft of this telegram to FDR on the evening of 10th, so the president definitely knew of it before he left Washington; but the PM then despatched the message to Stalin without Roosevelt's formal approval, telling the president, 'I feel sure the above is in accord with your views and wishes'. A second telegram from Churchill to Stalin made it clear that he was assuming FDR's endorsement, but had not yet received it.[51]

So Churchill was strictly playing fair with both sides. Nevertheless, he had never shared FDR's desire to have Chiang at Cairo, and perhaps suspected that by revealing the Chinese presence he might trigger a strong Soviet reaction. If so, he was right. Although Stalin had told Roosevelt on 10 November that Molotov would arrive in Cairo on the 22nd, two days later he informed the president and the PM that due to 'circumstances' of a 'serious character', Molotov would not be coming at all. The foreign minister himself told Harriman on 16 November that Chinese attendance at Cairo was 'a new circumstance of which we had no prior knowledge'. He added that 'Marshal Stalin was feeling poorly' and so, as Harriman put it, 'Molotov, had to hold receptions and generally to increase his workload'.[52]

Clark Kerr, however, saw through the word games, telling Eden that the prospect of Chiang in Cairo had probably 'frightened Molotov off'.[53] Even though Stalin had informed Hull confidentially during the Moscow conference that he intended to join the Pacific War once Germany had been defeated, he did not want any intimation of that in public, lest it give Tokyo any excuse to break the Soviet–Japanese neutrality treaty at a time when the Red Army was totally absorbed against Germany. Stalin's explicit reminder in his next message to both leaders that Tehran must be a Big Three affair with other powers 'absolutely excluded' was most likely prompted by fears that the Americans would seek to insinuate Chiang into that summit. 'Planned or not,' historian Warren Kimball has observed, 'Churchill thus had the private Anglo-American talks he so eagerly wanted.'[54]

On the morning of 12 November, Roosevelt boarded the battleship USS *Iowa* in Hampton Roads, Virginia. That afternoon, Churchill left Plymouth on the battlecruiser HMS *Renown*. Both leaders, especially the president, faced a long and gruelling journey, but the prize would be their first Big Three summit with Stalin.

*****

A week before, on 6 November, the Red Army had driven the Germans out of Kiev, capital of the Ukraine. Crossing the Dnieper, some 700 metres wide at Kiev, was a considerable feat, duly noted by the Western Allies. It was now clear that the Germans would not be able to hold the river line and would have to make a steady fighting withdrawal into Poland. The Soviet military successes, however, caused anxiety in some quarters. The South African leader, Jan Smuts, a confidant of Churchill who shared the PM's aversion to treating 'Overlord' as 'a fixed rigid code', told him on 14 November:

> Moscow is firing salvoes for great victories almost daily, while our progress makes people think that Russia alone is winning the war. The effect of this may be serious enough for the course of the war, but even more so for the post war world, in which Russia will stand forth as the great victor.[55]

On 20 November, the battleship *Iowa* arrived in Oran, where Roosevelt caught up with his mail. Belatedly replying to Stalin's message that the Soviets would not, after all, be going to Cairo, the president tactfully treated Molotov's 'serious circumstances' as medical and not diplomatic, and expressed the hope that he was 'all well again'. He also asked when Stalin expected to arrive in Tehran.[56]

On receiving this telegram, Molotov told the US embassy that 'at the moment Marshal Stalin is at the front, but he tells me that he will arrive at the appointed place no later than 28–29 November'; the foreign minister asked that this information be conveyed to the president.[57] In fact, Stalin was in Moscow, at the Kremlin or his 'Near Dacha', recovering from flu and methodically preparing for the upcoming conference; but the myth of the ubiquitous commander-in-chief, forever visiting his troops, was maintained for the benefit of the Allies, especially on the eve of Tehran.

On 22 November, the Soviet official train departed from Moscow, heading for Baku.[58] Despite careful preparations, things did not run smoothly. According to Soviet security documents declassified in 2007, during the journey Stalin had no connection with Moscow (the wires were down because of ice) and three criminals managed to sneak onto the tender of the locomotive before being apprehended.[59] Due to the poor state of the track, it was not possible to travel at speed, and so the train did not reach Baku until 9 a.m. on 26 November. Instead of having time for a stopover, the VIPs were whisked straight to the airfield because of concerns about the approach to Tehran.[60] According to Marshal Kliment Voroshilov, they left at 11.30 and 'arrived in Tehran on the British airfield at 15.00, from where we were driven to our embassy'. The two planes that transported the Soviet leadership were heavily protected with 'three groups of nine fighters each: one on each side and one to the front and above'. The technical staff for the conference did not fly to Tehran, but had to make a difficult journey by car from Astara, a border town in the Soviet republic of Azerbaijan.[61]

Roosevelt was now keen to pin down the details of the Tehran conference, especially to ensure time alone with Stalin. Also on his mind was where the Americans should stay, since the US legation in Tehran was situated on the outskirts of the city, about four miles from the British and Soviet missions – both walled enclosures in the centre, separated only by a narrow street. While the president was in Cairo, the head of his Secret Service detail, Mike Reilly, flew to Tehran to reconnoitre the three buildings and assess the security headaches of the teeming city. During his visit, he was troubled to learn from the NKVD that a detachment of German paratroopers had been dropped near the city, some of whom were still at large.[62]

Roosevelt to Stalin, sent 22 November 1943,
received 24 November 1943[63]

I have arrived in Cairo this morning and begin discussions with the Prime Minister. Conferences will follow with the Generalissimo by the end of the week. He will thereupon return to China. The Prime Minister and I with our senior staffs can then proceed to Teheran to meet you, Mr Molotov and your staff officers. If it suits your convenience I could arrive the afternoon of November 29. I am prepared to remain for two to four days depending upon how long you can find it possible to be away from your compelling responsibilities. I would be grateful if you would telegraph me what day you wish to set for the meeting and how long you can stay. I realize that bad weather sometimes causes delays in travel from Moscow to Teheran at this time of the year and therefore would appreciate your keeping me advised of your plans.

I am informed that your Embassy and the British Embassy in Teheran are situated close to each other whereas my Legation is some distance away. I am advised that all three of us would be taking unnecessary risks by driving to and from our meetings if we were staying so far apart from each other.

Where do you think we should live?

It is with keen anticipation that I look forward to our conversations.

The president's penultimate sentence could be read as a neutral question, but it sounds like a hint that he would welcome Soviet hospitality. This would fit with his long-standing desire to create real trust between him and Stalin and avoid any appearance of collusion with Churchill. In addition, he wanted to fathom the personality of the Soviet dictator, and he did not want to miss the unique opportunity to establish a human relationship. Roosevelt had travelled halfway round the world for this encounter: his phrase in the message, 'with keen anticipation', was an understatement. Hull, who saw the president on the eve of his long journey, noted that FDR was looking forward to meeting Stalin 'with the enthusiasm of a boy'.[64]

On the other hand, FDR did not conceal this message from Churchill. Seeking to pre-empt matters, the prime minister answered the president's 'where do you think we should live?' question before Stalin had a chance to reply.

Churchill to Stalin, sent 23 November 1943,
received 23 November 1943[65]

The President has shown me his telegram to you about our meeting. I understand that you wish to make your Headquarters at the Soviet Legation. It seems therefore best for the President to stay in the British Legation which is next door. Both Missions would then be surrounded by a cordon. It is most undesirable for the principals to make repeated journeys to and fro through the streets of Tehran. Better to fix a suitable place and stay inside.

The Foreign Secretary and the British Ambassador will accompany me. In addition, both the President and I are bringing our Chiefs of Staff. I hope we can be with you as long as possible so that there may be a real chance to get together and also to have a full inter-change of views on all aspects of the war between the Principals and High Staff.

It is interesting that, in his reply to Roosevelt, Stalin did not respond to the question about where FDR should stay – simply stating that he would be in Tehran and available on the evening of 28 November. An identical telegram was sent to Churchill.[66]

Stalin to Roosevelt, sent 25 November 1943, received 26 November 1943[67]

Your message from Cairo received. I will be at your service in Tehran the evening of November twenty-eight.

By the time Roosevelt read this brief message from Stalin, he had already received an invitation to stay at the Soviet residence, probably handed to him on 23 November by Vyshinskiy, who passed through Cairo en route to Algeria, where he was to participate in the Allied Commission on Italy. Roosevelt was intrigued by the invitation, but decided to ascertain whether it did come from Stalin himself, and asked the US minister in Tehran, Louis Dreyfus Jr, to find out discreetly. On 25 November, Dreyfus talked with the Soviet chargé d'affaires in Iran, Mikhail Maksimov. According to the latter's record, Dreyfus said that 'in a telegram to Marshal Stalin, Roosevelt, expressing his satisfaction with the upcoming meeting, hints that he wants to stay in the same place with Marshal Stalin'. Maksimov added, 'Dreyfus asked me to send a telegram, gently hinting at the President's wish, but not creating the impression that Roosevelt is angling for an invitation'.[68] In his cable asking for confirmation from the Foreign Ministry, Maksimov underlined the sensitivity of the request: 'Dreyfus added that if for whatever reason this cannot be done, this conversation must remain most secret'.[69]

On 26 November, Molotov, en route to Tehran, instructed Maksimov to tell Dreyfus 'that the Soviet government willingly accepts the President's proposal to accommodate him in the Soviet embassy in Tehran'[70] – the initiative being attributed entirely to Roosevelt. Dreyfus, General Patrick Hurley, the president's special representative, and US Secret Service staff inspected the proposed living quarters, consisting of a separate building with six rooms within the embassy compound. 'From the standpoint of your convenience and comfort, from the standpoint of conference communications and security, these quarters are far more desirable than your own Legation', Hurley cabled Roosevelt. Nevertheless, he told Maksimov that the President was still likely to lodge in the US legation in accordance with the official plan.[71]

After a six-hour flight from Cairo, Roosevelt and the US delegation arrived in Tehran in the afternoon of 27 November. Maksimov immediately met Harriman, who accompanied Roosevelt, and made this record of their conversation: 'The President, said Harriman, is very moved and grateful for being allowed to stay at the Embassy, but, unfortunately, he received the telegram only this morning' – too late to reply or change the arrangements.[72] That night, as Roosevelt and his retinue settled in the US legation, Molotov urgently invited Harriman to speak with him, stressing a threat of 'hostile actions' against the three leaders by 'pro-German elements', and suggesting that they should therefore 'take up on the initial proposal for President Roosevelt to stay at the Soviet Embassy'.[73]

The foreign minister did not back up his warning with specific evidence, and historians are still debating how well prepared was the German covert operation, codenamed 'Long Jump', to assassinate all three leaders of the anti-Hitler coalition.[74] Harriman was never entirely convinced, but promised to convey Molotov's advice to the president.[75] Next morning, 28 November, after a reiterated invitation from Stalin himself, Harriman stressed to FDR the potential danger to the Soviet leader if he had to be transported to and fro from the US legation, given the current security problems. Roosevelt duly accepted Stalin's offer and moved into the house in the Soviet embassy compound that afternoon. Harriman later recalled:

> Churchill, when consulted, was much relieved. He and his colleagues explained that they would have been glad to have the President stay in the British Embassy, but if he went there he would have only a bedroom and sitting room and could not have the privacy with visitors that he would wish.[76]

Within a few minutes of Roosevelt's arrival, Stalin paid a call. 'I am glad to see you,' Roosevelt declared warmly. 'I have tried for a long time to bring this about.' For three-quarters of an hour the two men talked, through interpreters, about the situation on the battlefronts and shared their dislike of de Gaulle in particular and the French in general. Both agreed that France should not be allowed to regain Indochina, favouring two or three decades of international trusteeship under Chinese tutelage for the region, aimed at 'preparing the people for independence'. Roosevelt also advised Stalin not to raise the future of India with Churchill, because he had 'no solution to the question', adding that he personally felt 'the best solution would be reform from the bottom, somewhat on the Soviet line'. Stalin, somewhat better informed, responded that India was a complex matter because of different levels of culture and the lack of relations between the castes, and added drily that 'reform from the bottom would mean revolution'. Just before they moved into the first plenary session, the president added that another reason why he was 'pleased to be in this house' was that it afforded the chance to meet Stalin 'more frequently' and in 'completely informal' circumstances.

Those comments underline the evidence above from previously unknown Soviet correspondence, which shows that, contrary to common belief, it was not so much Stalin who 'lured' Roosevelt to the Soviet embassy, as the president who invited himself to stay with the Soviet leader. The president had concealed his conspiratorial initiative even from close colleagues, to whom he claimed that the invitation had come from the Russians and that he accepted in order to show 'my trust, my full confidence in them. And it did please them. No question about it.' One reason for Soviet pleasure was that they were able to bug the rooms. Stalin assigned Sergo Beria, the son of his NKVD chief, to transcribe the recordings, and the Soviet leader got up unusually early during the conference to pore over the texts and ask detailed questions, even about the president's tone and emphasis. The Americans knew the rooms were probably bugged, but Roosevelt does not appear to have cared. Unlike Churchill in Moscow in August 1942, who unburdened himself of racist abuse about the Russians when warned of likely microphones, Beria gained 'the impression that Roosevelt quite simply said things he couldn't say to Stalin officially. That he conveyed a whole lot of information to him which it was impossible to convey at a state level.'[77]

During his second personal meeting with Stalin in Tehran on 29 November, Roosevelt handed over three documents about joint military planning against Germany and Japan. This initiative came from the Combined Chiefs of Staff who, at their meeting in Cairo on 26 November, had proposed a change of policy from simply 'explaining and defending' their position – as at the Moscow conference – to making 'specific requests on the Soviets'.[78] Apart from seeking to coordinate closer collaboration in operations against Germany, the Americans were particularly keen – picking up on Stalin's comment to Hull – to prepare for eventual Soviet belligerency against Japan. This was an issue that interested the president. During a meeting with his Joint Chiefs en route to Cairo, Roosevelt remarked that 'if Germany should be cleaned up, we must study how many bombers could be operated from the vicinity of Vladivostok'. General Bradley's outline plan in 1942 had suggested one hundred planes, supplied from Alaska.[79]

The first of the three papers FDR handed to Stalin on the 29th dealt with the construction on Soviet territory of US refuelling bases for the shuttle bombing of German military targets in Eastern Europe, which would allow the US Army Air Force significantly to increase its operational range. Agreement had already been reached in principle at the Moscow conference, and the Joint Staffs now wanted to hammer out concrete plans. On the Soviet side, the issues were complicated and it took a few months before preparations began in the Ukraine. Shuttle bombing commenced in the summer of 1944, but the launch bases for US bombers were located in Italy and not in Britain, as had originally been proposed by Roosevelt. The two other papers concerned the Asian war. The first sought Stalin's permission for the US military mission to undertake a detailed survey of possible air bases in the Soviet Maritime Province, from which the US could undertake bombing of Japan. The second requested a formal agreement on exchanging intelligence and plans about 'eventual operations against Japan'. Once again, the Americans were anxious to pin down the USSR on details, whereas the Kremlin did not want to rush into joint planning, let alone the deployment of a large US contingent in Siberia. Stalin promised to study the proposal and then discuss it with Harriman. Serious negotiations between the two countries about these issues would not open in earnest until the turn of 1944–45. But the proposals conveyed by the president at Tehran indicated the new atmosphere among the Big Three now that they and their advisers were finally meeting at the summit.[80]

The main issue at Tehran, however, was the war in Europe. For the first time, the Big Three were negotiating in person, and this changed the dynamics of their relationship. Angry at Churchill's deceptions over strategy, the Americans were determined to pin him down on 'Overlord', and Stalin's presence now provided the weight to outvote him. Invited during the first plenary session on 28 November to express his opinion on strategy, the Soviet leader plumped firmly for France as the best way of 'getting at the heart of Germany'. He not only supported the Americans on the priority of a cross-Channel attack, but insisted – against Churchill's pleas for a continued Italian campaign – that, after Rome had been captured, surplus troops should be sent to southern France to support the breakout from 'Overlord'.[81]

Emboldened by his success, in the plenary session the following day, 29 November, Stalin was even blunter, making three points from a prepared script. First, a firm date should be set for 'Overlord', so that the USSR could plan a complementary offensive from the east. Second, that the Western Allies mount a 'supporting' operation in southern France before or concurrent with 'Overlord' (in contrast with what he termed 'diversionary' operations north of Rome or in the Balkans). And, third, that Roosevelt and Churchill appoint a commander-in-chief for 'Overlord' as soon as possible, because 'nothing would come out of the operation unless one man was made responsible not only for the preparation but for the execution of the operation'. Stalin was following through on the Soviet position ever since the Moscow foreign ministers' conference: their overriding diplomatic priority was 'measures to shorten the war'. And when Churchill continued to huff and puff about 'great possibilities in the Mediterranean', the Soviet leader kept repeating that all such operations were 'diversions'. When the PM insisted that 'Overlord' could only be mounted under certain 'conditions', including the presence of no more than twelve mobile German divisions behind the front, Stalin cut in sarcastically: 'What if there are 13 divisions, not 12?' Finally, the Soviet leader said he wished to 'ask Mr Churchill an indiscreet question, namely do the British really believe in "Overlord" or are they only saying so to reassure the Russians?' Brooke was infuriated by the whole session – 'Winston was not good and Roosevelt even worse. Stalin meticulous' – but he conceded that the Soviet leader 'had a military brain of the highest order. Never once in any of his statements did he make any strategic error, nor did he ever fail to appreciate the implications of a situation with a quick and unerring eye.'[82]

Stalin carried on goading the PM that evening over dinner. He 'lost no opportunity to get in a dig at Mr. Churchill', noted Roosevelt's interpreter, 'Chip' Bohlen. 'Almost every remark that he addressed at the Prime Minister contained some sharp edge, although the Marshal's manner was entirely friendly'. Bohlen judged this to be payback for Churchill's obstructiveness over 'Overlord' during the afternoon. Insisting that without 'really effective measures' to control Germany there would be another war in fifteen to twenty years, Stalin suggested that Churchill had a 'secret liking' for the Germans, and at one point stated that at least 50,000 of the German officer corps should be 'liquidated'. When Churchill exploded at the idea of the 'cold blooded execution' of soldiers without trial, Roosevelt jokingly proposed a compromise: 49,000 executions. An exhausted PM lost his rag and flounced off into the next room. Stalin and Molotov had to run after him, saying that it had all been a bit of fun. 'Stalin has a very captivating manner when he chooses to use it,' Churchill wrote in his memoirs, 'and I never saw him do so to such effect as at this moment'. Mollified, but not entirely persuaded that 'all was chaff', Churchill returned to the dinner table. 'The conversation ended in a convivial embrace', according to Clark Kerr: 'The P.M. and Stalin stood with their hands on each other's shoulders, looking into each other's eyes.'[83]

What happened on 29 November was significant, but should not be over-stated. By now the Russians and Americans had become infuriated by Churchill's endless procrastination about 'Overlord', exacerbated in recent weeks by blatant deception. Both delegations were determined to pin him down to a firm commitment that the Allies would invade France in May 1944 – and on this they succeeded. Roosevelt, keen to build trust with Stalin, went out of his way not to side with Churchill, or to stay with him. But this did not mean that the president had abandoned his relationship with the prime minister; simply that he took it for granted in the context of his priorities for Tehran. Harry Hopkins, who played his usual role as go-between and fixer between FDR and Churchill, told the latter of the president's relief to discover that Stalin was 'get-atable'.[84] And although Roosevelt had three bilateral meetings with Stalin at Tehran, against Churchill's one, the PM and the Soviet leader had already held three meetings and a long Kremlin dinner in August 1942.

The following evening, 30 November, the atmosphere at the special dinner for Churchill's 69th birthday reeked of booze and bonhomie, with toasts abounding. Churchill paid a warm tribute to the president and also toasted 'Stalin the Great' as one of 'the great figures of Russian history'. The Soviet leader's teasing of Churchill did not abate: when the PM admitted that the political complexion of Britain was becoming, if not red at least 'a trifle pinker', Stalin responded instantly: 'That is a sign of good health.' The president claimed the last word, adroitly picking the theme of political 'complexion'. He acknowledged that their three countries had 'different customs and philosophies and ways of life'. But, he continued, 'we have proved here that the varying ideals of our nations can come together in a harmonious whole, moving unitedly for the common good of ourselves and of the world. So as we leave this historic gathering, we can see in the sky, for the first time, that traditional symbol of hope, the rainbow.'[85]

After the president had left, Stalin had a very amiable exchange with the prime minister.

'I want to call Mr Churchill my friend.'

'Call me Winston,' the PM responded. 'I call you Joe behind your back.'

'No, I want to call you my friend. I want to be allowed to call you my good friend.'

Once that had been agreed, Churchill declared: 'I drink to the Proletarian masses.'

'I drink to the Conservative Party,' Stalin replied, whereupon they tottered off to their beds around midnight.

('What piffle great men sometimes talk,' Clark Kerr observed *sotto voce.*)[86]

Undoubtedly Churchill felt less satisfied with Tehran than his two partners, who were delighted to reach agreement at last about 'Overlord'. The Americans were also pleased that Stalin was now talking about eventual entry into the Asian war, and Roosevelt had time to air some of his views about the four policemen and postwar peacekeeping in one of their private discussions. The PM was unable to draw out Stalin on his own territorial goals, receiving the somewhat ominous answer: 'There is no need to speak at the present time about any Soviet desires, but when the time comes, we will speak.'[87] Churchill, already feverish before the end of the conference, began to entertain dark fears about the future: 'I realised at Teheran for the first time,' he said later, 'what a small nation we are. There I sat with the great Russian bear on one side of me, with paws outstretched, and on the other side the great American buffalo, and between the two sat the poor little English donkey.' But it was the donkey, he added, 'who was the only one, the only one of the three, who knew the right way home'.[88]

Indeed, the 'donkey' soon was trotting again. The British regained some strategic freedom of manoeuvre by persuading the Americans at the second Cairo conference to abandon a proposed amphibious operation in the Andaman Islands in the Bay of Bengal ('Buccaneer') – an attempt by Roosevelt to placate Chiang Kai-shek. Cancellation would free up landing craft, with which the PM hoped to exploit opportunities in the Mediterranean. And his position was further strengthened when Roosevelt finally decided on 6 December, while still in Egypt, that Eisenhower, not Marshall, would command 'Overlord' – ostensibly on the grounds that he 'could not sleep easily' if the Army chief of staff were not at his side in Washington. Churchill was also content. The Americans had been pushing for a 'super supreme commander' for the whole of the European theatre, as a way to rein in British 'diversions' in the Mediterranean – a job suited to Marshall's stature. Once it became clear that Britain would not accept the 'super' idea, Eisenhower – vastly experienced as a commander thanks to North Africa and southern Italy – was the logical choice for 'Overlord'. And Britain's consolation prize – a British commander for the whole of the Mediterranean, in the ample person of General Sir Henry Maitland-Wilson (known as 'Jumbo') – suited Churchill just fine.[89]

Stalin was also pleased when he heard the news from Roosevelt. The Soviet leader had been insistent about the need to appoint a commander for

'Overlord', and he also esteemed Eisenhower as a tried and trusted war leader, unlike the strategist and planner Marshall. To Harriman's 'great relief', Stalin therefore approved and even added the explicit sentence 'I welcome the appointment of General Eisenhower' to Molotov's otherwise rather formulaic acknowledgement.[90]

*****

The Tehran conference was hailed in Allied capitals. The images of Allied unity were compelling (plate 1) and the 'Declaration of the Three Powers' featured in many major newspapers: 'We came here with hope and determination. We leave here, friends in fact, in spirit and in purpose.' *Pravda* called it a 'landmark meeting' and 'a clear indication of the increasing strength of the Anglo-Soviet–American fighting alliance, of a deeper cooperation between the three great powers.'[91] *The Times* of London said it showed that the Allies shared a 'common desire to bring the war to a quick and decisive end and return security and freedom to Europe'.[92] The *New York Times* dubbed Tehran the 'Victory Conference' and only a few formerly isolationist, Republican papers such as the *Chicago Tribune* warned about the advance of 'Red' power. At the end of 1943, 51 per cent of Americans expressed confidence about postwar cooperation with the USSR, compared with only 36 per cent before the Moscow and Tehran conferences.[93]

Stalin sought to underscore the USSR's positive view of the conference and its achievements. He personally amended the title of the report by the Soviet TASS news agency on the outcome from the 'The Conference of the Heads of Governments of the Soviet Union, United States and Britain' to, more positively, 'The Conference of the Leaders of the Three Allied Powers'.[94] And he revised Molotov's circular to Soviet ambassadors on the conference to smooth over certain differences between the Allies and strengthen the sense of agreement on basic issues.[95] The following two messages from Roosevelt, both dated 3 December, reflect his own positive impression of the conference – which, in the second, he called 'a great success'. The first was a handwritten letter in a sealed envelope, which Harriman was not able to give Stalin until 18 December, possibly because the Soviet leader was indisposed with flu.

Roosevelt to Stalin, sent 3 December 1943, received 18 December 1943[96]

The weather conditions were ideal for crossing the mountains the day of our departure from Tehran so that we had an easy and comfortable flight to Cairo. I hasten to send you my personal thanks for your thoughtfulness and hospitality in providing living quarters for me in your Embassy at Tehran. I was not only extremely comfortable there but I am very conscious of how much more we were able to accomplish in a brief period of time because we were such close neighbors throughout our stay.

I view those momentous days of our meeting with the greatest satisfaction as being an important milestone in the progress of human affairs. I thank you and the members of your staff and household for the many kindnesses to me and to the members of my staff.

I am just starting home and will visit my troops in Italy on the way.

Roosevelt to Stalin, sent 3 December 1943, received 4 December 1943[97]

Our party have arrived safely at our destination and we earnestly hope that by this time you also have arrived safely. The conference, I consider, was a great success and I feel sure that it was an historic event in the assurance not only of our ability to wage war together but also to work for the peace to come in utmost harmony. I enjoyed very much our personal talks together and particularly the opportunity of meeting you face to face. I look forward to meeting you sometime again. Until that time, I wish the greatest success to you and your Armies.

The response from Stalin to Roosevelt does not have the usual mark of approval from the 'Boss' or any traces of being edited by him. The text was drafted by Molotov and then revised on a typescript version (additions in italics).[98] It is possible that both the wording and the changes were agreed with Stalin over the phone. If so, the Soviet leader was clearly warming up the tone of his correspondence with Roosevelt in the more cordial post-Tehran atmosphere.

Stalin to Roosevelt, sent 6 December 1943, received 6 December 1943[99]

Thank you for your telegram.

I agree that the *Teheran* Conference was a great success and that our personal meetings were, in many respects, extremely important. I hope that the common foe of our peoples – Hitlerite Germany – will soon feel it. *Now there is confidence that* and our peoples will harmoniously act together *during the present time and after this war is over.*

I wish *the best* successes to you and your armed forces in the coming *important* operations.

I also hope that our meeting in Teheran should not be regarded as the last one, and that we shall meet again.

Having finally received Roosevelt's warm personal message of 3 December, Stalin expressed agreement with the president that their close association in Tehran had yielded positive results. In his reference to 'fate', Stalin probably had in mind the information about the assassination attempt on the leaders of the Big Three, which served as an incentive for Roosevelt's move to the Soviet embassy.

Stalin to Roosevelt, sent 20 December 1943, received 20 December 1943[100]

I thank you for Your letter, which Your Ambassador has extended to me on December 18.

I am glad that fate has given me an opportunity to render you a service in Teheran. I also attach important significance to our meeting and to the conversations taken place there which concerned such substantial questions of accelerating of our common victory and establishment of future lasting peace between the peoples.

Churchill was exhausted from several weeks of arduous travel and intense conferences. He had left London with a heavy cold and after Tehran this went onto his lungs, complicated by heart fibrillations on 14 December. 'Am stranded amid ruins of Carthage,' he told Roosevelt, 'with fever which has ripened into pneumonia.' For several days his condition seemed life-threatening, and his wife flew out to be with him. Such was the gravity of his condition that she was able to report to daughter Mary that he had 'consented not to smoke, and to drink only weak whisky and soda'.[101]

Nevertheless, diplomacy was not forgotten. Like Roosevelt carrying vivid impressions of Tehran, Churchill sent Stalin a generous birthday message in accordance with their now established custom. The novel salutation 'my friend' is perhaps an echo of their post-prandial exchange on 30 November.

Churchill to Stalin, sent 20 December 1943, received 20 December 1943[102]

Cordial greetings, my friend, upon the occasion of your birthday. May the coming year see the culmination of our struggle against the common foe.

Stalin responded warmly and Churchill reciprocated.

Stalin to Churchill, sent 22 December 1943[103]

Please accept my heartfelt thanks for your friendly greetings on the occasion of my birthday. With all my heart I wish you speedy recovery and return to complete health, which is so essential for delivering the decisive blow to the enemy.

Churchill to Stalin, sent 25 December 1943, received 26 December 1943[104]

Thank you so much for your message. I am making a good recovery and am already fully at work again on matters of common interest to us both. I send my best wishes to you and your gallant armies for further successes in 1944.

News of the resumption of the northern convoys (convoy JW55B sailed from Britain on 20 December) was followed by other good tidings: the sinking of the German battleship *Scharnhorst*, which had presented a serious threat to the convoys off the coast of Norway. The sailing of JW55B was detected by German aircraft on 22 December, and the *Scharnhorst* left port in pursuit on Christmas Day. But British intelligence knew this from Enigma intercepts, and Admiral Sir Bruce Fraser, commander-in-chief of the Home Fleet, dispatched a group of cruisers, which destroyed the German battleship's radar controls. He then entered the conflict on his flagship HMS *Duke of York* (which had carried Churchill to the first Washington conference in December 1941). After shells from the *Duke of York* struck its boilers, the *Scharnhorst* lost speed, and soon became a sitting duck for torpedoes from the British cruisers. Its destruction eliminated the last German capital ship operating off Norway – *Tirpitz* having been severely damaged by British midget submarines in September. The Battle of the North Cape, as it became known, also avenged the *Scharnhorst*'s impudent 'Channel Dash' from Brest to Wilhelmshaven in February 1942 which had so humiliated Churchill and the Royal Navy. The PM took pleasure in telling Stalin the news.

Churchill to Stalin, sent 27 December 1943, received 27 December 1943[105]

The Arctic convoys to Russia have brought us luck. Yesterday the enemy attempted to intercept with the battle cruiser *Scharnhorst*. The Commander-in-Chief, Admiral Fraser, with the *Duke of York* (35,000 ton battleship) cut off *Scharnhorst*'s retreat and after an action sank her.

Am much better and off to the south for convalescence.

The initial draft of Stalin's reply to this message was dry and terse: 'To you and the valiant British Navy, congratulations on the sinking of the German battle cruiser *Scharnhorst*.' In the final version, Stalin made the message warmer and friendlier, appreciating the importance of this success for Churchill personally, and for the future of the northern convoys.[106]

Stalin to Churchill, sent 27 December 1943, received 29 December 1943[107]

Thank you for the message regarding the *Scharnhorst*. I send you personally and also Admiral Sir Bruce Fraser and the valiant sailors of the *Duke of York* my congratulations on this splendid blow, the sinking of the German battleship *Scharnhorst*. I am glad you are recovering.

I shake your hand firmly.

Stalin's congratulations to the Royal Navy were appreciated by Churchill. On 29 December, he reciprocated by noting the Soviet recapture of Korosten in the northern Ukraine, after a tough struggle. The PM also mentioned the new Soviet state anthem, about which he had been informed by the Moscow embassy. The 'Internationale' had been banned from the BBC by Churchill in 1941 and remained a sensitive matter, because of its revolutionary lyrics ('Servile masses arise, arise ... And the last fight let us face', etc.) though, as Clark Kerr admitted to Stalin, even Tories often whistled its catchy tune. Stalin advised the ambassador that they should learn the new anthem: 'Its tune is a little more complicated.'[108]

Slavsya, Otechestvo nashe svobodnoye! ('Be glorious, our free Fatherland!') was played for the first time on Soviet radio on 1 January 1944. Despite laudatory references to 'great Lenin' and 'Stalin our leader', this was a hymn of praise above all to 'Great Russia' and to eventual 'victory' over the 'barbarian invaders' – infused not with ideology but patriotism. Its language was another sign of how wartime Russia seemed to be changing; its timing, at the start of a new year, underlined a growing sense that the end was finally in sight.

Churchill to Stalin, sent 29 December 1943, received 1 January 1944[109]

Thank you so much. I am informing Admiral Fraser, his officers and men of your congratulations. They will welcome the tribute from a gallant and honoured Ally. I am so glad you have retaken Korostet [sic], whose loss you told us about at Teheran. I only wish we could meet once a week. Please give my regards to

Molotov. If you will send me the music of the new Soviet Russian Anthem, I could arrange to have it played by the BBC on all occasions when important Russian victories were announced.

*****

The cordiality of the messages between the three leaders at the end of 1943 exemplified the new quality of their relationship, as a result of meeting face to face. Roosevelt had always been disposed to get on with Stalin, but even Churchill – despite the setbacks at Tehran for British policy – was affected. The PM's line to Stalin on 29 December, 'I only wish we could meet once a week', was no one-off: he would make similar comments to and about Stalin a month later, reflecting his deepening conviction about the 'two Stalins' – the human being with whom he could do business, and the man in the machine who could suddenly and inexplicably throw a spanner in the works.

Nevertheless, Tehran took its toll on all three of them, not just Churchill. Stalin returned to Moscow with a high temperature and serious flu, from which he took ten days to recover.[110] The first official visitor to his office after Tehran was received on 11 December and stayed only fifteen minutes; Stalin did not resume his regular schedule until the 15th.[111] FDR came off worst of all, having travelled the farthest and being the least robust member of the Big Three. He, too, contracted influenza in Tehran and could not shake it off. While Stalin's poor health remained a secret, Roosevelt's indisposition became very public. On 11 January 1944, he was obliged to cancel his traditional appearance on Capitol Hill to deliver the annual State of the Union address – reading it instead over the radio as a fireside chat from the White House. 'This "flu" is Hell,' he wrote to his cousin Polly Delano three days later. 'I am not over mine yet.'[112] Weeks later the Wheelchair President was still complaining of persistent headaches and exhaustion, frequently nodding off while reading official papers. In fact, the next year would see a steady decline in his health. For Franklin D. Roosevelt, in a very personal sense Tehran marked the beginning of the end.

11

THE SPIRIT OF TEHRAN EVAPORATES

(January to March 1944)

THE SPIRIT OF TEHRAN was palpable. It can be seen, for instance, in Churchill's reciprocation on 9 January of Stalin's 'handshake' in his message of 27 December 1943, and in his comment on 24 January: 'I am sure that if we had been together these difficulties would not have occurred.' In a message to Eden on 16 January 1944, the PM spoke of his changing attitude towards the Soviet Union: 'The tremendous victories of the Russian armies, the deep-seated changes in the Russian State and Government, the new confidence which has grown in our hearts towards Stalin – these have all had their effect.'[1] Churchill was conscious that those Russian victories meant that the USSR would inexorably become a force in Eastern Europe, and that London and Washington therefore needed to forge a working relationship with Moscow. In the opening months of 1944, his concern to do so was most evident over two issues – the fate of the Italian navy and the future of Poland. He devoted a substantial amount of time and energy to these issues, acting – as usual – as the front man for both Britain and America, and drafting most of the joint messages sent by himself and Roosevelt.

The Soviet demand for a share in the Italian navy and merchant fleet dated back to the previous autumn, when Italy surrendered, and developed into an irritating diplomatic argument for several reasons. Churchill and Roosevelt had handled the matter sympathetically, but casually, at Tehran, so Stalin, attentive as ever about details, pushed back persistently in the New Year. The Kremlin's pressure partly reflected its desire to be treated as a diplomatic equal – a refrain in Ambassador Clark Kerr's messages from Moscow – but was also an early marker about reparations for the losses and devastation that the country had suffered. This would be a major element of Soviet war aims. The Western response was greatly complicated by fears among the British and US military that any attempt to send Italian vessels to the USSR might precipitate the collapse of the Badoglio government and a mutiny among the Italian armed forces at a time when the country's 'co-belligerency' still mattered to Allied strategy. After the dramatic events of the previous autumn, the Italian campaign had stalled. From mid-January, Allied forces battered away unsuccessfully against Hitler's Gustav Line, anchored by Monte Cassino and its ancient Benedictine monastery. An amphibious landing at Anzio failed to break out towards Rome and also became bogged down. Rather than unsettle the Italian situation even further, Churchill and Roosevelt – faced with Stalin's persistence about the ships – decided to placate him with some of their own warships and merchant vessels, mostly obsolescent because of the imperatives of 'Overlord'. In the end, the bulk of the ships came from Britain.

While the British and Americans inched north in Italy, the Red Army was moving westward, fast – aided by an unusually mild winter and the more clement climate of the Ukraine. Stalin now felt increasingly confident about the military position. According to Marshal Zhukov's memoirs, on his return from Tehran the Soviet leader said 'Roosevelt promised to mount broad campaigns in France in 1944. I think that he will keep his word. And if he doesn't, we'll have enough power to finish off Hitler's Germany alone.'[2] The Red Army's advance was not without its setbacks and, as usual, victories were won at prodigious human cost; but by early 1944 – with Leningrad finally liberated – the Soviets were on the edge of the Baltic states and nearing the borders of Poland. The destiny of Eastern European countries that had been the subject of intense diplomatic debate between the three Allies in the spring of 1942, when the Anglo-Soviet treaty was being negotiated, was now about to be settled by force of arms.

Churchill knew the Allies could do nothing about the Baltics, but Poland was a different matter because of Britain's guarantee of Polish independence in 1939 and the presence in London of the Polish government-in-exile, led (since General Sikorski's mysterious death in July 1943) by the People's Party leader, Stanisław Mikołajczyk. Back home in mid-January after his enforced recuperation in North Africa, Churchill threw himself into an intense effort to broker a Polish–Soviet agreement, holding long meetings with the London Poles and composing intricate messages to Stalin, beginning on 28 January with one addressed to the Soviet leader as 'my friend and comrade', in the hope that they could solve the issue together. Churchill's aim was to persuade the Polish émigrés to accept, broadly speaking, the Curzon Line as the eastern border of the new Poland, in the hope that they would then work fairly amicably with

Stalin over a postwar government that was free yet also friendly to the USSR. Given the deep-rooted hostility on both sides – evident in Stalin's derisory comments and the determination of many London Poles to insist, in defiance of all military reality, on Poland's 1939 borders – Churchill's hopes were utopian. That he persisted for so long is testimony not only to his typical 'bulldog' traits, but also to that 'new confidence' about Stalin that stemmed from Tehran. Nevertheless, by the beginning of March, with the Soviet leader claiming that the Polish government clearly did not want 'normal relations' with the USSR and so the time was not yet ripe for a solution, the PM slumped into gloom about the future. Though real, the spirit of Tehran proved hard to sustain in the face of international realities.

Churchill's predominance at the Western end of the Stalin correspondence is even more evident than usual in early 1944. Of the forty-three messages exchanged among the Big Three in January and February, only seven emanated from Roosevelt – mostly State Department drafts that the president merely tweaked. As we have seen, FDR never evinced the same interest as Churchill in the epistolary relationship, but his detachment was accentuated by his chronic ill health after Tehran, with bouts of flu and bronchitis that he could not shake off, together with listlessness and at times exhaustion. In any case, on the Polish issue, FDR deliberately played only a supporting role – backing up at times Churchill's bid for a settlement. Good relations with Stalin were always his priority and he did not wish to have his fingerprints on any Polish settlement, for fear of antagonizing Polish-American voters ahead of the 1944 election. That said, some messages do reflect the president's deeper concerns: for instance, one on 25 February about bringing the USSR into the process of postwar economic planning. In his State of the Union message on 11 January, the president was at his most radical, calling on Congress to extend and enshrine New Deal principles such as employment, basic housing, medical care and education in a Second Bill of Rights. 'America's own rightful place in the world depends in large part upon how fully these and similar rights have been carried into practice for all our citizens,' he declared. 'For unless there is security here at home there cannot be lasting peace in the world.'[3]

Discussing relations with the USSR in the House of Commons on 22 February, Churchill again extolled the benefits of summitry. 'There would be very few differences between the three great Powers,' he declared, 'if their chief representatives could meet once a month. By such meetings, both formal and informal, all difficulties could be brought out freely and frankly, and the most delicate matters could be approached without the risk of jars or misunderstandings, such as too often arise when written communications are the only channel.' Nevertheless,

Churchill went on, 'geography imposes its baffling obstacles', which meant that correspondence was inescapable most of the time. But the PM tried to reinforce the messages via personal contacts through trusted intermediaries, especially Ambassador Clark Kerr, who had established a genuine rapport with Stalin. This was evident at Tehran when Stalin was puffing on a cigarette, only to be ticked off by Clark Kerr: 'It's cissy to smoke cigarettes.' Churchill sat quaking at the likely response, but Stalin stubbed out the cigarette almost sheepishly and fumbled for his pipe.[4] In February 1944, the PM wanted Clark Kerr to reinforce key messages with a personal interview, but this proved difficult to arrange because Stalin had gone reclusive again (officially said to be 'at the front', as in July 1943). As a result, a key message about the Italian ships was not delivered for two weeks, unnecessarily exacerbating friction over the issue.

Professional diplomats, however, were sceptical about the growing fascination with summitry and personal correspondence. Typical is this letter from Christopher Warner, head of the FO's Russia desk, to a colleague in Moscow:

> It is very important, we think, to try to get the great ones here out of their habit of 'extremes' about Russia. They must take things in their stride otherwise the Russian Government will be always pulling their legs. Besides, the attitude of mind which throws the hat high in the air when Molotov and Joe turn on their kindly and responsive mood for the benefit of the Prime Minister and Secretary of State, and gets in a flap whenever the Soviet press is a bit naughty, is most prejudicial to a sound conduct of policy, surely.

Warner said he was opposed to a policy of cooperation 'if on the Russian side it is going to be all take and no give'; he believed 'we must discover whether the Russians want real co-operation and we must make the attempt, surely, to show them what it means. I am afraid I think the Teheran and Moscow Conferences were dangerously wrong in this respect and we are now paying the penalty.'[5]

As the war neared its denouement, this debate about personal contacts versus formal diplomacy, about open-handedness versus hard bargaining, would become ever more salient in London and Washington.

*****

Stalin to Churchill, sent 2 January 1944, received 3 January 1944[6]

I am sending you the music of the new Soviet Anthem in the next mail. Monsieur Molotov conveys to you his gratitude for your greetings, and his best wishes. I fully share your idea of the desirability of our frequent meetings.

Gusev handed a copy of the anthem to the British on 10 January. When Clark Kerr returned to Moscow at the end of the month, he told Stalin that Churchill 'liked the new tune' and found it 'lively and inspiring'.[7]

Stalin's 'get well' message to Roosevelt, as usual in Gromyko's ponderous translation, was further evidence of the warm afterglow of Tehran.

Stalin to Roosevelt, sent 4 January 1944, received 4 January 1944[8]

I am glad to learn from the information published in the press that you feel better. I convey to you the best wishes, and mainly – the wishes of quick and complete recovery.

Churchill was pleased with what he called Stalin's 'further friendly message' of 2 January, and kept up the rhythm with a chatty reply, congratulating the Red Army on its recent 'splendid' advances and assuring Stalin that 'everything is going at full blast' for 'Overlord'. General Bernard Montgomery, the British hero of Alamein in November 1942, had now been appointed operational commander for the Normandy landings, serving as Eisenhower's deputy.[9]

Edvard Beneš, the premier of the Czechoslovak government-in-exile (whom Churchill called 'Beans' behind his back) had visited Moscow in December 1943 and found Stalin very warm about the new relationship among the Allies, as he told Churchill when they met in Marrakech on 4 January. The PM cabled Eden: 'He said he was instructed by Stalin to give me the most friendly greeting on his behalf. Beans said that we really all of us got together at Teheran, following on Moscow, and the atmosphere is absolutely friendly and quite different from former times.'[10] The Czech leader was convinced that the Soviets were ready to normalize relations with Poland and guarantee its independence, on condition that the Poles recognize the eastern borders along the Curzon Line and replace the most anti-Soviet figures in the London government. After poring over the map, Stalin had drawn up the new Polish borders, in a document which Beneš brought with him. As Churchill wrote to Roosevelt:

This gives the Poles a fine place to live in more than 300 miles square and with 250 miles of seaboard on the Baltic. As soon as I get home I shall go all out with the Polish government to close with this or something like it ... If I can get this tidied up early in February, a visit from them to you would clinch matters.[11]

However, on 5 January, without consulting the British or Americans, the Mikołajczyk government issued a declaration which offered no hint of recognition of the new borders, and urged the Polish underground to cooperate with the advancing Soviet troops only if Soviet–Polish relations had been restored. It was this démarche that Stalin mentioned in his response to Churchill. The cable was drafted in Molotov's office. The 'Boss' added one very pungent sentence about the Poles (italicized).[12]

Stalin to Churchill, sent 7 January 1944, received 8 January 1944[13]

I have received your message of January 5th. I am pleased by your information that the preparations for 'Overlord' are in full swing and that you are preparing other measures in the course of this month.

I feel bound to say, in as much as you have touched on this subject, that if one is to judge by the last declaration of the Polish emigrant Government and by other expressions of Polish representatives then, as is apparent, there is no foundation for reckoning on the possibility of bringing these circles to reason. *They are incorrigible.*

Please give my thanks and good wishes to Lord Beaverbrook.

Our attacks are continuing for the time being with definite success especially in the south although the Germans put up stubborn resistance wherever they can.

In his reply, Churchill alluded to the continued fighting in the Ukraine and, cryptically, to the planned landing at Anzio, on the west coast of Italy, southwest of Rome. Eden was unhappy about relying simply on Beneš's account of Stalin's opinion and about Churchill's reiterated pledge to 'bring [the] Poles to reason',[14] but the PM now had the bit between his teeth. He varied his usual refrain about bombing with another evocation of the spirit of Tehran. His final sentence about a 'handshake' warmly reciprocated the end of Stalin's message of 27 December 1943.

Churchill to Stalin, sent 9 January 1944, received 12 January 1944[15]

We are watching almost from hour to hour the marvellous advances of the Soviet Armies. To my lay mind it looks as if Jmerinka [Zhmerinka] might be very important. I am well enough to go home quite soon and propose to do utmost to bring Poles to reason, on lines of your talk with Benes. If we were in Tehran again, I would now be saying to you across the table: 'Please let me know in plenty of time when we are to stop knocking down Berlin so as to leave sufficient billeting accommodation for the Soviet armies.'

All plans for our Italian Battle have been satisfactorily settled here. I return your handshake well and truly.

Another important question concerned Yugoslavia. By the end of 1943, Churchill, despite his personal dislike of Josip Broz Tito's communist partisans, began to appreciate that they were the main force of resistance to the Germans, and fought them more effectively than the pro-royalist Chetniks under General Draža Mihailović. The British already had a liaison officer with Tito in the person of F.W. 'Bill' Deakin, Churchill's research assistant in the 1930s. In January 1944, they flew in a new mission to support Tito under the former British diplomat Fitzroy Maclean, followed by the PM's own son Randolph. Churchill did not, however, wish to abandon the Yugoslav monarch Peter II Karadordević and tried to persuade Tito to recognize the king. An agreement to send a Soviet mission to Tito was reached in Tehran. With British help, this arrived in Cyprus in mid-January and reached Yugoslavia a few weeks later. In a message from Churchill to Tito on 8 January, which he copied to Stalin, the PM expressed the hope that the Soviet military mission would work harmoniously with Maclean's legation. Perhaps by sharing this chatty letter with the Soviet leader Churchill wished to strengthen personal relations and political accord. As far as can be judged, however, the effect proved to be the opposite. The Soviet military already knew about the spectacular arrival of Randolph Churchill. When this news was relayed to Stalin, he said, 'Make no mistake, sons of premiers do not parachute in and show up in other people's headquarters for no reason.'[16]

Churchill was at pains to inform Stalin that the new Soviet anthem would be premiered on BBC radio on 16 January. This was not a one-off event. Churchill told Brendan Bracken, the minister of information, that the BBC should say the music 'has been sent to me personally at my request by Marshal Stalin'; he also instructed that it should be 'played on all occasions when news of Russian victories is received'.[17]

Churchill to Stalin, sent 13 January 1944, received 15 January 1944[18]

Music promised in your message of the 2nd January now received and will be played before the 9 p.m. News on Sunday night and by the full Symphony Orchestra of the BBC.

The winter of 1941–42 had been Russia's coldest for nearly a century and a half; by contrast, the winter of 1943–44 was the shortest and warmest in living memory. Furthermore, the southern Ukraine has a relatively mild climate which, despite sudden thaws and consequent *rasputitsa* quagmires, made it possible for the Red Army to continue its operations without a break.[19] In January and February 1944, the main focus of the offensive was the right bank of the Dnieper, pushing west and southwest from Kiev. The fighting ebbed and flowed: Stalin's next message mentioned the German counter-attack around the city of Vinnitsa, near the site of 'Werewolf', Hitler's forward headquarters in 1942–43. The Soviet leader maintained Churchill's playful tone regarding Berlin, as if continuing their chat in Tehran and, interestingly, talked of their forthcoming 'joint arrival' in Berlin. But keeping up the pressure about 'Overlord', he reminded the PM 'we still have a very long way to go'.[20]

Stalin's concern was not unjustified. On 7 January, the PM had learned that early June 1944, not May, was the likely date, in view of the necessary conjunction of moon and tides; but on the 14th, Roosevelt cautioned against sharing this with Stalin: 'I think the psychology of bringing this thing up at this time would be very bad in view of the fact that it is only a little over a month since the three of us agreed on the statement in Tehran.'[21]

Churchill continued to use convoys as a means of appeasing Stalin before 'Overlord' was mounted, squeezing in an additional one before the invasion – which he promised was his 'first care'. Stalin said this would be of 'considerable value to our front'.[22]

The Anglo-American landing at Anzio (codename 'Shingle') began on the night of 21–22 January. Churchill had become obsessed by the operation, seeing it as a splendid chance to seize Rome, break the deadlock in Italy and justify renewed concentration on the Mediterranean. The landing itself achieved complete surprise, but the cautious American commander, General John Lucas, dug in against a likely German counter-attack instead of pushing forward. In his memoirs, Churchill presented Anzio as 'a story of high opportunity and shattered hopes': instead of 'hurling a wild cat on to the shore', what resulted was just a 'stranded whale'. The ensuing four-month delay in breaking out of the beachhead provided what he called 'very adverse data for "Overlord"'. When conveying the initial news of Anzio to Stalin, however, Churchill's mood was still upbeat and expectant: 'I hope to have good news for you before long.'[23]

The joint message from Churchill and Roosevelt of 23 January on transferring Italian ships to the USSR goes back to an aside in Churchill's message to Stalin on 18 September 1941. Molotov formally raised this idea with Eden and Hull during the Moscow conference, seizing on a statement by Churchill that over a hundred naval vessels and 150,000 tons of merchant shipping had passed into Anglo-American hands. Since, Molotov said coyly, the three of them were 'to some extent businessmen as well as politicians', he proposed that one battleship, one cruiser, eight destroyers, four submarines and 40,000 tons of merchant shipping should be transferred from Italy to the USSR as part-payment for two years of devastating war against the Soviet people. Eden urged a positive answer – hoping to deflect the continuing pressure for a second front – and Clark Kerr argued that Western consent would have 'a stupendous psychological effect' on Soviet sentiment, opining that the request was 'based mainly upon reasons of prestige'.[24]

In other words, those responsible for conducting British diplomacy saw this proposal as another facet of the Soviet desire to be treated as equals. On 27 October, the Cabinet had agreed in principle that the Soviets should be given some share in the Italian fleet, but it discerned many practical difficulties, and so a formal answer was postponed until the Big Three met at Tehran.[25] When pressed there by Stalin and Molotov on 1 December, Churchill requested time to sort things out with the Italians. 'In two months, a battleship and a cruiser: would that do?' he asked. 'What about the end of January?' shot back Stalin, precise as ever.[26] Roosevelt was also sympathetic to the Soviet request and the motives behind it. With Harriman under pressure from the dogged Molotov, the president unilaterally decided just before Christmas that the USSR should get the use of a third of the Italian fleet for the duration of the war. This gesture of symbolic equity actually reflected the thinking behind Molotov's request: his list of ships had been calculated by the Soviet navy's high command as a rough approximation of one-third of the Italian fleet's combat power.[27] But the Combined Chiefs of Staff were vehemently opposed to such 'generosity'. They argued that such a blow to Italian pride might threaten Italian cooperation in the war effort (supplies, fleet repair facilities, etc.) in the run-up to 'Overlord' and 'Anvil', for which the ships might themselves be useful. In any case, the Italian vessels would take months to refit for northern waters, and the Admiralty insisted that its dockyards were full.[28]

Recuperating in Marrakech, Churchill dismissed most of these arguments as wrong or exaggerated. 'It is far more important', he told Eden, 'to convince Stalin that when we say a thing we mean business than to study the frills and flounces of the Italians.' He also had an ulterior motive: 'I am particularly anxious to make good on this Italian ship business with the Russians because I may want some easement you know of in respect of the "Overlord" dates, and we also want friendly consideration from the Russians in the Polish business.'[29] But the military remained obdurate, and so on 10 January Churchill came up with an alternative – to 'lend UJ at least one of our battleships which we have laid up for want of manpower'. By keeping faith in this way 'it would certainly show the greatest goodwill on our part which is indeed deserved by their splendid victories'.[30]

Although Eden believed Stalin's real aim was 'prestige accruing from the acquisition of Italian ships,'[31] Churchill's idea provided the basis for an agreement thrashed out with Roosevelt over the next two weeks, namely offering one British battleship and one US cruiser for immediate Soviet use. In a message prepared by Admiral Leahy, the president urged Churchill to add the eight destroyers and four submarines as originally requested by Molotov – either from Italy or from the Royal Navy – but the PM deprecated any attempt to pressure the Italians or deplete British naval resources. The president conceded, and the final version of the message was sent to Moscow from London on 23 January.[32]

Churchill and Roosevelt to Stalin, sent 23 January 1944, received 23 January 1944[33]

With regard to the handing over to the Soviets of Italian shipping asked for by the Soviet Government at the Moscow Conference and agreed to with you by us both at Tehran, we have received a memorandum by the Combined Chiefs of Staff contained in our immediately following telegram.[34] For the reasons set out in this memorandum, we think it would be dangerous to our triple interests actually to carry out any transfer or to say anything about it to the Italians until their cooperation is no longer of operational importance.

Nevertheless, if after full consideration you desire us to proceed, we will make secret approach to Badoglio with a view to concluding the necessary arrangements without their becoming generally known to the Italian naval forces. If in this way agreement could be reached, such arrangements with the Italian naval authorities as were necessary could be left to him. These arrangements would have to be on the lines that the Italian ships selected should be sailed to suitable Allied ports where they would be collected by Russian crews, who would sail into Russian northern ports which are the only ones open where any refitting necessary would be undertaken.

We are, however, very conscious of the dangers of the above course for the reasons we have laid before you and we have therefore decided to propose the following alternative, which, from military points of view, has many advantages.

The British battleship *Royal Sovereign* has recently completed refitting in the United States. She is fitted with radar for all types of armament. The United States will make one light cruiser available at approximately the same time.

His Majesty's Government and the United States Government are willing for their part that these vessels should be taken over at British ports by Soviet crews and sailed to North Russian ports. You could then make such alterations as you find necessary for Arctic conditions.

These vessels would be temporarily transferred on loan to Soviet Russia and would fly the Soviet flag until, without prejudice to military operations, the Italian vessels can be made available.

His Majesty's Government and the United States Government will each arrange to provide 20,000 tons of merchant shipping to be available as soon as practicable and until the Italian merchant ships can be obtained without prejudice to the projected essential operations 'Overlord', 'Anvil'.

This alternative has the advantage that the Soviet Government would obtain the use of vessels at a very much earlier date than if they all had to be refitted and rendered suitable for Northern waters. Thus, if our efforts should take a favourable turn with the Turks and the Straits become open, these vessels would be ready to operate in the Black Sea. We hope you will very carefully consider this alternative, which we think is in every way superior to the first proposal.

On 17 January 1944, *Pravda* published a report from Cairo, stating that, according to 'reliable sources', the British had held secret talks with Joachim Ribbentrop, Hitler's foreign minister, in Spain or Portugal about a possible separate peace. This claim infuriated the Allied capitals. Diplomats and journalists were at a loss, trying to guess a pretext for such a rumour. Was it a Soviet demonstration of discontent with the Allies? Or had German propaganda planted disinformation in Moscow, in an attempt to drive a wedge between the USSR and its Western partners? In Washington, the British ambassador, Lord Halifax, publicly refuted the rumour; in Moscow, the British chargé, 'Jock' Balfour, even suggested during a conversation at the Foreign Ministry that *Pravda* should retract this report. Roosevelt refrained from addressing Stalin on these issues, but Secretary of State Hull sent an alarmed message via Ambassador Harriman, which stressed that such incidents weakened the post-Tehran atmosphere of trust and, he said, 'play into the hands of the sceptics in our country who persistently reiterate that "one cannot deal with Russia".'[35]

Roosevelt and Churchill, whose secret services had penetrated the Japanese diplomatic codes (operation 'Magic'), believed that *Pravda*'s source might have been a dispatch to Tokyo from Japan's ambassador in Madrid, which the Soviets intercepted.[36] Although precise information on this issue is not available, there is no doubt that, thanks to its own agents, Moscow had excellent opportunities for reading the cables of Japanese foreign missions.[37] Churchill decided to protest directly to Stalin, especially after being informed that *Pravda* did not have a special correspondent in Cairo and that the Soviet government had ordered wide publicity for the report. He also let off steam about pieces critical of Britain in *War and the Working Class*, a fortnightly journal founded in June 1943 under the close supervision of Stalin and Molotov.[38] In high dudgeon, the PM referred to 1940, when Britain was fighting Hitler alone and yet did not make a separate deal with the aggressor, and expressed deep regret that the Soviet leader had let these complaints go public. Once again that telling line: 'I am sure that if we had been together these difficulties would not have occurred.'

This message from Churchill might be seen as the point when the 'spirit of Tehran' evaporated.

Churchill to Stalin, sent 24 January 1944, received 25 January 1944[39]

We are sending Ambassador Clark Kerr back to you at once in order that he may explain a series of difficulties which, although they appear trifling at the outset, may ripen into the greatest embarrassment for us both.

I have been much impressed and also surprised by the extraordinarily bad effects produced here by the *Pravda* story to which so much official publicity was given by the Soviet Government. Even the best friends of Soviet Russia in England have been bewildered. What makes it so injurious is that we cannot understand it. I am sure you know that I would never negotiate with the Germans separately and that we tell you every overture they make, as you have told us. We never thought of making a separate peace even in the year when we were all alone and could easily have made one without serious loss to the British Empire and largely at your expense. Why should we think of it now, when our triple fortunes are marching forward to victory? If anything has occurred or been printed in the English newspapers annoying to you, why can you not send me a telegram or make your Ambassador come round and see us about it? In this way all the harm that has been done and the suspicions that have been aroused could be avoided.

I get every day long extracts from *War and the Working Classes* [*sic*] which seem to make continuous Left-Wing attacks on our administration in Italy and politics in Greece. Considering that you have a representative on the Commission for Italy we should hope that these complaints would be ventilated there and we should hear about them and explain our point of view between governments. As these attacks are made in public in Soviet newspapers which, on foreign affairs, are believed rightly or wrongly not to diverge from the policy of the Soviet Union, the divergence between our Governments becomes a serious Parliamentary issue. I have delayed speaking to the House of Commons until I see the results of the battle in Italy, which is not going too badly but in a week or ten days I shall have to address the House of Commons and deal with the matter to which I have referred in this telegram as I cannot allow charges and criticism to go unanswered.

I have been very much buoyed up with the feeling brought back from Tehran of our good relations and by the message you sent me through Benes and I try night and day to make things go the way you wish them and the way our triple interests require. I am sure that if we had been together these difficulties would not have occurred. I am working now constantly at making the second front a success and on an even larger scale, and my work is rendered more difficult by the kind of pin-pricking to which I have referred. Of course a few words spoken by you would blow the whole thing out of the water. We have always agreed to write frankly to each other so I do so now but I hope you will see Clark Kerr when he arrives and let him explain more at length the position as between Allies not only fused together in war but linked by our Twenty Years' Treaty.

I have not yet been able to telegraph about the talks with the Poles because I must, in matters of such far-reaching importance, know where I am with the United States. I hope, however, to send you a message in a few days.

Brigadier Maclean and my son Randolph have safely parachuted into Tito's headquarters.

*****

By mid-January 1944, the Red Army was reaching what had been the 1939 borders of Poland. Churchill, restored to health, made a determined bid to get the London Poles to hammer out an agreement with Moscow before their country's fate was decided on the battlefield. On 20 January, he held a meeting with Mikołajczyk and his colleagues, and then reported at length to Stalin a week later. The PM said he had pressed the Poles to accept the Curzon Line as the future eastern border of Poland, with appropriate compensation from Germany in the west, but he rejected any attempt by Stalin to interfere in the composition of a future Polish government. He also conveyed the understandable doubts of the London Poles. What would be the relationship between the Red Army and the Polish underground movement? And would the Red Army pull out after the war, allowing the Poles to have a 'free and independent' state? To anyone who took seriously the history of Russo-Polish relations, not least the bitter war of 1920, the idea of an amicable accord between the two sides was utopian. But Churchill was animated not only by his sense of duty towards Poland, stemming from Britain's hollow guarantee of 1939, but also by his new mood after Tehran – appealing to Stalin as 'my friend and comrade'. The evening before he sent the message, he told a journalist, à propos of Russo-Polish relations, 'If only Stalin and I could meet once a week, there would be no trouble at all. We get on like a house on fire.'⁴⁰ No one else shared his confidence about making such an appeal to Stalin. Mikołajczyk and his colleagues were sceptical of the whole idea; likewise most of the FO. On Churchill's orders, Cadogan had produced a draft only to learn, as he put it in his diary, that 'the silly old man had dictated one of his own'. Cadogan and Eden were allowed to make only minor 'tinkerings'.⁴¹

Churchill to Stalin, sent 28 January 1944, received 1 February 1944⁴²

On Thursday last, accompanied by the Foreign Secretary and with the authority of the War Cabinet, I saw representatives of the Polish Government in London. I informed them that the security of the Russian frontiers against Germany was a matter of high consequence to His Majesty's Government and that we should certainly support the Soviet Union in all measures we considered necessary to that end. I remarked that Russia had sustained two frightful invasions with immense slaughter and devastation at the hands of Germany, that Poland had had national independence and existence restored after the first World War, and that it was the policy of the great Allies to restore Poland once again after this war. I said that although we had gone to war for the sake of Poland we had not gone for any particular frontier line but for the existence of a strong, free, independent Poland which Marshal Stalin declared himself as supporting. Moreover although Great Britain would have fought on in any case for years until something happened to Germany, the liberation of Poland from Germany's grip is being achieved mainly by the enormous sacrifices of the Russian armies. Therefore, the Allies had a right to ask that Poland should be guided to a large extent about the frontiers of the territory she would have.

I then said that I believed from what had passed at Tehran that the Soviet Government would be willing to agree to the easterly frontiers of Poland conforming to the Curzon Line subject to the discussion of ethnographical considerations, and I advised them to accept the Curzon Line as a basis for discussion. I spoke of the compensations which Poland would receive in the North and in the West. In the North there would be East Prussia; but here I did not mention the point about Konigsberg. In the West they would be secure and aided to occupy Germany up to the line of the Oder. I told them it was their duty to accept this task and guard their frontiers against German aggression towards the east in consequence of their liberation by the Allied forces. I said in this task they would need a friendly Russia behind them and would, I presume, be sustained by the guarantee of the three great Powers against further German attack. Great Britain would be willing to give such a guarantee if it were in harmony with her Ally, Soviet Russia. I could not forecast the action of the United States but it seemed that the three Great Powers would stand together against all disturbers of the peace, at any rate until a long time after the war was ended. I made it clear that the Polish Government would not be committed to agree to the Curzon Line as a basis of examination except as part of the arrangement which gave them the fine compensations to the North and to the West which I had mentioned.

Finally I said that if the Russian policy was unfolded in the sense I had described, I would urge the Polish Government to settle on that basis and His Majesty's Government would advocate the confirmation of such a settlement by the Peace Conference or by the Conferences for the settlement of Europe following the destruction of Hitlerism, and would support no territorial claims from Poland which went beyond it. If the Polish Ministers were satisfied that agreement could be reached upon these lines, it would be their duty at the proper time not merely to acquiesce in it but to commend it to their people with courage, even though they ran the risk of being repudiated by extremists.

The Polish Ministers were very far from rejecting the prospects thus unfolded, but they asked for time to consider the matter with the rest of their colleagues, and as a result of this they have asked a number of questions, none of which seem to me to be in conflict with the general outline of my suggestions to them. In particular they wish to be assured that Poland would be free and independent in the new home assigned to her; that she would receive the guarantee of the great Powers against German revenge effectively; that these great Powers would also assist in expelling the Germans from the new territories to be assigned to Poland; and that in the regions to be incorporated in Soviet Russia such Poles as wished would be assisted to depart for their new abodes. They also inquired about what their position will be if a large part of Poland west of the Curzon Line is soon occupied by the advancing Soviet Armies. Will they be allowed to go back and form a more broad-based government in accordance with the popular wish and allowed to function administratively in the liberated areas in the same way as other governments who have been overrun? In particular they are of course deeply concerned about the relations between the Polish Underground Movement and the advancing Soviet forces, it being understood that their prime desire was to assist in driving out the Germans. This Underground Movement raises matters important to our common war effort.

We also attach great importance to assimilating our action in the different regions which we hope to liberate. You know the policy we are following in Italy. There we have taken you fully into our councils, and we want to do the same in regard to France and the other countries to whose liberation we look forward. We believe such uniformity of action is of great importance, now and in the future, to the cause of the United Nations.

The earliest possible agreement in principle on the frontiers of the new Polish State is highly desirable to allow of a satisfactory arrangement regarding these two very important points.

While, however, everyone will agree that Soviet Russia has the right to recognise or refuse recognition to any foreign government, do you not agree that to advocate changes within a foreign government comes near to that interference in internal sovereignty to which you and I have expressed ourselves as opposed? I may mention that this view is strongly held by His Majesty's Government.

I now report this conversation, which expresses the policy of His Majesty's Government at the present time upon this difficult question, to my friend and comrade Marshal Stalin. I earnestly hope these plans may be helpful. I had always hoped to postpone discussions of frontier questions until the end of the war when the victors would be round the table together. The dangers which have forced His Majesty's Government to depart from this principle are formidable and imminent. If, as we may justly hope, the successful advance of the Soviet armies continues and a large part of Poland is cleared of German oppressors, a good relationship will be absolutely necessary between whatever forces can speak for Poland and the Soviet Union. The creation in Warsaw of another Polish Government different from the one we have recognised up to the present, together with disturbances in Poland, would raise an issue in Great Britain and the United States detrimental to that close accord between the three Great Powers upon which the future of the world depends.

I wish to make it clear that this message is not intended to be any intervention or interference between the Governments of the Soviet Union and Poland. It is a statement in broad outline of the position of His Majesty's Government in Great Britain in regard to a matter in which they feel themselves deeply concerned.

I should like myself to know from you what steps you would be prepared to take to help us all to resolve this serious problem. You could certainly count on our good offices for what they would be worth.

I am sending a copy of this message to the President of the United States with a request for complete secrecy.

As Eden had predicted, a demonstration of Allied 'goodwill' on the issue of the transfer of the Italian ships was not enough for Stalin. It must have been particularly galling for him that Roosevelt and Churchill were paying more deference to the feelings of a country that had been their enemy until six months before, while giving the runaround to an ally of two and a half years that had borne the brunt of the land war against Hitler. Yet status was not the only issue: as is clear from a memo from the naval staff before the Moscow conference, the Soviets also sought immediate 'partial compensation' for the massive damage inflicted by the Axis.[43] Given the continued diplomatic impasse, however, on 29 January Stalin accepted the temporary compromise of replacing the Italian ships he desired with British and American vessels. But he pounced on the fact that in the joint message of 23 January there was no mention of destroyers and submarines (deliberately omitted at British insistence), and demanded that his allies cover these as well. He made the whole issue one of Allied fidelity to their promises: 'After your joint affirmative reply at Tehran,' he told Roosevelt and Churchill, 'I considered this matter settled and the thought never entered my mind of any reconsideration of this decision.'[44]

'What can you expect from a bear but a growl?' Churchill commented to Roosevelt.[45] Stalin and Molotov also growled back about the PM's criticism of *Pravda*, claiming that far more English press reports about the USSR were deserving of an official denial (*démenti*). The original Russian text of Stalin's message referred carefully to *Pravda*'s 'agents' in Cairo, rather than using the term 'correspondents', whose non-existence in Cairo had somehow to be circumvented – but the latter word appeared in the FO's translation. The message also directly contested Churchill's interpretation of 1940, quoting back at him some of his statements at the time, while skirting judiciously around Stalin's relationship with Hitler in 1940–41.

Stalin to Churchill, sent 29 January 1944, received 29 January 1944[46]

I have received your message of the 24th January.

My reply has been delayed somewhat as I have been greatly overburdened with affairs on the Front.

As regards the *Pravda* report, undue importance should not be attached to it as there is no ground to contest the right of a newspaper to publish reports of rumours received from trustworthy newspaper correspondents. We ourselves at least never laid claim to that kind of interference in the affairs of the British press, even though we have had, and still have, incomparably more serious cause to do so. Our Tass Agency deny only a very small proportion of the reports meriting a dementi from what is published in the English newspapers.

If we must come to the essence of the question, I cannot agree with you that England could at one time easily have concluded a separate peace with Germany, largely at the expense of the USSR and without serious loss to the British Empire. It seems to me that this was said in the heat of the moment, like[47] other statements of yours of another character which I remember. I remember, for instance, in the difficult time for England until the Soviet Union joined in the war, you admitted the possibility of the British Government having to move over to Canada and to carry on the struggle against Germany from across the ocean. On the other hand, you admitted that it was precisely the Soviet Union which, having developed its struggle with Hitler, removed the danger which undoubtedly threatened Great Britain from Germany. If nevertheless we admit that England could have managed without the USSR, then surely it is no less possible to say the same of the Soviet Union. I do not like talking about all this, but I am compelled to have my say and remind you of the facts.

About the journal 'War and the Working Class' I can only say is that it is a trades-union journal and that the Government cannot accept responsibility for articles appearing in it. Furthermore the journal, like our other journals, is true to a fundamental principle – the strengthening of friendship with the Allies – which does not exclude but rather presupposes friendly criticism.

As with you so with me, pleasant impressions have remained of our meetings in Tehran and of our joint labours.

I will of course see Mr Kerr on his arrival.

Faced with Stalin's firm reply, Churchill decided to avoid continued debate about 1940–41. He did, however, draft a brief acknowledgement: 'Thank you for your telegram. I liked the last sentence but one much the best. I agree that we had better leave the past to history, but remember if I live long enough I may be one of the historians' – an intriguing aside about the war memoirs he was already planning to write. The PM then asked Eden for his opinion. 'I like it,' the foreign secretary replied, 'but I don't know how it will go down in Russian, or how the strange animal will understand it. He seems to lack humour on paper.'[48]

In the end, Churchill sent no response, but he let off steam to the king's private secretary on 2 February. 'If my shirt were taken off now,' he exclaimed, 'it would be seen that my belly is sore from crawling to that man. I do it for the good of the country, and for no other reason.'[49] He also cabled Clark Kerr, now back in Moscow: 'I am deeply discouraged by the tone of the telegrams about *Pravda* and Italian ships received from Stalin.' He added: 'I have laboured long upon this subject, and now so far as I am concerned I have reached the end.' Here was Churchill at his most mercurial – devoting hours excitedly to his three messages on *Pravda*, the Italian ships and Poland, and then slumping into the dumps at Stalin's reaction. This was just the yo-yo mood swings that Christopher Warner and the FO's Northern Department deplored when dealing with the Russians. At the end of his message, the PM told Clark Kerr that he was waiting to see Stalin's reaction to his message about Poland: 'If this is conceived in the same spirit as the other two, then indeed I think the future dark.'[50]

There was a foretaste of the reaction when Clark Kerr visited the Kremlin on 2 February to deliver Churchill's message. The ambassador found Stalin and Molotov immovable about getting rid of the 'intransigents' from the London Polish government, but willing to resume relations if that government 'took a new form'. Churchill latched onto the second point – telling Roosevelt 'I am more hopeful than I have yet been' – whereas the FO considered his attitude 'over optimistic'.[51] Stalin's formal reply was received on 5 February. He made clear that the Poles had to publicly accept the Curzon Line and, equally publicly, disavow the frontier forced on the Russians by the Treaty of Riga in 1921. He also expressed his desire to acquire the city of Königsberg from Germany, as an ice-free port on the Baltic; he had raised this briefly at Tehran in what Eden regarded as an unacceptable try-on.[52] Furthermore, Stalin hammered on about the unfriendly element in the Polish government, singling out General Kazimierz Sosnkowski, the commander-in-chief of the Polish armed forces and a vehement anti-Soviet nationalist. The message brazenly cited the 'Katyn story' as an example of the London Poles' 'pro-Fascist' activities. On 26 January, *Pravda* and *Izvestiya* had both front-paged the report of the government's 'special commission' on Katyn which confirmed 'the truth' that the shootings had been committed by the Germans in 1941 and that the London Poles had acted 'in unison with Hitler' in scurrilously blaming the USSR for the crime.[53] At the end of the message, Stalin offered a breezy one-sentence assurance about the London Poles' doubts: 'I do not think that it would be difficult to reach agreement.'

Stalin to Churchill, sent 4 February, received 5 February 1944[54]

I received your message on the Polish question from Sir A. Clark Kerr who arrived in Moscow the other day and with whom I have already had a useful talk.

I see you are giving much attention to the problem of Soviet–Polish relations. We value these efforts very highly.

It seems to me that the first question on which there ought to be full clarification is the question about the Soviet Polish frontier. You have of course rightly remarked that Poland ought on this question to be guided by the Allies. As far as the Soviet Government is concerned, it has already openly and clearly given its opinion of the question of the frontier. We have declared that we do not consider the 1939 frontier to be unalterable and have agreed on the Curzon Line, thereby making very great concessions to the Poles. But in the meantime the Polish Government has evaded answering our proposal about the Curzon Line and continues in its official statements to declare that the frontier imposed upon us by the Riga Treaty is unalterable. One can infer from your letter that the Polish Government is ready to acknowledge the Curzon Line but as is known the Poles have nowhere made a declaration about this.

It is my opinion that the Polish Government ought to make an official declaration that the line of the frontier established by the Riga Treaty admits of alteration and that the Curzon Line constitutes the new frontier between the USSR and Poland. It ought to make its declaration about this as officially as the Soviet Government when it declared that line of the 1939 frontier admitted of change and that the Curzon Line ought to be the Soviet Polish frontier.

As regards your statement to the Poles to the effect that Poland could move its frontier considerably to the West and North, we are as you know in agreement with this subject to one amendment. About that amendment I spoke to you and the President at Tehran. We claim that the north-eastern portion of East Prussia, including the port of Koenigsberg, as an ice-free one, should go to the Soviet Union. That is the only portion of German territory which we claim. Without the satisfaction of that minimum claim of the Soviet Union, the concession of the Soviet Government expressed in its acknowledgment of the Curzon Line loses all meaning as I have already told you at Tehran.

Finally about the actual composition of the Polish Government. You understand that we cannot renew relations with the present Polish Government and indeed what sense would there be in renewing relations with a Government when there was no certainty that we should not tomorrow again be obliged to break off these relations as a result of some fresh Fascist provocation, from their side such as the 'Katyn story'. During the most recent period the Polish Government, where Sosnkowski sets the tone, has not put an end to hostile statements against the Soviet Government. The statements, extremely hostile to the Soviet Government, of the Polish Ambassadors in Mexico and Canada and of General Anders in the Near East, the publication of Polish underground papers on German occupied territory which overstep all bounds in hostility to the USSR, the destruction at the direction of the Polish Government of Polish partisans fighting against the German occupying forces, and many other pro-Fascist acts of the Polish Government are well-known. In this situation, without the fundamental improvement in the composition of the Polish Government it is impossible to expect any amelioration. The exclusion of pro-Fascist imperialist elements and the inclusion of people of democratic turn of mind, it may be hoped, would provide the necessary conditions for a renewal of good Soviet Polish relations, the settlement of the question of the Soviet Polish frontier and generally for the regeneration of Poland as a strong, free and independent state. In this improvement of the composition of the Polish

Government the Poles above all are interested and the broad layers of the Polish people. I remember, by the way, that in May last year you wrote to me that the composition of the Polish Government could be improved and that you would busy yourself in that direction. At that time you did not think that this would be interference in the internal sovereignty of Poland.

As regards the question put by the Polish Ministers mentioned in the 4th point of your letter, I do not think that it would be difficult to reach agreement.

*****

On 6 February, Churchill and Eden spent a long lunch at Chequers putting Stalin's points to Mikołajczyk and his senior colleagues. The PM told them they had 'these alternatives: a fine land of security and peace, or the certainty either that an Anglo-Russian agreement would be made apart from the Polish Government, or that things would be left to drift into chaos'. Mikołajczyk, however, was immovable, declaring that Stalin's demands over the Curzon Line and the composition of his government could not be accepted 'without abandoning Poland's moral right and losing the support of his people'.[55] Oliver Harvey noted grimly: 'The Poles still determined to do their usual suicide act'.[56]

Roosevelt was perfectly content for Churchill to take the lead in the Sisyphean bid to break the Polish–Soviet impasse. At Tehran on 1 December 1943 FDR had told Stalin in private that, although supporting the idea of moving Poland westward, he was looking ahead to the 1944 election, in which he 'might have' to run again and needed to bear in mind the votes of 6–7 million Polish-Americans. For that reason, said the president, he could not take a public position. Ambassador Harriman, however, was unhappy about his government's fence-sitting. He raised the Polish issue with Stalin on 2 February and pressed Washington on several occasions to support Churchill's search for a settlement before the advancing Red Army resolved things by force.[57] Under this pressure, Roosevelt finally added his voice – characteristically expressing the hope that the London Poles could be persuaded to reconstruct their government without too much evidence of foreign 'dictation' and stressing that this controversy should not jeopardize 'our long-range objective' of achieving 'international collaboration' among the great powers. The message was drafted by the State Department; FDR approved it, adding only the last paragraph.[58]

Roosevelt to Stalin, sent 7 February 1944, received 11 February 1944[59]

I have followed with the closest attention the recent developments in your relations with Poland. I feel that I am fully aware of your views on the subject and am therefore taking this opportunity of communicating with you on the basis of our conversations at Tehran. First of all, let me make it plain that I neither desire nor intend to attempt to suggest much less to advise you in any way as to where the interests of Russia lie in this matter since I realize to the full that the future security of your country is rightly your primary concern. The observations which I am about to make are prompted solely by the larger issues which affect the common goal towards which we are both working.

The overwhelming majority of our people and Congress, as you know, welcomed with enthusiasm the broad principles subscribed to at the Moscow and Tehran conferences, and I know that you agree with me that it is of the utmost importance that faith in these understandings should not be left in any doubt. I am sure that a solution can be found which would fully protect the interests of Russia and satisfy your desire to see a friendly, independent Poland, and at the same time not adversely affect the cooperation so splendidly established at Moscow and Tehran. I feel it is of the utmost importance that we should bear in mind that the various differences which inevitably arise in the conduct of international relations should not be permitted to jeopardize all important questions of cooperation and collaboration among nations which is the only sound basis for a just and lasting peace.

I have given careful consideration to the views of your Government as outlined by Mr Molotov to Mr Harriman on January 18 regarding the impossibility from the Soviet point of view of having any dealings with the Polish Government-in-exile in its present form and Mr Molotov's suggestion that the Polish Government should be reconstituted by the inclusion of Polish elements at present in the United States, Great Britain, and the Soviet Union. I fully appreciate your desire to deal only with a Polish Government in which you can repose confidence and which can be counted upon to establish permanent friendly relations with the Soviet Union, but it is my earnest hope that while this problem remains unsolved nothing should be done to transform this special question into one adversely affecting the larger issues of future international collaboration. While public opinion is forming in support of the principle of international collaboration, it is especially incumbent upon us to avoid any action which might appear to counteract the achievement of our long-range objective. I feel I should ill serve our common interest if I failed to bring these facts to your attention.

Prime Minister Churchill tells me that he is endeavoring to persuade the Polish Prime Minister to make a clean-cut acceptance as a basis for negotiation of the territorial changes which have been proposed by your Government. Is it not possible on that basis to arrive at some answer to the question of the composition of the Polish Government which would leave it to the Polish Prime Minister himself to make such changes in his government as may be necessary without any evidence of pressure or dictation from a foreign country?

As a matter of timing it seems to me that the first consideration at this time should be that Polish guerrillas should work with and not against your advancing troops. That is of current importance and some assurance on the part of all Poles would be of great advantage as a first step.

On the continuing saga of the Italian ships, the British chiefs of staff were reluctantly willing to satisfy Stalin's demand for destroyers and submarines, so long as these were 'over-age' vessels used for training, which could be supplied without directly affecting Allied strength for 'Overlord'.[60] After some haggling with Washington, where the US Navy refused to release any American vessels, Churchill took up the chiefs of staff's offer and the two leaders conveyed the news to Stalin in a joint message of 7 February. Ironically, the 'over-age' British destroyers were originally 'over-age' American destroyers from the First World War, transferred by Roosevelt under the so-called 'Destroyers-for-Bases' deal which had heartened the British in the dark summer of 1940. Recycled yet again, they would now serve a similar diplomatic purpose in Western relations with the USSR. Churchill told Clark Kerr that, when delivering the message to Stalin, 'you should say quite bluntly that the destroyers are old but I don't want to be reproached on that score. They are serviceable and will steam and fight.'[61]

Roosevelt and Churchill to Stalin, sent 7 February 1944, received 24 February 1944[62]

The receipt is acknowledged of your message in regard to handing over Italian shipping to the Soviet.

It is our intention to carry out the transfer agreed to at Tehran at the earliest date practicable without hazarding the success of 'Anvil' and 'Overlord', which operations we all agree should be given the first priority in our common effort to defeat Germany at the earliest possible date.

There is no thought of not carrying through the transfers agreed at Tehran. The British battleship and American cruiser can be made available without any delay and an effort will be made at once to make available from the British Navy the eight destroyers. Four submarines will also be provided temporarily by Great Britain.

We are convinced that disaffecting Italian Navy at this time would be what you have so aptly termed an unnecessary diversion and that it would adversely affect the prospects of our success in France.

Meanwhile, the Red Army continued its advance, with news beamed around the world on 27 January 1944 that Leningrad had been completely liberated – ending a siege of nearly 900 days that began on 8 September 1941. It claimed more Russian lives than all the British and American war dead combined.

Churchill alluded to that when writing to Stalin on 8 February. By contrast, he had to admit that the Italian campaign had not lived up to his high hopes, but made as much as possible of the news that he was sending another Arctic convoy. On the 10th, he also told Stalin that the 'stirring music' of the new Russian anthem had been played by the BBC 'on several occasions, and will continue to be played in celebration of Russian victories'. Next day the Soviet leader sent a cordial and chatty reply with his 'best wishes'. Tensions seemed to be easing.[63]

Churchill to Stalin, sent 8 February 1944, received 9 February 1944[64]

Very many thanks for your full telegram about Polish affairs. Eden and I had a long day with the Poles on Sunday and are working hard. In two or three days I shall report to you further.

My military advisers are profoundly impressed with recent developments on your front. I offer my sincere congratulations.

The battle in Italy has not gone as I hoped or planned. Although the landing was a brilliant piece of work and achieved complete surprise, the advantage was lost and now it is a question of hard slogging. However the enemy has brought five additional divisions to the south of Rome and we are now actively engaging seventeen. We have good hopes of a satisfactory outcome, and anyhow the front will be kept aflame from now on.

I have now succeeded in arranging with the British Admiralty and the American War Shipping Administration for another additional convoy of ships to go to North Russia in March. I should hope that the actual number of ships would be eighteen or twenty, nearly all of which are American. Although this does not increase the amount of supplies due under the protocol, it conveys them to you a good deal quicker and along the northern route which I understand you greatly prefer to the Persian. The Arctic convoys have been getting through well and the U-boats were much knocked about on the last occasion by our escorts.

Every good wish.

On 16 February, Stalin replied to Roosevelt's message about Poland, essentially trotting out the same arguments he had deployed on the 4th to Churchill. He apologized for the delay, citing 'pressing duties at the front'.[65] This fiction was becoming increasingly frequent to excuse slow replies to Churchill and Roosevelt or unavailability to meet their ambassadors.

Like Churchill, Roosevelt was sending plenty of cheery telegrams. On the 17th, a formal message of congratulations for Red Army Day – 'the heroic defense of Leningrad has been crowned and rewarded by the recent crushing defeat of the enemy before its gates' – was accompanied by another cable that day giving details of a couple of US merchantmen and a cruiser that would be transferred for 'temporary use' by the Soviet navy until 'adequate Italian tonnage' was available. Two days later, FDR sent a brief message of 'deep satisfaction' about 'the recent successes of your armies in the Ukraine and in the Northwest', while the PM chipped in to say 'Mr Eden and I rejoice in your liquidation of the southern pocket' and to offer reassurance that 'all preparations for "Overlord" are moving forward well'.[66]

This flurry of emollient telegrams probably reflected the anxiety felt by both Roosevelt and Churchill about achieving a modus vivendi over Poland. Churchill's latest bout of 'wrestling' with the Poles, led by Mikołajczyk and Foreign Minister Tadeusz Romer, had taken place at 10 Downing Street on 16 February. The Polish leader was willing to admit privately that the 1921 Treaty of Riga borders were no longer tenable and to accept the idea of a temporary 'demarcation line' somewhere between the Curzon and the Riga Lines, in order to handle the administration of the liberated territories – without prejudice to decisions at the eventual peace conference. But he insisted that, since such a line would inevitably to some extent prejudge the eventual settlement, it must at least run east of Wilno (Vilna/Vilnius) and Lwów – two cities that in his view were historically Polish, dating back to the heyday of late-medieval Greater Poland.[67]

Mikołajczyk's position, therefore, was nuanced, but he dared not reveal much of this in public because of the implacable opposition from much of his government, the Home Army leadership and Poles serving in the Allied forces to the transfer of any piece of pre-1939 Poland to the 'Bolsheviks'. In any case, the premise of the demarcation line – that the Red Army would be content to sweep on westward into Germany, while leaving an independent government in control of its lines of communications – was, to say the least, implausible given the bloodstained history of Russo-Polish relations. Nevertheless, the PM tried the idea of a temporary wartime demarcation on Stalin. Churchill's reference in the cable to 'this war against German aggression' as 'part of a thirty years' war from 1914 onward' is one of the earliest examples of what would become a trope of his subsequent memoirs.

Clark Kerr was instructed by Churchill to deliver this message in person to Stalin, so that he could reinforce its arguments in person. The Soviet leader was, however, in one of his 'at-the-front' moods, so the meeting was deferred until 28 February. The ambassador did, however, send the message and a Russian translation to Molotov the day before, so that the Kremlin was acquainted with its contents in advance.

Churchill to Stalin, sent 20 February 1944, received 27 February 1944[68]

The following telegram from me to you has been seen by the Polish Prime Minister and Minister for Foreign Affairs, has been written in close consultation with them and is despatched with their agreement, and I earnestly hope that it may be the means of reaching a working arrangement between Poland and Soviet Russia during the war, and that it may become the foundation of a lasting peace and friendship between the two countries as part of the general settlement of Europe.

I am sending a copy of it to the President of the United States.

Mr Eden and I send you our best wishes.

Churchill to Stalin, sent 20 February 1944, received 27 February 1944[69]

The Foreign Secretary and I have had numerous long discussions with the Polish Prime Minister and the Minister for Foreign Affairs. I shall not attempt to repeat all the arguments which were used, but only to give what I conceive to be the position of the Polish Government in the upshot.

The Polish Government are ready to declare that the Riga Line no longer corresponds to realities and, with our participation, to discuss with the Soviet Government, as part of the general settlement, a new frontier between Poland and the Soviet Union, together with the future frontiers of Poland in the north and west. Since, however, the compensations which Poland is to receive in the North and West cannot be stated publicly or precisely at the present time the Polish Government clearly cannot make an immediate public declaration of their willingness to cede territory as indicated above because the publication of such an arrangement would have an entirely one-sided appearance with the consequence that they would immediately be repudiated by a large part of their people abroad and by the Underground Movement in Poland with which they are in constant contact. It is evident therefore that the Polish–Soviet territorial settlement, which must be an integral part of the general territorial settlement of Europe, could only formally be agreed and ratified when the victorious Powers are gathered round the table at the time of an armistice or peace.

For the above reasons the Polish Government, until it has returned to Polish territory and been allowed to consult the Polish people, can obviously not formally abdicate its rights in any part of Poland as hitherto constituted, but vigorous prosecution of the war against Germany in collaboration with the Soviet armies would be greatly assisted if the Soviet Government will facilitate the return of the Polish Government to the territory of liberated Poland at the earliest possible moment; and in consultation with their British and American allies, as the Russian armies advance, arrange from time to time with the Polish Government for the establishment of the civil administration of the Polish Government in given districts. This procedure would be in general accordance with those to be followed in the case of other countries as they are liberated. The Polish Government are naturally very anxious that the districts to be placed under Polish civil administration should include such places as Vilna and Lwow, where there are concentrations of Poles, and that the territories to the east of the demarcation line should be administered by Soviet Military authorities with the assistance of representatives of the United Nations. They point out that thus they would be in the best position to enlist all such able-bodied Poles in the war effort. I have informed them and they clearly understand that you will not assent to leaving Vilna and Lwow under Polish administration. I wish on the other hand to be able to assure them that the area to be placed under Polish civil administration will include at least all Poland west of the Curzon Line.

At the frontier negotiations contemplated in paragraph 2 above, the Polish Government, taking into consideration the mixed character of the population of Eastern Poland, would favour a frontier drawn with a view to assuring the highest degree of homogeneity on both sides, while reducing as much as possible the extent and hardships of an exchange of populations. I have no doubt myself, especially in view of the immediate practical arrangements contemplated by the Polish Government set out in paragraph 3 above, that these negotiations will inevitably lead to the conclusion you desire in regard to the future of the Polish–Soviet frontier, but it seems to me unnecessary and undesirable publicly to emphasise this at this stage.

As regards the war with Germany which they wish to prosecute with the utmost vigour, the Polish Government realise that it is imperative to have a working agreement with the Soviet Government in view of the advance of the liberating Russian armies on to Polish soil, from which these armies are driving the German invader. They assure me emphatically that they have at no time given instructions to the Underground Movement to attack 'partisans'. On the contrary, after consultation with the leaders of their Underground Movement and with their accord they have issued orders for all Poles now in arms or about to revolt against Hitlerite tyranny as follows: when the Russian army enters any particular district in Poland, the underground movement is to disclose its identity and meet the requirements of the Soviet commanders, even in the absence of a resumption of Polish–Soviet relations. The local Polish military commander, accompanied by the local civilian Underground authority, will meet and declare to the commander of incoming Soviet troops that, following the instructions of the Polish Government, to which they remain faithful, they are ready to co-ordinate their actions with him in the fight against the common foe. These orders, which are already in operation, seem to me, as I am sure they will to you, of the highest significance and importance.

For the first time on February 6th I told the Polish Government that the Soviet Government wished to have the frontier in East Prussia drawn to include, on the Russian side, Konigsberg. The information came as a shock to the Polish Government, who see in such a decision substantial reduction in the size and in the economic importance of the German territory to be incorporated in Poland by way of compensation. But I stated that, in the opinion of His Majesty's Government, this was a rightful claim on the part of Russia. Regarding, as I do, this war against German aggression as all one and as a thirty years' war from 1914 onwards, I reminded M. Mikolajczyk of the fact that the soil of this part of East Prussia was dyed with Russian blood expended freely in the common cause. Here the Russian armies advancing in August 1914 and winning the battle of Cumbinnen and other actions had with their forward thrusts and with much injury to their mobilisation forced the Germans to recall two army corps from the advance on Paris, which withdrawal was an essential part in the victory of the Marne. The disaster at Tannenberg did not in any way undo this great result. Therefore it seemed to me that the Russians had a historic and well-founded claim to this German territory.

As regards the composition of the Polish Government, the Polish Government cannot admit any right of a foreign intervention. They can, however, assure the Russian Government that by the time they have entered into diplomatic relations with the Soviet Government they will include among themselves none but persons fully determined to co-operate with the Soviet Union. I am of the opinion that it is much better that such changes should come about naturally and as a result of further Polish consideration of their interests as a whole. It might well be, in my opinion, that the moment for a resumption of these relations in a formal manner would await the reconstitution of a Polish Government at the time of the liberation of Warsaw when it would arise naturally from the circumstances attending that glorious event.

It would be in accordance with the assurances I have received from you that, in an agreement covering the points made above, the Soviet Government should join with His Majesty's Government in undertaking vis-a-vis each other and Poland, first to recognise and respect the sovereignty, independence and territorial integrity of reconstituted Poland and the right of each to conduct its domestic affairs without interference, secondly, to do their best to secure in due course the incorporation in Poland of the Free City of Danzig, Oppeln, Silesia, East Prussia, west and south of a line running from Konigsberg and of as much territory up to the Oder as the Polish Government see fit to accept; thirdly, to effect the removal from Poland including the German territories to be incorporated in Poland of the German population; and fourthly, to negotiate the procedure for the exchange of population between Poland and the Soviet Union and for the return to their mother country of the nationals of the Powers in question. All the undertakings to each other on the part of Poland, the Soviet Union and the United Kingdom should in my view be drawn up in such a form that they could be embodied in a single instrument or exchange of letters.

I informed the Polish Ministers that should the settlement which has now been outlined in the various telegrams that have passed between us become a fact and be observed in spirit by all the parties to it, His Majesty's Government would support that settlement at the Conference after the defeat of Hitler and also that we would guarantee that settlement in after years to the best of our ability.

Roosevelt, at Churchill's request, backed up this message with one of his own. The original draft made reference to the number of Americans of Polish descent, but the president removed this rather lame argument for speedy agreement and replaced it with a final paragraph reiterating the value for their common war effort of close cooperation between the Polish underground and the Red Army. With FDR's permission, Harriman delayed transmission of the message until 28 February, waiting – like Clark Kerr – for Stalin's 'return' in order to synchronize delivery of both telegrams.[70]

Roosevelt to Stalin, sent 21 February 1944, received 28 February 1944[71]

I am informed as to the text of the message sent to you on February 20th by Mr Churchill on the subject of a tentative settlement of the Polish post war boundary by agreement between the Soviet and the Polish Governments.

This suggestion by the Prime Minister, if accepted, goes far toward furthering our prospects of an early defeat of Germany and I am pleased to recommend that you give to it favorable and sympathetic consideration.

As I intimated before, I think that the most realistic problem of the moment is to be assured that your armies will be assisted by the Poles when you get into Poland.

Stalin was still exercised about the deal over the Italian ships. That same day he sent a reminder about the destroyers and submarines to Roosevelt and also to Churchill – managing to annoy them both.

Stalin to Roosevelt, sent 21 February 1944, received 21 February 1944[72]

I have received your message of February 18.[73] Thank you for the information.

It, however, does not exhaust the question, since there is nothing mentioned in it about the Anglo-American destroyers and submarines instead of the Italian ones (8 destroyers, 4 submarines), as it was agreed upon at Teheran. I hope to receive speedy reply regarding these questions, touched on in my communication of January 29th.

Stalin to Churchill, sent 21 February 1944, received 21 February 1944[74]

I have received your message of February 19th. Thank you for your communications.

At the same time I must remind you that up to now I have not had an answer about the eight Anglo-American destroyers and the other ships which should be put at the temporary disposal of the Soviet Union in place of the Italian naval and merchant vessels, according to the decision jointly reached by yourself, the President and myself at Tehran. I cannot understand the long delay.

I await a reply to my message of January 29th.

Even before receiving this blunt cable from Stalin, the PM had asked Clark Kerr on 19 February why he had received no reply, 'let alone a word of appreciation', to the joint Roosevelt–Churchill letter of 7 February about the ships. Clark Kerr replied that Stalin had still not returned from the front and reiterated that he was waiting for a personal meeting in order to deliver the message. He added, 'Molotov is aware that I have something to say about the ships and that the news is good but I have not wished to content myself with seeing him about it, because I have felt the matter to be one for Stalin himself and one upon which he could be usefully talked to.' The ambassador asked to 'hold on for some days yet in the hope that Stalin may soon return' and Churchill agreed.[75]

So when, on the 21st, Churchill received not thanks from Stalin but a reproachful reminder, he was naturally furious. 'I am much grieved that this matter which I hoped would cause pleasure and which cost us so much should have miscarried,' he cabled Clark Kerr. 'It is your duty now to put things right.'[76] The premier also sent Stalin the following telegram.

Churchill to Stalin, sent 22 February 1944, received 24 February 1944[77]

Italian Ships:

I sent you a message on February 7th signed by the President and myself and also a private one to Ambassador Clark Kerr, the substance of which he was to deliver personally. The upshot was that I will supply from British resources the eight destroyers and four submarines as well as a battleship and twenty thousand tons of merchant shipping. The United States will supply a cruiser and twenty thousand tons of merchant shipping. I have been wondering why I had not received a message from you acknowledging this, as I was hoping you would be pleased with the efforts I had made. I gather Ambassador Clark Kerr wanted to deliver the message to you personally and that you were away at the front. I have telegraphed to him to put things right. No time has been lost in preparing the ships.[78]

That same day Churchill commented publicly on the state of relations with the USSR during his speech to the House of Commons about the war. Alluding to controversies like the *Pravda* statement about a possible compromise peace, he said that it was being asked in some quarters whether there had been a 'cooling off' in the 'good relations' established at the recent conferences. 'None of the ground made good at Moscow and Teheran has been lost,' he assured the House. 'The three great Allies are absolutely united in their action against the common foe . . . It is upon such a prolonged, intimate and honourable association that the future of the world depends.'[79]

On 23 February, Clark Kerr duly delivered Churchill's telegram to Molotov, together with the ill-fated joint message from both leaders, now more than two weeks old. In an unusually lengthy cover letter to the foreign minister, he explained why he had held back delivery because Stalin was at the front:

I confess that, in doing so, I did not foresee that he would be absent for so long. I kept hoping that he would be back and ready to receive me. Now I hold myself responsible for such a long delay, and I kindly ask you to convey to Marshal Stalin my regrets and apologies.[80]

While awaiting Stalin's reply on Poland, both leaders kept up their friendly noises. Like Roosevelt, Churchill sent a message of congratulation on Red Army Day – as did the British chiefs of staff.[81]

The president also sent a message that, for once, did not react to Stalin's agenda, but instead addressed an issue close to his own heart: the postwar order. On 9 November 1943, representatives of forty-four countries, including the USSR, had signed an agreement in Washington to establish the United Nations Relief and Rehabilitation Administration. This was intended to help war-ravaged countries rebuild their economies and to alleviate food crises. The initiative came from the USA, which first raised the issue at the Moscow conference of foreign ministers. In early 1944, the Americans, together with the British, also began to develop the foundations of a new international monetary system that would be agreed at Bretton Woods, New Hampshire, in July. The president was keen to involve Stalin in these and other international bodies, as part of his effort to bring the Soviets into the 'family circle' of nations: hence this message, drafted by the State Department. Stalin responded only on 10 March, after consulting his diplomats and economists.

Roosevelt to Stalin, sent 23 February 1944, received 25 February 1944[82]

In recent months a number of important steps have been taken by the Governments of the United Nations toward laying the foundations for post-war cooperative action in the various fields of international economic relations. You will recall that the United Nations Conference on Food and Agriculture, held in May 1943, gave rise to an Interim Commission which is now drafting recommendations to lay before the various governments for a permanent organization in this field. More recently, there has been established – and is now in operation – the United Nations Relief and Rehabilitation Administration. For nearly a year, there have been informal technical discussions at the expert level among many of the United Nations on mechanisms for international monetary stabilization; these discussions are preparatory to a possible convocation of a United Nations Monetary Conference. Similar discussions have been taking place, though on a more restricted scale, with regard to the possibility of establishing mechanisms for facilitating international developmental investment. To some extent, informal discussions have taken place among some of the United Nations with regard to such questions as commercial policy, commodity policy, and cartels. Discussions are in contemplation on such questions as commercial aviation, oil, and others. In April a conference of the International Labor Organization will take place, in part for the purpose of considering its future activities.

In a document presented by the Secretary of State at the Moscow meeting of Foreign Ministers entitled 'Bases of Our Program for International Economic Cooperation', the need was emphasized for both informal discussions and formal conferences on various economic problems. It was suggested that 'the time has come for the establishment of a commission comprising representatives of the

THE SPIRIT OF TEHRAN EVAPORATES

principal United Nations and possibly certain others of the United Nations for the joint planning of the procedures to be followed in these matters'.

It is clear to me that there is a manifest need for United Nations machinery for joint planning of the procedures by which consideration should be given to the various fields of international economic cooperation, the subjects which should be discussed, the order of discussion, and the means of coordinating existing and prospective arrangements and activities. I do not mean to raise at this time and in this connection the broader issues of international organization for the maintenance of peace and security. Preliminary discussions on this subject are currently in contemplation between our three Governments under the terms of the Moscow Protocol. What I am raising here is the question of further steps toward the establishment of United Nations machinery for post-war economic collaboration, which was raised at the Moscow meeting by the Secretary of State and was discussed by you, Prime Minister Churchill and myself at Teheran.

I should appreciate it very much if you would give me your views on the suggestion made by the Secretary of State at Moscow, together with any other thoughts as to the best procedure to be followed in this extremely important matter.

On 26 February, Stalin commented on the joint Churchill–Roosevelt message of 7 February. He was not satisfied about the destroyers, picking up on the point about their obsolescence which Churchill had insisted on 5 February that Clark Kerr must underline. Stalin was trying it on and did not have high hopes: 'we shouldn't expect to get more modern vessels', he told Admiral Kuznetsov.[83]

Stalin to Roosevelt and Churchill, sent 26 February 1944, received 26 February 1944[84]

I received through Ambassador Harriman your two messages of February 24 and 25 regarding the Italian vessels. I have also received your joint with Mr Prime-Minister message of February 7, transmitted to me by the British Ambassador Kerr on February 24. Thank you and Mr Prime-Minister for the communication about your decision to accomplish the transference for temporary use to the Soviet Union by Great Britain of 8 destroyers and 4 submarines, and also as a battleship and 20,000 tons of merchant shipping, and by the United States of a cruiser and 20,000 tons of merchant vessels. Since Mr Kerr specially warned that all the destroyers are old, I have a certain fear regarding the fighting qualities of these destroyers. Meanwhile, it seems to me that for the British and American fleets it will not present much difficulty to allot in the number of eight destroyers at least half of them modern and not old ones. I still hope that you and Mr Prime-Minister will find it possible that among the destroyers being transferred there be at least four modern ones. In the issue of military operations on the part of Germany and Italy we lost a considerable part of our destroyers. Therefore it is quite important for us to have at least a partial replacement of these losses.

On 3 March, Churchill met Ambassador Gusev for the first time since he handed back Stalin's message about Arctic convoys on 18 October 1943. During breakfast at 10 Downing Street Gusev asked the PM for his reactions to Stalin's latest letter. 'We can't give other destroyers instead of those that have already been allocated,' Churchill snapped. 'We are preparing for a big operation, and you will not have a big operation in the north.'[85]

Stalin's initial reaction to Churchill's message about Poland was expressed to Clark Kerr on 28 February. His attitude was totally negative, asserting that the émigré Polish government 'does not want an agreement with Russia. It wants to drive a wedge between the Soviet Union and England.' Stalin was particularly vexed by the Polish proposal for United Nations' administration of the liberated regions of Western Ukraine and the Baltic states, including Vilna and Lwów where many Poles resided. 'We most certainly cannot endure such insults,' he exploded. 'Are we not the masters of our own land? Why insult us! Do we deserve this?'[86] In his report to Churchill, Clark Kerr stated that 'this dreary and exasperating conversation lasted for well over an hour. No argument was of any avail.' Stalin, he said, 'snorted from time to time' at the points the PM had made and, when pressed for 'constructive suggestions', simply reiterated his demands for the Curzon Line and for a reconstructed Polish government.[87]

On 3 March, Harriman received a similar response when he asked Stalin for his reaction to the president's latest message. 'Again the Poles,' the Soviet leader exclaimed. 'Is this the most important issue?' The Russian transcript of the conversation noted: 'Comrade Stalin remarks that all he does is deal with Polish affairs: writes, requests, clarifies. He even completely forgoes military affairs.' As in the interview with Clark Kerr, Stalin sharply denounced the London Poles. Harriman, though himself not exactly a fan, responded that 'there are also good people among them'. Stalin was not impressed: 'Good people can be found everywhere,' he snorted, 'even among the Bushmen' (*bushmeny*) – adding 'Churchill will not be able to do anything with the Poles. The Poles deceive Churchill.'[88]

In his formal reply to the message from Churchill and Roosevelt, Stalin confined himself to a concise rebuttal.[89]

Stalin to Churchill, sent 3 March 1944, received 3 March 1944[90]

I received both your messages of the 20th February on the Polish question from Sir A. Clark Kerr on the 27th February.

I have studied the detailed account of your conversations with members of the emigre Polish Government and have come more and more to the conclusion that such people are not capable of establishing normal relations with the USSR. Suffice it to point to the fact that not only do they not wish to recognise the Curzon Line but they lay claim to Lwow as well as Vilna. As regards designs to place under foreign control the administration of certain Soviet territories, we cannot accept for discussion such aspirations since we consider even the very raising of a question of such a kind insulting to the Soviet Union.

I have already written to the President that the solution of the question of Soviet–Polish relations has not ripened yet.

It is necessary once more to affirm the justness of this conclusion.

After reading Stalin's message Roosevelt noted, 'No reply necessary'. But Churchill called it 'most discouraging'.[91] If, as Stalin claimed, the time was not yet ripe for a diplomatic solution to the Polish question, then the solution would likely come by force – as the Red Army marched west. And the PM was getting tired of these bruising exchanges with the Soviet leader. When Eden suggested another message to Stalin about the treatment of British naval personnel, Churchill told him to stir up some publicity on the issue through parliamentary questions. 'I cannot send such a telegram,' the PM told Eden. 'It would only embroil me with the Bruin on a small point when so many larger ones are looming up. He would only send an insulting, argumentative answer.'[92]

On Saturday evening, 4 March, as he unwound at Chequers, the PM was in sombre mood. 'Stalin refuses to be moderate about the Poles,' noted his private secretary, Jock Colville. 'He said that he felt like telling the Russians, "Personally I fight tyranny in whatever uniform it wears or slogans it utters".' Puffing on Turkish cigarettes and listening to Gilbert and Sullivan records, his mood became increasingly melancholic: 'We live in a world of wolves – and *bears*.'[93]

Churchill's weekend blues were another passing phase. He had not abandoned his efforts to achieve a Polish settlement. But by the spring of 1944 it seemed that Tehran was a fond but faded memory.

12

'FORCE AND FACTS'

(March to June 1944)

IN THE SPRING OF 1944, the Red Army continued its steady advance, while the British and Americans were initially bogged down in Italy – unable to break out of the Anzio beachhead or overcome the daunting Benedictine monastery on the heights of Monte Cassino. But the tempo in the west increased dramatically from mid-May, as the Allies finally surged north to take Rome on 5 June and the long-awaited second front finally dawned the following morning on the beaches of Normandy. Meanwhile, in a sign of cooperation totally lacking among the Axis powers, Stalin timed his main 1944 offensive in Belorussia ('Bagration') to strike at the Germans a couple of weeks after D-Day. Soviet participation in ancillary operations such as 'Bodyguard' (the strategic deception campaign to divert German attention from Normandy) and 'Frantic' (the shuttle bombing of occupied Eastern Europe, using refuelling bases on Soviet soil) also testified to a new level of collaboration.

Among the Big Three correspondents, familiar patterns became even more pronounced. Roosevelt was very much the third party, sending only ten of the forty-five messages exchanged during the three months from 3 March to 5 June 1944 – many of those largely the work of his staff. The president had been unable to shake off the bronchitis and lassitude left by his exhausting trip to Tehran, and was finally prevailed upon by his daughter Anna to have a proper medical check-up. Conducted at Bethesda Naval Hospital on 28 March, this revealed an alarming list of problems, topped by hypertension and incipient heart failure. FDR took the next month off on the estate of his old friend Bernard Baruch in South Carolina. He arrived on 9 April, Easter Sunday, and did not return to the White House until 7 May: this was the most complete vacation of his whole presidency. Although dealing with regular mail pouches from the White House, Roosevelt kept work to a minimum and spent most of his time fishing, driving around the estate and sleeping ten or twelve hours a night.[1] One might discern evidence of his poor health in the botched handling of a press conference on 3 March about the Italian ships and in the bizarre appeal to the German people he proposed to issue on D-Day – which was rapidly shot down by both his partners. Yet the ailing president kept his eye on issues that mattered to him – for instance, sending Stalin several messages seeking to draw the USSR into institutions to shape the postwar world, such as the International Labour Organization, and trying to build solidarity between the American and Russian peoples, as in the case of the Leningrad and Stalingrad scrolls. He also looked for any opportunity to paper over the cracks in the Alliance concerning Poland – as in the Lange–Orlemanski visit to the USSR.

As before, Churchill drafted most of their joint messages to Stalin and handled the major controversies with the Kremlin. This period saw resolution of the long-running argument about the Italian ships, an angry deadlock over the Polish border, and a testy little row about leakage of Stalin–Churchill messages to the British press – each of which was revealing of the personalities beneath the words. Stalin's grudging acceptance of ageing British destroyers instead of surrendered Italian naval vessels finally drew a line under a relatively minor dispute that he had built up into an issue of principle – the USSR's equality within the Alliance – and on which he had shown real intransigence once personally engaged. Churchill's handling of the leakage issue – which the British had initially blamed (wrongly) on the Soviet embassy and then refused to retract – was even more of an ego trip. Their biggest row, over the postwar frontiers of Poland, marked the failure of Churchill's intense efforts since January to broker a deal that satisfied both Stalin and the London Poles by offering *de facto* but not *de jure* acceptance of the Curzon Line as the new Poland's eastern border. The PM's eloquent appeal on 7 March – 'Force can achieve much but force supported by the good will of the world can achieve more' – was characteristic of Churchill the correspondent, trying to use his rhetorical skill in epistolary argument. Stalin's response was equally typical of his forensic style, twisting Churchill's reference to 'force' into an imputation that the USSR was behaving unjustly and using that legalistically to insinuate that the British were trying to break the 'Tehran Agreement' on Poland. As with the Katyn revelations in April 1943, Stalin's response when backed into a corner was to come out fighting in a different direction.

In such cases, these two men wrote to win: once locked in a correspondence that mattered to him, neither was inclined to back down graciously. Roosevelt, by contrast, was altogether more detached – partly because of his health, but also because his was a more feline character, rarely putting his cards on the table. His persistence in trying to avoid Tehran as the venue for the Big Three summit had been a notable exception.

In fact, Churchill and Stalin had more than a touch about them of what we might call the 'alpha male' or, in Foreign Office parlance at the time, the 'prima donna'. So the FO was keen to pull some of these prickly problems back into diplomatic channels, as was the norm in Washington. In mid-May, Geoffrey Wilson of the FO's Northern Department offered Ambassador Clark Kerr his appraisal of where things had gone wrong:

> What has happened, I think, is that the P.M. thought he could conduct a personal correspondence with Stalin on the same sort of family basis as that on which he conducted his personal correspondence with the President. Owing mainly to Stalin's failure to respond, it didn't come off, and instead of this being merely regarded as a difference of method and approach, it was interpreted as deliberate discourtesy, or worse, as an indication that the Russians had the most sinister designs. Our hopes were pitched too high. Provided your real interests don't clash with those of another chap, you can get along quite well with him even if you don't see much of him and don't call him by his Christian name.[2]

Wilson's critique of the prime minister may have had some point, but even if – stretching imagination to its utmost – Stalin and Churchill had both been Old Harrovians, differences of place and distance would have been enormous barriers to meaningful communication in 1944. After the intense directness of Tehran, the business of composing intricate messages and sending them off into the ether proved deeply frustrating. On 5 March, the PM lamented to Ambassador Gusev the lack of direct contact with the Soviet leader, echoing sentiments he had expressed to the Commons on 22 February. Personal meetings, said Churchill, 'give an opportunity to understand each other better, without the aid of paper formulas. My meetings with Stalin were sincere and did not have the tone of these "pieces of paper".'[3]

It did not help matters that Gromyko and Gusev had not grown into subtle intermediaries like Litvinov and Maisky, which of course was Stalin and Molotov's firm intention. The British developed a particular aversion to Gusev

('Frogface') – which did not help in the 'leakage' affair. But there were more substantive concerns about his command of English and his apparent lack of insight. 'One misses Maisky very much,' noted Eden on 28 March, 'for it was always possible to have a heart to heart with him.'[4] In Moscow, Harriman was a figure of substance – because of his own personality and also thanks to his known closeness to the president. FDR had always liked to despatch VIP visitors to Moscow in the hope of developing a vicarious closeness to Stalin; now, perhaps, the president felt he had a VIP permanently on the spot. But proximity did not guarantee access. Clark Kerr – an equally effective envoy – found it very taxing to navigate between his own leader and the man in the Kremlin. Churchill was now issuing strict instructions about reinforcing prime ministerial messages by a personal conversation with Stalin. But the Soviet leader had become adept at fending off people he did not want to see: as Molotov finally confessed to an insistent Clark Kerr on 19 March, the familiar excuse, 'at the front', did not mean that the Boss was out of Moscow; merely that his mind was on the war, not diplomacy.[5]

By May, Churchill had done a volte-face and was reprimanding the ambassador for the 'manner' he had 'picked up in Moscow', namely that 'he personally delivers every telegram to Molotov and Stalin, sometimes waiting for days, while these leaders are not available or are not willing to give audience. Of course, some of the telegrams he must deliver personally, but wouldn't it be more prudent to send others by courier?' Churchill considered it 'much better – for example, when we send a very harsh message – if our man would not have to wait to be run over by a bulldozer and forced to give extenuating explanations which only weakens the argument'.[6]

Working with Churchill meant living with inconsistencies, and the PM's moods were particularly volatile in the spring of 1944. In April, aggrieved at the breakdown over Poland, he adopted what he called 'a moody silence' towards Stalin and the Russians, averring that 'force and facts are their only realities'. As a result, only four messages were exchanged among the Big Three in the whole of April. And in early May, the PM became positively apocalyptic about the future for a week or so, telling Eden that the Russians were 'drunk with victory' and that there was 'no length they may not go to'. (All this was in marked contrast to his talk in January about the 'new confidence which has grown in our hearts towards Stalin'.)[7] Eden's attempt to assuage Churchill's anger by a loose agreement with Gusev on 5 May that the Soviets should 'take the lead' in trying to get Romania out of the war, while the British did the same in Greece, laid the basis for the more substantive 'percentages agreement' on influence in the Balkans that the prime minister would conclude with Stalin in October.

All three leaders were tired and tense that spring, aware that the summer offensives would decide the fate of the war. It is not, perhaps, too far-fetched to imagine Stalin using his 'at the front' interludes to recharge his batteries and ponder the endgame of his struggle with Hitler, so different from what had seemed likely a couple of years earlier. Churchill's agitation and temper reflected his continued fears about the cost of 'Overlord', even though he was now 'hardening' on the operation, as he told FDR in a moment of candour in March.[8] The president had in fact talked of coming over to Britain for the landings, and although some of that may have been the usual FDR soft-soap, the two men exchanged especially cordial messages just before D-Day, with Roosevelt sending a warm personal letter thanking Churchill for a picture of him that was now on the president's bedroom wall, and the PM responding that 'our friendship is my greatest stand-by amid the ever-increasing complications of this exacting war'.[9] This exchange is a reminder that the Churchill–Roosevelt relationship, though no longer as close and animated as in 1940–41, remained axiomatic for each of them, despite their efforts to build new ties with the Kremlin. Here was a diplomatic fact, amid the fields of force, that Stalin certainly did not forget.

*****

Churchill struggled to deal with Stalin's blunt message of 3 March that the time was not ripe for a solution to the Polish question. When the War Cabinet debated the issue on 6 March, Beaverbrook was alone in suggesting that the PM should not reply, because the correspondence was getting 'acrimonious'. Although recognizing that the outcome in Poland would be decided by events, most of the Cabinet agreed that the British government had 'undertaken obligations' and should ensure that its attitude was 'on record', to avoid any impression 'that we had washed our hands of this matter'. Stated more bluntly, to quote Cadogan, London feared accusations of 'another Munich'.[10] Churchill duly revised his draft message to Stalin and sent it on 7 March, with a copy to Roosevelt, who called it 'a very clear and concise statement of the British attitude in the Polish controversy'.[11] The PM made clear that *de facto* Stalin would get a border on the Curzon line which the British would support at the peace conference; but he was equally firm that the Cabinet would not abandon the Polish government in London. He ended by reiterating that all his hopes for the world rested on Big Three 'friendship and cooperation'.

Churchill to Stalin, sent 7 March 1944, received 12 March 1944[12]

I thank you for your message of March 3 about the Polish question.

I made it clear to the Poles that they would not get either Lwow or Vilna and the references to these places, as my message shows, merely suggested a way in those areas in which the Poles thought they could help the common cause. They were certainly not intended to be insulting either by the Poles or by me. However, since you find them an obstacle, pray consider them withdrawn and expunged from the message.

The proposals I submitted to you make the occupation by Russia of Curzon Line a *de facto* reality in agreement with the Poles from the moment your armies reach it, and I have told you that, provided the settlement you and we have outlined in our talks and correspondence was brought into being, His Britannic Majesty's Government would support it at the armistice or peace conferences. I have no doubt that it would be equally supported by the United States. Therefore you would have the Curzon Line *de facto* with the assent of the Poles as soon as you get there, and with the blessing of your Western Allies at the general settlement.

Force can achieve much but force supported by the good will of the world can achieve more. I earnestly hope that you will not close the door finally to a working arrangement with the Poles which will help the common cause during the war and give you all you require at the peace. If nothing can be arranged and you are unable to have any relations with the Polish Government, which we shall continue to recognise as the government of the ally for whom we declared war upon Hitler, I should be very sorry indeed. The War Cabinet ask me to say that they would share this regret. Our only comfort will be that we have tried our very best.

You spoke to Ambassador Clark Kerr of the danger of the Polish question making a rift between you and me. I shall try earnestly to prevent this. All my hopes for the future of the world are based upon the friendship and cooperation of the Western democracies and Soviet Russia.

Churchill also sent Clark Kerr meticulous instructions – no fewer than seven points – about how the message should be delivered and verbally reinforced. Summing up, he said: 'You should not fail to emphasise the gravity of divergence in its bearing on the future but you should also avoid anything that could be construed as a change of policy or change of heart, let alone anything like a threat.' 'It may well be, however,' Churchill added sombrely, 'that the Russian treatment of Poland will prove to be a touchstone and make all sorts of far more important things more difficult.'[13]

It was testimony to the effectiveness of his relationship by now with both Churchill and Stalin that on 8 March Clark Kerr decided to suggest some modifications to the PM's message. In particular, he proposed softening the fourth paragraph about the use of force, which might otherwise leave Stalin with the impression that Britain felt there was 'no justice in his case', and also avoid any remark about the 'casting of a shadow over the coming operations', which would 'suggest to Stalin's suspicious mind that we were not going to live up to our promises made at Tehran'. The ambassador apologized to Churchill for his temerity – 'if I had to choose I should rather take on Stalin than you' – but stated that the matter was so important that 'I feel bound to tell you of the dangers I foresee'.[14] In the FO, Oliver Harvey shared Clark Kerr's concerns, noting in his diary that Churchill and Eden were 'both in very anti-Soviet mood – rather dangerously so, I think'. The prime minister, however, was not moved. 'You have authority to tell Marshal Stalin that I should like to be able to say in Parliament that the door is still open,' he told the ambassador, 'but whether I can do so will depend on his reply.' He would not accept any changes in the message, declaring 'Appeasement has had a good run.'[15]

Clark Kerr waited to hand the PM's message about Poland to Stalin in person, so he could underline the essential points. Encouraged by Molotov to think that a meeting was imminent, on 12 March he gave the foreign minister a translation of the message. This was standard practice just before any audience at the Kremlin, but the ambassador was soon to regret what he had done.

Meanwhile, the Italian naval saga continued to run. Roosevelt had not helped matters by getting himself into a real tangle on the matter in a press conference on 3 March, when he said it was 'about half decided' that Russia would get Italian ships 'or the equivalent' and would do so 'roughly on a – what? – a one-third basis, because there were three great nations involved'. Aware that he had made a mess of things, FDR immediately despatched evasive explanations to both Stalin and Churchill.[16] The Soviet leader sent a brief thank-you, but Churchill was furious, bombarding the president with a series of messages about this 'complete departure' from previous agreements and reminding him that Britain had 'suffered at least twenty times the naval losses of your Fleet in the Mediterranean'. The president did not disavow his 'one-third' statement, but quietly buried it, telling Churchill 'I do not think there is any essential conflict', and agreed to the PM's proposed joint message to Stalin. Although gilding the lily in places – for instance, on the Japanese threat from Singapore – this explanation by Churchill and the Admiralty of Britain's need for destroyers was essentially accurate.[17]

Roosevelt and Churchill to Stalin, sent 9 March 1944, received 9 March 1944[18]

Although the Prime Minister instructed Ambassador Clark Kerr to tell you that the destroyers we are lending you were old, this was only for the sake of absolute frankness. In fact they are good, serviceable ships, quite efficient for escort duty. There are only seven fleet destroyers in the whole Italian Navy, the rest being older destroyers and torpedo-boats. Moreover, these Italian destroyers, when we do get them, are absolutely unfitted for work in the North without very lengthy refit. Therefore we thought the eight which the British Government had found would be an earlier and more convenient form of help to you. The Prime Minister regrets that he cannot spare any new destroyers at the present time; he lost two the week before last, one in the Russian convoy, and for landing at 'Overlord' alone he has to deploy for close inshore work against batteries no fewer than 42 destroyers, a large proportion of which may be sunk. Every single vessel that he has of this class is being used to the utmost pressure in the common cause. The movement of the Japanese Fleet to Singapore creates a new situation for us both in the Indian Ocean. The fighting in the Anzio bridgehead and generally throughout the Mediterranean is at its height. The vast troop convoys are crossing the Atlantic with the United States Army of Liberation. The Russian convoys are being run up to the last minute before 'Overlord' with very heavy destroyer escorts. Finally there is 'Overlord' itself. The President's position is similarly strained but in this case mainly because of the great scale and activity of the operations in the Pacific. Our joint intentions to deliver to you the Italian ships agreed on at Moscow and Tehran remain unaltered, and we shall put the position formally to the Italian Government at the time the latter is broadened and the new Ministers take over their responsibilities. There is no question of our right to dispose of the Italian Navy, but only of exercising that right with the least harm to our common interests. Meanwhile all our specified ships are being prepared for delivery to you on loan as already agreed.

The Kremlin, in turn, had been exercised about how to deal with Roosevelt's letter of 23 February about cooperation in postwar reconstruction – eventually replying on 10 March. Cordell Hull's memo, which Stalin mentioned in his message, had been given to Molotov during the Moscow conference of 1943 and had won enthusiastic support from the foreign trade commissar, Anastas Mikoyan. On 14 October 1943, in a letter to Molotov, Mikoyan not only supported involvement in the proposed international stabilization fund, but also urged that the USSR be involved in its administration:

In order to safeguard the Soviet Union's proper participation in the Fund's governing bodies it should be suggested that the core members of the United Nations – the United States, Great Britain, the USSR and China – have at least about 10% of the total number of votes each, regardless of the size of their quotas, and agree that a representative of the USSR will sit on the Fund's Executive Committee.[19]

All this, of course, represented uncharted terrain for the USSR, hitherto largely insulated from the global economy, and it sparked considerable debate among planners in Moscow. There were clear material benefits, for instance the prospect of financial aid to 'restore quickly the war-ravaged economy of the liberated regions of the USSR, to advance further the entire socialist economy of the country and to improve the living standards of the population'.[20] Yet the issue was not just about domestic economic recovery, but also equality of status in the world, as shown by Mikoyan's reference to the United Nations Big Four. And until early 1945, at least, the Soviet government maintained a positive attitude to developing postwar economic cooperation with its allies. This was reflected in Stalin's vague but warm reaction to Roosevelt's proposal.

Stalin to Roosevelt, sent 10 March 1944, received 10 March 1944[21]

I have received your message on the question of post-war economic collaboration. Undoubtedly, the questions touched upon in Mr Hull's note regarding international collaboration in the sphere of economics are of great importance and demand attention. I consider as quite expedient the establishment at the present time of a United Nations apparatus for the working out of these questions and also for the establishment of conditions and order of consideration of various problems of the international economic collaboration in accordance with the decisions of the Moscow and Teheran Conferences.

Stalin did not rush to make a detailed response to Churchill's letter of 7 March about Poland. Molotov did prepare a draft response, but the Boss struck out a brief assessment of that message, and instead added some irate words about revelations in the British press of his correspondence with Churchill. What infuriated Stalin was that his 3 March reply to Churchill about Poland had been the subject of a detailed article in the left-wing *Daily Herald* and also a piece in *The Times* by its diplomatic correspondent, Iverach McDonald. The ever suspicious Stalin saw here at least negligence and at worst deliberate leakage by the British government. Yet his anger was probably exaggerated for the occasion –

following his practice, when under pressure, of mounting his own attack at another point.

Stalin to Churchill, sent 16 March 1944, received 18 March 1944[22]

I received from Sir A. Clark Kerr on March 12th your message of March 7th on the Polish question.

Thank you for the explanations which you made in this message.

In spite of the fact that our correspondence is considered secret and personal the contents of my letter to you have for some time begun to appear in the English press, and, moreover, with many distortions which I have no possibility of refuting.

I consider this to be a breach of secrecy. This fact makes it difficult for me to express my opinion freely. I hope that you have understood me.

Churchill and his entourage certainly saw Stalin's complaint about the British press as a tactical ploy. 'It is quite obvious that the Bear proposes to reach no agreement and accept no compromises' on Poland, noted Jock Colville, 'and is fabricating all sorts of excuses to this end'. The PM decided to send no reply, blaming the leakage on the Soviet embassy; but according to Colville, he said 'that it was now obvious our efforts to forge a Soviet–Polish agreement had failed and that he would soon have to make a cold announcement in Parliament to that effect'.[23]

Meanwhile, on the Italian ships, Stalin finally conceded this protracted controversy with a message of grudging acceptance of the aged British destroyers. At the same time, he reiterated the principle of Soviet equality of rights as an ally – the issue that had driven him all along.

Stalin to Churchill and Roosevelt, sent 17 March 1944, received 17 March 1944[24]

I have received your message about the transfer to the Soviet Union by the British Government of eight destroyers. I am prepared to agree that these destroyers are fully suitable for escort duty, but it is, of course, known to you, that the Soviet Union needs destroyers suitable also for other warlike operations. The right of the Allies to dispose of the Italian Navy is, of course, entirely beyond dispute and the Italian Government should be given so to understand in the particular case of the Italian ships which are liable to be handed over to the Soviet Union.

In another message prompted by his bureaucracy, Roosevelt urged Stalin to authorize Soviet participation in a conference of the International Labour Organization (ILO), an offshoot of the League of Nations. The USSR had been a member of the ILO before being expelled from the League at the end of 1939. The United States was now planning to revive the ILO and had asked the USSR to join in, but the Foreign Ministry's initial response to the proposal was negative. In a letter to Harriman on 7 March 1944, Molotov stated that the USSR was no longer 'in a relationship with the League of Nations' and that, in any case, the ILO 'lacks the authority' to be effective, 'which in present circumstances calls for more democratic forms of organisation of international cooperation in that sphere'.[25] Roosevelt hoped that a personal appeal to Stalin might change Soviet policy, fearing that the absence of the USSR would have a 'bad effect' on ILO prestige 'both here and among labor in occupied areas'.[26] The message was drafted by White House aide Isador Lubin, a specialist on labour statistics, and coordinated with the Labor and State Departments.

Roosevelt to Stalin, sent 20 March 1944, received 23 March 1944[27]

I have just been informed by Harriman that the Soviet Union is not planning to participate in the conference of the International Labor Organization to be held in Philadelphia starting April 2.

I have given considerable thought to the role that the International Labor Organization should play in constantly improving the labor and social standards throughout the world. I am anxious that you should know my thoughts about this matter.

It is my opinion that the International Labor Organization should be the instrument for the formulation of international policy on matters directly affecting the welfare of labor and for international collaboration in this field. I should like to see it become a body which will also serve as an important organ of the United Nations for discussing economic and social matters relating to labor and an important agency for the consideration of international economic policies which look directly toward improvement in standard of living. It would be unfortunate if both our Governments did not take advantage of the conference in Philadelphia to help develop our common objectives. We could thereby adapt the existing International Labor Organization to the tasks facing the world without loss of valuable time.

I am instructing the United States Government delegates to the Philadelphia Conference to propose measures to broaden the activities and functions of the

International Labor Organization and raise the question of its future relationship to other international organizations. In view of your interest in these matters and since there is a great range of social and economic problems that are of common interest to both our Governments, I greatly hope that your Government will participate in this conference.

Churchill now decided to respond to Stalin's insinuation that the British government had been leaking his messages on Poland. An inquiry authorized by the Cabinet into the leakage of Stalin–Churchill correspondence indicated that the most likely source of the leaks was the Soviet embassy in London, including the ambassador himself, who gave an interview to *The Times* correspondent on 7 March. In his message on the 21st, Churchill made this clear to Stalin, and Clark Kerr gave Molotov fuller details.[28] As for Polish affairs, Churchill decided to bring matters to a head, having still received no reply from Stalin to his important message of 7 March. So he rounded off his cable by warning the Soviet leader bluntly that he would soon have to tell Parliament that Soviet–Polish negotiations had collapsed. An opening pat on the back about the relative moderation of the peace terms that Moscow had offered to Finland did little to offset the hard punches that followed.

The message was worked over in fractious mood by Churchill, Eden and Cadogan – 'everyone exhausted', the latter scribbled in his diary. The FO had hoped to defuse relations with Moscow by getting discussions off 'this dangerous high-level of P.M.–Stalin down to a Molotov–Clark Kerr level', noted Harvey. 'If we can keep the old prima donnas off the stage, we believe we might be able to make progress.'[29] Fond hopes!

Churchill to Stalin, sent 21 March 1944, received 22 March 1944[30]

Your telegram of March 16.

First of all I must congratulate you again on all the wonderful victories your Armies are winning and also on the extremely temperate way in which you have dealt with the Finns. I suppose they are worried about interning nine German divisions in Finland for fear that the nine German divisions should intern them. We are much obliged to you for keeping us in touch with all your action in this theatre.

With regard to the Poles, I am not to blame in any way about revealing your secret correspondence. The information was given both to the American *Herald Tribune* correspondent and to the London *Times* correspondent by the Soviet Embassy in London. In the latter case, it was given personally by Ambassador Gusev.

I shall have very soon to make a statement to the House of Commons about the Polish position. This will involve my saying that attempts to make an arrangement between the Soviet and Polish Governments have broken down; that we continue to recognise the Polish Government, with whom we have been in continuous relations since the invasion of Poland in 1939; that we now consider all questions of territorial change must await the Armistice or Peace Conferences of the victorious Powers; and that in the meantime we can recognise no forcible transferences of territory.

I am repeating this telegram to the President of the United States. I only wish I had better news to give him for the sake of all.

Finally, let me express the earnest hope that the breakdown which has occurred between us about Poland will not have any effect upon our cooperation in other spheres where the maintenance of our common action is of the greatest consequence.

The fate of Churchill's 7 March letter on Poland offers a revealing insight into Stalin's handling of the correspondence as a whole. The message was unanswered because it had not yet been formally delivered. The audience with the Soviet leader that Clark Kerr had been led to expect by Molotov did not materialize. On pressing further, the ambassador was informed by the foreign minister in a letter on 17 March that 'Stalin of late has been much at the front' and that after a 'brief visit to Moscow has returned to his duties there'. Clark Kerr was not convinced, noting to Churchill that the Soviet leader had found time to host a dinner in the Kremlin for the high command of the Polish People's Army in the USSR, so 'I cannot but think that he is deliberately avoiding another talk about Poland'.[31]

The ambassador was also angry that Molotov had implied that a meeting with Stalin was imminent – thereby, he told Churchill, 'luring me into sending him a translation of your message'. Bearing in mind the unfortunate outcome after delaying the PM's messages about the Italian ships, Clark Kerr decided to be on the safe side and secured a meeting with the foreign minister, so as to ram home the essentials, as instructed by the PM, to Molotov if not to the Boss. Throughout this encounter, on 19 March, Clark Kerr tried to emphasize the gravity of the situation, while avoiding 'anything in the nature of a threat'. The foreign minister listened impassively – with what the ambassador called 'none of the interruptions and asides with which Stalin would have enlivened the proceedings – and promised to pass it all on. According to Molotov, Stalin 'had decided to divorce himself from politics' and 'was now entirely absorbed with the battle', leaving his foreign minister with 'the duty of dealing with the world'.

These were the remarks that finally illuminated that familiar but vague phrase 'at the front', which evidently signified Stalin's mental rather than physical absence. 'There seems nothing for it now,' Clark Kerr cabled Churchill wearily, 'but to await Stalin's reaction.'[32]

This finally arrived on 25 March and was even worse than expected.[33] Both sides could now see that there was little chance of an agreement between the Kremlin and the London Poles, and so Stalin, like Churchill, was preparing his position for the record. As over Katyn and the second front, Stalin and Molotov were masters of casuistry, exploiting vulnerable words in Churchill's message to suit their needs. The PM's line that 'force can achieve much but force supported by the good will of the world can achieve more' was interpreted as evidence that Churchill was breaching the 'Tehran Agreement' and impugning the credentials of the Soviet westward offensive as a war of liberation. And Clark Kerr's 19 March monologue to Molotov, which the foreign minister may well have exaggerated to Stalin, was treated as exemplifying the 'method of threats', which was not only 'incorrect' between allies but positively 'harmful'. The Soviet leader was able to round off the message by portraying the Soviet Union as holding true to the principles of cooperation, even if Churchill regrettably chose to lapse into defamation and intimidation.

Stalin to Churchill, sent 23 March 1944, received 25 March 1944[34]

I have recently received from you two messages on the Polish question and have studied the statement which Sir A. Clark Kerr made to V.M. Molotov on your instructions on the same question. I was unable to reply at the time as matters at the front often take me away from non-military matters.

I shall now reply on these questions.

It is patent that your messages, and especially the statement of Sir A. Clark Kerr, are full of threats concerning the Soviet Union. I should like to draw your attention to this fact, as the method of threats is not only incorrect in the mutual relations of allies but is also harmful and can lead to contrary results.

In one of your messages you qualified the efforts of the Soviet Union in the matters of the maintenance and realisation of the Curzon Line as a policy of force. This means that you now seek to qualify the Curzon Line as unlawful and the struggle for it as unjust. I can on no account agree with such an attitude. I cannot but remind you that at Tehran you, the President and I agreed as to the justice of the Curzon Line. You considered then the attitude of the Soviet Government regarding this question as perfectly just, and you said that the representatives of the emigre Polish Government would be mad to refuse to accept the Curzon Line. Now you maintain something that is directly to the contrary.

Does this not mean that you no longer acknowledge what we agreed upon at Tehran, and that by this very fact you are breaking the Tehran Agreement? I have no doubt that if you had continued to stand firmly, as before, by the attitude you adopted at Tehran, the dispute with the Polish émigré Government would already have been settled. As for myself and the Soviet Government, we continue to stand by the attitude we adopted at Tehran and have no intention of departing from it, since we consider that the realisation of the Curzon Line is not a manifestation of a policy of force but a manifestation of the policy of the restoration of the legal rights of the Soviet Union to those territories which even Curzon and the Supreme Council of the Allied Powers recognised in 1919 as being non-Polish.

You state in your message of the 7th March that the question of the Soviet–Polish frontier will have to be deferred until the summoning of the Armistice Conference. I think we have here some misunderstanding. The Soviet Union is not waging and has no intention of waging war against Poland. The Soviet Union has no dispute with the Polish people and considers itself the ally of Poland and the Polish people. For this very reason, the Soviet Union is shedding blood for the sake of the liberation of Poland from German oppression. For this reason, it would be strange to speak of an armistice between the U.S.S.R. and Poland. But the Soviet Union has a dispute with the émigré Polish Government, which does not represent the interests of the Polish people or express their aspirations. It would be even more strange to identify with Poland the emigre Polish Government in London separated (literally 'torn away') from Poland. I find it difficult even to point to the difference between the emigre Government of Poland and the similar emigre Government of Yugoslavia, or between certain Generals of the Polish emigre Government and the Serbian General Mikhailovich.

In your message of the 21st March you state that you intend to make a statement in the House of Commons to the effect that all territorial questions must await the armistice of the peace conference of the victorious Powers, and that, until then, you cannot recognise any transferences of territory <u>carried out by force</u>. I understand this to mean that you represent the Soviet Union as a power hostile to Poland, and that the essence of the matter is that you deny the emancipatory character of the war of the Soviet Union against German aggression. That is equivalent to attempting to ascribe to the Soviet Union what is not the case and to discrediting it thereby. I have no doubt that such a statement of yours will be taken by the peoples of the Soviet Union and world public opinion as an undeserved insult directed at the Soviet Union.

Of course you are free to make whatever statement you please in the House of Commons – that is your affair. But if you do make such a statement, I shall consider that you have committed an unjust and unfriendly act towards the Soviet Union.

In your message you express the hope that the failure over the Polish question will not influence our cooperation in other spheres. As for myself, I stood for, and continue to stand for collaboration. But I fear that the method of threats and discrediting, if it continues in the future, will not conduce to our collaboration.

'A violent reply from Joe,' noted Cadogan. Eden found Churchill 'very much perturbed' by this 'very bad message' and noted in his diary: 'I share his anxiety and truly don't know what course to advise with least damage to our affairs.'[35] The PM told the president on 1 April that the Cabinet felt that since Stalin was 'determined to find fault and pick a quarrel on every point', there was no point in further prime ministerial messages, but he personally had 'a feeling that their bark may be worse than their bite and that they have a great desire not to separate themselves from their British and American allies'. To make clear Britain's position, a message was sent for the record 'from the War Cabinet' to Molotov, stressing that the British government had not abandoned the position it had taken on the Curzon Line, but that, in current circumstances, it could 'only withdraw from the ungrateful role of mediator' and announce the 'failure' of its efforts. Roosevelt – now about to go off for recuperation following his alarming medical check-up at Bethesda – agreed with the British posture, deeming it 'correct in its purpose and considerate beyond reasonable expectation'.[36]

Churchill instructed Eden on 1 April that they should now adopt 'a moody silence so far as Stalin is concerned', dealing only with Molotov and then in 'the most urbane and detached way', without getting into any arguments or attempts to 'flatter or kowtow to them'. It was clear, he said, that 'our and especially *my* very courteous and even effusive personal approaches have had a bad effect'. Churchill observed darkly: 'Although I have tried in every way to put myself in sympathy with these Communist leaders, I cannot feel the slightest trust or confidence in them. Force and facts are their only realities.'[37]

Eden agreed that 'we should give personal messages between you and Stalin a rest'. But however 'exasperating' recent Russian behaviour had been, he urged Churchill 'not to jump to the conclusion that they have decided to go back on the policy of cooperation', emphasizing that 'the Polish affair stands in a category by itself'. Like Churchill, he dismissed a call from Hull for 'plain-speaking' as simply leading to yet more rows and was 'inclined to let matters drift a little longer before considering a showdown with Stalin'. This was also the view of the FO's senior officials, who wanted to put British–Soviet relations on the back-burner instead of being the subject of super-heated ego messages between the two leaders. Harvey was encouraged during April to learn of secret contacts between Soviet commanders and the Polish underground, and between the London and Moscow Poles – all of which were denied by Molotov. 'I am glad to say,' he noted in his diary, 'we are sitting back and taking no part.'[38]

By now, the USSR was making its own plans for Poland. At the end of 1943, a State National Council (*Krajowa Rada Narodowa*) had been set up in secret under the leadership of Bolesław Bierut, bringing together Polish leftist parties led by the communists, which became a political alternative to the London government. The State Council issued an appeal to the Polish people to 'support the Soviet government's policy in Soviet–Polish relations'.[39] The Kremlin also wanted to enlist pro-Soviet Poles living in America and Britain, in the hope of giving an international face to the alternative government. The Soviet embassy in Washington looked for leaders acceptable to Moscow, and identified two possible figures from the Polish-American community: the socialist Oskar Lange, who had emigrated from Poland to the USA in the 1930s and was now an economics professor at the University of Chicago, and an obscure Catholic priest from Springfield, Massachusetts, called Stanislaus Orlemanski. Both had a public profile of pro-Soviet sympathies and hostility towards the London government. The Kremlin decided to invite Lange and Orlemanski to Moscow to meet the Soviet leadership, and on 21 February 1944, under instructions from Moscow, Gromyko personally asked Roosevelt to facilitate their trip. The president said he would consult with Hull, but despite Soviet reminders, no further response followed.[40]

This was because the request had placed the administration in a quandary. 'These two men,' reported Hull's deputy, Edward Stettinius, to Roosevelt on 8 March, 'represent a specific and heavily slanted view of the Polish–Soviet question which is not shared by American citizens of Polish descent nor American public opinion in general.' If they travelled to the USSR with official US assistance, their visit would be 'widely interpreted as the first step in the abandonment by this Government of the Polish Government-in-exile'. On the other hand, Stettinius warned, it would be 'undesirable, if not impossible' to prohibit two American citizens from accepting an invitation from the Soviet government. As a way out of this predicament, the State Department therefore recommended making the trip an entirely private affair and emphasizing this in a message to Stalin, a draft of which was attached to Stettinius's memo. Roosevelt procrastinated before making a final decision. He knew full well the mood among Polish-Americans and was frustrated by its prevalently anti-Soviet attitude. Yet he had to take their feelings seriously, especially ahead of the presidential election in November. A couple of weeks later, FDR approved the issue of passports to Lange and Orlemanski and signed off the draft message to Stalin, with only minor changes. Denying the two men US transport was part of the administration's effort to avoid any official fingerprints on the trip. Stalin accepted Roosevelt's terms. In April, the two Polish-Americans were flown on Soviet planes to Moscow via Alaska and Siberia, arriving separately at different times, so as to minimize attention.[41]

Roosevelt to Stalin, sent 24 March 1944, received 25 March 1944[42]

In accordance with your suggestion Dr. Lange and Father Orlemanski will be given passports in order to accept your invitation to proceed to the Soviet Union. Due, however, to military movements our transportation facilities are greatly overcrowded at the present time and transportation, therefore, from the United States to the Soviet Union will have to be furnished by Soviet facilities. I know you will realize that Dr. Lange and Father Orlemanski are proceeding in their individual capacity as private citizens and this Government can assume no responsibility whatsoever for their activities or views and should their trip become the subject of public comment it might be necessary for this Government to make this point clear.

Stalin sent a polite but categorical refusal to Roosevelt's request for Soviet participation in the ILO conference in Philadelphia, reiterating arguments enumerated in an earlier letter from Molotov, as well as using (fictitious) objections from Soviet trade unions. The real reason was Stalin's deep hostility towards the League and all its organizations, which, back in the 1930s, he privately dubbed 'league-of-nations dung' (*lignatsovskiy navoz*). Although FDR sent a follow-up message on 31 March, expressing the hope that the ILO would soon break with the League and align itself with the United Nations, this was not done until after the war. The USSR did not join the ILO until 1954, after Stalin's death.[43]

Stalin to Roosevelt, sent 25 March 1944, received 25 March 1944[44]

I share your endeavor toward cooperation of our two Governments in studying economic and social matters connected with the tasks of improving working

conditions on a world scale. The Soviet Union is unable, however, to send its representatives to the International Labor Bureau conference in Philadelphia due to
the motives, stated in the letter to Mr Harriman, as the Soviet trades-unionist
organizations expressed themselves against such a participation and the Soviet
Government cannot but take account of the opinion of the Soviet trades-unionist
organisations.

It goes without saying that, if the International Labor Organization in
reality becomes an organ of the United Nations and not of the League of Nations,
with which the Soviet Union cannot have associations, then the participation in its
work of representatives of the Soviet Union would be possible. I hope that this will
become possible and that appropriate measures will be carried out already in the
near future.

Meanwhile, recriminations continued about the leakage of the Stalin–Churchill
correspondence in the British press. In response to Churchill's accusations
against Gusev and the Soviet embassy, the Kremlin instructed the ambassador to
conduct his own investigation. Gusev once again found himself in a difficult
situation, since he had indeed met McDonald of *The Times* on the eve of the
controversial publication, so in his report to Molotov he accused the British journalist of malicious distortion. But the main and most convincing argument in
Gusev's defence was that he was not privy to Churchill's messages to Stalin, also
discussed in the articles in question. Castigating the allegations against him
as a 'poorly prepared provocation', the ambassador craftily concluded his explanation by saying: 'Churchill and Eden would like to have another person as the
Soviet ambassador in London and with this démarche they have begun an official campaign to achieve this goal.'[45] Gusev was indeed disliked in London and
he now turned this to his advantage, since being undesirable in the eyes of the
British government would only underscore his independence in the eyes of the
Kremlin. It was the Poles who were most likely responsible for the leaks, having
been familiarized by the British with relevant parts of the Churchill–Stalin
correspondence, and Eden's entourage privately admitted such a possibility.[46]

Gusev's account clearly satisfied Stalin, who wrote sternly to Churchill the
day after receiving the ambassador's dispatch.

Stalin to Churchill, sent 25 March 1944, received 25 March 1944[47]

I have carried out a thorough enquiry into your statement that the disclosure of
the correspondence between us occurred through the fault of the Soviet Embassy
in London and of Ambassador F.T. Gousev personally.

This enquiry has shown that neither the Embassy nor F.T. Gousev personally were at all guilty in this matter and that they did not even have in their possession certain of the documents the contents of which were published in the English newspapers. Thus the leakage occurred not on the Soviet but on the English side.

Gousev is willing to undertake any investigation of this matter in order to prove that he and the members of his staff are in no way implicated in the matter of the disclosure of the contents of our correspondence. It seems to me that you have been led astray with regard to Gousev and the Soviet Embassy.

The War Cabinet, mindful of the general policy of avoiding further argument with the Kremlin, 'decided that nothing was to be gained by pursuing a correspondence which was bound to be controversial', but Stalin's accusations caught Churchill on the raw and he ordered another inquiry, telling the Cabinet secretary: 'I cannot leave the charge of being liars unrefuted.'[48]

The results of that inquiry proved embarrassing, eventually showing in July 1944 that the PM had been wrong to tell Stalin on 21 March that Gusev had leaked their correspondence to *The Times*. The PM wanted the FO to carry the can if there had to be any official apology to Moscow,[49] but both he and Eden tried to hush things up until *The Times*, which had found out about the controversy, insisted that its story was based on a report in the *New York Herald Tribune* and threatened to make this clear to the Soviet embassy. At the end of July, Clark Kerr was therefore instructed to deliver a special statement to Molotov curtly stating this background. The ambassador wanted to mitigate this text with some hint of 'an apology or regret' because otherwise the Russians might reopen the whole issue. But the Foreign Office stood firm: Orme Sargent cabled Clark Kerr to say that 'we have had the greatest difficulty over this matter', on the one hand because of strong hints from *The Times* that it would take up the matter directly with the Russians, and on the other because of Churchill's 'reluctance to do anything which might be interpreted as exoneration of the Soviet Embassy'. The ambassador was told 'to show clearly that we do not ourselves accept any responsibility', while also 'dropping a hint that we do not entirely absolve the Soviet Embassy'.[50] When Clark Kerr duly wrote in this vein to Molotov on 8 August, the foreign minister replied that it confirmed the Kremlin's insistence throughout that charges of leakage from Gusev and the embassy were 'without any foundation'. He also noted that, since it was 'not clear' from the ambassador's letter who had been responsible, 'I should be grateful for further information on this question.' After further cogitation in London, Clark Kerr was told on 4 September that it was 'not intended to send any reply'.[51]

The original Stalin–Churchill exchange about the leaks had taken place in mid-March, so this whole affair had dragged on for nearly six months. Although both the Soviet and the Polish embassies were clearly engaged in spin for the British press, on the specific issue of Gusev, the PM's accusation on 21 March had proved unfounded, but Churchill did not want to lose face by admitting it. There were parallels here with Stalin's ego trip over the Italian navy. Hence the FO's keen desire to keep diplomacy away from the 'prima donnas'.

*****

Churchill did indeed adopt what he called a 'moody silence' for several weeks. But by mid-April he was casting around for a positive issue on which to reset the relationship. 'Would it not be well for you and me,' he cabled Roosevelt on the 14th, 'to send a notice to Uncle J. about the date of OVERLORD?' Characteristically, he also sent a draft for consideration, phrased in very cordial tones and taking pains to praise the 'magnificent series of unforeseen victories' that Soviet troops had won 'for the common cause' during the winter months, when inactivity had been expected. During March and April, the Red Army had liberated much of the southern Ukraine and pushed into the Crimea.[52]

General Marshall prepared a reply, which Roosevelt, still recuperating, sent to London without change. This informed Churchill that the Combined Chiefs of Staff had recently instructed the US and British military missions in Moscow to inform the Soviet general staff in strictest confidence of the target date for 'Overlord' (31 May) and to seek confirmation of the complementary Soviet offensive that Stalin had promised at Tehran, but without asking for the operational details that Churchill was requesting in his draft message. This cable was delivered on 10 April.[53] The PM – though perhaps miffed that the Kremlin was already in the know and that his draft was not, as customary, being nodded through by the president – sought to justify the sending of an additional message from the two of them: 'This engages Stalin's direct personal attention and is more worthy of the tremendous event to which we are committing heart and soul than a Staff notification.' And, the PM added hopefully, 'it may even be followed by a friendly response'.[54]

Churchill sent the message virtually as amended and abbreviated by Roosevelt (in other words by Marshall).

Roosevelt and Churchill to Stalin, sent 19 April 1944, received 21 April 1944[55]

Pursuant to our talks at Teheran, the general crossing of the sea will take place around R date which Generals Deane and Burrows have recently been directed to give to the Soviet General Staff. We shall be acting at our fullest strength.

We are launching an offensive on the Italian mainland at maximum strength about mid-May.

Since Teheran your armies have been gaining a magnificent series of victories for the common cause. Even in the months when you thought they would not be active they have gained these great victories. We send you our very best wishes and trust that your armies and ours, operating in unison in accordance with our Teheran agreement, will crush the Hitlerites.

On 22 April, the day after this cable was received in the Kremlin, General Aleksey Antonov, deputy chief of the general staff, sent a formal reply to the CCS message: 'The General Staff of the Red Army is satisfied with your kind message about the start date of operation "Overlord", in accordance with the Tehran Agreement. The new Soviet offensive in support of the Allied Anglo-American troops will be launched at the same time.' On that day, Stalin also replied to Roosevelt and Churchill in similar terms, using a Molotov draft.[56]

The top-secret information on 'R', the start date for 'Overlord', apparently had a direct impact on the planning of military operations by the Soviet high command. On 12 April, two days after the receipt of the first precise news from the Americans and the British, a joint meeting of the Politburo, the State Committee for Defence (GKO) and Stavka took place, at which a series of 'successive strategic offensive operations' were plotted along the full extent of the Soviet–German front.[57] On 22 April, the day of Stalin's reply, a further meeting was convened at the Stavka with senior commanders. Puffing on his pipe, Stalin asked for a report on the problems they would encounter in the 1944 campaign. Zhukov duly began, but was soon interrupted by the supreme commander: 'These will not be the only problems. In June the Allies intend to finally conduct a major landing operation in France. Our allies are in a hurry.' Stalin smiled. 'They are afraid we will rout Nazi Germany without them.' He went on more soberly: 'Of course, it is in our interests to see Germany finally beginning to fight on two fronts. This will make things even more difficult for them.'[58]

A few days later, Stalin firmed up plans for the summer campaign, which would feature a major offensive into Belorussia against Hitler's Army Group

Centre – the biggest thorn in Russia's flesh ever since 'Barbarossa'. This would be timed as far as possible to coincide with 'Overlord'. The Soviet leader then sent the 'friendly response' that Churchill had hoped for to the joint message of 18 April.

Stalin to Roosevelt and Churchill, sent 22 April 1944, received 22 April 1944[59]

I have received your message of the 18th April. The Soviet Government is satisfied with your statement that, in accordance with the Tehran agreement, the crossing of the sea will take place on the date planned, regarding which Generals Deane and Burrows have already informed our General Staff, and that you will be acting at full strength. I express my confidence in the success of the planned operation.

I also hope for the success of the operation to be undertaken by you in Italy.

As agreed in Tehran, the Red Army will undertake at the same time its new offensive in order to give maximum support to the Anglo-American operations.

I beg you to accept my thanks for the wishes you express regarding the success of the Red Army. I subscribe to your declaration that your Armies and ours, supporting one another, will crush the Hitlerites and fulfil their historic mission.

The message – though stilted in tone – was enormously significant. It showed that, for all the acrimony at times, Stalin and his two Western counterparts were operating as allies in a fundamental sense – seeking to concert their separate war efforts against a common enemy – unlike Nazi Germany and Imperial Japan within the so-called 'Axis'.

Yet neither Roosevelt nor Churchill replied to Stalin. The White House sent the text in the mail pouch to FDR in South Carolina, but the president was barely looking at his mail; two weeks later, there was a note on the Map Room log sheet: 'Admiral Leahy says no reply or acknowledgment considered necessary.'[60] As for Churchill, he managed formally to maintain his 'moody silence' by tacking a note of appreciation onto the end of a message about other matters he sent to Molotov. (This was an avenue that had conveniently opened up because he was overseeing the Foreign Office for two weeks while the exhausted Eden was taking a vacation.) 'Pray convey to Marshal Stalin,' Churchill told the foreign minister, 'my acknowledgment of his reply sent to the message sent him by President Roosevelt and me. It is indeed an event which we may rightly describe as "an historic mission".' Playing the same game, Molotov appended to a message about Yugoslavia and Greece the comment: 'Marshal Stalin received your information with satisfaction.'[61] And so the 'prima donnas' managed to contrive, indirectly, a thaw in relations – without any loss of face.

Roosevelt was not sufficiently well even to return to Washington for the funeral of Frank Knox, the US secretary of the navy, who died from a heart attack, aged seventy, on 28 April. The Soviet embassy expressed condolences from the USSR, but Stalin also decided to do so personally – the only such occasion in his correspondence with Roosevelt and Churchill, apart from the president's own death in April 1945. This was despite the fact that Knox, like most of the top US military, did not enjoy a good reputation in Moscow and was considered frankly anti-Soviet. Perhaps Stalin felt the need to vary the negative tone of many of his spring 1944 messages. Roosevelt sent a formal note of thanks.[62]

Resuming direct communication with Stalin on 3 May, Churchill chose to strike another positive note by reviewing the Arctic convoys over the previous six months, in what reads almost like a report to the headmaster to show what good boys the British had been. The high delivery rate and relatively light losses of the six convoys totalling 180 ships underlined how the war at sea had shifted in favour of the Allies since 1942–43. Stalin sent a warm message of thanks, with his 'best wishes'.[63]

Lange and Orlemanski's visit to the Soviet Union was a great success from Stalin's point of view, although most of the Polish-American press damned it as a 'betrayal' of the Polish cause and dubbed the two of them 'agents of Moscow'. They not only met the 'Moscow' Poles – the Union of Polish Patriots (UPP) – but were also received by Stalin and Molotov for lengthy discussions on Polish–Soviet relations. Hence, perhaps, the unusually warm greeting – 'Dear Friend' – of the following message from Stalin to Roosevelt.

Stalin's emphasis on Father Orlemanski was probably because what hit the headlines in America were the latter's naive comments on returning home, about Stalin's benevolence towards the Poles and his desire to have dialogue with the Vatican. The priest was reprimanded by his superiors for breaching the papal ban on dealings with communists. Gromyko kept the Kremlin updated on Orlemanski's trials and tribulations[64] and Stalin did not forget the affair. Almost two years later, he asked the chairman of the American Slav Congress, 'How is Orlemanski? He has suffered a lot.' Molotov chimed in: 'Orlemanski was kicked around pretty badly when he returned to the US.'[65]

More meaningful talks were held with Professor Lange – a discreet and perceptive visitor – who after the war renounced his US citizenship and became the new Polish government's first ambassador to the United States. Both Stalin and Clark Kerr independently urged Lange to visit London and press Mikołajczyk to break with the reactionary elements of his government and work with the UPP.[66] Despite his pro-Soviet views, Lange also made an impression on Harriman as a 'thoughtful, intelligent and moderate man'.[67] On his return, the economist sent a detailed report of his Moscow conversations to the president and the State Department. Its overall tone was very upbeat: the Soviet leadership sought a constructive solution to the Polish question in cooperation with the Western Allies, and this would be possible if the London Poles stopped their anti-Soviet propaganda and worked with the UPP.[68] A copy of Lange's report was deceitfully obtained by agents of the Washington gossip columnist Drew Pearson, who hyped it up as evidence that 'Polish–Russian relations, one of the most troublesome problems of the war, are on the eve of a wholesome rapprochement.'[69]

Roosevelt's reaction to Lange's meticulous report has not been preserved in the archives, but the president eagerly responded to a transcript of Orlemanski's State Department debriefing, which ended: 'Be sure to tell the Big Fellow down in Washington that Stalin wants to work things out; it's just that he's awfully suspicious – suspicious of nearly everybody. He likes Roosevelt though.' These words coincided so perfectly with the president's perception of himself and of his rapport with Stalin – dating back to his letter to Churchill in March 1942 – that he called the report 'extremely interesting' and even asked Hull whether he should see Orlemanski 'off the record'. No such meeting took place, however: the State Department evidently managed to cool the Big Fellow's ardour. But the Lange–Orlemanski saga, though relatively small beer, reveals the continued hopes in Washington in mid-1944 that the Polish question could still be finessed.[70]

Stalin to Roosevelt, sent 6 May 1944, received 6 May 1944[71]

My dear friend:

I am extremely grateful for your assistance in permitting Reverent [sic] Stanislav Orlemańsky to come to Moscow.

I wish you good health and success.

Resuming contact with Stalin on a cordial note did not jolt Churchill out of the mood of deep gloom about the USSR that overcame him in early May. This despondency reflected not only his indifferent health and gnawing anxiety about 'Overlord', but also his unusually close acquaintance with the diplomatic cables while supervising the Foreign Office in Eden's absence. What particularly exercised the PM was the increasing interest that the Russians were taking in the Balkans, above all Greece and Romania. As usual with Churchill's rows, *amour propre* was not far below the surface – in this case a cable from Molotov about two Special Operations Executive (SOE) agents dropped into Romania at the end of 1943, which the foreign minister represented as 'a semi-official British mission' working behind the back of the USSR. In a paroxysm of rage late at night, the PM drafted a furious reply, with phrases such as 'you are absolutely mad if you suppose we are in any intrigue with Romania', and 'of course, if you do not believe a single word we say . . .' On 4 May, Churchill sent Eden a couple of scorching minutes asking, 'Are we going to acquiesce in the communization of the Balkans, and perhaps of Italy?' and inquiring 'whether it might not be wise for us to recall our Ambassador from Moscow for consultation' because 'evidently we are approaching a showdown with the Russians about their communist intrigues' in those countries.[72]

He also fumed to Averell Harriman, passing through London, about the efforts he had made over the previous few months to resolve the Polish question, for which all he had received was 'insults from Stalin – a barbarian', and going on about 'how hurt he was that Stalin had not believed in his good intentions'. By 8 May, the PM's tone was positively apocalyptic: 'I am afraid that very great evil may come upon the world. This time at any rate we and the Americans will be heavily armed. The Russians are drunk with victory and there is no length they may not go to.'[73]

Eden sought to head off a 'showdown' through a frank talk with Gusev on 5 May. Trying to clear up the contretemps about Romania, he suggested that, since that country was clearly in the Soviet theatre of operations, the USSR 'should take the lead in our joint efforts to get Romania out of the war'. But then, saying that he was 'gravely concerned' about Soviet press agitation about Greece, the foreign secretary asked the Soviets to let Britain take the lead there, since Greece was in the British theatre of command. Eden seems to have been thinking at this stage simply about short-term wartime practicalities, but the arrangement gradually assumed a more solid form. On 18 May, Gusev asked Eden whether the USA had been informed. The ambassador was clearly acting on instructions, though it is not clear whether the Kremlin was merely being prudent or saw here the embryo of a more lasting deal. At any event, on 19 May Churchill told Roosevelt *en passant* in a long message that the Soviets had just 'told us that they accepted the broad principle that they take the lead in the Rumanian business and give us the lead in Greece'. The State Department sniffed a territorial deal in the making as soon as it got wind of the business at the end of May and, after some testy exchanges between the PM and the president (meaning in reality the State Department), the two leaders agreed on 11 June that this mutual 'take the lead' arrangement would simply be trialled for three months. FDR warned Churchill, fatefully: 'We must be careful to make it clear that we are not establishing any post war spheres of influence.'[74]

Another area of friction between London and Washington was the proposed invasion of southern France, codenamed 'Anvil'. US strategists saw this as an essential complement to 'Overlord', opening up the major ports of Marseille and Toulon to improve supply lines to the Allied forces in France. For Churchill, by contrast, 'Anvil' would divert forces from the British-led campaign in Italy – which was indeed a subsidiary American motive. These arguments had dragged on ever since Tehran, and in the spring were far from resolved; but by May it was clear that, even if the operation did go ahead, it could not be mounted at the same time as the landings in Normandy. Fearing that Stalin would regard the delay as a failure of Allied will, Roosevelt felt it important to explain to the Soviets the reasons behind it. Leahy's draft was amended by the PM, after consultation with the chiefs of staff (insertions in italics), and the joint message was despatched from London.[75] Stalin, however, reacted calmly. Already in Tehran he had made it clear that, subject to 'Overlord' taking priority, the timing of 'Anvil' – before or after Normandy – should depend on British and American capabilities.[76]

Roosevelt and Churchill to Stalin, sent 13 May 1944, received 14 May 1944[77]

In order to give the maximum strength to the attack across the sea against northern France, we have transferred part of our landing craft from the Mediterranean to England. This, together with the need for using our Mediterranean land forces in the present Italian battle makes it impracticable to attack the Mediterranean coast of France in conjunction *simultaneously* with the 'Overlord' assault. We are ~~expecting~~ *planning* to make such an attack later, *for which purpose additional landing craft are being sent to the Mediterranean from the United States.* In order to keep the greatest number of German forces away from northern France and the Eastern Front, we are attacking the Germans in Italy at once on a maximum scale and, at the same time, are maintaining a threat against the Mediterranean coast of France.

Stalin to Roosevelt and Churchill, sent 15 May 1944, received 15 May 1944[78]

I have received your joint message. It is clearer to you how and in what order to dispose your forces. The main point of course consists in how to ensure the full success of 'Overlord'. I express my confidence in the success of the attack which has been started against the Germans in Italy.

In May, the tempo intensified on both Allied battlefronts. The liberation of the coastal areas of the Ukraine required close cooperation between the Red Army and the Black Sea Fleet in combined operations, for example, around the port of Nikolayev, which was finally liberated on 28 March. This victory in turn allowed Soviet forces to cross the southern Bug river and opened up the opportunity for operations in the Crimea. Hitler attached great importance to the defence of the Crimea, brushing aside pleas from some of his generals to withdraw from the peninsula, which was now hopelessly isolated after the Red Army had liberated Odessa on 10 April. The operation began on 5 May, and Sevastopol fell four days later. Although the Germans managed to evacuate about half of the 260,000 troops still remaining, of whom about 42,000 were subsequently lost at sea, this was a huge setback: aside from the propaganda disaster, the Wehrmacht had been driven from its key strategic position on the southern flank of the Eastern Front.

Meanwhile, in Italy the logjam finally broke: on 18 May, in their fourth major attempt, Allied troops took the heights of Monte Cassino. This was the key to the Gustav Line protecting Rome, whose northwest branch, the Adolf Hitler Line, was mentioned in Churchill's victory message to Stalin on the 19th. By then, however, Cassino had become almost a symbol of Allied ineptitude, given the sweeping extent of Soviet successes. The whole campaign had been dogged by friction and rivalry between British and American commanders. On the other hand, the final victory was a truly international achievement. Churchill singled out the Moroccan mountain troops of the Free French army, who traversed supposedly impossible terrain to attack with unparalleled ferocity, and more fulsomely the Polish soldiers of General Anders' corps. The PM's political subtext was clear, quietly reminding Stalin that the 'London Poles', whom the Soviets derided as traitors, were heroically laying down their lives against the common enemy.[79]

In his cable to Stalin, Churchill also played up the contribution made by the Italian campaign to support 'Overlord', by diverting German divisions that otherwise might have been deployed in Normandy. But belated success in Italy also opened up for the British possible opportunities in Central Europe and the Balkans. In the middle of June 1944, General Alexander proposed an operation codenamed 'Armpit', aimed at Vienna.[80] Churchill also had his eyes on Yugoslavia, where Britain's burgeoning relationship with Tito's communist partisans was consolidated by the totemic presence of his son, Randolph. In his reply on 22 May, Stalin echoed Churchill's hopes for a good accord between the British and Soviet missions to Tito.[81]

Roosevelt wanted to preface the beginning of 'Overlord' with an appeal to the German people, in the hope of undermining their will to fight on. He perhaps also had in mind the growing concern in Washington, and particularly London, that his statement in January 1943 that this time, unlike 1918, Germany must make an 'unconditional surrender' might have had the effect of strengthening German resistance. What FDR initially envisaged was a joint statement on behalf of all three Allied governments, but in a telegram to Churchill on 18 May, Roosevelt proposed to speak out alone. The prime minister sent a message of guarded support, but said he would bring the matter before the Cabinet.[82]

Roosevelt to Stalin, sent 23 May 1944, received 24 May 1944[83]

Instead of a tripartite statement to be issued by the Soviet, U.K. and U.S. Governments, what would you think of a statement by me along these lines, to be issued after D-day?

'It has been suggested that the Allied Governments join in a joint statement to the German people and their sympathizers emphasizing the landings recently made on the Continent of Europe. I have not been in agreement with this as it might over-emphasize the importance of these landings. What I want to impress upon the German people and their sympathizers is the inevitability of their defeat. What I want to emphasize to them is their continuation of the war from now on is unintelligent on their part. They must know in their hearts that under their present leadership and under their present objectives it is inevitable that they will be totally defeated.

'Every German life that is lost from now on is an unnecessary loss. From a cold-blooded point of view it is true that the Allies will suffer losses as well, but the Allies so greatly outnumber the Germans in population and in resources that on a relative basis the Germans will be far harder hit – down to every family – than the Allies. And in the long run mere stubbornness will never help Germany. The Allies have made it abundantly clear that they do not seek the total destruction of the German people. They do seek the total destruction of the philosophy of those Germans who have announced that they could subjugate the world.

'The Allies are seeking the long range goal of human freedom – a greater true liberty – political, intellectual, and religious; and a greater justice, economic and social.

'Our times are teaching us that no group of men can ever be strong enough to dominate the whole world. The Government and the people of the United States – with nearly twice the population of Germany – send word to the German people that this is the time to abandon the teachings of evil.

'By far the greater part of the world's population of nearly two billion people feel the same way. Only Germany and Japan stand out against all the rest of humanity.

'Every German knows this in his heart. Germany and Japan have made a terrible and disastrous mistake. Germany and Japan must atone reasonably for the wanton destruction of lives and property which they have committed; and they must give up an imposed philosophy, the falsity of which by now must be very clear to them.

'The more quickly the end of the fighting and the slaughter, the more quickly shall we come to a more decent civilization in the whole world.

'The attacks which are now being made in the European theater by the Americans, by the British, by the Russian armies and their associates will, we hope, continue with success, but the German people can well realize that they are only a part of a series of attacks which will increase in number and volume until the inevitable victory is completed.'

Churchill has agreed to follow up with a similar message along the same lines.

What seems striking today is the crassness of this proposed appeal. It is not clear whether FDR composed the text himself, or more likely, judging from the log sheet, issued a general instruction including the first and last paragraphs of the proposed cable and told Leahy to compose the appeal itself. Either way, the president's action seems to be further evidence of his deteriorating grip. The language of the appeal is contorted, ponderous and often repetitive – slipping at times into sermonizing, as in the invocation to 'abandon the teachings of evil'. Certainly it lacks the elegance and eloquence that one associates with FDR's speeches and fireside chats, not least his memorable D-Day 'prayer' a couple of weeks later. Little wonder that the idea got short shrift from both his allies, once they saw what the president proposed to say.

Meanwhile the prime minister, now buoyed up by success in Italy and the imminence of D-Day, sent an upbeat message to Stalin. He fed his fellow war buff detailed information on the Italian military situation as the Allies finally went all-out for Rome. He also talked of a resumption of the Arctic convoys, but added 'I must first see what we lose in destroyers and cruisers in the sea part of "Overlord"' – again revealing his fear that the Normandy landings would entail very heavy Allied losses. But Churchill also took pride in the scale of the armada and furthermore offered congratulations on Soviet successes in the Crimea.[84]

Stalin sent a cordial reply, editing Molotov's draft – additions (italicized) and deletions shown below – to make the comments on Italy more laudatory.[85]

Stalin to Churchill, sent 26 May 1944, received 26 May 1944[86]

I am grateful to you for the information about the battle in Italy which you communicated to me in your last message. We are all following ~~the developing events~~ *your successes* with ~~great attention~~ *admiration*.

Your communications about the development of preparations for 'Overlord' give us great hope. It is especially important that the British and American troops are filled with such ~~resoluteness~~ *determination*.

~~Your~~ *I welcome your* readiness to consider some time the preparation of a new programme of Arctic convoys ~~is highly evaluated by us~~.

Thank you for your congratulations. We are making strenuous preparations for new large-scale operations.

Meanwhile, as was his wont, Roosevelt again focused on the larger public relations aspect of alliance-building. It was his idea to award Stalingrad and Leningrad honorary scrolls. At the beginning of the year, he had instructed the War Department to produce diplomas for these Soviet Hero Cities, as well as for Chongqing, the capital of the Chinese Nationalists. But the Pentagon dragged its feet and the scrolls were only ready in May. The president, still lethargic, made no changes to the text proposed by the military. The document for Stalingrad stated that the victory on the Volga 'stopped the invasion tide and became a turning point in the war of the Allied nations against the forces of aggression'. Ambassador Harriman handed the scrolls to Stalin on 26 June 1944, and this was duly reported in the Soviet and American press.[87]

Roosevelt's proposal to address the German people was not supported in the Kremlin. The Russian translation of the message is dotted with bewildered annotations from Stalin and Molotov; they were also unhappy about the lack of proper recognition of the Soviet role in the forthcoming Allied onslaught on Hitler's Reich. It was Stalin who added to Molotov's reply the italicized phrase about inappropriate timing.[88]

Stalin to Roosevelt, sent 26 May 1944, received 26 May 1944[89]

I have received your message regarding the appeal to the German people.

Taking into consideration the whole experience of war with the Germans and the character of the Germans, I think that the proposed by you appeal cannot bring positive effect, since it is timed to the moment of the beginning of the landing *but not to the moment of sign of serious successes as a result of the landing of Anglo-American troops and as a result of the coming offensive of the Soviet Armies.*

We could return to the question of character of the appeal itself when favourable circumstances for such an appeal arrive.

Independently of Stalin, London also rejected Roosevelt's idea of a declaration to the German people. On 25 May, Churchill wrote to tell FDR that the Cabinet had not approved his initiative:

> I do not know what U.J. will say about your declaration, but we here earnestly hope you will not make it in its present form and, above all, at this present time. There was also a feeling that a document so grave addressed to the enemy, should emanate from the three principal Allies. I may add that nothing of this document would get down to the German pillboxes and frontline in time to affect the fighting troops.

This was a polite rendition of a unanimously scathing Cabinet discussion. Smuts, the South African premier, deplored the 'most casual and almost conversational tone' of the proposed message; Churchill himself thought the wording could be 'construed as almost a peace offer' and felt that any such message should be postponed 'until we had secured a victory'.[90] On 27 May, even before receiving the negative reaction from Stalin, FDR cabled both partners to say that he was withdrawing his proposal.[91]

*****

On 4 June, Allied forces finally liberated Rome – months later than Churchill and Roosevelt had confidently predicted in the autumn of 1943 and amid mutual recrimination between their two armies. Although General Alexander, the overall Allied commander in Italy, was well aware of the symbolic significance of Rome, his plans had focused on destruction of enemy forces and especially on the encirclement of the German 10th Army, retreating from the vicinity of Cassino, as Churchill made clear to Stalin on 28 May. The encirclement was to be effected by a frontal assault by the forces that had taken Cassino, assisted by the US Fifth Army, breaking out of the Anzio beachhead to cut off the Germans' retreat. However, the army commander, General Mark Clark, unilaterally directed his troops to go for Rome. Clark had little affection or respect for the Brits and believed they also had their eyes on the Italian capital. But, at root, he simply wanted to take Rome himself.[92] As a result, Allied hopes of encircling the 10th Army were frustrated.

Although Stalin politely described the liberation of Rome as 'a great victory' in identical messages to his allies, Moscow did not expect any marked change of tempo on the Italian front, regardless of specific operational successes or failures. A Soviet intelligence summary on 30 June predicted that 'in Italy the adversary will continue to retreat slowly to the Po River, while pursuing his main goal – wearing down the allied forces and dragging out hostilities. In the future, the enemy will retreat to the Alps.'[93]

Mark Clark's Roman triumph was short-lived. It hit the headlines on 5 June, but the following day was eclipsed by the news for which Hitler's enemies had long been yearning, from northern France. Because of weather conditions in the Channel, Eisenhower – the supreme Allied commander – was forced to postpone the Normandy landings for twenty-four hours, even though most of the troops were already at sea. Fortunately, the Luftwaffe was now only a shadow of its once-mighty self, so the armada was not attacked or even detected. Allied deception plans (operation 'Bodyguard') also kept Berlin's attention focused on the Pas de Calais, where the Channel was at its narrowest.

Given the fact that Stalin had been demanding a second front for nearly three years, and he had often been given duplicitous information by his two allies, it was important to keep him in the loop about an operation originally scheduled for May but then deferred to the following month. On 30 May, Ambassador Clark Kerr informed the Kremlin that final confirmation of the start date for 'Overlord' would be passed to Moscow on 1 June. But it was not until Churchill's letter on the night of 5 June – much of it justifying the attenuated campaign in Italy – that Stalin received confirmation that 'D-Day' would dawn the following morning.

Churchill to Stalin, sent 5 June 1944, received 6 June 1944[94]

You will have been pleased to learn of the Allied entry into Rome. What we have always regarded as more important is the cutting off of as many enemy divisions as possible. General Alexander is now ordering strong armoured forces northward on Terni, which should largely complete the cutting off of all the divisions which were sent by Hitler to fight south of Rome. Although the amphibious landing at Anzio and Nettuno did not immediately fructify as I had hoped when it was planned, it was a correct strategic move and brought its reward in the end. First it drew ten divisions from the following places: 1 from France, 1 from Hungary, 4 from Yugoslavia and Istria, 1 from Denmark and 3 from North Italy. Secondly, it brought on a defensive battle in which, though we lost about 25,000 men, the Germans were repulsed and much of the fighting strength of their divisions was broken with a loss of about 30,000 men. Finally, the Anzio landing has made possible the kind of movement for which it was originally planned, only on a far larger scale. General Alexander is concentrating every effort now on the entrapping of the divisions south of Rome. Several have retreated into the mountains leaving a great deal of their heavy weapons behind, but we hope for a very good round-up of prisoners and material. As soon as this is over we shall decide how best to use our armies in Italy to support the main adventure. Poles, British, Free French and Americans have all broken or beaten in frontal attack the German troops opposite them and there are various important options which will soon have to be considered.

I have just returned from two days at Eisenhower's Headquarters, watching troops embark. The difficulties of getting proper weather conditions are very great, especially as we have to consider the fullest employment of the Air, Naval and Ground forces in relation to the tides, waves, fog and cloud. With great regret General Eisenhower was forced to postpone for one night, but the weather forecast has undergone a most favourable change and tonight we go. We are using 5,000 ships and have available 11,000 fully-mounted aircraft.

The opening of the second front, which would be supported by the Red Army summer offensive against Hitler's Army Group Centre, brought Allied military cooperation to a new peak. It is no coincidence that the last stages of preparation for operation 'Bagration' occurred around the original start date of 'Overlord', 31 May. After a series of meetings with the military, Stalin approved the final plan at the end of May. According to Vasilevskiy 'it was simple and at the same time bold and grandiose'.[95] In a series of coordinated strikes starting later in June, Soviet troops were to eliminate a huge bulge east of Minsk – the so-called 'Belorussian balcony' – and encircle the retreating enemy forces. 'Overlord' and 'Bagration' would subject the Third Reich to simultaneous and pulverizing attack from two sides.

There were other signs of strengthening military cooperation between the Allies. At the beginning of June, the British military attaché in Moscow, General 'Bronco' Burrows, suggested establishing a special situation room in which the Soviet general staff would be provided with secret intelligence on how 'Overlord' was developing. The British chiefs of staff agreed, provided this would be a joint American–British initiative.[96] On 2 June, US heavy bombers from Britain carried out the first 'shuttle' bombing of Axis territory, refuelling at three specially prepared airfields in and around Poltava in the recently liberated Ukraine. This initiative had been proposed by Roosevelt at Tehran, and Stalin had formally agreed in a conversation with Harriman in February 1944.[97] Operation 'Frantic' allowed the Americans to strike at targets in eastern Germany, Hungary and Romania beyond the range of a round-trip from Britain. Both sides had ulterior motives, of course – the US Army Air Force hoped to use Poltava as a prelude to setting up bases in Soviet Siberia from which to bomb Japan, while Stalin probably hoped to find out more about US advanced technology. The whole operation was jeopardized by a devastating Luftwaffe raid on Poltava on 21 June, when forty-seven B-17s were destroyed on the ground. Nevertheless, 'Frantic' continued and was another sign of closer, if flawed, cooperation between the Allies.

The Soviets, whom London and Washington often castigated for their secretiveness, also provided valuable intelligence to the Western Allies. During its preparations for 'Overlord', the Anglo-American command received secret documents from the 302nd German Division, captured in the course of liberating the Ukraine. This was one of the units that had repulsed a trial landing at Dieppe in 1942. The material transferred included the German critique of the Allied operation, which offered useful insights for the D-Day planners.[98] Also indicative of the cooperative mood was Stalin's readiness at this time to demonstrate to the Allies new models of Soviet armoured vehicles, including self-propelled artillery pieces.[99] Overall, there was a clear desire for Big Three cooperation ahead of the impending offensives. As Molotov told Yugoslav envoys in April 1944, 'presently the situation on the fronts of the war against Germany is such that the Allies will be more active, and it is important for us to maintain good relations with them at this stage'.[100]

How long 'this stage' would last remained to be seen. But the mood on the eve of D-Day was positive and expectant, as the Grand Alliance stretched to its full height.

13

FROM EAST AND WEST

(June to September 1944)

ON 6 JUNE, ALMOST four years after France had signed an armistice, a western front was re-established on the continent of Europe. That morning, American, British and Canadian forces managed to secure five beachheads along the coast of Normandy. Although the breakout took almost two months, Allied progress thereafter was rapid, liberating Paris on 25 August and Brussels on 3 September. On the Eastern Front, the advance was even more dramatic. During the night of 22–23 June – the third anniversary of 'Barbarossa' – the Red Army launched 'Bagration', its main summer offensive. Over the next five weeks, while the Allies were still stuck in Normandy, Soviet troops advanced some 400 miles, driving the Germans out of Belorussia and eastern Poland, to the suburbs of Warsaw, and totally destroying Hitler's Army Group Centre. More than twenty divisions simply disappeared from the German order of battle (map 2).

'Overlord' finally satisfied Stalin's top demand in all his dealings with Churchill and Roosevelt since 1941 – a second front in France. On 11 June, the Soviet leader went out of his way to praise the D-Day landings, telling Churchill 'History will record this deed as an achievement of the highest order', which both Napoleon and Hitler had planned, but never accomplished. In the east, 'Bagration' had been deliberately timed to assist the Normandy landings, as Stalin promised at Tehran. Churchill made a point of thanking him for honouring that pledge (7 June) and Harriman later remarked that the 'Bagration' offensive 'convinced many of our military commanders, especially Eisenhower, that Stalin kept his word'.[1] Allied landings in southern France in mid-August (operation 'Anvil'), followed by a rapid advance up the Rhône valley led to the creation of a solid front line in Western Europe. A ring around Germany was closing relentlessly, from east and west, and it is no accident that the most significant attempt by conservative German officers to kill Hitler and seek a compromise peace – the so-called Stauffenberg Plot – was mounted on 20 July.

The new closeness between the Big Three can be seen in the cordial tone of the correspondence that summer, especially between Churchill and Stalin about military operations. It is also evident in their correspondence during July about decorating British and American figures who had played a leading role in facilitating the Arctic convoys, and also in what might be called the 'Debice Affair'. In this little-known episode, Churchill alerted Stalin to a V-2 missile launching site in southeast Poland, which Soviet and British experts later examined. Stalin, of course, was keen to gain access to German rocket technology, but the British considered that giving him the opportunity was less important than pooling intelligence about this new threat to London.

As usual, Roosevelt was less engaged in the detailed correspondence about waging war, but he weighed in strongly when the shape of the peace was at issue. Mindful of the interwar years, the president wanted a new world organization that would include both the United States and the Soviet Union. On 21 August 1944, delegations from the Big Three convened at Dumbarton Oaks, a mansion in the Georgetown district of Washington, DC, to develop the architecture of the new international organization. Although largely modelled on the League of Nations and its Covenant, the new body reflected the determination of the president and State Department planners – mindful of enduring isolationism at home – to give it an acceptably American face. The US delegation insisted on using the Rooseveltian title 'United Nations', rather than 'World Union' (one of the Soviet proposals), and on not calling its founding document a 'Covenant' (as with the League) but a 'Charter' – echoing the 'Atlantic Charter' of 1941.[2] Over six weeks, considerable progress was made, but on two issues the Soviet delegation dug in: the use of veto powers and the number of seats allocated to the USSR. These were the subject of correspondence between Roosevelt and Stalin in September.

Designing the postwar world was not easy, but filling in the territorial details was even more challenging, especially in Eastern Europe and the Balkans. There, borders had been in dispute since the end of the Great War, and the rapid advance of the Red Army reopened this Pandora's Box. The most intractable issue was Poland, where the success of 'Bagration' triggered an uprising by the Polish Home Army (AK) on 1 August, which became the predominant topic of Big Three correspondence and severely strained relations. The Red Army's passivity and, particularly, Stalin's refusal to let Allied planes use Soviet airfields to land and refuel aroused growing comment and indignation in London and Washington. While Roosevelt did not wish to force the issue – as usual seeing Poland in the light of his overriding imperative of cooperation with the Soviets – Churchill and Eden were less restrained. From late June, with the opening of 'Bagration', Stalin threw his weight strongly behind the Polish Committee of National Liberation (PCNL), established in Lublin. Although the Soviet leader, after representations from Roosevelt as well as Churchill, agreed to meet Mikołajczyk in Moscow at the end of July, what he and the PCNL now offered was a few seats for the London Poles in an ostensibly coalition government. The Warsaw Uprising, which went ahead without clear authorization from London, and which Stalin denounced on 22 August as the act of 'a group of criminals', was seen by him, with good reason, as an attempt by the AK to pre-empt Soviet hegemony in Poland.

By the time the AK surrendered to the Nazis on 3 October, the uprising had cost some 250,000 Polish lives – mostly civilians. With the Red Army now taking control in both Romania and Bulgaria, and with Stalin, as usual, batting away requests for another Big Three meeting, Churchill decided to take matters into his own hands – embarking on his second mission to Moscow.

*****

Churchill to Stalin, sent 6 June 1944, received 6 June 1944[3]

Everything has started well. The mines, obstacles and land batteries have been largely overcome. The air landings were very successful and on a large scale. Infantry landings are proceeding rapidly and many tanks and self-propelled guns are already ashore. Weather outlook is moderate to good.

This long-awaited announcement moved even the stolid Molotov beyond his usual terse acknowledgement. 'The news received with your letter,' he told Clark Kerr, 'is really very welcome and has now grabbed the attention of everyone.'[4] Stalin also sent a rapid reply, copied to Roosevelt,[5] expressing his appreciation of the good news and confirming the Soviet commitment to aid 'Overlord' with a broad offensive on its own front.

Stalin to Churchill, sent 6 June 1944, received 6 June 1944[6]

I have received your communication about the successes of the beginning of the OVERLORD operations. It gives joy to us all and hope of further successes.

The summer offensive of the Soviet forces, organised in accordance with the agreement at the Tehran Conference, will begin towards the middle of June on one of the most important sectors of the front. The general offensive of the Soviet forces will develop by stages, by means of the successive bringing of armies into offensive operations. At the end of June and during July offensive operations will become a general offensive of the Soviet forces.

I shall not fail to inform you in due course of the progress of the offensive operations.

Churchill was pleased with Stalin's message: 'It looks good,' he told Roosevelt.[7] He responded with a long account of the opening of what he admitted – after all his earlier attempts to talk up North Africa and Italy – was the 'second front'. It was full of detail about tank engagements, the use of artificial harbours and future strategic plans – intended to pique Stalin's interest. The PM ended by thanking the Soviet leader 'cordially' for his intimation about the Red Army's summer offensive. To underline the atmosphere of trust, he added, 'I hope you will observe that we have never asked you a single question because of our full confidence in you, your Nation and your Armies.'[8]

Roosevelt also replied to Stalin, composing the message himself.[9]

Roosevelt to Stalin, sent 7 June 1944, received 8 June 1944[10]

Thank you very much for your message of congratulation on the fall of Rome, and also for sending me the copy of your message to Mr Churchill.

All of this makes me very happy.

The news from Northern France is that everything is progressing according to schedule.

I send you my warm regards.

Churchill continued to keep Stalin abreast of the latest military developments. His optimism about rapid progress from now on in Italy, and his dismissal of Rommel's tactics in France were characteristic of the PM's propensity, once in battle, to accentuate the positives. In neither case, however, did he prove prophetic. Italy remained a slugging match. And although Rommel's conviction that the logistically powerful Allies could only be turned back by a vigorous counter-attack near the beaches was frustrated by Hitler's determination to retain key Panzer divisions for a possible invasion around Calais, stiff German resistance and Montgomery's caution would deny the British the city of Caen (which the planners had hoped would fall on D-Day itself) for over a month.

Churchill's reference to 'the Teheran design' was another effort to highlight the coherence and commitment of the Alliance.

Churchill to Stalin, sent 10 June 1944, received 11 June 1944[11]

I am delighted to receive your message which I have communicated to General Eisenhower. The whole world can see the Teheran design appearing in our concerted attacks upon the common foe. May all good fortune go with the Soviet armies.

By tonight, 10th, we ought to have landed nearly 400,000 men together with a large superiority in tanks and a rapidly growing mass of artillery and lorries. We have found three small fishing ports which are capable of taking unexpected traffic. In addition, the two great synthetic harbours are going ahead well. The fighting on the front is reported satisfactory. We think Rommel has frittered away some of his strategical reserves in tactical counter-attacks. These have all been held. We must expect the strategic reaction of the enemy in the near future.

General Alexander is chasing the beaten remnants of Kesselring's army northwards swiftly. They will probably make a stand on Rimini-Pisa position, on which some work has been done. Alexander reports fighting value of the twenty German divisions is greatly reduced. There are six or seven divisions retreating northwards under cover of rearguards and demolitions. He is on their track while mopping up the others.

On 16 April, a new Italian government had been formed, headed by Badoglio, which continued to cooperate with the unpopular monarch Victor Emmanuel III. Roosevelt wanted the king to abdicate, but the latter agreed only to cede the throne to his son, Crown Prince Umberto. Then after the liberation of Rome, without notifying the Allies, the Italians formed a new coalition government headed by the veteran socialist Ivanoe Bonomi: this spanned the political spectrum from the Christian Democrat Alcide de Gasperi to the communist leader Palmiro Togliatti, who had returned from wartime exile in Moscow. Bonomi and his colleagues said they would stick to the commitments made earlier, namely fulfilment of the terms of capitulation and no decision on the monarchy's future until final victory. Churchill was nevertheless furious about the ousting of Badoglio, which deprived London of its familiar partner: he had to accept this, but tried to impose conditions on Bonomi's government. Roosevelt and the State Department were pleased at the inclusion of their favourite, Count Carlo Sforza, whom Churchill despised. But to many American observers, in the words of one journalist, 'we run third in Italy' – after Britain and then Russia.[12] This was to be a growing bone of contention between London and Washington.

Asked by Churchill for his reaction to Badoglio's ouster, on 11 June Stalin agreed it was 'unexpected', but took a surprisingly relaxed attitude to events. In 1943, to the chagrin of the Allies, the USSR had abruptly established relations with the Badoglio government. Now the future of this cooperation was unclear. However, in contrast to the fuss made in the autumn of 1943, by mid-1944 the Kremlin had reconciled itself to Western predominance in Italy, and began to use it as a precedent for Soviet dominance in Eastern Europe and the Balkans. That is why, in his response to Churchill, Stalin gave the Allies virtually carte blanche for further changes in Italy. As evident from an earlier conversation with Togliatti in March 1944, Stalin, unlike some Foreign Ministry officials, was cautious about the prospects for revolution in Italy after the war. He believed that, for the moment, the best way to limit British influence in the country was a policy of 'national unity': the polarization of Italy into 'two camps', conservative and anti-fascist, would only strengthen London's position.[13]

In his message to Churchill on 11 June, Stalin also included a remarkable encomium about 'Overlord'. The draft of the most expressive passage does not bear any sign of his personal editing, but several days later it was reproduced almost verbatim in the leader's interview to *Pravda*: 'the history of war knows no other similar undertaking as regards breadth of design, vastness of scale, and high skill of execution'. Stalin also used similar language when speaking to Harriman on 10 June. It is therefore likely that these words came from the man himself, an avid student of history. His assessment was not far off Churchill's, given to the House of Commons on D-Day itself: 'This vast operation is undoubtedly the most complicated and difficult that has ever taken place.'[14]

Stalin to Churchill, sent 11 June 1944, received 11 June 1944[15]

I have received your message on the resignation of Badoglio. To me, too, the departure of Badoglio was unexpected. It seemed to me that without the consent of the Allies, the British and Americans, the removal of Badoglio and the appointment of Bonomi could not take place. From your message, however, it is evident that this took place regardless of the will of the Allies. One must assume that certain Italian circles purpose to make an attempt to change to their advantage the Armistice conditions. In any case, if for you and the Americans circumstances suggest that it is necessary to have another Government in Italy and not the

Bonomi Government, then you can count on there being no objections to this from the Soviet side.

I have also received your message of the 10th of June. I thank you for the information. As is evident, the landing, conceived on a grandiose scale, has succeeded completely. My colleagues and I cannot but admit that the history of warfare knows no other like undertaking from the point of view of its scale, its vast conception and its masterly execution. As is well known, Napoleon in his time failed ignominiously in his plan to force the Channel. The hysterical Hitler, who boasted for two years that he would effect a forcing of the Channel, was unable to make up his mind even to hint at attempting to carry out his threat. Only our Allies have succeeded in realising with honour the grandiose plan of the forcing of the Channel. History will record this deed as an achievement of the highest order.

Churchill reprinted Stalin's second paragraph in his war memoirs, commenting: 'The word "grandiose" is the translation from the Russian text which was given to me. I think "majestic" was probably what Stalin meant. At any rate, harmony was complete.'[16]

Churchill wrote his next message to Stalin while in Normandy. He had been desperate to get there with the first landing parties, but the king forbade him to take such risks. On 12 June, however, the PM took great pleasure in reviewing the bridgehead and visiting Montgomery's headquarters. To Stalin, he enthusiastically described the military situation, assuming his favourite roles of commander and commentator, and enlivening the detail with vivid word-pictures such as 'this city of ships' stretching along the coast for nearly fifty miles. Churchill returned to London from his day trip across the Channel 'sunburnt and contented'.[17]

The mood of euphoria in London was dispelled on the night of 12–13 June by the first attack from a new German weapon, the V-1 flying bomb. Some twenty-seven V-1s had been launched that night and another 150 on 15–16 June, though most fell south of the capital. During the latter raid, Churchill emerged from his bomb shelter to see for himself what was happening – exemplifying, as one private secretary put it, 'the PM's energy and (hair-raising!) disregard for his personal danger'.[18]

The Kremlin attached great importance to the new secret weapon. The Soviet embassy in London was ordered to inform Moscow Centre of its combat properties. 'There is still no reliable data on the structure of the unmanned aircraft used by the Germans,' Gusev reported on 16 June, 'but most observers agree that this is certainly a jet engine plane apparently radio-controlled. It is believed that they were launched from special platforms on the French coast of the English Channel in the region of Calais-Boulogne.'[19] Subsequently, the Soviet military mission was shown the models of the new German weapon.[20]

During the customary summer break in Arctic convoys, London was preparing for their resumption now that the naval demands of 'Overlord' had been addressed. On 17 June, Churchill told Stalin that he and Roosevelt hoped to send about thirty merchantmen in the middle of August. In another example of continuing Allied cooperation, convoy JW59 sailed on 15 August and consisted of thirty-six ships. As for the V-1, the PM was upbeat: 'Hitler has started his secret weapon upon London. We had a noisy night. We believe we have it under control. All good wishes in these stirring times.'[21]

In early June, Roosevelt finally agreed that Mikołajczyk could visit the USA. The Polish premier had long been seeking a meeting with the president – as the State Department put it, to 'very frankly' express 'his apprehension that the Soviet Government intends to communize Poland' or at least to set up a government 'under complete Soviet control'.[22] According to Hull, Roosevelt had deferred the visit till after D-Day because 'we could not afford to become partisan in the Polish question to the extent of alienating Russia at that crucial moment'.[23] But even when FDR let the visit go ahead, the same diplomatic priorities prevailed. The president asked Harriman to make it clear to the Kremlin that his position on the Polish question had not changed since Tehran, and that he wanted to mute discussion of Poland during the election campaign ('now is not the time to let the dogs bark'). In Washington, Hull also assured Gromyko that the visit was 'purely formal' and prompted largely by electoral considerations, in other words to appease the Polish vote. Mikołajczyk, Hull said, would not give any public speeches and there would be no joint communiqué with FDR.[24]

From 7 to 14 June, Roosevelt held four meetings with Mikołajczyk. He tried to persuade the Polish leader that Stalin was not an 'imperialist' and was willing to deal with the London government, provided it got rid of the four members deemed unacceptable by Moscow – which Mikołajczyk made clear he had no intention of doing. He considered Roosevelt's 'faith' in Stalin to be 'tragically erroneous'. As for the new Polish frontiers, FDR supported the idea of moving them westwards, but hoped that Poland would keep Lwów and get Königsberg, stating that he was ready to broker a deal with Stalin. But the Polish premier would have none of this. 'I said that Russia had no more right to half our country than it had to that portion of the United States from the Atlantic to the Mississippi.' The president nevertheless persuaded Mikołajczyk to go to Moscow for personal talks with Stalin – 'you Poles must find an understanding with Russia' – adding that 'on your own, you'd have no chance' and that 'the British and Americans had no intention of fighting Russia'.[25] Learning that Mikołajczyk wished to return to Washington in the event that his talks with Stalin failed, FDR said affably that his door was, of course, 'always open'.[26] Having indicated to Mikołajczyk that he would provide $20 million to maintain Polish missions in the Americas and help the underground in Poland, FDR later cut the sum back to $10 million and made it 'conditional on the Polish underground forces' activities being closely coordinated with the military operations of the Soviet army'.[27]

In a letter to Stalin about the Polish premier's visit, carefully drafted by the State Department, Roosevelt gave an optimistic picture of its results, maintaining his posture of friendly non-involvement in Soviet–Polish relations.[28]

Roosevelt to Stalin, sent 17 June 1944, received 19 June 1944[29]

As you know, the Polish Prime Minister Mr. Mikolajczyk has just completed a brief visit to Washington. For reasons which Ambassador Harriman has already explained to you I considered his visit at the time to be necessary and desirable.

You are aware, therefore, that his visit was not connected with any attempt on my part to inject myself into the merits of the differences which exist between the Polish Government-in-exile and the Soviet Government. Although we had a frank and beneficial exchange of views on a wide variety of subjects affecting Poland, I can assure you that no specific plan or proposal in any way affecting Polish–Soviet relations was drawn up. I believe, however, that you would be interested in my personal impression of Mr. Mikolajczyk and of his attitude toward the problems confronting his country.

Premier Mikolajczyk impressed me as a very sincere and reasonable man whose sole desire is to do what is best for his country. He is fully cognizant that the whole future of Poland depends upon the establishment of genuinely good relations with the Soviet Union and, in my opinion, will make every effort to achieve that end.

His primary immediate concern is the vital necessity for the establishment of the fullest kind of collaboration between the Red Army and the forces of the Polish underground in the common struggle against our enemy. He believes that coordination between your Armies and the organized Polish Underground is a military factor of the highest importance not only to your Armies in the East but also to the main task of finishing off by our combined efforts the Nazi beast in his lair.

My impression is that the Prime Minister is thinking only of Poland and the Polish people and will not allow any petty considerations to stand in the way of his efforts to reach a solution with you. In fact it is my belief that he would not hesitate to go to Moscow, if he felt that you would welcome such a step on his part, in order to discuss with you personally and frankly the problems affecting your two countries particularly the urgency of immediate military collaboration. I know you will understand that in making this observation I am in no way attempting to press upon you my personal views in a matter which is of special concern to you and your country. I felt, however, that you were entitled to have a frank account of the impressions I received in talking with the Polish Prime Minister.

The Foreign Ministry draft of Stalin's next message to Churchill was presented to the Boss by Molotov with a postscript: 'Perhaps something needs to be added about our offensive.'[30] The foreign minister was always wary of getting into purely military matters, which were the domain of the supreme commander. The last paragraph was added later by Molotov, presumably after talking with Stalin, and was repeated in a brief note of information sent on the same day to Roosevelt.[31]

'Our offensive' was the main Red Army summer assault in Belorussia – operation 'Bagration', named for one of the heroes of the war of 1812. Stalin had been obliged to postpone the start date from around 'the middle of June' (as he told Churchill on 6 June) because of logistical difficulties. On 14 June, Stalin decided that 'Bagration' would commence on 23 June – though for security reasons he told his allies 'in not more than a week'.[32]

Stalin's phrasing was typically low-key but telling. He casually dropped in a reference to employing '130 divisions' just four days after Churchill spoke of twenty Allied divisions being in action in Normandy. Even allowing for the smaller official size of a Soviet division in 1944 (12,000 men) compared to US or British divisions (respectively 14,000 and 18,000 men), the contrast in scale of the two operations was huge. And for a leader who generally talked about victories after the fact, rather than in anticipation (as was Churchill's wont), Stalin's prediction to both his allies of 'considerable' or 'serious' (*sereznyy*) success is striking.

Stalin to Churchill, sent 21 June 1944, received 21 June 1944[33]

Thank you for your communication about your and the President's intention to resume the northern convoys to the Soviet Union about August 10th. This will be of very considerable help to us.

As regards Italian affairs, you know of course already about the resolution of the Consultative Council in connexion with the new Italian Government. On the part of the Soviet Government there is no objection to this resolution.

We are all greatly pleased by the successful progress of the operations conducted in Normandy by British and American troops, which have already acquired such serious scope and strength. From my heart I wish your troops further successes.

In not more than a week will begin the second round of the summer offensive of the Soviet forces. 130 divisions will take part in this offensive, including armoured tank divisions. I and my colleagues expect considerable success. I hope our offensive will render essential support to the operations of the Allied armies in France and Italy.

Forwarding Stalin's message to Roosevelt, Churchill called it 'important and good'. The last paragraph had also been sent separately by the Kremlin to FDR. In a distinctly flat reply prepared by Leahy, the president told Stalin that 'your good action together with our efforts on the Western Front should quickly put the Nazis in a very difficult position'.[34]

Moscow closely monitored Mikołajczyk's visit to the USA, which, in conjunction with 'Bagration', proved a turning point in Soviet policy. Prior to this, clandestine communication had been going on between Viktor Lebedev, Soviet ambassador to the Allied governments-in-exile in London, a few members of the Polish Cabinet there, including Stanisław Grabski, and Mikołajczyk himself. Lebedev's instructions stated: 'Your main objective is to accelerate the split within the Polish government in London and to promote a more rapid formation of the Polish opposition which would advocate friendly relations with the USSR. Therefore, you should not raise the issue of Katyn, for it is not relevant.' Lebedev was also instructed to tell the London Poles to sever ties with General Kazimierz Sosnkowski and the three other Cabinet members on Moscow's 'no' list: 'This will certainly facilitate agreements on all issues of Soviet–Polish relations.'[35] But their membership of the London government and the border issue were both red lines for Mikołajczyk. The Kremlin, in turn, was irritated by his visit to the USA and complained to Harriman that he had made a statement to the press in defiance of FDR's prohibition (Harriman said that only formal speeches had been banned).[36]

It seems that by now the Kremlin had decided on the creation of the Polish Committee of National Liberation. On 22 June, Lebedev received instructions from Molotov about his next meeting with the London Poles, which revealed a toughening of the Soviet stance. While reiterating Moscow's position on the Curzon Line and on getting rid of the gang of four, Molotov also said it was 'necessary to clarify to Mikołajczyk that it is not about replacing several ministers in the Polish government, but the reorganization of the Polish government in which Mikołajczyk would still be prime minister'. This should include Poles from Britain, the USA and the USSR, as well as from Bolesław Bierut's pro-Soviet State National Council (*Krajowa Rada Narodowa*) within Poland. In addition, Moscow now took a more assertive line on Katyn: 'the reorganized Polish government should in the interest of justice admit the profound fallacy of the Polish government's actions relating to the Katyn murders which led to the break up between the Soviet government and the Polish government'. If these conditions were met, Molotov told Lebedev, the Soviet government would 'not object to the restoration of diplomatic relations and an agreement on the Polish administration'.[37]

Next day, 23 June, Lebedev acted on his new instructions – taking a tough line on Poland's borders and a reorganized government, demanding the inclusion of pro-Soviet representatives, among them members of the Union of Polish Patriots in Moscow. Both the London Poles and the British government were surprised at the new line. Reporting 'a set-back in the Polish–Soviet negotiations', Eden told Churchill that Lebedev, 'who had previously been most friendly and forthcoming', had suddenly 'changed his tone' by insisting on new 'absolute conditions'. The London Poles professed themselves 'at a loss' to explain Lebedev's new stance and his 'cold and curt' manner, but Eden opined 'that they may have neglected opportunities for conciliatory gestures towards the Russians'. He emphasized to Mikołajczyk the need for close cooperation between the Polish underground and the advancing Soviet forces and also for the reining-in of Sosnkowski, both as a 'President-substitute' and in his constitutional 'semi-independence' as commander-in-chief of the Polish forces, which seemed to British opinion as 'undemocratic and out-of-date' (Eden avoided the term 'fascist'). Beyond these private nudges to the Poles, however, Eden told Churchill, 'I am quite sure that it would be a mistake for us to intervene in any way at Moscow'.[38]

It was not, therefore, surprising that Stalin's reply to the president on 24 June avoided giving a firm answer about Mikołajczyk's visit to Moscow and once again raised the question of a much broader Polish government.

Stalin to Roosevelt, sent 24 June 1944, received 24 June 1944[39]

Thank you for the information regarding your meeting with Mr. Mikolajczyk.

If to bear in mind the establishment of military cooperation between the Red Army and the fighting against Hitlerite invaders forces of the Polish underground movement, then this, undoubtedly, is now an essential matter for the final rout of our common foe.

Great significance, of course, has in this respect the correct solution of the question of Soviet–Polish relations. You are familiar with the point of view of the Soviet Government and its endeavor to see Poland strong, independent and democratic, and the Soviet–Polish relations – good-neighborly and based upon durable friendship. The Soviet Government sees the most important premises of this in the reorganization of the émigré Polish Government, which would provide the participation in it of Polish statesmen in England, as well as Polish statesmen in the United States and the USSR, and especially Polish democratic statesmen in Poland itself, and also in the recognition by the Polish Government of the Curzon Line as the new border between the USSR and Poland.

It is necessary to say, however, that from the statement of Mr. Mikolajczyk in Washington it is not seen that he makes in this matter any steps forward. That is why it is difficult for me at this present moment to express any opinion in respect to Mr. Mikolajczyk's trip to Moscow.

Your opinion on the question of Soviet–Polish relations and your efforts in this matter are highly valued by all of us.

*****

'Bagration' commenced on the night of 22–23 June, the third anniversary of 'Barbarossa' – though the coincidence was fortuitous. The Red Army's four 'fronts' (*fronty* – army groups) achieved almost total surprise: the Wehrmacht had been led to expect a major assault in the Ukraine, just as they had been deceived about Normandy, rather than Calais, a few weeks earlier. By 26 June, the German defence line was breached, the city of Vitebsk had fallen and Soviet troops were across the Dnieper and Dvina rivers. In the first six days of the operation, thirteen German divisions were surrounded and destroyed.[40] By 4 July, the city of Minsk had been liberated, with 100,000 German troops encircled. The pace and dynamism of 'Bagration' were reminiscent of 'Barbarossa' – rapid armoured advances and lethal pincer operations – in terrain and places that had hit the headlines three years before. There was a further parallel. In the brutal vanguard of 'Barbarossa' was Hitler's Army Group Centre. Now, in the maelstrom of 'Bagration', Army Group Centre was simply wiped off the German order of battle. Between 22 June and 10 July, '28 divisions were so shattered or weakened as to be no longer operational' – a greater loss than at Stalingrad eighteen months earlier. The destruction of Army Group Centre has been called 'the greatest single defeat of the Wehrmacht in World War II' and even 'the heaviest defeat in German military history'.[41]

But victory was purchased at a heavy price for the Red Army, driven on as usual by Stalin regardless of losses, in a way that was not true of the Allied forces in Normandy. Roosevelt and especially Churchill were far more worried about their own 'body count'. In only the first eight days of fighting, the four Soviet *fronts* lost 19,600 men killed and 74,600 wounded and missing. The Red Army's victory was marked on 17 July by parading through the centre of Moscow some 57,000 enemy soldiers and officers captured in Belorussia.[42] Ambassador Clark Kerr remarked with some surprise that the Muscovites watching the procession 'behaved with admirable self-restraint' and that many 'were in fact moved to compassion at the sight'.[43]

Churchill kept up his chatty news bulletins to Stalin. On 25 June, he applauded the initial news of 'Bagration' and pledged all possible support in the west. He highlighted the logistical benefits that should accrue from the imminent fall of Cherbourg, although noting the short-term setback because of damage to the Mulberry harbours in the recent summer gales. On Italy, he was again hugely over-optimistic: in fact, Florence was not liberated 'in June', as he anticipated, but on 4 August, while the Pisa–Rimini ('Gothic') Line – which Churchill expected to have reached in July – remained intact until the spring of 1945. These delays were in part because the Americans, as usual, did not share the PM's estimate of 'the various strategic possibilities' in Italy, preferring to concentrate forces on southern France.

Churchill also told Stalin that he could

> safely disregard all the German rubbish about the results of their flying bomb. It has had no appreciable effect upon the production or the life of London. Casualties during the seven days it has been used are between ten and eleven thousand. The streets and parks remain full of people enjoying the sunshine when off work or duty. Parliament debates continue throughout the Alarms.[44]

His breezy assurances were largely justified. And also prudent, because of the very negative view taken by the Soviet embassy in London – located in Kensington Palace Gardens, just west of Hyde Park and right in the target area. Gusev sent Moscow some agitated reports in mid-June, when the embassy was evacuating women and children:

> the British do not yet possess an effective means to combat unmanned machines ... All the aristocracy and bigwigs have already been evacuated. The number of evacuees increases as the bombardment intensifies ... Each explosion in London leaves about three or four thousand people homeless.[45]

In reality, between 5 June and 31 July, 5,735 flying bombs landed, destroying about 17,000 houses and killing 4,735 people.[46]

For his part, Stalin sided with Churchill, not Gusev, in his estimation of the V-1, which, he said, could 'have no serious importance either for operations in Normandy or for the population of London whose bravery is known to all'. On 27 June, the Soviet leader also sent 'warm congratulations' to both his allies on their 'brilliant success' in liberating Cherbourg.[47] They in turn congratulated him on the fall of Vitebsk (Roosevelt) and then Minsk (Churchill), to which he sent more cordial acknowledgements.[48] As a variant in this amicable game of ping-pong diplomacy, Stalin sent a special D-Day portrait photograph in a silver frame to both his partners. The inscription to each leader read: 'In memory of the day of the invasion of Northern France by the Allied American and British [or British and American] liberating forces. From his friend Joseph V. Stalin.'[49]

Behind the jolly exchanges, however, June 1944 had a darker side. The speed and scope of the Red Army's victories had profound diplomatic implications, which were explored by Churchill in a long message to Stalin on 11 July. The loose understanding between Eden and Gusev on 5 May – that, for a trial period of three months, the Soviets would take the lead in dealing with Romania and the British with Greece – had run into problems. Some of these were caused by the State Department's allergy to anything that smacked of 'spheres of influence', exacerbated by some muddled handling of the issue between the FO and the Washington embassy. But Stalin also seems to have been happy to drag his feet on the deal, in order to see whether his army's advance made it unnecessary to tie his hands diplomatically. So Churchill now tried to sniff out Stalin's position.[50]

The Soviet drive along the Black Sea coast, coupled with the success of D-Day, also had an effect on Turkey, whose canny neutrality had previously tilted towards Berlin. On 15 June, Numan Menemencioğlu, the country's pro-German foreign minister, was forced out, precipitating a shift in Britain's hitherto hardline stance. London's new policy was to urge Turkey to break off relations with Germany and, in the case of the FO, to try to build up Turkey as a friendly buffer to 'counter the spread of Russian influence in the Balkans', if that proved necessary. Without revealing such thinking, Churchill sounded out Stalin on Turkey. The Soviet position since Tehran, reiterated in a memo of 10 July, was that the only way for Turkey to establish friendly relations with the USSR was to declare war on Germany. So Churchill, following Eden's advice, played up the negative consequences for Allied military logistics and operations if Turkey did formally join the Grand Alliance.[51]

On both the Balkans and Turkey, Churchill expounded his views with unusual diffidence – aware, perhaps, that the Red Army's rapid progress left Stalin in a strong diplomatic position. In the rest of the telegram he put the best face on the failure so far to break out of Normandy and also emphasized the impact of the V-1 raids.

In his message on 11 July, Churchill – as usual – also talked up prospects in Italy. This followed a long Cabinet discussion on 7 July, when General Alexander, the commander-in-chief in Italy, argued bullishly that once the Pisa–Rimini line was breached they should push northeast from Bologna and the Po Valley 'through the Ljubljana Gap towards the Danube Valley'. This, he said,

> would threaten the whole of the enemy's position in the Balkans and we should be approaching the advancing Russians, who would almost certainly shortly develop a thrust towards Lemberg [Lwów] and possibly through or round the Carpathians. Once we reached the Danube valley, the enemy will have to abandon his positions in the Balkans, which would result in his satellites in that theatre dropping out of the war. It would also open possibilities for a march to Vienna.

Churchill warmly supported Alexander's proposals.[52]

It should be noted that there was no talk here of forestalling the Russians – rather to cap the sluggish Italian campaign with a strategic triumph; but even so, the whole idea was far-fetched. The so-called 'Ljubljana Gap' was actually a col some 2,000 feet high and 30 miles wide, completely commanding the slopes that the Allies would have to traverse. The route onwards to Vienna lay through narrow mountain passes, easily defensible; what's more, the Austrian capital was 600 miles from Rome, from where Alexander's armies had still hardly moved. That was about three times the distance from Naples to Rome, which it had taken the Allies six months to cover. Little wonder that the Americans thought the idea was crazy, as did Brooke, who dismissed Churchill and Alexander's talk of a march to Vienna as 'futurist dreams'.[53]

Churchill to Stalin, sent 11 July 1944, received 12 July 1944[54]

Some weeks ago it was suggested by Eden to your Ambassador that the Soviet Government should take the lead in Roumania and the British should do the same in Greece. This was only a working arrangement to avoid as much as possible the awful business of triangular telegrams, which paralyses action. Molotov then suggested very properly that I should tell the United States Government, which I did and always meant to, and after some discussion the President agreed to a three-months' trial being made. These may be three very important months, Marshal Stalin, July, August and September. Now, however, I see that you find some difficulties in this. I would ask whether you should not tell us that the plan may be allowed to have its chance for three months. No one can say it affects the future of Europe or divides it into spheres. But we can get a clear-headed policy in each theatre, and we will all report to the others what we are doing. However, if you tell me it is hopeless I shall not take it amiss.

There is another matter I should like to put to you. Turkey is willing to break relations immediately with the Axis Powers. I agree with you that she ought to declare war, but I fear that if we tell her to do so she will defend herself by asking both for aircraft to protect her towns, which we shall find it hard to spare or put there at the present moment, and also for joint military operations in Bulgaria and the Aegean for which we have not at present the means. And in addition to all this she will demand once again all sorts of munitions, which we cannot spare because the stocks we had ready for her at the beginning of the year have been drawn off in other directions. It seems to me therefore wiser to take this breaking of relations with Germany as a first instalment. We can then push a few things in to help her against a vengeance attack from the Air and, out of this, while we are together, her entry into the war might come. The Turkish alliance in the last war was very dear to the Germans, and the fact that Turkey had broken off relations would be a knell to the German soul. This seems to be a pretty good time to strike such a knell.

I am only putting to you my personal thoughts on these matters, which are also being transmitted by Eden to Molotov.

We have about a million and 50 thousand in Normandy, with a vast mass of equipment, and rising by 25 thousand a day. The fighting is very hard and before the recent battles, for which casualties have not yet come in, we and the Americans had lost 64 thousand men. However there is every evidence that the enemy has lost at least as many and we have besides 51 thousand prisoners in the bag. Considering that we have been on the offensive and had the landing from the sea to manage, I consider that the enemy has been severely mauled. The front will continue to broaden and the fighting will be unceasing.

Alexander is pushing very hard in Italy also. He hopes to force the Pisa–Rimini line and break into the Po Valley. This will either draw further German divisions on to him or yield up valuable strategical ground.

Londoners are standing up well to the bombing which has amounted to 22 thousand casualties so far and looks like becoming chronic.

Once more congratulations on your glorious advance to Wilna.

Behind the V-1 flying bombs loomed the spectre of the V-2 long-range ballistic rocket. A massive RAF raid in August 1943 on Peenemunde, where they were being developed, forced the Germans to relocate the V-2 test site (named 'Debice') to the Blizna region in southeast Poland. Here, in May 1944, Polish Home Army soldiers discovered a V-2 rocket launched by the Germans and managed to hide it from an SS unit that came to collect the debris.[55] On the night of 25 July 1944, the missile was flown to Britain on a plane specially sent over for the purpose. Along with evidence from another V-2 that landed in Sweden and failed to detonate, the sample from Debice became London's main source of information about the new German weapon. Attaching great importance to the issue, Churchill decided to write to Stalin on 13 July: on the one hand giving away important secret information; yet on the other, hoping to gain access to far more, if the Soviets were willing to collaborate.

Churchill to Stalin, sent 13 July 1944, received 13 July 1944[56]

There is firm evidence that the Germans have been conducting trials of the flying rocket from an experimental station at Debice in Poland for a considerable time. According to our information, this missile has an explosive charge of about 12,000 pounds and the effectiveness of our counter-measures largely depend on how much we can find out about this weapon before it is launched against this country. Debice is in the path of your victorious advancing armies and it may well be that you will overrun this place in the next few weeks.

Although the Germans will almost certainly destroy or remove as much of the equipment at Debice as they can, it is probable that a considerable amount of information will become available when the area is in Russian hands. In particular, we hope to learn how the rocket is discharged, as this will enable us to locate the launching sites.

I should be grateful therefore, Marshal Stalin, if you could give appropriate instructions for the preservation of such apparatus and installations at Debice as your armies are able to ensure after the area has been overrun, and that thereafter you would afford us facilities for the examination of this experimental station by our experts.

Churchill to Stalin, sent 13 July 1944, received 14 July 1944[57]

Thank you very much for your message of congratulation. I have repeated it to General Montgomery and told him he may tell his troops.

Stalin took care over his response to Churchill regarding Romania and Turkey. On the former, he was not opposed to the proposed deal, but wanted Washington's explicit consent to ensure Allied harmony. As for Turkey's entry into the war, the Kremlin had by now defined its position: namely that Turkish entry was no longer of much use to the Allies because of the Soviet advance and the opening of the second front. In Stalin's view, the Turks should have entered the war at the end of 1943, as set down at the Moscow conference, and for the consequences of not doing so 'the Turks have only themselves to blame'.[58] His letter now clearly hinted that those consequences would include no seat at the peace conference, which would strengthen his hand in traditional issues of Soviet–Turkish contention, such as access through the Straits and the delineation of the Anatolian border. Aware of their weakening position, in August the Turks broke off diplomatic relations with Berlin, but they did not declare war until February 1945.

Stalin to Churchill, sent 15 July 1944, received 15 July 1944[59]

I have received your message of 12 July.

As regards the question of Roumania and Greece, it is not necessary here to repeat what is already known to you from the correspondence between our Ambassador in London and Mr Eden. One thing is clear to me: it is that the American Government have some doubts regarding this question, and that it would be better to revert to this matter when we receive the American reply to our enquiry. As soon as the observations of the American Government are known, I shall not fail to write to you further on this question.

The question of Turkey should be considered in the light of those facts which have been well known to the Governments of Great Britain, the Soviet Union and the U.S.A. from the time of the negotiations with the Turkish Government at the end of last year. You, of course, will remember how insistently the Governments of our three countries proposed to Turkey that she should enter the war against Hitlerite Germany on the side of the Allies as long ago as November and December of 1943. Nothing came of this. As you know, on the initiative of the Turkish Government in May–June of this year we again entered into negotiations with the Turkish Government and twice we proposed to them the same thing that the three Allied Governments had proposed to them at the end of last year. Nothing came of this either. As regards these or other half-measures on the part of Turkey, at the present time I see no benefit in them for the Allies. In view of the evasive and vague attitude with regard to Germany adopted by the Turkish Government, it is better to leave Turkey in peace and to her own free will and not to exert fresh pressure on Turkey. This, of course, means that the claims of Turkey, who has evaded war with Germany, to special rights in post-war matters also lapse.

We should like to meet your request, which is stated in the message of 13th July, regarding the experimental station at Debice if this station falls into our hands. Please define precisely which Debice is referred to, as in Poland, I am told, there are several places of this name.

I thank you for the information regarding the situation in Normandy and Italy and for your congratulations on the occasion of our advance in the Vilno sector.

The rapid developments on the battlefield prompted Roosevelt – always keener to meet than to write – to seek another Big Three conference to discuss the end of the war and the postwar settlement. This was becoming even more pressing, because of Churchill's insistent requests for another meeting with Roosevelt to thrash out various issues, especially strategy in the Mediterranean. Both of them agreed in mid-July that, to quote Churchill, 'it would be better that U.J. came too', and FDR duly sent an invitation to Stalin – 'purely as a feeler', he told Churchill. The president added: 'If he feels he cannot come, you and I should meet anyway.'[60] As FDR hinted on 27 July, the publicity generated by a summit would also yield domestic benefits in an election year.

Originally Roosevelt's message contained another sentence, successfully queried by Harriman. It implied, the ambassador argued, that Stalin 'should fly over the enemy-occupied territory' which, given the dangers, might arouse 'resentment on the part of Stalin's principal advisors' and thereby 'jeopardize the prospects of the meeting itself'.[61] This rather quaint reading of how decision-making in the USSR was conducted – reminiscent of Churchill's 'two Stalins' theory – is all the more striking because it came from someone with such good access to the Kremlin.

Roosevelt to Stalin, sent 17 July 1944, received 19 July 1944[62]

Things are moving so fast and so successfully that I feel there should be a meeting between you and Mr. Churchill and me in the reasonably near future. The Prime

Minister is in hearty accord with this thought. I am now on a trip in the Far West and must be in Washington for several weeks on my return. It would, therefore, be best for me to have a meeting between the tenth and fifteenth of September. The most central point for you and me would be the north of Scotland. I could go by ship and you could come either by ship or by plane. ~~Your Army is doing so magnificently that the hop would be much shorter to Scotland than the one taken by Molotov two years ago.~~ I hope you can let me have your thoughts. Secrecy and security can be maintained either aboard ship or on shore.

Responding to Stalin's request about the V-2, Churchill clarified the location of the German missile station in Poland, and once again stressed the importance of this issue for the British.

Churchill to Stalin, sent 19 July 1944, received 20 July 1944[63]

Your telegram of July 15 about the experimental station at Debice. The following is the British official location of the said station:

(Begins:) The area in which we are interested and where the experimental firing of large rockets takes place is North East of Debice or Debica, which is situated on the main railway line between Cracow and Lwow. Latitude 50 degrees 05 minutes North; longitude 21 degrees 25 minutes East. The actual area is some 10 by 3½ miles, and lies between the following points:

A. 50 degrees 07 minutes North, 21 degrees 27 minutes East.
B. 50 degrees 12 minutes North, 21 degrees 36 minutes East.
C. 50 degrees 11 minutes North, 21 degrees 39 minutes East.
D. 50 degrees 04 minutes North, 21 degrees 32 East. (Ends)

It is possible that they have a thousand of these things, each of which carries about five tons. If this be true it would become an undoubted factor in the life of London. Our present killed and wounded are about 30,000, but everyone is taking it very well. Parliament will require me to convince them that everything possible is done. Therefore it would be a help if you could lay your hands on any evidence that may be available and let us know so that some of our people may come and see it. We have got a good deal out of the bomb that fell in Sweden and which did not detonate, but traces of the Polish experiments will give an invaluable supplement. There is one particular part of the radio work out of the rocket that fell in Sweden which we should particularly like to find although it looks quite a petty thing. If you will put your officers in touch with Generals Burrows and Deane and order them to help them, the matter need not be of any more trouble to you.

You will no doubt have been rejoiced to know that we have broken out into the plains of Normandy in a strong force of seven or eight hundred tanks with a number of highly mechanized brigades and artillery, and that we are behind their line, and that their lines are already stretched by many days of battle to the last limit. I am therefore sanguine enough to hope that we may derange the entire enemy front. However everybody has had disappointments in this war, so all I will say is that I hope to report good news to you before long. I am going over tomorrow to be there for a few days myself.

This last paragraph signalled the long awaited breakout from the Normandy beachhead by Eisenhower's armies. Despite continuing recriminations between British and US commanders, their forces virtually encircled Hitler's 7th Army in the 'Falaise Pocket'. By the time this battle ended in August, 60,000 German troops were dead or prisoner. After nearly two months of hard slogging in Normandy, the Western Front started to move with a speed that matched the earlier progress of 'Bagration', as Eisenhower's armies raced towards Paris and the German border.

Amid this deteriorating situation for the Reich, on 20 July dissident German officers attempted to assassinate Hitler at his headquarters in East Prussia. Interestingly there was no discussion of this in the Big Three's correspondence, apart from a passing reference by Roosevelt to Stalin on the 21st that the recent 'difficulties' in Germany were 'all to the good'.[64] Behind the scenes, however, views of the Stauffenberg Plot diverged. In London, the failure came as something of a relief: had it been successful, the conservatives and officers taking power would have tried to negotiate peace terms, thereby posing a challenge to the official Allied policy of unconditional surrender. In Moscow, according to one Soviet account, Stalin opined that

> while Hitler is alive, he will not strike a separate deal with the West. And there can be no question of a deal for the United States and Britain while Hitler is at the helm. It is a different matter if Hitler disappears. There is a possibility of Goering or Papen coming to power, with whom the Western powers may come to an arrangement.

The Kremlin continued to receive occasional intelligence reports of Anglo-American contacts with the Germans and of a possible separate peace agreement.[65] And in a report that was passed up to the president, Allen Dulles, head of the Office of Strategic Services (OSS) field station in Berne – a key source of intelligence on Germany – stated that, despite its failure, 'this attempt to revolt should contribute to the undermining of the German army's will to continue the struggle'. But Dulles also warned of the possibility 'that the next attempt to overthrow Hitler's regime from within will be undertaken by a group oriented to the East'. In other words, the failure of the Stauffenberg Plot could 'further strengthen Russian influence in Germany'.[66]

Stalin evaded Roosevelt's proposal for another Big Three meeting. He rolled out his usual excuse of being absorbed in 'front matters' – and, for good measure, invoked the will of his 'colleagues'. This polite '*nyet*' pre-empted a plea from Churchill for a Scottish summit at Invergordon, urging on the Soviet leader 'the great advantage and simplification of all our joint affairs which would flow as at Tehran from a threefold meeting'.[67]

Stalin to Roosevelt, sent 22 July 1944, received 22 July 1944[68]

I share your thought about the desirability of a meeting between you, Mr Churchill and myself.

However, I must say that now, when the Soviet Armies are involved in battles on such a wide front, it would be impossible for me to leave the country and depart for a certain period of time from the conducting of front matters. All my colleagues consider it absolutely impossible.

Well aware of the importance of the V-2 rocket, Stalin responded positively to Churchill's request for an inspection of the experimental station in Debice. The assurance that he would take the case under his 'personal control' was not mere words. The Soviet leader displayed great interest in the issue and, after receiving Churchill's letter, ordered a thorough investigation to be carried out.

Stalin to Churchill, sent 22 July 1944, received 22 July 1944[69]

In connexion with your last message, I have given the necessary instructions about the experimental station in Debice. General Slavin, the representative of the General Staff, will arrange the necessary liaison on this matter with Generals Burrows and Deane. I fully appreciate that the British Government is seriously concerned about this question, and for that reason I promise you that I will take the matter under my personal control, so that everything possible may be done in accordance with your request.

I learned with great satisfaction from your message of the fact that your troops in Normandy had got into the rear of the Germans. I wish you further success.

By the time Stalin sent the following reply to Churchill,[70] the situation with the Polish government had changed markedly – as prefigured in Lebedev's volte-face in London on 22–23 June. On 21 July in Chełm, in Polish territory occupied by Soviet forces, the Polish Committee of National Liberation was formally founded and then rapidly recognized by the USSR. Headed by Bolesław Bierut, a communist loyal to Moscow, the PCNL became a real alternative to the London government. The importance Stalin attached to this is shown by the concurrent change in Soviet strategy. Zhukov's original plan on 8 July for a quick liberation of East Prussia was pushed aside, and a breakthrough towards the Vistula was given priority. On 21 July, Stalin also ordered his forces to make rapid progress in capturing Lublin: 'The political situation and the interests of an independent democratic Poland urgently demand it.'[71] Lublin became the PCNL's seat of government.

Stalin's explanation to Churchill for why he had recognized the PCNL was deftly phrased. He said it was necessary to establish local administration and oversee liberated Polish territory; he also represented recognition as a principled decision not to interfere in Polish affairs by imposing a Soviet government. But he did not deny that he envisaged the new body as the embryo of a future Polish government. For the first time, Stalin gave consent for Mikołajczyk's visit to Moscow but made it clear that the leader of the London Poles would have to deal primarily with the new pro-Soviet Polish authorities. Given the importance of the issue, Stalin sent a copy of the message to Roosevelt, who learned about it from Churchill as well.

Stalin to Churchill, sent 23 July 1944, received 23 July 1944[72]

I have received your message of the 20th July. I am writing to you now only on the Polish question.

Events on our front are proceeding at an extremely rapid tempo. Lublin, one of the large towns of Poland, was occupied today by our troops, who are continuing their advance.

In these circumstances the question of administration on Polish territory has arisen for us in a practical form. We do not wish to have and shall not set up our administration on the territory of Poland, for we do not wish to interfere in the internal affairs of Poland. The Poles themselves must do this. We therefore considered it necessary to establish contact with the Polish Committee of National Liberation, which was recently set up by the National Council of Poland, which was itself constituted in Warsaw at the end of last year out of representatives of the democratic parties and groups, as you must have already been informed by your Ambassador in Moscow. The Polish Committee of National Liberation intends to undertake the setting up of administration on Polish territory, and this, I hope, will be accomplished. In Poland we have not found any other forces which could have set up a Polish administration. The so-called underground organisations, directed by the Polish Government in London, proved short-lived and devoid of influence. I cannot consider the Polish Committee as the government of Poland, but it is possible that, in due course, it will serve as a nucleus for the formation of a Provisional Polish Government out of democratic forces.

As regards Mikolajczyk, I shall of course not refuse to receive him. It would, however, be better if he were to address himself to the Polish National Committee, whose attitude would be friendly to Mikolajczyk.

Stalin's message was discussed at a Cabinet meeting the next day, 24 July. Too late, the British were waking up to the diplomatic implications of 'Bagration'. Churchill said it was now imperative that Mikołajczyk go immediately to Moscow:

> At the pace at which the campaign was going, the Russians might very soon be in Warsaw, and every day's delay thus strengthened the position of the local Poles, and placed the Polish government in London at a greater disadvantage if no contact was established. If contact was not made now, the alternative government, with Russian backing, would be well in the saddle when the peace settlement was reached and would claim with some plausibility to be representative of Poland.

Agreeing, the Cabinet instructed Eden to speak urgently to Mikołajczyk and convince him to go to Moscow. On Churchill's recommendation, it was also decided not to show Stalin's message to the Polish premier, who instead should be told simply that Stalin would now see him, but that he must deal direct with the PCNL.[73]

Eden did manage to persuade Mikołajczyk, who expected nothing to come of this difficult mission. The Polish National Council in London had already denounced the PCNL, which did not help the situation. Churchill immediately informed Stalin of Mikołajczyk's impending departure. 'It may well be they will receive a friendly welcome,' he cabled Roosevelt, 'but of course their outburst last night about "Usurpers" et cetera may have worsened the situation. However we still have hope, and aim at fusion of some kind.'[74]

Churchill to Stalin, sent 25 July 1944, received 26 July 1944[75]

Monsieur Mikolajczyk is starting tomorrow night in response to the suggestion in the last paragraph of your message of July 23rd. He is bringing with him Monsieur Romer and Monsieur Grabski. His Majesty's Government are making arrangements for his transport to Tehran or to Moscow as may be required. He desires a full and friendly conversation with you personally. He commands the full support of all his colleagues in the Polish Government, which of course we continue to recognise.

Our heartfelt wish is that all Poles may be united in clearing the Germans from their country and in establishing that free, strong and independent Poland working in friendship with Russia which you have proclaimed is your aim.

I have told the President of the United States of your telegram to me and have sent him also a copy of this. He will no doubt communicate with you.

Prodded by Eden, Churchill sent a follow-up message, urging Stalin to accommodate the Poles in order to preserve the unity of the Alliance. Also at Eden's behest, he asked Roosevelt to weigh in as well.[76] For his part, the president kept up the pressure about another Big Three meeting as soon as possible.

Churchill to Stalin, sent 27 July 1944, received 27 July 1944[77]

Mikolajczyk and his colleagues have started. I am sure Mikolajczyk is most anxious to help a general fusion of all Poles on the lines on which you and I and the President are, I believe, agreed. I believe that the Poles who are friendly to Russia should join with the Poles who are friendly to Britain and the United States in order to establish a strong, free, independent Poland, the good neighbour of Russia, and an important barrier between you and another German outrage. We will all three take good care that there are other barriers also.

It would be a great pity and even a disaster if the Western democracies find themselves recognising one body of Poles and you recognising another. It would lead to constant friction and might even hamper the great business which we have to do the wide world over. Please, therefore, receive these few sentences in the spirit in which they are sent, which is one of sincere friendship and our Twenty Years Alliance.

Roosevelt to Stalin, sent 27 July 1944, received 28 July 1944[78]

I have received your telegram about the Polish situation and I hear from the Prime Minister that Mikolajczyk is leaving to call on you. It goes without saying that I greatly hope you can work this whole matter out with him to the best advantage of our common effort.

Roosevelt to Stalin, sent 27 July 1944, received 28 July 1944[79]

I can fully understand the difficulty of your coming to a conference with the Prime Minister and me in view of the rapid military progress now being made but I hope you can keep such a conference very much in mind and that we can meet as early as possible. Such a meeting would help me domestically and we are approaching the time for further strategical decisions.

Moscow now moved decisively on the Polish question. On 25 July, the PCNL released its manifesto announcing Lublin as the provisional capital of Poland; next day the Soviet government signed an agreement transferring administrative control of the liberated Polish territory to the PCNL. On the 27th, the two parties signed another agreement affirming a common border along the Curzon Line, with some deviations in favour of Poland. The Kremlin also promised to support the Polish demand for a western border along the Oder–Neisse line, though this point was concealed from the Allies for the moment. And Soviet military authorities in Poland were instructed to cooperate only with the PCNL, treating persons 'posing as representatives of the Polish government in exile' as 'impostors'.[80]

Writing to Churchill, however, Stalin professed his willingness to mediate between the rival Polish factions. The prime minister, always seeking signs of hope on the intractable Polish question, forwarded the message to Roosevelt, adding implausibly 'this seems to me the best ever received from UJ'.[81]

Stalin to Churchill, sent 28 July 1944, received 28 July 1944[82]

I have received your messages of the 25th and 27th July on the subject of the departure of Mikolajczyk. M. Mikolajczyk and his party will be given the necessary assistance on arrival in Moscow.

You know our point of view on the question of Poland, which is our neighbour and relations with whom have a special importance for the Soviet Union. We welcome the National Committee, which has been created on the territory of

Poland from democratic forces, and I think by the creation of this Committee a good start has been made for the unification of Poles friendly disposed towards Great Britain, the U.S.S.R. and the United States and for the surmounting of opposition on the part of those Polish elements who are not capable of unification with democratic forces.

I understand the importance of the Polish question for the common cause of the Allies, and for this very reason I am prepared to give assistance to all Poles and to mediate in the attainment of an agreement between them. The Soviet troops have done and are doing everything possible to hasten the liberation of Poland from the German usurpers and to help the Polish people in the restoration of their freedom and in the matter of the welfare of their country.

By the end of July 1944 the Red Army's offensives, launched a month before, had redrawn the map of Eastern Europe. In the north, Soviet forces reached the Finnish border on 21 July. The 3rd Belorussian *Front* was ordered to capture the city of Kaunas in southern Lithuania no later than 1–2 August (which they duly did) and then push on to the border of East Prussia (by 10 August), in preparation for a future offensive into German territory.[83] Further south, in Belorussia, the second phase of 'Bagration' was being unveiled. The 27 July directive to General Konstantin Rokossovskiy's 1st Belorussian *Front* stated that once the area around Brest had been seized, 'the right flank of the front is to move ahead in the general direction of Warsaw' and, by 5–8 August, should take the city's east-bank suburb of Praga (scene of a brutal battle between Russian and Polish forces in 1794 which triggered the Second Partition of Poland); meanwhile Rokossovskiy's left flank should establish bridgeheads on the western bank of the Vistula to the south of Warsaw in the area of Demblin, Zwoleń and Solec.[84] This would allow him to attack the Polish capital in a pincer operation.

Churchill told Stalin on 29 July 'your advances become more magnificent every day',[85] but Whitehall – now actively engaged in postwar planning – was urgently reflecting on what those advances portended. There was a general consensus that, after victory, Britain had to build a strong Western European bloc for its own self-defence. But the chiefs of staff believed that Foreign Office planners were too hopeful of maintaining the twenty-year alliance with the Soviet Union, whereas much of the FO considered the British military to be anti-Bolshevik diehards. The gist of their arguments undoubtedly got back to Moscow via well-placed Soviet agents. Brooke set out the military view starkly in his diary:

Germany is no longer the dominating power of Europe, Russia is. Unfortunately Russia is not entirely European. She has however vast resources and cannot fail to become the main threat in 15 years from now. Therefore foster Germany, gradually build her up and bring her into a federation of Western Europe. Unfortunately [until Hitler has been defeated] this must be done under the cloak of a holy alliance between England, Russia and America.

'Not an easy policy,' Brooke added, in an apparent sideswipe at Eden, 'and one requiring a super Foreign Secretary!'[86]

Stalin to Roosevelt, sent 2 August 1944, received 2 August 1944[87]

I have received your messages of July 28.

I share your opinion regarding the significance which our meeting could have, but circumstances, connected with military operations on our front about which I wrote previously, do not allow me, to my regret, to count on an opportunity of such a meeting in the nearest future.

As regards the Polish question, the matter depends, first of all, on the Poles themselves and on the capability of these or other persons from the Polish emigre government to cooperate with the already functioning in Poland Polish Committee of National Liberation around which more and more are rallying the democratic forces of Poland. On my part, I am ready to render to all Poles any possible assistance in this matter.

There had been a delay in issuing visas to the British experts travelling from Tehran to Blizna in Poland to inspect the Debice V-2 launch site. 'Since,' as Eden observed rather naively, 'it looks as if Marshal Stalin's instructions may not have penetrated to the Soviet authorities dealing with the granting of visas', he asked Churchill to send Stalin 'a personal message on the subject'. This the PM duly did on 4 August, receiving a reply the same day that the Soviet ambassador in Tehran had been 'instructed to give visas without delay' to the British.[88] Once again, direct contact at the top cut through the red tape underneath, on a matter where both leaders saw eye to eye – unlike Poland.

On 4 August, the GKO ordered the dispatch to the Debice site of a special mission headed by General Petr Fedorov, head of the Scientific Research Institute 1 (NII-1, formerly the Rocket Research Institute).[89] They arrived well ahead of the Allied mission, comprising mostly British experts and led by Colonel Thomas Sanders, and were able to find a good deal on the test site, including a combustion chamber, pieces of fuel tanks and rocket body parts. All the finds were taken to NII-1.[90] Nevertheless, the arrival of the Allies had its benefits. According to Boris Chertok, a member of the Soviet mission: 'Our group had been working in Poland for about a week when British experts arrived, including a representative of British intelligence, who had a detailed map of the area', which 'never let them down'. Chertok concluded that 'Churchill's appeals to Stalin were truly crucial for our further search. If not for his letter, our army would have triumphantly traversed these Polish swamps and forests, without delving into what the Germans had been doing.'[91] Some parts of the rocket were delivered to London, apparently via the British military mission in Moscow, and Clark Kerr and Harriman told Stalin 'British and American experts have managed to obtain very valuable results.'[92] On 16 October, Churchill would write a warm letter of thanks on the results of the mission to Debice.

*****

By the end of July, the 1st Belorussian *Front* had reached the left bank of the Vistula, 15–18 kilometres south of Warsaw. The leadership of the underground Home Army decided to try to liberate the capital unilaterally, ahead of the advancing Soviet troops. Mikołajczyk's Cabinet issued authorization for operation 'Tempest' on 25 July, but left the exact start date to the discretion of the Home Army commander, Tadeusz Bór-Komorowski. Despite the small chance of success, on 1 August Bór ordered it to go ahead. Mikołajczyk, who had just arrived in Moscow, learned of Bór's decision after the fact, though during a meeting with Molotov on 31 July he did mention that 'the Polish government was considering a general uprising in Warsaw and would like to ask the Soviet government to bomb the airfields near Warsaw'.[93] From the very first, the fears of the sceptics were confirmed: badly armed rebels clashed with superior German forces. The AK command and the Polish government in London appealed to the Allies for assistance, including the supply of munitions and a supporting attack by the Red Army.[94] In other words, the Soviets, whom the rebels had hoped to pre-empt, were now being asked to help. The RAF, with the participation of Polish pilots, prepared a plan to deliver equipment and ammunition to the Warsaw area, located far away from the Allied airfields in Italy. Reporting this to Stalin, Churchill hoped for the Red Army's assistance.

Churchill to Stalin, sent 4 August 1944, received 4 August 1944[95]

At urgent request of Polish Underground Army we are dropping, subject to weather, about sixty tons of equipment and ammunition into the southwest quarter of Warsaw, where it is said a Polish revolt against the Germans is in fierce struggle. They also say that they appeal for Russian aid which seems very near. They are being attacked by 1½ German divisions. This may be of help to your operations.

Stalin kept a close eye on developments in Warsaw. As the documents show, an order suspending the offensive of the 2nd Tank Army, advancing into the suburb of Praga, was issued by its commanders on 1 August at 04.10 Moscow time, prior to the start of the Warsaw Uprising. Seven days later, Zhukov and Rokossovskiy, commander of the 1st Belorussian *Front*, told Stalin that, 'given the necessary time to prepare', the operation to take Warsaw could be launched on 25 August 1944.[96] A Polish scholar has noted that 'it is still unknown how Stalin reacted to these proposals. What is clear is that no appropriate orders followed and the Warsaw operation was not in practice carried out.'[97]

How far the reasoning behind this was military or political – Red Army overstretch or a desire to let the Germans eliminate the AK – puzzled Western policymakers at the time, and still preoccupies historians today.[98] Arguably, we need to pay closer attention to another element in the story, the Wehrmacht. The Soviet order on 1 August calling off the assault on Warsaw reflects the sudden and devastating counter-attack by German armoured divisions, launched out of the blue and at great risk by General Walter Model, the hard-driving commander of Army Group Centre, that morning, just as the Warsaw Uprising began. This not only stopped the Soviet thrust on Warsaw, virtually destroying the 2nd Tank Army, but also saved the German front from complete collapse, which would have allowed the Red Army to drive on to the Baltic. In the light of all this, the official history of the German army in the Second World War offers a more nuanced estimate of Kremlin thinking: 'at first the Soviets wanted to take Warsaw but could not' – because of the German counter-attack; later, after the uprising got going, 'they could have taken Warsaw but no longer wanted to'.[99]

In his reply to Churchill about Warsaw, Stalin questioned the PM's information and disparaged the Polish underground. His additions to Molotov's draft (in italics) made this assessment even more patronizing.

Stalin to Churchill, sent 5 August 1944, received 5 August 1944[100]

I have received your message about Warsaw.

I think that the information which has been communicated to you by the Poles is greatly exaggerated and does not inspire confidence. One could reach that conclusion even from the fact the Polish emigrants have already claimed for themselves that they all but captured Vilna with a few stray units of the home army and even announced that on the radio. But that, of course, does not in any way correspond with the facts. *The home army of the Poles consists of a few detachments which they incorrectly call divisions. They have neither artillery nor aircraft nor tanks. I cannot imagine how such detachments can capture Warsaw, for the defence of which the Germans have produced four tank divisions among them the Hermann Goering Division.*

On 3 August, Stalin and Molotov held the first meeting with Mikołajczyk and his colleagues. They strongly encouraged the Poles to reach an agreement with the PCNL on establishing a new government, heavily hinting that otherwise they would deal only with the 'Lublin' group. The border issue arose once again: Mikołajczyk said that the loss of Lwów and Vilna would 'insult the Polish people', and urged Stalin to 'make a generous gesture' in order to receive 'the gratitude of the Polish people' and enable them to see him as an 'ally'.[101] Stalin was unyielding. Despite all this, the London Poles agreed to meet the PCNL, but the two sides failed to reach an agreement on a new government based on the PCNL, in which the Londoners would have four ministerial portfolios out of eighteen, including the post of prime minister for Mikołajczyk. In a final meeting with the London Poles on 9 August, Stalin appealed for Slavic solidarity in the face of future German revanchism, and played down any ideological ambitions on his part, memorably stating that 'communism suits Germany like a saddle suits a cow'.[102] He also promised to assist the Warsaw Uprising with weapons and ammunition. The atmosphere was 'much more cordial' than in previous meetings, Mikołajczyk told Clark Kerr, who then informed Churchill, in a cable relayed to Roosevelt, 'that this talk has put cheerfulness where there had been gloom in the hearts of the Poles'.[103]

Stalin to Churchill, sent 8 August 1944, received 8 August 1944[104]

I wish to inform you about my meeting with Mikolajczyk, Grabski and Romer. My talk with Mikolajczyk convinced me that he has unsatisfactory information about the situation in Poland. At the same time, I was left with the impression that Mikolajczyk is not opposed to the finding of ways to unite the Poles.

As I do not think it possible to impose any decision on the Poles, I suggested to Mikolajczyk that he and his colleagues should meet and themselves discuss their problems with representatives of the Polish Committee of National Liberation and, above all, the question of the speediest possible union of all democratic forces on liberated Polish territory. These meetings have already taken place. I have been informed about them by both sides. The delegation of the National Committee proposed that the 1921 Constitution should be taken as the basis of the activity of the Polish Government and, in the event of agreement, offered Mikolajczyk's group four portfolios, among them the post of Prime Minister for Mikolajczyk. Mikolajczyk, however, could not bring himself (literally: did not decide) to accept. Unfortunately, these meetings have not led to the desired results, but they have all the same had a positive significance, inasmuch as they have permitted Mikolajczyk and also Morawski and Bierut, who had only just arrived from Warsaw, to inform each other in a broad way about their points of view and especially of the fact that both the Polish National Committee and Mikolajczyk expressed the wish to work together and to seek the practical possibilities to that end. One may consider this as the first stage in relations between the Polish Committee and Mikolajczyk and his colleagues. We shall hope that the business will get better in the future.

Stalin's report of the talks for Churchill was also transmitted to Roosevelt – together with an additional paragraph about the socialist economics professor Oskar Lange, which shows Stalin's continuing desire to produce a Polish government beholden to himself, but also cosmetically acceptable in the West. Prompted by Stalin, the PCNL asked Roosevelt on 8 August to assist Lange in relocating to Poland, so that he could become head of its foreign affairs section, 'which will grow into the Ministry of Foreign Affairs of the future Polish government'. Stalin's own letter to the president reinforced the committee's request.[105]

London and Washington were satisfied with the Moscow consultations on Poland. 'The mood is more agreeable than we have sometimes met,' the PM told the president, 'and I think we should persevere.' Roosevelt, likewise, welcomed the 'pleasing news of the Soviet–Polish conversations'.[106] Churchill therefore sent an upbeat message to Moscow, nudging Stalin about aid to Warsaw, but dwelling mostly on the impending encirclement of German troops in the 'Falaise Pocket' and opining that 'a victory of first class proportions is not beyond our hopes'. He told Stalin that there were now in France a million GIs and 750,000 British, Canadian and Allied troops.[107]

On 9 August, the commander of the German 9th Army told Army Group Centre that 'resistance strengthens in Warsaw. Initially an improvised uprising, it is now governed by military discipline. The forces currently at our disposal will not be sufficient to suppress the uprising'.[108] The Germans therefore diverted large forces to the city and set about eliminating both the buildings and their inhabitants. In a crescendo of protest in Britain and America, the press wrote of Warsaw being abandoned by the Allies; criticism was rife in both Parliament and Congress. The RAF was now sustaining serious losses delivering goods to Warsaw,[109] but a large part of the supplies ended up in German hands. Moreover the aircrews, mostly Polish volunteers, did not have enough fuel to get back to their bases in Italy, and were often forced to eject or crash-land. Soviet airfields were much closer to Warsaw, and an increasingly agitated Churchill now begged Stalin to deliver arms and ammunition, incorporating in his communication a 'distressing message' from the AK's commanders to the Polish government in London, which expressed near despair at their isolation:

> the soldiers and the population of the capital look hopelessly at the skies expecting help from the Allies. On the background of smoke they see only German aircraft ... Have you discussed in Moscow help for Warsaw? I repeat emphatically that without immediate repeat immediate support consisting of drops of arms and ammunition, bombing of objectives held by the enemy, and air landing, our fight will collapse in a few days.

Clark Kerr gave Molotov Churchill's message on 13 August, but the document itself has not been preserved in the Stalin archive.[110]

On 14 August, two days after sending this message and without any answer, Churchill cabled Eden from Italy:

> It certainly is very curious that the Russian Armies should have ceased their attack on Warsaw and withdrawn some distance at the moment when the underground army had revolted. It would only be a flight of 100 miles for them to send in all the necessary quantities of ammunition and machine-guns the Poles need for their heroic fight.

But, to avoid overloading his correspondence with Stalin, the PM asked Eden to underline the point in a message to Molotov, because this was 'more impersonal'.[111]

Initially, Roosevelt reacted positively to the Kremlin's request to help Oskar Lange to return to Poland in order to join the new Polish government. 'It is my thought', he noted on 11 August, 'that we can raise no objection to Professor Lange's going as he is really a free agent and we let him go once before.' But

Under-Secretary of State Edward Stettinius warned that this time the stakes were much higher. 'I do not see how this government can lend its support or offer any facilities to an American citizen – even should he renounce such citizenship – accepting an official position in a Committee which is frankly and openly a rival to a government which we officially recognize.' Stettinius saw the desire to include Lange as 'obviously a tactical move to strengthen the claims of the Polish Committee to be recognized as the legal government of Poland'. His draft reply to Stalin was accepted by Roosevelt, but the president softened its tone with minor additions (italicized) and deletions.[112]

Roosevelt to Stalin, sent 12 August 1944, received 12 August 1944[113]

I am most grateful for your telegram of August 9 in which you were good enough to give me a resume of Prime Minister Mikolajczyk's conversations in Moscow both with you and the Polish Committee.

As you know it is my earnest hope that some solution satisfactory to all concerned will emerge out of these conversations and which will permit the formation of an interim legal and truly representative Polish Government.

In regard to Lange, *I am sure you will recognize the difficulty of this Government taking official action at this stage. Of* of course he as a private citizen has every right under our law to do what he sees fit, including the renunciation of his American citizenship. You will, I am sure, understand why, under the circumstances and particularly pending the outcome of the conversations between Premier Mikolajczyk, whose Government we *still* recognize *officially*, and the Polish Committee, the Government of the United States *does not want to* ~~cannot in any way~~ become involved in nor express any opinion concerning the request of the Polish Committee that Professor Lange join it as head of the section on Foreign Affairs.

Although Poland was the main topic of Big Three altercation over Eastern Europe, Yugoslavia was also a sensitive issue. Moscow kept Tito at arm's length in the summer of 1944. His requests for a personal meeting with Stalin remained unanswered, although Soviet shipments of weapons and other aid continued. The Kremlin was treading carefully in view of Churchill's personal interest in Yugoslavia and continuing British recognition of King Peter II as legitimate ruler of the country. Britain's support for Tito and his partisans was intended to help win the war, rather than to provide a basis for the peace. 'I know you appreciate our plight,' Tito wrote to Stalin on 5 July, 'since different parties are trying to intervene in our internal affairs, and we must still be careful not to aggravate relations with the Allies, maintaining at the same time our political and military independence.'[114]

While in Italy, Churchill met Tito for the first time, on 12–13 August in Naples. There the PM tried to broker an agreement between Tito and Ivan Šubašić, prime minister of the royal government-in-exile. Tito assured Churchill that he had no intention of imposing communism on Yugoslavia. But this was a tactical ploy – he had already formulated his position in April: 'While all our peoples desire it, still at the moment it seems inappropriate to emphasize it, since some of the Allies are wary of it and might think that this is done under the influence of the Soviet Union.'[115] Under Churchill's pressure, however, he accepted a public deal with the royal government. The Tito–Šubašić agreement was signed on the Adriatic island of Vis on 16 August, outlining an interim coalition prior to democratic elections. To the British, Yugoslavia seemed more manageable than Poland – at least for the moment.

Churchill to Stalin, sent 14 August 1944, received 15 August 1944[116]

I have had meetings during the last two days with Marshal Tito and the Yugoslav Prime Minister. I told both Yugoslav leaders that we had not thought but that they should combine their resources so as to weld the Yugoslav people into one instrument in the struggle against the Germans. Our aim was to promote the establishment of a stable and independent Yugoslavia, and the creation of a united Yugoslav Government was a step towards this end.

The two leaders reached a satisfactory agreement on a number of practical questions. They agreed that all Yugoslav naval forces will now be united in the struggle under common flag. This agreement between the Yugoslav Prime Minister and Marshal Tito will enable us with more confidence to increase our supplies of war material to Yugoslav forces.

They agree between themselves to issue [a] simultaneous declaration in a few days' time which I hope will reduce the internal fighting and will strengthen and intensify Yugoslav war effort. They are going off together today to Vis to continue their discussions.

I am informing President Roosevelt of results of these meetings.

Since the RAF could not cope with additional aid to the Polish insurgents, Roosevelt approved plans of the US Army Air Forces to deliver goods to Warsaw and attack German positions using heavy bombers under fighter escort. It was intended that the planes would fly from France and then, after their mission, land on Soviet airfields in Poltava, which served as a base for US shuttle bombers. A request to this effect was reiterated by Harriman, who kept reminding the Kremlin of Stalin's 9 August promise to Mikołajczyk of material help. But on 15 August, Vyshinskiy told both Allied ambassadors that the Warsaw Uprising was 'a purely adventuristic affair to which the Soviet Government could not lend a hand'. After the meeting, a sombre Harriman cabled the president: 'I am for the first time since coming to Moscow gravely concerned by the attitude of the Soviet government.' Judging from Vyshinskiy, the Kremlin's refusal to send aid to those fighting the Germans was 'based on ruthless political considerations'.[117] The ambassador urged the president to send Stalin a blunt message, warning that persistence with such a policy would leave the American public's hopes for postwar cooperation 'profoundly shaken'. But FDR did not want to escalate the issue and, on Hull's advice, told Harriman to maintain pressure through diplomatic channels. On 15 August, when Clark Kerr transmitted a message from Eden expressing hope that the US proposal would be accepted, Molotov noted: 'We should respond in the same vein as Vyshinskiy to Harriman.'[118]

Stalin also took the same line with Churchill. The distinctly harsher assessment of the uprising now current in the Kremlin probably reflected recent information from Bierut, who emphasized its anti-Soviet nature.[119]

Stalin to Churchill, sent 16 August 1944, received 16 August 1944[120]

After a conversation with M. Mikolajczyk I gave orders that the Command of the Red Army should drop arms intensively in the Warsaw area. A parachutist liaison officer was also dropped who, according to the report of the Command, did not reach his objective as he was killed by the Germans.

Further, having familiarised myself more closely with the Warsaw affair, I am convinced that the Warsaw action represents a reckless and terrible adventure which is costing the population large sacrifices. This would not have been if the Soviet Command had been informed before the beginning of the Warsaw action and if the Poles had maintained contact with them.

In the situation which has arisen, the Soviet Command has come to the conclusion that it must dissociate itself from the Warsaw adventure as it cannot take either direct or indirect responsibility for the Warsaw action.

I have received your communication regarding the meeting with Marshal Tito and Prime Minister Subasic. I thank you for the communication.

I am very pleased at the successful landing of Allied forces in the South of France. I wish success from my heart.

Not only did the Kremlin refuse to help the Home Army, but it also declined to let the Allies use bases on Soviet territory for their own supply missions. The USSR, Molotov informed Clark Kerr, 'decidedly object to American or British aircraft landing on the Soviet territory after dropping arms in the centre of Warsaw, since the Soviet government does not wish to associate themselves either directly or indirectly with the adventure in Warsaw'.[121] These messages from Stalin and Molotov were discussed at length by the War Cabinet on 16 and 18 August, with Eden taking the lead because of Churchill's absence in Italy. He particularly feared the effect on British and American opinion of Stalin abruptly 'going back on his promise' to Mikołajczyk to provide aid. He also drew attention to Soviet broadcasts, right up to the end of July, urging patriotic Poles in Warsaw to rise up against the Germans. Churchill, in turn, pressed Roosevelt about this 'episode of profound and far reaching gravity', warning, with apocalyptic vagueness, that if a 'wholesale massacre' ensued with Soviet troops only 'a few score miles away', then 'no measure can put upon the full consequences that will arise'. He urged a joint protest to Stalin.[122]

Roosevelt, however, viewed Warsaw in a global context. In early August, General Deane held consultations in Moscow on the Far East with representatives of the general staff. The Soviets remained wary of provoking Japan too early, and discussions were sticky. So, on the 14th, with Harriman's support, Deane asked the US Joint Chiefs to arrange an appropriate message to Stalin from the president, in order to 'accelerate our negotiations'. Roosevelt, then in Hawaii to confer about strategy in the Pacific, approved Leahy's draft without significant amendment and sent the message on 19 August.[123]

On 17 August, Molotov received Harriman and Clark Kerr, who had been instructed to make a joint protest about the Soviet ban on using their airfields to aid the Warsaw Uprising. The foreign minister stuck to the now established line that his government 'considers the Warsaw adventure a reckless scheme' and 'does not wish to take responsibility for it, including for the aircraft that will be sent to help Warsaw'. He not only rejected all their arguments about Stalin's promise to Mikołajczyk and about the damaging effect of inaction on Allied public opinion, but also said that the Soviet government intended to return the airfields to the Soviet armed forces because of the supposedly limited use that the USA had made of them.[124]

This unexpected message sounded like a threat linking the Polish question to the shuttle bombing, and alarmed the US Army Air Forces (USAAF), which doubted the effectiveness of airborne aid to Warsaw and feared for the fate of its shuttle operations. Harriman, now very suspicious about Soviet motives, urged the president to send a 'firm message' to Stalin, stressing that 'we cannot agree with the Soviet position when they, without lifting a finger, allow the killing of the Poles in Warsaw and prevent us from helping them'. However, the State Department told him to ease off on Warsaw because the smooth running of the shuttle bombing 'should not in any way be allowed to be imperilled by this question'. Hull sent Harriman the president's instructions: continue making verbal protests to the Soviet side while deferring any direct presidential appeal to Stalin.[125] Nevertheless, during an election year FDR could not afford to ignore public opinion, especially Polish-Americans, and therefore accepted Churchill's proposal to send a joint telegram to Stalin asking him to reconsider assisting the USAAF operations. The message, drafted by Leahy, was not very expressive – perhaps deliberately – but Churchill, with other problems on his mind in Italy, simply endorsed the text: 'Our thoughts are one,' he cabled FDR.[126] Harriman and Clark Kerr were instructed to deliver the message jointly to the Kremlin. This they duly did, after securing agreement on a small but significant amendment (italicized), intended to pin down the Kremlin more tightly.[127]

Roosevelt and Churchill to Stalin, sent 20 August 1944, received 20 August 1944[128]

We are thinking of world opinion if anti-Nazis in Warsaw are in effect abandoned. We believe that all three of us should do the utmost to save as many of the patriots there as possible. We hope that you will drop immediate supplies and munitions to the patriot Poles of Warsaw, ~~or will agree that our planes should do it very quickly~~ *or you will agree to help our planes in doing it very quickly.* We hope you will approve. The time element is of extreme importance.

This limp appeal had no effect on Stalin. He merely supplemented his main argument about the Polish 'criminals' with one of a military nature: that the uprising had only led to German reinforcement of Warsaw and thereby made the Red Army's task even more difficult. Stalin's editing of Molotov's draft again demonstrates the close attention he paid to the Polish affairs, as well as both men's mounting anger about the uprising – dismissing its leaders as nothing less than 'a group of criminals'.

Stalin to Churchill and Roosevelt, sent 22 August 1944, received 22 August 1944[129]

I have received the message from you and Mr Churchill. I wish to express my opinions.

Sooner or later the truth about the group of criminals, who have embarked on the Warsaw adventure in order to seize power, will become known to everybody. These people have exploited the good faith of the inhabitants of Warsaw, throwing many almost unarmed people against the German guns, tanks and aircraft. A situation has arisen in which each new day serves not the Poles for the liberation of Warsaw but the Hitlerites who are inhumanly shooting down the inhabitants of Warsaw.

From the military point of view, the situation which has arisen, by increasingly directing the attention of the Germans to Warsaw, is just as unprofitable for the Red Army as for the Poles. Meanwhile the Soviet troops which have recently encountered new and notable efforts by the Germans to go over to the counter-attack, are doing everything possible to smash these counter-attacks and go over to a new wide-scale attack in the region of Warsaw. There can be no doubt that the Red Army is not sparing its efforts to break the Germans round Warsaw and to free Warsaw for the Poles. That will be the best and most effective help for the Poles who are anti-Nazi.

After receiving this message, an irate Churchill urged Roosevelt that they tell Stalin, 'unless you directly forbid it', that they would go ahead and use the bases already provided on Soviet territory in the Ukraine to refuel US planes that had supplied Warsaw. But the president – again seeing Poland within his larger agenda – told the PM: 'I do not consider it advantageous to the long range general war prospect for me to join with you in the proposed message to U.J.' Nor did FDR respond to Stalin's message of 22 August: 'I do not think this needs an answer,' he told Leahy.[130] After discussing Stalin's cable on 28 August, the British War Cabinet likewise concluded that 'in the light of this telegram it was difficult to see what could be secured by a further approach to Premier Stalin'.[131]

In the end, Moscow did agree to Allied aircraft landing at Ukrainian airfields – but only on 9 September, once the main rebel forces had been defeated (although fighting continued in Warsaw). By then the War Cabinet had concluded that the continuation of air-drop operations from Italy by RAF Bomber Command – which was incurring 15 per cent losses – was 'militarily unjustifiable'.[132] But in mid-September, when Rokossovskiy's 1st Belorussian *Front* had regrouped and resumed its offensive against Warsaw, it began inten- sive night drops of arms, ammunition, food and medicine for the insurgents. Between 14 September and 1 October, Rokossovskiy's men made 2,243 flights over Warsaw and dropped far more supplies in key categories than the RAF had managed from long range in August and September: for instance, 156 mortars (the British delivered 13), 42,000 hand grenades (14,000), 113 tons of food (45 tons).[133] The Soviets also claimed that much of the British aid, delivered from high altitude, fell into German hands: 'The British and American aircraft dropping the cargo actually do not help the insurgents but supply the Germans,' Rokossovskiy reported to Stalin.[134]

Replying to Roosevelt on the Far East, Stalin limited himself to general assurances – perhaps with a veiled hint in the last sentence that the Americans would be wise not to keep making a fuss about Warsaw.

Stalin to Roosevelt, sent 22 August 1944, received 22 August 1944[135]

I have received your message on the Pacific Ocean matters.

I understand the significance you attach to these matters.

We also attach great importance to your successes there. I am confident at the same time that you are well aware to what an extent our forces are strained in order to secure success for the unfolding struggle in Europe. All this allows to hope that the time is not far off when we shall attain a solution of our urgent task and will be able to take up other questions. I hope nothing will interfere with General Deane's successful cooperation with our Army General Staff.[136]

Following agreement on leasing British warships to the USSR in lieu of the promised Italian ones, a contingent of Soviet sailors arrived in Britain in May to receive the vessels. The first batch – a battleship and four submarines – was formally handed over on 30 May at the Rosyth naval base in Scotland. The aged British destroyers required a lengthy refit, and it was not until August that they were ready to set sail, as part of the escort for the next Arctic convoy (JW59). On 17 August, the squadron, led by the battleship *Arkhangelsk*, formerly *Royal Sovereign*, left Scapa Flow. 'The Stavka inquired about the sailing daily,' recalled Admiral Nikolay Kuznetsov, then Soviet navy minister. 'I had to report all the details.'[137] Despite U-boat harassment, on 24 August the squadron anchored in Kola Bay and Stalin immediately cabled the news to Churchill, expressing his gratitude with due formality. 'Permit me to tender to you and to the Government of Great Britain my sincere thanks and those of the Soviet Government for this important assistance which has been afforded to the armed forces of the Soviet Union.' Churchill called this a 'very pleasant telegram' – doubtless finding it a relief from the tone of recent Kremlin missives.[138]

Meanwhile, on 15 August, Allied forces – predominantly US and French – landed along the Côte d'Azur in southern France. Originally intended to coincide with D-Day, the operation – then codenamed 'Anvil' – was postponed because of lack of resources and because of Churchill's tenacious insistence on 'nourishing' the campaign in Italy, where the British were in overall command, and even advancing into Slovenia. Resisted by the US military, who wanted to take Toulon and Marseilles and thereby expand Allied supply lines at a time when few major ports in northern France had been captured, Churchill had dug in for what proved one of the roughest Anglo-American strategic arguments of the war. But this time, the president sided with his own military advisers – unlike in 1942, over North Africa – and the landings, renamed 'Dragoon', eventually went ahead. Contrary to the PM's vocal forebodings, they were a complete success – quickly driving the weak German defenders up the Rhône valley and linking up with Eisenhower's forces in mid-September.

*****

The postwar world was also becoming an issue. In September, Roosevelt raised with Stalin the Dumbarton Oaks discussions about the new world organization. Gromyko, leading the Soviet delegation, had dropped what his US counterpart Stettinius called a 'bombshell' by asking for a seat in the General Assembly for each of the sixteen Soviet republics.[139] Gromyko was following strict instructions from the Politburo.[140] Remembering how it had been isolated and marginalized during the League of Nations era, the Kremlin sought to maximize its representation in the new organization. The February 1944 reforms to the Soviet constitution accorded foreign policy credentials to the republics, thereby providing a certain legal basis to this request. But Roosevelt called the idea 'absurd', telling Stettinius that 'it would be just as logical for the United States to demand forty-eight memberships, one for each state'. Fearful of the effect on American opinion, FDR insisted that the matter 'should be kept as quiet as possible': within the US delegation, it was referred to as the 'X matter'.[141] In London, Attlee's Armistice and Post-War Committee considered the Soviet proposal to be 'highly undesirable', while recognizing that, however hollow the 1944 constitutional reforms were in practice, theoretically the Kremlin's arguments were strong: 'On paper, therefore, the Soviet republics have greater autonomy in foreign policy, than India.' Unwilling to confront Moscow on the issue, the British happily passed the buck to the Americans.[142]

Roosevelt's message to Stalin followed a draft from Stettinius. The president added the final paragraph.[143] In reply, the Soviet leader underlined the importance he attached to the issue, adhering to his maximum agenda, although his emphasis on the Ukraine and Belarus hinted at a possible adjustment of the Soviet position in the ensuing diplomatic bargaining.

Roosevelt to Stalin, sent 31 August 1944, received 1 September 1944[144]

I am much concerned at the reference made by your delegation at Dumbarton Oaks that the Soviet Government might desire to have the sixteen constituent republics considered for individual membership in the new International Organization. Although it was made clear by your delegation that this subject would not be raised again during this present stage of the conversations, I feel I must tell you that to raise this question at any stage before the final establishment and entry into its functions of the international organization would very definitely imperil the whole project, certainly as far as the United States is concerned and undoubtedly other important countries as well. I hope you will find it possible to reassure me on this point.

This would not prejudice later discussion of the question after the organization came into being. The Assembly would then have fully authority to act.

Stalin to Roosevelt, sent 7 September 1944, received 7 September 1944[145]

I have received your message on the question of participation of the Union of Soviet Republics in the International Security Organization.

I attach exceptional importance to the statement of the Soviet Delegation on this question. After the known constitutional reforms in our country in the beginning of this year, the governments of the Union Republics are extremely alert as to what attitude the friendly States will take toward the adopted in the Soviet constitution broadening of their rights in the sphere of international relations. You, of course, know that for instance the Ukraine, Byelorussia, which are constituent parts of the Soviet Union, by the number of their population and by their political importance are surpassing certain countries in respect to which all of us agree that they should belong to the number of initiators of the establishment of the International Organization. Therefore, I hope to have an opportunity to explain to you the political importance of the question brought up by the Soviet Delegation at Dumbarton Oaks.

The other problem at Dumbarton Oaks was the principle of unanimity among the great powers – the permanent members of the future Security Council. The Soviet delegation had strict instructions to interpret this principle as widely as possible, including a blanket veto for each permanent member, even when itself involved in a dispute. The Americans and British dissented. The difference of approach was revealed during a conversation Roosevelt had with Gromyko on 8 September. The ambassador reported to Moscow: 'jokingly he illustrated the fact that under the US law, as well as the laws of other countries, "the jury may not include the husband testifying against his wife, and vice versa". Thus Roosevelt wanted to emphasize that the party involved in the dispute should not take part in its resolution.'[146] The president also raised this matter with Stalin, again using a State Department draft, to which he added only one sentence, italicized below.

Roosevelt to Stalin, sent 8 September 1944, received 9 September 1944[147]

I have just had a pleasant and interesting talk with your Ambassador in the regard to the progress of the Dumbarton Oaks talks. There is apparently only one issue of importance on which we have not yet reached agreement and that is the question of voting in the Council. The British and ourselves both feel strongly that parties to a dispute should not vote in the decisions of the Council even if one of the parties is a permanent member of the Council, whereas I gather from your Ambassador that your Government holds the opposite view.

Traditionally since the founding of the United States parties to a dispute have never voted in their own case and I know that public opinion in the United States would neither understand nor support a plan of international organization in which this principle is violated. Furthermore I know that this same view is held by many nations of the world and I am entirely convinced that the smaller nations would find it difficult to accept an international organization in which the great powers insisted upon the right to vote in the Council in disputes in which they themselves were involved. They would most certainly see in that an attempt on the part of the great powers to set themselves up above the law. *Finally, I would have real trouble with the Senate.* For these reasons I hope that you will find it possible to instruct your delegation to agree to our suggestion on voting. If this can be done the talks at Dumbarton Oaks can be speedily concluded with complete and outstanding success.

On 14 September, Stalin emphatically rejected Roosevelt's proposal (underlining in the original). Molotov reminded Gromyko why the USSR was adamant about the principles of unanimity and great-power veto:

> We do not want a repeat of the story that happened in the League of Nations at the end of 1939 regarding Finland. Then, as you know, the powers controlling the League assembled a bloc hostile to the Soviet Union and expelled it from the League. In the future international organization, we must not allow any possibility for manoeuvres against the Soviet Union. The British and Americans must give in on this matter.[148]

Stalin to Roosevelt, sent 14 September 1944, received 14 September 1944[149]

I have received your message regarding the discussions at Dumbarton Oaks.

I also hope that these important discussions may end successfully. This may be of serious significance for the further strengthening of cooperation of our countries and for the whole cause of future peace and security.

I must say that, for the success of the activities of the international security organization, of great significance will be the order of voting in the council, having in mind the importance that the council work on the basis of the principle of coordination and unanimity of the four leading powers on all questions, including and those which directly relate to one of these nations. The initial American proposal that there should be established a special procedure of voting in case of a dispute in which one or several members of the council, who have the statute of permanent members, are directly involved, seems to me correct. Otherwise will be brought to naught the agreement achieved among us at the Teheran Conference which is proceeding from the principle of provision, first of all, the unanimity of agreement of four powers necessary for the struggle against aggression in the future.

Such a unanimity proposes, of course, that among these powers there is no room for mutual suspicions. As to the Soviet Union, it cannot also ignore the presence of certain absurd prejudices which often hinder an actually objective attitude toward the USSR. And the other nations also should weigh the consequences which the lack of unanimity among the leading powers may bring about.

I hope that you will understand the seriousness of the considerations expressed here and that we shall find a harmonious solution of this question as well.

After Stalin's 26 July message again postponing another Big Three meeting, Roosevelt agreed with Churchill's proposal to hold a further Anglo-American conference on military and strategic matters. The PM suggested inviting Molotov instead, but the president did not reply.[150] The conference, codenamed 'Octagon', was held in Quebec from 11 to 16 September 1944 and ranged widely over the war in Europe and the Pacific, as well as the postwar issues. A summary of the decisions taken at the conference was prepared by the Combined Chiefs of Staff. Roosevelt and Churchill signed this document and instructed their ambassadors in Moscow to deliver it to Stalin jointly, in view of its special importance.[151] The instruction makes it all the more surprising – given the ill feeling caused by other conference reports largely composed by the military – that they, and especially Churchill, did not take more trouble over the composition and tone of the message.[152]

The information relayed to Stalin represented only a small part of the decisions taken in Quebec.[153] There was no mention of important policy issues such as international control over the Ruhr and Saar or the 'Morgenthau Plan' for the deindustrialization of Germany. Relatively little was said about the extensive discussions about military action against Japanese forces, probably because the USSR was not yet at war with Japan. The report on Italy deliberately smoothed over Anglo-American disagreements – Churchill's hopes of continuing the Italian campaign, possibly branching out to the Balkans, and the American desire to concentrate Allied forces in France rather than Italy. And the two Western leaders remained completely silent about another key decision taken after Quebec, during their private meeting in Roosevelt's home at Hyde Park, New York. This was the signing, on 18 September, of a memorandum on the continuation after the war of Anglo-American cooperation in developing nuclear energy for military and commercial purposes ('Tube Alloys'), keeping the project secret from the rest of the world. To avoid leaks about this project – 'particularly to the Russians' – Roosevelt and Churchill agreed to establish surveillance of the leading Danish nuclear physicist Niels Bohr, who had called on them to establish international control over the new weapon.[154]

Roosevelt and Churchill to Stalin, sent 19 September 1944, received 23 September 1944[155]

In our Conference at Quebec just concluded we have arrived at the following decisions as to military operations.

Operations in North West Europe

It is our intention is to press on with all speed to destroy the German armed forces and penetrate into the heart of Germany. The best opportunity to defeat the enemy in the west lies in striking at the Ruhr and the Saar since it is there that the enemy will concentrate the remainder of his available forces in the defence of these essential areas. The northern line of approach clearly has advantages over the southern and it is essential that we should open up the northwest ports, particularly Rotterdam and Antwerp, before bad weather sets in. Our main effort will therefore be on the left.

Operations in Italy

As a result of our present operations in Italy

(a) Either Kesselring's forces will be routed, in which case it should be possible to undertake a rapid regrouping and a pursuit towards the Ljubljana gap; or

(b) Kesselring's army will succeed in effecting an orderly withdrawal, in which event we may have to be content with clearing the Lombardy Plains this year.

Our future action depends on the progress of the battle. Plans are being prepared for an amphibious operation on the Istrian Peninsula to be carried out if the situation so demands.

Operations in the Balkans

Operations of our air forces and Commando type operations will continue.

Operations against Japan

We have agreed on further operations to intensify the offensive against the Japanese in all theatres, with the ultimate objective of invading the Japanese homeland.

Plans for the prompt transfer of power to the Pacific theatre after the collapse of Germany were agreed upon.

Harriman and Clark Kerr delivered this message during an unusually long and cordial meeting in the Kremlin on 23 September. Clark Kerr reported to London:

Stalin said that the operations in France have no parallel counterpart in the east. They had been very fast and completely successful. This was not a compliment. It was the truth. The isolation of Brittany and the capture of Paris had been magnificent operations, risky and bold.

The ambassador added: 'there was no doubt of his sincerity here'. Churchill greatly appreciated this praise, as he indicated in his next message. Stalin showed considerable interest in Allied plans for the war against Japan and inquired whether they still wanted Soviet participation. The ambassadors confirmed that this was indeed the case, but said that nothing concrete could be done until Stalin approved proper military conversations. He immediately said that these should start in a few days. Harriman also raised the issue of a Big Three summit in the Mediterranean, as proposed by Roosevelt, but Stalin, although admitting this would be 'very desirable', declined on the grounds of age, deteriorating health and his doctors' ban on air travel. He said he didn't possess the vigour of Churchill – 'that desperate fellow'. Pressed by the ambassadors light-heartedly – perhaps he could get some new doctors? – Stalin went through the usual repertoire of excuses: he hadn't recovered from his last trip to the front; he could of course send Molotov; oh, no, said Molotov, no one could replace Marshal Stalin; and so on.[156]

Since another Big Three summit was not on the cards, Churchill decided he must go to Moscow himself – convinced that the crunch questions could only be addressed in person. Yet his message of 27 September broached the idea carefully. The PM first thanked Stalin for his praise of the Allied victories, and then paid an even more striking tribute to the Red Army. He went on to express concern for Stalin's health, made clear his desire for a meeting of all three of them in the interests of all the world, and then threw in some gossip about FDR's oft-stated hope to visit Britain and about the presidential election, before emphasizing – perhaps in view of Stalin's quizzing of the ambassadors – that Soviet entry into the war against Japan was indeed 'earnestly' desired by London and Washington. His offer to pop over to Moscow came only in an almost casual sentence at the end of that paragraph, which seemed to hint that the Asian war could be a major topic of discussion.

Churchill to Stalin, sent 27 September 1944, received 27 September 1944[157]

I was gratified to hear from Ambassador Clark Kerr the praise which you gave to the British and American operations in France. We value very much such expressions from the leader of the heroic Russian armies. I shall take occasion to repeat tomorrow in the House of Commons what I have said before, that it is the Russian Army that tore the guts out of the German military machine and is at the present moment holding by far the larger portion of the enemy on its front.

I have just returned from long talks with the President and I can assure you of our intense conviction that on the agreement of our three nations, Britain, the United States of America and the U.S.S.R. stand the hopes of the world. I was very sorry to learn that you had not been feeling well lately and that your doctors did not like your taking long journeys by air. The President had the idea that the Hague would be a good place for us to meet. We have not got it yet but it may be that the course of the war even before Christmas may alter the picture along the Baltic shore to such an extent that your journey would not be tiring or difficult. However we shall have much hard fighting to do before any such plan can be made.

Most Private. The President intends to visit England and thereafter France and the Low Countries immediately after the Election, win or lose. My information leads me to believe that he will win.

I most earnestly desire, and so I know does the President, the intervention of the Soviets in the Japanese war as promised by you at Tehran as soon as the German army was beaten and destroyed. The opening of a Russian military front against the Japanese would force them to burn and bleed, especially in the air, in a manner which would vastly accelerate their defeat. From all that I have learnt about the internal state of Japan and the sense of hopelessness weighing on their people, I believe it might well be that once the Nazis are shattered a triple summons to Japan to surrender coming from our three Great Powers might be decisive. Of course we must go into all these plans together. I would be glad to come to Moscow in October if I can get away from here. If I cannot Eden would be very ready to take my place. Meanwhile I send you and Molotov my most sincere good wishes.

The Asian war was indeed one of the two major topics Churchill wished to raise in Moscow – as he explained to Roosevelt on 29 September: 'Our two great objects would be, first, clinch his coming in against Japan and, secondly, to try to effect a friendly settlement with Poland. There are other points too about Greece and Yugoslavia which we would also discuss.' Yet Eastern Europe and the Balkans were not even hinted at in the PM's message to Stalin, perhaps because the stakes were so high and Britain's hand had suddenly become extremely weak on account of Red Army successes in the past few weeks.[158]

A coup in Romania on 23 August had brought it over to the Allied side and into collaboration with the Red Army. As Churchill told the chiefs of staff on 8 September:

The turning over of Rumania has given the Russians a great advantage, and it may well be that they will enter Belgrade and Budapest, and possibly Vienna, before the Western Allies succeed in piercing the Siegfried Line. However desirable militarily such a Russian incursion may be, its political effect upon Central and Southern Europe may be formidable in the last degree.[159]

By this time the USSR had declared war on Bulgaria (5 September), prompting a coup four days later in the capital, Sofia, which brought the Bulgarians over to the Allies as well. Molotov informed Clark Kerr and Harriman only a few hours before the actual declaration of war. Both ambassadors expressed satisfaction and tried to conceal their anxieties. When Harriman asked, 'will Soviet troops enter Bulgaria?' Molotov blandly replied: 'this will depend on the military situation'.[160]

The arrival of Soviet troops in Romania and then Bulgaria in quick succession threw into confusion Whitehall's rather leisurely planning for the Balkans, where, it had been assumed, the three Allies would collectively negotiate armistices. The crux for the British was Greece. In late August, Churchill had instructed the chiefs of staff to prepare a British landing in Greece by 11 September, to ensure an orderly German surrender to pro-British partisans.[161] But after the bouleversement in Sofia, the Foreign Office became alarmed that the Red Army, with its new Bulgarian allies, might move into Greece, against which Bulgaria had territorial claims. 'It is essential,' the FO told the chiefs of staff on 9 September, 'that we should leave the Soviet Government in no doubt about the importance we attach to Greece', and suggested that they should inform Moscow 'of our intention to send in a British force'.[162] But paper plans to send a large contingent of British troops (46,000) – to ensure, as the FO put it, 'the retransfer of territory taken by Bulgaria from Yugoslavia and Greece and also to demonstrate British interest in Bulgaria' – had been overtaken by events. Now, as Attlee remarked with his usual crispness, 'the Russians were certain to play the major role in Bulgaria'.[163] Soviet intelligence monitored the growing British anxiety, notifying Moscow on 7 November that 'at the HQ of the High Command of the British Army in the Middle East there is much vexation and dissatisfaction with the Soviet government's action, since it disrupts British plans in the Balkans'.[164]

Hungary was another area of British interest. Richard Law, parliamentary under-secretary at the FO, told Attlee's committee in August that, even if the USSR occupied the country, 'it would perhaps be desirable to send a token force of 1,200 to demonstrate our interest and show the Flag'.[165] In a similar vein, Harvey told the chiefs of staff on 19 September that in Hungary 'we think we ought to stand out for a larger share in the control mechanism than in Roumania. We would like the Control Commission to be tripartite and responsible to Governments rather than to the Soviet High Command; and we might even suggest that the chairmanship should rotate.'[166] By October, such talk would sound utopian.

The last straw for the British was Tito's sudden visit to Moscow on 21–27 September, which seemed to cast doubt on his agreement with Šubašić in August. The Kremlin agreed to the visit in order to convince the wily Yugoslav leader of its support. The Foreign Policy Archive contains an expressive undated telegram to Tito from one 'Alekseyev' (Molotov's pseudonym):

> We have no commitments to the Allies regarding Yugoslavia. We are not bound by anything and could act, but, unfortunately, we do not have enough troops to do so. We can reinforce you with arms, and we'll do that ... If you want to fly to Craiova, you can do so with the help of our people.[167]

Tito did just that. On 19 September, he flew from the island of Vis on a Soviet aircraft to Red Army positions in Craiova (southern Romania), and thence to the Soviet capital. Tito's meetings with Stalin were followed anxiously in London. From the information communicated in Molotov's letters to Clark Kerr and Harriman on 26 September – about an agreement on the temporary deployment of Soviet troops in Yugoslavia 'for the purpose of carrying out operations against German and Hungarian forces in Hungary'[168] – it could be concluded that the Soviet position in the Balkans was strengthening. The prospect that Tito might 'throw himself completely into the hands of the Russians', Churchill told Eden,

> has now become not only possible but probable owing to the surprising changes which have taken place in Roumania and Bulgaria. The position can only be dealt as you propose, namely by conversation in Moscow. We must ask Russians plainly what their policy is.[169]

In response to the joint message from the Allied leaders about the Quebec conference, Stalin sent an identical letter to both, sketching out Soviet plans to clear its exposed flanks before the invasion of Germany.[170]

Stalin to Roosevelt, sent 29 September 1944, received 29 September 1944[171]

I have received your and Mr. Churchill's message on the Conference in Quebec with information regarding your further military plans. It is clear from your message what important tasks are to be solved by the American and British armed forces. Allow me to wish you and your troops all success.

At the present time the Soviet forces are busy with the annihilation of the Baltic group of German troops hanging over our right flank. Without the liquidation of this group it is impossible for us to advance into Eastern Germany. Besides, our troops have two immediate tasks: to knock Hungary out of war and feel through the German defenses on the Eastern front by an onslaught of our troops, and, under favorable circumstances – to smash them.

Stalin responded warmly to the PM's offer to come to Moscow. On the question of Soviet plans for Japan, Stalin merely confirmed his Tehran position, which was to enter the Asian war once Germany had been defeated. He deleted the final phrase of Molotov's draft,[172] not wanting to drop any advance hint of Soviet claims in the Far East.

Stalin to Churchill, sent 30 September 1944, received 30 September 1944[173]

I have received your message of September 27th.

I share your conviction that firm agreement between the three leading Powers constitutes a true guarantee of future peace and answers to the best hopes of all peace-loving peoples. The continuation of our Governments in such a policy in the post-war period as we have achieved it during this great war, will, it seems to me, have a decisive influence.

Of course I have a great desire to meet with you and the President. I attach great importance to it from the point of view of the interests of our common cause. But, as far as I am concerned, I must make one reservation. The Doctors advise me not to undertake long journeys. For a certain period I must take account of this.

I warmly welcome your desire to come to Moscow in October. We shall have to consider military and other questions which are of great importance. If anything prevents you from coming to Moscow we should of course be very ready to meet Mr Eden.

Your information about the President's plans for a journey to Europe is of great interest to me. I am also sure of his success in winning the Election.

As regards Japan, our position is the same as it was at Teheran. ~~It is time now, however, to consider this matter in greater detail than last year.~~

I and Molotov send you our best wishes.

'This is encouraging,' Eden noted in his diary, 'but we shall have a tough battle over Polish business. Talked to W[inston] twice on phone. He was highly excited.'[174] From Moscow, Clark Kerr cabled: 'The Russians and I are delighted that you have decided to come here and that Anthony will be with you. The iron stands hot for the hammering.'[175]

14

'ONLY THE THREE OF US'

(October to December 1944)

CHURCHILL'S SECOND VISIT TO Moscow was an important milestone in Allied relations. Codenamed 'Tolstoy', it lasted from 9 to 19 October 1944. Conversations were conducted in a consistently friendly atmosphere – with none of Stalin's alternations of mood that had characterized their first meeting in August 1942 – and there were also frank and productive talks about future military plans. Through his bombshell 'percentages' proposal for Southeast Europe, Churchill sought to secure Britain's position in Greece and agreement on a joint policy in Yugoslavia, in exchange for conceding Soviet predominance in Romania and Bulgaria. This cynical deal implied the division of Europe into spheres of influence between the two countries. Stalin, for his part, firmed up his commitment to enter the war against Japan after the defeat of Germany, while signalling that the USSR would also make territorial claims in the Far East. All this, combined with Stalin's amplified hospitality and courtesy, left a strong impression on the prime minister, who reaffirmed his conviction of how important it was to deal with Uncle Joe face to face.

Stalin played along with Churchill's sometimes conspiratorial tone, emphasizing the intimate nature of their talks, but he was constantly wary of Roosevelt's reactions. Primed by Harry Hopkins, the president used Ambassador Harriman as an observer at some of the meetings, and also reserved America's full freedom of decision for the future. FDR's stated conviction that 'the three of us, and only the three of us' could resolve the great issues of war and peace – expressed to Stalin on 4 October – energized him into planning their next summit. As with Tehran in 1943, Yalta in 1945 was not FDR's preferred venue

– he wanted somewhere more accessible in the Mediterranean – but Hopkins had broached the Black Sea coast in his efforts to secure an early summit, and Stalin then exploited the opportunity. In a series of unyielding messages in October and November, reminiscent of the pre-Tehran pattern of a year before, he got his way once again on the venue of his choice.

The military situation was less propitious for the Allies than in the heady days of late summer. Although the Red Army made steady, if costly, progress in Hungary, the situation in the west was more difficult. After the race into Belgium, a daring operation to seize the bridges over the Lower Rhine through a combination of paratroop drops supported by armoured thrusts failed at Arnhem (17–25 September). The Wehrmacht then regrouped, and Churchill had to admit to Stalin on 25 November that the combination of stern German resistance and harsh winter weather made it unlikely that they would get across the Rhine in 1944. The surprise German counter-attack just before Christmas (Battle of the Bulge) was a further setback, creating a brief crisis on Eisenhower's front, until the cloud lifted and the Allied air supremacy again proved decisive.

During the panic, Stalin acceded to requests from Roosevelt and Churchill to let Eisenhower's deputy – Air Chief Marshal Sir Arthur Tedder – visit Moscow for urgent sharing of military plans. Another example of his punctiliousness about the formalities of inter-Allied cooperation, where they did not affect key Soviet interests, was his continued willingness to share military information. Collaboration over the V-2 rocket site in Poland (Debice) in the summer was followed by a supportive attitude in December to Churchill's request for information about German T-5 acoustic torpedoes from a U-boat sunk in the Baltic. The PM's direct dealing with Stalin himself on these issues reflected the fact that the American and especially British military missions in Moscow had stiff and often frictional relations with their Soviet counterparts – innate Russian suspicion being reinforced by the openly anti-Bolshevik attitude of many senior Western officers.

Roosevelt's longest messages again concerned plans for the postwar United Nations – essential in his mind as the forum for drawing both the Soviet government and the American people permanently into the international community. At the end of the year, there was a flurry of correspondence about the Soviet insistence on the principle of great-power unanimity in the future Security Council. Fear of having its interests overridden was a major factor – the Soviet experience of its time in the League of Nations was still raw – but 'prestige' was a further consideration: Moscow had fought hard on this issue and did not want to lose face by compromising. Perhaps Stalin had in mind his protracted argument and eventually rather humiliating climb-down in 1943–44 over a share of the Italian navy.

In late 1944, for the first time, France and especially General Charles de Gaulle took up a good deal of space in the Big Three correspondence. How to handle the prickly French leader had hitherto been largely an issue for Churchill and Roosevelt, but matters changed with the formal recognition in October of de Gaulle's FCNL as the government of France – Roosevelt being finally obliged to accept facts on the ground, despite his rooted antipathy towards de Gaulle. The general then set about rehabilitating France, after the humiliation of 1940, as a great power – first hosting Churchill when the PM made an emotional return to Paris in November and then throwing a surprise by his Moscow visit in December, when de Gaulle signed a pact of mutual assistance with Stalin. This trip occasioned a good deal of correspondence among the Big Three, with Stalin keen to show his somewhat anxious allies that he was not trying to play a double game. Although the pact was of limited significance, due to France's continued weakness as a power, the French were becoming a new factor in the Big Three relationship because of Britain's concern to rebuild them as a power in Western Europe. This idea of a 'Western bloc', always more attractive to the Foreign Office than to Churchill, remained largely a matter of speculation in Whitehall, but it was discussed in messages between the PM and Stalin. What is more, the anti-Soviet spin put on it by the British military was well known to the Kremlin, thanks to Soviet agents in Whitehall.

De Gaulle was the prime example in Western Europe of what was now becoming a major challenge for the Big Three – the jockeying for power within states that were being liberated from Nazism. The issue was particularly vexed in Eastern Europe, because of – on the one hand – the presence of the Red Army and the Soviet determination for security against a third German war and – on the other – Britain's desire to maintain its waning influence as a great power in the region and ensure settlements that did not egregiously flout its wartime rhetoric about freedom and democracy. 'At this time every country that is liberated or converted by our victories is seething with communism,' Churchill told Eden on 10 November. 'All are linked together and only our influence with Russia prevents their actively stimulating this movement, deadly as I conceive it to be to peace and also to the freedom of mankind.'[1] With little or no power projection in the region, Churchill was reduced to finding plausible émigré politicians – preferably monarchists – who he hoped would also satisfy Stalin, as the basis of future governments. In addition, he also resorted to the desperate gambit of the percentages deal, which ring-fenced Greece and

Yugoslavia but at the price of effectively telling Stalin that he had a free hand elsewhere.

In Greece, Churchill exploited his leeway to try to sort out the royalist–communist confrontation on his terms, using British troops to put down communist protests in December. His actions aroused intense public criticism in Washington, but the Kremlin kept conspicuously quiet, with Stalin honouring what he agreed in Moscow. In Yugoslavia, the percentages deal initially seemed to be working, thanks to Tito–Šubašić agreements for a coalition government and Stalin's continued commitment in his messages to a joint policy in the country. But Churchill became increasingly suspicious of Tito, denouncing his non-cooperation in a long message on 3 December that he copied to the Soviet leader.

The great rift, as before, occurred over Poland. Churchill had demanded that the London Poles come to Moscow, so that he could help broker what he hoped would be a fifty-fifty deal with the Lubliners on the composition of a new Polish government. But his combination of patient explanation and volcanic denunciation got nowhere: Mikołajczyk was unable to make his colleagues accept the Curzon Line as the Polish–Soviet border – the concession which Stalin insisted was a precondition for any deal on the future government. On 24 November, Mikołajczyk resigned, to be replaced by a more hardline leadership. Churchill's expressions of hope that 'Mick' would soon return to power and sort out a satisfactory settlement must now have shown Stalin the hollowness of Britain's policy on Poland. With the Lubliners in control, backed by the Red Army, he caustically told Churchill that Mikołajczyk was now irrelevant – indeed simply a front for 'criminal' anti-Soviet elements – and pushed ahead with recognition of the Lublin committee (PCNL) as the new Polish government. This was despite two rare and lengthy forays into the Polish correspondence at the end of the year by Roosevelt, who now felt freer to speak out on Poland after his re-election.

The president had accepted his party's nomination in July, even though his health remained shaky. During the campaign, while conserving his energies as much as possible, FDR was able to deliver some telling speeches when it mattered, and on 7 November he gained another massive victory: 432 electoral votes to 99, winning 36 of the 48 states. Afterwards he had more time and energy for correspondence with Stalin, not just on Poland, as is evident from the series of messages in December. His fourth term would run until January 1949 – assuming nothing unforeseen happened.

*****

Churchill's second Moscow odyssey was much easier than the first, because he did not have to take the circuitous route around Spain, across North Africa to Tehran and then over the Caucasus. With Western Europe liberated, he could fly direct across France to Naples, then Cairo and on to Moscow. Even so, the journey would be a test of Churchill's health and stamina but he cabled Stalin on 4 October, 'I am looking forward to returning to Moscow under the much happier conditions created since August 1942.'[2]

When Churchill first informed Roosevelt on 29 September that he and Eden intended to go to Moscow – adding 'we would of course welcome Averell's assistance' – the president did not seem particularly concerned. Next day he told Churchill, 'I will direct Harriman to give you any assistance that you may desire', and, after another message from the PM about the likely agenda, Leahy drafted a brief reply, approved by the president, which began: 'I wish you every success in your visit to U.J.'. But both 'Chip' Bohlen, the State Department's leading Russianist, and Harry Hopkins, recently returned to the president's side after a long illness, worried that FDR seemed to be giving Churchill carte blanche in handling relations with Stalin. Hopkins took it upon himself to stop Leahy's cable and then raised the matter with Roosevelt, who became rather agitated once he was forced to think things through. As a result, Bohlen and Hopkins prepared longer messages to Churchill and to Stalin, which the president approved. These stated grandly that America had an interest in everything about 'this global war' and asked that Harriman sit in on the meetings as an 'observer'. They also reserved the president's full freedom of action ahead of the next Big Three meeting. Roosevelt specifically told Churchill not to discuss the controversial question of the number of votes each power should have at the United Nations until they all met. The PM agreed, but did remark that Harriman's role should not preclude 'private tête-a-têtes' with Stalin or Molotov.[3]

Significantly, Roosevelt's message to Stalin was not copied to Churchill.

Roosevelt to Stalin, sent 4 October 1944, received 5 October 1944[4]

While I had hoped that the next meeting could have been between you, Churchill, and myself, I appreciate that the Prime Minister wishes to have an early conference with you.

You, naturally, understand that in this global war there is literally no question, political or military, in which the United States is not interested. I am firmly convinced that the three of us, and only the three of us, can find the solution to the still unresolved questions. In this sense, while appreciating the Prime Minister's desire for the meeting, I prefer to regard your forthcoming talks with Churchill as preliminary to a meeting of the three of us which, so far as I am concerned, can take place any time after the elections here.

In the circumstances, I am suggesting, if you and Mr. Churchill approve, that our Ambassador in Moscow be present at your coming conference as an observer for me. Naturally, Mr. Harriman would not be in position to commit this Government relative to the important matters which you and the Prime Minister will, very naturally, discuss.

You will, by this time, have received from General Deane the statement of our Combined Chiefs of Staff position relative to the war against Japan and I want to reiterate to you how completely I accept the assurances which you have given us on this point. Our three countries are waging a successful war against Germany and we can surely join together with no less success in crushing a nation that I am sure in my heart is as great an enemy of Russia as she is of ours.

Roosevelt's message caused some confusion in the Kremlin. The evident lack of coordination between London and Washington did not fit the Soviet stereotype of an Anglo-American axis. In his reply, Stalin was at pains to explain his side of the story and dispel any impression of Anglo-Soviet collusion.

Stalin to Roosevelt, sent 8 October 1944, received 8 October 1944[5]

Your message of October 5 somewhat puzzled me. I supposed that Mr. Churchill was going to Moscow in accordance with the agreement reached with you at Quebec. It happened, however, that this supposition of mine does not seem to correspond to reality.

It is unknown to me with what questions Mr. Churchill and Mr. Eden are going to Moscow. So far I have not been informed about this by either one. Mr. Churchill, in his message to me, expressed a desire to come to Moscow, if there would not be any objections on my part. I, of course, gave my consent. Such is the matter in connection with Mr. Churchill's trip to Moscow.

In the future I will keep you informed about the matter, after the meeting with Mr. Churchill.

Churchill and Eden arrived in Moscow on 9 October, and they met Stalin and Molotov in the Kremlin at 10 p.m. for the first meeting of the 'Tolstoy' conference. Picking up on Clark Kerr's earlier idiom, the PM was determined to 'strike while the iron is hot'.[6] Both the British and the Russians kept detailed records of how the conversation developed, and these provide a revealing glimpse into this side of the Big Three triangle.[7]

Voicing his firm belief ever since Tehran, Churchill opened with the comment that 'by talking to each other he and Stalin could avoid innumerable telegrams and letters' and thereby hopefully 'clear away many questions' about which they had been writing 'for a long time'. Within a few minutes (and after a couple of Polish 'jokes') the two leaders agreed that the London Poles should be flown to Moscow for an attempted shotgun marriage with the Lublin committee. Churchill had a plane on standby back in Britain for this purpose.

Then the PM turned to the Balkans. Mindful of the imminent despatch of British troops to Greece, he stressed that this was a country in which Britain had 'particular interest' because 'Britain must be the leading Mediterranean power'. By contrast, he said he was 'not worrying much about Roumania. That was very much a Russian affair.' Stalin agreed that 'Britain should have the first say in Greece.' Churchill said it was 'better to express these things in diplomatic terms and not use the phrase "dividing into spheres", because the Americans might be shocked. But as long as he and Marshal Stalin understood each other he could explain matters to the President.'

At this point, Stalin – anxious to cover himself – interrupted to convey the gist of Roosevelt's message, namely that Harriman should act as an observer and that any decisions reached in Moscow should be 'of a preliminary nature'. Churchill said that this should not preclude some 'intimate talk' between the two of them, but promised to keep Roosevelt informed. Then, apparently cosying up to Churchill, Stalin added that 'on the whole' he did 'not like the message' from FDR, because it 'seemed to demand too many rights for the United States, leaving too little for the Soviet Union and Great Britain who, after all, had a treaty of common assistance' – unlike the USA and the USSR.

Getting back to the Balkans, Churchill – according to the original minutes by the British interpreter, Major Arthur Birse – 'then produced what he called a "naughty document" showing a list of Balkan countries and the proportion of interest in them of the Great Powers'. Clearly in a mischievous mood, Churchill added 'that the Americans would be shocked if they could see how crudely he had put it'. But, he said jocularly, 'Marshal Stalin was a realist. He himself was not sentimental while Mr Eden was a bad man. He had not consulted his Cabinet or Parliament.'[8]

The PM's 'naughty' list reflected discussions between the two governments dating back to the Eden–Gusev agreement of May 1944. In Romania, Churchill allotted Russia 90 per cent and 'the others' 10 per cent; in Greece, Britain would have 90 per cent and 'the others' 10 per cent. In Bulgaria, the proportions should be Russia 75 per cent and 'the others' 25 per cent, while in Yugoslavia and Hungary he proposed a 50:50 split. According to Churchill, Stalin put a tick on the document and pushed it back across the table to Churchill. They moved onto the future of Turkey and Italy but then the Soviet leader reverted to Bulgaria, suggesting that Britain's interest there 'was not, in fact, as great as the Prime Minister had claimed' – to which Eden remarked bluntly that 'Britain wanted more in Bulgaria than in Roumania'. After some inconclusive haggling, they agreed that Eden and Molotov should 'go into details' next day.[9]

Percentages had come totally out of the blue. Churchill had not broached the idea even with Eden, as became clear on the 10th, when the two foreign ministers tried to work out their meaning. Did percentages have a territorial significance, Molotov asked – for example, connoting in Yugoslavia, the coast versus the interior? Or did they indicate the proportion of seats each ally would have on the control commissions for these countries? Eden said testily that he 'did not care much about the figures', but he was now saddled with them and the rest of their discussions were about percentages, even though neither man knew what quite they meant.[10]

Nor, it would seem, did Churchill. Asked by a sceptical Cabinet, he said the 'system of percentages' was intended 'to express the interest and sentiment with which the British and Soviet Governments approach the problems of these countries', so that 50:50 would imply 'joint action and an agreed policy', whereas 90:10 would indicate that one power would 'play a leading part'. But he had never used percentages before, and nor would he do so again. Perhaps the PM thought that numbers would give some precision to his proposals, unlike vague terms such as 'predominance' or 'influence'. Possibly he imagined that quantification would appeal to Marxist-Leninists, as men of calculation rather than emotion. Maybe he saw it as almost a piece of theatre, to grab Stalin's attention – a ploy which would only work when performed in person.[11]

The Cabinet Office, however, thought the script had shown extremely poor taste. Ian Jacob, Churchill's military secretary, later rewrote some passages which seemed 'most inappropriate for a record of this importance' and 'would give the impression to historians that these very important discussions were conducted in a most unfitting manner'. Despite Jacob's attempt to sanitize history, we know of the 'naughty document' thanks to separate preservation of the interpreter's summary and to Churchill's account of the evening in his memoirs.[12]

The next morning, 10 October, over lunch Churchill showed Stalin a draft telegram to Roosevelt on the progress of negotiations, which contained a phrase on an agreed policy about the Balkan countries, 'having regard to our varying duties towards them'. Stalin felt this was too transparent an allusion to spheres of influence and he was seconded by Harriman, also at lunch. The ambassador reminded Stalin of FDR's wish to leave all the important issues for the Big Three to consider. 'Stalin said he was glad to hear this,' Harriman told Roosevelt, 'and, reaching behind the Prime Minister's back, shook my hand.'[13] Even so, the phrase remained in the message but Stalin added an important clarification on the Polish discussions (in italics). This proved to be the only joint message by Churchill and Stalin in the history of the Big Three correspondence. It was turned into clean English at the British embassy and sent to Roosevelt via Gromyko in Washington.

Churchill and Stalin to Roosevelt, sent 10 October 1944, received 11 October 1944[14]

In an informal discussion we have taken a preliminary view of the situation as it affects us and have planned out the course of our meetings, social and others. We have invited Messrs. Mikolajczyk, Romer and Grabski to come at once for further conversations with us *and with the Polish National Committee*. We have agreed not to refer in our discussions to the Dumbarton Oaks issues, and that these shall be taken up when we three can meet together. We have to consider the best way of reaching an agreed policy about the Balkan countries, including Hungary and Turkey, having regard to our varying duties towards them. We have arranged for Mr Harriman to sit in as an observer at all the meetings, where business of importance is to be transacted, and for General Deane to be present whenever military topics are raised. We have arranged for technical contacts between our high officers and General Deane on military aspects, and for any meetings which may be necessary later in our presence and that of the two Foreign Secretaries together with Mr Harriman. We shall keep you fully informed ourselves about the progress we make.

We take this occasion to send you our heartiest good wishes and to offer our congratulations on the prowess of the United States forces and upon the conduct of the war in the West by General Eisenhower.

On 11 October, Churchill dictated a very long letter to Stalin, further seeking to clarify and qualify the meaning of percentages in a way that suggested he had acted on impulse and was now realizing the complexities he had created. Eden and Harriman persuaded him not to send the letter, but Churchill later printed it in his memoirs 'as an authentic account' of his thought at the time. Near the end, the PM made a striking comment about eventual Soviet–British convergence:

> We have the feeling that, viewed from afar and on a grand scale, the differences between our systems will tend to get smaller, and the great common ground which we share of making life richer and happier for the mass of the people is growing every year. Probably if there were peace for fifty years the differences which now might cause such grave troubles to the world would become matters for academic discussion.[15]

It is not clear what to make of such apparently un-Churchillian sentiments, but the PM had evidently been much affected by the mood of the moment.

The conference was to include a full-scale discussion of both sides' military plans. This would make up for the terse, almost brusque, account of the Quebec conference conveyed earlier to Moscow, and would take account of the recalibration of Allied plans in the west, after the failure at Arnhem, and the Red Army's consolidation of its summer gains by completing the conquest of the Baltic states and the protracted siege of Budapest. The meeting lasted for three and a half hours on the night of 14 October. Brooke gave an overview of the Western Front since D-Day, explaining the recent slowing of the Anglo-American advance by reference to logistical problems, especially the continuing battle to open the port of Antwerp. Deane focused on developments in the Pacific and made several inquiries about the start date of the Soviet–Japanese hostilities and the pace of the Soviet military build-up. Antonov reported on a new Red Army offensive in the areas between Riga and Memel. Next evening, the discussion continued without Churchill, taken ill with a tummy bug. It concerned only the Pacific theatre of operations and was conducted mainly between the Soviets and the Americans.[16]

Even the usually testy Brooke was satisfied: 'We had a really nice conversation on the whole of the German Eastern Front, including future moves. The whole was on a most open and free basis of discussion', he wrote in his diary on 14 October. As in 1942, he was impressed by Stalin's grasp of strategic detail: at one point, when Antonov was flummoxed by a probing question from Brooke about the capacity of the Trans-Siberian railway, the Boss launched into a precise and detailed answer about the number of trains, their type and size, etc. On the war against Japan, Brooke noted, 'there was never any doubt that the Russians were coming in as soon as they could, and that they were prepared to discuss plans now'. But, he added, Stalin did mention that 'there was a political aspect to this problem that must also be tackled. What was Russia to get for her help?'[17] This was clearly a matter for the Big Three as a whole, but Churchill already felt 'it will be absolutely necessary to offer Russia substantial war objectives in the Far East'.[18]

Brooke also penned some interesting general observations on the eleven days in Moscow. Although gratified by the new openness in official discussions, he found it 'very distressing' to learn from the British military mission 'how impossible it is to build any sort of social relations with the local inhabitants. They will never come for meals, and never ask any of our representatives to come out. A vast gap exists which apparently cannot be bridged.' As for Russian banquets, with binge drinking and extravagant toasts, these drove the austere Brooke up the wall. After a lunch in the Kremlin that started at 2.30 p.m. and did not end till 6.15 p.m., he fumed in his diary about 'listening to half-inebriated politicians and diplomats informing each other of their devotion and affection, and expressing sentiments very far detached from veracity. Are international friendships based on such frothy products of drunken orgies? If so, God help the future.'[19]

Outwardly, in a brief response to their joint report, composed by Leahy, Roosevelt welcomed Churchill's opening talks with Stalin. However, he suspected that other matters were also discussed in the Kremlin, which Harriman soon confirmed – having been gradually informed by Churchill about the percentages. Hopkins unburdened himself to Gromyko on 13 October. 'Hopkins said that he did not like the idea of the current meeting between Comrade Stalin and Churchill,' the ambassador told Moscow. 'Roosevelt believes that the United States should not stay out of the more or less important events, in whatever corner of the globe these events unfold' and 'it would be very regrettable, Hopkins said, if an agreement on the Balkans is achieved without Roosevelt's participation. He would not want to be presented with a fait accompli.'[20] Nevertheless, thanks to Hopkins, the president had reserved the US position on all major issues until the next Big Three meeting. The main consequence of 'Tolstoy' in Washington was to strengthen Roosevelt's determination to arrange another summit.

Roosevelt to Churchill and Stalin, sent 11 October 1944, received 12 October 1944[21]

Thank you for your joint message No. 794 of October 10.

It is most pleasing to know that you are reaching a meeting of your two minds as to international policies in which we are all interested because of our common, current and future efforts to prevent international wars.

After intense pressure from Churchill, Mikołajczyk and two colleagues arrived in Moscow on the evening of 12 October. Over the next few days, they held a series of fraught discussions with Churchill and Stalin, with Churchill alone, and with the Soviet-backed PCNL from Lublin. The PM's ambition was a fifty-fifty deal over the Polish government, with Mikołajczyk as prime minister. In various conversations, Stalin and Molotov indicated that some sort of deal on the government might well be possible, but only if the London Poles formally accepted the Curzon Line as Poland's new eastern frontier. This remained the fundamental sticking point. Shuttling to and fro between Stalin and Mikołajczyk, Churchill tried various forms of words, including 'demarcation line' and 'basis of a frontier'; but nothing, it seemed, would bridge the gap. At times, the PM became absolutely furious with the London Poles and their insistence that they could not 'deprive' themselves of any Polish territory, even though much of the land at issue was populated by Ukrainians and already controlled by the Red Army. 'Because of quarrels between Poles we are not going to wreck the peace of Europe,' Churchill exploded on 14 October. 'Unless you accept the frontier, you are out of business forever. The Russians will sweep through your country and your people will be liquidated. You are on the verge of annihilation.' Later he fumed to Mikołajczyk: 'I feel as if I were in a lunatic asylum . . . You are absolutely incapable of facing facts.' Eden's private secretary Oliver Harvey watched the spectacle: 'Nothing would move Mick who sat impassive while the P.M. raged,' he noted in his diary. 'Up and down the room he paced, threatening and cursing.'[22]

Some of this was for theatrical effect; but Churchill was genuinely angry – and also incredulous at the obduracy of the Poles: so rigid about a border that had already been lost that they were losing the chance of any role in Poland's government. Even so, the PM felt some sympathy for Mikołajczyk's predicament, caught between his own militants and the sinister embrace of Bierut's Lubliners. 'Our lot from London are a decent but feeble lot of fools,' he told the king, 'but the delegates from Lublin seem to be the greatest villains imaginable' who 'recited their parts with well-drilled accuracy'.[23] Eden referred to the Lublin trio as 'the Skunk, the Rat and the Snake'.[24]

At Churchill's request, Stalin met Mikołajczyk alone on 18 October. As at the previous meeting in August, he assured the Polish leader that Moscow had no plans to Sovietize Poland and promised that the Poles would gain new lands in the west from Germany. Then he demanded recognition of the Curzon Line, which Mikołajczyk refused. Consequently, there was no agreement. But according to the Foreign Ministry's report sent to Soviet ambassadors abroad, 'at the end of negotiations Mikołajczyk said that he personally agreed on recognizing the Curzon Line as the Soviet–Polish border but that he must discuss the matter with his colleagues in London . . . he intended to return very quickly'.[25]

Churchill and his party left Moscow on 19 October. Just before his departure, the PM received gifts from Stalin, together with this letter.

Stalin to Churchill, sent 19 October 1944, received 19 October 1944[26]

Dear Mr Churchill,

On the day of your departure from Moscow, I beg you to accept from me in memory of your stay in the Soviet capital these modest presents – for Mrs Churchill a vase 'Steersman on a boat', and for yourself a vase 'Hunter with bow against a Bear'.

Again I wish you health and good spirits.

Stalin had a keen sense of diplomatic protocol, but also a mischievous sense of humour. Is it inappropriate to discern a subtext to his gift to Churchill, especially given the PM's known propensity to refer to Russia as 'Ursus Major' or 'the Bear'? And what of the present to Clementine – who was always trying to keep the PM on a steady course?

At any event, Churchill took the gifts at face value and immediately sent a warm message of thanks for them and for his whole time in Moscow.

Churchill to Stalin, sent 19 October 1944, received 19 October 1944[27]

My dear Marshal Stalin,

I have just received the two beautiful vases which you have given to me and my Wife as a souvenir of this memorable visit to Moscow. We shall treasure them among our most cherished possessions.

I have had to work very hard here this time and also have received an Air Courier every day entailing decisions about our own affairs. Consequently I have not been able to see any of the City of Moscow, with all its historic memories. But in spite of this, the visit has been from beginning to end a real pleasure to me on account of the warm welcome we have received, and most particularly because of our very pleasant talks together.

My hopes for the future alliance of our peoples never stood so high. I hope you may long be spared to repair the ravages of war and lead All The Russias out of the years of storm into glorious sunshine.

Your friend and war-time comrade

Out of respect for his ally, Stalin not only attended a reception at the British embassy for the very first time but also came to see Churchill off at the airport. 'A great honour that he should come himself,' Brooke remarked. 'Joe had his new uniform on with red tabs and collar and a little gold lace,' noted Elizabeth Layton, Churchill's personal secretary, 'and he certainly looks impressive. He is much shorter than you would think, but has a very special dignity about him.' As the plane taxied along the runway, Stalin took out a handkerchief and waved it.[28] Another example of his sense of humour: during the conference, when someone spoke of the Big Three as the Holy Trinity, Stalin quipped, 'If that is so, Churchill must be the Holy Ghost. He flies around so much.'[29]

Churchill was certainly gratified by the tone of the conversations, and he also enjoyed the badinage. In one boozy late-night session in Stalin's apartment which lasted until 4.30 a.m., the two leaders got onto Churchill's 'private war' against Russia in 1919, albeit in a joshing way. 'I'm glad now that I did not kill you,' remarked Churchill. 'I hope you are glad that you did not kill me?' Stalin readily agreed, quoting a Russian proverb: 'A man's eye should be torn out if he can see only the past.' All in all, the PM's confidence in the Soviet leader had been strengthened by this second visit to Moscow. As his physician, Lord Moran, observed, 'he still makes his plans in the faith that Stalin's word is his bond'.[30] But the PM also sensed 'strong pressures in the background, both party and military', and he could not shake off his earlier idea about 'two Stalins'. 'There is no doubt,' he cabled the War Cabinet,

> that within our narrow circle we have talked with an ease, freedom and beau gest[e] never before attained between our two countries. Stalin has made several expressions of personal regard which I feel sure were sincere. But I repeat my conviction that he is by no means alone. 'Behind the horseman sits dull care.'[31]

For his part, Stalin was also pleased with the Moscow conference. Although he had acknowledged Britain's primary role in Greece, that country had never been of major concern to him – whereas Romania, effectively conceded by Churchill, definitely was. In any case, as Stalin had concluded back in the spring of 1942, the balance of power in postwar Europe would be decided on the battlefield rather than at the conference table. Or, more exactly – since he wished to maintain a relationship with his wartime allies – the spoils of battle would be sanctified by diplomatic agreement. With regard to the Poles, the Soviet leader had played along with Churchill's efforts to forge consensus, while knowing that he was in the box seat because the Red Army was taking control of the country. And, now clearly aware of Churchill and Roosevelt's keenness for the Soviets to enter the war against Japan, Stalin had indicated that this would come at a price.

When writing to Roosevelt about the talks, Stalin did not go into detail – knowing that the president had been well informed by Churchill and Harriman. Instead he chose to highlight the capacity of their three governments for flexible negotiation and also to underline that the Moscow discussions were a prelude to 'definite decisions' that only the Big Three could take. He was now ready to talk concretely about their next meeting – not least because Hopkins had put him in a very advantageous position to do so.

Stalin to Roosevelt, sent 19 October 1944, received 19 October 1944[32]

During the stay of Mr. Churchill and Mr. Eden in Moscow we have exchanged views on a number of questions of mutual interest. Ambassador Harriman has, certainly, informed you of all the important Moscow conversations. I also know that the Prime Minister had to send you his estimate of the Moscow conversations. On my part I can say that our conversations were extremely useful for the mutual ascertaining of views on such questions as the attitude towards the future of Germany, Polish question, policy in regard to the Balkan States, and important questions of further military policy. During the conversations it has been clarified that we can, without great difficulties, adjust our policy on all questions standing before us, and if we are not in a position so far to provide an immediate necessary decision of this or that task, as for example, on the Polish question, but nevertheless, more favourable perspectives are opened. I hope that these Moscow conversations will be of some benefit from the point of view that at the future meeting of three of us, we shall be able to adopt definite decisions on all urgent questions of our mutual interest.

Ambassador Gromyko has informed me of his recent conversation with Mr. Hopkins, in which Mr. Hopkins expressed an idea that you could arrive in the Black Sea at the end of November [and] meet with me on the Soviet Black Sea coast. I would extremely welcome the realization of this intention. From the conversation with the Prime Minister, I was convinced that he also shares this idea. Thus the meeting of three of us could take place at the end of November in order to consider the questions which have been accumulated since Teheran. I would be glad to receive a message from you on this matter.

Stalin was referring to Gromyko's conversation on 13 October, when Hopkins tried to signal American dissatisfaction with Churchill's mission to Moscow and pressed for a proper Big Three meeting. Hopkins suggested late November – after Roosevelt had recovered from the presidential election – and also actually proposed the Crimea. He had previously told the president that, in view of the situation on the Eastern Front, 'there was not a chance of luring Stalin out of Russia at this time': so, rather than 'wind up with a lot of long-winded and irritating cables back and forth' (as happened before Tehran), Hopkins said, 'we might as well make up our minds first at least to go to some convenient port in Russia – preferably in the Crimea'. At the 13 October meeting, when Hopkins broached the idea, Gromyko said that Stalin was ready for a meeting of all three leaders, but then gave the usual excuses that the Boss would not be able to leave the USSR in view of the latest offensive, etc. Whereupon, according to Hopkins, 'I asked Gromyko whether there was any place in the Crimea at which it was fit to hold a conference, and he said he was sure there was but made no further comment.'[33]

Hopkins' remarks about the Crimea were seized on in Moscow: the relevant paragraph in Gromyko's dispatch was underlined.[34] Stalin was in favour of the idea – naturally, since Hopkins had conceded a venue that suited the Soviet leader without any of the haggling that took place before Tehran – and he discussed it with Churchill while the PM was in Moscow. 'I was delighted to hear from U.J. that you had suggested a triple meeting towards the end of November in a Black Sea port,' Churchill cabled FDR on 21 October. 'I think this is a very fine idea, and hope you will let me know about it in due course. I will come anywhere you two desire.'[35]

En route home, Churchill sent a thank-you letter to Stalin from Cairo, again lauding the constructive atmosphere of their meetings.

Churchill to Stalin, sent 20 October 1944, received 21 October 1944[36]

Eden and I have come away from the Soviet Union refreshed and fortified by the discussions which we had with you, Marshal Stalin, and with your colleagues. This memorable meeting in Moscow has shown that there are no matters that cannot be adjusted between us when we meet together in frank and intimate discussion. Russian hospitality, which is renowned, excelled itself on the occasion of our visit. Both in Moscow and in the Crimea, where we spent some enjoyable hours, there was the highest consideration for the comfort of myself and our mission. I am most grateful to you and to all those who were responsible for these arrangements. May we soon meet again.

*****

Roosevelt had continued to maintain his opposition to recognizing de Gaulle's French Committee of National Liberation (FCNL) as the provisional government of France. But the question became more urgent once much of France had been freed from Nazi rule; both the Foreign Office and the State Department wanted to move things along. While still in Moscow, Eden handed Molotov a memorandum about recognition, to which the foreign minister responded positively, and Churchill pressed Roosevelt hard to come around.[37] Eisenhower, anxious to free his command from as much civil administration as possible, was ready to announce a Zone of the Interior, including Paris, under the FCNL's control on 23 October. This finally forced FDR's hand. He let Stalin know, in a cable prepared by the State Department to make the whole business sound smooth and carefully calculated.[38]

The president was also giving thought to the forthcoming Big Three meeting. Writing to Stalin, he again underlined the preliminary nature of the Moscow discussions and also now tried to extricate himself from the near-commitment to a Crimean venue that Hopkins' unilateral diplomacy had set up. Having canvassed alternatives with Churchill, the president asked Stalin about Cyprus or Malta – but not in a categorical tone. (In all, he toyed with at least ten possible locations in October and November.)[39]

Roosevelt to Stalin, sent 24 October 1944, received 25 October 1944[40]

I am delighted to learn from your message dated October 19 and from reports by Ambassador Harriman of the success attained by you and Mr. Churchill in approaching an agreement on a number of questions that are of high interest to all of us in our common desire to secure and maintain a satisfactory and a durable peace. I am sure that the progress made during your conversations in Moscow will facilitate and expedite our work in the next meeting when the three of us should come to a full agreement on our future activities and policies and mutual interests.

We all must investigate the practicability of various places where our meeting in November can be held, such as accessibility, living accommodations, security, etc., and I would appreciate suggestions from you.

I have been thinking about the practicability of Malta, Athens, or Cyprus if my getting into the Black Sea on a ship should be impracticable or too difficult. I prefer travelling and living on a ship.

We know that the living conditions and security in Malta and Cyprus are satisfactory.

I am looking forward with much pleasure to seeing you again. Please let me have your suggestions and advice.

In reply, Stalin nailed things down briskly – obliquely noting that it was the Americans who had first proposed the Crimea and playing the health card by again invoking his doctors.

Stalin to Roosevelt, sent 29 October 1944, received 29 October 1944[41]

I have received your message of October 25.

If the idea that was expressed earlier about the possibility of our meeting on the Soviet Black Sea coast appears to be acceptable for you I would consider it extremely desirable to realize this plan. The conditions for a meeting there are absolutely favorable. I hope that by that time it will be also possible to provide a safe entrance of your vessel into the Black Sea. Since the doctors do not recommend to undertake any big trips at the present time, I have to give consideration to that.

I shall be glad to see you as soon as you find it possible to undertake the trip.

Meanwhile Churchill was enjoying the fruits of his trip to Moscow. Boxes full of traditional Soviet gifts had now been unpacked in London, and this time the vodka, cognac and caviar were particularly abundant.

Churchill to Stalin, sent 29 October 1944, received 30 October 1944[42]

It is only since my arrival in London that I have realised the great generosity of your gifts of Russian products to myself and members of my Mission. Please accept the warmest thanks of all who have been grateful recipients of this new example of Russian hospitality.

On 5 November, Churchill sent another chatty message to Stalin, mentioning the long-awaited opening of the Scheldt river into Antwerp, which relieved Eisenhower's logistical bottleneck, and the stalling of the Italian campaign in mud that reminded senior officers of Flanders in 1914–18. On Poland, the PM was deliberately vague – trying to conceal from Stalin that the Polish government in London had refused to accept the decisions taken during 'Tolstoy' and blaming Mikołajczyk's delay in returning to Moscow on his difficulties in consulting Roosevelt amid the election endgame. In fact, the Polish premier never went back to Moscow: on 24 November, he resigned after failing to persuade his Cabinet to accept the Curzon Line.

The PM could, however, take comfort from Yugoslavia, where the fifty-fifty approach agreed in Moscow seemed to be working. Eden persuaded Molotov to send a joint telegram to Tito and Šubašić on 13 October, urging them to meet as soon as possible for discussions on forming a government.[43] In general,

Soviet policies in Yugoslavia that autumn were flexible. 'The English are concerned about the growing Soviet influence in Yugoslavia,' stated a Moscow Foreign Ministry circular after 'Tolstoy'.

> We sought to dispel these fears, clarifying that we do not pursue the Sovietization of Yugoslavia, but at the same time stressing the importance of an accurate evaluation of the national liberation struggle of the Yugoslav national forces led by Marshal Tito and the importance of uniting all democratic national forces of Yugoslavia.[44]

It is significant that Stalin corresponded with Šubašić at this time and also advised Tito to take the extraordinary step of offering an amnesty to the Chetnik guerrillas, against whom his partisans had bitterly fought.[45] Šubašić's visit to Moscow, of which Stalin informed Churchill on 9 November, fitted within this diplomatic strategy.[46]

Churchill to Stalin, sent 5 November 1944, received 6 November 1944[47]

Many congratulations on your advance to Budapest.

We have now got effective control of the approaches to Antwerp, and I hope that coasters will be through in about ten days and ocean-going ships in three or four weeks. This solves the problem of the northern flank of the advance into Germany. There has been very hard fighting in Belgium and Holland and the British 21st Army Group have lost in British and British-controlled over 40,000 men since taking Brussels. When the various pockets and ports that are still holding out have been reduced, we shall have a far larger number of prisoners than that.

During the quiet spell on the Anglo-American front, all preparations have been made for a major offensive.

Tremendous torrential rains have broken a vast number of our bridges on the Italian front and all movement is at present at a stand-still.

About Yugoslavia, I am awaiting Dr. Subasic's return and the result of his report to King Peter. I was very glad to learn that King Peter was favourably impressed with such accounts as had hitherto reached him. Brigadier Maclean is with me now and tells me how much the atmosphere improved at Partisan headquarters when it was known that Russia and Britain were working together.

Although I have not said anything to you about the Poles you may be sure that I have not been idle. At present they are still talking to the United States Government and I do not know what answer I shall be able to extract. However, I take this opportunity of assuring you that I stand exactly where I stood when we parted

and that His Majesty's Government will support at any Armistice or Peace Conference the Soviet claims to the line we have agreed upon. It will be a great blessing
when the election in the United States is over.

Every good wish.

Another sign of the times was Churchill's congratulations on the birthday of
the state he had tried to strangle in its cradle – duly acknowledged with equal
politeness by Stalin.[48]

Churchill to Stalin, sent 7 November 1944, received 7 November 1944[49]

It gives me great pleasure to send you my congratulations on the anniversary of
the foundation of the Soviet State. I wish your country and yourself all success in
peace as in war, and pray that the Anglo-Soviet Alliance may be the cause of
much benefit to our two countries, to the United Nations and to the world.

On 8 November, Gromyko asked urgently: 'Roosevelt has been re-elected. Does
Comrade Stalin think it appropriate to send him greetings on this occasion?'[50]
Stalin hardly needed any prompting and sent formal congratulations. The pres-
ident replied with a thank-you prepared by Leahy.

Stalin to Roosevelt, sent 9 November 1944, received 9 November 1944[51]

I am sending you my congratulations on the occasion of your re-election. I am sure
that under your tried leadership the American people will complete, together
with the peoples of the Soviet Union, Great Britain and the other democratic
countries, the cause of struggle against a common foe and will guarantee victory
in the name of liberation of mankind from Nazi tyranny.

Roosevelt to Stalin, sent 10 November 1944, received 11 November 1944[52]

I am very pleased to have your message of congratulations and happy that you
and I can continue together with our Allies to destroy the Nazi tyrants and establish a long period of peace in which all of our peace-loving peoples, freed from
the burdens of war, may reach a higher order of development and culture, each in
accordance with its own desires.

Britain's long hunt for the German battleship *Tirpitz* finally bore fruit: it was
sunk by RAF Lancaster bombers on 12 November near Tromsø in Norway.

Although already severely damaged and barely operational, the *Tirpitz* bore a famous name and had terrorized the Arctic convoys in 1942, so the news was sweet. 'It is a great relief to us to get this brute where we have long wanted her,' Churchill told Roosevelt.[53] He also hastened to inform Stalin.

Churchill to Stalin, sent 12 November 1944, received 13 November 1944[54]

Royal Air Force bombers have sunk the *Tirpitz*. Let us rejoice together. Everything has gone very well here, and the great operations which I mentioned in my last telegram are rapidly unfolding. I am off tonight first to French and then to United States Headquarters. Every good wish.

Stalin had long believed that the British could have been more decisive in dealing with the *Tirpitz*; as so often, suspecting ulterior motives. In October 1943, he had even suggested to Eden that 'the British want to capture the *Tirpitz* intact and are thus reluctant to damage her'.[55] Nevertheless, the PM's message was well received.

Stalin to Churchill, sent 13 November 1944, received 13 November 1944[56]

The news that British aeroplanes have sunk the Tirpitz has greatly delighted us. The British airmen may legitimately pride themselves on this deed.

I wish success to the great operations of whose opening you have informed me.

I send you best wishes.

On 10–12 November, Churchill and Eden visited Paris for the first time since its liberation. It was an emotional moment, as the PM and de Gaulle marked Armistice Day together and walked amid cheering crowds along the Champs-Elysées. The visit eased some of the tension caused by de Gaulle's anger at being marginalized by Roosevelt and Churchill. It also allowed the British to start rebuilding France's position in Europe and, thereby, a European balance of power. Reporting in general terms on the visit to Stalin – who received a detailed report of the discussions via intelligence channels[57] – Churchill pressed France's case for a share in the Allied occupation of Germany. He emphasized that he had promised nothing, because 'all this must be settled at an inter-Allied table', but added that this 'reinforced the desirability of a meeting between us three and the French in the fairly near future. In this case the French would be in on some subjects and out on others.'[58] Stalin had no objection to Churchill's proposal that de Gaulle attend some sessions of their Big Three conference, but Roosevelt told Churchill firmly on 18 November that he did not agree, remarking caustically that 'such a debating society would confuse our essential issues'.[59]

Apart from lobbying Churchill, de Gaulle pressed behind the scenes for a visit to Moscow. Although having no illusions about Soviet policy, he nevertheless saw Russia – France's main traditional ally before 1914 – as an important future partner which could help him pursue a more independent policy. In early November, through diplomatic channels, he began to probe the ground for a visit to Moscow. De Gaulle's feelers were extended just when the Kremlin was receiving reports that Britain wanted to build a postwar 'Western bloc', centred on France but including some smaller European states. Drawing on press reports and conversations with British and French diplomats, Gusev told Moscow that after the war 'only one great power will remain on the continent – the Soviet Union, which will assume the leading role in European politics. This prospect goes against British foreign policy interests, which have never really abandoned the policy of the "balance of power in Europe".' Gusev, however, noted that 'France also wants to revive an alliance with Russia', and offered his opinion that 'a regional pact in Western Europe will not challenge the regional security system that the Soviet Union is building along its borders together with the Slavic nations, but, on the contrary, will complete the encirclement of Germany and make it possible to nip in the bud the next act of aggression'.[60]

Stalin, previously in no hurry to invite de Gaulle, now eagerly responded to his overtures. A Franco-Soviet accord offered the prospect of keeping France out of any Western bloc and, as a quid pro quo, he might be able to secure French recognition for the PCNL in Poland. On 13 November, de Gaulle received a formal invitation to visit the USSR, which he promptly accepted. Stalin was careful to notify Churchill, just back from Paris, and promised to keep the PM informed of the talks. At this point, however, Moscow still had little information about the French agenda.[61]

Roosevelt's detailed letter to Stalin on 18 November was penned by the president himself – a rare occurrence. This demonstrated his keen desire to meet Stalin, and his mounting anxiety about the venue. His reservations about meeting in the Crimea were now stated more strongly, and he also asked to defer the meeting until late January, after his State of the Union message and his Fourth Inaugural. Replying on 23 November, Stalin accepted the new date, but stuck tight on the place.

Roosevelt to Stalin, sent 18 November 1944,
received 19 November 1944[62]

All three of us are of one mind – that we should meet very soon, but problems chiefly geographical do not make this easy at this moment. I can, under difficulties, arrange to go somewhere now in order to get back here by Christmas but, quite frankly, it will be far more convenient if I could postpone it until after the Inauguration which is on January twentieth.

My Navy people recommend strongly against the Black Sea. They do not want to risk a capital ship through the Aegean or the Dardanelles, as it would involve a very large escort much needed elsewhere. Churchill has suggested Jerusalem or Alexandria, and there is a possibility of Athens, though this is not yet sure.

Furthermore, I have at this time a great hesitation in leaving here while my old Congress is in its final days, with the probability of its not adjourning finally until December fifteenth. Also, I have to be here, under the Constitution, to send the Annual Message to the new Congress which meets here in early January.

What I am suggesting is that we should all meet about the twenty-eighth or thirtieth of January, and I should hope that by that time you will have rail travel to some port on the Adriatic and that we should meet you there or that you could come across in a few hours on one of our ships to Bari and then motor to Rome, or that you should take the same ship a little further and that we should all meet at some place like Taormina, in eastern Sicily, which should provide a fairly good climate at that time.

Almost any place in the Mediterranean is accessible to me so that I can be within easy air distance of Washington in order to carry out action on Legislation – a subject with which you are familiar. I must be able to get Bills or Resolutions sent from here and returned within ten days.

I hope that your January military operations will not prevent you from coming at that time, and I do not think that we should delay the meeting longer than the end of January or early February.

Of course, if in the meantime the Nazi Army or people should disintegrate quickly, we would have to meet earlier, although I should much prefer the meeting at the end of January.

A further suggestion as to a place would be one on the Riviera but this would be dependent on withdrawal of German troops from northwestern Italy. I wish you would let me know your thoughts on this.

I hope to talk over many things with you. We understand each other's problems and, as you know, I like to keep these discussions informal, and I have no reason for formal agenda.

My Ambassador in China, General Hurley, is doing his best to iron out the problems between the Generalissimo and the forces in Northern China. He is making some progress but nothing has been signed yet.

My warmest regards to you.

Stalin to Roosevelt, sent 23 November 1944, received 24 November 1944[63]

It is greatly regretted that your naval organs doubt the expedience of your initial supposition that the Soviet coast of the Black Sea should be chosen as the meeting place for the three of us. The suggested by you date of the meeting at the end of January or beginning of February has no objections on my part, but at the same time I have in mind that we shall succeed in choosing as a meeting place one of the Soviet port cities. I still have to take into consideration the advice of the doctors about the danger of long trips.

I still hope, however, that we shall succeed, if not right now, then somewhat later to agree finally upon an acceptable for all of us meeting place.

I am sending you my very best wishes.

Amid the flux of southeastern Europe, Yugoslavia was an area of Soviet–British cooperation, building on the fifty-fifty deal agreed in Moscow. The Tito–Šubašić talks produced an agreement signed on 1 November, which paved the way for the formation of a coalition government. A central provision was that King Peter II was not to return to the country 'until the people decide on it'; in his absence, the regency council exercised his royal power, but the new government would not have to swear the oath of loyalty.[64] Three weeks later, Šubašić flew to Moscow with a few colleagues. At the Kremlin on 22 November, Stalin urged them to speed up the process of creating a federation with Bulgaria and to negotiate on all matters relating to Yugoslavia with the British. He also endorsed the Tito–Šubašić agreement and warned against an early return of the king to Yugoslavia, mentioning with approval the stance of George II of Greece, who had agreed not to return to Athens until after a referendum on the monarchy.[65] Churchill, however, evaluated the agreement differently. He felt that Šubašić had 'sold out on pretty cheap terms to Tito', in whom the PM was losing confidence.[66]

Stalin to Churchill, sent 24 November 1944,
received 24 November 1944[67]

Today Dr. Subasic leaves Moscow after a short stay. I have had a conversation with him and also with the Deputy President of the National Committee, Kardel, and the Yugoslav Ambassador, Simic. In the conversation it was clear that the agreement which Marshal Tito and Subasic have reached about a United Yugoslav Government could be of use to Yugoslavia and that it would not do to put off the bringing into operation of this agreement. You are of course informed about this agreement and will be, I hope, in agreement with it, especially after a conversation with Subasic who is returning immediately to London. Now, when Belgrade has been freed from the Germans and the Yugoslavs – Serbs, Croats, Slovenes and the rest – are ready to unite and work together, support of these united efforts of the peoples of Yugoslavia on the part of our Governments will be a new blow to the Hitlerites and will be of not a little assistance to the common work of the Allies.

In his next letter to Stalin, Churchill alluded to the 'Western bloc'. Conscious that this phrase was in the air, Churchill sought to reassure the Kremlin by brushing it aside and reiterating his overriding faith in the Big Three Alliance. In private, he disparaged talk of a Western bloc as vacuous and imprudent. 'Until a really strong French army is again in being, which may well be more than five years or even ten,' he told Eden on 25 November, 'there is nothing in these countries but hopeless weakness.' The foreign secretary accepted that it would be both 'absurd and highly dangerous' to make such continental commitments, except in conjunction with a strong France and 'as part of some general plan for containing Germany evolved under the aegis of a World Organisation'. But, he argued that if France and the smaller states of Western Europe 'have the impression that we are not in the future going to accept any commitments on the Continent', they might conclude that 'their only hope' lay in 'making defence arrangements, not with us, but with the Russians'.[68] Eden envisaged the Western bloc primarily as a bulwark against a resurgent Germany, but the chiefs of staff also saw it as possible insurance in the longer term against the USSR. The FO lamented 'the difficulty and futility of such speculation', and deplored the idea of 'building up Germany, which is at present unthinkable', urging instead reiteration of 'the significance of the Anglo-Soviet alliance'. There was also concern in the FO that if the chiefs' anti-Soviet spin on the idea leaked out, it could damage relations with Moscow.[69]

This was no empty fear. In fact, an NKVD report at the end of 1944 cited the exchange between Churchill and Eden in late November, summarizing the latter's argument as follows: 'If we do not make a commitment to protect the smaller western nations, they will fall into the hands of the Soviet Union. The Chiefs of Staff agree that we must have a defence in depth.'[70]

Churchill to Stalin, sent 25 November 1944, received 26 November 1944[71]

Your message of November 20th. I am glad that de Gaulle is coming to see you and I hope you will talk over the whole field together. There has been some talk in the Press about a Western bloc, I have not yet considered this. I trust first of all to our Treaty of Alliance and close collaboration with the United States to form the mainstay of a World Organisation to ensure and compel peace upon the tortured world. It is only after and subordinate to any such world structure that European arrangements for better comradeship should be set on foot and in these matters we shall have no secrets from you, being well assured that you will keep us equally informed of what you feel and need.

The battle in the West is severe and the mud frightful. The main collision is on the axis Aix-la-Chapelle–Cologne. This is by no means decided in our favour yet, though Eisenhower still has substantial reserves to throw in. To the North-west, Montgomery's armies are facing north holding back the Germans on the line of the Dutch Maas. This river permits us an economy in force on this front. To the East we are making slow but steady progress and keeping the enemy in continual battle. One must acclaim the capture of Metz and the driving of the enemy back towards the Rhine as a fine victory for the Americans. In the South the French have had brilliant success particularly in reaching the Rhine on a broad front and in taking Strasbourg, and these young French soldiers, from 18 to 21 years old, are showing themselves worthy of the glorious chance to cleanse the soil of France. I think highly of General de Lattre de Tassigny. De Gaulle and I travelled there in order to see the opening of this battle from a good view-point. However, a foot of snow fell in the night and everything was put off for three days.

In a week or ten days it should be possible to estimate whether the German Armies will be beaten decisively West of the Rhine. If they are, we can go on in spite of the weather. Otherwise there may be some lull during the severity of the Winter, after which one more major onslaught should break organised German resistance in the West.

Do you think it is going to be a hard winter and will this suit your strategy? We all greatly liked your last speech. Please do not fail to let me know privately if anything troublesome occurs so that we can smooth it away and keep the closing grip on Nazidom at its most tense degree.

The speech mentioned by Churchill was Stalin's address on the twenty-seventh anniversary of the October Revolution, which indeed prompted much positive comment in the Allied capitals. In Washington, Gromyko reported, particular note was taken that Stalin for the first time named Japan as an aggressor and that he also paid tribute to Allied military successes. 'Until recently people here (and apparently also in England)', observed the ambassador, 'have been of the opinion that the Allied war effort has not been adequately recognized by the Soviet Union.'[72] According to Gusev, what attracted most attention in the British press was Stalin's statement that it was 'not some random and momentary motives but vital and lasting interests that lie at the core of the alliance between the Soviet Union, Britain and the United States.'[73]

On 30 November, Churchill turned seventy. Among the many greetings there was a telegram of 'affectionate regards' from Roosevelt which recalled 'the party with you and UJ a year ago' at Tehran, and added 'we must have more of them that are even better.'[74] Stalin, too, sent congratulations.

Stalin to Churchill, sent 29 November 1944, received 29 November 1944[75]

Heartfelt congratulations on your birthday. I send you my friendly wishes for long years of good health and good cheer for the benefit of our common cause.

Churchill responded cordially, also recalling Tehran, and said, 'I most particularly welcomed in your message the wish you expressed that our comradeship and personal relations may continue in the future, not only in the hazards of war but also in solving the problems of peace.'[76]

Despite his formidable stamina, Churchill was beginning to show the strain of more than four years of war and thousands of miles of shuttle diplomacy. His private secretary Jock Colville noted in his diary:

The P.M.'s box is in a frightful state, with scores of urgent papers demanding a decision. He has frittered away his time in the last week and has seemed unable or unwilling or too tired to give his attention to complex matters. He has been reading the first paragraph or so and referring papers to people without seeing what is really required of him. Result: chaos.[77]

Yet the prime minister did find time on his birthday to write to Stalin about what he called 'a small but important matter' – his fascination with gadgetry being as strong as ever. The acoustic homing torpedo T-5 had been used on German U-boats since summer 1943. Its sonar equipment could detect the noise of a ship's propellers at a distance of a thousand metres.[78] Two T-5 torpedoes were found intact on the U-250, which was sunk by the Russians in shallow water near Tallinn and then raised to the surface. The Soviet Navy Ministry duly informed the British military mission in Moscow. Although the Royal Navy had developed counter-measures against the T-5, it was keen to see a specimen of the weapon, and the Admiralty asked Churchill to expedite matters by asking Stalin direct.

Churchill to Stalin, sent 30 November 1944, received 1 December 1944[79]

The Admiralty have asked me to seek your assistance in a small but important matter. The Soviet Navy have informed the Admiralty that two German T.5 acoustic torpedoes have been found in a U-boat captured at Tallinn. This is the only known type of torpedo directed by acoustic principles and is very effective against not only merchant ships, but escort vessels. Although not yet in use on a very large scale, it has sunk or damaged twenty-four British escorts, five of them in convoys to North Russia.

Our experts have invented one special device which provides some protection against the torpedo and is fitted to British destroyers now operated by the Soviet Navy. Study of an actual specimen of the T.5 torpedo would however be of the utmost value in developing counter-measures. Admiral Archer has asked the Soviet naval authorities that one of the two torpedoes should immediately be made available for examination and practical tests in the United Kingdom. I understand that they do not rule out the possibility but that the question is still under consideration.

You will, I am sure, recognise the great assistance that the Soviet Navy can render to the Royal Navy by facilitating the immediate transport of one torpedo to the U.K., when I remind you that the enemy have for many months past been preparing to launch fresh U-boat campaigns on a large scale with new boats specially fast under water. From this there would follow all the increased difficulties of transporting U.S. troops and supplies across the ocean to both theatres of war. We regard the obtaining of a T.5 torpedo as of such urgency that we should be ready to send a British aircraft to any convenient place designated by you to fetch the torpedo.

I therefore ask you to give your kind attention to this matter, the importance of which is increased by the probability that the Germans have given the designs of the torpedo to the Japanese Navy. The Admiralty will gladly give to the Soviet Navy all the results of their researches and experiments with the torpedo and the benefit of any new protective equipment subsequently devised.

The PM had to wait two weeks for an answer, but when this came it showed the value of the top-level correspondence in cutting through obstacles lower down. The same was true of another message he sent to Stalin on 1 December. This concerned an incident in Yugoslavia three weeks before, when US P-38 Lightning fighters mistakenly attacked a Red Army troop convoy; several Soviet soldiers were killed and twenty vehicles destroyed. While adding his regrets for the American action, caused by navigational error, Churchill used the affair to press for clearer bomb lines as their armies converged on the same enemy areas, and also for more effective liaison between their army staffs. He sent a further message along similar lines next day. As with the cable about the acoustic torpedo, Churchill was mostly relaying memoranda prepared by his commanders. But messages on such matters signed by the PM himself, if not too frequent, packed a special punch. Stalin agreed with the need for a clear demarcation line and instructed his general staff to expedite arrangements with the Allied military missions in Moscow.[80]

As for the Western bloc, the Soviet leader sent an anodyne reply – which did not mean that he underestimated the issue.

Stalin to Churchill, sent 1 December 1944, received 1 December 1944[81]

As regards a Western bloc, so far I am scantily informed on the subject and Press reports are conflicting. I am grateful to you for promising to inform me how this question will develop and am prepared to do the same myself.

I was interested to read your report on military operations in the West. The weather, certainly, is now hampering terribly the development of operations.

I shall not fail to profit by your good advice and to inform you if anything of special importance arises.

*****

De Gaulle and his entourage arrived in Moscow on 2 December. Before the first formal conversation, Stalin sent a message to both his partners about the agenda, which by then had been discussed by Soviet and French diplomats. In doing so, Stalin showed his fidelity as an ally. But he was also trying to ascertain Roosevelt and Churchill's general views before he started to talk with de Gaulle – aware of FDR's distaste for the general and of Churchill and Eden's desire to build up postwar France. Overall, the Kremlin wanted to foster friendly relations with France, provided this did not compromise cooperation with the Anglo-Americans. It was also aware of France's likely territorial claims against Germany in the Rhineland.[82]

Stalin to Roosevelt, sent 2 December 1944, received 2 December 1944[83]

According to all data General De-Gaulle and his friends who arrived in the Soviet Union, will put two questions.

1. About the conclusion of Franco-Soviet pact of mutual assistance similar to Anglo-Soviet pact.

   It is difficult for us to object. But I would like to know your opinion on this question. I ask you to give me your advice.

2. Probably General De-Gaulle will raise a question about the change of the eastern frontier of France with the expansion of the French frontier to the left bank of the Rhine. It is also known that there is a project about the establishment of the Rhine-Westphalian region under the international control.

   It is possible that this control provides the participation of France. Thus the proposal of the French concerning the shift of the frontier to the Rhine will compete with the project of establishment of the Rhine region under the international control.

   I ask your advice on this question as well.

   I sent a similar message to Mr. Churchill.

Despite Mikołajczyk's resignation and the formation of a new Polish government-in-exile that was even more hardline towards the USSR, Churchill hoped that 'Mick' would return to power, considering him the only political figure capable of reaching the deal with Moscow that they believed to be essential. The PM dismissed warnings from Clark Kerr that failing to break off relations with the new government risked a 'head-on collision' with Moscow. If there was any danger of that happening, he told Eden, Stalin 'presumably would blow his whistle, as at present our relations are most friendly'.[84] Writing to Stalin, the PM again tried to present the Polish imbroglio in the most positive light possible.

Churchill to Stalin, sent 3 December 1944, received 3 December 1944[85]

I have seen Mr Mikolajczyk, who has explained to me the reason for his resignation. Briefly, the position is that he could not count on the support of important sections of his Cabinet for his policy and was therefore unable at this stage to conclude an agreement on the basis of the discussions between us at our recent Moscow meeting.

Attempts are now being made to form an alternative Polish Government, in which M. Mikolajczyk or M. Romer and the Ambassador, M. Raczynski, have refused to participate. A change of Prime Ministers does not affect the formal relations between States. The desire of His Majesty's Government for the reconstitution of a strong and independent Poland, friendly to Russia, remains unalterable. We have practical matters to handle with the Polish Government, and more especially the control of the considerable Polish armed forces, over 80,000 excellent fighting men, under our operational command. These are now making an appreciable contribution to the United Nations' war effort in Italy, Holland and elsewhere. Our attitude towards any new Polish Government must therefore be correct, though it will certainly be cold. We cannot of course have the same close relations of confidence with such a government as we have had with Mr Mikolajczyk or with his predecessor, the late General Sikorski, and we shall do all in our power to ensure that its activities do not endanger the unity between the Allies.

It is not thought that such a government, even when formed, will have a long life. Indeed, after my conversations with M. Mikolajczyk, I should not be surprised to see him back in office before long with increased prestige and with the necessary powers to carry through the programme discussed between us in Moscow. This outcome would be all the more propitious because he would by his resignation have proclaimed himself and his friends in the most convincing way as a champion of Polish good relations with Russia.

I trust, therefore, that you will agree that our respective influence should be used with the Poles here and with those at Lublin to prevent any steps on either side which might increase the tension between them and so render more difficult M. Mikolajczyk's task when, as I hope, he takes it up again in the not far distant future. He is himself in good heart and remains anxious, as ever, for a satisfactory settlement. I see no reason why he should not emerge from this crisis as an even more necessary factor than before for the reconstruction of Poland.

In view of the strengthening Soviet position in Yugoslavia, Churchill was intent on ensuring adherence to the Moscow agreement about joint policies. He believed that this would not only contain the spread of Soviet influence, but also tame Tito's ambitions through pressure from Stalin. To complement this diplomacy, plans were developed at Alexander's headquarters for a landing on the Yugoslav coast (operation 'Gelignite'). Although primarily intended as a way for the Allies to break out of the impasse in Italy by a right hook around the top of the Adriatic to Trieste and Fiume to help cut off the German forces, this would also have the political benefit of projecting British power into the Balkans.

Churchill also conveyed his growing displeasure directly to Tito. On 3 December, he sent a long message of complaint referencing 'several instances of lack of co-operation on the part of your officers' in dealings with British representatives, and reminding him that he and Stalin had arranged 'to pursue as far as possible a joint policy towards Yugoslavia' to ensure an 'equal balance' between Soviet and British influence, whereas 'you seem to be treating us in an increasingly invidious fashion'. He told Tito he was copying this telegram to Stalin. But the Soviet leader replied coyly on the 14th that, before responding in detail, he wanted to 'learn the opinion of the Marshal himself on these matters'.[86]

The PM's close attention to the Balkans at that time was prompted above all by the situation in Greece. The Germans had pulled out in the middle of October and – utilizing the free hand Churchill felt he had secured in Moscow – a new government was established under Georgios Papandreou in coalition with the communists of the National Liberation Front (EAM), backed up by British troops. But when Papandreou ordered the communist guerrillas of the Greek People's Liberation Army (ELAS) to lay down their arms, EAM resigned from the government on 1 December, and the ensuing leftist protests in Athens were met with violence. Churchill authorized the use of British troops to keep order and control the escalating civil war. Much now depended on Stalin's reaction: hence the PM's concern to uphold their percentages agreement.

Immediately after his first conversation with de Gaulle, Stalin duly notified both Roosevelt and Churchill, maintaining the posture of studious openness he had adopted in this delicate situation. On the two main agenda issues – a Franco-Soviet pact and France's bid for a frontier on the Rhine – he again tried to draw out the views of his partners.[87]

Stalin to Churchill, sent 3 December 1944, received 3 December 1944[88]

The meeting with General de Gaulle has provided the opportunity for a friendly exchange of views on questions of Franco-Soviet relations. In the course of the talks General de Gaulle persisted, as I had expected, with two main questions: the frontier of France on the Rhine and the conclusion of a Franco-Soviet Pact of mutual assistance of the type of the Anglo-Soviet Treaty.

As regards the frontier of France on the Rhine, I expressed myself to the effect that it was impossible to decide this question without the knowledge and consent of our chief allies, whose armies are waging a battle of liberation against the enemy on the territory of France. I emphasised the complexity of a solution to this question.

With regard to the proposal for a Franco-Soviet Pact of mutual assistance, I pointed out the necessity of a study of this question from all sides and on the necessity for clarification of the juridical aspects of such a pact, in particular of the question who would ratify such a pact in France in present conditions.

Consequently the French would still have to offer a number of explanations which we had up till now not received from them.

In sending you this information I shall be grateful for a reply from you and for your comments on these questions.

I have conveyed the same message to the President.

I send you my best wishes.

Stalin's message was discussed by the War Cabinet on 4 December. Churchill 'expressed satisfaction with the cordial tone' and appreciated Stalin's 'request for our advice'. He recommended a reply similarly framed in 'cordial terms'. Eden then explained the preference of the FO for a tripartite pact that included Britain – mainly, he explained, because 'the fact that France had no treaty with the United Kingdom might create misunderstanding' if the French signed a bilateral pact of mutual assistance with the USSR. In other words, it might seem that Paris was closer to Moscow than to London.[89] The Cabinet approved a reply along these lines. In it, the PM expressed the hope that it might be possible in due course to modify Roosevelt's opposition to any French presence at the Big Three summit.

Churchill to Stalin, sent 5 December 1944, received 5 December 1944[90]

Your telegram about de Gaulle's visit and the two questions he will raise. We have no objection whatever to a Franco-Soviet Pact of Mutual Assistance similar to the Anglo-Soviet pact. On the contrary, His Majesty's Government consider it desirable and an additional link between us all. Indeed it also occurs to us that it might be best of all if we were to conclude a tripartite treaty between the three of us which would embody our existing Anglo-Soviet Treaty with any improvements. In this way the obligations of each one of us would be identical and linked together. Please let me know if this idea appeals to you as I hope it may. We should both of course tell the United States.

The question of changing the eastern frontier of France to the left bank of the Rhine, or alternatively of forming a Rhenish-Westphalian province under international control, together with the other alternatives, ought to await settlement at the peace table. There is, however, no reason why, when the three heads of government meet, we should not come much closer to conclusions about all this than we have done so far. As you have seen, the President does not expect General de Gaulle to come to the meeting of the three. I would hope that this could be modified to his coming in later on when decisions specially affecting France were under discussion.

Meanwhile would it not be a good thing to let the European Advisory Commission sitting in London, of which France is a member, explore the topic for us all without committing in any way the heads of government.

I am keeping the President informed.

Roosevelt was not enthusiastic about a tripartite pact. He told Churchill it 'might be interpreted by public opinion here as a competitor to a future world organization, whereas a bilateral arrangement between France and the Soviet Union similar to the Soviet–British Pact would be more understandable'. In his letter to Stalin, prepared by the State Department, the president therefore simply confined himself to supporting a Franco-Soviet pact.[91]

With regard to the planned United Nations: faced since Dumbarton Oaks with Soviet resistance on voting procedure in the new Security Council, the State Department came up with a compromise formula in a memo of 14 November.[92] Permanent members of the Council would have the right to veto enforcement action against them, but could not restrict the right of the Council to discuss a particular dispute. In this case, it was proposed that the permanent member who was party to the conflict refrain from voting. This wording did not prevent the great powers from blocking the adoption of undesirable security decisions, and the Americans hoped that it would be acceptable to Moscow. Roosevelt decided to wait for Harriman to return to Moscow, so that he could deliver a message to Stalin in person. The text was prepared by Stettinius who, four days earlier, had replaced the ailing Hull as secretary of state. He sent Roosevelt a draft cable to Harriman with the text of the letter and instructions for the ambassador on how to present the matter to the Soviet leader – all of which were approved by FDR. 'We have great confidence in your ability to convince Marshal Stalin of the reasonableness of our views,' wrote Stettinius, adding that

> even if you are not entirely successful at this time in persuading the Marshal to adopt as his own the views expressed in the President's message, it is essential to keep the issue open and to avoid any crystallization of a negative attitude on the part of the Soviet government on this vitally significant matter.[93]

The message was sent to Churchill for information. Harriman, however, was not able to secure a meeting with Stalin until 14 December.

Roosevelt to Stalin, sent 5 December 1944, received 14 December 1944[94]

In view of the fact that prospects for an early meeting between us are still unsettled and because of my conviction, with which I am sure you agree, that we must move forward as quickly as possible in the convening of a general conference of the United Nations on the subject of an international organization, I am asking Ambassador Harriman to deliver this message to you and to discuss with you on my behalf the important subject of voting procedure in the Security Council. This and other questions will, of course, have to be agreed between us before the general conference will be possible. I am also taking up this matter with Mr. Churchill.

After giving this whole subject further consideration, I now feel that the substance of the following draft provision should be eminently satisfactory to everybody concerned:

PROPOSAL FOR SECTION C OF THE
CHAPTER ON THE SECURITY COUNCIL

C. Voting

1. Each member of the Security Council should have one vote.
2. Decisions of the Security Council on procedural matters should be made by an affirmative vote of seven members.
3. Decisions of the Security Council on all other matters should be made by an affirmative vote of seven members including the concurring votes of the permanent members; provided that, in decisions under Chapter VIII, Section A, and under Paragraph One of Chapter VIII, Section C, a party to a dispute should abstain from voting.

You will note that this calls for the unanimity of the permanent members in all decisions of the Council which relate to a determination of a threat to the peace and to action for the removal of such a threat or for the suppression of aggression or other breaches of the peace. I can see, as a practical matter, that this is necessary if action of this kind is to be feasible, and I am, therefore, prepared to accept in this respect the view expressed by your Government in its memorandum on an international security organization presented at the Dumbarton Oaks meeting. This means, of course, that in decisions of this character each permanent member would always have a vote.

At the same time, the Dumbarton Oaks proposals also provide in Chapter VIII, Section A, for judicial or other procedures of a recommendatory character which the Security Council may employ in promoting voluntary peaceful settlement of disputes. Here, too, I am satisfied that recommendations of the Security Council will carry far greater weight if they are concurred in by the permanent members. But I am also convinced that such procedures will be effective only if the Great Powers exercise moral leadership by demonstrating their fidelity to the principles of justice, and, therefore, by accepting a provision under which, with regard to such procedures, all parties to a dispute should abstain from voting. I firmly believe that willingness on the part of the permanent members not to claim for themselves a special position in this respect would greatly enhance their moral prestige and would strengthen their own position as the principal guardians of the future peace, without in any way jeopardizing their vital interests or impairing the essential principle that in all decisions of the Council which affect such interests of [sic] the Great Powers must act unanimously. It would certainly make the whole plan, which must necessarily assign a special role to the Great Powers in the enforcement of peace, far more acceptable to all nations.

Neither the Soviet nor the American memoranda presented at Dumbarton Oaks contained specific provisions for voting procedure on questions of this nature. Our representatives there were not, of course, in a position to reach a definite agreement on the subject. You and I must now find a way of completing the work which they have so well carried forward on our behalf.

If you should be inclined to give favorable consideration to some such approach to the problem of voting in the Council as I now suggest, would you be willing that there be held as soon as possible a meeting of representatives designated by you, by me, and by Mr. Churchill to work out a complete provision on this question and to discuss the arrangements necessary for a prompt convening of a general United Nations conference?

Stalin dealt briskly with Churchill's ineffectual attempts to talk up Mikołajczyk, blasting the former Polish leader as mere cover for anti-Soviet 'criminal' elements in Poland. The Kremlin did have intelligence evidence about the Polish Home Army's hostile actions against Soviet troops,[95] but the message was largely bombast to help secure early recognition of the Polish National Committee as the interim government of Poland. In the translation prepared for Churchill, the Russian word *emigranty* was in places rendered 'emigrants' rather than 'émigrés'. Stalin's brutal dismissal of Mikołajczyk and the London Poles as yesterday's men who were irrelevant to the actual facts on the ground underlined the increasing hollowness of Churchill's Polish policy. The PM could only reply somewhat lamely: 'We must make sure that our permanent and loyal relations are not disturbed by awkward movements of subordinate events.'[96]

Stalin to Churchill, sent 8 December 1944, received 8 December 1944[97]

I have received your message about M. Mikolajczyk.

In the time that has passed since my last meeting with M. Mikolajczyk in Moscow, it has become clear that he is unable to help in the solution of Polish affairs. On the contrary his negative role has become apparent. It is now apparent that his conversations with the Polish National Committee serve as a cover for those elements which behind his back have carried on criminal terroristic work against Soviet officers and generally against Soviet people on the territory of Poland. We cannot reconcile ourselves with such a position. We cannot reconcile ourselves with the fact that terrorists encouraged by the Polish emigrants kill our people in Poland and carry on a criminal fight against the Soviet troops who are liberating Poland. In these people we see allies of our common enemy, and their radio communications with M. Mikolajczyk which we have intercepted on agents of the Polish emigrants arrested on Polish territory expose not only their cunning plans but also throw a shadow on M. Mikolajczyk himself and his people.

The ministerial changes in the Polish emigre Government are not now of serious interest. That is still the same process of marking time by people who have lost touch with the national soil and have no contact with the Polish people. At the same time the Polish Committee of National Liberation has achieved notable successes in strengthening its national democratic organisations on Polish soil, in the practical carrying out of land reform for the benefit of the peasants and in broadening the organisation of its Polish forces, and it exercises great authority among the Polish population.

I think that now our task consists in backing up the Polish National Committee at Lublin and all who are willing and able to work with them. That is especially important for the allies, having in view the task of hastening the destruction of the Germans.

The Moscow talks with de Gaulle ended on 10 December with the signing of a treaty of alliance and mutual assistance similar to the Anglo-Soviet treaty of 1942. De Gaulle totally rejected the British idea of a tripartite pact. His trip to Moscow was all about restoring France – still stung by the humiliation of 1940 – to what he deemed its rightful rank as 'one of the greatest states'. The general bristled at Churchill's proposal, writing later in his memoirs: 'Why did he address himself exclusively to Stalin in a matter concerning France as much as London or Moscow?'[98]

During their meeting on 8 December, Stalin did advance various arguments in favour of a tripartite pact. 'A Franco-Soviet Pact is a good thing,' he said. But 'a tripartite pact that would involve England is a better option. France and Russia would absorb the first blows, but it is difficult to win a war without England.' Stalin also argued that he had already assented to Churchill's proposal, so the PM would be 'offended' if his offer were rejected. However, there seemed to be an ulterior motive here: by eventually presenting acceptance of a bilateral pact as a major concession to de Gaulle, the Soviet leader thereby prodded him to make a counter-concession on something vital for the Soviets, namely the establishment of relations between the French government and the PCNL. 'Let the French do us a favour, and we will do one for them,' he declared. 'Churchill will be offended, but what can you do?'[99]

De Gaulle was conscious that full recognition of Lublin would put him out of step with the 'Anglo-Saxons' and also betray France's interwar commitments to Poland, so he dug in against that proposal. Eventually a compromise was reached. 'After a repeated exchange of views on this question,' an internal Soviet Foreign Ministry memo stated, 'de Gaulle has agreed to accept a representative of the Polish Committee of National Liberation in Paris and send a representative of the French Provisional Government to Lublin.'[100] For Moscow, this was its first breakthrough – albeit limited – in overcoming the diplomatic isolation of their Polish allies – though Stalin deleted from the messages to Roosevelt and Churchill a paragraph about de Gaulle's meeting with members of the PCNL and the agreement between them on exchanging representatives. London and Washington were aware of these developments through Clark Kerr and Harriman's contacts with Georges Bidault of the French delegation, but Stalin apparently did not want to spoil the positive tone of his message, knowing his allies' antipathy to the Lubliners.

De Gaulle had gained some status by inviting himself to Moscow, but in the process he overplayed France's hand. Stalin conceded nothing on France's postwar demands for territory and status – making clear that these would be discussed by the Big Three. As de Gaulle's biographer Jean Lacouture observes, 'all he brought back from Moscow was a face-saving pact – and a few splendid pages of his *Mémoires de guerre*'.[101] Stalin, by contrast, now not only had an alliance with France – whereas Britain did not, despite all Whitehall's talk about a Western bloc – but he had also managed to seem punctilious about informing his allies.

Stalin to Churchill, sent 10 December 1944, received 10 December 1944[102]

I communicated to General de Gaulle your opinion about your preference for an Anglo-French-Soviet pact of mutual assistance and spoke in favour of accepting your proposal. However, General de Gaulle insisted on concluding a Franco-Soviet pact, saying that a three party should be concluded at the next stage as that question demanded preparation. At the same time a message came from the President, who informed me that he had no objection to a Franco-Soviet pact. In the result, we reached agreement about concluding a pact and it was signed to-day. The pact will be published after General de Gaulle's arrival in Paris.

I think that General de Gaulle's visit has had positive results and will assist not only in strengthening Franco-Soviet relations, but will also be a contribution to the common cause of the Allies.

Stalin to Roosevelt, sent 10 December 1944, received 10 December 1944[103]

Thank you for your reply on the French question. Together with General De-Gaulle we came to a decision that the conclusion of the Franco-Soviet Pact of mutual assistance will be beneficial to the cause of the French–Soviet relations as well as for the European security in general. Today the Franco-Soviet Pact was signed.

As to the post-war border of France, the consideration of this question, as I have already written to you, has been postponed.

Stalin also met Churchill's request for data on the captured German T-5 torpedo. The Navy Ministry put together some material for the response, but

Stalin made important additions (shown in italics). Clearly, he was willing to be more responsive than his subordinates. As with the V-2 site in Debice, Stalin showed particular consideration in meeting the Allies' requests for information on the latest German weapons. In this case he was even more cooperative than the text given to Churchill suggests, because the first option was mistranslated: Stalin actually offered that, after Soviet examination and experiment, 'the torpedo itself could be placed at the disposal of the British Admiralty'. In his reply on 23 December, however, Churchill accepted the option that ensured Britain the most rapid information, namely to send one of its own experts over to the USSR to examine the torpedo on the spot.[104]

Stalin to Churchill, sent 14 December 1944, received 14 December 1944[105]

I have received your message concerning the German torpedo T-5. Two German acoustic torpedoes were in fact captured by Soviet sailors and are now being studied by our experts. Unfortunately we are unable to send one of these torpedoes immediately to England, since both of them have been damaged by explosion and it would consequently be necessary for the purpose of examination and experiment to replace the damaged parts of one torpedo by parts of the other, otherwise examination and experiment will be impossible. *There are thus two alternatives: either* the drawings and descriptions which are made in the course of examining the torpedo can be forwarded immediately to the British Military Mission and placed at the disposal of the British Admiralty when examination of and experiment with the torpedo is completed, *or British experts could come immediately to the Soviet Union to make a detailed examination of the torpedo on the spot and make drawings from it. We are ready to facilitate either alternative.*

*****

Conscious that everything pointed to the establishment of the PCNL as the new government of Poland, London and Washington sought to prevent, or at least defer, its formal recognition by the USSR. On 15 December, Churchill spoke in sombre tone in a special Commons debate on Poland, stressing readiness to accept the Curzon Line but also refusal to recognize the Lubliners. What pricked Washington was the PM's remark: 'I find great difficulty in discussing these matters, because the attitude of the United States has not been defined with the precision which His Majesty's Government has thought it wise to use.'[106] That spurred the State Department and the president – who now felt freer to speak out on Polish matters after the election – to send a telegram to Churchill stating that he was thinking of asking Stalin to postpone any recognition of the PCNL until the three of them could discuss the matter. Supported by the Cabinet, Churchill warmly welcomed FDR's 'most valuable' proposal and urged him to act fast. The president's letter was hastily prepared by the State Department and, as desired by the Cabinet, it included a four-point general statement of US policy. Churchill told FDR 'it can do nothing but good'. However, the message was not delivered until Harriman was able to meet Stalin on 20 December.[107]

Roosevelt to Stalin, sent 16 December 1944, received 20 December 1944[108]

In view of the interest raised in this country by Prime Minister Churchill's statement in the House of Commons yesterday and the strong pressure we are under to make known our position in regard to Poland, I believe it may be necessary in the next few days for this government to issue some statement on the subject. This statement, if issued, will outline our attitude somewhat along the following lines:

'1. The United States Government stands unequivocally for a strong, free, independent and democratic Poland.

2. In regard to the question of future frontiers of Poland, the United States, although considering it desirable that territorial questions await the general postwar settlement, recognizes that a settlement before that time is in the interest of the common war effort and therefore would have no objection if the territorial questions involved in the Polish situation, including the proposed compensation from Germany, were settled by mutual agreement between the parties directly concerned.

3. Recognizing that the transfer of minorities in some cases is feasible and would contribute to the general security and tranquility in the areas concerned, the United States Government would have no objection if the Government and the people of Poland desire to transfer nationals and would join in assessing such transfers.

4. In conformity with its announced aim, this Government is prepared to assist, subject to legislative authority, and in so far as may be practicable, in the economic reconstruction of countries devastated by Nazi aggression. This policy applies equally to Poland as to other such devastated countries of the United Nations.'

The proposed statement, as you will note, will contain nothing, I am sure, that is not known to you as the general attitude of this Government and is I believe in so far as it goes in general accord with the results of your discussion with Prime Minister Churchill in Moscow in the autumn, and for this reason, I am sure, you will welcome it.

I feel it is of the highest importance that until the three of us can get together and thoroughly discuss this troublesome question there be no action on any side which would render our discussions more difficult. I have seen indications that the Lublin Committee may be intending to give itself the status of a provisional government of Poland. I fully appreciate the desirability from your point of view of having a clarification of Polish authority before your armies move further into Poland. I very much hope, however, that because of the great political implications which such a step would entail you would find it possible to refrain from recognizing the Lublin Committee as a government of Poland before we meet, which I hope will be immediately after my inauguration on January 20. Could you not until that date continue to deal with the Committee in its present form? I know that Prime Minister Churchill shares my views on this point.

Having signed his 1 November agreement with Tito to create a coalition, Šubašić was quizzed by both King Peter II, whose government he officially headed, and the Foreign Office about the deal reached with Tito. Šubašić insisted that he had gone as far as he could and that there was no alternative to the agreement, given the actual situation in Yugoslavia, where the National Liberation Army was the sole authority. 'Let there be no illusions,' he told the king. 'The Commander-in-Chief of this Army is Tito, and he is at the same time the embodiment of every other authority within Yugoslavia. It would prove impossible to wreck his authority in the country to-day.'[109] On 19 December, reporting positively to Stalin on developments in Yugoslavia, Churchill reiterated the importance of their 'joint policy' and emphasized the need for free elections in Yugoslavia.[110]

After sending the Kremlin some weighty messages of state, the PM evidently enjoyed discussing the 1943 film *Kutuzov* – about Russia's 1812 hero against Napoleon – which Stalin had sent him. His words of praise have a lyrical quality, and he was also able to get in a dig at de Gaulle in the last paragraph. By linking *Kutuzov* with one of the PM's favourite movies – *That Hamilton Woman*, starring Vivien Leigh and Laurence Olivier, which recounted the story of Emma Hamilton's romance with Admiral Lord Nelson – this allowed the PM to remind Stalin that Britain and Russia had experienced difficulties with France in the past, as well as the present. He also underlined that their two countries had fought against would-be continental dictators both in the nineteenth century and in what Churchill was already calling the 'thirty years' war' against Germany since 1914. The tone of the message was deliberately light.[111]

Churchill to Stalin, sent 19 December 1944, received 20 December 1944[112]

I saw last night for the second time the film which you have given me called Kutuzov. The first time I greatly admired it but, as it was all in Russian, I could not understand the exact meaning of each situation. Last night I saw it with the English captions, which made exactly intelligible the whole thing, and I must tell you that in my view this is one of the most masterly film productions I have ever witnessed. Never has the conflict of two will-powers been more clearly displayed. Never has the importance of fidelity in commanders and men been more effectively inculcated by the film pictures. Never have the Russian soldiers and the Russian nation been presented by this medium so gloriously to the British nation. Never have I seen the art of the camera better used.

If you thought it fit privately to communicate my admiration and thanks to those who have laboured in producing this work of art and high morale, I should thank you. Meanwhile I congratulate you.

I like to think we were together in that deadly struggle, as in this 30 years' war. I do not suppose you showed the film to de Gaulle, any more than I shall show him 'Lady Hamilton' when he comes over here to make a similar treaty to that which you have made with him, and we have made together. Salutations.

In late December, it was Churchill's turn to send birthday wishes. He did so in the spirit of Stalin's formal greetings, but the PM's assurances about the 'value' of the leader's longevity for the 'Grand Alliance' were not just *politesse*: in line with his 'two Stalins' theory, he sincerely believed that there was no one else in the Kremlin with whom he could do business. Later, at Yalta, Churchill would raise a similar toast about how 'precious' was Stalin's life.[113]

Churchill to Stalin, sent 18 December 1944, received 20 December 1944[114]

I send you my most sincere congratulations on your birthday. I believe that your life is very precious to the future of the world and to the constant strengthening of the ties which unite our two countries. It is therefore no figure of speech when I wish you 'Many happy returns of the day'.

With a new summit approaching, Roosevelt decided for the first time to send a birthday greeting to Stalin.

Roosevelt to Stalin, sent 21 December 1944, received 22 December 1944[115]

It gives me great pleasure on this anniversary of your Excellency's birth to extend to you my sincere congratulations and best wishes.

By this time, the war in the west had changed dramatically. On 16 December, Hitler mounted a surprise counter-offensive in the Ardennes, along the German–Belgian border around St Vith. Eisenhower's command was taken by surprise as two Panzer armies thrust into some weak US divisions, taking advantage of the bad weather which neutralized the Allies' overwhelming advantage in the air. Ike had been wrong-footed, but he rapidly rushed re-inforcements to the front at Bastogne, including the crack US 82nd and 101st Airborne Divisions. Conscious that several of the German divisions had recently been moved from the Eastern Front, Ike asked for closer strategic coordination between him and the Red Army. 'If, for instance, it is the Russian intention to launch a major offensive in the course of this or the next month,' he cabled the CCS on 21 December, 'knowledge of the fact would be of the utmost importance to me and I would condition my plans accordingly.' He added: 'I am aware that a request of this nature would inevitably entail my giving reciprocal information to the Russians, which I am quite ready to do.'[116]

Churchill and the British chiefs of staff considered it 'hopeless' to try to obtain this information via the military missions or in writing. The PM cabled Roosevelt proposing 'a joint telegram to U.J. suggesting that he should allow us to send a high-ranking officer, nominated by General Eisenhower', in order to share information. Churchill sent a draft text, but Roosevelt decided to despatch the message to Stalin himself. Leahy used much of the PM's draft and the president added a sentence (in italics) seeking to play down any sense of panic in Belgium. Churchill supported this request in a separate telegram and Stalin readily agreed.[117]

The immediate crisis was short-lived. Once the weather cleared on 23 December, Allied airpower pulverized Hitler's columns – already running out of fuel. But the Soviet leader's prompt and positive response to Eisenhower's request was noteworthy. Later, even those who had become critics of Stalin acknowledged his gesture. Khrushchev said it was 'a demonstration of friendship and help to the Allies, who had found themselves in a tight spot. Stalin conducted himself in a dignified manner.'[118]

Roosevelt to Stalin, sent 23 December 1944, received 24 December 1944[119]

I wish to direct General Eisenhower to send to Moscow a fully qualified officer of his staff to discuss with you Eisenhower's situation on the Western Front and its relation to the Eastern Front, in order that all of us may have information essential to our coordination of effort. We will maintain complete secrecy.

I hope you will see this officer of Eisenhower's Staff and arrange to exchange with him information that will be of mutual benefit. *The situation in Belgium is not bad but it is time to talk of the next phase.*

In view of the emergency an early reply to this proposal is requested.

Eisenhower decided to send his trusted British deputy, Air Chief Marshal Sir Arthur Tedder, to Moscow. Churchill – then on his surprise visit to Athens and obsessed with the Balkans – wanted to send along as well his favourite, Field Marshal Sir Harold Alexander, who in December 1944 had taken over as supreme Allied commander in the Mediterranean. He hoped that 'Alex' could use the opportunity to discuss with the Soviet command a simultaneous attack on Vienna, and even prepared a letter to Stalin to that effect; but it was shot down by the chiefs of staff when Churchill returned home. Brooke found the PM exhausted and 'confused' – dictating a succession of minutes 'based on misconceptions due to faulty reading of documents' and propounding 'the wildest of strategy' aimed at 'ensuring that British troops were retained in the lime light if necessary at the expense of the Americans and quite irrespective of any strategic requirements!'[120]

The 25 December not being a holiday in the USSR, Stalin seems to have spent some time catching up on his thank-you letters – aware, like his Western counterparts, of the need to lubricate the sometimes grinding wheels of diplomacy.

Stalin to Churchill, sent 25 December 1944, received 27 December 1944[121]

Thank you for your congratulations and good wishes for my birthday. I always value highly your friendly sentiments.

Stalin to Churchill, sent 25 December 1944, received 27 December 1944[122]

I shall of course welcome the conclusion of an Anglo-French treaty.

I value highly your praise of the film KUTUZOV and shall not fail to inform those who worked on the film of your appreciation.

I send you my best wishes.

Stalin to Roosevelt, sent 26 December 1944[123]

Please accept my thanks for your congratulations and good wishes on the occasion of my birthday.

In reply to Roosevelt's message of 5 December about voting in the United Nations Security Council, Stalin firmly insisted on the principle of unanimity of the great powers in absolutely all matters. Here, Gromyko's recommendations were taken into account. The ambassador had cabled on 22 December that although the American proposal represented 'a retreat from their original position' and precluded 'the possibility of international sanctions against the USSR', he believed it should be rejected:

> Acceptance of the offer means that on all the questions of dispute resolution in which the Soviet Union could be directly involved, it would still oppose the Council and the organization. Politically, we might be put into uncomfortable situations when the Council adopts decisions against us with regard to a peaceful settlement of disputes.

Gromyko also made some tactical points. He emphasized that 'a concession in such a serious matter, after lengthy negotiations, is undesirable from the point of view of our prestige' (these words were heavily underlined in the Kremlin). He also calculated that if the Soviet Union persisted, 'the Americans and the British will be forced to adopt our proposals on the vote' – not least because of time pressures: 'in case there is a delay in the creation of an international organization, we have nothing to lose. Here at least, the press and the public will always hassle the US government in the event of such a delay. This may eventually force Roosevelt to consent.'[124]

Stalin to Roosevelt, sent 26 December 1944,
received 26 December 1944[125]

On December 14 I have received from Mr. Harriman your message. I fully share your opinion that prior to convocation of the general conference of the United Nations on the question of establishment of an International Organization we should agree upon the principal questions not agreed upon in the course of the Dumbarton Oaks conversations and, in the first place, on the question of the procedure of voting in the Security Council. I have to remind you that in the original American draft was specially marked the necessity to work out special rules in regard to the procedure of voting in case of a dispute which involves directly one or several permanent members of the Council. In the British draft it was also stated that the general order of settlement of disputes between great powers, should such disputes arise, may prove unfit.

In this connection the first and second points of your proposal meet with no objections and can be accepted, bearing in mind that point two deals with procedure questions mentioned in chapter VI, subdivision 'D'.

As regards point three of your proposal I have, to my regret, to inform you that with the proposed by you wording of this point I see no possibility of agreeing. As you yourself admit the principle of unanimity of permanent members is necessary in all decisions of the Council in regard to determination of a threat to peace as well as in respect to measures of elimination of such a threat or for suppression of aggression or other violations of peace. Undoubtedly, that when decisions on questions of such a nature are made there must be full agreement of powers which are permanent members of the Council bearing upon themselves the main responsibility for maintenance of peace and security.

It goes without saying that the attempt to prevent, on a certain stage, one or several permanent members of the Council from participating in voting on said questions, and theoretically it is possible to assume also a case when the majority of permanent members will find themselves prevented from participation in making decisions on a question, can have fatal consequences for the cause of preservation of international security. Such a situation is in contradiction with the principle of agreement and unanimity of decisions of the four leading powers and can lead to a situation when some great powers are put in opposition to other great powers and this may undermine the cause of universal security. In prevention of this small countries are interested not less than great powers since a split among great powers, united for tasks of maintenance of peace and security for all peace-loving countries is pregnant with the most dangerous consequences for all these nations.

Therefore I have to insist on our position on the question of voting in the Security Council. This position, as it seems to me, will provide the new International Organization with the unanimity of four powers, contributing to avoiding of attempts to put certain powers in opposition to other great powers which (unanimity) is necessary for their joint fight against aggression in the future. Naturally, such a situation would secure the interests of small nations in the cause of preservation of their security and would correspond to the interests of universal peace.

I hope that you will estimate the importance of the above-stated views in favor of the principle of unanimity of decisions of the four leading powers and that we shall find an agreed upon decision of this question as well as certain other questions which remain still unsolved. On the basis of such an agreed upon decision our representatives could work out a full draft on this question and discuss the measures necessary for an early convocation of a general conference of the United Nations.

Stalin's objections prompted further reflection in Washington. Roosevelt confessed to Lord Halifax, the British ambassador, in early January that, after thinking it through again and 'putting himself in Stalin's position', he felt 'a good deal of sympathy' with the Soviet position. How would we feel, he said, if a conflict between Mexico and Guatemala broke out, in which the United States could be involved? The American people would hardly be satisfied if the US had no say in the matter. The president spoke in similar vein to Secretary of War Henry Stimson.[126] Thus, Gromyko's tactic of playing tough with the Americans proved shrewd.

Stalin ignored the Allies' request to postpone recognition of the PCNL. On 27 December, the Presidium of the Supreme Soviet announced that it intended to recognize the provisional government of Poland as soon as it had been formally constituted.[127] That same day Molotov and Stalin prepared a long and detailed statement of the Soviet position. Of particular importance was the final paragraph about the USSR's special interests in Poland, which Stalin would then reiterate many times in the correspondence and at Yalta. Tomasz Arciszewski was Mikołajczyk's hardline successor as prime minister of the London government.

Stalin to Roosevelt, sent 27 December 1944, received 27 December 1944[128]

I have received your message on Polish matters on December 20.

As regards Mr. Stettinius' statement of December 18, I would prefer to express myself about this during our personal meeting. In any case the events in Poland have considerably moved ahead than it is reflected in the said statement.

A number of facts which took place during the time after the last visit of Mikolajczyk to Moscow and, in particular the radio-communications with Mikolajczyk's government intercepted by us from arrested in Poland terrorists – underground agents of the Polish émigré government – with all palpability proves that the negotiations of Mr. Mikolajczyk with the Polish National Committee served as a screen for those elements who conducted from behind Mikolajczyk's back criminal terrorist work against Soviet officers and soldiers on the territory of Poland. We cannot reconcile with such a situation when terrorists instigated by Polish emigrants kill in Poland soldiers and officers of the Red Army, lead a criminal fight against Soviet troops which are liberating Poland, and directly aid our enemies, whose allies they in fact are. The substitution of Mikolajczyk by Arzyshevsky [sic] and, in general, transpositions of ministers in the Polish émigré government have made the situation even worse and have created a precipice between Poland and the émigré government.

Meanwhile the Polish National Committee has made serious achievements in the strengthening of the Polish state and the apparatus of government power on the territory of Poland, in the expansion and strengthening of the Polish army, in carrying into practice of a number of important governmental measures and, in the first place, of the agrarian reform in favor of the peasants. All this has lead [sic] to consolidation of democratic powers of Poland and to powerful strengthening of authority of the National Committee among the wide masses on Poland and among wide social Polish circles abroad.

It seems to me that now we should be interested in the support of the Polish National Committee and all those who want and are capable to work together with it and that is especially important for the Allies and for the solution of our common task – the speeding of the defeat of Hitlerite Germany. For the Soviet Union, which is bearing the whole burden for the liberation of Poland from German occupationists, the question of relations with Poland under present conditions is the task of daily close and friendly relations with a power which has been established by the Polish people on its own soil and which has already grown strong and has its own army which together with the Red Army is fighting against the Germans.

I have to say frankly that if the Polish Committee of National Liberation will transform itself into a Provisional Government then, in view of the above-said, the Soviet Government will not have any serious ground for postponement of the question of its recognition. It is necessary to bear in mind that in the strengthening of a pro-Allied and democratic Poland the Soviet Union is interested more than any other power not only because the Soviet Union is bearing the main brunt of the battle for liberation of Poland but also because Poland is a border state with the Soviet Union and the problem of Poland is inseparable from the problem of security of the Soviet Union. To this we have to add that the successes of the Red Army in Poland in the fight against the Germans are to a great degree dependent on the presence of peaceful and trustworthy rear in Poland, and the Polish National Committee fully takes into account this circumstance while the émigré government and its underground agents by their terroristic actions are creating a threat of civil war in the rear of the Red Army and counteract the successes of the latter. On the other hand, under the condition which exist in Poland at the present time there are no reasons for the continuation of the policy of support of the émigré government, which has lost all confidence of the Polish population in the country and besides creates a threat of civil war in the rear of the Red Army, violating thus our common interests of a successful fight against the Germans. I think that it would be natural, just and profitable for our common cause if the governments of the Allied countries as the first step have agreed on an immediate exchange of representatives with the Polish National Committee so that after a certain time it would be recognized as the lawful government of Poland after the transformation of the National Committee into a provisional government of Poland. Otherwise I am afraid that the confidence of the Polish People in the Allied powers may weaken. I think that we cannot allow the Polish people to say that we are sacrificing the interests of Poland in favor of the interests of a handful of Polish emigrants in London.

Roosevelt asked Churchill for his comments on Stalin's letter. Having consulted Eden and the Cabinet about it, the PM replied on 30 December proposing no change in their non-recognition policy towards the Lublin Committee, but adding: 'The matter should be reserved for the coming conference.'[129] The president, however – mindful of the domestic sensitivity of the issue he had tried to downplay for so long – decided to send Stalin a warning message now. This letter, drafted by 'Chip' Bohlen, head of the East European Department of the State Department – as with most of Roosevelt's messages on Poland in 1944–45 – made a last attempt to persuade Stalin to defer recognition of the PCNL. All possible political and military arguments were cited as justification. Like Churchill before him, the president urged Stalin not to write off Mikołajczyk, whom the Western Allies continued to see as the key figure in the future Polish government. The last sentence of the document was dictated to Bohlen by Roosevelt himself. He had it copied to Churchill with a note: 'You will see that we are in step.'[130]

Roosevelt to Stalin, sent 30 December 1944,
received 31 December 1944[131]

I am disturbed and deeply disappointed over your message of December 27 in regard to Poland in which you tell me that you cannot see your way clear to hold in abeyance the question of recognizing of the Lublin Committee as the provisional government of Poland until we have had an opportunity at our meeting to discuss the whole question thoroughly. I would have thought no serious inconvenience would have been caused your Government or your Armies if you could have delayed the purely juridical act of recognition for the short period of a month remaining before we meet.

There was no suggestion in my request that you curtail your practical relations with the Lublin Committee nor any thought that you should deal with or accept the London Government in its present composition. I had urged this delay upon you because I felt that you would realize how extremely unfortunate and even serious it would be at this period in the war in its effect on world opinion and enemy morale if your Government should formally recognize one Government of Poland while the majority of the other United Nations including the United States and Great Britain continue to recognize and to maintain diplomatic relations with the Polish Government in London.

I must tell you with a frankness equal to your own that I see no prospect of this Government's following suit and transferring its recognition from the Government in London to the Lublin Committee in its present form. This is in no sense due to any special ties or feelings for the London Government. The fact is that neither the Government nor the people of the United States have as yet seen any evidence arising either from the manner of its creation or from subsequent developments to justify the conclusion that the Lublin Committee as at present constituted represents the people of Poland. I cannot ignore the fact that up to the present only a small fraction of Poland proper west of the Curzon Line has been liberated from German tyranny, and it is therefore an unquestioned truth that the people of Poland have had no opportunity to express themselves in regard to the Lublin Committee.

If at some future date following the liberation of Poland a provisional government of Poland with popular support is established, the attitude of this Government would of course be governed by the decision of the Polish people.

I fully share your view that the departure of Mr. Mikolajczyk from the Government in London has worsened the situation. I have always felt that Mr. Mikolajczyk, who I am convinced is sincerely desirous of settling all points at issue between the Soviet Union and Poland, is the only Polish leader in sight who seems to offer the possibility of a genuine solution of the difficult and dangerous Polish question. I find it most difficult to believe from my personal knowledge of Mr. Mikolajczyk and my conversations with him when he was here in Washington and his subsequent efforts and policies during his visit at Moscow that he had knowledge of any terrorist instructions.

I am sending you this message so that you will know the position of this Government in regard to the recognition at the present time of the Lublin Committee as the provisional government. I am more than ever convinced that when the three of us get together we can reach a solution of the Polish problem, and I therefore still hope that you can hold in abeyance until then the formal recognition of the Lublin Committee as a government of Poland. I cannot, from a military angle, see any great objection to a delay of a month.

Stalin, however, would brook no delay. The scene was set for a climactic argument when the Big Three finally met.

15

YALTA AND AFTER

(January to April 1945)

IN RETROSPECT, THE BATTLE of the Bulge seems like a temporary blip on the Western Front, but at the time it unsettled Allied complacency. Concerned that further German assaults might be in the offing, Churchill asked Stalin directly on 6 January when a new Soviet offensive would be mounted, and Eisenhower sent his own emissary to Moscow to share strategic and operational plans. Not only did this open up a direct, if informal, channel for him with the Kremlin, but it also had some influence in Stalin's decision to bring forward his Vistula offensive by eight days to 12 January – which he presented as a further sign of solidarity with his allies.

Roosevelt and Churchill were preoccupied with the Big Three conference at Yalta, planning for which was a feature of the correspondence throughout January. The president's health, now in evident decline, would not be helped by such a long journey – by sea to Malta, then plane to Saki on the west of the Crimea, and finally a difficult car ride across snowy mountains down to its southern coast. The Yalta conference, held on 4–11 February, later became notorious in some Western circles – a sell-out of Eastern Europe to Moscow, in the view of the American right; a cynical superpower partition of Europe, according to French Gaullists. In reality, Yalta resulted in a series of compromises, from which each of the Big Three came away with something. Roosevelt firmed up Soviet commitments to enter the Asian war and join the new United Nations organization; Churchill blocked Russian demands for massive reparations from Germany and secured an equal role for France in the Allied occupation; and Stalin obtained most of his territorial demands in Asia and also a loosely phrased agreement about the future government of Poland that gave him plenty of room for manoeuvre. Overall, as Secretary of State Edward R. Stettinius wrote in his 1949 account of Yalta, Roosevelt 'did not "surrender" anything significant at Yalta which was in his power to withhold'.[1] The concessions to Stalin on Poland were not the result of Anglo-American diplomatic errors in 1945, but the consequence of Anglo-American strategy in 1942–43, when they delayed their invasion of France; this meant that if the Red Army defeated the Wehrmacht, it would end the war in control of Eastern Europe.

This was not how Churchill and Roosevelt saw things at the time, however. Both leaders were pleased with what had been achieved at Yalta – and especially with the positive and constructive atmosphere. Each went out on a limb when back home in talking up the significance of the conference for future relations and postwar peace in major speeches to the House of Commons and to a joint session of the Congress. But they faced serious disquiet in both capitals about the ambiguities of the Polish settlement, with Churchill in particular under intense criticism from members of his own party and, indeed, government. Convinced that Poland was becoming a 'test-case' for the Alliance, the PM became increasingly agitated as the Soviet grip tightened on the country and Western influence, even access, was blocked. Already talking of a 'veil' or 'curtain' coming down in Eastern Europe, he begged FDR for a joint message to Stalin, holding the Soviet leader to what they felt had been agreed at Yalta. But the president, anxious to avoid a top-level confrontation in the interests of the relationship as a whole – especially ahead of the founding conference of the United Nations at San Francisco in late April – hoped to resolve matters at the ambassadorial level, and the joint message was not sent until 31 March.

Partly in preparation for that, Churchill held his fire on correspondence with Stalin – sending only three messages in March and two more in the first week of April. During this period, by contrast, the president sent eight cables: a rare instance of him being a more prolific correspondent than the prime minister. Most of the messages were of considerable length, and all dealt with matters of grave importance: not just the future of Poland, but also the treatment of American prisoners of war in Poland, the sudden Soviet refusal to send Molotov to San Francisco for the inauguration of the UN, and Stalin's insinuation that the Americans were trying to negotiate behind his back a compromise peace with the Germans in Italy. In these weeks, the White House was taking the lead in relations with Moscow; the messages from Number Ten were at best supportive. But Churchill and Roosevelt were also at odds on these key issues – FDR taking a harder line than Churchill on POWs and the Italian negotiations, whereas the PM pushed the Polish issue and also wanted a concentrated drive to Berlin. But on all matters, Churchill deferred to Roosevelt. That reflected the changing balance at the Western end of the Big Three as the war entered its endgame. 'Our Armies are about one-half the size of the American and will soon be little more than one-third,' Churchill told Smuts in December. 'It is not so easy for me as it used to be to get things done.'[2] He knew Roosevelt was now the senior partner.

Even more striking, virtually none of the 3,400 words emanating from the White House during this period was written or dictated by the president. Drained by Yalta, close to death, he depended on the words of others: General Marshall, Admiral Leahy, FDR's chief of staff, and 'Chip' Bohlen in the State Department. Yet those last eight messages unquestionably expressed Roosevelt's authentic voice. At the climax of the Big Three's epistolary relationship, the now almost wordless president still had no doubt that, as he told Churchill in 1942: 'I can handle Stalin.'

*****

Contrary to the hopes of his allies in January 1945, Stalin did not delay recognition of the PCNL as the provisional government of Poland until after the Big Three meeting. As when breaking off diplomatic relations with the Polish government in London over Katyn in 1943, Stalin presented Roosevelt and Churchill with a fait accompli, again citing implausible reasons to justify his haste. This time he claimed the recent vote for recognition by the Supreme Soviet had forced his hand. Churchill observed wryly to FDR: 'it is interesting to see that the "Presidium of the Supreme Soviet of the USSR" has now been brought up into line'. The president did not reply to Stalin's message and Churchill alluded to it only briefly in his cable of 5 January. On Poland, both were keeping their powder dry for the summit.[3]

On the big issue of the summit's venue: for much of December, Roosevelt had urged Harriman to press the Mediterranean option, but it proved impossible to pull the president out of the Crimean hole that Hopkins had dug for him back in October. On 26 December, the ambassador had a last-ditch discussion with Molotov, but the latter was under strict instructions not to yield on this matter of prestige and convenience – citing Roosevelt's original proposal (Harriman said Hopkins had simply been sounding out the idea himself) and pleading the strict requirements of Stalin's doctors (Roosevelt's far graver medical condition was never mentioned in the correspondence). Molotov added that, if the Crimea were not acceptable, then Stalin had delegated him to meet Roosevelt and Churchill wherever they wished. Next day the Americans accepted Yalta. The Kremlin's Tehran-tested method of soft blackmail worked once again.[4]

With his schoolboy love of codewords, the PM gave the summit its name –
picking up on the Greek myth of Jason and the Argonauts, who travelled along
the Black Sea coast in search of the Golden Fleece. In his reply to Stalin, the PM
also alluded to the situation on the Western Front. The Americans had now
turned the tide at Bastogne, but it would take three weeks – and more bickering
between Montgomery and US generals – to pinch out the German bulge. The
PM also mentioned operation 'Nordwind' in Alsace, which began on 1 January.
It proved to be the Wehrmacht's brief final fling in the west, but that was far
from clear to the Western Allies in that dark New Year.

Churchill to Stalin, sent 5 January 1945, received 6 January 1945[5]

Your personal and secret message of January 3rd:

I thank you for sending me your two messages to the President on the Polish
question. Naturally I and my War Cabinet colleagues are distressed at the course
events are taking. I am quite clear that much the best thing is for us three to meet
together and talk all these matters over, not only as isolated problems but in relation to the whole world situation both of war and transit to peace. Meanwhile, our
attitude, as you know it, remains unchanged.

I look forward very much to this momentous meeting and I am glad that the
President of the United States has been willing to make this long journey. We have
agreed, subject to your concurrence, that the code name shall be called 'Argo-
naut' and I hope that you will use that in any messages that may be interchanged
by the Staffs who will be consulting about arrangements.

I have just come back from General Eisenhower's and Field Marshal Montgomery's separate Headquarters. The battle in Belgium is very heavy but it is
thought that we have the mastery. The dispersionary attack which the Germans
are making into Alsace also causes difficulties with the French and tends to pin
down American forces. I still remain of the opinion that weight and weapons,
including Air, of the Allied forces will make von Rundstedt regret his daring and
well organised attempt to split our front and, if possible, lay hands on the now
absolutely vital Antwerp port.

I reciprocate your cordial wishes for the New Year. May it shorten the agony
of the great nations we serve and bring about a lasting peace on our joint
guarantee.

The Ardennes crisis called into question the Allies' carefully calibrated approach
to manpower mobilization: the British had already reached their limit in
effective reserves, while the Americans hastily 'combed out' supply units for

replacement frontline troops, even resorting to the use of black troops in combat – hitherto unprecedented in the US Army during the Second World War because of white Southerners' 'racial etiquette'. Ike feared that more 'German fury' offensives in the west would follow. Aware that Hitler had moved key forces for the Ardennes offensive from the Eastern Front, and lacking hard intelligence about the Red Army's plans for the New Year, Ike told the Combined Chiefs that his situation 'would be much relieved if the Russians launched a large offensive' because all the German reserves 'would then have to be divided between the east and the west'.[6] With Ike's personal envoy, Air Chief Marshal Tedder, delayed in Cairo, Churchill took matters into his own hands by asking Stalin personally about Soviet plans.

Churchill to Stalin, sent 6 January 1945, received 7 January 1945[7]

The battle in the West is very heavy and, at any time, large decisions may be called for from the Supreme Command. You know yourself from your own experience how very anxious the position is when a very broad front has to be defended after temporary loss of the initiative. It is General Eisenhower's great desire and need to know in outline what you plan to do, as this obviously affects all his and our major decisions. Our Envoy, Air Chief Marshal Tedder, was last night reported weather-bound in Cairo. His journey has been much delayed through no fault of yours. In case he has not reached you yet, I shall be grateful if you can tell me whether we can count on a major Russian offensive on the Vistula front, or elsewhere during January, with any other points you may care to mention. I shall not pass this most secret information to anyone except Field Marshal Brooke and General Eisenhower, and only under conditions of the utmost secrecy. I regard the matter as urgent.

The Stavka had been preparing for a large-scale New Year offensive since November 1944, but no details had yet been provided to the Western Allies. Its main thrust would be the Vistula–Oder operation carried out by forces of the 1st Belorussian and 1st Ukrainian *Fronty*. This was finally to take Warsaw, drive across the rest of Poland to the German border, cross the River Oder and seize the industrial region of Silesia. The precise date was somewhat flexible. In his memoirs, the commander of the 1st Ukrainian *Front*, Marshal Konev, stated that 'the operation was to begin on 20 January', but on 9 January he was contacted by Antonov, acting chief of the general staff,

who said that given the Allies' difficult situation on the Western Front in the

Ardennes, they appealed to us with a request, if possible, to accelerate the beginning of our offensive; after this appeal, the Supreme Headquarters of the Supreme Command revised the timing of the offensive operation. The 1st Ukrainian *Front* should start the offensive not on 20 January, but on 12 January.[8]

Yet on Christmas Eve 1944, German intelligence on the Eastern Front had already predicted that the Soviet offensive would start around 12 January. The schedule had been left somewhat flexible, and Stalin had good reasons to start earlier rather than later – not least to control as much of Poland as possible before he met his allies at Yalta, and before the icy ground – well suited to tanks – was turned into mud by February's predicted thaw. But Churchill's cable allowed Stalin to present the accelerated timetable as a gesture of Allied solidarity.[9]

Stalin to Churchill, sent 7 January 1945, received 8 January 1945[10]

I received your message of January 6th 1945 on the evening of January 7th. Unfortunately Air Marshal Tedder has not yet arrived in Moscow.

It is most important that we should be able to take advantage of our supremacy over the Germans in artillery and in the air. This demands clear flying weather and an absence of low mists which hinder aimed artillery fire. We are preparing an offensive, but the weather is at present unfavourable. Nevertheless, taking into account the position of our Allies on the Western Front, G.H.Q. of the Supreme Command have decided to accelerate completion of our preparation, and, regardless of the weather, to commence large-scale offensive operations along the whole Central Front not later than the second half of January. Rest assured we shall do everything possible to render assistance to the glorious forces of our Allies.

Churchill thanked Stalin for his 'thrilling' response and immediately forwarded it to Eisenhower, asking him in conspiratorial tones to read and then 'burn' it. Ike did so but, after the Red Army offensive began, he sent Antonov an effusive cable of thanks for 'the momentous news that the magnificent Red Army has surged forward in a new and powerful campaign', pledging that 'under our blows from both the east and west, the enemy will bleed and die and his dwindling resources will be blasted until Nazi Germany is completely crushed'. The almost Churchillian tone of the message to the Russians earned Eisenhower a stern rebuke from his mentor, General Marshall, who reminded Ike of his Kansas roots: 'In future I suggest you approach them in simple Main Street

Abilene style. They are rather cynically disposed toward the diplomatic phrasing of our compliments and seem almost to appreciate downright rough talk of which I give them a full measure.'[11]

The Yugoslav monarch-in-exile, King Peter II, continued to obstruct Britain's wish to implement the Tito–Šubašić agreement. Eden tried to impress on him that, whatever its deficiencies, the agreement offered the king's 'best chance to preserve the monarchy and his own position, given the dominant situation which Marshal Tito had achieved in Yugoslavia'.[12] But on the 11th, without consulting the British, the king issued a public communiqué rejecting the agreement 'in its present form'. At a hastily convened session, the War Cabinet agreed to treat what Churchill called his 'most ill-considered and unfortunate' action as unconstitutional, and therefore 'null and void', and approved a message assuring Stalin that Britain would proceed with the agreement. Eden urged that it was 'desirable to carry the United States with us in this matter' and so Churchill added a final paragraph to this effect.[13] Stalin urged Churchill to implement the Tito–Šubašić agreement immediately, rather than consulting further with Washington. But Churchill, now detecting some signs of movement on the king's part about the proposed Regency Council, played for time, despite Stalin's protests – as subsequent exchanges showed.[14] The PM managed to string things out until Yalta: as with Poland, he thought it much better to discuss Yugoslavia face to face and in the context of the whole Allied relationship.

The meeting between Stalin and Tedder finally took place on 15 January and proved both unusually relaxed, by Kremlin standards, and very constructive. This was the first one-on-one between the Soviet supreme commander and an authoritative representative of the Allied high command, and the businesslike Tedder – with his avoidance of rhetoric and fulsome compliments – appealed to Stalin, especially since the Soviets regarded the Royal Air Force (unlike the British Army) with real respect. Stalin also liked Tedder's humour: handing over an untidy paper parcel, the air marshal stated dead-pan that it did not contain a bomb. Stalin unwrapped a box of cigars from Ike – and appreciated the joke. Both parties informed each other of the situation on their fronts, and Stalin assured his visitor of the continuation of the Soviet offensive. Map to hand, he detailed the main elements of the Red Army offensive towards the Oder, talking with unusual animation and good humour. Major Birse, the British interpreter, felt that the Soviet leader 'was meeting us more than half-way, judging by the way such problems have been treated in the past', and concluded that this was 'one of the most successful and encouraging meetings with Marshal Stalin'.[15]

Stalin's appreciation was evident in the identical messages he sent to the two Western leaders, as well as in a letter that Tedder took back to Eisenhower.[16]

Stalin to Roosevelt, sent 15 January 1945, received 15 January 1945[17]

Today, on January 15, I had a conversation with Marshal Tedder and the generals who accompanied him. As it seems to me, mutual information is sufficiently complete. The exhaustive answers have been given on the matters in question by both sides. I should say that Marshal Tedder makes the most favourable impression.

After four days of offensive operations on the Soviet German front, now I have a possibility to inform you that in spite of unfavourable weather the offensive of the Soviet troops is going on satisfactorily. The whole Central Front from the Carpathians to the Baltic Sea is moving westward. Although the Germans are resisting desperately, they, however, are forced to retreat. I have no doubt that the Germans will have to disperse their reserves between two fronts, as a result they will be obliged to abandon the offensive on the Western Front. I am glad that these circumstances will relieve the situation of the Allied troops in the West and will accelerate the preparation of the offensive planned by General Eisenhower.

As to the Soviet troops, you may be sure that they in spite of existing difficulties will do everything in their power so that the blow undertaken by them against the Germans would be most effective.

The Red Army offensive, launched on 12 January, progressed rapidly – benefiting from Hitler's wilful dismissal of any serious threat from the east and the movement of much of the Wehrmacht's mechanized forces and fuel supplies to the Ardennes. Zhukov and Konev's tank divisions destroyed the German 9th Army and 4th Panzer Army and surged west: by 31 January, their forward elements had reached the river Oder, 400 kilometres from the start line and only 60 kilometres short of Berlin. But, as with 'Bagration' the previous summer, the spearheads outran their supply lines and became dangerously vulnerable to flanking attacks. On 2 February, the Stavka officially postponed the advance to Berlin.[18]

Nevertheless, the relief in the West was palpable, as Churchill acknowledged – thanking Stalin 'from the bottom of my heart'.[19] Like the PM, Roosevelt also sent thanks about the Tedder mission and the new Soviet offensive. In this message, prepared by his naval aide Admiral Wilson Brown, reference was also made to the scale of the US offensive against Japan – probably to show Stalin that the GIs were doing their bit, and possibly to put pressure on him about not delaying too long before joining the fight.

Roosevelt to Stalin, sent 17 January 1945, received 18 January 1945[20]

Thank you for your encouraging message dated January 15 in regard to Air Marshal Tedder's conference with you, and in regard to the offensive of your Armies on the Soviet–German front.

The past performances of your heroic soldiers and their already demonstrated efficiency in this offensive, give high promise of an early success to our armies on both fronts.

By skillful coordination of our combined efforts, the time required to force a surrender upon our barbarian enemies will be radically reduced.

As you know, America is putting forth a great effort in the Pacific at a distance of 7,000 miles, and it is my hope that an early collapse of Germany will permit the movement of sufficient forces to the Pacific Area to destroy quickly the Japanese menace to all of our Allied Nations.

By late January, rumours of the upcoming meeting of the Big Three were surfacing in the Western press, but its location was kept secret. Fearing leaks during their talks, Churchill proposed that they ban journalists from Yalta; Roosevelt and Stalin concurred. But all three understood how important it was to capture the historic meeting for propaganda purposes (and indeed posterity), so they also agreed with Churchill to bring a few trusted photographers and cameramen. Among them were Harry Hopkins' son Robert, an army captain, and the Soviet government's official photographer Boris Kosarev.[21]

Having received Roosevelt's birthday wishes in December, Stalin did not fail to reciprocate.

Stalin to Roosevelt, sent 30 January 1945[22]

I beg you to accept, Mr President, my sincere congratulations and best wishes on the occasion of your birthday.

Stalin arrived in Yalta by train on 1 February, well before his allies. He settled into the Yusupov Palace in Koreiz, the residence of the Soviet delegation, about halfway between the residences of Stalin's two allies. Some six miles along the coast to the west was the Vorontsov Palace – a bizarre Moorish-Gothic edifice where Churchill and the British resided. To the east stood the Livadia Palace – built for the last tsar, Nicholas II, and now to serve as home for Roosevelt and the Americans, as well as the venue for the plenary meetings of the conference.

On 29 January, the British delegation, headed by Churchill, flew to Malta. There they awaited the American flotilla, which arrived on the morning of 2 February. That day, the two sets of military staffs held various meetings but all Churchill's efforts to discuss the summit with FDR proved unavailing: the president – who called 2 February 'an awful day' – was exhausted from the trip and his health was in rapid and evident decline.[23] Also, as in the lead-up to Tehran, he did not wish to reinforce Stalin's suspicion of an Anglo-American common front ahead of the summit. Late that night, the US delegation flew off to Saki in the Crimea, followed shortly by the British – both delegations in a series of planes. The flight took about seven hours (plate 20).

The Allied leaders were met at Saki by Molotov and Vyshinskiy. A car journey over the mountains on bad roads was still ahead of them, which proved to be very taxing for both Roosevelt and Churchill. Fortunately, the weather was clear and there were no blizzards on the mountain passes, as on the previous day.[24] Along the entire route, two hundred metres apart, sentries were stationed, many of them young women soldiers who cheerfully saluted the passing convoys. The trip was brightened up by rest stops, during which caviar, champagne and other delicacies were served. Late on the evening of 3 February, the Allied leaders arrived at their destination and settled in their residences.

The Crimea had only recently been liberated from the Germans, who had systematically looted the area. The Soviets had to pull out the stops to get the palaces ready in time, stripping major Moscow hotels of their staff, furnishings and tableware. Even so, the facilities were often rather primitive – with frequent complaints from the British and particularly the Americans about the profusion of bed bugs and the paucity of bathrooms. Churchill joked to Hopkins that, 'if we had spent ten years on research, we could not have found a worse place in the world'.[25] And the journey there had been exhausting, especially for the Wheelchair President – who struck the British as having aged greatly since Tehran (plate 22).

The conference lasted eight working days, from Sunday 4 February through Sunday 11th. Each day, around 4 p.m., there was a plenary meeting at the Livadia, often taking four hours, supplemented by meetings of the foreign ministers and of the military delegations at the three venues, usually at lunchtime. For Roosevelt and the Americans, two issues were uppermost: resolving the remaining problems about the United Nations organization, so that a founding conference could be convened as soon as possible, and firming up the planning for Soviet entry into the Pacific War. Churchill and the British focused more on Europe – feeling special obligations to ensure an independent and democratic Poland because of their 1939 guarantee, and also concerned to avoid what they deemed the mistakes made after the last war by imposing a punitive peace and massive reparations on Germany. Britain's position on both these matters was potentially at odds with Stalin's, because the Soviet leader was determined to control Poland and to exploit Germany, after all that the Russians had suffered in two world wars. Other issues also came to the surface. The Soviets were fishing for large-scale postwar credits from the USA. The Foreign Office was keen to rebuild France as a European power and potential ally, in case the USA once again reverted to isolationism after the war was over. And all three powers were anxious to repatriate their soldiers who had been captured by the Germans or liberated by one or other ally. So the agenda was complex, with each country playing a stronger hand on some issues than on others. For the first couple of days, they put their cards on the table and then they started to do deals.

On the war against Japan, the US military continued to press for detailed planning. Knowing that their Soviet counterparts would do nothing without authorization from Stalin himself, they persuaded the president to give him a formal letter.

Roosevelt to Stalin, sent 5 February 1945, received 5 February 1945[26]

The following are two basic military questions to which the United States Chiefs of Staff would appreciate an early answer at this conference:

  (a) Once war breaks out between Russia and Japan, is it essential to you that a supply line be kept open across the Pacific to Eastern Siberia?
  (b) Will you assure us that United States air forces will be permitted to base in the Komsomolsk-Nikolayevsk or some more suitable area providing developments show that these air forces can be operated and supplied without jeopardizing Russian operations?

Stalin did not respond in writing. But the Far East was the main topic of conversation at his one-on-one meeting with Roosevelt on 8 February. The president began by saying that he would only invade the Japanese home islands 'if absolutely necessary' and that 'he hoped by intensive bombing to destroy Japan and its army and thus save American lives'. (Possibly this reflected his knowledge of progress on the atomic bomb project; more likely it simply testified to his long-standing belief in airpower as a decisive strategic weapon.) At any event, Stalin readily consented to the JCS's request for US air bases along the Amur river. He also noted the president's warning that the existing air and sea bridge from Alaska to Siberia might be difficult to defend and sustain once Japan was at war with the USSR. 'All that is good,' Stalin went on, 'but what about the political conditions on which the Soviet Union is entering the war with Japan?' Harriman had already established Stalin's desiderata in a conversation on 15 December, and Roosevelt said that 'he felt there would be no difficulty in regard to the southern half of Sakhalin and the Kurile Islands going to Russia at the end of the war'. On the question of a warm-water port, such as Dairen on the Kwantung Peninsula, and Stalin's request to use the Manchurian railways, however, the president said on several occasions that he would have to discuss those questions with Chiang Kai-shek. Whereupon Stalin dug in hard and said – apparently with a straight face – that without these political conditions of 'national interest' being met, it would be difficult for him to explain to the Soviet people and the Supreme Soviet why Russia was entering the war against Japan. With Roosevelt starting to relent, he added that 'he did not think it was necessary yet to speak to the Chinese' and that it would be well to leave the conference 'with these conditions set out in writing agreed to by the three powers'. The president said he 'thought this could be done'.[27]

And it was. On 11 February, the Big Three signed an agreement stating that within two or three months after Germany had surrendered, the USSR would enter the war against Japan, on condition that in Outer Mongolia – under effective Soviet control since 1921 – the 'status quo shall be preserved', that the 'former rights of Russia violated by the treacherous attack of Japan in 1904 shall be restored' and that the Kurile Islands 'shall be handed over to the USSR'. Although not privy to Roosevelt's talk with Stalin, Churchill readily signed the document – against the advice of Eden and the FO, who did not see any need to 'buy' Soviet entry into the war. The State Department was also unhappy. Its experts favoured internationalization of both Sakhalin and the Kuriles, because of the competing claims of Russia and Japan, and also queried the loose way in which most of Russia's territorial demands were packaged as recompense for its humiliating defeat by Japan in 1904–05. What is more, as the agreement stated, most of these issues still had to be discussed with the Chinese. That's why the document was not published with the conference communiqué.[28]

At the third plenary meeting, on 6 February, the Big Three engaged seriously on the Polish question, rehearsing arguments they had deployed in many messages over the previous few months. Roosevelt and Churchill lobbied for a new provisional government of Poland, emphasizing Lublin's unrepresentative nature. Before leaving London, the PM had told his Cabinet colleagues that recognition was 'the one counter that remained in our hands' on Poland and 'we should not give it up save in return for something worth having'. For his part, Roosevelt had told senior senators on 11 January 'that the Russians, had the power in Eastern Europe, that it was impossible to have a break with them and that, therefore, the only practicable course was to use what influence we had to ameliorate the situation'.[29]

In the face of their statements on 6 February, Stalin made a lengthy presentation of the Soviet position, stressing the strategic importance of Poland for Soviet security, expressing scepticism about reaching any agreement with the London Poles, and denouncing the anti-Soviet activities of the Home Army in Poland, which threatened 'order and stability' in the rear of the Red Army. He set out these arguments with unusual passion, and there was clearly no point in pursuing matters further that evening – it now being time for dinner.[30]

That night, however, Roosevelt asked Bohlen to prepare a letter to Stalin. This was revised in consultation with Harriman, Churchill and Eden, and then given to Molotov next morning. Conceding the power of some of Stalin's arguments, especially the importance of a secure rear for the Red Army, it nevertheless held firm on non-recognition of the Lublin government and pressed a compromise proposal – namely to invite to Yalta representatives of Lublin plus some non-communists in Poland, to see if a temporary provisional government could be formed prior to free elections.[31]

Roosevelt to Stalin, sent 6 February 1945, received 7 February 1945[32]

I have been giving a great deal of thought to our meeting this afternoon, and I want to tell you in all frankness what is on my mind.

In so far as the Polish Government is concerned, I am greatly disturbed that the three great powers do not have a meeting of minds about the political set up in Poland. It seems to me that it puts all of us in a bad light throughout the world to have you recognizing one government while we and the British are recognizing another in London. I am sure this state of affairs should not continue and that if it does it can only lead our people to think there is a breach between us, which is not the case. I am determined that there shall be no breach between ourselves and the Soviet Union. Surely there is a way to reconcile our differences.

I was very much impressed with some of the things you said today, particularly your determination that your rear must be safeguarded as your army moves into Berlin. You cannot, and we must not, tolerate any temporary government which will give your armed forces any trouble of this sort. I want you to know that I am fully mindful of this.

You must believe me when I tell you that our people at home look with a critical eye on what they consider a disagreement between us at this vital stage of the war. They, in effect, say that if we cannot get a meeting of minds now when our armies are converging on the common enemy, how can we get an understanding on even more vital things in the future.

I have had to make it clear to you that we cannot recognize the Lublin Government as now composed, and the world would regard it as a lamentable outcome of our work here if we parted with an open and obvious divergence between us on this issue.

You said today that you would be prepared to support any suggestions for the solution of this problem which offered a fair chance of success, and you also mentioned the possibility of bringing some members of the Lublin Government here.

Realizing that we all have the same anxiety in getting this matter settled, I would like to develop your proposal a little and suggest that we invite here to Yalta at once Mr. Bierut and Mr Osobka-Morawski from the Lublin Government and also two or three from the following list of Poles, which according to our information would be desirable as representatives of the other elements of the Polish people in the development of a new temporary government which all three of us could recognize and support: Bishop Sapieha of Cracow, Vincente Witos, Mr Zurlowski, Professor Buyak, and Professor Kutzeba. If, as a result of the presence of these Polish leaders here, we could jointly agree with them on a provisional government in Poland which should no doubt include some Polish leaders from abroad such as Mr Mikolajczyk, Mr Grabski and Mr Romer, the United States Government, and I feel sure the British Government as well, would then be prepared to examine with you conditions in which they would dissociate themselves from the London government and transfer their recognition to the new provisional government.

I hope I do not have to assure you that the United States will never lend its support in any way to any provisional government in Poland that would be inimical to your interests.

It goes without saying that any interim government which could be formed as a result of our conference with the Poles here would be pledged to the holding of free elections in Poland at the earliest possible date. I know this is completely consistent with your desire to see a new free and democratic Poland emerge from the welter of this war.

Stalin responded to the letter during the plenary meeting on the afternoon of 7 February – with considerable deftness. He said he had tried to reach the Lublin Poles by phone, but was told they were away in Kraków and Łódź. 'As to the others, he was not sure they could be located in time for them to come to the Crimea.' Stalin added that Molotov had 'worked out some proposals on the Polish question which appeared to approach the President's suggestions, but that these proposals were not typed out'. In the meantime, he therefore proposed that they consider the results of the foreign ministers' discussion that day about the continuing logjam over the United Nations.[33]

This gave Molotov the opportunity to state that the USSR was now satisfied with US clarifications of the Dumbarton Oaks proposals, which had so troubled the Kremlin in the autumn. Consequently it would no longer insist on sixteen seats in the General Assembly – one for each republic – but would be satisfied simply with 'admission of three or at least two of the Soviet Republics as original members' of the UN. Roosevelt called this 'a great step forward'; Churchill agreed, expressing 'heartfelt thanks' to Stalin and Molotov. Perhaps the Russians were genuinely reassured by State Department explanations of what had been a somewhat fuzzy proposal. More probably, they never expected to gain sixteen seats, but intended to withdraw that claim at an opportune tactical moment to secure Anglo-American concessions on an area that really mattered.[34]

That is indeed what happened over the next three days with regard to Poland. First, the two Western leaders retreated on the question of a genuinely new interim government – instead accepting the formula that the existing regime would be 'reorganized on a broader democratic basis'. By 9 February, Roosevelt had decided that what mattered was the principle of 'free elections': these were to be held within a couple of months and had to be validated as 'free and unfettered' by the British and US ambassadors. But the president then backed away from that: the best Churchill could manage – in a private meeting with Stalin on 10 February – was a line in the conference communiqué that London and Washington would be 'kept informed about the situation in Poland' by their ambassadors once these had been accredited to the government in Warsaw. (Accreditation, of course, could only take place once London and Washington had recognized that government.) Seeking some compensation for his failure to do more on the political question, the PM reopened the territorial issue at the final plenary, held that day, and secured a statement in the communiqué that, in return for conceding the Curzon Line with minor modifications in the east, 'Poland must receive substantial accessions of territory in the north and west'. For their part, the Americans tried to compensate by persuading the others to sign the 'Declaration on Liberated Europe', which stated that the principles of 'sovereign rights and self-government' should prevail in all countries freed from Axis rule. But, by the end of the conference, both Churchill and Roosevelt were looking for fig-leaves to show sceptics back home. The Polish 'settlement' they had agreed was framed in loose words, interpretable in various ways, whose implementation would depend on mutual trust.[35]

The military conversations at Yalta were much more constructive than at Tehran. But, as before, the Soviets referred most decisions to the Boss. In the military meeting on 6 February, Marshall sounded out Antonov on the idea of projecting US airpower much closer to the heart of the Reich by building two bases for heavy bombers and fighters near Budapest – which finally fell to the Red Army on 13 February. Antonov seemed favourably disposed, but indicated that this issue should be submitted to Stalin himself by Roosevelt.[36]

Roosevelt to Stalin, sent 7 February 1945, received 8 February 1945[37]

The full potential of the United States air forces now based in South-eastern Italy is not being realized due to excessive distances from the only available bases to targets in enemy territory and bad weather that is frequently encountered over the Alps and the Northern Adriatic. The staging or basing of fighters in the Budapest area would be of particular importance in providing the heavy fighter escort which is now required on deep penetrations and which may be increasingly necessary with the recent revival of German fighter strength employing jet-propelled aircraft. Also, the staging of heavy bombers in the Budapest area would considerably increase the radius of action and bomb tonnage delivered against targets north of the Alps by United States air forces.

Therefore your agreement is requested to the provision of two airdromes in the Budapest area for use by United States air units. If you agree, our military staffs can begin work on this project at once.

The Allies were also keen to analyse the effectiveness of their bombing campaign. In November 1944, on Stimson's suggestion, Roosevelt set up the US Strategic Bombing Survey. Given that Germany's oil supplies had been a priority target, it is not surprising that the survey was especially interested in the Romanian oil refineries at Ploesti, but this was now under Red Army control. Again the matter had to be referred to Stalin.

Roosevelt to Stalin, sent 7 February 1945, received 8 February 1945[38]

An urgent need exists for the earliest possible survey of targets bombed by the U.S. Strategic Air Forces, similar to the survey made of Ploesti. To be effective, investigation must be instituted before tangible evidence is destroyed and personnel present during the bombing are removed from the area.

Details of the survey requirements are being passed to Marshal Khudyakov.

I request your agreement to the conduct of these surveys.

Roosevelt handed both these requests to Stalin during their bilateral meeting on 8 February. The Soviet leader agreed to both without discussion and said he would give the necessary orders. Taking advantage of Roosevelt's gratitude, Stalin raised a suggestion made by Stettinius to Molotov that the USA would have surplus shipping after the war which might be sold to the USSR. Roosevelt said that he hoped to work this without cash payment by some version of extended credit, as with Lend-Lease. This allowed Stalin to make a little speech lauding 'the extraordinary contribution of the Lend-Lease to the winning of the war'.[39]

Had Roosevelt wanted, this would have been an opportunity to exert one of the few clear sources of leverage that the United States enjoyed: namely the Soviets' desire for financial aid to help rebuild their ravaged economy. In January, responding to a request from Molotov, the US Treasury had proposed offering up to $10 billion in postwar credits for the purchase of US industrial equipment, as a carrot to induce cooperation at Yalta. Harriman favoured a quid pro quo approach, tying offers of aid more closely to Soviet concessions. But both sides assumed that the aid issue would come up at Yalta, and on 19 January the president told Stettinius that he 'thought it a mistake to communicate with Russia on postwar financing and would prefer holding the question until he saw Stalin personally and could discuss the matter with him at that time'. On 5 February, at the opening meeting of foreign ministers, Molotov duly highlighted the issue of economic aid, together with reparations from Germany, as key issues. 'Now that the end of the war was in sight,' he said, 'it was most important that agreements be reached on these economic questions.'[40]

But at their meeting on 8 February, despite Stalin clearly giving him an opening, FDR did not raise the issue of financial aid. Nor was it discussed at any time during the conference – unlike reparations from Germany, over which Stalin and Churchill locked horns on several occasions. The British did not want a repeat of the international debt tangle that had enmeshed and debilitated the world economy after the last war; Stalin saw substantial reparations as the USSR's just reward for bearing the brunt of the German war. Churchill's manoeuvring to defer the whole issue was a major British success of the conference, and also a source of real irritation to Stalin. Roosevelt, however, chose not to play the economic card in any way – perhaps because he did not rate it highly as a bargaining tool,[41] most certainly because his whole approach to the

Soviets was to avoid hardball dollar diplomacy and seek to build a relationship of trust.

Even during the conference, Churchill maintained his practice of feeding Stalin juicy updates on the war situation – perhaps to make more palatable heavy policy papers.

Churchill to Stalin, sent 9 February 1945, received 9 February 1945[42]

I send you herewith

(i) the latest news received from London regarding the fighting on the Western Front, and

(ii) a memorandum setting out the latest position in Greece.

I trust that these notes may be of interest to you.

The first enclosure comprised a military update on two new offensives, which Marshall had outlined at the first plenary meeting on 4 February.[43] Now that the Ardennes bulge had been eliminated, on 8 February Montgomery's 21st Army Group, together with the Ninth US Army, began pushing towards the Rhine north of Düsseldorf, as preparation for crossing the river and thrusting into the Ruhr. Further south, in Alsace, the Sixth United States Army Group under General Jake Devers had just completed elimination of the 'Colmar Pocket' – formed by long-standing resistance by the German 19th Army. By 9 February, Devers' American and French units held the west bank of the Rhine from the Swiss border to Strasbourg. Both operations were facets of Eisenhower's 'broad front' strategy for moving into Germany, in contrast with the British preference for a 'narrow thrust' that privileged Monty's forces but would have left much of the US Army relatively idle. Ike – now a consummate soldier-diplomat – shaped Allied strategy in part to avoid such political ructions in either country.

Churchill's second enclosure concerned Greece. At the end of the plenary meeting on 8 February, when there had been much heated discussion about the murky situation in Poland, Stalin said deadpan: 'there are all sorts of rumours with regard to Greece. I have no criticism to make but I should like to know what is going on.' Caught on the raw, Churchill said Greece would take a great deal of time to explain and he would reserve the matter for next day's meeting. In the event, he chose to send Stalin a memo about the Greek situation – perhaps anxious to avoid airing an issue on which Britain was being openly criticized by its American ally, and also aware that everything there was still in flux. His memo documented the negotiations between the British-backed

Greek government and the communist-led guerrillas that were now going on in Athens. Some progress had been made towards 'general disarmament' and on an amnesty. But the communists had demanded an immediate end to martial law, and when this was rejected, the memo stated, 'the Conference was adjourned and did not meet on February 7'. In the end, an agreement was signed at Varkiza, near Athens, on 12 February, but that came too late to save Churchill from further needling from Stalin at the plenary session on the 9th, with the PM saying huffily at one point that the Soviets were welcome to send an observer to Greece. According to the minutes, Stalin replied grandly that he had 'complete confidence in British policy in Greece'. In private, the Soviet leader was highly critical of London's actions, but at Yalta he used Greece to remind Churchill that he was honouring their percentages agreement of October – thereby again inviting concessions elsewhere.[44]

On the UN, Stalin's acceptance on 7 February of just three Soviet seats in the new UN General Assembly had broken the deadlock. But the State Department was worried about reaction back home if it seemed that the Big Three would have unequal representation in the new body: the USA with only one seat, the USSR with three and the British Empire with six – the UK, India and the four self-governing dominions of Canada, Australia, New Zealand and South Africa. Churchill had been careful at Yalta to ensure the inclusion of India – not self-governing, but a member of the old League of Nations – which is why he was happy to support Stalin's position. 'I did not see how I could oppose Russian request for Ukraine and White Russia in view of our having six representatives,' he told Cabinet critics, 'and I still think our six will be safer if Russia is also a multiple voter.'[45]

Hopkins and others raised the issue with the president, noting that US opponents of the League in 1919 had cited the 'six British votes' as one argument against American membership. Surely the president did not want to risk that happening again in 1945?[46] But nor did FDR want to risk alienating the USSR, which might refuse to join the UN if its reduced demands were not met. So he decided to cover his bases by asking for Stalin's consent in principle to Assembly seats for the USA, should that prove politically necessary. He sent a similar request to Churchill.

Roosevelt to Stalin, sent 10 February 1945, received 10 February 1945[47]

I have been thinking, as I must, of possible political difficulties which I might encounter in the United States in connection with the number of votes which the Big Powers will enjoy in the Assembly of the World Organization. We have agreed, and I shall certainly carry out that agreement, to support at the forthcoming United Nations Conference the admission of the Ukrainian and White Russian Republics as members of the Assembly of the World Organization. I am somewhat concerned lest it be pointed out that the United States will have only one vote in the Assembly. It may be necessary for me, therefore, if I am to insure whole-hearted acceptance by the Congress and people of the United States of our participation in the World Organization, to ask for additional votes in the Assembly in order to give parity to the United States.

I would like to know, before I face this problem, that you would perceive no objection and would support a proposal along this line if it is necessary for me to make it at the forthcoming conference. I would greatly appreciate your letting me have your views in reply to this letter.

Stalin did not object to the president's proposal. He simply proposed an equal number of seats for the USA and the USSR.[48] Churchill also gave his consent, but unlike Stalin, left the president to propose how the USA should express what the PM called its 'undisputed equality' in the General Assembly.[49] The Yalta communiqué was therefore able to proclaim that the founding conference of the United Nations would convene in San Francisco on 25 April – a major achievement for the president. But, in deference to requests from him and Churchill, it said nothing about the three Soviet votes, simply stating blandly that, although 'the important question of voting procedure' had not been agreed at Dumbarton Oaks, 'the present conference has been able to resolve this difficulty'.[50] In fact, Roosevelt dropped the idea of three US seats at the end of March when leaks surfaced in the US press, provoking fierce criticism of the White House's 'secret diplomacy'.

Yalta was never intended to be a definitive conference. Rather, it was convened to address immediately urgent issues and to keep the Alliance on course towards the final peace conference. Although later often stigmatized as a sell-out of Poland and Eastern Europe, the discussions on these issues reflected the decisive importance of the Red Army's presence in most of the region, just as the Anglo-American armies in the west had allowed their leaders to keep Stalin at arm's length over Italy and France. And, to offset their 'surrender' on Poland, Roosevelt and Churchill chalked up gains of their own. The president secured his top priorities of the United Nations and Soviet entry into the war against Japan. The PM managed to defer serious discussion of German dismemberment and reparations – to Stalin's visible irritation – and also obtained for France a zone of occupation in defeated Germany and a place on the Allied Control Council there, despite the doubts of his two allies.

Taken in the round, Yalta therefore seemed like a satisfactory piece of complex diplomatic bargaining. Roosevelt and Churchill's thank-you letters reflected their genuine satisfaction about the conference's outcome and its generally warm and businesslike tone. The president's was published in *Pravda* on 16 February. As usual, Churchill's message was fuller and more emotional. But the sentiments expressed there were familiar, especially his belief in personal meetings and the faith he reposed in Stalin personally (plate 21). Hopkins summed up in similar vein for the American side: 'The Russians had proved that they could be reasonable and farseeing and there wasn't any doubt in the minds of the President or any of us that we could live with them and get along with them peacefully for as far into the future as any of us could imagine.' But, he added, 'I think we all had in our minds the reservation that we could not foretell what the results would be if anything should happen to Stalin' because 'we could never be sure who or what might be in the back of him there in the Kremlin'.[51]

Roosevelt to Stalin, sent 12 February 1945, received 13 February 1945[52]

Upon leaving the hospitable shores of the Soviet Union, I wish again to tell you how deeply grateful I am for the many kindnesses which you showed me while I was your guest to the Crimea. I leave greatly heartened as a result of the meeting between you, the Prime Minister and myself. I am sure that the peoples of the world will regard the achievements of this meeting, not only with approval, but as a genuine assurance that our three great nations can work as well in peace as they have in war.

Churchill to Stalin, sent 17 February 1945, received 18 February 1945[53]

On behalf of H.M. Government I send you grateful thanks for all the hospitality and friendship extended to British delegation to the Crimea Conference. We were deeply impressed by the feats of organisation and of improvisation which enabled the Conference to meet in such agreeable and convenient surroundings, and we all take back with us most happy recollections. To this I must add a personal expression of my own thanks and gratitude. No previous meeting has shown so clearly the results which can be achieved when the three Heads of Government meet together with the firm intention to face difficulties and solve them. You yourself said that cooperation would be less easy when the unifying bond of the fight against a common enemy had been removed. I am resolved, as I am sure the President and you are resolved, that the friendship and cooperation so firmly established shall not fade when victory has been won. I pray that you may long be spared to preside over the destinies of your country which has shown its full greatness under your leadership, and I send you my best wishes and heartfelt thanks.

What did Stalin make of Yalta? Toasts at summit banquets are not necessarily a good guide to sober realities, but the Soviet leader – even in his cups – usually chose his words with care. Here are two intriguing observations he made during dinner on 8 February. First, he said, 'I want to drink to our Alliance, that it should not lose its character of intimacy, of its free expression of views. In the history of diplomacy I know of no such close alliance of three great powers as this, when Allies had the opportunity of so frankly expressing their views.' But then Stalin went on, in what appears a gentle warning to the other two that would prove prophetic for them all:

> In an alliance the Allies should not deceive each other. Perhaps that is naive? Experienced diplomatists may say: 'Why should I not deceive my Ally?' But I as a naive man think it best not to deceive my Ally even if he is a fool. Possibly our alliance is so firm just because we do not deceive each other. Or is it because it is not so easy to deceive each other?[54]

*****

Both Western leaders faced a substantial job selling Yalta back home. With the deals on UN voting and Soviet gains in the Far East still secret for the moment, public attention focused mostly on the Polish settlement. On 1 March, Churchill defeated a Commons motion deploring 'the decision to transfer to one ally the territory of another ally' by 396 votes to 25, but that overwhelming margin concealed the depth and significance of the opposition: eleven government ministers abstained and one resigned. In the preceding debate, Churchill admitted at length the deficiencies of the Polish settlement but stuck out his neck with pledges about Soviet fidelity – 'I feel their word is their bond' – and, in private, about Stalin himself. To a special meeting of government ministers he made the remarkable statement that 'Poor Neville Chamberlain believed he could trust Hitler. He was wrong. But I don't think I'm wrong about Stalin.'[55]

Under the American system, Roosevelt did not face that kind of grilling. But he had to endure his own highly public ordeal in the form of a speech to a joint session of the Congress – also on 1 March. This was only one day after FDR had returned to Washington after a detour via the Middle East and his exhaustion was evident. When addressing the Congress in the past, he had walked stiffly down the aisle on an aide's arm, his useless legs locked in place by iron braces. This time, however, he not only allowed himself to be wheeled into the House Chamber but also delivered the speech from a chair, admitting his tiredness after 'a fourteen thousand-mile trip' and asking the legislators' indulgence for his 'unusual posture' because it 'makes it a lot easier for me not to have to carry about ten pounds of steel around on the bottom of my legs'. This was the most public sign FDR had ever given of his infirmity. In his remarks, with frequent ad-libbing, the president admitted that no country got its way 'one hundred percent' at the conference – citing Poland's eastern boundary as one issue on which he did not entirely agree with the outcome – but said that international peacemaking decisions would 'often be a result of give-and-take compromise'. Overall, he hyped Yalta as 'a turning point in American history' and indeed 'in the history of the world', declaring that it 'ought to spell the end of the system of unilateral action, the exclusive alliances, the spheres of influence, the balances of power, and all the other expedients that have been tried for centuries – and have always failed. We propose to substitute for all these a universal organization in which all peace-loving Nations will finally have a chance to join.'[56] Like Churchill, Roosevelt had given many hostages to fortune.

By March, the prime minister was beginning to have second thoughts. On the 8th and 10th, he sent FDR lengthy messages about what seemed like the creeping Sovietization of Eastern Europe in defiance of the Declaration on Liberated Europe. On Romania, the PM effectively admitted that his hands were tied by his percentages agreement, because Stalin had not interfered with British actions in Greece, so he hoped the president would take the lead in pressing Stalin to adhere to the 'principles of Yalta' over Romania. Churchill's main concern, however, was Poland – especially after extensive backstairs protests by MPs of all parties during and after the Commons debate. 'I think you will agree with me,' he told FDR, 'that far more than the case of Poland is involved. I feel that this is the test case between us and the Russians of the meaning which is to be attached to such terms as Democracy, Sovereignty, Independence, Representative Government and free and unfettered elections.' Angry that Molotov was closing down all consultation with 'Non-Lublin Poles', he wanted to send a 'personal message' to Stalin underlining what was at stake and enclosed a lengthy draft. Otherwise, he said, if Molotov were allowed to 'make a farce out of consultations' and 'we do not get things right now', he and the president would be 'seen by the world' to have 'under-written a fraudulent prospectus' for Poland at Yalta.[57]

Roosevelt, however, persuaded Churchill not to send the message. There was, he told the PM, no disagreement between the two of them about the principles at stake: 'the only difference as I see it is one of tactics'. Rather than put Polish issues 'squarely to the Soviet Government' at this stage through a message to Stalin, thereby risking 'certain refusal', Roosevelt felt it would be more productive to proceed quietly but firmly through their ambassadors, as agreed at Yalta – 'under the guise of a general political truce'.[58] The president, though ailing, never lost track of the fact that the Yalta agreements on Poland and Eastern Europe had been essentially cosmetic: seeking to put an acceptable face on the harsh reality of Soviet control. Churchill also knew this – his claim that Britain and the USSR might have comparable notions of 'democracy' and 'representative government' was ludicrous – but his mood swings, always more volatile than Roosevelt's, became particularly pronounced as the exhaustion of five years of war took hold. Shaken by the depths of the parliamentary revolt, he could see that his historical reputation might be at stake. Poland was indeed now a test case, not of British and Russian political theory, but of Churchill's faith in Stalin.

With Poland therefore the elephant in room, correspondence between the Big Three for most of March revolved around the treatment of US and British POWs. Here, Roosevelt took the lead. The president was now under intense pressure from Harriman, Deane and the military mission in Moscow about alleged poor treatment of American POWs, recently liberated from the Nazis, in Soviet camps in Poland. The Red Army, for its part, pleaded shortage of resources and, as usual, also the sensitivity of its rear areas. Eventually the Pentagon proposed an airlift of supplies to the POWs and the immediate evac-uation of those who were sick and wounded, using their air base at Poltava in the Ukraine. They also prodded the president to flag up the issue in a special message to Stalin. The War Department draft was handed by Secretary Stimson to Roosevelt, who dictated the last three sentences about POWs in Germany. The message was then sent to Deane for delivery to the Kremlin, and was copied to Churchill.[59]

Roosevelt to Stalin, sent 3 March 1945, received 4 March 1945[60]

I have reliable information regarding the difficulties which are being encountered in collecting, supplying, and evacuating American ex-prisoners of war and Amer-ican aircraft crews who are stranded east of the Russian lines. It is urgently requested that instructions be issued authorizing ten American aircraft with Amer-ican crews to operate between Poltava and places in Poland where American ex-prisoners of war and stranded airmen may be located. This authority is requested for the purpose of providing supplementary clothing, medical and food supplies for all American soldiers, to evacuate stranded aircraft crews and liberated prisoners of war, and especially to transfer the injured and sick to the American hospital at Poltava. I regard this request to be of the greatest importance not only for humanitarian reasons but also by reason of the intense interest of the American public in the welfare of our ex-prisoners of war and stranded aircraft crews. Secondly on the general matter of prisoners of war in Germany I feel that we ought to do something quickly. The number of these prisoners of war, Russian, British and U.S., is very large. In view of your disapproval of the plan we submitted, what do you suggest in place of it?

Stalin replied with a firm refusal, assuring FDR that on Polish territory and other areas liberated by the Red Army 'there are no groups of American prisoners of war, as all of them, except the single sick persons who are in the hospitals, have been sent to the gathering point in Odessa, where 1200 American prisoners of war have already arrived and the arrival of the rest is expected in the nearest future'. Consequently, he added, 'there is not necessity to carry on flights of American planes from Poltava to the territory of Poland on the matters of American prisoners of war'.[61]

The controversy escalated during March. On the 12th, the Soviet authorities revoked permission for General Deane to visit Poland, asserting that there were no longer any US POWs in the country. American 'contact officers', sanctioned under the Yalta agreement, were also being excluded from Poland. Harriman told Washington that 'the Soviets have been attempting to stall us off by misinformation from day to day'. In order to induce Moscow to 'live up to our interpretation of the agreement', he and Deane urged another Roosevelt–Stalin message backed up by possible 'retaliatory measures', such as Eisenhower restricting the movements of Soviet contact officers in the West and cutting back on Lend-Lease supplies that were not essential to the Soviet war effort.[62] The draft message to Stalin, prepared by Stettinius and Stimson, was approved by the president, with minor amendments (italicized).

Roosevelt to Stalin, sent 17 March 1945, received 18 March 1945[63]

With reference to the question of evacuation of American prisoners from Poland I have been informed that the arrangement for General Deane with a Soviet Army officer to make a survey the U.S. prisoners of war situation has been cancelled. In your last message to me you stated that there was no need to accede to my request that American aircraft be allowed to carry supplies to Poland and to evacuate the sick. I have information that I consider positive and reliable that there are *very* considerable number of sick and injured Americans in hospitals in Poland and also numbers of liberated U.S. prisoners in good health who are awaiting entrainment in Poland to transit camps in Odessa, or are at large in small groups that have not yet made contact with Soviet authorities.

Frankly I cannot understand your reluctance to permit American officers and means to assist their own people in this matter. This Government has done everything to meet *each of* your requests. I now request you to meet mine in this particular matter. *Please call Harriman to explain my desires in detail.* ~~Harriman can explain our desires in detail.~~

The British were also worried about the treatment of their prisoners of war. During March, Churchill, too, came under pressure from his diplomats and military to take up the matter with Stalin himself, but he twice insisted that Eden should handle things with Molotov. 'I had better keep my wire to Stalin clear at the moment,' he told the foreign secretary on 1 March. And on the 21st, he again rejected another draft message on the matter to Stalin 'as it would only make a row between us after a month's silence'. Clearly the PM had decided, especially after his exchange with FDR over Poland, to save up his channel to Stalin for that 'test case'. Instead he sent what he called 'a friendly and informal message to Stalin' which gave 'no excuse for a rough answer' by simply asking the Soviet leader on 21 March to 'give the matter your personal attention' – a ploy that had worked for him before, as over the Debice V-2 rocket site the previous summer. He then fed the Soviet leader the latest war news as Eisenhower's armies neared the Rhine, before ending with a familiar refrain: 'We seem to have a lot of difficulties now since we parted at Yalta but I am quite sure that all these would soon be swept away if only we could meet together.'[64] The PM was quite open about his tactics. 'At present I do not want to touch on political issues in correspondence with the Marshal,' he told Gusev during a breakfast meeting at the Soviet embassy on 21 March. 'Let the ambassadors and diplomats deal with political issues, while we concentrate on combat.'[65]

But Stalin did not relent over the POWs. Faced with Roosevelt's second appeal, he adopted his customary posture when pressed, using attack as the best form of defence by repeating counter-claims – which London and Washington regarded as largely spurious – about the treatment of Soviet POWs in US and British camps. This dispute was really about the larger situation in Poland itself. Stalin had no desire to have Western observers loose along the Red Army's line of communications and in a country where his Lublin government was tightening its hold. Churchill alluded to this in a message to Roosevelt on 16 March. 'At present,' he stated, 'all entry into Poland is barred to our representatives', adding in a pregnant phrase: 'An impenetrable veil has been drawn across the scene.'[66]

Harriman, in particular, treated POWs almost entirely as a facet of what he considered the bigger picture. By now deeply distrustful of Soviet good faith and convinced that only a tough line by Roosevelt would pay any dividends, he sent increasingly emotional messages about the POWs, apparently in the hope that this 'American' issue would finally spur the president into vigorous action in a way that the governance of Poland had so far not done.

Stalin to Roosevelt, sent 22 March 1945, received 22 March 1945[67]

I have received your message concerning the evacuation from Poland of former American prisoners of war.

In regard to the information which you have about a seemingly great number of sick and wounded Americans who are in Poland, and also those who are awaiting for departure for Odessa or who did not get in touch with Soviet authorities, I must say that that information is not exact. In reality, on the territory of Poland by March 16 there were only 17 sick Americans, except a number of Americans who are on the way to Odessa. Today I have received a report that very soon they (17 persons) will be taken to Odessa by planes.

In regard to a request contained in your message I must say that if that request concerned me personally I would be ready agree even to the prejudice of my interests. But in this case the matter concerns the interests of the Soviet armies at the front and Soviet commanders, who do not want to have extra officers with them, having no relation to military operations but at the same time requiring care for their accommodation, for the organization of meetings and all kinds of connections for them, for their guard from possible diversions on the part of German agents who have not yet been caught, and other measures diverting commanders and officers under their command from their direct duties.

Our commanders pay with their lives for the state of matters at the front and in the immediate rear and I do not consider it possible to limit their rights in any degree.

In addition to this I have to say that former American prisoners of war liberated by the Red Army are in Soviet prisoner-of-war camps in good conditions, at any rate in better conditions than former Soviet prisoners of war in American camps where they have been partially placed together with German prisoners of war and where some of them were subjected to unfair treatment and unlawful inconvenience up to beating as it was reported to the American Government more than once.[68]

Churchill did not persist on the POW question. Saving his fire for a really big salvo on Poland, he sent another news bulletin from the front while eagerly awaiting Monty's crossing of the Rhine. On 26 March, the PM relished his chance to urinate into Germany's iconic river – having already enjoyed peeing on the Siegfried Line. One cannot imagine either of his august counterparts doing the same – not just because they did not share what Brooke called 'Winston's boyish humour', but also because Roosevelt couldn't go near the front and Stalin wouldn't.[69]

Churchill to Stalin, sent 24 March 1945, received 24 March 1945[70]

I am at Field Marshal Montgomery's H.Q. He has just given orders to launch the main battle to force the Rhine on a broad front centring about Wesel supported by the landing of an Airborne Corps and by about 2,000 guns.

It is hoped to pass the river tonight and tomorrow and establish bridgeheads. A very large reserve of armour is available to exploit the assault once the river is crossed.

I shall send you another message tomorrow. Field Marshal Montgomery asks me to present his respects to you.

*****

The message Churchill promised to send on 25 March never materialized. That weekend relations between the Soviet Union and its allies suddenly seemed close to total rupture. The president – still exhausted from Yalta and desperately in need of a break – spent most of Saturday the 24th discussing two draft messages to Stalin on issues that had boiled up into major diplomatic crises. The second of these concerned plans for the United Nations, lynchpin of FDR's postwar planning. Even more pressing were Stalin's claims that the Western Allies were trying to do a deal with the Nazis behind his back.

On 8 March, General Karl Wolff – the Waffen SS commander in northern Italy, who had close links with Himmler – had made contact with the American OSS station in Bern, Switzerland, about the possible surrender of German forces in Italy – an operation known as 'Crossword' in Britain and 'Sunrise' in America.[71] Field Marshal Alexander, the Allied commander-in-chief in Italy, proposed first to send representatives to Switzerland to establish the *bona fides* of the Nazi emissaries, and then, if satisfied, to arrange surrender negotiations at his headquarters in Caserta, near Naples. The Combined Chiefs approved, on condition that the Soviet government was informed before Alexander took any further action, and on 12 March this information was relayed to Molotov in separate letters from Harriman and Clark Kerr. The Allies were acting with propriety in accordance with the Moscow agreement of 1943, which stipulated inter-Allied consultations in the event of such appeals by the enemy; but in any case, it was likely Moscow would find out about these contacts. Molotov promptly replied that his government did not object but wished to send three Soviet officers to Bern 'to take part in these conversations'. The British chiefs of staff and FO agreed, though intending to limit the Soviets to observer status, and instructions to that effect were sent to Alexander and also to Clark Kerr for communication to Molotov.[72]

However, Harriman took the highly unusual step of asking Clark Kerr to delay delivery of this *British* message until he had consulted Washington. Harriman and Deane then sent cables to Stettinius and Marshall, vehemently opposing any Soviet participation and framed along parallel lines of argument. Of course, they said, the USSR would naturally have a place if these purely military discussions turned political and developed into 'the capitulation of a government'. But they claimed that Allied representatives would not be invited to a similar situation on the Eastern Front, for instance the surrender of thirty divisions cut off in Latvia, and that any Soviet presence now could deter the Germans from surrendering – an argument to which the president was receptive.[73] (FDR was, in fact, peeved at the attempted British intervention. Russia has 'nothing to do with the campaign in Italy', he told the Canadian premier, William Lyon Mackenzie King, on 13 March, adding that 'Winston had made the situation very difficult'.)[74] But Harriman and Deane's core argument against acceding to Molotov's request seems to have been tactical, in line with the overall policy they now fervently advocated, namely that 'the Soviets would consider it a sign of weakness', as Harriman put it, prompting 'even more untenable demands from them in the future'. Deane was even blunter: acceptance would be 'an act of appeasement'. Clark Kerr relayed Harriman's main points to Churchill, who took them seriously.[75]

The American Joint Chiefs used these messages from Moscow to treat Bern as purely exploratory discussions, to which the Soviets would not be invited. They would, of course, be present if any formal talks were conducted at Alexander's HQ, though only as observers, since the negotiations would be about the surrender of German forces in an Anglo-American theatre. Any arrangements for their attendance would be conducted entirely by the US and British military missions in Moscow because, the JCS stated, the 'cumbersome' procedure of going through the State Department and Foreign Office 'introduces into what is almost entirely a military matter an unavoidable political element' which could 'tie Marshal Alexander's hands'. The State Department and the president accepted this position, and Churchill and Eden felt obliged to concur. Molotov was duly informed, but sent back a furious message on 16 March to both ambassadors, denouncing the change of tack as 'utterly unexpected and incomprehensible from the point of view of Allied relations between our countries'. He insisted that 'the negotiations already begun in Bern be broken off' and that 'from now on all possibility of separate negotiations by one or two of the Allied Powers' without the participation of all three should be 'ruled out'.[76]

'The speed and nature of Molotov's reply indicate keen displeasure', Clark Kerr remarked to the FO with dry understatement.[77] Facing now a serious rift, British and American reactions diverged. Continuing to regret that the Russians had not been allowed to go to Bern, 'so that they would know all about what was going on', the FO drafted a joint Churchill–Roosevelt message of explanation for Stalin, intended to clear up the 'misunderstanding' before it was too late. But Harriman, determined to defend his position, sent Washington another cable making it clear that he treated Bern as further evidence for his 'growing impression' since Yalta 'that the Soviet leaders have come to believe that they can force their will on us on any issue'. He also instanced the way they had 'arbitrarily, and in disregard of the facts, placed their own interpretation on the Yalta agreements' regarding Poland, Romania and POWs. In Washington, Leahy and the JCS decided that Harriman 'must be supported' and advised that Roosevelt should not send a message to Stalin but should continue to deal with Molotov. The US military composed a brisk message, stating that the USA was 'surprised at the tenor' of Molotov's communication, which it attributed to 'a misunderstanding on the part of the Soviet Government'. The tone was almost condescending.[78]

This evoked a blistering response from Molotov on 22 March, stating that what was at stake was not a question of 'misunderstanding' but of 'something worse', namely that, for the previous two weeks in Bern, US and British representatives had been 'carrying on negotiations' with the Germans 'behind the back of the Soviet Government', which was carrying 'the main burden of the war against Germany'. This, he said, was 'absolutely inadmissible'. Such a message could only have been sent with Stalin's agreement, and it was now clear in Washington that a response from the president could no longer be deferred. A draft was prepared by the War Department and Leahy, to which Roosevelt made some deletions and additions (in italics).[79]

Roosevelt to Stalin, sent 24 March 1945, received 25 March 1945[80]

I have received from Ambassador Harriman a letter addressed to him by Mr. Molotov regarding an investigation being made by Field Marshal Alexander into a reported possibility of obtaining the surrender of part or all of the German army in Italy, in which letter Mr. Molotov demands that this investigation to be undertaken in Switzerland be stopped forthwith because of the non participation therein of Soviet officers.

I am sure that the facts of this matter, through a misunderstanding, have not been correctly presented to you.

The facts are as follows: Some few days ago unconfirmed information was received in Switzerland that some German officers were considering the possibility of arranging for the surrender of German troops that are opposed to the British–American Armies in Italy commanded by Field Marshal Alexander.

When this information reached Washington, Field Marshal Alexander was *authorized* ~~directed~~ to send an officer, or officers, of his staff to Switzerland to ascertain the accuracy of the report, and if it appeared to be of sufficient promise, to arrange with any competent German officers for a conference with Field Marshal Alexander at his headquarters in Italy to discuss details of the surrender. *Soviet representatives would, of course, be present if such a meeting could be arranged.*

The Soviet Government was immediately informed of this investigation to be made in Switzerland and was later informed that it will be agreeable for Soviet officers to be present at Field Marshal Alexander's meetings with German officers when and if such a meeting is finally arranged *in Berne* to discuss details of a surrender *at Caserta.*

Attempts by our representatives to arrange a meeting with German officers have met with no success up to the present time, but there still appears to be a possibility of such a meeting.

You will, of course, understand that my government must give every assistance to all officers in the field in command of American Forces who believe there is a possibility of forcing the surrender of enemy troops in their area. It would be completely unreasonable for me to take any other attitude or to permit any delay which must cause additional and avoidable loss of life in the American Forces. You as a military man will understand the necessity for prompt action to avoid losing an opportunity. *It is in the same category as would be the sending of a flag of truce to your general at Konigsberg or Danzig.*

In such a surrender of enemy forces in the field, there can be no political implications whatever and no violation of our agreed principle of unconditional surrender.

At any discussion of details of surrender by our commander of American Forces in the field, I will be pleased to have the benefit of the experience and advice of any of your officers who can be present, but I cannot agree to suspend investigation of the possibility because of objection on the part of Mr. Molotov for some reason completely beyond my understanding.

I do not expect much from the reported possibility, but I hope you will, with the purpose of preventing misunderstanding between our officers, point out to the Soviet officials concerned the desirability and necessity of our taking prompt and effective action without any delay to accomplish the surrender of any enemy military forces in the field that are opposed to American Forces.

I am sure that when a similar opportunity comes on the Soviet front you will have the same attitude and will take the same action.

Roosevelt's other headache on Saturday, 24 March was a sudden intimation that the USSR might be backing away from the new United Nations, whose founding conference in San Francisco was scheduled for 25 April. On 13 March, the Politburo had approved a top-level Soviet delegation, including not only Molotov, but also Stalin's right-hand man in the party, Andrey Zhdanov. The list had apparently been intended to showcase the Soviet Union's special role in the creation of the UN and the Kremlin's eagerness to launch it. A few days later, Molotov confirmed his participation to both the Foreign Office and the State Department. But then the list was abruptly downgraded by another Politburo decision, on 22 March – the same day Molotov sent his message about Bern, virtually accusing the Allies of treachery.[81] Commenting on the revised Soviet delegation, Joseph Grew of the State Department told the president that, 'with the exception of the Ambassador himself, this is not a high-ranking delegation. There is not even a Vice Commissar of Foreign Affairs or any member of the Government of Cabinet rank.'[82]

In fact, the Soviets had been probing the Yalta agreements on the UN for some weeks.[83] But that had been on relatively low-key issues, whereas the absence of the Soviet foreign minister, an international celebrity, from what was known to be the centrepiece of Roosevelt's postwar vision would be a public relations disaster. Harriman called it an example of 'the usual Soviet tactics', when feeling crossed in one area, of retaliating in another.[84] Despite State Department fears about overloading the Roosevelt–Stalin channel, Washington saw no option but to respond at the highest level.

Roosevelt to Stalin, sent 24 March 1945, received 25 March 1945[85]

Ambassador Gromyko has just informed the State Department of the composition of the Soviet Delegation to the San Francisco Conference. While we have the highest regard for Ambassador Gromyko's character and capabilities and know that he would ably represent his country, I cannot help being deeply disappointed that Mr. Molotov apparently does not plan to attend. Recalling the friendly and fruitful cooperation at Yalta between Mr. Molotov, Mr. Eden and Mr. Stettinius, I know that the Secretary of State has been looking forward to continuing the joint work in the same spirit at San Francisco for the eventual realization of our mutual goal, the establishment of an effective international organization to insure a secure and peaceful future for the world.

Without the presence of Mr. Molotov the Conference will be deprived of a very great asset. If his pressing and heavy responsibilities in the Soviet Union make it impossible for him to stay for the entire Conference, I very much hope that you will find it possible to let him come at least for the vital opening sessions. Since all sponsoring powers and the majority of other countries attending will be represented by their Ministers of Foreign Affairs, I am afraid that Mr. Molotov's absence will be construed all over the world as a lack of comparable interest on the part of the Soviet Government in the great objectives of this Conference.

But Stalin batted back the president's message with the facile excuse that Molotov's presence was vitally needed at the Supreme Soviet and a prediction that Gromyko would replace him at San Francisco 'with great success' – all of which only enhanced the impression that the Kremlin didn't care a damn about the UN.

Stalin to Roosevelt, sent 27 March 1945, received 27 March 1945[86]

We extremely value and attach great importance to the forthcoming Conference in San Francisco, called to found the international organization of peace and security for peoples, but circumstances have developed in such a way that Mr. V.M. Molotov, really, is not able to participate in the Conference. I and Mr. Molotov regret it extremely but the convening, on request of the deputies of the Supreme Soviet, in April, of a sessions [sic] of the Supreme Soviet of the USSR where the presence of Mr. Molotov is absolutely necessary, is excluding the possibility of his participation even in the first meetings of the Conference.

You also know that Ambassador Gromyko has quite successfully accomplished his task in Dumbarton Oaks and we are confident that he will with great success head the Soviet delegation in San Francisco.

As regards various interpretations, you understand, this cannot determine the decisions which are to be made.

The Soviet leader also rebutted Roosevelt's main theses about the Bern affair, in a text unchanged from Molotov's draft. One key question was raised here for the first time: if the Allies had nothing to hide from the USSR, why were the

Soviets being excluded from the Bern contacts and given little information about them? As the British archives confirm, contrary to instructions, Alexander's HQ did not keep Moscow informed via the British military mission about the Swiss discussions, the next round of which took place on 19 March between Wolff and Dulles in Ascona on Lake Maggiore, near the Swiss–Italian border. When the chiefs of staff and Churchill belatedly discovered this ten days later, they were concerned that the talks were going far beyond the purely credential-validating process originally outlined to Moscow. 'We have decided to ignore the insulting telegrams which Molotov has sent,' Churchill told Eden. 'This, however, does not relieve us from our obligation as Allies on any matter which might involve peace negotiations.'[87] Soviet intelligence had meanwhile informed the Kremlin of these contacts, casting them in the most negative possible light for the Allies.

In his message, Stalin also rejected the president's analogy with Königsberg and Danzig, and highlighted the essential point from the Soviet perspective, which was not narrowly military (what might happen on the Italian front) but the larger political implications – breezily dismissed by the JCS on 13 March. Moscow feared that the Western Allies might sign a separate peace, allowing Germany to move troops to the Eastern Front. That was indeed in the minds of many top figures in the Reich by that stage in the war.

Stalin to Roosevelt, sent 29 March 1945, received 29 March 1945[88]

I gave consideration to the question you raised before me in the letter of March 25, 1945, and have found that the Soviet Government could not have given a different answer after the Soviet representatives were refused participation in the discussions in Bern with the Germans regarding the possibility of capitulation of German troops and opening the front to Anglo-American troops in Northern Italy.

I am not against and, more than this, I am fully for using the opportunity of disintegration in the German armies and to hasten their capitulation in any section of the front, to encourage them in the opening of the front for the Allies.

But I agree to negotiations with the enemy on such matter only in the case when these negotiations will not make the situation of the enemy easier, if there will be excluded a possibility for the Germans to maneuvre [sic] and to use these negotiations for shifting of their troops to other sections of the front and, first of all, to the Soviet front.

Only with the purpose of creating a guarantee was the participation of representatives of the Soviet Military Command in such negotiations with the enemy considered necessary by the Soviet Government, no matter where they would take place – in Bern or Caserta. I cannot understand why representatives of the Soviet Command were refused participation in these negotiations and in what way could they cause inconvenience to the representatives of the Allied Command.

For your information I have to tell you that the Germans have already made use of the negotiations with the Allied Command and during this period have succeeded in shifting three divisions from Northern Italy to the Soviet front.

The task of coordinated operations with a blow upon the Germans from the West, South and East, announced at the Crimea Conference is to bind the troops of the enemy to the place of their location and not to give the enemy any possibility to maneuver and shift troops in the necessary for him direction. This task is being carried out by the Soviet Command. This is being violated by Fieldmarshal Alexander.

This circumstance is irritating the Soviet Command and creates ground for distrust.

'As a military man', you write me, 'you will understand, that it is necessary to act quickly in order not to miss an opportunity. It would be the same if your general at Koenigsberg or Danzig would be approached by the enemy with a white flag.' It is regretted that an analogy does not suit this case. German troops at Koenigsberg and Danzig are surrounded. If they surrender they will do it in order to avoid annihilation but they cannot open a front to the Soviet troops as the front has moved away from them far to the West, to the Oder. An entirely different situation is that of the German troops in Northern Italy. They are not surrounded and they do not face annihilation. If the Germans in Northern Italy, in spite of this, seek negotiations in order to surrender and to open the front to Allied troops, this means that they have different, more serious aims relating to the fate of Germany.

I have to tell you, that if on the Eastern front, somewhere on the Oder, similar conditions of a possibility of capitulation of the Germans and opening the front to Soviet troops would arise, I would not hesitate to inform immediately the Anglo-American Military Command and to request it to send their representatives for participation in negotiations as in such cases the Allies should have no secrets from each other.

On the advice of his military, Roosevelt decided to challenge Stalin's arguments about Bern. But he did promise that the Soviets would be kept informed of any further contacts through Alexander, whose instructions to this effect had just been reiterated.[89] However, when the British field marshal passed the relevant information to the Soviet side, it was withheld by the heads of the Allied military missions in Moscow – with Deane clearly taking the lead – because it would seem to confirm Soviet suspicions about the ongoing negotiations in Bern. Alexander was asked by the Americans to 'amend the message which you desire us to give to the Soviet Authorities to conform to the assurances already given by our respective governments and by our Heads of States'.[90] This he duly did, but of course the Soviets knew from their own intelligence the extent of the contacts – if not their detailed content. All of which further increased the fears of the innately suspicious Kremlin.

Roosevelt to Stalin, sent 31 March 1945, received 1 April 1945[91]

It seems to me in the exchange of messages we have had on possible future negotiations with the Germans for surrender of their forces in Italy, that although both of us are in agreement on all the basic principles, the matter now stands in an atmosphere of regrettable apprehension and mistrust.

No negotiations for surrender have been entered into, and if there should be any negotiations they will be conducted at Caserta with your representatives present throughout. Although the attempt at Bern to arrange for the conduct of these negotiations has been fruitless, Marshal Alexander has been directed to keep you informed of his progress in this matter.

I must repeat that the meeting in Bern was for the single purpose of arranging contact with competent German military officers and not for negotiations of any kind.

There is no question of negotiating with the Germans in any way which would permit them to transfer elsewhere forces from the Italian front. Negotiations, if any are conducted, will be on the basis of unconditional surrender. With regard to the lack of Allied offensive operations in Italy, this condition has in no way resulted from any expectation of an agreement with the Germans. As a matter of fact, recent interruption of offensive operations in Italy has been due primarily to the recent transfer of Allied forces, British and Canadian divisions, from that front to France. Preparations are now made for an offensive on the Italian front about April 10th, but while we hope for success, the operation will be of limited power due to the lack of forces now available to Alexander. He has seventeen dependable divisions and is opposed by twenty-four German divisions. We intend to do everything within the capacity of our available resources to prevent any withdrawal of the German forces now in Italy.

I feel that your information about the time of the movements of German troops from Italy is in error. Our best information is that three German divisions have left Italy since the first of the year, two of which have gone to the Eastern front. The last division of the three started moving about February 25, more than two weeks before anybody heard of any possibility of a surrender. It is therefore clearly evident that the approach made of German agents in Bern occurred after the last movement of troops began and could not possibly have had any effect on the movement.

This entire episode has arisen through the initiative of a German officer reputed to be close to Himmler and there is, of course, a strong possibility that his sole purpose is to create suspicion and distrust between the Allies. There is no reason why we should permit him to succeed in that aim. I trust that the above categorical statement of the present situation and of my intentions will allay the apprehension which you express in your message of March 29.

In reality, deception was being practised on the Soviet side as well as the American. On 31 March, just before receiving this message from FDR, Harriman and Deane had delivered to Stalin a cable from Eisenhower setting out revisions in his strategic plans. This indicated that once the Ruhr pocket had been eliminated, his forces would drive east towards Leipzig, to link up with the Red Army, and south into Bavaria to prevent the consolidation of an Alpine redoubt. The British, not informed in advance, objected vehemently, but Eisenhower insisted that he was simply following the military logic of seeking and destroying the enemy's forces, in order to end the war as quickly as possible, and also building on the Tedder visit in January by ensuring clear lines of demarcation between his forces and the Red Army. Churchill, however, high-lighted the diplomatic implications of Ike's action: it would marginalize Monty's million-strong British–Canadian army group in north Germany and also greatly benefit the Soviet Union. 'The Russian armies will no doubt overrun all Austria and enter Vienna,' he told Roosevelt on 1 April. 'If they also take Berlin, will not their impression that they have been the overwhelming contributor to our common victory be unduly imprinted in their minds, and may this not lead them into a mood which will raise grave and formidable difficulties in the future?'[92]

By the time the PM sent this message, however, the die was cast. When Harriman and Deane delivered Ike's message about targeting Leipzig not Berlin, both were struck that Stalin seemed pleased with the news. Of course he was, with Soviet planning for the drive to Berlin almost ready and intelligence snippets about Bern magnifying fears that the Wehrmacht might surrender in the west and let Eisenhower's forces roll unimpeded to the German capital. On 1 April, the morning after receiving Ike's message, Stalin called in Zhukov and

Konev – his two top commanders (and also bitter rivals). 'Well, then,' he asked, 'who is going to take Berlin: are we or are the Allies?' There was, naturally, only one answer. And so Stalin unleashed the race for Berlin – a race against the West, and also between Konev and Zhukov. That same day he sent a polite reply to Eisenhower, agreeing with Ike's strategic assessment and stating: 'Berlin has lost its former strategic importance. The Soviet High Command therefore plan to allot secondary forces in the direction of Berlin.' Historian Antony Beevor has called this cable 'the greatest April Fool in modern history'.[93]

During 31 March, the president also laboured over a message about Poland. For several weeks he had resisted pressure from Churchill, even telling his Cabinet on 16 March that the British seemed 'perfectly willing for the United States to have a war with Russia,'[94] but now he finally agreed to bring matters to a head with Stalin himself. At issue were the slippery legacies of Yalta.

The immediate post-Yalta goal had been that the existing provisional government should be 'reorganised on a broader democratic basis with the inclusion of democratic leaders from Poland itself and from Poles abroad'. Harriman, Clark Kerr and Molotov would comprise a 'commission' to coordinate consultations.[95] But the Yalta agreements on Poland had resorted to deliberately vague wording in order to gain acceptance all round. When Leahy remonstrated with Roosevelt about their verbal elasticity, the president told him: 'I know, Bill. I know it. But it's the best I can do for Poland at this time.'[96] So the Soviets had tried to stretch the words in the direction they preferred, while the Western Allies did the opposite. In order to maintain a clear pro-Soviet majority, the Kremlin let the Warsaw government vet all the candidacies, whereas London and Washington insisted on a radical renewal of that government including members of the Polish opposition. But this, declared Molotov, would not be a 'reorganization' of the government but rather its 'liquidation'.[97] The situation was aggravated by Moscow's reluctance to allow official US and British representatives into Poland to ascertain the political situation at first hand. The offer of such a trip – made by Stalin in Yalta and then by Molotov at the end of February[98] – was soon retracted on the pretext of needing to obtain Warsaw's consent.

'Of course Molotov doesn't want a breakdown,' Eden observed to Churchill on 24 March, 'he wants to drag the business out while his stooges consolidate their power. We cannot be parties to this and must force the issue.' The foreign secretary even wondered 'is it any value to go to San Francisco in these conditions?' Churchill agreed that the time was now ripe for another overture to Roosevelt about a joint message to Stalin, perhaps covering all the problems now on the boil. The PM warned Eden that 'we cannot press the case against Russia beyond where we can carry the United States', but added, 'Nothing is more likely to bring them into line with us than any idea of the San Francisco Conference being imperilled.'[99] It was along these lines that a message to Roosevelt was drafted in the FO and sent by Churchill on 27 March. The president was not entirely persuaded, noting that the Yalta agreement on Poland was a 'compromise' that placed 'somewhat more emphasis on the Lublin Poles than on other groups' and also urging that matters should be handled as much as possible at ambassadorial level. But, conscious of all the friction with Moscow over the previous week or so, he agreed that 'the time has come to take up directly with Stalin the broader aspects of the Soviet attitude (with particular reference to Poland)' – though again, as was Washington's general line in the spring of 1945, he decided to act on his own. On 29 March, he sent a draft telegram for Stalin to Churchill, whose comments resulted in a few amendments – indicated in italics – in the final version. (Underscore indicates changes made before the US draft was sent to London.) The president's tone, less combative than Churchill would have liked, was one of careful explanation, tinged with pained anxiety about whether Stalin fully grasped the impact of his various recent actions on American opinion.[100]

Churchill sent his own message to Stalin, likewise shown in draft to Roosevelt. In this, he reinforced the president's arguments, while keeping off Romania because of its sensitive place in the percentages agreement over Greece. He included the pregnant phrase about 'a veil of secrecy' coming down over the Polish scene and warned that he might soon have to tell Parliament about the failure to agree on Poland. Like Roosevelt, the PM was trying to play the 'public opinion' card with Stalin – either in hope or desperation.

Roosevelt to Stalin, sent 31 March 1945, received 1 April 1945[101]

I cannot conceal from you the concern with which I view the development of events of mutual interest since our fruitful meeting at Yalta. The decisions we reached there were good ones and have for the most part been welcomed with enthusiasm by the peoples of the world who saw in our ability to find a common basis of understanding the best pledge for a secure and peaceful world after this war. Precisely because of the hopes and expectations that these decisions raised, their fulfillment is being followed with the closest attention. We have no right to let them be disappointed. So far there has been a discouraging lack of progress made in the carrying out, which the world expects, of the political decisions which we reached at the Conference particularly those relating to the Polish question. I am frankly puzzled as to why this should be and must tell you that I do not fully understand in many respects the <u>apparent indifferent</u> attitude of your Government. Having understood each other so well at Yalta, I am convinced that the three of us can and will clear away any obstacles which have developed since then. I intend, therefore, in this message to lay before you with complete frankness the problem as I see it.

Although I have in mind primarily the difficulties which the Polish negotiations have encountered, I must make a brief mention of our agreement embodied in the declaration on liberated Europe. I frankly cannot understand why the recent developments in Rumania should be regarded as not falling within the terms of that agreement. I hope you will find time personally to examine the correspondence between our Governments on this subject.

However, the part of our agreements at Yalta which has aroused the greatest popular interest and is the most urgent relates to the Polish question. You are aware of course that the Commission which we set up has made no progress. I feel this is due to the interpretation which your Government is placing upon the Crimea decisions. In order that there shall be no misunderstanding I set forth below my interpretations of the points of the agreement which are pertinent to the difficulties encountered by the Commission in Moscow.

In the discussions that have taken place so far your Government appears to take the position that the new Polish Provisional Government of National Unity which we agreed should be formed should be little more than a continuation of the present Warsaw Government. I cannot reconcile this either with our agreement or our discussions. While it is true that the Lublin Government is to be reorganized and its members play a prominent role it is to be done in such a fashion as to bring into being a new Government. This point is clearly brought out in several places in the text of the agreement. I must make it quite plain to you that any such solution which would result in a thinly disguised continuance of the present Warsaw regime would be unacceptable and would cause the people of the United States to regard the Yalta agreement as ~~a fraud~~ having failed. It is equally apparent that for the same reason the Warsaw Government cannot under the agreement claim the right to select or reject what Poles are to be brought to Moscow by the Commission for consultation. Can we not agree that it is up to the Commission to select the Polish leaders to come to Moscow to consult in the first instance and invitations be sent out accordingly. If this could be done I see no great objection to having the Lublin group come first in order that they may be fully acquainted with the agreed interpretation of the Yalta decisions on this point. *It is of course understood that if the Lublin group come first no arrangements would be made independently with them before the arrival of the other Polish leaders called for consultation.* In order to facilitate the agreement the Commission might first of all select a small but representative group of Polish leaders who could suggest other names for the consideration of the Commission. We have not and would not bar or veto any candidate for consultation which Mr. Molotov might propose being confident that he would not suggest any Poles who would be inimical to the intent of the Crimea decision. I feel that it is not too much to ask that my Ambassador be accorded the same confidence *and that any candidate for consultation presented by any one of the Commission be accepted by the others in good faith.* It is obvious to me that if the right of the Commission to select these Poles is limited or shared with the Warsaw Government the very foundation on which our agreement rests would be destroyed. While the foregoing are the immediate obstacles which in my opinion have prevented our Commission from making any progress in this vital matter there are two other suggestions which were not in the agreement but nevertheless have a very important bearing on the result we all seek. Neither of these suggestions has been as yet accepted by your Government. I refer to (1) that there should be the maximum of political tranquility in Poland and that dissident groups should cease any measures and counter-measures against each other. That we should respectively use our influence to that end seems to me eminently reasonable. (2) It would also seem entirely natural in view of the responsibilities placed upon them by the agreement that representatives of the American and British members of the Commission should be permitted to visit Poland. *As you will recall Mr. Molotov himself suggested this at an early meeting of the Commission and only subsequently withdrew it.*

I wish I could convey to you how important it is for the successful development of our program of international collaboration that this Polish question be settled fairly and speedily. If this is not done all of the difficulties and dangers to Allied unity which we had so much in mind in reaching our decisions at the Crimea will face us in an even more acute form. You are, I am sure, aware that the genuine popular support in the United States is required to carry out any Government policy foreign or domestic. The American people make up their own mind and no Government action can change it. I mention this fact because the last sentence of your message about Mr. Molotov's attendance at San Francisco made me wonder whether you give full weight to this factor.

Churchill to Stalin, sent 1 April 1945, received 1 April 1945[102]

You will by now, I hope, have received the message from the President of the United States which he was good enough to show to me before he sent it. It is now my duty on behalf of His Majesty's Government to assure you that the War Cabinet desire me to express to you our wholehearted endorsement of this message of the President's, and that we associate ourselves with it in its entirety.

There are two or three points which I desire specially to emphasise. First, that we do not consider we have retained in the Moscow discussions the spirit of Yalta, nor indeed, at points, the letter. It was never imagined by us that the Commission which we all three appointed with so much goodwill would not have been able to carry out their part swiftly and easily in a mood of give and take. We certainly thought that a Polish Government, 'new' and 'reorganised' would by now have been in existence, recognised by all the United Nations. This would have afforded a proof to the world of our capacity and resolve to work together for its future. It is still not too late to achieve this.

However, even before the forming of such a new and reorganised Polish Government it was agreed by the Commission that representative Poles should be summoned from inside Poland and from Poles abroad, not necessarily to take part in the government but merely for free and frank consultation. Even this preliminary step cannot be taken because of the claim put forward to veto any invitation, even to consultation, of which the Soviet or the Lublin Governments do not approve. We can never agree to such a veto by any one of us three. This veto reaches its supreme example in the case of Monsieur Mikolajczyk, who is regarded throughout the British and American world as the outstanding Polish figure outside Poland.

We also have learned with surprise and regret that Monsieur Molotov's spontaneous offer to allow observers or missions to enter Poland has now been withdrawn. We are, therefore, deprived of all means of checking for ourselves information often of a most painful character, which is sent us almost daily by the Polish Government in London. We do not understand why a veil of secrecy should thus be drawn over the Polish scene. We offer fullest facilities to the Soviet Government to send missions or individuals to visit any of the territories in our military occupation. In several cases this offer has been accepted by the Soviets and visits have taken place to mutual satisfaction. We ask that the principle of reciprocity shall be observed in these matters, which would help to make so good a foundation for our enduring partnership.

The President has also shown me messages which have passed between him and you about Monsieur Molotov's inability to be present at the Conference at San Francisco. We had hoped the presence there of the three Foreign Ministers might have led to a clearance of many of the difficulties which have descended upon us in a storm since our happy and hopeful union at Yalta. We do not however question in any way the weight of public reasons which make it necessary for him to remain in Russia.

Like the President I too was struck with the concluding sentence of your message to him. What he says about the American people also applies to the British people and to nations of the British Commonwealth with the addition that His Majesty's present advisers only hold office at the will of a universal suffrage parliament. If our efforts to reach an agreement about Poland are to be doomed to failure I shall be bound to confess the fact to Parliament when they return from the Easter recess. No one has pleaded the cause of Russia with more fervour and conviction than I have tried to do. I was the first to raise my voice on June 22nd, 1941. It is more than a year since I proclaimed to a startled world the justice of the Curzon Line for Russia's western frontier and this frontier has now been accepted by both the British Parliament and the President of the United States. It is as a sincere friend of Russia that I make my personal appeal to you and to your colleagues to come to a good understanding about Poland with the Western democracies and not to smite down the hands of comradeship in the future guidance of the world which we now extend.

POWs and the UN, Poland and Bern – the intensity of Big Three correspondence over the previous few weeks had been unprecedented. Most of the messages were lengthy and required hours of thought and attention from leaders who were exhausted from years of war and also anxious about the future. On 3 April, Stalin finally let rip.

His second message on Bern was in a tone reminiscent of his diatribes about Katyn and Warsaw – except this time it was directed not at Polish 'criminals' but at the president of the United States. The draft, as usual, came from Molotov, but Stalin's limited additions (in italics) sharpened the tone.

Stalin to Roosevelt, sent 3 April 1945, received 4 April 1945[103]

I have received your message on the question of negotiations in Bern. You are absolutely right that in connection with the affair regarding negotiation of the Anglo-American Command with the German Command somewhere in Bern or some other place 'has developed an atmosphere of fear and distrust deserving regrets.'

You insist that there have been no negotiations yet.

It may be assumed that you have not been fully informed. As regards my military colleagues, they, on the basis of data which they have on hand, do not have any doubts that the negotiations have taken place and that they have ended in an agreement with the Germans, on the basis of which the German commander on the Western front – Marshal Kesselring, has agreed to open the front and permit the Anglo-American troops to advance to the East, and the Anglo-Americans have promised in return to ease for the Germans the peace terms.

I think that my colleagues are close to truth. Otherwise one could not have understood the fact that the Anglo-Americans have refused to admit to Bern representatives of the Soviet Command for participation in the negotiations with the Germans.

I also cannot understand the silence of the British who have allowed you to correspond with me on this unpleasant matter, and they themselves remain silent, although it is known that the initiative in this whole affair with the negotiations in Bern belong to the British.

I understand that there are certain advantages for the Anglo-American troops as a result of these separate negotiations in Bern or in some other place since the Anglo-American troops get the possibility to advance into the heart of Germany almost without any resistance on the part of the Germans, but why was it necessary to conceal this from the Russians, and why your Allies – the Russians, were not notified?

As a result of this at the present moment the Germans on the Western front in fact have ceased the war against England and the United States. At the same time the Germans continue the war with Russia, the Ally of England and the United States. It is understandable that such a situation can in no way serve the cause of preservation of the strengthening of trust between our countries.

I have already written to you in my previous message and consider it necessary to repeat it here that I personally and my colleagues would have never made such a *risky* step, being aware that a momentary advantage, no matter what it would be, is fading before the principle [*sic*] advantage on *the preservation and* strengthening of trust among the Allies.

The president was now in Warm Springs, Georgia, where he arrived on Good Friday, 30 March, for what his medical advisers fervently hoped would be a period of rest and recuperation as he prepared for his keynote address to the founding conference of the United Nations Organization in San Francisco on 25 April. In Washington, his advisers were shaken by Stalin's tone and language. 'It may be assumed that you have not been fully informed' sounded like diplomatic parlance for calling Roosevelt a liar. Leahy felt it 'clearly shows Soviet suspicion and distrust of our motives of our promises, a sad prospect of [for] any successful cooperative agreement at the approaching political conference at San Francisco'. He forwarded Stalin's message to Roosevelt, who instructed him to 'take the necessary steps for the preparation of an immediate reply'.

Using a draft from Marshall's office, which Leahy revised, a text was sent to FDR, who approved it unchanged. In his diary, Leahy called it 'a sharp reply' to Stalin's message, which 'approaches as closely to a rebuke as is permitted in diplomatic exchanges between States'.[104]

Phrases such as 'bitter resentment' and 'vile misrepresentations' catch the eye. Yet it is also clear that these bold assertions masked some economy with the truth. Take, for instance, the statement, 'No negotiations were held at Bern.' This was literally true in the formal sense of 'negotiations', but the White House files contain a 'triple priority' dispatch from the OSS in Bern, on 1 April, Easter Sunday, which summarized recent contacts and stated that, assuming no further delays, 'Wolff should come to a meeting sometime Monday or early Tuesday.'[105]

Roosevelt to Stalin, sent 4 April 1945, received 5 April 1945[106]

I have received with astonishment your message of April 3 containing an allegation that arrangements which were made between Field Marshals Alexander and Kesselring at Bern, 'permitted the Anglo-American troops to advance to the East and the Anglo-Americans promised in return to ease for the Germans the peace terms.'

In my previous messages to you in regard to the attempts made in Bern to arrange a conference to discuss a surrender of the German Army in Italy, I have told you that,

(1) No negotiations were held in Bern;
(2) That the meeting had no political implications whatever;
(3) That in any surrender of the enemy army in Italy there could be no violation of our agreed principle of unconditional surrender;
(4) That Soviet officers would be welcomed at any meeting that might be arranged to discuss surrender.

For the advantage of our common war effort against Germany, which today gives excellent promise of an early success in a disintegration of the German armies, I must continue to assume that you have the same high confidence in my truthfulness and reliability that I have always had in yours.

I have also a full appreciation of the effect your gallant army has had in making possible a crossing of the Rhine by the forces under General Eisenhower and the effect that your forces will have hereafter on the eventual collapse of the German resistance to our combined attacks.

I have complete confidence in General Eisenhower and know that he certainly would inform me before entering into any agreement with the Germans. He is instructed to demand and will demand unconditional surrender of enemy troops that may be defeated on his front. Our advances on the Western Front are due to military action. Their speed has been attributable mainly to the terrific impact of our air power resulting in destruction of German communications, and to the fact that Eisenhower was able to cripple the bulk of the German Forces on the Western Front while they were still West of the Rhine.

I am certain that there were no negotiations in Bern at any time, and I feel that your information to that effect must have come from German sources which have made persistent efforts to create dissension between us in order to escape in some measure responsibility for their war crimes. If that was Wolff's purpose in Bern your message proves that he has had some success.

With a confidence in your belief in my personal reliability and in my determination to bring about together with you an unconditional surrender of the Nazis, it is astonishing that a belief seems to have reached the Soviet Government that I have entered into an agreement with the enemy without first obtaining your full agreement.

Finally I would say this, it would be one of the great tragedies of history if at the very moment of the victory, now within our grasp, such distrust, such lack of faith should prejudice the entire undertaking after the colossal losses of life, materiel and treasure involved.

Frankly I cannot avoid a feeling of bitter resentment toward your informers, whoever they are, for such vile misrepresentations of my actions or those of my trusted subordinates.

The tone of Roosevelt's message delighted Churchill, who had become distressed at the growing weakness of his 'poor friend'. The PM told his wife on 6 April: 'Many of the telegrams I get from him are clearly the work of others around him.' However, said Churchill, the message to Stalin 'certainly ends up with a flash of his old fire, and is about the hottest thing I have seen so far in diplomatic intercourse.' Later he made the same point in his memoirs: 'I felt that although Mr. Roosevelt did not draft the whole message he might well have added this final touch himself ... it seemed like Roosevelt himself in anger.'[107] Little did Churchill know that the ending, like most of the 'personal' telegrams he received from FDR in 1945, had been penned by presidential aides.[108]

Contrary to Stalin's suspicions about the British origins of 'Crossword', London was actually playing second fiddle and indeed was being kept out of the loop. The British embassy in Washington was simply told that the State Department and the US Joint Chiefs were 'ignoring Molotov's letter' of the 22nd. Not until after Stalin and Roosevelt's blistering exchange about Bern on 3–4 April was Churchill copied in – and only then after a formal request by Leahy to the president himself. All this suggests that Britain may have been deliberately excluded by the USA because of its preference for a more transparent approach to the Soviets, and perhaps because of fears about Soviet agents in high places in London. When Churchill discovered his exclusion, he did not conceal his irritation from the Cabinet on 5 April. But he rallied round FDR by sending Stalin a verbose message of explanation, which ended by repudiating the aspersions of bad faith and stating: 'I associate myself and my colleagues with the last sentence of the President's reply.'[109]

The coordinated messages from Roosevelt and Churchill on the Polish question did not alter the Soviet stance. The next meeting of the Molotov–Harriman–Clark Kerr commission on 2 April got nowhere and the Western ambassadors questioned the point of continuing its work, given what Clark Kerr called Molotov's 'obstinacy and perversity'.[110] But Churchill proposed waiting for Stalin's response to the 'very serious telegrams' he and Roosevelt had sent. 'If the responses are wholly hostile,' he told Lord Cranborne – a hawkish Cabinet critic of his policy towards the USSR – 'I think it is most unlikely that Russia will come to San Francisco. She will prefer to fight it out on the side of the Lublin Poles.' In which case, Churchill continued, the Conference should definitely go ahead. 'Anthony and I consider that it would be a great blow to our cause and prestige and also to the cause of a free Poland if the mere sulkiness of Russia prevented this World Conference from going ahead. The Russians would feel that their mere abstention paralysed world action.' Indeed, Churchill admitted that although 'never been at all keen on this Conference' – it being very much the president's obsession – if the Soviets tried to block it 'I would in that event become very keen upon it', in order to demonstrate that 'all the United Nations, with Britain and the United States at their head' were not 'put off their stroke by a mere gesture of insolence by Stalin and Molotov'.[111] The Americans also did not want to postpone the conference and were on tenterhooks for Stalin's response. Harriman – now desperate to return to Washington to drum up support for his tough line towards the Soviets – was told by Stettinius to stay in Moscow till Stalin's replies were received.[112]

On Poland, the Soviet leader responded with two separate messages on 7 April – in detail to the president, more briefly to the PM plus a copy of the message to Roosevelt. Stalin was unyielding, and blamed the face-off on the Western ambassadors, who had 'departed from the principles of the Crimea

Conference' by effectively repudiating the Provisional Government and trying to draw in Poles who did not accept what had been agreed at Yalta.

Stalin to Roosevelt, sent 7 April 1945, received 9 April 1945[113]

In connection with your message of April 1 I consider it necessary to make the following remarks on the question of Poland.

Matters on the Polish question have really reached a dead end.

Where are the reasons for it? The reasons for it are that the Ambassadors of the United States and England in Moscow – members of the Moscow Commission have departed from the principles of the Crimea Conference and have introduced into the matter new elements not provided by the Crimea Conference.

Namely: a) At the Crimea Conference all three of us considered the Provisional Government of Poland as the government functioning in Poland at the present time which is subject to reconstruction and which should serve as kernel of the new government of national unity. But the Ambassadors of the United States and England in Moscow depart from this principle, ignore the existence of the Provisional Polish Government, do not notice it, at the best – put a sign of equality between singletons from Poland and from London and the Provisional Government of Poland. Besides, they consider that the reconstruction of Provisional Government should be understood as its liquidation and formation of an entirely new government. Besides, the matter reached such a state when Mr. Harriman stated in the Moscow Commission: 'It is possible that no member of the Provisional Government will be included in the composition of the Polish government of national unity.'

Naturally, such a position of the American and British Ambassadors cannot but cause indignation on the part of the Polish Provisional Government. As regards the Soviet Union, it certainly cannot agree with such a position, as it would mean direct violation of the decisions of the Crimea Conference.

b) At the Crimea Conference all three of us agreed that not more than five persons from Poland and three persons from London should be called for consultation. But the Ambassadors of the United States and England in Moscow have departed from this position and demand that each member of the Moscow Commission be given the right to invite an unlimited number of people from Poland and from London.

Naturally, the Soviet Government could not agree with this as the summons of people should be carried out according to decisions of the Crimea Conference, not by individual members of the Commission, but by the Commission as a whole, namely by the Commission as such. But the request of an unlimited number of persons summoned for consultation contradicts the plans of the Crimea Conference.

c) The Soviet Government proceeds from the fact that in accordance with the meaning of the decisions of the Crimea Conference such Polish leaders should be invited for consultations who, firstly, recognize the decisions of the Crimea Conference, including the decision on the Curzon Line, and, secondly, are really striving to establish friendly relations between Poland and the Soviet Union. The Soviet Government insists on this as blood of the Soviet troops abundantly shed for the liberation of Poland and the fact that in the course of the last 30 years the territory of Poland has been used by the enemy twice for attack upon Russia, – all this obliges the Soviet Government to strive that the relations between the Soviet Union and Poland be friendly.

But the Ambassadors of the United States and England in Moscow do not take this into consideration and strive that Polish leaders should be invited for consultation regardless of their attitude towards the decisions of the Crimea Conference and the Soviet Union.

Such, in my opinion, are the reasons hindering the solution of the Polish question on the basis of mutual agreement.

In order to leave the dead end and reach a harmonious decision it is necessary, in my opinion, to undertake the following steps:

1) To agree that the reconstruction of the Provisional Polish Government means not its liquidation but just its reconstruction by way of broadening it, bearing in mind that the kernel of the future Polish Government of National Unity should be the Provisional Polish Government.

2) To return to the projectings of the Crimea Conference and to summon only eight Polish leaders, five of whom should be called from Poland and three from London.

3) To agree that, under any conditions, a consultation with representatives of the Provisional Polish Government should be carried out, bearing in mind that this consultation with them should be carried out first of all as the Provisional Polish Government is the greatest force in Poland as compared to those singletons who will be called from London and from Poland and whose influence on the population of Poland cannot be compared with the tremendous influence which the Provisional Polish Government enjoys in Poland.

I draw your attention to this point as, in my opinion, any other decision on this point can be perceived in Poland as an insult to the Polish people and as an attempt to force upon Poland a government formed without taking into consideration the public opinion of Poland.

4) To summon for consultation from Poland and from London only such leaders who recognize decisions of the Crimea Conference on Poland and are really striving to establish friendly relations between Poland and the Soviet Union.

5) To carry out the reconstruction of the Provisional Polish Government by substituting some of the present ministers of the Provisional Government by new ministers from among Polish leaders not participating in the Provisional Government.

As regards the numerical correlation of old and new ministers in the composition of the Polish Government of national unity, there could be established approximately a similar correlation which was realized in respect to the Government of Yugoslavia.

I think that, taking into consideration the above-stated remarks, a harmonious decision on the Polish question can be reached in a short time.

Stalin sent Churchill a copy of this cable, plus a briefer message answering some point the PM had made. In this he hinted at a possible opening, by offering to receive Mikołajczyk in Moscow (subject to his public recognition of the Yalta decisions on Poland). Interestingly, this offer appeared only in the message to Churchill – seen as the main broker over the London Poles – and the relevant paragraph was inserted late in the second draft.[114] Mikołajczyk was still disliked in Moscow: writing from the Soviet mission in London, Lebedev told Molotov that intercepted correspondence between Mikołajczyk and the leaders of the Polish Home Army had 'exposed him as an ardent enemy of the USSR'.[115] But Stalin clearly assumed he could make a token gesture to Churchill on his favourite Pole without affecting the preponderance of Moscow's men in the Warsaw government.

The final paragraph of this message to Churchill struck a different note. It was inserted by Molotov, apparently as dictation from Stalin. 'I had an agreeable conversation with Mrs Churchill who made a deep impression upon me. She gave me a present from you. Allow me to express my heartfelt thanks for this present.'[116]

Clementine Churchill visited the USSR from 2 April to 11 May as head of her Aid to Russia Fund, on which she had worked for most of the wartime alliance. At the end of March, Churchill had considered postponing her trip because of all the tensions, but he decided to let it go ahead as 'a sign of personal good will', he told Eden.[117] The first visit of this kind raised delicate protocol issues, which the Soviets resolved with great courtesy. The PM's wife was assigned a special train on which she toured the country – visiting Leningrad, Stalingrad, Odessa, Kursk, the Caucasus and the Crimea. Before leaving Moscow, she was received 'most amiably' on 3 April by Molotov, who 'referred to present difficulties but said they would pass and Anglo-Soviet friendship remain' and was then the guest of honour at a 'lovely banquet' hosted by the Molotovs. On 7 April, Stalin himself welcomed Clementine, offering warm thanks for all her fundraising. This was the day he sent his message to Churchill, so the paragraph must have been added at the last minute. The PM's gift, mentioned there, was a gold fountain pen. 'My husband,' Clementine declared, 'wishes me to express the hope that you will write him many more friendly messages with it.' According to her testimony, Stalin accepted it with a smile, but added: 'I only write with a pencil.' The PM was much flattered by his wife's reception in Moscow but found it all hard to square with the fraught state of diplomacy – cabling her on 6 April: 'What puzzles me is the inconsistency.'[118]

In his other message of 7 April, on the Bern affair, Stalin was more conciliatory – assuring the president that he had never doubted his integrity. The accusations of a secret Allied deal with the Nazis were also dropped. Information showing Moscow that the OSS's Swiss contacts had by then stalled – obtained via both Alexander and Soviet intelligence – apparently played a role. Nevertheless, Stalin continued to treat this as an issue of principle: transparency between allies. He also defended the reputation of his 'informers' and reminded Roosevelt of mistakes by US agents – citing specifically information provided by General Marshall that was later refuted by Soviet intelligence.

Stalin to Roosevelt, sent 7 April 1945, received 9 April 1945[119]

I have received your message of April 5.

In my message of April 3 I spoke not about honesty and dependability. I never doubted your honesty and dependability, as well as the honesty and dependability of Mr. Churchill. I speak about the fact that in the course of this correspondence between us has been revealed a difference of opinions as to what can an Ally allow himself to do in respect to the other Ally and what he should not allow himself to do. We, Russians, believe that in the present situation at the fronts when the enemy is confronted by the inevitability of capitulation, at any meeting with the Germans on questions of capitulation by representatives of one of the Allies arrangements have to be made for the participation in this meeting of representatives of the other Ally. At any rate this is absolutely necessary if this Ally is seeking participation in such a meeting. Americans, however, and the Englishmen think differently, considering the Russian point of view wrong. Proceeding from this fact they rejected the Russians the right of participation in the meeting with the Germans in Switzerland. I have already written to you and consider it not unnecessary to repeat that the Russians in a similar situation under no circumstances would have refused the Americans and Englishmen the right for participation in such a meeting. I continue to consider the Russian point of view as the only right one as it excludes any possibility of mutual distrust and does not permit the enemy to sow distrust among us.

It is difficult to agree that lack of resistance on the part of the Germans on the Western front can be explained only that they are defeated. The Germans have on the Eastern Front 147 divisions. They could without harm to their cause take from the Eastern front 15–20 divisions and shift them to the aid of their troops on the Western front. However, the Germans did not do it and are not doing it. They continue to fight savagely with the Russians for some unknown junction Zemlianitsa in Czechoslovakia which they need as much as a dead man needs poultices, but surrender without any resistance such important towns in Central Germany as Osnabrük [sic], Mannheim and Kassel. Don't you agree that such a behavior of the Germans is more than strange and incomprehensible.

As regards my informers, I may assure you that they are very honest and modest people who carry out their duties accurately and have no intentions of insulting anyone. These people have been manyfold [sic] tested by us by their deeds. Judge for yourself. In February, 1945, General Marshal has given a number of important information to the General Staff of the Soviet troops, where he, on the basis of data he had on hand, warned the Russians that in March there will be two serious counter-attacks of the Germans on the Eastern front one of which will be directed from Pomerania on Torun and the other from the region of Moravska Ostrava on Lodz. In fact, however, it proved that the principal blow of the Germans was being prepared and was realized not in the above-mentioned regions but in an entirely different region, namely in the region of Lake Balaton, to the South-West of Budapest. As it is known the Germans have concentrated in this region up to 35 divisions, including 11 tank divisions. This was one of the most serious blows in the course of the war with such great concentration of tank forces. Marshal Tolbukhin succeeded in avoiding a catastrophe and in complete defeat of the Germans later, because my informers have uncovered, true a little late, this plan of the main blow of the Germans and immediately informed Marshal Tolbukhin. Thus I had another occasion to convince myself in the accuracy and knowledge of Soviet informers.

For your orientation in this matter I am enclosing a letter of the Chief of the General Staff of the Red Army, Army General Antonov, addressed to Major-General Dean [sic].[120]

A copy of this message was sent to Churchill, along with a brief separate message telling the PM that it would be 'very difficult' to continue their 'confidential communications' if he treated 'every frank statement of mine as offensive'. It was a neat put-down. In short, the Soviet leader definitely did not recant, but decided to defuse the Bern incident, lest it rupture Big Three relations.

Stalin to Churchill, sent 7 April 1945, received 7 April 1945[121]

Your message of 5th April received. In my message of 7th April to the President, which I am sending to you also, I have already replied to all the fundamental points raised in your message in relation to the negotiations in Switzerland. On the other questions raised in your message I consider it necessary to make the following remarks.

Neither I nor Molotov had any intention of 'blackening' anyone. It is not a matter of wanting to 'blacken' anyone but of our having developed differing points of view as regards the rights and obligations of an ally. You will see from my message to the President that the Russian point of view on this question is the correct one, as it guarantees each ally's rights and deprives the enemy of any opportunity of sowing discord between us.

My messages are personal and strictly confidential. This makes it possible to speak one's mind clearly and frankly. That is the advantage of confidential communications. If, however, you are going to regard every frank statement of mine as offensive, it will make this kind of communication very difficult. I can assure you that I had and have no intention of offending anyone.

In all three capitals, one senses that the leaders drew breath. It had been a torrid few weeks.

*****

Churchill was the first to make a move. He wanted to exploit the possible opening about Mikołajczyk, asking Eden to urge the Pole to publicly state that he accepted the Yalta decisions about borders and that his attitude to the USSR was friendly. But he did not want to reply to Stalin until he knew the president's reaction to the 7 April telegram on Poland. 'We forced the pace and did most of the drafting last time,' he told Eden – referring to the 31 March message – 'and now I think it would be good for him to let us know how he feels.' So on 11 April, the PM asked Roosevelt for his 'views about how we should answer Stalin as soon as possible' – noting that he had to address the Commons on Poland on the 19th. He added, 'I have a feeling that they do not want to quarrel with us, and your telegram about CROSSWORD may have seriously and deservedly perturbed them.' Forwarding Stalin's message about Bern the same day, Churchill judged this 'as near as they can get to an apology'.[122]

Roosevelt also wanted to heal the breach, although not without some hesitation – as is shown by some neglected documents in the US archives. The president's first response to Stalin's message about Bern was to instruct Leahy on the 9th: 'I think no reply necessary unless you or General Marshall want to make reply.'[123] By now the military's position had softened somewhat under the sobering effect of the Soviet reaction to 'Crossword'. On 5 April, the Joint Strategic Survey Committee (JSSC) – whose role was to think beyond operations and consider the broad interface of security and foreign policies – expressed grave doubts about the recent trajectory of relations with the USSR. The committee emphasized that the preservation of the wartime alliance must remain the overriding goal and spoke out against the retaliatory approach advocated by Harriman and Deane which had underpinned the JCS's tough line over POWs and Bern. On 5 April, the JSSC even suggested that the president should send Stalin a supplementary message about the 'highly regrettable and profound misunderstanding between us' and invite a group of senior Soviet officers to visit the Western Front to observe operations and satisfy themselves about the integrity of the Allied leadership. Leahy rejected the idea of another presidential missive: that would weaken the force of Roosevelt's letter of 4 April. But he was sympathetic to the JSSC's concerns.[124]

This new mood affected reactions to Stalin's 7 April letter about Bern, which was received two days later. On the 11th, Leahy sent Roosevelt a draft response and the president approved it without amendment. The cable confirming approval, sent by his secretary in Warm Springs, arrived at the White House just after midnight and the message was immediately despatched to Harriman for delivery to the Kremlin. A couple of hours later, the White House also despatched an answer to Churchill's inquiries about how to respond to Stalin. But this message had been composed by the president himself at Warm Springs – one of the very few Big Three messages he authored in 1945. In it Roosevelt told Churchill: 'I would minimize the general Soviet problem as much as possible because these problems, in one form or another, seem to arise every day as in the case of the Bern meeting. We must be firm, however, and our course thus far is correct.'[125]

Just two sentences, and not entirely coherent – the double use of 'problem' – but nevertheless both eloquent and authentic. On one level, the president was urging the PM to play down recent tensions as much as possible in the Commons, bearing in mind that the San Francisco conference was only two weeks away. But more generally, Roosevelt was expressing his consistent view that the big issue was an enduring relationship with the USSR; all else was secondary. He had made his point about Bern, and Stalin had backed off; so it was time to move on. This was also the line Leahy had taken in the cable for Stalin that the president had just approved. We do not know whether the president and the chief of staff had communicated over the phone, but they were certainly working in concert.

Roosevelt to Stalin, sent 11 April 1945, received 13 April 1945[126]

Thank you for your frank explanation of the Soviet point of view of the Bern incident which now appears to have faded into the past without having accomplished any useful purpose.

There must not, in any event, be mutual distrust and minor misunderstandings of this character should not arise in the future. I feel sure that when our armies make contact in Germany and join in a fully coordinated offensive the Nazi Armies will disintegrate.

There was a revealing sequel, because Harriman had the audacity to query the content of the message. The ambassador had by now decided that Roosevelt's policy towards the Soviets was fundamentally wrong. It was he who had urged 'our interpretation' of the Yalta accords on Poland; he had also turned the murky issue of POWs into a test of confidence. That in turn had emboldened the JCS deception of both the Soviets and the British over Bern. Whereas Roosevelt did not want the succession of 'problems' with Moscow to poison relations, Harriman believed those relations were now irredeemably poisoned by the Kremlin. He was obsessed by the idea that US policy had become driven by 'fear of the Soviet Union' – a phrase that kept recurring in a long telegram for the State Department that he drafted on 10 April. In this he also wrote: 'The President at great inconvenience and risk to himself paid the highest possible compliment to the Soviet Union by coming to Yalta. It seems clear that this magnanimous act on his part has been interpreted as a sign of weakness and Stalin and his associates are acting accordingly.'[127]

In the end, the ambassador did not send his diatribe. But he did take it upon himself to hold up delivery of Roosevelt's message to Stalin. In a cable sent from Moscow on Thursday morning, 12 April, he suggested that the president might wish to concert a joint response with Churchill and also change the wording and thrust of his message by deleting the word 'minor' in the second sentence. 'I must confess,' declared Harriman, 'that the misunderstanding appeared to me to be of a major character and the use of the word "minor" might well be misinterpreted here.' Leahy, however, had little doubt of the president's mind – especially after seeing FDR's own message to Churchill the previous night. He quickly drafted a brisk reply telling Harriman there was no reason to delay delivery, or to amend the content: 'I do not wish to delete the word "minor" as it is my desire to consider the Berne misunderstanding a minor incident.' Roosevelt sent his approval and the rebuke was duly transmitted to the ambassador that afternoon. The messages to Stalin, Churchill and Harriman – composed via this bizarre teamwork by Roosevelt and Leahy – encapsulate the president's policy towards the Soviet Union.[128]

The Map Room log sheet for the cable to Harriman on 12 April contains the following brief historical note: 'Of interest is the fact that this is the last message sent by President Roosevelt. Approved by the President at approximately 12:45 CWT [Central War Time], it was transmitted to the Map Room at 13:06 CWT, at about the same time the President was stricken.'[129]

EPILOGUE

THE NEWS OF ROOSEVELT's death reached Churchill around midnight on 12 April, as he worked on his papers. The PM's distress was evident to all around him. He wrote to Eleanor Roosevelt, the president's widow, 'I have lost a dear and cherished friendship which was forged in the fire of war.' Churchill's first reaction was to fly to the United States to pay his respects at the funeral and also to bend the ear of the new president, Harry S. Truman – a former senator with no executive experience, whom the ailing Roosevelt, characteristically, had done nothing to prepare for possible succession. A plane was scheduled to leave at 8.30 p.m. on the 13th, but at 7.45 p.m. Cadogan noted in his diary, 'no decision reached – P.M. said he would decide at aerodrome'. At the last minute, Churchill made up his mind not to go – for reasons that have never been entirely clear. He told the king it was because he and Eden would have been out of the country simultaneously – the foreign secretary was going to the San Francisco conference – and he also mentioned the ceremonies in London to commemorate the president and 'the press of work' which was 'very great'. But in December 1941 Churchill had felt no qualms about being out of the country at the same time as Eden, after Pearl Harbor, when they embarked on their simultaneous missions to Washington and Moscow. Domestic politics may have been more of a factor than he admitted, because the Labour party had given notice that it would not continue the wartime coalition once Germany had been defeated. Churchill wrote to Clementine on 9 April: 'I think there is very little doubt that the Government will break up shortly.' At any event, in his memoirs Churchill expressed regret that he had not attended the funeral, or talked to Truman when the new president was still finding his feet. But that was written with Cold War hindsight.[1]

In Moscow, Ambassador Harriman heard the news just after 1 a.m. on 13 April. He immediately phoned Molotov, who insisted on coming to the US embassy. He arrived at 3 a.m. and stayed for some time, talking about Roosevelt's role in the war and his plans for the peace. The foreign minister 'seemed deeply moved and disturbed', Harriman cabled Washington. 'I have never heard Molotov talk so earnestly.' At 8 p.m. that evening, the ambassador went to the Kremlin. 'When I entered Marshal Stalin's office,' he told Washington,

> I noticed that he was obviously deeply distressed at the news of the death of President Roosevelt. He greeted me in silence and stood holding my hand for about 30 seconds before asking me to sit down. He then asked many questions about the President and the circumstances which brought about his death.

Harriman explained in general terms about Roosevelt's heart problems. (Reading between the lines, one wonders if the suspicious dictator sensed foul play.) At any event, Harriman emphasized that Truman would continue Roosevelt's policies and said that the new president was 'a man Marshal Stalin would like – he was a man of action and not of words'. Stalin interjected, 'President Roosevelt has died but his cause must live on. We shall support President Truman with all our forces and all our will.' Seizing the moment, Harriman made a suggestion that he had been mulling over all day. He said that 'the most effective way to assure the American public and the world at large of the desire to continue collaboration with us and the other United Nations would be for Mr Molotov to go to the United States at this time' – calling on the new president in Washington and then attending, however briefly, the opening ceremonies of the UN in San Francisco. Stalin and Molotov had a brief discussion about the dates of the conference and of the Supreme Soviet and then asked Harriman if he was speaking purely personally. 'I made it clear that I was,' the ambassador noted, 'but added that I felt completely confident that I was expressing the views of the President and the Secretary of State.' On the basis of those assurances, Stalin said that Molotov's trip to the USA – 'though difficult at this time' – would be arranged.[2]

It was an adroit piece of diplomacy by the ambassador, using the shock caused by Roosevelt's death to jolt Soviet–American relations out of the confrontational mode that had developed during March. Molotov duly attended the founding conference of the United Nations on 25 April, together with Eden and Stettinius, and Truman delivered the opening address in Roosevelt's stead. Of course, the UN soon became moribund as a peace-keeping organization during the Cold War, because the 'policemen' fell out with each other. But the fact that the USSR had joined the organization in that brief window of good-will after Roosevelt's death meant that the Soviets were formally part of the postwar international order, rather than outsiders, as had been the case with the League of Nations after the Bolshevik Revolution. To bring Russia in from the cold had always been Roosevelt's dream while he lived. He achieved a part of it in and through his death.

The president had died less than a month before victory in Europe. That climactic moment of the Alliance was not, however, without controversy. By 7 May, the German armies in the west were ready to surrender and Eisenhower signed the appropriate documents at Reims in the early hours of that morning, with all fighting to cease at one minute past midnight on 8–9 May. Mindful of the Bern furore, he made sure that a Soviet representative was present, albeit without official authority from Moscow. Ike wanted to make a public announcement that evening, because the orders to lay down their arms would be transmitted *en clair* and could not be kept secret. Churchill was also keen to do so, because the news was leaking out in Britain and crowds were beginning to gather in London. But Stalin was determined that there should be a single grand surrender in Berlin, where the Red Army was still dealing with considerable German resistance. According to Zhukov, Stalin phoned him in Berlin on 7 May to say that Reims should be treated as 'preliminary' surrender. 'It was the Soviet people who bore the main brunt of the war, not the Allies,' he told Zhukov. 'Therefore the Germans should sign the surrender before the Supreme Command of all the countries of the anti-Hitler coalition, and not just before the Supreme Command of the Allied Forces.' And this must be done in Berlin, 'the centre of Nazi aggression'. With Churchill unwilling to restrain popular celebrations any further, Victory in Europe (VE) Day was celebrated in Britain and America on 8 May – as indeed it was informally by Soviet troops in Berlin. But the formal surrender at Zhukov's headquarters in the Berlin suburb of Karlshorst did not take place until just after midnight on 9 May, as Stalin had decreed. Henceforth, the Western Allies have commemorated 8 May as victory day, not 9 May as in the USSR and its successor states. In 1945, as in 1941, the Big Three powers were still fighting their own separate wars.[3]

The downfall of the Third Reich was marked by an exchange of grandiloquent messages. Churchill sent Stalin 'heartfelt greetings' from 'our island home' on the Soviet Union's 'splendid victory' and reiterated his 'firm belief that on friendship and understanding between the British and Russian peoples depends the future of mankind'. Stalin replied by expressing his 'confidence in continued successful and happy development in the post-war period of the friendly relations that have taken shape between our countries during the war'. Truman, in his message to Stalin, extolled 'the ability of a freedom-loving and supremely courageous people to crush the evil forces of barbarism', while the Soviet leader said that the coalition of the three powers would 'go down in history as a model military alliance between our peoples'.[4]

Behind the gilded rhetoric, however, the mood was darkening. In Washington, on 23 April, Truman gave Molotov a stern dressing-down on Poland, instructing him to stick to the Yalta agreements. This piece of diplomatic theatre reflected the advice of Harriman – who flew back home specially to push his tough-line policy – but also the new president's psychological need, having suddenly stepped into a dead man's shoes, to show he wasn't going to be pushed around. 'I let him have it,' Truman bragged afterwards: 'A straight one-two to the jaw.'[5] In similar vein a few weeks later, on 18 May, Churchill gave Ambassador Gusev a 'brisk talking to' about Poland. He then instructed his chiefs of staff to prepare a contingency plan for the use of force to get 'a square deal for Poland'. The hypothetical start date for hostilities against the USSR was 1 July 1945. The astonished planners labelled this 'Operation Unthinkable'. Not only because it was inconceivable less than two weeks after victory to imagine turning against one of Britain's wartime allies, in the process even rearming the former German enemy, but also because the chances of success were zero. The planners explained that a surprise attack by forty-seven British and US divisions around Dresden might force Soviet concessions over Poland, but it would result in a full-scale war, from which victory was 'quite impossible', to quote Brooke.[6]

That Churchill could even entertain such an amazing idea – in total defiance of the lessons of the Eastern Front in 1941–45 – surely reveals his utter exhaustion after five years of war leadership. And it also hints, perhaps, at the loss of Roosevelt as a balancing element in the PM's relations with Moscow. Their constructive tension over Poland had been a case in point – Churchill recurrently pressing the 'debt of honour' to the Poles, Roosevelt focusing almost cynically on the imperatives of Big Three cooperation. Many of their messages to Stalin had been drafted transatlantically, with the president often tempering the PM's addiction to words and impulse for action. Churchill's affection for the courageous Wheelchair President was unquestioned. Talking about Roosevelt on one occasion in 1947, he broke off, looked out of the window and murmured, 'How I loved that man!'[7] As for Stalin, the emotional 13 April volte-face about San Francisco hints at a particular respect for Roosevelt that is evident at times in the correspondence – both in the positive touches and also in the rarity of those tetchy, sarcastic or even rude messages that Stalin often sent to Churchill. Blasts such as 13 January 1943 or 3 April 1945 were very much the exception in his correspondence with Roosevelt. Stalin never trusted anyone, but FDR seemed a reliable factor in an uncertain world. In short, even though the president had often been the silent partner in their epistolary triangle, his sudden death seems to have exposed his importance for the other two.

Yet that is no reason to exaggerate the transition from Roosevelt to Truman.[8] Despite the dressing-down of Molotov and the concept of operation 'Unthinkable', in reality Big Three relations in 1945 were erratic. When Truman finally found time in May to read the Yalta agreements, he realized how elastic they were. Veering now under the influence of Roosevelt's old buddy Joseph E. Davies, the president decided to defuse the long-running argument over Poland. He sent the ailing Harry Hopkins to Moscow to agree a token enlargement of the Polish government with a few non-communists, which paved the way for US recognition. Churchill had no choice but to offer grudging acquiescence. And the PM, for all his sombre talk of an 'iron curtain' coming down across Europe – a phrase he used in a cable to Truman on 12 May – had not abandoned his personal faith in Stalin. He and other British policymakers blamed recent problems on Molotov or the 'Party Bosses' or the 'Army Marshals'. At root, Churchill's goal was to reach a settlement with the Soviet leader at another summit, negotiating from what he hoped would be a position of strength.[9]

Yet that meeting was postponed through the summer, and by the time it did take place at Potsdam at the end of July 1945, British influence was on the wane (plate 24). The principal deals, over German reparations and Poland's western borders, were stitched up by Truman's secretary of state, Jimmy Byrnes, a political fixer, with Britain on the sidelines. And Churchill himself was no longer in power. The result of the British election was announced on 26 July, right in the middle of the Potsdam conference. It was a surprise landslide victory for Attlee and the Labour party, and a humiliating defeat for the Tories. Churchill was devastated. But the outcome was understandable. As he lamented during the election campaign, 'I have no message for them now'. Having given 'the lion's roar' in 1940, he had lost his voice for a people who yearned for peace and a 'New Jerusalem'. Yet, digging deep, he told one aide after the election: 'They are perfectly entitled to vote as they please. This is democracy. This is what we've been fighting for.'[10]

To Stalin, of course, such a concept of democracy was inconceivable, and the abrupt political demise of Churchill – so soon after the death of

Roosevelt – removed another 'known known' from the international scene. It has been justly observed that the Soviet leader had 'lost his two equals', his two familiar partners, just as the war ended and what had been a game of 'classic trilateral diplomacy' degenerated into a complex 'international morass', with a plethora of new faces and new issues. Pre-eminent among the unsettling novelties was the news on 6 August that the USA now possessed the atomic bomb, thereby rendering obsolete all conventional notions of the balance of power.[11]

For Churchill, the election defeat seemed almost like a sentence of death. As the family lunched in sepulchral gloom on 26 July, Clementine – aware of her husband's utter weariness – declared brightly that 'it may well be a blessing in disguise'. Looking at her, he grunted, 'At the moment it seems quite effectively disguised.'[12] Yet Clemmie was right. After a few months of recuperation, Winston found his voice again. First, with speeches in 1946 that echoed around the world, notably Fulton (about relations with America and Russia) and Strasbourg (on Franco-German rapprochement and European unity). And then with six volumes of war memoirs between 1948 and 1954, grandly entitled *The Second World War*, which left an enduring Churchillian imprint on recent history. These also prompted Stalin to embark on publication of the Big Three's full correspondence – a project that he had intimated to de Gaulle in December 1944[13] – as a way of getting on record the Soviet side of the story. And so the battle for history was joined.

*****

Yet the Churchill–Stalin epistolary relationship did not end in July 1945, and this story provides a fascinating coda to 1941–45. Aware that Stalin had been taken ill during the Potsdam conference, the defeated Churchill sent him a farewell message of good wishes from London. 'Thank you for your telegram,' the Soviet leader replied on 1 August. 'My indisposition was slight and I am again feeling well. Greetings. J. Stalin.' As we shall see, Churchill did not forget that message. He also kept up the wartime practice of sending birthday greetings, cabling 'Many happy returns of the day' in December 1945. 'I thank you for your good wishes on my birthday,' Stalin replied. 'I was on leave and I regret that I am only now sending you belatedly my best wishes on your birthday.'[14]

The idea of Stalin going 'on leave' was, of course, something of an eyebrow-raiser. But the war had taken its toll of the Soviet leader, just as it had of his two wartime allies. He was suffering from arteriosclerosis – the disease which reduces the flow of blood to the brain and had caused Roosevelt's fatal stroke – and this accentuated Stalin's obsessive suspiciousness and oscillations of mood. On 9 October 1945, he voted himself a vacation and took off to his cliff-top dacha near Sochi on the Black Sea for a couple of months. As news leaked out, the Western press was full of speculation about his health, including reports of a heart attack, and about a possible successor – as Stalin soon knew, being an avid reader of summaries of the foreign press. Molotov was left in charge in Moscow but he had to account for his actions every day to the Boss, who kept him under 'remote control', just as during the foreign minister's 'go-between' visits to Churchill and Roosevelt in 1942. Always ready to assume the worst, Stalin began to brood about the ambitions of 'Comrade Molotov'. And it was Churchill who unwittingly brought matters to a head.

On 7 November 1945, the former PM spoke in the Commons in a debate on relations with the USA and especially its possession of the atomic bomb – what he called 'a sacred trust for the maintenance of peace'. But on what was the anniversary of the 1917 revolution, Churchill carefully prefaced his remarks with a lengthy passage about 'the deep sense of gratitude we owe to the noble Russian people and valiant Soviet Armies, who, when they were attacked by Hitler, poured out their blood and suffered immeasurable torments until absolute victory was gained' and urged that 'these feelings of comradeship and friendship, which have developed between the British and Russian peoples, should be not only preserved but rapidly expanded'. Churchill went on:

> I wish to say how glad we all are to know and feel that Generalissimo Stalin is still strongly holding the helm and steering his tremendous ship. Personally, I cannot feel anything but the most lively admiration for this truly great man, the father of his country, the ruler of its destinies in times of peace, and the victorious defender of its life in time of war.[15]

Churchill had expressed such sentiments in florid messages over the past few years, especially on special Soviet anniversaries. Equally familiar was Molotov's response, which was to publish excerpts from Churchill's speech in *Pravda*. But Stalin's reaction was very different from the days of wartime: on 10 November, he sent a scorching cable from Sochi to his quartet of lieutenants, telling 'comrades Molotov, Beria, Malenkov and Mikoyan' that

> I consider the publication of Churchill's speech, with its praise of Russia and Stalin, was a mistake. Churchill does all of this because he needs to soothe his bad conscience and camouflage his hostile attitude to the USSR, in particular the fact that he and his pupils from the Labor Party are organizers of a British–American–French bloc against the USSR.

Stalin insisted that 'against this servility before foreigners we must struggle tooth and nail' and warned that publishing such speeches would simply 'implant servility and fawning'. Back came a dutiful apology from Molotov, parroting his master's voice: 'I consider it a mistake, because, even in our printed version, it came through that the praise of Russia and Stalin served Churchill to camouflage his hostile anti-Soviet aims. In any case the speech should not have been printed without your consent.'[16]

The stinging rebuke from Sochi was no mere whim.

More likely it was a deliberate design by Stalin to use the *Pravda* article as a pretext for setting a new and tougher tone against the West, to shake off his colleagues' residual respect towards the Allies by rekindling the old Bolshevik spirit of vigilance and contempt for the class enemy.'[17]

But Molotov seems not to have got the point. Over the next few weeks, he eased some censorship restrictions on the foreign press, which culminated in a despatch from the Moscow correspondent of the London *Daily Herald* relaying speculation about Stalin's health and especially his possible replacement by Molotov. Stalin was furious about such 'lies and slanderous fabrications about our government'; he now set about totally humiliating Molotov. He told the other three members of the inner circle: 'I am convinced that Molotov does not cherish the interests of our state and the prestige of our government, all he wants is to achieve popularity in certain foreign circles. I cannot regard such a comrade as my First Deputy any more.' Hauled over the coals by Beria, Mikoyan and Malenkov, on 7 December Molotov sent Stalin a cable of ritual humiliation, confessing his 'serious political mistakes', including his 'display of false liberalism' towards foreign correspondents in Moscow. 'Your telegram is imbued with a deep mistrust of me as a Bolshevik and as a person, which I accept as the most serious party warning for all my future work,' he cabled Sochi, promising to try to win back Stalin's trust, 'which I cherish more than my life itself.' Molotov's abject *mea culpa* was reminiscent of his grovelling in May 1942 when Stalin executed his volte-face over the terms of the Anglo-Soviet treaty.[18]

This 1945 furore was part of a larger pattern. Stalin had already taken Molotov to task during the London conference of foreign ministers in September, when Molotov's inclination to compromise with America and Britain on issues ranging from a Soviet trusteeship in Tripolitania to a full role for Moscow in the occupation of Japan ran up against Stalin's implacable obduracy. As with the saga of the Italian warships in 1943–44, the Soviet leader was obsessed about equal rights and status among the Big Three: 'The Allies are pressing on you to break your will,' he fumed to Molotov, 'they lack a minimal respect for their Ally.'[19] The altercations over the London conference, Churchill's speech and the *Daily Herald* article were all signs that Stalin was moving away from pragmatic wartime cooperation into treating the West as a potential enemy – a posture that would also justify a new crackdown on political deviation and 'cosmopolitanism' at home. And here another speech from Churchill in 1946 gave him even more valuable ammunition.

The former prime minister, chafing at his loss of power, had accepted an invitation to speak at an obscure Presbyterian college in Missouri because this was in Truman's home state and the president had offered to introduce him. Churchill's address at Fulton on 5 March 1946 has gone down in history as his 'Iron Curtain' speech, but that phrase was only one of several soundbites. He also warned that the growing problems with the USSR would not be removed 'by a policy of appeasement' and called for a permanent 'special relationship between the British Commonwealth and Empire and the United States', including military cooperation, interchangeable weaponry, shared bases and eventually common citizenship. All this, however, was not a clarion call for war with the Soviets, but a plea for negotiation from a position of strength: he said he sought 'a good understanding on all points with Russia under the general authority of the United Nations Organisation' backed by 'the whole strength of the English-speaking world'. This, said Churchill in his peroration, 'is the solution which I respectfully offer to you in this Address to which I have given the title "The Sinews of Peace"'.[20]

Of the soundbites, the special relationship was, he told the audience, 'the crux' of his message. Because it was not just on the Soviet side of the triangle that the wartime alliance had weakened: Churchill was deeply concerned that America was now disengaging itself from Britain. The Combined Chiefs of Staff atrophied, Lend-Lease had been terminated abruptly, and a nationalist Congress was pulling back from cooperation on atomic weapons. At Fulton, therefore, Churchill's eyes were on Washington as much as, if not more than, on Moscow: he was invoking the Iron Curtain to justify the special relationship.[21]

What defined the place of the 'Sinews of Peace' speech in history was not Churchill's intention but Stalin's reaction. The USSR was already in the news because of its failure to withdraw its troops, as agreed, from northern Iran – another legacy of 1941. Then, on 11–12 March, *Pravda* and *Izvestiya* attacked Churchill's speech; this was followed on the 13th by a remarkable question and answer in *Pravda* with Stalin himself, denouncing Churchill's speech as a 'call to war with the Soviet Union' and an assertion that the English-speaking peoples, 'being the only valuable nations, should rule over the remaining nations of the world'. This, he declared, was 'racial theory' based on language – 'one is reminded of Hitler and his friends'. This became front-page news in the West – captured, for instance, in the *New York* Times headlines on 14 March:

STALIN SAYS CHURCHILL STIRS WAR
AND FLOUTS ANGLO-RUSSIAN PACT;
SOVIET TANKS APPROACH TEHERAN

SEES RACE THEORY

Russian Leader Likens Churchill to Hitler for Plea to U.S.

SAYS SOVIETS CAN WIN WAR[22]

Historians have speculated about Stalin's motives. By exaggerating Churchill's words into a full-scale 'call to war', perhaps he hoped to shake the West, while mobilizing his own people? Maybe he wanted to show Truman that he was not cowed by US possession of the atomic bomb?[23] At any event, Washington and London hastily distanced themselves from the Fulton speech, even though Attlee had privately endorsed its thrust in advance and Truman had read the whole text with approval en route to Fulton. Indeed the president may well have seen it as a trial balloon for a new and tougher policy towards the USSR, which the administration gradually rolled out in 1946–47.[24] As a result, Churchill received all the opprobrium for the speech in the short term – and then all the credit as the Cold War deepened and Fulton came to be seen as another instance of his statesmanlike prescience (just as over rearmament in the 1930s). Stalin's vituperation did not upset him. Words deleted from the draft of a speech in New York on 15 March betray his glee at hitting the headlines:

It is extraordinary that the head of a mighty, victorious government should descend from his august seat of power to enter into personal controversy with a man who has no official position of any kind and had been particu-larly careful to say that he spoke without the authority of any government. I shall not let the implied compliment turn my head. Nor am I dismayed by harsh words, even from the most powerful of dictators. Indeed I had years of it from Hitler and managed to get along all right.[25]

Rejuvenated by the oxygen of global publicity, Churchill found his zest for politics returning, fired by a belief that the Labour party was selling off the empire and selling out the country. He told his doctor on 27 June: 'A short time ago I was ready to retire and die gracefully. Now I'm going to stay and have them out.' His crony Brendan Bracken summed up the new mood in typically colourful language. Churchill, he said, was 'determined to continue to lead the Tory party till he becomes Prime Minister on earth or Minister of Defence in Heaven.'[26]

Yet Churchill did not take Stalin's diatribe about Fulton personally. On 21 December 1946, he asked the Soviet ambassador in London to transmit a brief message to Stalin: 'All personal good wishes on your birthday, my wartime comrade.' Three days later came the reply: 'My warm thanks for your good wishes on my birthday.' With Moscow's consent, Churchill duly published his message to Stalin, which appeared in several British papers, often featuring the phrase 'my wartime comrade.'[27] In January 1947, Field Marshal Montgomery visited Moscow, picking up a long-standing invitation in the hope of reducing what Attlee called 'the cloud of suspicion' hanging over Anglo-Soviet relations. Monty spent a cordial evening with Stalin on 10 January. He later told Churchill that the Soviet leader had inquired as to Churchill's health and then said that 'you disagreed with him now on many political matters, but he would always have the happiest memories of his work with you as the great war leader of Britain; he added that he had the greatest respect and admiration for what you had done during the war years'. Stalin said he would be 'delighted' if Monty would convey these words to Churchill.[28]

On 3 February 1947, Churchill replied to Stalin in what he called 'a similar spirit':

My dear Stalin

I was very glad to receive your kind message through Field Marshal Montgomery. About political differences, I was never very good at Karl Marx.

I always look back on our comradeship together, when so much was at stake, and you can always count on me where the safety of Russia and the fame of its armies are concerned.

I was also delighted to hear from Montgomery of your good health. Your life is not only precious to your country, which you saved, but to the friend-ship between Soviet Russia and the English-speaking world.

Believe me,
Yours very sincerely,
Winston S. Churchill[29]

Of course, too much should not be made of such diplomatic pleasantries. Nevertheless, these exchanges remind us that the Fulton speech was not intended as a personal attack on Stalin, and they suggest that Churchill had retained something of his wartime faith in the Soviet leader. In this regard, it is striking that throughout his war memoirs, written between 1947 and 1953, Churchill avoided personal attacks on Stalin. Even where bluntly critical of Soviet wartime conduct, as over the Warsaw Uprising in 1944, he referred generally to 'men in the Kremlin' who, he said, were 'governed by calculation and not by emotion'. In notes for volume six, Churchill suggested that the breach of the Yalta agreements 'probably was due not to bad faith on the part of Stalin and Molotov, but that when they got back home they were held up by their colleagues'. This intriguing observation echoes his wartime comments about Stalin not being an entirely free agent.[30] Volume six actually contains some very positive asides about the Soviet leader. Concerning autumn of 1944 in 'Prelude to a Moscow Visit', drafted in November 1950 at the nadir of the Korean war, Churchill wrote: 'I felt acutely the need to see Stalin, with whom I always considered one could talk as one human being to another.' And at the end of May 1951, revising his account of Stalin at Potsdam, he referred to him as an 'amazing and gigantic personality'.[31]

For Churchill, this past was a springboard to the future. On 4 November 1951, little over a week after returning to Downing Street for a second term, he sent a cable to the Soviet leader: 'Now that I am again in charge of His Majesty's Government, let me reply to your farewell telegram from Potsdam in 1945, "Greetings. Winston Churchill."' Stalin replied next day with a short note of thanks, whereupon Churchill cabled Truman, 'we are again on speaking terms'. On 6 November, he read to the House of Commons a message he had sent to Stalin on 29 April 1945, warning that a quarrel between 'the English-speaking peoples' and 'you and the countries you dominate' would 'tear the world to pieces'. He promised MPs he would now make 'a supreme effort to bridge the gulf between the two worlds, so that each can live its life, if not in friendship at least without the fear, the hatreds and the frightful waste of the "cold war"'.[32] The 1945 documents were fresh in his mind from working on the memoirs, and his November 1951 message to Stalin was almost saying: 'Let us resume from where we were so rudely interrupted six years ago.'

In February 1950, when still leader of the opposition, Churchill had called for another 'parley at the summit' with the USSR – coining a further slogan for the diplomatic lexicon to complement 'iron curtain' and 'special relationship'.[33] Summitry became the overriding passion of the old man's second term, and on several occasions during 1952 he spoke privately of his desire for an

Anglo-American approach to Stalin, leading perhaps to a modern Congress of Vienna, at which the Potsdam conference would be reopened and then properly concluded. He also observed in June 1952 that 'while Stalin was alive we were safer from attack than if he died and his lieutenants started scrambling for the succession'. Reminiscing with Soviet Ambassador Andrey Gromyko in February 1953 about wartime summits, he said his 'percentages' meeting with Stalin in Moscow in October 1944 was 'the highest level we ever reached'.[34]

But a few weeks later, the Soviet leader suffered a massive stroke, caused – like Roosevelt's – by arteriosclerosis. The Politburo quartet watched him die an agonizing death on 5 March 1953 and then gave him a grand state funeral, before laying his embalmed body in the mausoleum with Lenin himself. 'The whole of Russia wept. So did I,' wrote the poet Yevgeniy Yevtushenko. 'Trained to believe that Stalin was taking care of everyone, people were lost and bewildered without him.' Yet within weeks, signs of a thaw were apparent. The new collective leadership of old men was 'positively unfolding', wrote journalist Edward Crankshaw – 'blossoming like leathery cactuses'. There was general agreement in the Politburo, in which Georgiy Malenkov initially emerged as *primus inter pares*, about reducing the Gulag of political prisoners, improving living standards and easing relations with the West.[35]

Churchill saw Stalin's death as an opportunity, at last, to do what he had advocated at Fulton – to meet again with the Soviet leadership at the summit. 'He seems to think of little else,' his doctor noted on 7 March.[36] On the 11th, the PM wrote to President Dwight D. Eisenhower, another wartime colleague, urging joint or separate approaches to 'the new regime'. The PM felt that, 'now there is no more Stalin', the two of them could be 'called to account if no attempt was made to turn over a leaf so that a new page would be started'. He reminded Ike that he and Eden – now back in his wartime post as foreign secretary – had 'done a lot of business with Molotov'. However, the State Department and the Foreign Office were unenthusiastic, preferring to wait and watch developments in Moscow; but Churchill kept up the pressure. On 4 May, he sent the president the draft of a letter he wished to send to Molotov, asking the Soviet foreign minister:

> I wonder whether you would like me to come to Moscow so that we could renew our own war-time relation and so that I could meet Monsieur Malenkov and others of your leading men. Naturally I do not imagine that we could settle any of the grave issues which overhang the immediate future of the world, but I have a feeling that it might be helpful if our intercourse proceeded with the help of friendly acquaintance and goodwill instead of impersonal diplomacy and propaganda.[37]

Eisenhower reacted with 'a bit of astonishment' as he put it diplomatically. 'Uncle Joe used to plead ill health as an excuse for refusing to leave the territory under the Russian flag or controlled by the Kremlin,' he reminded Churchill. But 'that excuse no longer applies' and 'I do have a suspicion that anything the Kremlin could misinterpret as weakness or over-eagerness on our part would militate against success in negotiation.' The president warned the ageing PM that the 'solitary pilgrimage' he proposed could arouse unsettling speculation, and stated his own firm belief that conference diplomacy should await 'some evidence, in deeds, of a changed Soviet attitude'.[38]

Churchill's rather huffy response was again rooted in 1941–45:

> According to my experience of these people in wartime we should gain more goodwill on the spot by going as guests of the Soviets than we should lose by appearing to court them. This was particularly the case when Anthony and I spent a fortnight in Moscow in October, 1944.

Resurrecting elements of his old 'two Stalins' trope, the PM added 'I am fully alive to the impersonal and machine-made foundation of Soviet policy' and reminded Ike that none of the collective leadership 'has any contacts outside Russia, except Molotov. I am very anxious to know these men and talk to them as I think I can frankly and on the dead level'.[39]

A few days later, on 11 May 1953, Churchill went public, telling the Commons and the world that, given the 'change of attitude' and the 'amicable gestures' from the new Soviet government, 'a conference on the highest level should take place between the leading Powers without long delay', conducted 'with a measure of informality and a still greater measure of privacy and seclusion'. He told the House that if there were sufficient 'will' at 'the summit of the nations' such a meeting might at least establish 'more intimate contacts'. At best, he added, 'we might have a generation of peace'.[40]

Churchill's grand design got nowhere. In part this was because on 23 June 1953 he, too, suffered a serious stroke – not fatal, but sufficient to undermine the rest of his second premiership. Yet the root problem was that, whatever the PM's state of health, neither Eisenhower nor the new Soviet leadership had any intention of reprising the roles of Roosevelt and Stalin for Churchill's gratification on a global stage very different from wartime. Eisenhower, increasingly peeved by the PM's verbose messages, planned to write his own script as leader of the 'Free World' in an age of bipolarity. And in the eyes of Molotov and his colleagues, Churchill was the man of Fulton: meaning 'Iron Curtain' not 'Sinews of Peace'. They suspected he wanted to exploit the post-Stalin transition for Cold War advantage.[41]

Yet Churchill did not give up. On 4 July 1954, acting off his own bat, he sent a letter to Molotov proposing 'a friendly meeting, with no Agenda' between himself and the Soviet leadership in some neutral capital, which might prepare the ground for 'a wider reunion where much might be settled'. Again nothing came of the idea: although Malenkov was interested in the hope of bolstering his flagging position, Molotov and most of his colleagues saw Britain now as a minor player. Yet when Churchill's family finally persuaded him to let go of the reins of power in April 1955, one of the PM's last 'Dear Friend' messages to the president contained a striking expression of regret that now 'we shall never meet on a Top Level confrontation of our would-be friends'.[42]

'Our would-be friends' reminds us that Churchill never forgot his wartime relationship with Stalin, and indeed clung on to it in the confrontational postwar world. He also remained remarkably positive about the late Soviet leader. There were occasional blips, of course. In a speech in his constituency on 23 November 1954, commenting on West Germany's postwar transformation from enemy to ally, he said that this

> vast reversal of British, American and of European opinion was brought about only by the policy of Soviet Russia itself and above all by Stalin, the Dictator, who was carried away by the triumphs of victory and acted as if he thought he could secure for Russia and Communism the domination of the world.

That was his most direct personal attack on Stalin.[43] Yet in April 1956, he told Eisenhower that 'Stalin always kept his word with me', again recalling the Moscow percentages meeting of 1944, when he said he had told the Soviet leader, 'You keep Romania and Bulgaria in your sphere of influence, but let me have Greece.' To this bargain, Churchill told Ike, 'he scrupulously adhered during months of fighting with the Greek Communists'. This was Churchill's abiding refrain in later life, right up to his death in January 1965 – that Stalin 'never broke his personal word to me'. Years later, Winston's last private secretary was unable to explain what he termed Churchill's 'remarkable blind spot in judging Stalin'.[44]

*****

Given what we know now about Stalin's rule, it was indeed a blind spot. The 'two Stalins' fantasy cherished by Churchill and others in London and Washington – not least FDR, who regularly gave Stalin the benefit of the doubt – was the product of wishful thinking. Even though Stalin ran a team, he was unquestionably the Boss; as Molotov – his closest colleague – knew the hard way. And once the common enemy had been defeated, Stalin's increasingly paranoid mentality about matters foreign and domestic poisoned whatever chance might have existed for the continued cooperation that all three wartime leaders had repeatedly said they wanted.

Perhaps Churchill and Roosevelt's blind spot about Stalin was a necessary fiction – essential to hold their unholy alliance together in order to beat Hitler. Of course, the world of 1945 was very different from that of 1941, and the break-up of the Alliance was in considerable measure the result of what might be termed structural factors: two new 'superpowers' born through the midwifery of war, facing off against each other in Germany amid the ruins of Europe, with one possessing the atomic bomb and the other intent on developing it. So in some ways the Cold War has an air of inevitability about it, regardless of personal relations at the top.

Yet *The Kremlin Letters* offer tantalizing evidence of Stalin gradually entering into a relationship of competitive cooperation that was not necessarily doomed to Cold War extinction. He seems to have been genuinely unsettled by the rapid demise in 1945 of his two Western partners. Churchill, as we have seen, represented a country that was soon seen by Moscow as no longer a key player in international affairs, whereas the United States was crucial. So the great intangible in all this is Roosevelt. His sudden death on the eve of victory in Europe leaves fascinating what-ifs about how US policy might have evolved had FDR lived. Would he have maintained his wartime line that America's role was to act as mainly a global force, while leaving Europe to balance itself? Would he, like Truman, have finally felt obliged to respond to Stalin's hardening sphere of influence in Eastern Europe? Or might Roosevelt's continued presence in the White House have modified Stalin's suspicions to some degree?

Such questions are impossible to answer – not least because they assume a president still capable of decision and action, whereas all the signs in April 1945 indicated that FDR's days were numbered. Nevertheless, the transition from World War alliance to Cold War confrontation remains to this day a matter of debate and speculation. One even catches this in a question Molotov posed to Churchill in July 1954: 'One may ask why during the years of war there existed between our countries the relations which had a positive significance, not only for our own peoples but for the destinies of the whole world, and why such relations cannot be developed in the same good direction now.'[45]

Churchill's answer was, and remained, personal diplomacy. During the war, he invested a huge amount of time and energy in fostering an epistolary relationship with Stalin, paving the way for his solitary pilgrimages to Moscow in

1942 and 1944. Stalin, too, entered into the business of letter-writing and, after a clumsy start in 1941, showed increasing finesse in international diplomacy – despite bouts of status anxiety (as over a share in the Italian fleet) and obsessive suspicion (as in the Bern affair), not to mention his own white-hot blind spot: Poland. Roosevelt was much less hands-on as a correspondent – relying more on the tactile reports from trusted envoys than on cold words that got lost or twisted in translation. But all this was for the same end: to reach the point where they were able, in Churchill's quaint phrase, to 'parley at the summit' at Tehran and Yalta.

Their shared belief in the potency of personal diplomacy still endures in the twenty-first century. But in our era of mobile phones, emails and video-conferencing, not to mention tweets, it is of course far easier for leaders to get acquainted without having to become assiduous pen-pals. And in a world not engulfed in war, with the assistance of jet aeroplanes, the business of meeting at the summit is spared the difficulties and dangers of 1941–45. As a result, there is less evidence about how leaders conduct the business of personal diplomacy. That is why the epistolary relationship of Stalin, Churchill and Roosevelt is not only historically interesting but has enduring value. *The Kremlin Letters* opens a window into the minds of three men at the top, as they made history – engaging with each other in a world war that none had anticipated and winning a victory that – for good or ill – changed the course of the twentieth century.

ENDNOTES

Introduction

1. We found five additional messages, plus a few paragraphs that seem to have been omitted by chance.
2. For fuller discussion see Vladimir Pechatnov, 'How Soviet cold warriors viewed World War II: The inside story of the 1957 edition of the Big Three correspondence', *Cold War History*, 14 (2014), 109–25.
3. WM 142 (43) 2 CA, 18 Oct. 1943, CAB 65/40.
4. RGASPI f.558, op.11, d.257, ll.82–4.
5. Richardson wrote *Pamela* (1740) and *Clarissa* (1747–48), Rousseau *Julie, ou la nouvelle Héloise* (1761), and Goethe made his name with *Die Leiden des jungen Werthers* (1774).
6. Stephen Kotkin, *Stalin: Paradoxes of power, 1878–1928*, London, 2014, 736.
7. Sheila Fitzpatrick, *On Stalin's Team: The years of living dangerously in Soviet politics*, Princeton, 2015, 2.
8. Strictly 'minister' did not replace 'commissar' until 1946 – for foreign affairs and for other government departments. But for ease of comprehension, the terms 'ministry' and 'minister' are used throughout the book.
9. Albert Resis (ed.), *Molotov Remembers: Inside Kremlin politics. Conversations with Felix Chuev*, Chicago, 1993, 57.
10. Thomas Jones, *A Diary with Letters, 1931–1950*, London, 1954, entry for 22 May 1936, 204.
11. Harriman, 362.
12. Churchill to Stalin, draft 31 Jan. 1944, PREM 3/396/11/320.
13. Colville, 553.
14. *SWW*, 3: 331.
15. Speech of 12 Nov. 1942 in Gilbert 7, 254.
16. William D. Leahy, *I Was There*, London, 1950, 125; Bohlen memcons, 15 and 29 March 1945, in Charles E. Bohlen papers, box 4, Memcons, President, 1945 (NARA).
17. David Reynolds, 'The Wheelchair President and his special relationships', in Reynolds, *From World War to Cold War: Churchill, Roosevelt and the international history of the 1940s*, Oxford, 2006, 165–76.
18. Bohlen, minutes, Roosevelt–Stalin meeting, 28 Nov. 1943, in *FRUS Cairo and Tehran*, 483.

19. Address to the American Youth Congress, 10 Feb. 1940 (APP); see generally Mary Glantz, *FDR and the Soviet Union: The president's battles over foreign policy*, Lawrence, KS, 2005.
20. Warren F. Kimball, *The Juggler: Franklin Roosevelt as wartime statesman*, Princeton, 1991, 83ff.
21. Sherwood, 227.
22. Interview with FDR's physician, Dr Howard Bruenn, quoted in Robert H. Ferrell, *The Dying President: Franklin D. Roosevelt, 1944–1945*, Columbia, MO, 1998, 85.
23. Examples include Herbert Feis, *Churchill, Roosevelt, Stalin: The war they waged, the peace they sought*, Princeton, 1957; Robin Edmonds, *The Big Three: Churchill, Roosevelt and Stalin in peace and war*, London, 1991.
24. Milovan Djilas, *Conversations with Stalin*, London, 1962, 70.
25. Staff Meeting, 8 Dec. 1943, Harriman papers, box 171 (LC).
26. Spellman memo, quoted in Robert I. Gannon, *The Cardinal Spellman Story*, Garden City, NY, 1962, 223–4.
27. See Dennis J. Dunn, *Caught between Roosevelt and Stalin: America's ambassadors to Moscow*, Lexington, KY, 1998, 3–6; and more generally Eduard Mark, 'October or Thermidor? Interpretations of Stalinism and the perception of Soviet foreign policy in the United States, 1927–1947', *American Historical Review*, 94:4 (1989), 937–62.
28. Roosevelt to Churchill, 11 April 1945, in Kimball, 2: 630.
29. Minutes to Eden, 16 Jan. and 1 April 1944, CHAR 20/152.
30. Geoffrey Wilson to Sir Archibald Clark Kerr, 15 May 1944, 3, FO 800/302.
31. Winston S. Churchill, *Into Battle: Speeches, 1938–40*, London, 1941, 131.
32. Letter of 8 Feb. 1945, in Cadogan, 706.
33. Churchill to Eden, 18 March 1943, CHAR 20/108.
34. The complete Churchill–Roosevelt correspondence, edited by Warren F. Kimball, has been a fundamental resource in preparing this volume.
35. Moran, 160, 162, 166 – entries for 29 Nov. and 2 Dec. 1943.
36. A.A. Gromyko, I.N. Zemskov et al. (eds), *Sovetskiy Soyuz na mezhdunarodnykh konferentsiyakh perioda Velikoy Otechestvennoy voyny 1941–1945 gg.*, Moscow, 1984, 4: 94.
37. A theme developed in David Reynolds, 'The diplomacy of the Grand Alliance', in Ewan Mawdsley (ed.), *The Cambridge History of the Second World War*, 3 vols, Cambridge, 2015, 2: 301–23.

1 Strange Encounters

1. In his memoirs, Churchill presented the letter of 25 June 1940 as his own initiative (*SWW*, 2: 119–20); on the FO's role, see Gabriel Gorodetsky, *Stafford Cripps' Mission to Moscow, 1940–42*, Cambridge, 1984, 51–3.
2. Horst Boog et al. (eds), *Germany and the Second World War*, Vol. 4: *The Attack on the Soviet Union*, Oxford, 1998, 47–8.
3. *SWW*, 3: 319–23, quoting p. 323.
4. Georgiy Zhukov, *Reminiscences and Reflections*, 2 vols, Moscow, 1985, 1: 281; see generally Gabriel Gorodetsky, *Grand Delusion: Stalin and the German invasion of Russia*, New Haven, CT, 1999, esp. chs 12–14.
5. Glantz/House, 37, 49; Richard Overy, *Russia's War*, London, 1998, 77–9.
6. Welles to Steinhardt, 4 July 1941, *FRUS 1941*, 1: 892–3; COS (41) 224th mtg, 25 June 1941, CAB 79/12.
7. Gorodetsky, *Cripps' Mission*, 184–6; *SWW*, 3: 340; Churchill to Cripps, 8 July 1941, PREM 3/403/6.
8. CD 1941, 903.
9. *SANO*, 1: 69–71.
10. Moscow to FO, 8 July 1941, PREM 3/403/6.
11. Eden to Churchill, 9 July 1941, PREM 3/403/6.
12. WM 67 (41) 1, 9 July 1941, CAB 65/19; Cadogan, 392.

13. And also, as Eden recalled from his time as foreign secretary in 1937–38, the way Neville Chamberlain – another enthusiast of personal diplomacy – had excluded him from dealings with Mussolini. See Harvey, 17–18.
14. CD 1941, 920.
15. *SANO*, 1: 77–81.
16. *Pravda*, 14 July 1941; *Hansard Parliamentary Debates*, HC Deb 373 col. 463.
17. Gorodetsky, *Cripps' Mission*, 194.
18. 'Zapisnaya knizhka marshala F.I. Golikova. Sovetskaya voyennaya missiya v Anglii i SShA v 1941 godu', *Novaya i Noveyshaya Istoriya*, 2 (2004), 92–3.
19. CHAR 20/41/24–5.
20. Gorodetsky, 372–4; cf. the official despatch in *SANO*, 1: 85–8.
21. Gorodetsky, 375.
22. CD 1941, 964–5.
23. To Maisky in London, 25 July 1941, AVP RF f.059, op.1, p.365, d.2487, ll.110–11.
24. Beaumont, 32–3.
25. WM 41 (72) 2, 21 July 1941, CAB 65/19; Harris to Hap Arnold, 2 Aug. 1941, and Lyon to Echols, 'Notes on Soviet Aircraft Production', 17 Oct. 1941, RG 218, Central Decimal Files, 1942–1945, Foreign, Russia 400–B (NARA).
26. CD 1941, 981.
27. Moscow to Foreign Office, 26 July 1941, PREM 3/401/1.
28. Harvey, 24.
29. CD 1941, 991.
30. Gorodetsky, 375; Sherwood, 236.
31. Gorodetsky, 376.
32. Roosevelt to Hopkins for Stalin, 26 July 1941, printed in Sherwood, 321–2.
33. Sherwood, 321–2.
34. Memo of meeting, 31 July 1941, part 3, enclosed in Hopkins to Roosevelt, 20 Aug. 1941, PSF(S) box 5: Russia, 1939–41.
35. Quoted in Sherwood, 344.
36. FDR to Wayne Coy, 2 Aug. 1941, PSF(D) box 49: Russia, 1941.
37. CD 1941, 1016–17; M. Komarov, 'Postavki po lend-lizu dlya VMF', *Morskoy Sbornik*, 3 (2002), 76.
38. AVP RF f.059, op.1, p.365, d.2485, ll.61–3.
39. AVP RF f.059, op.1, p.365, d.2484, l.46.
40. Butler, 40.
41. Umanskiy to Molotov, 19 Aug. 1941, *SAMO*, 1: 106; cf. Welles, memo, 18 Aug. 1941, *FRUS 1941*, 1: 56–7.
42. WP (41) 202, CAB 65/19; David Reynolds, *The Creation of the Anglo-American Alliance, 1937–1941: A study in competitive cooperation*, London, 1981, 258–9.
43. CD 1941, 1065–6.
44. See *FRUS 1941*, 1: 819–22.
45. CD 1941, 1127–8.
46. Ashley Jackson, *The British Empire and the Second World War*, London, 2006, 157–9; V.P. Puzyrev, 'Iranskiy koridor lend-liza' in *Lend-liz i Rossiya*, Arkhangelsk, 2006, 171–83.
47. Eden to Cripps, 26 Aug. 1941, FO 954/24B, SU/41/74; Gorodetsky, 381; cf. *SANO*, 1: 106.
48. AVP RF f.059, op.1, p.365, d.2488, ll.45–6. Partially published in *SAMO*, 1: 109; see also summary in Gorodetsky, 381–2.
49. AVP RF f.059, op.1, p.365, d.2486, ll.146–8. See summary of this telegram in Gorodetsky, 382–3.
50. Stalin Archive, RGASPI f.558, op.11, d.255, ll.76–8.
51. Gorodetsky, 384.
52. CHAR 20/42A/64–7.
53. FO 371/29490, N5105/78/38.
54. Eden to Cripps, 4 Sept. 1941, FO 954/24B/388; cf. Colville, 381.
55. Gorodetsky, 387.

56. PREM 3/403/6, reprinted in CD 1941, 1171–2.
57. Gorodetsky, 388.
58. WM 90 (41) 1 CA, 5 Sept. 1941, CAB 65/23.
59. Cadogan, 405.
60. Memo to PM, 5 Sept. 1941, PREM 3/403/6/156–7.
61. Eden, 276.
62. CD 1941, 1170–1.
63. Cripps to FO, 7 Sept. 1941, PREM 3/403/6. When sending FDR copies of Stalin's message and his reply, Churchill noted that, although nothing had been said explicitly, 'we could not exclude the impression that they might be thinking of separate terms' – in other words a negotiated peace with Germany. See Kimball, 1: 238.
64. Cf. David French, *Raising Churchill's Army: The British Army and the war against Germany, 1919–1945*, Oxford, 2000, 188.
65. FO 954/24B/403.
66. Gorodetsky, 390–1; *SANO*, 1: 119–22.
67. *SWW*, 3: 411.
68. CD 1941, 1231–2.
69. Churchill to Eden, 19 Sept. 1941, PREM 3/403/6/112; *SANO*, 1: 123–6.
70. Harriman, 79; Beaverbrook report, 18 Sept. 1941, DO (41) 11, CAB 69/3.
71. DO (41) 62nd mtg, 19 Sept. 1941, CAB 69/2; DO (41) 12, CAB 69/3, quoting para. 15.

2 'Two Relatively Unrelated Wars'

1. Herring, 18–21.
2. Harriman, 89; see also Harriman papers, box 872, Feis files, 21 Oct. 1953 (LC); L.F. Sotskov (ed.), *Agressiya. Rassekrechennye dokumenty sluzhby vneshney razvedki Rossiyskoy Federatsii 1939–1941*, Moscow, 2011, 525–31.
3. PREM 3/401/7/175–9.
4. Text in *FRUS 1941*, 1: 836; for background see PSF(D) box 49: Russia, 1941.
5. *SAMO*, 1: 158; Kimball, 1: 371.
6. *FRUS 1941*, 1: 836.
7. Sherwood, 390.
8. PSF(D) box 49: Russia, 1941.
9. *SWW*, 3: 415–16; cf. Beaumont, 52–3; A.J.P. Taylor, *Beaverbrook*, London, 1974, 626–7.
10. Ismay, military report, 6 Oct. 1941, in WP (41) 238, CAB 66/19.
11. Stalin to Churchill, 3 Oct. 1941, *Corr 1957*, 1: 29.
12. WM 100 (41) 2, CAB 65/19.
13. CD 1941, 1308.
14. CD 1941, 1329.
15. Rodric Braithwaite, *Moscow 1941: A city and its people at war*, London, 2006, ch. 12, esp. pp. 243, 249; Gorodetsky, *Cripps' Mission*, 251–4.
16. Roosevelt, memo to Hopkins, 25 Oct. 1941, PSF(D) box 49: Russia, 1941.
17. Memo, 30 Oct. 1941, Harry Hopkins papers, Sherwood Collection, Box 309 (FDRL).
18. PSF(S) box 5: Russia, 1939–41.
19. Although FDR sent a copy to Churchill for information and Maisky was then given a copy by Beaverbrook – see *Corr 1957*, 1: 6.
20. *Corr 1957*, 2: 22, 286.
21. PSF(D) box 49: Russia, 1941.
22. Reception of American Ambassador Steinhardt, 2 Nov. 1941, RGASPI f.558, op.11, d.363, l.23.
23. A.Yu. Borisov, *SSSR i SShA: soyuzniki v gody voyny, 1941–1945*, Moscow, 1983, 59; Mikoyan to Stalin, 13 Aug. 1941, AP RF f.3, op.66, d.295, ll.9–10.
24. PSF(S) box 5: Russia, 1939–41.
25. Steinhardt to Vyshinskiy, 5 Nov. 1941, RGASPI f.558, op.11, d.363, ll.44–8.

26. In fact the list was sent by Hopkins, after Roosevelt's 'OK'; see PSF(S) box 5: Russia, 1939–41 – Berney to Tully, 31 Oct. 1941 and list (which is reproduced in full in Butler, 49–51).
27. PSF(D) box 49: Russia, 1941.
28. Reception of American Ambassador Steinhardt, 6 Nov. 1941, RGASPI f.558, op.11, d.363, ll.49–50.
29. G.N. Sevostyanov (ed.), *Sovetsko-amerikanskiye otnosheniya, 1939–1945*, Moscow, 2004, 167–8.
30. *SAMO*, 1: 139.
31. *Izvestiya*, 9 November 1941.
32. Kimball, 1: 253, 255–6; Harriman, 107–8.
33. Churchill to Cripps, 28 Oct. 1941, and Cripps to Churchill, 30 Oct. 1941, FO 954/24B/476–7 and 481–2.
34. Cripps handed Vyshinskiy the text on 6 November; a copy of the message with Stalin's remarks on it was dated similarly (Vyshinskiy diary, 5 Nov. 1941, RGASPI f.558, op.11, d.255, l.131 and ll.136–8). But Stalin referred to it as Churchill's message of 7 November when he replied on the 8th.
35. WM 108 (41) 6 CA, CAB 65/24.
36. Quoted in Eden to Cripps, 21 Oct. 1941, FO 954/24B/441.
37. In the draft approved by the Cabinet, the second paragraph opened 'We told you in my message of September 6th that we were willing to declare war on Finland' – but it was later decided not to remind Stalin of that. Cf. text in WM 108 (41) 6 CA, CAB 65/24.
38. FO 954/24B/488–9.
39. Roosevelt to Stalin, 6 Nov. 1941, *FRUS 1941*, 1: 856–7 and Stalin to Roosevelt, 21 Nov. 1941, PSF(D) box 49: Russia, 1941.
40. AVP RF f.059, op.1, p.365, d.2468, ll.250–8.
41. *SANO*, 1: 138; DVP, 24: 374.
42. RGASPI f.558, op.11, d.255, l.146.
43. WM 111 (41) 8, CAB 65/24.
44. Gorodetsky, 400–2.
45. Eden, 281.
46. WM 111 (41) 8, CAB 65/24; Harvey, 62–3.
47. Cripps to Eden, 13 and 15 Nov. 1941, PREM 3/395/6/131–2.
48. Harvey, 63.
49. WM 114 (41) CA, CAB 65/24.
50. Record of Eden–Maisky conversation, 12 Nov. 1941, PREM 3/395/17/481–4.
51. Maisky to NKID, 19 Nov. 1941, AVP RF f.059, op.1, p.365, d.2486, ll.288–90 and 296–8; cf. Eden, 282.
52. Eden to Cripps, 17 Nov. 1941, approved by War Cabinet, WM 111 (41) 1, CAB 65/24.
53. RGASPI f.558, op.11, d.255, ll.144–5.
54. Harvey, 65; *SWW*, 3: 470–1.
55. Eden, 282–3.
56. CD 1941, 1486–7.
57. FO 954/24B/521.
58. DO 71 (41)2, CAB 69/2; Alanbrooke, 206.
59. CD 1941, 1562–3.
60. FO 954/24B/523.
61. AVP RF f.059, op.1, p.352, d.2406, l.238.
62. RGASPI f.558, op.11, d.256, l.2.
63. FO 954/24B/523.
64. See PREM 3/170/1, esp. Cranborne to Eden, 2 Dec., Eden to PM, 29 Nov. and minutes by Churchill, 4 Dec. 1941; also Harvey, 68. See more generally Markuu Ruotsila, *Churchill and Finland: A study in anticommunism and geopolitics*, London, 2006, 103–43.

3 'I Can Handle Stalin'

1. The phrase of Robert Sherwood: see Sherwood, 264, 269–70; on 8 Dec. 1941 see Eden, 285–6.
2. Alfred E. Eckes Jr, *The United States and the Global Struggle for Minerals*, Austin, TX, 1979, 75, 84.
3. Forrest C. Pogue, *George C. Marshall: Ordeal and hope, 1939–42*, New York, 1966, 275–6.
4. Sherwood, 442.
5. Eden had visited Moscow in March 1935 when parliamentary under-secretary at the FO.
6. Eden memo, 28 Jan. 1942, WP (42) 48, CAB 66/21.
7. Doris Kearns Goodwin, *No Ordinary Time: Franklin and Eleanor Roosevelt, the home front in World War II*, New York, 1994, 312–13, 319–20, quoting FDR to Russell Leffingwell, 16 March 1942 on 320.
8. *SAMO* 1: 143; also see *FRUS 1941*, 1: 662–3.
9. *SAMO* 1: 145.
10. *FRUS 1941*, 4: 752–3, 760.
11. To Stalin from Washington, 19 Dec. 1941, AVP RF f.059, op.1, p.346, d.2366, ll.179–81.
12. RGASPI f.82, op.2, d.1091, l.104.
13. From Moscow to Foreign Office, 17 Dec. 1941, CHAR 20/47/30.
14. CHAR 20/50/7.
15. CHAR 20/47/105.
16. Northern Dept. minute for Sargent, 11 Jan. 1942, FO 371/32874, N716.
17. CD 1942, 11–12.
18. Horst Boog et al. (eds), *Germany and the Second World War*, Vol. 4: *The Attack on the Soviet Union*, Oxford, 1998, 716–17.
19. G.K. Zhukov, *Vospominaniya i razmyshleniya*, 2 vols, Moscow, 2002, 2: 42–4.
20. Stavka Directive, 10 Jan. 1942, Dmitriy Volkogonov Papers, reel 4, Manuscripts Division, LC.
21. Glantz/House, 91.
22. There was a further round of hortatory platitudes on 8 and 14 February – see CD 1942, 232, 248–9.
23. Gerhard Schreiber et al., *Germany and the Second World War*, Oxford, 1995, 3: 751.
24. A.S. Lukicheva (ed.), *Moskovskaya bitva v khronike faktov i sobytii*, Moscow, 2004, 468.
25. CD 1942, 57.
26. CHAR 20/132.
27. Secretary of War to President, 30 Dec. 1941, RG 218, Geographic File, 1942–1945, CCS 400.3295 USSR (2-27-42), Sec.1, Pt.1 (NARA); Report on War Aid furnished by USA to USSR, PSF, Subject File, Russia – Lend-Lease (HSTL).
28. PSF(S) box 5: Russia, 1942–45.
29. Welles to President, 10 Feb. 1942, PSF(D) box 49: Russia, 1942–43.
30. Beaverbrook's notes on 3rd meeting, 30 Sept. 1941, Harriman papers, box 160 (LC); David Mayers, *FDR's Ambassadors and the Diplomacy of Crisis*, Cambridge, 2013, 221–2.
31. PSF(D) box 49: Russia, 1942–43.
32. *SAMO*, 1: 192, 196.
33. *SAMO*, 1: 216.
34. PSF(S) box 5: Russia, 1942–45.
35. PSF(S) box 5: Russia, 1942–45.
36. Roosevelt, memo for Hopkins, 23 Feb. 1942, PSF(D) box 49: Russia, 1942–43.
37. PSF(S) box 5: Russia, 1942–45.
38. CD 1942, 299; amended draft in FO 371/32876, N1081/5/38.
39. Hinsley, 2: 88–99.
40. *SWW*, 4: 81; Yasmin Khan, *The Raj at War: A people's history of India's Second World War*, London, 2015, 113.
41. Harvey, 91.

42. Quoted in Max Hastings, *Finest Years: Churchill as warlord, 1940–1945*, London, 2009, 238.
43. Quotations from CD 1942, 321–2.
44. Kimball, 1: 362.
45. Draft in CHAR 20/71A/4; Cadogan, 437–8, 440; DO 7 (42) 4, CAB 69/4.
46. Eden to Halifax, 22 Jan. 1942, FO 954/29A; CD 1942, 47–8.
47. WM 17 (42) 5 CA, CAB 65/29. Beaverbrook claimed that Attlee, in the heat of argument, said that he would resign if the borders were affirmed, see Kenneth Young, *Churchill and Beaverbrook*, London, 1966, 235.
48. Kimball, 1: 394. See also Steven M. Miner, *Between Churchill and Stalin: The Soviet Union, Great Britain, and the origins of the grand alliance*, Chapel Hill, NC, 1988, 201–13.
49. CD 1942, 370–1.
50. DVP, 25/1: 190–1.
51. AVP RF f.43z, op.10, p.71, d.10, l.55.
52. CD 1942, 395–6.
53. Gorodetsky, 417–21.
54. Personal message from Beaverbrook to Comrade Stalin, 19 March 1942, RGASPI f.558, op.11, d.256, l.41; Comrade Stalin's reply of 26 March to Beaverbrook, ibid., l.46.
55. CD 1942, 417.
56. RGASPI f.558, op.11, d.284, l.5, and Clark Kerr to Warner, 11 June 1942, FO 800/300/22–4; see also Beaumont, 110, 233, and Clark Kerr to FO, 29 March 1942, PREM 3/395/18/674–5.
57. CD 1942, 451 and 503.
58. Henry Morgenthau Jr, Presidential Diaries, 5: 1075, 11 March 1942 (FDRL).
59. Kimball, 1: 420.
60. Kimball, 1: 400–4, 446–8.
61. Kimball, 1: 441.
62. Roosevelt to Stalin, 11 April 1942, and drafts and notes of 31 March and 1 April, PSF(S) box 5: Russia, 1942–45.
63. *SAMO*, 1: 158–9.
64. Kimball, 1: 437.
65. PSF(S) box 5: Russia, 1942–45.
66. See correspondence in *SAMO*, 1: 159–63.
67. Butler, 65.
68. William H. Standley and Arthur A. Ageton, *Admiral Ambassador to Russia*, Chicago, 1955, 151–8. Butler, 66, chose to distil Standley's memoir account of his conversation into a formal message from the president.
69. Kimball, 1: 448, 458–9.
70. Stoler, 75–6.
71. Alanbrooke, 248–9; Pogue, *George C. Marshall*, 319–20.
72. *SAMO*, 1: 164–5.

4 Molotov the Go-Between

1. *SWW*, 4: 344.
2. See US Dept. of Agriculture leaflet on 'Mitchell Monument' www.fs.usda.gov/Internet/FSE_DOCUMENTS/stelprdb5374039.pdf
3. Glantz/House, 283, 292.
4. Mark Harrison (ed.), *The Economics of World War II: Six great powers in international comparison*, Cambridge, 1998, 283, 287; Lisa A. Kirschenbaum, *The Legacy of the Siege of Leningrad, 1941–1945: Myth, memories, and monuments*, Cambridge, 2006, 60.
5. This paragraph follows the account in Beaumont, ch. 4, esp. pp. 88–9 and 92. Hopkins is quoted in Richard M. Leighton and Robert W. Coakley, *Global Logistics and Strategy, 1940–1943*, Washington, DC, 1955, 556.
6. For fuller background on the British side, see Ross, 18–25.

7. WM 44 (42) 4 CA, CAB 65/30; see also WP (42) 144, CAB 66/23.
8. CD 1942, 555–6.
9. CD 1942, 589.
10. Roosevelt to Stalin, 4 May 1942, PSF(S) box 5: Russia, 1942–45.
11. PSF(S) box 5: Russia, 1942–45.
12. WM 52 (42) 5, CAB 65/26.
13. Kimball, 1: 473, 482–3.
14. WM 52 (42) 5, CAB 65/26.
15. Beaumont, 101–2; *SAMO*, 1: 172.
16. CD 1942, 634.
17. CHAR 20/75/7.
18. CD 1942–43, 669.
19. Rzheshevsky, 63.
20. PSF(S) box 5: Russia, 1942–45.
21. CD 1942, 679; see also James Levy, 'The needs of political policy versus the reality of military operations: Royal Navy opposition to the Arctic convoys, 1942', *Journal of Strategic Studies*, 26 (2003), 36–52, quoting Pound on p. 46.
22. CD 1942, 688–9.
23. *SWW*, 4: 301; cf. the draft in CHUR 4/271, fo. 35.
24. The full run of Stalin–Molotov correspondence during the visit is printed, with commentary, in Rzheshevsky, 63–161. See also, more recently, the discussion of Molotov's visit in *Velikaya Otechestvennaya voyna 1941–1945 godov* (12 vols), Vol. 8: V.G. Titov et al. (eds), *Vneshnyaya politika i diplomatiya Sovetskogo Soyuza v gody voyny*, Moscow, 2014, 166–78.
25. Rzheshevsky, 103–4.
26. CD 1942, 705–6.
27. Stalin to Churchill, 23 May 1942, CD 1942, 706; I. Inozemtsev, 'Zashchita s vozdukha severnykh morskikh kommunikatsiy', *Voyenno-Istoricheskiy Zhurnal*, 8 (1982), 15–16.
28. WP (42) 198, 18 May 1942, CAB 66/24.
29. Rzheshevsky, 121–3, 138–9.
30. WP (42) 198; Harvey, 127–9.
31. WM 68 (42) 68 CA, 26 May 1942, CAB 65/30; Kimball, 1: 490.
32. Steven M. Miner, *Between Churchill and Stalin: The Soviet Union, Great Britain, and the origins of the grand alliance*, Chapel Hill, NC, 1988, 246–51 stresses the American role. On the military situation, see Glantz/House, 114–16.
33. CD 1942, 707.
34. Rzheshevsky, 148.
35. *Pravda*, 12 June 1942.
36. CHAR 20/75/83.
37. CHAR 20/75/108.
38. Rzheshevsky, 174–5, 177, 224.
39. *FRUS 1942*, 3: 577; Rzheshevsky, 205–6.
40. *FRUS 1942*, 3: 571, 579, 583.
41. Rzheshevsky, 204, 210–11, 218–20. In Russian: 'V khode peregovorov bylo dostignuto polnoye ponimaniye v otnoshenii neotlozhnykh zadach sozdaniya vtorogo fronta v Evrope v 1942 godu.'
42. Sherwood, 577; Kimball, 1: 504; Charles E. Bohlen, *Witness to History, 1929–1969*, New York, 1973, 128.
43. Rzheshevsky, 221, 266 (quote).
44. Rzheshevsky, 269, 274, 281–2, 298–9.
45. Sherwood, 561.
46. MR box 8.
47. PSF(D) box 49: Russia, 1942–43.

48. Churchill to Stalin, 16 June 1942, and reply, 20 June 1942, CD 1942, 798–9, 814.
49. FDR to Stalin, 17 June 1942, MR box 8; *SAMO*, 1: 198–202.
50. CD 1942, 729; see more generally Christopher Mann, *British Policy and Strategy Towards Norway, 1941–45*, Basingstoke, 2012, 76–7.
51. CD 1942, 781.
52. Hollis to Eden, 10 July 1942, with draft reply, FO 954/23B/519–21.
53. WM (42) 73 CA, CAB 65/30.
54. Kimball, 1: 515.
55. Churchill to Stalin, 20 June 1942, CD 1942, 809–10; see also Clark Kerr to Molotov, 21 June 1942 in RGASPI f.558, op.11, d.256, l.104.
56. FDR to Stalin, 23 June 1942, and reply, 1 July 1942, MR box 8; see also *SAMO*, 1: 211–13 and *FRUS 1942*, 3: 604–6.
57. FDR to Stalin, 6 July 1942, MR box 8.
58. Kimball, 1: 518.
59. Stalin to FDR, 18 July 1942, and FDR to Stalin, 22 July 1942, MR box 8.
60. MR box 8.
61. *Corr 1957*, 2: 29.
62. MR box 8.
63. CD 1942, 939.
64. S.W. Roskill, *The War at Sea*, London, 1956, vol. 2, esp. pp. 115, 138, 143; Correlli Barnett, *Engage the Enemy More Closely: The Royal Navy in the Second World War*, London, 2000, 710–22.
65. DO 14 (42), 10 July 1942, CAB 69/2.
66. CD 1942, 798.
67. DO 15 (42), 13 July 1942, CAB 69/2.
68. Kimball, 1: 528–33.
69. Gorodetsky, 447–50.
70. See drafts in PREM 3/393/3.
71. DVP, 25/1: 505. For fuller discussion of Anders' Army, see *Russkiy Arkhiv: Velikaya Otechestvennaya*, Vol. 14: *SSSR i Polsha, 1941–1945*, Moscow, 1994.
72. CHAR 20/78/26–8.
73. Welles to President, 18 July 1942, and copy of letter signed by Roosevelt for Stalin, 20 July 1942, PSF(D), box 49: Russia, 1942–43.
74. Harold Shukman (ed.), *Stalin's Generals*, London, 1993, 281.
75. Glantz/House, 117–21, quoting p. 120; Antony Beevor, *Stalingrad*, London, 1998, 84–5.
76. Gorodetsky, 451–3; DVP, 25/2: 58–9.
77. CD 1942, 985.
78. This sentence was omitted – apparently by mistake – from the translation in the British files, though it appears in the original Russian text: see *Corr 1957*, 1: 56.
79. Gorodetsky, 453; WM 95 (42) 2, CA, 24 July 1942, CAB 65/31.
80. Gorodetsky, 454.
81. Kimball, 1: 545.
82. Stoler, 79–90, quoting p. 88.
83. Clark Kerr to Eden, 28 July 1942, and Cadogan, minute for Eden, 29 July 1942, PREM 3/76A/1.
84. Eden, 338; WM 100 (42) CA, CAB 65/27; Cadogan, 464–5. Churchill was specially tested for high-altitude flying before leaving.
85. Gorodetsky, 456–7.
86. CD 1942, 1019.
87. CD 1942, 1021–2.
88. CD 1942, 1021.
89. Molotov to Maisky, 31 July 1942, RGASPI f.558, op.11, d.256, l.141.
90. Gorodetsky, 456–7.

5 Churchill's 'Lump of Ice'

1. *SWW*, 4: 428. In an early draft (Jan. 1949) Churchill said his mission was 'like carrying cold weather to the North Pole' – CHUR 4/279/446.
2. Donald Gillies, *Radical Diplomat: The life of Archibald Clark Kerr, Lord Inverchapel, 1882–1951*, London, 1999, 136: Moran, 82.
3. Kimball, 1: 566.
4. Clark Kerr to Eden, 20 Aug. 1942, FO 954/25B/382.
5. Dennis J. Dunn, *Caught between Roosevelt and Stalin: America's ambassadors to Moscow*, Lexington, KY, 1998, 139, 169.
6. Ian Jacob diary, 8 Aug. 1942, Jacob papers JACB 1/15.
7. See Hinsley, 2: 103–8.
8. CD 1942, 1255; Kimball, 1: 643.
9. CD 1942, 1031.
10. Kimball, 1: 553; Harriman, 146–7; FDR to Harriman, 4 Aug. 1942, Harriman papers, box 163 (LC).
11. MR box 8.
12. Roosevelt to Standley, 8 Aug. 1942, MR box 8. For a more detailed discussion of Willkie's visit, see V.O. Pechatnov, 'Vizit V. Villki [W. Willkie] v SSSR (po novym dokumentam)', in *SShA – Kanada: ekonomika, politika, kultura*, 7 (1999), 73–90.
13. MR box 8.
14. *Corr 1957*, 2: 32.
15. Gilbert 7, 217.
16. See minutes of the conversation in CAB 127/23; also *SANO*, 1: 265–71 and DVP, 25/2, 106–11. The British transcripts and records of the conference were printed for the War Cabinet as WP (32) 373, CAB 66/28.
17. *SWW*, 4: 430.
18. Text in RGASPI f.558, op.11, d.257, ll.9–12; printed in *Corr 1957*, 1: 59–60.
19. CHAR 20/79A/28.
20. Sentence in square brackets omitted in English translation: cf. *Corr 1957*, 1: 60–1 and CHAR 20/79A/28.
21. British minute in CAB 127/23; Moran, 75–6. On the interpreters, see Ian Jacob diary, 13 Aug. 1942, Jacob papers JACB 1/17; for Churchill on Pavlov, see Kimball, 1: 569–70.
22. Churchill to War Cabinet, 14 Aug. 1942, CD 1942, 1077.
23. Arthur Bryant, *The Turn of the Tide, 1939–1942*, London, 1957, 461.
24. DVP, 25/2: 58.
25. *SAMO*, 1: 221.
26. OGB, 3/2: 84. There was in fact only one meeting of the Cabinet's Defence Committee in July 1942, on the 13th, and that discussed convoys – see DO 15 (42) in CAB 69/4.
27. Albert Resis (ed.), *Molotov Remembers: Inside Kremlin politics. Conversations with Felix Chuev*, Chicago, 1993, 45–6.
28. See O.A. Rzheshevskiy, *Stalin i Cherchill*, Moscow, 2010, 258, 268.
29. Ibid., 380–1.
30. Stalin had insisted on this phrasing: 'full understanding was reached ... with regard to the urgent tasks of creating a second front in Europe in 1942'. He alluded to the communiqué when talking with Churchill on 13 August.
31. CD 1942, 1077–8.
32. CD 1942, 1087.
33. *Corr 1957*, 1: 63; Maurice Matloff and Edwin M. Snell, *Strategic Planning for Coalition Warfare, 1941–1942*, Washington, DC, 1953, 308–9.
34. Moran, 77–9.
35. Clark Kerr diary, FO 800/300/138–45; extracts also in Gillies, *Radical Diplomat*, 134–6.
36. Kimball, 1: 571. See also A.H. Birse, *Memoirs of an Interpreter*, London, 1967, 97–105, quoting p. 101.

37. *SWW*, 4: 445–9; also Birse's notes in PREM 3/76A/12/35–7, and Birse, *Memoirs*, 103. For Maisky's advice, see Gorodetsky, 458–9, 461.
38. Clark Kerr to Molotov, 17 Aug. 1942 in RGASPI f.558, op.11, d.257, l.24.
39. CD 1942, 1089.
40. CD 1942, 1087; DVP, 25/2: 158: The Russian word 'dusha' could be a translation of 'soul' or 'heart' in English – the latter being perhaps a more Churchillian word – but in any event it connotes 'the essence of a person'.
41. After meeting Putin for the first time in Slovenia in 2001, Bush told a reporter: 'I found him to be very straightforward and trustworthy. We had a very good dialog. I was able to get a sense of his soul, a man deeply committed to his country and the best interests of his country.' Bush, News Conference in Kranj, 16 June 2001 (APP).
42. W. Averell Harriman and Elie Abel, *Special Envoy to Churchill and Stalin*, New York, 1975, 160.
43. PSF(S) box 5: Russia, 1942–45.
44. MR box 8.
45. Deliveries of trucks amounted to less than half of what had been promised – see Herring, 66.
46. MR box 8.
47. Butler, 86.
48. Churchill to Stalin, 31 Aug. 1942, CD 1942, 1136.
49. See Correlli Barnett, *Engage the Enemy More Closely: The Royal Navy in the Second World War*, London, 2000, 724. This section of the message was amended in detail by the chiefs of staff – see record by Jacob, 5 Sept. 1942, PREM 3/393/4.
50. *SANO*, 1: 271.
51. Kimball, 1: 570; CD 1942, 988. See also Nicholas Tamkin, 'Britain, the Middle East, and the "Northern Front," 1941–42', *War in History*, 15 (2008), 314–36.
52. CD 1942, 1159–60.
53. CD 1942, 1163.
54. Churchill to Stalin, 12 Sept. 1942, CD 1942, 1197; on Willkie see DVP, 25/2: 214.
55. *SAMO*, 1: 286.
56. Maisky to Eden, 16 Sept. 1942, PREM 3/401/21; Eden to Churchill, 17 Sept. 1942, FO 954/3A/128–30; DVP, 25/2: 190–2.
57. Eden to PM, 23 Sept. 1942, FO 954/3A/136.
58. Eden to PM, 25 Sept. 1942, FO 954/3A/140.
59. *Hansard Parliamentary Debates*, HC Deb 383, col. 95.
60. *SAMO*, 1: 286.
61. Stalin to Maisky, 28 Oct. 1942 cited in Rzheshevskiy, *Stalin i Cherchill*, 378.
62. J. Burns to H. Arnold, 31 Oct. 1942, RG 18, Central Decimal Files, Oct. 1942–1944, Foreign, Russia 452.1–B (NARA).
63. Eisenhower to Marshall, 21 Sept. 1942, in Eisenhower, 1: 570–3.
64. Kimball, 1: 602–6, C-151 and draft to Stalin C-154.
65. Kimball, 1: 606.
66. Churchill to Stalin, 22 and 30 Sept. 1942, CD 1942, 1227, 1241–2.
67. A.M. Samsonov, *Stalingradskaya bitva*, 4th edn, Moscow, 1989, 178.
68. RGASPI f.558, op.11, d.257, l.74.
69. *SAMO*, 1: 233.
70. Mikoyan to Stalin, Molotov, 20 Sept. 1942 in AP RF f.3, op.63, d.220, l.101.
71. *SANO*, 1: 236.
72. CD 1942, 1245.
73. For more detail, see Baker B. Beard, 'The Bradley Mission: The evolution of the Alaska–Siberia route', in Fern Chandonnet (ed.), *Alaska at War, 1941–1945: The forgotten war remembered*, Fairbanks, AK, 2008, 311–18.
74. DVP, 25/2: 235.
75. *SAMO* 1: 244–9.

76. Herring, 72; *Mirovye voyny XX veka*, Book 3: *Vtoraya mirovaya voyna: Istoricheskiy ocherk*, Moscow, 2002, 249.
77. Warren F. Kimball, 'Stalingrad: A chance for choices', *Journal of Military History*, 60 (1996), 105.
78. PSF(D) box 49: Russia, 1942–43.
79. *FRUS 1942*, 3: 655–8; Hurley to President, 8 Dec. 1942, PSF(S) box 5: Russia, 1942–45.
80. PSF(D) box 49: Russia, 1942–43.
81. As he had to admit to Stalin – see *SAMO*, 1: 248. Standley devoted a chapter of his memoirs to a caustic account of his treatment by Willkie: William H. Standley and Arthur A. Ageton, *Admiral Ambassador to Russia*, Chicago, 1955, ch. 17.
82. *SAMO*, 1: 235, 248–50.
83. Washington – Soviet Ambassador, 8 Oct. 1942 in AVP RF f.059, op.1, p.369, d.2512, l.131.
84. MR box 8.
85. Kimball, 1: 617, 621.
86. MR box 8.
87. Kimball, 1: 617, 621; cf. WM 135 (42) 1 CA, CAB 65/32.
88. CHAR 20/81/18–20.
89. MR box 8.
90. Maisky to Molotov, 9 Oct. 1942, AVP RF f.059, op.8, p.2, d.7, ll.322–3.
91. AVP RF f.059, op.1, p.369, d.2509, l.39.
92. Hopkins to Marshall, 10 Oct. 1942, Hopkins papers, box 217 (FDRL).
93. MR box 8.
94. FO 954/3A/176.
95. Sargent, minute, 28 Oct. 1942, FO 954/3A/188.
96. Kimball, 1: 637, 643.
97. RGASPI f.558, op.11, d.257, ll.82–4.
98. RGASPI f.558, op.11, d.257, l.93.
99. Roosevelt to Stalin, 14 Oct. 1942, MR box 8.
100. MR box 8.
101. MR box 8.
102. Antony Beevor, *Stalingrad*, London, 1998, 192–7.
103. CHAR 20/132.
104. MR box 8.
105. Stalin to Roosevelt, 28 Oct. 1942, MR box 8; RGASPI f.558, op.11, d.364, l.96.
106. *SANO*, 1: 294.
107. Maisky to Stalin, 24 Oct. 1942 in DVP 25/2: 293.
108. Rzheshevskiy, *Stalin i Cherchill*, 378.
109. OGB, 3/2: 407–8.
110. L.F. Sotskov (ed.), *Agressiya. Rassekrechennye dokumenty sluzhby vneshney razvedki Rossiyskoy Federatsii 1939–1941*, Moscow, 2011, 380.
111. *SANO*, 1: 294.
112. *Pravda*, 19 October 1942.
113. *Vneshnyaya politika Sovetskogo Soyuza v period Otechestvennoy voyny*, Moscow, 1946, 1: 318.
114. Harvey, 172.
115. DVP, 25/2: 290–3; Eden to Clark Kerr, 25 Oct. 1942, FO 954/25B/449–50.
116. WM 145 (42) 2, CA, 26 Oct. 1942, CAB 65/32.
117. Churchill to Eden, 27 Oct. 1942, CHAR 20/67, printed in CD 1942, 1318–19.

6 Casablanca

1. Harvey, 165; Eric Larrabee, *Commander in Chief: Franklin Delano Roosevelt, his lieutenants, and their war*, New York, 1987, 140.
2. Glantz/House, 134.
3. CHAR 20/82/51 and 55.

4. *SANO*, 1: 270.
5. CD 1942, 1358.
6. CHAR 20/82/77.
7. CD 1942, 1371–2.
8. *SANO*, 1: 303–8, quoting pp. 303, 307.
9. Kimball, 1: 671–3.
10. See R.C. Lukas, *Eagles East: The Army Air Forces and the Soviet Union, 1941–1945*, Tallahassee, FL, 1970, 153–8.
11. *SANO*, 1: 307.
12. CD 1942, 1401–2.
13. The message to Churchill is printed in CD 1941, 1402–3.
14. AP RF f.45, op.1, d.374, l.15.
15. Transcript of a conversation of I.V. Stalin with British Ambassador Clark Kerr, 24 Feb. 1943, RGASPI f.558, op.11, d.284, l.49.
16. *FRUS 1942*, 3: 655–8; Butler, 94–7.
17. Henderson to Molotov, 14 Dec. 1942, RGASPI f.558, op.11, d.364, l.141.
18. MR box 8.
19. MR box 8.
20. The message to Roosevelt is in MR box 8.
21. CD 1942, 1426.
22. Clark Kerr to Eden, 25 Nov. 1942, FO 181/969/6.
23. CD 1942, 1430–2.
24. On 10 August 1941, the Soviet and British governments, through their ambassadors in Ankara, proclaimed their respect for Turkey's territorial integrity and their readiness to assist her in the event of an attack by a European power.
25. MR box 8; cf. *SAMO*, 1: 58, 63.
26. H. Freeman Matthews, acting US head of mission in Algiers, told his former boss, Admiral William Leahy, by then FDR's chief of staff: 'Only Darlan could order the cease-fire and ensure its implementation throughout North Africa.' Matthews to Leahy, 10 Dec. 1942, Leahy diaries, reel 3 (LC).
27. Molotov to Maisky, 27 Nov. 1942 in RGASPI f.558, op.11, d.257, ll.149–51, with Stalin's amendments at ll.154–5.
28. CD 1942, 1446–7.
29. 'This is a strong Russian proverb,' Maisky added on the translation sent to Churchill.
30. Maisky to NKID, 3 Dec. 1942, AVP RF f.059, op.1, p.372, d.2533, l.205.
31. Steven Casey, *Cautious Crusade: Franklin D. Roosevelt, American public opinion, and the war against Nazi Germany*, Oxford, 2001, 114.
32. Baggallay to Eden, 27 Dec. 1942, FO 181/969/6.
33. Clark Kerr to Eden, minute, 10 Dec. 1942, FO 954/16/210.
34. WM 162 (42), CAB 65/28, fo. 149.
35. WSC to Ismay for COS Committee, 29 Nov. 1942, PREM 3/499/7.
36. MR box 8.
37. FO memo, 29 Dec. 1942, quoted in Martin H. Folly, *Churchill, Whitehall and the Soviet Union, 1940–45*, London, 2000, 84. For the 6 Nov. speech to the Moscow Soviet of Workers' Deputies, see J. Stalin, *On the Great Patriotic War of the Soviet Union*, Moscow, 1944, 61–77, quoting pp. 69, 74.
38. *Corr 1957*, 1: 81, 83.
39. Kimball, 2: 42–3.
40. Kimball, 2: 54–5; cf. Sherwood, 661.
41. MR box 8.
42. CD 1942, 1475.
43. The message to FDR is in MR box 8.
44. Warren F. Kimball, *Forged in War: Roosevelt, Churchill, and the Second World War*, New York, 1997, 185.
45. Meeting with Churchill, 8 Feb. 1943, in Gorodetsky, 481–2.

46. CD 1942, 1488.
47. *SANO*, 1: 321.
48. A draft of this message suggested 1 or 15 February: MR box 8.
49. MR box 8.
50. CD 1942, 1522.
51. MR box 8.
52. DVP, 25/2: 418–20.
53. Roosevelt to Stalin, 16 Dec. 1942, and Stalin to Roosevelt, 18 Dec. 1942, MR box 8.
54. Exchange of messages on 21 Dec. 1942 in Kimball, 2: 85–6.
55. CD 1943, 42.
56. CD 1942, 1556.
57. Leahy, memo for the President, 30 Dec. 1942, MR box 8.
58. MR box 8.
59. RGASPI f.558, op.11, d.365, l.2.
60. Stalin to Roosevelt, 5 January 1943, *Corr 1957*, 2: 48.
61. *FRUS W and C*, 506–7.
62. MR box 8.
63. CD 1942, 1557–8; Gilbert 7, 285.
64. Kimball, 1: 648–51 and 2: 44–7.
65. *SANO*, 1: 326–7.
66. Churchill to Foreign Secretary, 9 Jan. 1943, FO 954/3/262. Churchill cited his message to Stalin on 29 Dec. 1942, which promised 'thirty or more ships' in January – in one 'portion' or two – and did not mention February. See also S.W. Roskill, *The War at Sea*, London, 1956, 2: 397–8.
67. Ivan M. Maisky, *Dnevnik diplomata*, ed. A.O. Chubaryan, 2 vols, Moscow, 2009, 2: 190.
68. CD 1943, 126.
69. CD 1943, 85.
70. RGASPI f.558, op.22, d.365, ll.12–13.
71. Entry for 18 Jan. 1943 in Gorodetsky, 468.
72. MR box 8.
73. Meeting of 8 Feb. 1943 in Gorodetsky, 481.
74. Kimball, 2: 108–9.
75. *FRUS W and C*, 628.
76. *FRUS W and C*, 796 (CCS Final Report), 591 (Arnold and Brooke).
77. *FRUS W and C*, 583 (Marshall) and 584–5 (Brooke).
78. Stoler, 103.
79. Entry for 26 Aug. 1941 in Gorodetsky, 381.
80. *FRUS W and C*, 640, 672, 732, 782–5, 803–7; Churchill to War Cabinet, 20 Jan. 1943, CD 1943, 164.
81. *FRUS W and C*, 848; cf. APP, Casablanca communiqué, 26 Jan. 1943.
82. Churchill to War Cabinet, 26 Jan. 1943, CD 1943, 235.
83. CD 1943, 230–1.
84. *SAMO*, 1: 273–4.
85. RGASPI f.558, op.11, d.365, l.31.
86. For Prime Minister from Foreign Secretary, 28 Jan. 1943, PREM 3/333/3; William H. Standley and Arthur A. Ageton, *Admiral Ambassador to Russia*, Chicago, 1955, 327–8; cf. *SAMO*, 1: 273.
87. Churchill to Stalin, 27 and 29 Jan. 1943, CD 1943, 244–5, 260; Tamkin, 84–6; cf. *FRUS W and C*, 659–60.
88. The (poorly translated) British version of the message is printed in CD 1943, 286.
89. MR box 8.
90. Antony Beevor, *Stalingrad*, London, 1998, 383.
91. Nicholas Stargardt, *The German War: A nation under arms, 1939–1945*, London, 2015, 329–37.
92. Entry for 7 Feb. 1943, in Gorodetsky, 477.

7 Second Front When?

1. For example, CD 1943, 428, 558, 938.
2. Kimball, 2: 189.
3. See Sherwood, 707–21, quoting pp. 717, 719.
4. Excerpts from Presidential Press Conference, 30 March 1943 (APP website).
5. Churchill to Stalin, 1 Feb. 1943, and Stalin to Churchill, 6 February 1943, CD 1943, 316–18, 357–8.
6. Churchill to Stalin, 1 Feb. 1943, CD 1943, 316–18.
7. Press conference, Cairo, 1 Feb. 1943, in CD 1943, 307–8.
8. Stalin's reply, sent on 5 February, is in MR box 8.
9. PPPR 1943, 63.
10. Churchill's message and Roosevelt's reply are in Kimball, 2: 132–5; but see also the original documentation in MR box 3: Roosevelt–Churchill, esp. pp. 31–6, and PREM 3/333/3.
11. The 29th Infantry Division, which would spend twenty months in Britain before finally receiving its baptism of fire on Omaha beach on the morning of D-Day.
12. Gorodetsky, esp. pp. 478–80; cf. Ivan M. Maisky, *Dnevnik diplomata*, ed. A.O. Chubaryan, 2 vols, Moscow, 2009, 2: 211–19.
13. Maisky to NKID, 9 Feb. 1943, AVP RF f.059, op.10, p.8, d.64, ll.15–17. Also printed in DVP, 26: 97–8.
14. CD 1943, 438.
15. CD 1943, 377.
16. The 16 Feb. message to FDR is in MR box 8.
17. Glantz/House, 143.
18. CD 1943, 447–8.
19. Eden, memo, 17 Feb. 1943, circulated to the Cabinet's Defence Committee as DO (43) 3, CAB 69/5.
20. From London, 18 Feb. 1943, AVP RF f.059, op.10, p.8, d.64, ll.29–30; also in DVP, 26: 130–1; Eden, memo, 17 Feb. 1943, 2.
21. President to Stalin, draft, 19 Feb. 1943, MR box 8.
22. MR box 8.
23. Bracken, memo, 22 Jan. 1943, WP (43) 37, CAB 66/33; P.M.H. Bell, *John Bull and the Bear: British public opinion, foreign policy and the Soviet Union, 1941–1945*, London, 1990, 68–9; Gorodetsky, 487.
24. CD 1943, 502, 547, 553, 562, 584, 589.
25. Kimball, 2: 151–4.
26. Maisky to NKID, 9 March 1943, AVP RF f.059, op.10, p.8, d.64, l.47.
27. Ismay for PM, 18 Feb. 1943. After the war, captured German documents indicated that seventeen divisions moved from France to Russia in the period Nov. 1942 to Feb. 1943, while three divisions had been transferred in the opposite direction en route for Tunisia. Hinsley, 2: 617.
28. CHAR 20/107/94–6.
29. CD 1943, 618; *SWW*, 4: 661–2.
30. Churchill to FO, 12 March, and Churchill to Stalin, 13 March 1943 in CD 1943, 626, 632–3.
31. Glantz/House, 144–7, quoting p. 144; Horst Boog et al. (eds), *Germany and the Second World War*, Vol. 6, *The Global War*, Oxford, 2001, 1184–93.
32. RGASPI f.558, op.11, d.260, l.29.
33. The message to FDR is printed in *Corr 1957*, 2: 58–9.
34. CHAR 20/108/25.
35. Stalin to Churchill, 15 March 1943 and Churchill to Stalin, 20 March 1943, CD 1943, 655–6, 719.
36. CHAR 20/108/24.
37. Churchill to Eden, 17 March 1943, CHAR 20/108/26.

38. Churchill to Eden, 18 March 1943, CHAR 20/108/32.
39. WM 42 (43) CA, 18 March 1943, CAB 65/37, fo. 89. Also CD 1943, 686–7.
40. RGASPI f.558, op.11, d.260, l.114.
41. CD 1943, 823.
42. CD 1943, 844–5.
43. Transcript of Stalin's conversation with Martel and Clark Kerr, 12 April 1943, RGASPI f.558, op.11, d.277, l.56.
44. Gorodetsky, 502–3.
45. Warner to Clark Kerr, 9 April 1943, FO 800/301, fo. 24.
46. AVP RF f.059a, op.7, p.13, d.6, ll.255–6.
47. Churchill to Ismay for COS, 13 March 1943, CD 1943, 633–4.
48. Churchill to Eden, 25 March 1943, CD 1943, 783–4.
49. Kimball, 2: 172–7.
50. CD 1943, 854.
51. CD 1943, 852–3.
52. Maisky to NKID, 31 March 1943, AVP RF f.059a, op.7, p.13, d.6, ll.258–60. See also Gorodetsky, 503–4.
53. CD 1943, 888.
54. Gorodetsky, 504.
55. Maisky to NKID, 3 April 1943, AVP RF f.059, op.10, p.8, d.64, ll.182–3; cf. Gorodetsky, 497, 504.
56. Cadogan, 518; Kimball, 2: 179–80.
57. Churchill to Clark Kerr, 4 April 1943, and replies 4 and 5 April 1943, FO 954/3B, fos 387–8, 390.
58. See CD 1943, 918–20.
59. CD 1943, 932.
60. CD 1943, 916.
61. PREM 3/401/16/29–30.
62. CD 1943, 951–2.
63. Mary Soames, *Clementine Churchill*, revised edn, London, 2002, 340–1, 360–3.
64. *Vneshnyaya torgovlya*, 3–4 (1943), 6.
65. Transcript of Stalin's conversation with Martel and Clark Kerr, 12 April 1943, RGASPI f.558, op.11, d.277, l.54.
66. CD 1943, 956.
67. CD 1943, 967–8.
68. Maisky to NKID, 14 April 1943, AVP RF f.059, op.10, p.8, d.64, l.107.
69. Message of 15 April 1943 in Kimball, 2: 191.
70. E.M. Spiers, *Chemical Warfare*, Chicago, 1986, 76–7.
71. Clark Kerr to FO, 14 April 1943, FO 800/301, fo. 26.
72. Maisky to NKID, 21 April 1943, AVP RF f.059, op.10, p.8, d.64, l.113; also see Maisky, *Dnevnik diplomata*, 2: 262–3.

8 Poles Apart

1. Lawrence Rees, *World War Two Behind Closed Doors: Stalin, the Nazis and the West*, London, 2008, 51–5. Extensive documentation has been published in a joint American–Russian–Polish volume: Anna M. Cienciala, Natalia Lebedeva and Wojciech Materski (eds), *Katyn: A crime without punishment*, New Haven, CT, 2007.
2. Molotov to Bogomolov, 22 April 1943, AVP RF f.059, op.10, p.23, d.182, l.145.
3. CD 1943, 1066. The message of 21 April to FDR is in MR box 8.
4. *SWW*, 4: 679–80; memo of Maisky visit, 23 April 1943, FO 954/19B/487–9.
5. Gorodetsky 508–9; Maisky to NKID, 24 April 1943, AVP RF f.059, op.10, p.8, d.54, ll.115–20.
6. WM 56 (43) 5, 19 April 1943, CAB 65/34.

7. O'Malley's despatch is in FO 371/34568, C4230/258/55; cf. P.M.H. Bell, *John Bull and the Bear: British public opinion, foreign policy and the Soviet Union, 1941–1945*, London, 1990, 116 and more generally FCO, *Katyn: British reactions to the Katyn Massacre, 1943–2003*, London, 2003.

8. Harvey, 249; Eden to PM, 20 April 1943, with draft, and PM to Eden, 23 April 1943, PREM 3/354/8.

9. CD 1943, 1100.

10. Cienciala et al., *Katyn*, 219–20.

11. Churchill to Stalin, 25 April 1943, CD 1943, 1106–7.

12. CD 1943, 1107.

13. President to Hull and Hull to Capt. Hammond, both 26 April 1943, MR box 8.

14. Which was how it was translated in *Corr 1957*, 2: 62.

15. MR box 8.

16. MR box 8.

17. Maisky to NKID, 29 April 1943, AVP RF f.059, op.10, p.8, d.54, ll.117–22 (DVP, 26: 361); similarly in Gorodetsky, 514; Harvey, 251. Eden was referring to Edvard Beneš, who was browbeaten by Hitler during the Sudeten crisis.

18. Clark Kerr to Foreign Office, 26 April 1943, PREM 3/354/8/416.

19. WM 59 (43) 1, CAB 65/34; cf. Bell, *John Bull and the Bear*, 120–5.

20. Cadogan, 525; cf. Gorodetsky, 515–17.

21. Cadogan, 524; Clark Kerr to FO, tel. 317, 29 April 1943 and FO to Clark Kerr, tel. 450, 30 April 1943, in FO 800/301, Pol/43/29 and Pol/43/26. Because of the late revision, the opening paragraph was not in the message sent to FDR: see Kimball, 2: 199.

22. As did Molotov, vehemently, when handed Churchill's message: Clark Kerr to FO, tel. 327, 1 May 1943, FO 800/301, Pol/43/27. See also Barker, 250.

23. CD 1943, 1137–8.

24. Rees, *World War Two: Behind Closed Doors*, 185.

25. For more on the vicissitudes of the families see Olga Kucherenko, *Soviet Street Children and the Second World War: Welfare and social control under Stalin*, London, 2016, 79–81.

26. Kimball, 2: 202–5.

27. Churchill to Clark Kerr, 2 May 1943, CD 1943, 1177.

28. Clark Kerr to Churchill, 3 May 1943, CD 1943, 1182.

29. Clark Kerr to Churchill, 8 May 1943 about Kremlin meeting on 7 May, CD 1943, 1238; Pavlov's rendition is in RGASPI f.558, op.11, d.284, ll.66–7.

30. Churchill to Stalin, 2 May 1943, CD 1943, 1178–9. See also Order of the Day no. 195, 1 May 1943, www.marxists.org/reference/archive/stalin/works/1943/05/01.htm

31. Stalin to Churchill, 4 May 1943, CHAR 20/111/25–6.

32. CHAR 20/111/66–7.

33. Kimball, 3: 202–3, 206.

34. MR box 8.

35. Davies was the third husband of Marjorie Merriweather Post, heiress to the General Foods empire. One of her estates – Mar-a-Lago in Florida – later became notorious as the biliously grandiose 'Southern White House' of billionaire president Donald J. Trump.

36. *SAMO*, 1: 314–15.

37. AVP RF f.06, op.5, d.327, ll.16–17.

38. Halifax to Eden and Churchill, 25 April 1943, FO 954/26A/58.

39. PSF(D) box 49: Russia, 1942–43.

40. The message to Churchill is printed in CD 1943, 1236.

41. MR box 8. As the file copy indicates, the telegram was sent *en clair* via RCA radio tele-communications from Moscow at 04.49 on 8 May and received by the White House at 23.15 on 7 May.

42. Churchill to Stalin, 9 May 1943, CD 1943, 1240.

43. Eden to Clark Kerr, 6 May 1943, FO 954/19B/520–1.

44. Churchill to Eden, 10 May 1943, CD 1943, 1255.

45. W.M. 67 (43) 3, annex, 10 May 1943, CAB 65/34; cf. Churchill's draft of 10 May in CHAR 20/128/9.
46. Cadogan, 529.
47. CD 1943, 1258.
48. Churchill to Stalin, 14 May 1943, CD 1943, 1291.
49. Beaumont, 142–57; Mikoyan to Stalin and Molotov, 27 June 1943, AP RF f.3, op.63, d.218, ll.90–1.
50. Roosevelt to Stalin, 18 May 1943, MR box 8; RGASPI f.558, op.11, d.365, l.110.
51. Dennis J. Dunn, *Caught between Roosevelt and Stalin: America's ambassadors to Moscow*, Lexington, KY, 1998, 185–6; William H. Standley and Arthur A. Ageton, *Admiral Ambassador to Russia*, Chicago, 1955, 369.
52. G.A. Koltunov and B.G. Solovev, *Kurskaya bitva*, Moscow, 1970, 40.
53. Dunn, *Caught between Roosevelt and Stalin*, 187–9; Clark Kerr to Warner, 3 June 1943 and Warner to Clark Kerr, 1 July 1943, FO 800/301/33–4, 53.
54. Quoted in Mary E. Glantz, *FDR and the Soviet Union: The president's battles over foreign policy*, Lawrence, KS, 2005, 128.
55. MR box 8.
56. PM to Deputy PM, 23 May 1943, CHAR 20/128/40.
57. Ivo Banac (ed.), *The Diary of Georgi Dimitrov, 1933–1949*, London, 2003, 275–6.
58. Warner to Clark Kerr, 28 May 1943, FO 800/301, fo. 30.
59. On which see Alex Danchev, *Very Special Relationship: Field Marshal John Dill and the Anglo-American Alliance, 1941–44*, London, 1986, 118–21.
60. *FRUS W and C*, esp. pp. 44–5, from CCS meeting of 13 May.
61. *FRUS W and C*, 282; Alanbrooke, 410.
62. *SWW*, 4: 729; cf. CD 1943, 1488–91, 1501.
63. *SWW*, 4: 726.
64. Churchill to Roosevelt, 26 May 1943, and FDR's revisions to Marshall's draft, both in MR box 8.
65. The draft preamble is in *FRUS W and C*, 379–80.
66. MR box 8.
67. MR box 8.
68. Standley to President, 5 June 1943, MR box 8.
69. MR box 8.
70. For the message to Churchill see CD 1943, 1573.
71. MR box 8.
72. Warner to Clark Kerr, 8 July 1943, FO 800/301, fo. 60.
73. Clark Kerr to FO, 15 June 1943, FO 954/26A/91; Churchill to Eden, 16 June 1943, CD 1943, 1624.
74. FDR to Arnold, memo, 10 June 1943, MR box 8 – where FDR's two messages of 16 June are also to be found.
75. Kimball, 2: 244–7 and 259–61.
76. Churchill to Clark Kerr, 19 June 1943, CD 1943, 1624–5. On the original copy dated 16 April in Eden's files (FO 954/26A/93–4), Churchill corrected the typo 'Channel reaches' to read 'Channel beaches', but this was not done in the telegram sent to Moscow.
77. MR box 8.
78. CD 1943, 1651–2.
79. FDR's message of 22 June 1943 may be found on the APP website and Stalin's reply on 26 June 1943 in MR box 8.
80. Churchill to Attlee and Eden, 21 May 1943, CD 1943, 137; Eden, 390.
81. Kimball, 2: 254–7.
82. *SANO*, 1: 398.
83. Stalin to Churchill, 26 June 1943, CD 1943, 1720–1; cf. Molotov to Maisky, 25 June 1943, AVP RF f.059, op.10, p.23, d.183, ll.96–9 (DVP, 26: 505–6).
84. CHAR 20/113/108.
85. Stalin to Roosevelt, 24 June 1943, MR box 8.

86. CD 1943, 1704–6.
87. Ismay to Churchill and Churchill to Clark Kerr, both 26 June 1943, PREM 3/333/5/252–3.
88. CD 1943, 1719–20.
89. Kimball, 2: 278–9, 283–4; cf. W. Averell Harriman and Elie Abel, *Special Envoy to Churchill and Stalin*, New York, 1975, 216–18. On 26 June a still-angry Churchill mused to Harriman that Stalin wanted to tie the Allies down by a second front in France because of his own designs on the Balkans.
90. Kimball, 2: 285–90.
91. Churchill to Clark Kerr, 29 June 1943, PREM 3/333/5/245.
92. Clark Kerr to Churchill, 1 July 1943, PREM 3/333/5/443–4.
93. Churchill, minute, 3 July 1943, PREM 3/333/5/240–2; cf. Eden to Clark Kerr, 5 July 1943, FO 954/26A/107.
94. Maisky to NKID, 3 July 1943, AVP RF f.059a, op.7, p.13, d.6, ll.293–8.
95. Molotov to Maisky, 25 June 1943, AVP RF f.059, op.10, p.22, d.177, l.29.
96. Maisky to NKID, 29 June 1943, AVP RF f.059, op.10, p.7, d.59, ll.130–2; Eden to Clark Kerr, 29 July 1943, FO 954/26A/108.
97. CD 1943, 1835.
98. CD 1943, 1862.
99. Text of Eden to Clark Kerr, with Churchill minute, 29 July 1943, FO 954/26A/109.
100. Halifax to Churchill, 8 July 1943, CD 1943, 1840.
101. MR box 8.
102. Davies to Stalin, 22 July 1943; Hopkins to Gromyko, 22 July 1943, MR box 8.
103. From Washington, 23 June 1943, AVP RF f.059, op.10, p.3, d.25, l.41.
104. RGASPI f.558, op.11, d.366, l.1.

9 Fighting Back

1. Cited in *Velikaya Otechestvennaya voyna 1941–1945 godov* (12 vols), Volume 3: V.P. Baranov et al. (eds), *Bitvy i srazheniya, izmenivshiye khod voyny*, Moscow, 2012, 531.
2. Glantz/House, 176
3. *SWW*, 5: 230.
4. Frieser, 150–7, 168–70.
5. Ibid., 138–40, 145–6.
6. Eisenhower, 2: 1261–2; Kimball, 2: 331–2; CD 1943, 2076–80.
7. Alanbrooke, 433, entry for 25 July 1943.
8. Yee Wah Foo, *Chiang Kaishek's Last Ambassador to Moscow: The wartime diaries of Fu Bingchang*, Basingstoke, 2011, 43–4, 94.
9. Churchill to King George VI, 11 Aug. 1943, CD 1943, 2237–8.
10. Harvey, 291 (quote), 295.
11. Diary entry for 1 Sept. 1943 in Eden, 405.
12. Wilson to Clark Kerr, 8 Aug. 1943, FO 800/301/110.
13. See Gorodetsky, 536–40, quoting p. 538.
14. Clark Kerr to Warner, 5 Sept. 1943, FO 954A/139; Alanbrooke, 464.
15. Roosevelt to Stalin, 5 Aug. 1943, MR box 8.
16. Memo of conversation with Churchill, 7 Aug. 1943, Harriman papers, box 164 (LC).
17. Sobolev to NKID, 27 July 1943, AVP RF f.059a, op.7, p.13, d.6, l.304 (DVP, 26: 600).
18. Harvey, 277, 281 – diary entries for 20 and 29 July. For fuller discussion of Churchill's downgrading of 'Overlord' in the light of success in Sicily see Reynolds, 374–6.
19. Clark Kerr to Eden, 30 July 1943, Eden to Churchill, 31 July 1943 and Churchill to Eden, 1 Aug. 1943, FO 954/26A/111–15; also Cadogan, 549.
20. See annotations by Cadogan and Eden on FO 954/26A/114; cf. Eden, 401.
21. CHAR 20/133/1. The version in CD 1943, 2206–7 prints the text as if it was a direct Churchill–Stalin message.
22. MR box 8.

23. The PM passed the message on to FDR, together with his reply of 12 August – Kimball, 2: 385–7.
24. CD 1943, 2226.
25. Eden to Churchill, 10 Aug. 1943, CD 1943, 2229.
26. WM 114 (43) 2 CA, 11 Aug. 1943, CAB 65/39.
27. Churchill to Stalin, 12 Aug. 1943, CD 1943, 2236–7.
28. Kimball, 2: 421.
29. Churchill to Sir Ronald I. Campbell, 18 Aug. 1943, CD 1943, 2284.
30. Eden, minute for Cadogan, 19 Aug. 1943, FO 954/2/39.
31. MR box 8.
32. Telegrams of 25 and 26 July in Kimball, 2: 347–8.
33. Standley to Hull, 30 July 1943, reprinted in Hull, memo for the President, 31 July 1943, MR box 8 – S-R messages.
34. Winant to FDR and Hull, 26 July 1943, *FRUS 1943*, 2: 335.
35. Sobolev to NKID, 27 July 1943, AVP RF f.059a, op.7, p.13, d.6, l.302.
36. *SANO*, 1: 410.
37. *SANO*, 1: 412–13.
38. Churchill to Attlee and FO, 18 Aug. 1943, CD 1943, 2283–4.
39. Kimball, 2: 423–4.
40. Roosevelt and Churchill to Stalin, 19 Aug. 1943, CHAR 20/132/1/57–8 and 58–9. They were printed as a single message in *Corr 1957*, 1: 79–82.
41. Stalin came back from a short visit to the Western and Kalinin *Fronts* on 5 August. In his office ledger there are two entries on 17 and 21 August, in both cases listing Molotov among the visitors. See A.A. Chernobayev (ed.), *Na priyeme u Stalina. Tetradi (zhurnaly) zapisey lits, prinyatykh I.V. Stalinym (1924–1953 gg.). Spravochnik*, Moscow, 2008, 416.
42. Clark Kerr to Eden, 28 Aug. 1943, and minute by Warner, 30 Aug. 1943, FO 954/26A/125–7.
43. Maisky to Molotov, 31 Aug.1943, AVP RF f.059, op.10, p.8, d.64, ll.182–9.
44. CD 1943, 2315–16.
45. Harriman, 225–6. See also his original memo of the dinner on 24 Aug. 1943 in Harriman papers, box 164 (LC).
46. Eden, 404, diary entry for 26 Aug. 1943.
47. Churchill to War Cabinet, 25 Aug. 1943, CD 1943, 2343–4; cf. WM 119 (43) 1 CA, CAB 65/39.
48. From Washington, 25 Aug. 1943, AVP RF f.059, op.10, p.3, d.26, l.2 (DVP, 26: 693).
49. CD 1943, 2338–9.
50. Clark Kerr to Eden, 24 Aug. 1943, FO 965/13B/396–7; WM 119 (43) 1 CA, CAB 65/39.
51. Kimball, 2: 432–4; Roosevelt and Churchill to Stalin, 29 Aug. 1943, MR box 8.
52. Brooke and Leahy to President and Prime Minister, 24 Aug. 1943, MR box 8.
53. Alanbrooke, 437–51, esp. p. 437, 440, 442, 448, 450–1.
54. Martin J. Sherwin, *A World Destroyed: The atomic bomb and the grand alliance*, New York, 1977, 85, 89.
55. V.I. Lota, GRU. *Ispytanie voynoy. Voyennaya razvedka Rossii nakanune i v gody Velikoy Otechestvennoy voyny 1941–1945 gg.*, Moscow, 2010, 648. The Soviet government had formally decided on 12 April 1943 to set up its own atomic project under Igor Kurchatov but, despite considerable intelligence from British and American sources, they were a long way behind 'Manhattan' – see David Holloway, *Stalin and the Bomb: The Soviet Union and atomic energy, 1939–1956*, New Haven, CT, 1994, 96–105.
56. MR box 8.
57. *SANO*, 1: 426–7, 440.
58. Churchill to Stalin, 30 Aug. 1943, and Stalin to Churchill, 31 Aug. 1943, CD 1943, 2358, 2370; see also CD 1943–44, 13.
59. On operation 'Achse', see Frieser, 1123–5.
60. See draft 2 Sept. 1943 marked 'For Col. Hammond' in MR box 8.
61. *SANO*, 1: 427–39, 442.

62. Roosevelt and Churchill to Stalin, 2 Sept. 1943, in MR box 8 and CD 1943–44, 6–7.
63. CD 1943–44, 44, 45–6, 54.
64. CD 1943–44, esp. 61–2.
65. MR box 8.
66. Eden to Churchill, 2 Sept. 1943, PREM 3/172/1/73A.
67. CD 1943–44, 47–8.
68. Stalin to Roosevelt and Churchill, 7 Sept. 1943, MR box 8.
69. RGASPI f.558, op.11, d.263, l.2. The message of 8 Sept. 1943 to Churchill is in CD 1943, 84–5.
70. Subsequently, as relations with the Allies warmed up after the Tehran conference, Soviet military missions were sent to Italy and France. For more details, see V.I. Lota, *Taynye operatsii Vtoroy mirovoy voyny: kniga o voyennoy razvedke, 1944 god*, Moscow, 2006, ch.2.
71. MR box 8.
72. From Washington, 9 Sept. 1943, AVP RF f.059, op.10, p.3, d.26, l.126.
73. MR box 8.
74. Roosevelt to Stalin, 9 Sept. 1943, MR box 8; Churchill to Stalin, 10 Sept. 1943, CD 1943–44, 104–6.
75. Stalin to Roosevelt and Churchill, 10 Sept. 1943, MR box 8.
76. N.G. Kuznetsov, *Kursom k pobede*, Moscow, 2003, 316.
77. MR box 8.
78. The word 'Tegeran' in the translation in the White House files is probably another sign of Gromyko's work: the Russian alphabet does not include any approximation to the letter 'h' (voiceless glottal fricative), which is therefore usually rendered as a 'g' – notoriously in the case of 'Garry Gopkins'.
79. CD 1943–44, quoting pages 156 and 152–3.
80. Kimball, 2: 447–8, 491, 492.
81. Eisenhower, 2: 1430–3; Kimball, 2: 456–63.
82. CD 1943–44, 213–14.
83. Stalin to Churchill, 22 Sept. 1943, CD 1943–44, 229.
84. *SAMO*, 1: 368–9, 371–2. Molotov's message dated 26 Sept. 1943 is in MR box 8.
85. Warren F. Kimball, *Forged in War: Roosevelt, Churchill, and the Second World War*, New York, 1997, 223.
86. Draft message, 25 Sept. 1943, RGASPI f.599, op.11, d.263, l.81.
87. Frieser, 294, 1255, drawing on the study edited by G.F. Krivosheyev, *Grif sekretnosti snyat*, Moscow, 1993 on the 'secret' losses of the Soviet forces.
88. V.P. Istomin, *Smolenskaya nastupatelnaya operatsiya (1943 g.)*, Moscow, 1975, 21.
89. CD 1943–44, 261 and note.
90. Cordell Hull, *The Memoirs of Cordell Hull*, 2 vols, New York, 1948, 2: 1255.
91. FDR's amendments to draft message, 25 Sept. 1943, and Opnav to Alusna, Moscow, 30 Sept. 1943, MR box 8. See also Frank Costigliola, *Roosevelt's Lost Alliances: How personal politics helped start the Cold War*, Princeton, NJ, 2012, 186–90.
92. MR box 8.
93. CD 1943–44, 273.
94. CD 1943–44, 258.
95. MR box 8.

10 Face to Face

1. *SAMO*, 1: 373.
2. WM 142 (43) 2 CA, 18 Oct. 1943.
3. Roosevelt and Churchill were worrying about interpreters for the Tehran conference as early as mid-September 1943 – see CD 1943–44, 153.
4. CD 1943–44, 760. For background, see Keith Sainsbury, *The Turning Point: The Moscow, Cairo, and Teheran conferences*, Oxford, 1986, chs 1–5.

5. Eisenhower, 3: 1469–70; Roosevelt to Stalin, 1 Oct. 1943, MR box 8.
6. Kimball, 2: 471–4, 484, quoting p. 473; Churchill to Stalin, 1 Oct. 1943, CHAR 20/132/1/68.
7. Stalin to Churchill, 2 Sept. 1943, CD 1943–44, 339, and Stalin to Roosevelt, 5 Sept. 1943, MR box 8.
8. Clark Kerr to FO, 23 Sept. 1943, FO 954/3B/485.
9. CD 1943–44, 266, 282.
10. CD 1943–44, 266.
11. CD 1943–44, 322–4.
12. OGB, 4/2: 618; O.A. Rzheshevskiy, *Stalin i Cherchill*, Moscow, 2010, 389; Michael Reilly (as told to William J. Slocum), *Reilly of the White House*, New York, 1947, 179.
13. CD 1943–44, 348.
14. MR box 8.
15. Hinsley, 3/1: 114–17, 173–7.
16. MR box 8.
17. Clark Kerr to Eden, 14 Oct. 1943, FO 954/3B/503; Kimball, 2: 533.
18. A.A. Gromyko, I.N. Zemskov et al. (eds), *Sovetskiy Soyuz na mezhdunarodnykh konferentsiyakh perioda Velikoy Otechestvennoy voyny 1941–1945 gg.*, Moscow, 1984, 1: 121.
19. CD 1943–44, 500–1.
20. CD 1943–44, 521–2, 554–5; WM 142 (43) 2 CA, CAB 65/40.
21. Churchill note, 18 Oct. 1943, CD 1943–44, 556–7; paraphrased in *SWW*, 5: 241–2.
22. From London, 19 Oct. 1943, AVP RF f.059, op.10, p.8, d.62, ll 74–7.
23. Cadogan, 568–9.
24. Gromyko et al., *Sovetskiy Soyuz na mezhdunarodnykh konferentsiyakh*, 1: 122; CD 1943–44, 609–10; Eden, 412–13.
25. Beaumont, 165.
26. WM 142 (43) 2 CA, CAB 65/40; CD 1943–44, 565–6.
27. From London, 22 Oct. 1943, AVP RF f.059, op.10, p.8, d.62, ll.105–7.
28. Warner to Secretary of State, 21 Oct. 1943, FO 371/37030.
29. Churchill to Roosevelt and Stalin, 12 Oct. 1943, CD 1943–44, 486–7; cf. WM 137 (43) 2, 8 Oct. 1943, CAB 65/36.
30. SecState to Embassy Moscow, 18 Oct. 1943, RG 84, US Embassy Moscow, Ambassador's Top Secret Records, 1943–50, Box 8 (NARA).
31. Gromyko et al., *Sovetskiy Soyuz na mezhdunarodnykh konferentsiyakh*, 1: 336–7.
32. Roosevelt to Stalin, 14 Oct. 1943, MR box 8.
33. MR box 8.
34. Stalin to Roosevelt, 17 Oct. 1943, MR box 8; Molotov to Gromyko, 12 Oct. 1943, AVP RF f.059, op.10, p.19, d.150, l.64.
35. MR box 8.
36. Roosevelt to Hull, 21 Oct. 1943, MR box 8.
37. MR box 8.
38. Kimball, 2: 547, 550–1.
39. CD 1943–44, 612.
40. *FRUS Cairo and Tehran*, 44–7.
41. Kimball, 2: 561.
42. CD 1943–44, 736, 760; *FRUS Cairo and Tehran*, 35, 52.
43. MR box 8.
44. Kimball, 2: 563; Stoler, 166.
45. Kimball, 2: 541, 555–7, 565
46. Harvey, 317–18. On Churchill's attempts to deceive Eden and Stalin about his strategic rethink and his cover-up of all this in his war memoirs, see Reynolds, 378–82.
47. MR box 8.
48. Stalin to Roosevelt, 10 Nov. 1943, MR box 8.
49. CD 1943–44, 872–3. The draft of the 8 Nov. message in the White House files is marked 'Will notify Prime tomorrow.'

50. Messages in Kimball, 2: 596–7.
51. Kimball, 2: 595. For texts of the two telegrams to Stalin on 12 November, see CD 1943–44, 864, 872–3.
52. Stalin to FDR, 12 Nov. 1943, MR box 8, and Stalin to Churchill, same date, CD 1943–44, 877; *SAMO*, 1: 438.
53. Quoted in Eden to Churchill, 14 Nov. 1943, FO 800/410/39.
54. Kimball, 2: 600. Stalin's messages to Churchill, 12 Nov. 1943, and to Roosevelt, 13 Nov. 1943, are in CD 1943–44, 877 and MR box 8.
55. Smuts to Churchill, 14 Nov. 1943, FO 800/410/35.
56. Roosevelt to Stalin, 20 Nov. 1943, MR box 8.
57. Molotov to Hamilton, 22 Nov. 1943, RGASPI f.558, op.11, d.367, l.23.
58. OGB, 4/2: 613.
59. V. Zhilyayev and A. Gamov, 'V poezde Stalina "zaytsami" ekhali ugolovniki', *Komsomolskaya Pravda*, 7 May 2007.
60. A.E. Golovanov, *Dalnyaya bombardirovochnaya . . .*, Moscow, 2004, 354.
61. RGASPI f.74, op.2, d.123, l.16 (first quotation); S.M. Shtemenko, *Generalnyy shtab v gody voyny*, b.1, Moscow, 1975, 148; OGB, 4/2: 613 (second quotation); on the itinerary of the support team, see V.M. Loginov, *Zhivoy Stalin. Otkroveniya glavnogo telokhranitelya Vozhdya*, Moscow, 2010, 123.
62. Michael F. Reilly (as told to William J. Slocum), *Reilly of the White House*, New York, 1947, 174–6.
63. MR box 8.
64. Cordell Hull, *The Memoirs of Cordell Hull*, 2 vols, New York, 1948, 2: 1313.
65. CD 1943–44, 940.
66. Stalin to Churchill, 25 Nov. 1943, CD 1943–44, 974.
67. MR box 8.
68. Minutes of Maksimov–Dreyfus conversation, 25 Nov. 1943, AVP RF f.06, op.5, p.23, d.248, ll.107–8.
69. From Tehran, 25 Nov. 1943, AP RF f.3, op.63, d.222, l.6.
70. Molotov to Dekanozov, 26 Nov. 1943, AP RF f.3, op.63, d.222, l.7.
71. *FRUS Cairo and Tehran*, 439–40.
72. Minutes of Maksimov–Harriman conversation, 27 Nov. 1943, AVP RF f.06, op.5, p.23, d.248, l.114.
73. *SAMO*, 1: 442–3.
74. Yu. L. Kuznets, *Tegeran 43*, Moscow, 2003; Donal O'Sullivan, *Dealing with the Devil: Anglo-Soviet intelligence cooperation in the Second World War*, New York, 2010, 200–5.
75. *SAMO*, 1: 463–7.
76. *FRUS Cairo and Tehran*, 463–4, quoting Harriman letter of 25 May 1954.
77. Quotations from Frances Perkins and Sergo Beria in Frank Costigliola, *Roosevelt's Lost Alliances: How personal politics helped start the Cold War*, Princeton, NJ, 2012, 196.
78. *FRUS Cairo and Tehran*, 426–7.
79. *FRUS Cairo and Tehran*, 258.
80. For the three documents see *FRUS Cairo and Tehran*, 617–19.
81. *FRUS Cairo and Tehran*, 490, 494.
82. *FRUS Cairo and Tehran*, 535, 537, 539, also 546–8; Alanbrooke, 483.
83. *FRUS Cairo and Tehran*, 552–5; *SWW*, 5: 330; Moran, 163.
84. Moran, 164.
85. *FRUS Cairo and Tehran*, 582–5.
86. Moran, 163 (Clark Kerr), 165.
87. *FRUS Cairo and Tehran*, 554–5.
88. As recalled by Violet Bonham Carter, quoted in John Wheeler-Bennett (ed.), *Action This Day: Working with Churchill*, London, 1968, 96.
89. WM 174 (43) CA, CAB 65/40. See also Reynolds, 384–7.
90. Roosevelt to Stalin, 6 Dec. 1943, and Stalin to Roosevelt, 10 Dec. 1943, both MR box 8; cf. Harriman, 285.

91. *Pravda*, 7 Dec. 1943.
92. *Times*, 6 Dec. 1943.
93. Andrew Buchanan, *American Grand Strategy in the Mediterranean during World War II*, Cambridge, 2013, 164; Ralph B. Levering, *American Opinion and the Russian Alliance, 1939–1945*, Chapel Hill, NC, 1976, 205.
94. Geoffrey Roberts, *Stalin's Wars: From world war to cold war, 1939–1953*, London, 2006, 187.
95. RGASPI f.558, op.11, d.234, ll.103–4.
96. *Corr 1957*, 2: 111.
97. MR box 8.
98. RGASPI f.558, op.11, d.367, l.44.
99. MR box 8.
100. MR box 8.
101. CD 1943–44, 1169.
102. *Corr 1957*, 1: 179.
103. *Corr 1957*, 1: 179.
104. CD 1943–44, 1217.
105. CD 1943–44, 1243.
106. RGASPI f.558, op.11, d.264, ll.110–11.
107. CD 1943–44, 1262.
108. Minutes of conversation between Comrade Stalin and British Ambassador Kerr, 2 Feb. 1944, RGASPI f.558, op.11, d.284, l.81.
109. CD 1943–44, 1271.
110. Zhilyayev and Gamov, 'V poezde Stalina'; Golovanov, *Dalnyaya bombardirovochnaya*, 366.
111. A.A. Chernobayev (ed.), *Na priyeme u Stalina. Tetradi (zhurnaly) zapisey lits, prinyatykh I.V. Stalinym (1924–1953 gg.). Spravochnik*, Moscow, 2008, 424.
112. Elliott Roosevelt (ed.), *FDR: His personal letters, 1928–1945*, 2 vols, New York, 1950, 2: 1483.

11 The Spirit of Tehran Evaporates

1. CD 1943–44, 1423.
2. G.K. Zhukov, *Vospominaniya i razmyshleniya*, 2 vols, Moscow, 2002, 2: 191.
3. State of the Union radio address to the nation, 11 Jan. 1944 (APP website).
4. Donald Gillies, *Radical Diplomat: The life of Archibald Clark Kerr, Lord Inverchapel, 1882–1951*, London, 1999, 156.
5. Warner to Balfour, 25 Jan. 1944, FO 800/302/1–3.
6. CD 1943–44, 1317.
7. Transcript of Comrade Stalin's conversation with British Ambassador Kerr, 2 Feb. 1944, RGASPI f.558, op.11, d.284, l.81.
8. MR box 9.
9. Churchill to Eden, and to Stalin, both 4 Jan. 1944, CD 1943–44, 1322 and 1323.
10. CD 1943–44, 1324.
11. Kimball, 2: 651.
12. RGASPI f.558, op.11, d.265, ll.25–6.
13. CD 1943–44, 1362.
14. Eden to Churchill, 10 Jan. 1944, FO 954/20A/7.
15. CD 1943–44, 1374–5.
16. A.E. Golovanov, *Dalnyaya bombardirovochnaya . . .*, Moscow, 2004, 490; cf. Churchill to Stalin, 10 Jan. 1944, CD 1943–44, 1368.
17. CD 1943–44, 1412.
18. CD 1943–44, 1406.
19. Frieser, 394; Glantz/House, 185–6.
20. Stalin to Churchill, 12 Jan. 1944, CD 1943–44, 1414.

21. Kimball, 2: 653–4, 662. That sentence was added to the draft by FDR.
22. Churchill to Stalin, 17 Jan. 1944, and Stalin to Churchill, 20 Jan. 1944, CD 1943–44, 1420, 1454.
23. Churchill to Stalin, 21 Jan. 1944, CD 1943–44, 1460; *SWW*, 5: 432, 437.
24. WM 147 (43) 2 CA, CAB 65/40, quoting fo. 47, Eden to Churchill, tel. 64 Space, 23 Oct. 1943.
25. CD 1943–44, 680–2, 700–1.
26. CD 1943–44, 1041–2; cf. *FRUS Cairo and Tehran*, 597.
27. Kimball, 2: 625; N.G. Kuznetsov, *Kursom k pobede*, Moscow, 2003, 337.
28. Chiefs of Staff to Britman, Washington, 23 Dec. 1943, PREM 3/240/3.
29. Churchill to Eden, 7 Jan. 1944, CD 1943–44, 1358–9.
30. Churchill to Eden, 10 Jan. 1944, CD 1943–44, 1380.
31. Eden to Churchill, 11 Jan. 1944, CD 1943–44, 1393.
32. Kimball, 2: 664–6, 669–71, 675–6; see also document on the background to the two messages to Stalin, 23 Jan. 1944, MR box 9 – R-S messages, and the summary in Woodward, 2: 586–7, 604–11.
33. CD 1943–44, 1469–70.
34. Printed in CD 1943–44, 1470.
35. SecState to Moscow Embassy, 25 Jan 1944, RG 84, Poles — State Cables, January–July 1944 (NARA).
36. Kimball, 2: 672–3, 677.
37. See Hiroaki Kuromiya and Andrzej Pepłoński, 'Kōzō Izumi and the Soviet breach of Imperial Japanese diplomatic codes', *Intelligence and National Security*, 28 (2013), 769–84.
38. Geoffrey Roberts, *Stalin's Wars: From world war to cold war, 1939–53*, London, 2006, 173–4.
39. CD 1943–44, 1487–8.
40. Conversation with journalist Colin Coote, 27 Jan. 1944, CD 1943–44, 1534.
41. Cadogan, 599.
42. CD 1943–44, 1535–8.
43. Preliminary requirements of the USSR regarding the Italian fleet, AVP RF f.07, op.4, p.26, d.13, l.54.
44. Stalin to Churchill and Roosevelt, 29 Jan. 1944, CD 1943–44, 1554–5.
45. Kimball, 2: 694, 698.
46. PREM 3/396/10/325–6.
47. A mistranslation of the original Russian, which should have been rendered 'unlike'.
48. Churchill to Stalin (draft), and Eden note, both 31 Jan. 1944, PREM 3/396/11/319–20.
49. Duff Hart-Davis (ed.), *King's Counsellor. Abdication and War: The diaries of Sir Alan Lascelles*, London, 2007, 198.
50. Churchill to Clark Kerr, 2 Feb. 1944, CD 1943–44, 1589.
51. Kimball, 2: 701–2; cf. FO comments on FO 954/20A/45–6, quoting Harvey.
52. Eden believed that Stalin may have raised the issue as 'an afterthought' and argued that the Curzon Line would be more than enough compensation for Stalin. Eden to Churchill, 24 Dec. 1943, FO 954/19B/587.
53. See Harriman to SecState, 27 Jan. 1944, *FRUS 1944*, 3: 1238–40.
54. CHAR 20/156/18–19.
55. British record of the meeting in CD 1943–44, 1649–55, quoting from p. 1655; copied to Roosevelt on 11 Feb. 1944 – Kimball, 2: 715–23.
56. Harvey, 331, entry for 15 Feb. 1944.
57. *FRUS Cairo and Tehran*, 594; Harriman, 320–4.
58. Message of 7 Feb. 1944, MR box 9.
59. MR box 9.
60. Ismay to PM, 2 Feb. 1944, CD 1943–44, 1592.
61. Churchill to Clark Kerr, 5 Feb. 1944, CD 1943–44, 1630.
62. CD 1943–44, 1664–5; MR box 9.

63. Churchill to Stalin, 10 Feb. 1944, and Stalin to Churchill, 11 Feb. 1944, CD 1943–44, 1713 and 1724.
64. CD 1943–44, 1675–6.
65. Stalin to Roosevelt, 16 February 1944, MR box 9.
66. Butler, 206; Roosevelt to Stalin, 17 Feb. 1944, and Mathewson to President, 19 Feb. 1944, and amended draft – all in MR box 9; Churchill to Stalin, 18 Feb. 1943, CD 1943–44, 1792.
67. CD 1943–44, 1773–82, quoting Churchill on p. 1779.
68. CD 1943–44, 1807.
69. CD 1943–44, 1807–10.
70. Harriman to President, and reply, both 23 Feb. 1944, MR box 9.
71. MR box 9.
72. MR box 9.
73. Roosevelt's telegram sent on 17 February offering two US merchantmen and a cruiser for 'temporary use'.
74. CD 1943–44, 1814.
75. Churchill to Clark Kerr, and reply, both 19 Feb. 1944, CD 1943–44, 1797, 1798–9.
76. Churchill to Clark Kerr, 22 Feb. 1944, CD 1943–44, 1836.
77. CD 1943–44, 1837.
78. The president sent a similar message on 23 Feb. 1944, MR box 9.
79. CD 1943–44, 1831.
80. Clark Kerr to Molotov, 23 Feb. 1944, RGASPI f.558, op.11, d.266, l.61.
81. Churchill to Stalin, 22 Feb. 1944, CD 1943–44, 1839; for the COS see RGASPI f.558, op.11, d.266, l.57.
82. MR box 9.
83. Kuznetsov, *Kursom k pobede*, 338. For the British version see CD 1943–44, 1891–2.
84. MR box 9.
85. From London, 3 March 1944, AVP RF f.059a, op.12, p.39, d.248, ll.255–7.
86. Transcript of Comrade Stalin's conversation with British Ambassador Kerr, 28 Feb. 1944, RGASPI f.558, op.11, d.284, l.101.
87. Clark Kerr to Churchill, 29 Feb. 1944, FO 954/20A/119–20; text also copied to FDR – see Kimball, 2: 763–5.
88. Transcript of Comrade Stalin's conversation with US Ambassador Harriman, 3 March 1944, RGASPI f.558, op.11, d.377, ll.40–6.
89. The response to Roosevelt on 3 March 1943, virtually identical, is in MR box 9.
90. CHAR 20/158/58.
91. Note dated 15 March on Stalin's message of 3 March 1944, MR box; Kimball, 3: 20–1.
92. Churchill to Eden, 2 March 1944, CD 1943–44, 1949–50.
93. Colville, 476.

12 'Force and Facts'

1. Doris Kearns Goodwin, *No Ordinary Time: Franklin and Eleanor Roosevelt, the home front in World War II*, New York, 1994, 497–501.
2. Wilson to Clark Kerr, 19 March [Eton] and 15 May 1944, FO 800/302, fos 30 and 73.
3. From London, 5 March 1944, AVP RF f.059a, op.7, p.13, d.6, l.318.
4. Eden, 450.
5. Clark Kerr to Churchill, 20 March 1944, FO 954/20A, fos 144–6.
6. Churchill to Eden, 7 May 1944, PREM 3/403/10.
7. CD 1943–44, 1423 and 2267–8; Churchill to Eden, M537/4, 8 May 1944, CHAR 20/152/5.
8. Message of 18 March. He also told Marshall: 'I am hardening very much on this operation as the time approaches in the sense of wishing to strike if humanly possible even if the limiting conditions we laid down at Moscow are not exactly fulfilled.' See Kimball, 3: 53–4.
9. Kimball, 3: 139, 162.

10. WM 28 (44) 1 CA, CAB 65/45; Cadogan, 609.
11. Kimball, 3: 33.
12. CD 1943–44, 1987.
13. CD 1943–44, 1986.
14. Messages of 8 March, CD 1943–44, 2006–8.
15. Harvey, 335; CD 1943–44, 2029.
16. Presidential press conference, no. 939, 3 March 1944, 6–9. The press conference started at 10.58; the messages were sent at 12.04 (Churchill) and 12.05 (Stalin) – see Kimball, 3: 14–15 and MR box 9.
17. Stalin to Roosevelt, 6 March 1943, MR box 9; Kimball, 3: 15–16, 19, 23–8.
18. CD 1943–44, 2020.
19. AVP RF f.06, op.5b, p.41, d.35, l.58. See also Armand van Dormael, *Bretton Woods: Birth of a monetary system*, London, 1978, 124–6.
20. AVP RF f.07, op.9, p.61, d.24, ll.7–8.
21. MR box 9.
22. CHAR 20/159/114.
23. Colville, 479, entry for 18 March 1944; Kimball, 3: 54.
24. CD 1943–44, 2110–11.
25. *Corr 1957*, 2: 293, note 55.
26. Message to Churchill, 3 April 1944 (also prepared by Lubin), in Kimball, 3: 75.
27. MR box 9.
28. FO to Moscow, 19 and 23 March 1944, FO 954/20A/142–3, 151.
29. Cadogan, 611–12; Harvey, 336.
30. CD 1943–44, 2153–4.
31. Clark Kerr to Churchill, 18 March 1944, FO 954/20A/139.
32. Clark Kerr to Churchill, 20 March 1944, FO 954/20A/144–6.
33. A copy was also sent to Roosevelt – text in MR box 9.
34. CHAR 20/160/72–4.
35. Cadogan, 613; Eden, 439.
36. WM 40 (44) 1 CA, 27 March 1944, CAB 65; Kimball, 3: 68–74, quoting pp. 69 and 73, also 79.
37. CD 1943–44, 2267–8.
38. Eden to Churchill, 5 April 1944, FO 954/26B, fo. 567; Harvey, 338–9; see also FO 371/43304, N2128.
39. *Russkiy Arkhiv: Velikaya Otechestvennaya*, Vol. 14: *SSSR i Polsha, 1941–1945*, Moscow, 1994, 151–3.
40. Transcript of conversation between Stalin and Harriman, 3 March 1944, RGASPI f.558, op.11, d.377, l.44.
41. Stettinius to President, 8 March 1944, and related correspondence, PSF(D) box 48: Poland, Orlemanski–Lange Reports; Stalin to Roosevelt, 28 March 1944, MR box 9. See also Steven Miner, *Stalin's Holy War: Religion, nationalism, and alliance politics, 1941–1945*, Chapel Hill, NC, 2003, 164–8.
42. PSF(D) box 48: Poland, Orlemanski–Lange Reports.
43. Roosevelt to Stalin, 31 March 1944, and reply of 4 April, MR box 9. Stalin quote from his letter to Kaganovich and Molotov, 12 September 1935, in O.V. Khlevnyuk et al., *Stalin and Kaganovich. Perepiska, 1931–1936*, Moscow, 2001, 564; cf. Victor-Yves Ghebali, *The International Labour Organisation: A case study on the evolution of UN specialised agencies*, Boston, 1989, 105–6.
44. MR box 9.
45. From London, 24 March 1944, AVP RF f.059, op.12, p.28, d.165, l.29–30, 33.
46. See Harvey, 331.
47. CD 1943–44, 2203.
48. WM 40 (44) 1 CA, CAB 65/24; CD 1943–44, 2227–8.
49. Churchill to Eden, 15 July 1944, M 865/4, CHAR 20/153/1.
50. See correspondence in FO 800/302, esp. fos 142–3, 147, 153–4.

51. FO 800/302/156–60, 164.
52. Kimball, 3: 90–1.
53. CCS to Deane and Burrows, 6 April 1944, RG 218, Geographical File 42–45, CCS 092 USSR (NARA).
54. Kimball, 3: 93–4, 100; see also Marshall to Roosevelt, 15 April 1944, MR box 6: R-C, from which it seems that neither FDR nor Churchill knew of the CCS initiative.
55. CD 1943–44, 2472.
56. Antonov to Deane, 22 April 1944, RG 218, Geographical File 42–45, CCS 092 USSR (NARA); RGASPI f.558, op.11, d.267, ll.57–8.
57. I.P. Makar, 'Operatsiya "Bagration" ', Voyenno-Istoricheskiy Zhurnal, 6 (2004), 3.
58. Georgiy Zhukov, Reminiscences and Reflections, 2 vols, Moscow, 1985, 2: 261.
59. CD 1943–44, 2527.
60. Stalin–Roosevelt/Churchill message, 22 April 1944, action sheet, MR box 9.
61. Churchill to Molotov, 23 April 1944, CHAR 20/163/46, and Molotov to Churchill, 28 April 1944, CHAR 20/164/5.
62. Stalin to Roosevelt, 29 April 1944, and Roosevelt to Stalin, 5 May 1944, MR box 9.
63. Churchill to Stalin, 3 May 1944, and Stalin to Churchill, 8 May 1944, CHAR 20/164/32–3 and 67.
64. From Washington, 15 May 1944, AVP RF f.059, op.12, p.33, d.209, ll.67–8.
65. Transcript of Stalin's conversation with Leo Krzycki, head of American Slav Congress, 3 Jan. 1946, RGASPI f.558, op.11, d.374, l.131.
66. Lange report, conversations with Stalin, 17 May 1944, p. 4, and with Clark Kerr, 14 May, PSF(D) box 48: Poland, Orlemanski–Lange Reports.
67. SecState, 19 May 1944, Moscow Post Files, RG 84, CGR, Poles — State cables, Jan.–July 1944 (NARA).
68. Lange to President, 12 June 1944, PSF(D) box 48: Poland, Orlemanski–Lange Reports.
69. Drew Pearson, 'Washington merry-go-round', Washington Post, 3 July 1944, p. 4; cf. Lange to J. Edgar Hoover, 5 July 1944, PSF(D) box 48: Poland, Orlemanski–Lange Reports.
70. DeWitt Poole, memo of conversation with Orlemanski, 27 May 1944, and FDR to Hull, 31 May 1944, PSF(D) box 48: Poland, Orlemanski–Lange Reports.
71. MR box 9.
72. Barker, 277; Churchill to Eden, M497/4 and M498/4, 4 May 1944, CHAR 20/152/5. On Churchill's health see Harvey, 339.
73. Harriman, 327–8; Churchill to Eden, M537/4, 8 May 1944, CHAR 20/152/5.
74. Barker, 278–81; Kimball, 3: 137, 181–2.
75. Kimball, 3: 126–8; see also text showing deletions and insertion in MR box 9.
76. A.A. Gromyko, I.N. Zemskov et al. (eds), Sovetskiy Soyuz na mezhdunarodnykh konferentsiyakh perioda Velikoy Otechestvennoy voyny 1941–1945, Moscow, 1984, 2: 128.
77. MR box 9.
78. CHAR 20/164/95.
79. Churchill to Stalin, 19 May 1944, CHAR 20/164/12–13.
80. For more detail, see Thomas M. Barker, 'The Ljubljana Gap Strategy: Alternative to Anvil/Dragoon or Fantasy?', Journal of Military History, 56 (1992), 57–86.
81. Stalin to Churchill, 22 May 1944, CHAR 20/164/112–13.
82. Kimball, 3: 134–5, 142.
83. MR box 9.
84. Churchill to Stalin, 23 May 1944, CHAR 20/165/16.
85. RGASPI f.558, op.11, d.267, l.93.
86. CHAR 20/165/40.
87. Corr 1957, 2: 143; Cf. Memo for the President, 29 March 1944, Official File OF 220 (Russia), Roosevelt–Stalin messages (FDRL).
88. RGASPI f. 558, op. 11, d.368, l.77.
89. MR box 9.
90. Kimball, 3: 143; WM 68 (44) 2, 24 May 1944, CAB 65/46.

91. Roosevelt to Stalin, 27 May 1944, MR box 9; Kimball, 3: 145–6.
92. Jon B. Mikolashek, *General Mark Clark: Commander of US Fifth Army and liberator of Rome*, Philadelphia, 2013, 134.
93. OGB, 5/1: 568. Stalin's messages of 5 June 1944 are in MR box 9 and CHAR 20/166/5.
94. CHAR 20/165/109.
95. A.M. Vasilevskiy, *Delo vsey zhizni*, 2nd edn, Moscow, 1975, 400.
96. WX-45590, 3 June 1944, WO 229/30.
97. *SAMO*, 2: 17.
98. Bradley F. Smith, *Sharing Secrets with Stalin: How the Allies traded intelligence, 1941–1945*, Lawrence, KS, 1996, 193.
99. N.I. Biryukov, *Tanki – frontu*, Smolensk, 2005, 408.
100. *Otnosheniya Rossii (SSSR) s Yugoslaviyey*, Moscow, 1998, 239.

13 From East and West

1. Harriman comments on Churchill's account of Tehran in 'Closing the Ring', Harriman papers, box 872, Feis files.
2. Elizabeth Borgwardt, *A New Deal for the World: America's vision for human rights*, Cambridge, MA, 2005, 163–7.
3. CHAR 20/166/4.
4. Molotov to Clark Kerr, 6 June 1944, in RGASPI f.558, op.11, d.267, l.110.
5. Stalin to Roosevelt, 6 June 1944, MR box 9.
6. CHAR 20/166/15.
7. Kimball, 3: 173.
8. Churchill to Stalin, 7 June 1944, CHAR 20/166/22–3. On 9 June, Stalin also tipped off his allies about the opening of the Soviet offensive against Finland the following day: see CHAR 20/166/51.
9. Note on log sheet for 7 June message, MR box 9: R-S.
10. MR box 9.
11. CHAR 20/155/54.
12. Allen Raymond, *Saturday Evening Post*, 17 June 1944, quoted in David W. Ellwood, *Italy 1943–1945: The politics of liberation*, Leicester, 1985, 97.
13. Silvio Pons, 'Stalin, Togliatti, and the origins of the cold war in Europe', *Journal of Cold War Studies*, 3:2 (2001), 9. Churchill's message to Stalin, dated 10 June, is in CHAR 20/166/56.
14. *Pravda*, 14 June 1944; Harriman, 314; *SWW*, 6: 5.
15. CHAR 20/166/76.
16. *SWW*, 6: 8. The adjective twice transliterated as 'grandiose' is essentially a borrowed word in Russian: more appropriate translations would be 'colossal' or, as Churchill said, even 'majestic'.
17. Gilbert 7, 808. For Churchill's message of 14 June 1944 and Stalin's reply next day, see CHAR 20/166/96–7 and 116.
18. Gilbert 7, 808–9.
19. From London, 16 June 1944 in AVP RF f.059, op.12, p.40, d.252, ll.210–19.
20. N.M. Kharlamov, *Trudnaya missiya*, Moscow, 1983, ch. 17.
21. Churchill to Stalin, 17 June 1944, CHAR 20/167/3–4.
22. Summary of Mikołajczyk letter of 18 March 1944, attached to memo from Hull to President, 26 March 1944, PSF(D) box 47: Poland, January–July 1944.
23. Cordell Hull, *The Memoirs of Cordell Hull*, 2 vols, New York, 1948, 2: 1441–2.
24. Conversation with Molotov, 3 June 1944, Harriman papers, box 172 (LC); From Washington, 6 June 1944 in AVP RF f.059, op.12, p.34, d.210, l.99. See also the US records of these conversations in *FRUS 1944*, 3: 1273–4, 1276–7.
25. Stanisław Mikołajczyk, *The Rape of Poland: The pattern of Soviet aggression*, London, 1948, 59–60.

26. Conference with Polish Prime Minister and President, 14 June 1944, RG 59, Decimal Files, 711.60C/6–1444 (NARA).
27. FDR, memo for the Director, Bureau of the Budget, 6 July 1944, and amended draft, PSF 47(D): Poland, January to June 1944, fos 136–7.
28. *SAMO*, 2: 102.
29. MR box 9.
30. RGASPI f.558, op.11, d.267, ll.161–2.
31. Stalin to Roosevelt, 21 June 1944, MR box 9.
32. A.M. Vasilevskiy, *Delo vsey zhizni*, 2nd edn, Moscow, 1975, 410.
33. CHAR 20/167/39.
34. Kimball, 3: 200; Roosevelt to Stalin, 22 June 1944, MR box 9: R-S. See also log sheet attached to Stalin to Roosevelt, 21 June 1944, MR box 9: S-R.
35. To Lebedev in London, 26 May 1944 in AVP RF f.059, op.12, p.27, d.149, ll.7–9.
36. *FRUS 1943*, 3: 1290–1.
37. To Lebedev in London, 22 June 1944 in AVP RF f.059, op.12, p.11, d.65, ll.114–15.
38. Eden to PM, 4 July 1944, enclosing O'Malley memo, 29 June 1944, FO 954/20A/197–9.
39. MR box 9.
40. *Velikaya Otechestvennaya voyna 1941–1945 godov* (12 vols), Vol. 4: M.A. Gareyev et al. (eds), *Osvobozhdeniye territoriy SSSR*, Moscow, 2012, 378.
41. Steven J. Zaloga, *Bagration 1944: The destruction of Army Group Centre*, Oxford, 1997, 71; Frieser, 554, 591.
42. V.A. Zolotarev (ed.), *Istoriya Velikoy Otechestvennoy voyny 1941–1945*, Moscow, 2010, 1: 552–6.
43. Clark Kerr to Eden, 19 July 1944, FO 371/43432.
44. Churchill to Stalin, 25 June 1944, CHAR 20/167/64–5.
45. From London, 17 June 1944; 24 June 1944 in AVP RF f.059, op.12, p.40, d.252, ll. 232–4; d.253, l.25.
46. Churchill's speech to the Commons, 2 August 1944, in Gilbert 7, 867.
47. Stalin to Churchill, 27 June 1944, CHAR 20/167/82 and 85; Stalin to Roosevelt, 27 June 1944, PSF(D) box 49: Russia, 1944.
48. Stalin to Roosevelt, 27 June 1944, and reply, 30 June, MR box 9; Churchill to Stalin, 4 July 1944, and reply, 7 July, CHAR 20/168/10 and 28.
49. Cf. Harriman to President, 12 June 1944, PSF(D) box 49: Russia, 1944.
50. Barker, 278–81.
51. Tamkin, 144–54; Eden, 'Soviet policy in the Balkans', 7 June 1944, WP (44) 304, CAB 66/51; *SANO*, 2: 121–4; Eden to Churchill, 11 July 1944, FO 954/28B/452.
52. WM 88 (44) 1 CA, 7 July 1944, CAB 65/47.
53. Alanbrooke, 566, 4 July 1944; see also Michael Howard, *The Mediterranean Strategy in the Second World War*, London, 1968, 66–7.
54. FO 954/28B/454–5.
55. For background, see Jonathan Walker, *Poland Alone: Britain, SOE and the collapse of the Polish resistance, 1944*, Stroud, 2008, 97–108.
56. CHAR 20/168/44.
57. CHAR 20/168/46.
58. To London, Washington, Algiers, 25 Jan. 1944 in AVP RF f.059, op.12, p.10, d.61, l.112.
59. CHAR 20/168/66–67.
60. Kimball, 3: 249–50.
61. Harriman to President, and President to Harriman, 18 July 1944, MR box 9.
62. MR box 9.
63. CHAR 20/168/84–5.
64. Roosevelt to Stalin, 21 July 1944, PSF(D) box 49: Russia, 1944.
65. L.A. Bezymenskiy, *Operatsiya 'Mif', ili skolko raz khoronili Gitlera*, Moscow, 1995, 78; OGB, 5/2: 48, 193–4.
66. Theodore S. Hamerow, *On the Road to the Wolf's Lair: German resistance to Hitler*, Cambridge, MA, 1997, 342.

67. Churchill to Stalin, 25 July 1944, CHAR 20/169/106–7.
68. MR box 9.
69. CHAR 20/168/101.
70. Also copied to Roosevelt: see MR box 9.
71. *Russkiy Arkhiv: Velikaya Otechestvennaya*, Vol. 14: *SSSR i Polsha, 1941–1945*, Moscow, 1994, 192, 198.
72. CHAR 20/168/104.
73. WM 95 (44) 3 CA, 24 July 1944, CAB 65/47.
74. Kimball, 3: 253.
75. CHAR 20/168/112.
76. Eden to Churchill, 26 July 1944, FO 954/20B/221; Kimball, 3: 255.
77. CHAR 20/169/6.
78. MR box 9.
79. MR box 9.
80. AVP RF f.06, op.6, p.49, d.667, l.8.
81. Kimball, 3: 261.
82. CHAR 20/169/28.
83. Gareyev, *Osvobozhdeniye territoriy SSSR*, 416.
84. *Russkiy Arkhiv: Velikaya Otechestvennaya*, Vol. 14: *SSSR i Polsha, 1941–1945*, 201.
85. Churchill to Stalin, 29 July 1944, CHAR 20/169/26.
86. Alanbrooke, 575, 27 July 1944; cf. Julian Lewis, *Changing Direction: British military planning for post-war strategic defence, 1942–47*, 2nd edn, London, 2003, 116–22, 349–50.
87. MR box 9.
88. Eden to Churchill, 3 Aug. 1944, FO 954/20B/232; Churchill to Stalin, and reply, both 4 Aug. 1944, CHAR 20/169/51 and 73.
89. For more detail see G.V. Dyadin and D.N. Filippovykh, *Pamyatnye starty*, Moscow, 2001.
90. B.P. Konovalov, *Tayna sovetskogo raketnogo oruzhiya*, Moscow, 1992, 6.
91. B.E. Chertok, *Rakety i lyudi*, Moscow, 1999, 1: 87. On Sanders' mission, see Christy Campbell, *Target London: Under attack from the V-weapons during World War II*, London, 2012, chs 42 and 46.
92. Konovalov, *Tayna*, 7; *SANO*, 2: 174.
93. *Russkiy Arkhiv: Velikaya Otechestvennaya*, Vol. 14: *SSSR i Polsha, 1941–1945*, 206. On the British side, see Hinsley, 3/2: 283–4.
94. AVP RF f.06, op.6, p.6, d.56, ll.2–3.
95. CHAR 20/169/50.
96. Quotations from *Russkiy Arkhiv: Velikaya Otechestvennaya*, Vol. 14: *SSSR i Polsha, 1941–1945*, 209–10, 218–19.
97. E. Durachinskiy, 'Varshavskoye vosstaniye', in *Drugaya voyna 1939–1945*, Moscow, 1996, 349.
98. For instance, Glantz/House, 213–14, argue that purely military considerations took precedence.
99. Frieser, 569, 579–84, quoting p. 583. See also documents in David M. Glantz, 'The Red Army's Lublin–Brest offensive and advance on Warsaw (18 July–30 September 1944): An overview and documentary survey', *Journal of Slavic Military Studies*, 19 (2006), 401–41.
100. CHAR 20/169/79.
101. Transcript of Stalin–Mikołajczyk conversation, 3 Aug. 1944 in AVP RF f.06, op.6, p.42, d.550, ll.6–15.
102. Transcripts of Stalin–Mikołajczyk conversation, 9 Aug. 1944 in AVP RF f.06, op.6, p.42, d.550, ll.25–9.
103. Clark Kerr to Churchill, in Kimball, 3: 273.
104. CHAR 20/169/101.

105. Osóbka-Morawski to Roosevelt, 8 Aug. 1944, Moscow Post Files, RG 84, CGR, box 40 (NARA); Stalin to Roosevelt, 9 Aug. 1944, MR box 9.
106. Kimball, 3: 269, 273.
107. Churchill to Stalin, 10 Aug. 1944, CHAR 20/170/4.
108. *Varshavskoye vosstaniye v dokumentakh iz arkhivov spetssluzhb*, Moscow/Warsaw, 2007, 74.
109. According to one authoritative assessment, 41 of the 306 planes that flew on these missions were lost (13.3 per cent), which was significantly higher than the average losses sustained in raids on Germany. Norman Davies, *Rising '44: The battle for Warsaw*, London, 2003, 381.
110. Churchill to Stalin, 12 Aug. 1944, PREM 3/396/6; Clark Kerr to Molotov, 13 Aug. 1944, RGASPI f.558, op.11, d.268, l.129. On the debate in Britain, see P.M.H Bell, *John Bull and the Bear: British public opinion, foreign policy and the Soviet Union, 1941–1945*, London, 1990, 130–72.
111. Churchill to Eden, 14 Aug. 1944, CHAR 20/180/9.
112. Stettinius to President, 11 Aug. 1944, and accompanying log sheet, MR box 9.
113. MR box 9.
114. *Otnosheniya Rossii (SSSR) s Yugoslaviyey, 1941–1945 gg.*, Moscow, 1998, 279–80, 289, 293.
115. Ibid., 555.
116. CHAR 20/170/22.
117. Quotations from Harriman, 339–40.
118. AVP RF f.06, op.6, p.30, d.352, l.26.
119. *Velikaya Otechestvennaya voyna 1941–1945 godov* (12 vols), Vol. 8: V.G. Titov et al. (eds), *Vneshnyaya politika i diplomatiya Sovetskogo Soyuza v gody voyny*, Moscow, 2014, 421.
120. CHAR 20/170/33–4.
121. AVP RF f.06, op.6, p.30, d.352, l.14, published in *Russkii Arkhiv: Velikaya Otechestvennaya*, 14 (3–1): 231–2.
122. WM 107 (44) CA and WM 108 (44) CA, CAB 65/47; Kimball, 3: 282–4.
123. Memorandum for JCS, 14 Aug. 1944, RG 165, OPD Executive 10, Item 69 (NARA); log sheet for message of 19 Aug. 1944, MR box 9.
124. *SAMO*, 2: 572–81.
125. Harriman to SecState, 17 Aug. 1944, and SecState to Harriman, 17 Aug. 1944, Moscow Post Files, RG 84, CGR, respectively boxes 40 and 39 (NARA); also Harriman, 342.
126. Kimball, 3: 284.
127. See log sheet to 20 Aug. 1944 message, MR box 9.
128. MR box 9.
129. CHAR 20/170/74–5.
130. Kimball, 3: 295–6; FDR note for Leahy, 28 Aug. 1944, MR box 9.
131. WM 111 (44) 7 CA, 28 Aug. 1944, CAB 65/47.
132. WM 122 (44) 7 CA, 11 Sept. 1944, CAB 65/47.
133. Data on Soviet and British aid in Geoffrey Roberts, *Stalin's Wars: From world war to cold war, 1939–1953*, London, 2006, 216.
134. AVP RF f.5, op.66, d.66, ll.70–6.
135. MR box 9.
136. Russian embassy translation as amended by Col. Park of Roosevelt's staff – see text in MR box 9: Stalin.
137. N.G. Kuznetsov, *Kursom k pobede*, 3rd edn, Moscow, 1989, 341.
138. Note to Private Office, 1 Oct. 1944, PREM 3/240/2.
139. From 1940 to 1956, Soviet Karelia was counted as a separate republic.
140. Directives for negotiations on the establishment of the international security organization in RGASPI f.17, op.162, d.37, l.131; Thomas M. Campbell and George C. Herring (eds), *The Diaries of Edward R. Stettinius, Jr. 1943–1946*, New York, 1975, 111, 113.
141. Borgwardt, *A New Deal for the World*, 163–4.

142. WP (45) 12, 5 Jan. 1945, CAB 66/60.
143. Campbell and Herring, *Stettinius Diaries*, 118, entry for 31 Aug. 1944.
144. MR box 9.
145. MR box 9.
146. A.A. Gromyko, I.N. Zemskov et al. (eds), *Sovetskiy Soyuz na mezhdunarodnykh konferentsiyakh perioda Velikoy Otechestvennoy voyny 1941–1945 gg.*, Moscow, 1984, 3: 178–9.
147. MR box 9.
148. To Soviet Ambassador in Washington, 16 Sept. 1944 in AVP RF f.059, op.12, p.6, d.31, l.20.
149. MR box 9.
150. Message of 4 Aug. 1944, in Kimball, 3: 262; see also *FRUS Quebec*, 12.
151. CCS 681/2 (Octagon), 15 Oct. 1944, PREM 3/329/2.
152. Churchill did say he wanted to add 'a word on the political dangers of divergences between the Russian and the Western Allies in respect of Poland, Greece and Yugoslavia', but FDR disagreed on the grounds that 'the communication was purely military in character'. *FRUS Quebec*, 382.
153. *FRUS Quebec*, 466–76.
154. Aide-mémoire, 18 Sept 1944, in Martin J. Sherwin, *A World Destroyed: The atomic bomb and the grand alliance*, New York, 1975, 284.
155. MR box 9.
156. Clark Kerr to Foreign Office, 24 Sept. 1944, FO 954/26B/458; Harriman to President only, 23 Sept. 1944, Harriman papers, box 174 (LC).
157. CHAR 20/172/45–6.
158. Kimball, 3: 341.
159. Minute D (O) 1/4, 8 Sept. 1944, CHAR 20/153/3.
160. *SAMO*, 2: 201.
161. Minute 942/4, 30 Aug. 1944, CHAR 20/153/2.
162. COS (44) 824 (O), 9 Sept. 1944, CAB 80/87.
163. Minutes of Armistice and Post-War Planning Commt, APW 14 (44) 1, CAB 87/1.
164. OGB, 5/2: 560.
165. APW 14 (44) 1, CAB 87/1.
166. COS (44) 843 (O), 19 Sept. 1944, CAB 80/87.
167. AVP RF f.07, op.5, p.53, d.234, l.20a.
168. *Otnosheniya Rossii (SSSR) s Yugoslaviyey*, 318.
169. Churchill to Eden, 21 Sept. 1944, CHAR 20/257/4.
170. The message to Churchill, also dated 29 Sept. 1944, is in CHAR 20/172/79.
171. MR box 9.
172. RGASPI f.558, op.11, d.269, l.22.
173. CHAR 20/172/71–2.
174. Eden, 479.
175. Clark Kerr to Churchill, 2 Oct. 1944, CHAR 20/172/85.

14 'Only the Three of Us'

1. Churchill to Eden, 10 Nov. 1944, CHAR 20/153/5.
2. CHAR 20/172/109.
3. Kimball, 3: 341–5; Sherwood, 832–4; Charles E. Bohlen, *Witness to History, 1929–1969*, New York, 1973, 162–3.
4. MR box 9.
5. MR box 9.
6. Churchill to Smuts, 9 Oct. 1944, CHAR 20/173/17.
7. See the records in PREM 3/434/2 and O.A. Rzheshevskiy, *Stalin i Cherchill*, Moscow, 2010, 420–1.
8. The typescript of Birse's record, with manuscript amendments by the Cabinet Office, is in FO 800/302/227–35.

9. Churchill's memoirs include an abbreviated but colourful account of the meeting, which he dictated six years later. See *SWW*, 6: 199 and CHUR 4/356/152.

10. Eden–Molotov meeting, 10 Oct. 1944, PREM 3/434/2. On the 11th, they settled on 80:20 for the USSR in Bulgaria and Romania, in return for conceding the British demand for 50:50 in Yugoslavia.

11. *SWW*, 6: 204; cf. Reynolds, 460.

12. Jacob, note, 6 Nov. 1944, CAB 120/158. Pierson Dixon of the FO also lamented the 'frivolities' and 'bad passages' in the original record.

13. Harriman, 357.

14. MR box 9.

15. *SWW*, 6: 203; Harriman, 358.

16. Rzheshevsky, 460–8.

17. Alanbrooke, 607–8.

18. Churchill to Eden, M.1025/4, 23 Oct. 1944, CHAR 20/153/4.

19. Alanbrooke, 603, 606.

20. Gromyko to Molotov, 13 Oct. 1944, AVP RF f.059, op.12, p.34, d.213, ll.284–5. See also *SAMO*, 2: 233–4.

21. MR box 7.

22. General Sikorski Historical Institute, *Documents on Polish-Soviet Relations 1939–1945*, Vol. 2: *1943–1945*, London, 1967, 416–24; Harvey, 361.

23. Churchill to King George VI, 15 Oct. 1944, CHAR 20/181/17.

24. 'I liked that,' Churchill added in an early draft of his war memoirs, but the passage was amended and then deleted from the final text in 1952 at the suggestion of the Cabinet secretary – see CHUR 4/356, fos 56, 138, 154.

25. To all ambassadors and ministers (to London), 21 Oct. 1944, AVP RF f.059, op.12, p.12, d.69, l.147.

26. CHAR 2/497/54.

27. CHAR 2/497/55.

28. Alanbrooke, 610; Gilbert 7, 1032 (Layton).

29. Harriman, 362.

30. Quotations from Moran, 225, 227–8.

31. Churchill to Attlee and War Cabinet, 17 Oct. 1944, CHAR 20/181/8–9. The quotation is a famous tag from one of Horace's Odes: *post equitem sedet atra cura.*

32. MR box 9.

33. Sherwood, 844, quoting from a memo written by Hopkins in October 1945, as he was thinking about his memoirs. The dating is somewhat fuzzy – Hopkins claimed that he talked to Gromyko after the election – but the gist of what he wrote seems accurate.

34. Gromyko to Molotov, 13 Oct. 1944, AVP RF f.059, op.12, p.34, d.213, ll.284–5.

35. Kimball, 3: 362.

36. CHAR 20/173/62.

37. AVP RF f.06, op.6, p.22, d.225, l.35; Kimball, 3: 365.

38. Roosevelt to Stalin, 20 Oct. 1944, and Stalin to Roosevelt, 22 Oct. 1944, MR box 9.

39. Kimball, 3: 366, 368; see also S.M. Plokhy, *Yalta: The price of peace*, New York, 2011, 26–7.

40. MR box 9.

41. MR box 9.

42. CHAR 20/173/130.

43. *SANO*, 2: 189–90.

44. To all ambassadors and ministers (to London), 21 Oct. 1944, AVP RF f.059, op.12, p.12, d.69, ll.147–8.

45. *Otnosheniya Rossii (SSSR) s Yugoslaviyey, 1941–1945 gg.*, Moscow, 1998, 320, 370.

46. Stalin to Churchill, 9 Nov. 1944, CHAR 20/175/12.

47. CHAR 20/174/82–3.

48. Stalin to Churchill, 16 Nov. 1944, CHAR 20/175/44.

49. CHAR 20/174/91.

50. Gromyko to Molotov, 8 Nov. 1944, AVP RF f.059, op.12, p.34, d.214, l.250.

51. MR box 9.
52. MR box 9.
53. Kimball, 3: 390.
54. CHAR 20/175/19.
55. Transcript of a conversation between Comrade Stalin and British Foreign Minister A. Eden, 21 Oct. 1943 in RGASPI f.558, op.11, d.281, l.4. This remark was not included in the published rendition of the meeting: see A.A. Gromyko, I.N. Zemskov et al. (eds), *Sovetskiy Soyuz na mezhdunarodnykh konferentsiyakh perioda Velikoy Otechestvennoy voyny 1941–1945 gg.*, Moscow, 1984, 1: 120–3.
56. CHAR 20/175/21.
57. OGB, 5/2: 568–77, 636–7.
58. Churchill to Stalin, 16 Nov. 1944, CHAR 20/175/32–3.
59. Stalin to Churchill, 20 Nov. 1944, CHAR 20/175/68; Kimball, 3: 394.
60. Gusev to Molotov, 18 Nov. 1944, AVP RF f.059, op.12, p.34, d.214, l.250.
61. Stalin to Churchill, 20 Nov. 1944, CHAR 20/175/68.
62. MR box 9.
63. MR box 9.
64. *Otnosheniya Rossii (SSSR) s Yugoslaviyey*, 586–7.
65. Ibid., 378.
66. Churchill to Gen. Wilson, 20 Nov. 1944, CHAR 20/175/53.
67. CHAR 20/175/100.
68. Churchill to Eden, 25 Nov. 1944, and Eden to Churchill, 29 Nov. 1944, PREM 4/30/8, fos 488–90, 452–8.
69. FO minutes, FO 954/22A, 260–1, quoting Harvey, 30 Nov. 1944.
70. OGB, 5/2: 633.
71. CHAR 20/175/106–7.
72. To Molotov, 15 Nov. 1944, AVP RF f.059, op.12, p.34, d.214, ll.309–10.
73. From London, 13 Nov. 1944, AVP RF f.050, op.12, p.41, d.258, ll.42–6.
74. Kimball, 3: 425.
75. *Corr 1957*, 1: 274.
76. Churchill to Stalin, 2 Dec. 1944, CHAR 20/176/48.
77. Colville, 530, entry for 30 Nov. 1944.
78. D.A. Vershinin et al., *Deystviya nemetskikh podvodnykh lodok vo vtoruyu mirovuyu voynu na morskikh soobshcheniyakh*, Moscow, 1956, 325–6.
79. CHAR 20/176/26.
80. Churchill to Stalin, 1 and 2 Dec. 1944, CHAR 20/176/36–7 and 51, and Stalin to Churchill, 8 Dec. 1944, CHAR 20/177/8.
81. CHAR 20/176/51.
82. The message to Churchill is in CHAR 20/176/50.
83. MR box 9.
84. Churchill to Eden, 26 Nov. 1944, CHAR 20/153/5.
85. CHAR 20/176/38.
86. Churchill to Tito, 3 Dec. 1944, and to Stalin, 3 Dec. 1944, CHAR 20/176/69–71 and 72; Stalin to Churchill, 14 Dec. 1944, CHAR 20/177/65.
87. The message to Roosevelt, also dated 3 Dec. 1944, is in MR box 9.
88. CHAR 20/176/76.
89. WM 161 (44) 10 CA, 4 Dec. 1944, CAB 65/48.
90. CHAR 20/176/83–4.
91. Kimball, 3: 445; Roosevelt to Stalin, 6 Dec. 1944, MR box 9.
92. *FRUS Yalta*, 50–1.
93. Stettinius to Harriman, 5 Dec. 1944, MR box 9.
94. MR box 9.
95. Yu.V. Ivanov, *Ocherki istorii rossiysko (sovetsko)-polskikh otnosheniy v dokumentakh, 1914–1945 gg.*, Moscow, 2014, 285–6.
96. Churchill to Stalin, 10 Dec. 1944, CHAR 20/177/12.

97. CHAR 20/177/4–5.
98. Stalin to Churchill, 7 Dec. 1944, CHAR 20/176/123; Charles de Gaulle, *The Complete War Memoirs of Charles de Gaulle*, translated by Jonathan Griffin and Richard Howard, New York, 1998, 730, 744.
99. *Sovetsko-frantsuzskiye otnosheniya vo vremya Velikoy Otechestvennoy voyny, 1941–1945*, 2 vols, Moscow, 1983, 2: 199–200.
100. To Soviet ambassadors, 14 Dec. 1944, AVP RF f.059, op.12, p.6, d.33, ll.129–31.
101. Jean Lacouture, *De Gaulle: The ruler, 1945–70*, New York, 1993, 46.
102. CHAR 20/177/37.
103. MR box 9.
104. Churchill to Stalin, 23 Dec. 1944, CHAR 20/178/27.
105. CHAR 20/177/66.
106. Winston S. Churchill, *The Dawn of Liberation: War speeches, 1944*, London, 1945, 297.
107. WM (44), 169 CA, 16 Dec. 1944, CAB 65/48; Kimball, 3: 462–3, 468.
108. MR box 9.
109. Aide-memoire to the King from Dr. Subasić, 17 Dec. 1944, annex 6 to WP (45) 4, 6 Jan. 1945, 66/60.
110. Churchill to Stalin, 19 Dec. 1944, CHAR 20/177/103.
111. David Reynolds, *From World War to Cold War: Churchill, Roosevelt and the international history of the 1940s*, Oxford, 2006, 26.
112. CHAR 20/177/103.
113. WP (45) 111, 18 Feb. 1945, CAB 66/62.
114. *Corr 1957*, 1: 287.
115. *Corr 1957*, 2: 177.
116. Eisenhower, 4: 2367.
117. Kimball, 3: 468–9; Churchill to Stalin, 23 Dec. 1944, CHAR 20/178/27; Stalin to Roosevelt, 25 Dec. 1944, MR box 9.
118. N.S. Khrushchev, *Vremya. Lyudi. Vlast: Vospominaniya*, Moscow, 1999, 1: 610.
119. MR box 9.
120. Churchill to Ismay, 29 Dec. 1944, PREM 3/398/3; Alanbrooke, 641–2.
121. CHAR 20/178/39.
122. CHAR 20/178/40.
123. *Corr 1957*, 2: 178.
124. From Washington, 22 Dec. 1944, AVP RF f.059, op.12, p.35, d.215, ll.387–91.
125. MR box 9.
126. Halifax to FO, 5 Jan. 1945, PREM 4/30/11/693; Stimson diary, 31 Dec. 1944, Sterling Library, Yale University.
127. V.S. Parsadanova, *Sovetsko-polskiye otnosheniya v gody Velikoy Otechestvennoy voyny 1941–1945 gg.*, Moscow, 1982, 209.
128. MR box 9.
129. Kimball, 3: 475–7, 480–1.
130. White House note following Roosevelt to Stalin, 30 Dec. 1944, MR box 9.
131. MR box 9.

15 Yalta and After

1. Edward R. Stettinius, *Roosevelt and the Russians: The Yalta Conference*, New York, 1949, 306.
2. Churchill to Smuts, 3 Dec. 1944, CHAR 20/176/53–4.
3. Kimball, 3: 496–7; Stalin to Roosevelt, 1 Jan. 1945, MR box 9; Stalin to Churchill, 3 Jan. 1945, CHAR 20/210/30.
4. *FRUS Yalta*, 20–3; see also Harriman memcon, 26 Dec. 1944, Harriman papers, box 176 (LC).
5. CHAR 20/210/39–40.
6. Eisenhower, 4: 2407–8.

7. CHAR 20/210/47–8.

8. I.S. Konev, *Zapiski komanduyushchego frontom*, Moscow, 2003, 366.

9. Antony Beevor, *Berlin: The downfall, 1945*, London, 2002, 6, 19–20; Hinsley, 3/2: 643.

10. CHAR 20/210/69.

11. Churchill to Stalin, 9 Jan. 1945, CHAR 20/210/73; Eisenhower, 4: 2412, 2428.

12. WM 2 (45) 6 CA, 8 Jan. 1945, CAB 65/51.

13. WM 4 (45) 2 CA, 11 Jan. 1945, CAB 65/51; Churchill to Stalin, 11 Jan. 1945, CHAR 20/210/9.

14. See CHAR 20/210/107–8 and 115, CHAR 20/211/10, 12, 14, 34, 47, 51.

15. Notes on Tedder's meeting with Stalin, 15 Jan. 1945, PREM 3/398/3/151–3; A.H. Birse, *Memoirs of an Interpreter*, London, 1967, 176–7.

16. RGASPI f.558, op.11, d.381, l.4. The message to Churchill is in CHAR 20/210/117.

17. MR box 9.

18. Glantz/House, ch. 15, esp. pp. 233, 241–2, 246–7.

19. Churchill to Stalin, 17 Jan. 1945, CHAR 20/211/10.

20. MR box 9.

21. Churchill to Stalin, 21 Jan. 1945, and reply, 23 Jan. 1945, CHAR 20/211/25 and 40; Roosevelt to Stalin, 22 Jan. 1945, and Stalin to Roosevelt, 23 Jan. 1945, MR box 9.

22. MR box 9.

23. David B. Woolner, *The Last Hundred Days: FDR at war and at peace*, New York, 2018, 43, 60.

24. Kimball, 3: 519.

25. *FRUS Yalta*, 39–40.

26. MR box 170: Naval Aide's Files A16/3 Warfare Russia, 1944–45.

27. *FRUS Yalta*, 766–71. There is no evidence for the claim in a chatty passage from Gromyko's memoirs that FDR had already told Stalin in a letter that the USA would accommodate his claims to South Sakhalin and the Kuril Islands: see Andrei Gromyko, *Memories*, London, 1989, 114–16, and S.M. Plokhy, *Yalta: The price of peace*, New York, 2011, 216, 223.

28. *FRUS Yalta*, 984; cf. Russell D. Buhite, *Decisions at Yalta: An appraisal of summit diplomacy*, Wilmington, DE, 1986, ch. 5. When the details leaked out, the issue became another element in accounts of the Yalta 'sellout'.

29. WM 10 (45) 1 CA, 26 Jan. 1945, CAB 65/51; Thomas C. Campbell and George C. Herring (eds), *The Diaries of Edward R. Stettinius Jr., 1943–1946*, New York, 1975, 214.

30. *FRUS Yalta*, 667–71, 677–81, 686.

31. Charles E. Bohlen, *Witness to History, 1929–1969*, New York, 1973, 188; Eden, 516–17; *FRUS Yalta*, 726–8.

32. *FRUS Yalta*, 727–8.

33. *FRUS Yalta*, 711.

34. *FRUS Yalta*, 711–13; cf. David Reynolds, *Summits: Six meetings that shaped the twentieth century*, London, 2007, 117.

35. Quotations from *FRUS Yalta*, 973–4; see generally Reynolds, *Summits*, 126–8.

36. *FRUS Yalta*, 647.

37. *Corr 1957*, 2: 189.

38. MR box 170: Naval Aide's Files A16/3 Warfare Russia, 1944–45.

39. *FRUS Yalta*, 767–8.

40. *FRUS Yalta*, 309–24, 610; Campbell and Herring, *Stettinius Diaries*, 216.

41. This was his line when meeting senators on 11 January 1945: Campbell and Herring, *Stettinius Diaries*, 214.

42. *Corr 1957*, 1: 304.

43. *Corr 1957*, 1: 396; cf. *FRUS Yalta*, 575–6.

44. *Corr 1957*, 1: 396; *FRUS Yalta*, 781, 790, 849; *Otnosheniya Rossii (SSSR) s Yugoslaviyey*, 394.

45. Churchill to Attlee for War Cabinet, 10 Feb. 1945, PREM 3/51/10.

46. Plokhy, *Yalta*, 195.

47. *FRUS Yalta*, 966.
48. Stalin to Roosevelt, 11 Feb. 1945, *FRUS Yalta*, 967–8.
49. Kimball, 3: 532–3.
50. *FRUS Yalta*, 971.
51. Sherwood, 870 – quoting remarks by Hopkins to him after the conference. They also sent the now customary messages about Red Army Day: see Churchill to Roosevelt, 20 Feb. 1945, CHAR 20/211/180 and Roosevelt to Stalin, 23 February 1945, MR box 9.
52. MR box 9.
53. CHAR 20/211/116.
54. Birse, notes on some of the speeches at dinner, Yusupov Palace, 8 Feb 1945, PREM 3/51/10/24.
55. *Hansard Parliamentary Debates*, HC Deb 408, col. 1284; Ben Pimlott (ed.), *The Second World War Diary of Hugh Dalton, 1940–1945*, London, 1986, 836.
56. George McJimsey (ed.), *Documentary History of the Franklin D. Roosevelt Presidency*, Vol. 14: *The Yalta Conference, October 1944–March 1945*, New York, 2003, doc. 144, esp. pp. 631, 633, 639.
57. Kimball, 3: 547–51, 553–9.
58. Kimball, 3: 560–2.
59. Notes after conference with the President, 3 March 1945, Stimson diary (LC).
60. MR box 9.
61. Stalin to Roosevelt, 5 March 1945, MR box 9.
62. *FRUS 1945*, 5: quoting 1074, 1078, 1081.
63. MR box 9.
64. Churchill to Eden, 1 and 21 March, FO 954/22B/486 and 498; Churchill to Stalin, 21 March 1945, CHAR 20/213A/14–15.
65. From London, 22 March 1945, AVP RF f.59, op.1, p.53, d.313, ll.205–8.
66. Kimball, 3: 572. See also the discussion in Frank Costigliola, '"Like animals or worse": Narratives of culture and emotion by US and British POWs and airmen behind Soviet lines, 1944–1945', *Diplomatic History*, 28 (2004), 749–80.
67. MR box 9.
68. For the briefer message to Churchill on 23 March 1945, similarly phrased, see CHAR 20/213A/52.
69. Alanbrooke, 667–8, 678.
70. CHAR 20/213A/40.
71. For background see Bradley F. Smith and Elena Aga Rossi, *Operation Sunrise: The secret surrender*, New York, 1979.
72. FO to Moscow, tel. 1234, 13 March 1945, FO 954/17A/129.
73. Cf. *FRUS 1945*, 3: 727.
74. Woolner, *Last Hundred Days*, 203–4.
75. Clark Kerr to FO, tel. 797, 14 March 1945, with Churchill annotations, PREM 3/198/2; Harriman to Stettinius and Deane to Marshall, both 13 March 1945, MR box 35: Germany, Italian negotiations, 1945.
76. *FRUS 1945*, 3: 727–32.
77. Clark Kerr to FO, tel. 837, 17 March 1945, FO 954/17A/154.
78. *FRUS 1945*, 3: 735–6; Stimson diary, 17 March 1945.
79. See drafts and log for message of 24 March 1945, MR box 9. Molotov's message is in *FRUS 1945*, 3: 786–7.
80. MR box 9.
81. Politburo decrees dated 13 and 22 March 1945, RGASPI f.17, op.13, d.1052, ll.10, 13.
82. Grew to President, 23 March 1945, *FRUS 1945*, 1: 151–2.
83. *FRUS 1945*, 1: 113–14, 132–4.
84. *FRUS 1945*, 5: 822.
85. MR box 9.
86. MR box 9.

87. Chiefs of Staff to Joint Staff Mission, Washington, 29 March 1945, and Churchill to Eden, 30 March 1945, FO 954/17A/180–2. See also Neal H. Petersen (ed.), *From Hitler's Doorstep: The wartime intelligence reports of Allen Dulles, 1943–1945*, University Park, PA, 2010, 478ff.
88. MR box 9.
89. See FO 954/17A/201, docs 62–5.
90. Moscow to Alexander, 2 April 1945, FO 954/17A/202, doc. 67. Churchill was not, of course, a head of state – as any British official would have known.
91. MR box 9.
92. Kimball, 3: 603–5; see more generally Forrest C. Pogue, *The Supreme Command*, Washington, DC, 1954, 441–7
93. Georgiy Zhukov, *Reminiscences and Reflections*, 2 vols, Moscow, 1985, 2: 346–9; Eisenhower, 4: 2583–4; Beevor, *Berlin*, 146–7.
94. Woolner, *Last Hundred Days*, 204.
95. *FRUS Yalta*, 980.
96. According to William D. Leahy, *I Was There*, London, 1950, 370; cf. Leahy diary, 7 Feb. 1945 (LC).
97. Fifth Session of the Polish Commission, 23 March 1945, copy in Harriman papers, box 178 (LC).
98. Cf. Churchill to Clark Kerr, 28 Feb. 1945, FO 954/20B/423.
99. Eden to Churchill, 24 March 1945, and Churchill to Eden, 25 March 1945, FO 954/26C/586–90.
100. Kimball, 3: 593–8, 601–2.
101. MR box 9.
102. CHAR 20/213A/97–98.
103. MR box 9.
104. Log sheet for 4 April message, MR box 9; entry for 4 April 1945, Leahy diaries (LC); cf. Leahy, *I Was There*, 392: '. . . between friendly states'.
105. Donovan, memo for the President, 1 April 1945, PSF OSS, 1945 in Declassified Holdings (FDRL).
106. MR box 9.
107. Mary Soames (ed.), *Speaking for Themselves: The personal letters of Winston and Clementine Churchill*, London, 1999, 522; *SWW*, 6: 394.
108. The evidence of how the message was composed and where Roosevelt was is hard to reconcile with what is claimed by Bohlen in his 1973 memoirs to be his recollection of the president 'seated at his White House desk, his eyes flushed, outraged that he should be accused of dealing with the Germans behind Stalin's back'. Bohlen, *Witness to History*, 209.
109. See log for message to Stalin, 4 April 1945, MR box 9, and *FRUS 1945*, 3: 735–6, note 69 (Leahy); Halifax to FO, 26 and 27 March 1945, FO 954/17A/178–9; WM 40 (45) CA, 5 April 1945, CAB 65/52. The message Churchill to Stalin, 5 April 1945, CHAR 20/214/10–12.
110. Clark Kerr to FO, 3 April 1945, PREM 3/356/5.
111. PM, minute to Dominions Secretary, 3 April 1945, copy in FO 954/20C/531–4.
112. *FRUS 1945*, 5: 824.
113. MR box 9.
114. RGASPI f.558, op.11, d.272, ll.71–4; cf. Stalin to Churchill, 7 April 1945, CHAR 20/214/48–9.
115. Lebedev to Molotov, 3 March 1945, AVP RF f.06, op.7, p.39, d.588, ll.15–16.
116. Stalin to Churchill, 7 April 1945, CHAR 20/214/48–9; cf. RGASPI f.558, op.11, d.370, l.128.
117. Churchill to Eden, 25 March 1945, FO 954/26C/591.
118. Soames, *Speaking for Themselves*, 521–4.
119. MR box 9.
120. Printed in *Corr 1957*, 2: 210, this is largely the same as the summary in Stalin's letter.

121. CHAR 20/214/33.
122. Churchill to Eden, 11 April 1945, CHAR 20/209/4; Kimball, 3: 624–5, 628–9.
123. From the President to Marshal Stalin, 11 April 1945, log sheet, MR box 9.
124. Arrangements with the Soviets: Report by the Joint Strategic Survey Committee, 5 April 1945, and Leahy to JCS, 6 April 1945, RG 218, Geographical File 42–45, CCS 092 USSR, (3–27–45), Sec.1 (NARA).
125. MR box 23: Warm Springs, 1945 messages, esp. OUT–402, and IN–196 and 197; cf. Kimball, 3: 630, and Woolner, *Last Hundred Days*, 264.
126. MR box 9.
127. Harriman, draft telegram, 10 April 1945, Harriman papers, box 178 (LC).
128. MR box 23: Warm Springs, 1945 messages, 12 April 1945, esp. OUT–409 and 411, and IN–198.
129. Log sheet for President to Harriman, 12 April 1945, MR box 35: Germany, Italian negotiations.

Epilogue

1. Gilbert 7, 1293–4; Mary Soames (ed.), *Speaking for Themselves: The personal letters of Winston and Clementine Churchill*, London, 1999, 524; *SWW*, 6: 418.
2. Harriman to SecState, 13 April 1945, and memcon 13 April 1945, *FRUS 1945*, 5: 825–9; see also Harriman papers, box 178 (LC).
3. Georgiy Zhukov, *Reminiscences and Reflections*, 2 vols, Moscow, 1985, 2: 396–7; Antony Beevor, *Berlin: The downfall*, London, 2002, 402–5.
4. *Corr 1957*, 1: 352–3, 2: 230–1.
5. Frank Costigliola, 'After Roosevelt's death: Dangerous emotions, divisive discourses, and the abandoned alliance', *Diplomatic History*, 34 (2010), 21.
6. Clark Kerr, note of meeting with Gusev, 18 May 1945, PREM 3/396/12/363–5; report by Joint Planning Staff, 'Operation Unthinkable', 22 May 1945, CAB 120/691; Alanbrooke, 693.
7. Daniel Longwill to Henry Laughlin, 8 Sept. 1953, Houghton Mifflin Trade Editorial papers, 318/1: Life, 1952–3 (Houghton Library, Harvard University).
8. See for example Geoffrey Roberts, 'Sexing Up the Cold War: New Evidence on the Molotov–Truman Talks of April 1945', *Cold War History*, 4/3 (April 2004), 105–25.
9. Robert L. Messer, *The End of the Alliance: James F. Byrnes, Roosevelt, Truman, and the origins of the Cold War*, Chapel Hill, NC, 1982, 71–84; Sargent to Churchill, 14 May 1945, PREM 3/396/14/585–6.
10. Moran, 277; Gilbert 8, 111.
11. Vladislav Zubok and Constantine Pleshakov, *Inside the Kremlin's Cold War: From Stalin to Khrushchev*, Cambridge, MA, 1996, 39–43.
12. *SWW*, 6: 583.
13. *Sovetsko-frantsuzskiye otnosheniya vo vremya Velikoy Otechestvennoy voyny, 1941–1945*, 2 vols, Moscow, 1983, 2: 200.
14. CHUR 2/142/136–40.
15. *Hansard Parliamentary Debates*, HC Deb 414, cols 1291, 1300.
16. Vladimir O. Pechatnov, '"The Allies are pressing on you to break your will . . .": Foreign policy correspondence between Stalin and Molotov and other Politburo members, September 1945 – December 1946', *Cold War International History Project Working Paper*, no. 26 (Sept. 1999), 10–11.
17. Alexander O. Chubariyan and Vladimir O. Pechatnov, eds, 'Molotov "the Liberal": Stalin's Criticism of his Deputy', *Cold War History*, 1 (2000), 130.
18. Quotations from ibid., 132–8.
19. Pechatnov '"The Allies"', 6.
20. Winston S. Churchill, *Winston Churchill, His Complete Speeches*, ed. Robert Rhodes James, 8 vols, New York, 1974, 7: 7285–93; cf. speech drafts in CHUR 5/4.

21. This argument is developed in David Reynolds, *From World War to Cold War: Churchill, Roosevelt and the international history of the 1940s*, Oxford, 2006, 259–60.
22. Quotations from reports of the speech in *New York Times*, 14 March 1946, 1 and 4.
23. See William Taubman, *Stalin's American Policy: From entente to détente to cold war*, New York, 1982, 141, 144; David Holloway, *Stalin and the Bomb: The Soviet Union and atomic energy, 1939–1956*, New Haven, CT, 1994, 168–71.
24. Reynolds, *From World War to Cold War*, 261–2; Fraser Harbutt, *The Iron Curtain: Churchill, America, and the origins of the cold war*, New York, 1986, 280–5.
25. Second draft of 15 March 1946 speech, p. A2, in CHUR 5/4.
26. Moran, 339; Bracken to Beaverbrook, 16 Oct. 1946, Beaverbrook papers, C/56 (House of Lords Record Office).
27. See CHUR 2/156/90–102.
28. Montgomery to Churchill, 21 Jan. 1947, CHUR 2/143/95. See also B.L. Montgomery, *The Memoirs of Field-Marshal the Viscount Montgomery of Alamein, KG*, London, 1958, 446–56, quoting Attlee on p. 446.
29. Churchill to Montgomery, 23 Jan. 1947, and to Stalin, 3 Feb. 1947, CHUR 2/143/96, 100.
30. 'Notes on Volume VI', p. 15, Ismay papers, 2/3/296 (Liddell Hart Centre, King's College, London).
31. *SWW*, 6: 186; cf. CHUR 4/355/8. On Potsdam see CHUR 4/380B/187.
32. Gilbert 8, 659; Churchill, *Speeches*, 8: 8296–7; John W. Young, *Winston Churchill's Last Campaign: Britain and the cold war, 1951–5*, Oxford, 1996, 46–7.
33. Speech in Edinburgh, 14 Feb. 1950, in Churchill, *Speeches*, 8: 7944.
34. Colville, 650, 655; Young, *Churchill's Last Campaign*, 130.
35. Quotations from Sheila Fitzpatrick, *On Stalin's Team: The years of living dangerously in Soviet politics*, Princeton, 2015, 226.
36. Moran, 427.
37. Messages of 11 March and 4 May 1953 in Peter Boyle (ed.), *The Churchill–Eisenhower Correspondence, 1953–1955*, Chapel Hill, NC, 1990, 31, 48. The originals of the correspondence are in PREM 11/1074 and Whitman Files: International Series, boxes 16–17, Dwight D. Eisenhower Library, Abilene, KS.
38. Eisenhower to Churchill, 5 May 1953, in Boyle, *Correspondence*, 49–50.
39. Churchill to Eisenhower, 7 May 1953, in Boyle, *Correspondence*, 50–1.
40. Churchill, *Speeches*, 8: 8475–85, quoting pp. 8484–85. The speech notes are in CHUR 5/51C/260–320.
41. Klaus Larres, *Churchill's Cold War: The politics of personal diplomacy*, New Haven, CT, 2002, 217–19, and generally chs 10–11.
42. Churchill messages of 7 and 9 July 1954 and 18 March 1955 in Boyle, *Correspondence*, 152–3, 157–8, 200. On Soviet attitudes see Uri Bar-Noi, 'The Soviet Union and Churchill's appeals for high-level talks, 1953–54', *Diplomacy and Statecraft*, 9:3 (1998), 110–33.
43. Churchill, *Speeches*, 8: 8604; also CHUR 5/56A/156.
44. Churchill to Eisenhower, 16 April 1956, CHUR 2/217/98–9; Anthony Montague Browne, *Long Sunset*, London, 1996, 158.
45. Molotov to Churchill, 7 July 1954, CHUR 6/3A/42.

INDEX